THE DEVELOPMENT OF SOCIOLOGICAL THEORY

THE DEVELOPMENT OF SOCIOLOGICAL THEORY

READINGS FROM THE ENLIGHTENMENT TO THE PRESENT

Edited by

A. Javier Treviño
Wheaton College

Los Angeles | London | New Delhi
Singapore | Washington DC | Melbourne

FOR INFORMATION:

SAGE Publications, Inc.
2455 Teller Road
Thousand Oaks, California 91320
E-mail: order@sagepub.com

SAGE Publications Ltd.
1 Oliver's Yard
55 City Road
London EC1Y 1SP
United Kingdom

SAGE Publications India Pvt. Ltd.
B 1/I 1 Mohan Cooperative Industrial Area
Mathura Road, New Delhi 110 044
India

SAGE Publications Asia-Pacific Pte. Ltd.
3 Church Street
#10-04 Samsung Hub
Singapore 049483

Publisher: Jeff Lasser
Editorial Assistant: Adeline Wilson
Production Editor: David C. Felts
Copy Editor: Jared Leighton
Typesetter: Hurix Systems Pvt. Ltd.
Proofreader: Pam Suwinsky
Cover Designer: Anupama Krishnan
Marketing Manager: Kara Kindstrom

Printed in the United States of America

Library of Congress Cataloging-in-Publication Data

Names: Treviño, A. Javier, 1958– editor.

Title: The development of sociological theory : readings from the Enlightenment to the present / [edited] by A. Javier Treviño.

Description: Thousand Oaks, California : Sage, [2018]

Identifiers: LCCN 2016041096 | ISBN 978-1-5063-0406-9 (pbk. : alk. paper)

Subjects: LCSH: Sociology—History.

Classification: LCC HM435 .D48 2018 | DDC 301—dc23

LC record available at https://lccn.loc.gov/2016041096

This book is printed on acid-free paper.

17 18 19 20 21 10 9 8 7 6 5 4 3 2 1

CONTENTS

Preface x

PART I **The Nature, Structure, and Types of Sociological Theory** **1**

C. Wright Mills (American, 1916–1962), *On Intellectual Craftsmanship* 5

Talcott Parsons (American, 1902–1979), *The Importance of General Theory* 10

Robert K. Merton (American, 1910–2003), *Middle-Range Theories* 22

George C. Homans (American, 1910–1989), *Theory as Explanation* 31

Dennis H. Wrong (American, 1923–), *The Oversocialized View of Human Nature* 38

Alvin W. Gouldner (American, 1920–1980), *The Theoretical Infrastructure* 46

PART II **The Enlightenment Roots of Sociological Theory** **53**

Thomas Hobbes (English, 1588–1679), *The Problem of Order* 55

Jean-Jacques Rousseau (French, 1712–1778), *The Social Contract* 58

Charles de Montesquieu (French, 1689–1755), *Laws, Mores, and Manners* 60

PART III **Protosociology** **63**

Henri de Saint-Simon (French, 1760–1825), *An Unjust Social Order* 65

Henri de Saint-Simon (French, 1760–1825), *The Hierarchical Structure of Society* 67

Auguste Comte (French, 1798–1857), *Order and Progress* 69

Auguste Comte (French, 1798–1857), *Law of the Three Stages* 71

Herbert Spencer (British, 1820–1903), *Social Progress* 73

Herbert Spencer (British, 1820–1903), *The Evolution of Society* 76

Harriet Martineau (British, 1802–1876), *The General Happiness* 78

William Graham Sumner (American, 1840–1910), *Folkways and Mores* 80

William Graham Sumner (American, 1840–1910),
In-Groups, Out-Groups, and Ethnocentrism 82

PART IV The Classical Tradition 85

Karl Marx (German, 1818–1883), *Commodity Fetishism* 89

Karl Marx (German, 1818–1883), *Alienated Labor* 91

Karl Marx (German, 1818–1883), *Historical Materialism* 98

Émile Durkheim (French, 1858–1917), *Mechanical and Organic Solidarity* 104

Émile Durkheim (French, 1858–1917), *Types of Suicide* 106

Émile Durkheim (French, 1858–1917), *Social Facts* 112

Max Weber (German, 1864–1920), *The Rationalism of Western Civilization* 114

Max Weber (German, 1864–1920), *The Spirit of Capitalism* 121

Max Weber (German, 1864–1920), *Types of Authority* 126

Georg Simmel (German, 1858–1918), *The Stranger* 132

Georg Simmel (German, 1858–1918), *Dyad and Triad* 136

Georg Simmel (German, 1858–1918), *The Metropolis and Mental Life* 141

PART V The Interstitial Statements 147

Gaetano Mosca (Italian, 1858–1941), *The Ruling Class* 151

Vilfredo Pareto (Italian, 1848–1923), *The Circulation of the Elites* 154

Robert Michels (German, 1876–1936), *The Iron Law of Oligarchy* 159

Gustave Le Bon (French, 1841–1931), *The Crowd Mind* 162

Gabriel Tarde (French, 1843–1904), *The Laws of Imitation* 164

Sigmund Freud (Austrian, 1856–1939), *The Herd Instinct* 167

Sigmund Freud (Austrian, 1856–1939), *The Conscience of Society* 170

Thorstein Veblen (American, 1857–1929), *Conspicuous Consumption* 173

William F. Ogburn (American, 1886–1959), *Cultural Lag* 175

PART VI The Second Generation 181

Pitirim A. Sorokin (Russian/American, 1889–1968), *Ideational, Sensate, and Idealistic Cultures* 185

Pitirim A. Sorokin (Russian/American, 1889–1968), *Imminent Sociocultural Change* 190

Talcott Parsons (American, 1902–1979), *The Pattern Variables* 195

Talcott Parsons (American, 1902–1979), *The Social System* 197

Talcott Parsons (American, 1902–1979), *The AGIL Schema* 200

Robert K. Merton (American, 1910–2003), *Manifest and Latent Functions* 203

Robert K. Merton (American, 1910–2003), *Social Structure and Anomie* 207

Robert K. Merton (American, 1910–2003), *The Self-Fulfilling Prophecy* 213

Hans H. Gerth (German/American 1908–1978) and C. Wright Mills (American, 1916–1962), *Structural Integration and Change* 223

David Riesman (American, 1909–2002), *Character and Conformity* 229

PART VII The Critical Edge 235

Lewis A. Coser (German/American, 1913–2003), *Social Structures, Social Conflicts, and Safety-Valve Institutions* 239

Ralf Dahrendorf (German/British, 1929–2009), *Class Conflict and Structural Change* 242

Karl Mannheim (Hungarian, 1893–1947), *The Sociology of Knowledge* 247

Antonio Gramsci (Italian, 1891–1937), *Hegemony* 253

Georg Lukács (Hungarian, 1885–1971), *The Reification of Consciousness* 256

Max Horkheimer (German, 1895–1973), *Critical Theory* 261

Theodor W. Adorno (German, 1903–1969), *The Culture Industry* 266

C. Wright Mills (American, 1916–1962), *The Designer as Cultural Worker* 271

PART VIII The Self, Interactions, and Exchanges 279

W. I. Thomas (American, 1863–1947), *The Definition of the Situation* 283

George Herbert Mead (American, 1863–1931), *Self and Society* 285

Charles Horton Cooley (American, 1864–1929), *The Looking-Glass Self* 289

Charles Horton Cooley (American, 1864–1929), *Primary Groups* 291

Erving Goffman (Canadian, 1922–1982), *Performances in Everyday Life* 294

Erving Goffman (Canadian, 1922–1982), *Managing Stigma* 301

Alfred Schütz (Austrian/American, 1899–1959), *The Meaningfully Produced Social World* 309

Peter L. Berger (Austrian/American, 1929–) and Thomas Luckmann (Austrian/American, 1927–2016), *Society as Objective Reality* 317

Harold Garfinkel (American, 1917–2011), *Ethnomethodology* 324

Marcel Mauss (French, 1872–1950), *Obligatory Exchange* 329

George C. Homans (American, 1910–1989), *Social Behavior as Exchange* 334

Peter M. Blau (Austrian/American, 1918–2002), *Reciprocity, Power Imbalance, and Dialectical Change* 343

James S. Coleman (American, 1926–1995), *Individual Interests and Systems of Exchange* 348

PART IX Community and Civil Society 355

Ferdinand Tönnies (German, 1855–1936), *Gemeinschaft and Gesellschaft* 357

Robert A. Nisbet (American, 1913–1996), *The Quest for Community* 363

Robert N. Bellah (American, 1927–2013), *Civil Religion in America* 369

Philip Selznick (American, 1919–2010), *A Normative Theory of Moral Community* 380

Amitai Etzioni (Israeli/American, 1929–), *Communitarianism* 384

Norbert Elias (German/British, 1897–1990), *The Civilizing Process* 392

PART X Race and Gender 395

W. E. B. Du Bois (American, 1868–1963), *The Veil and Double Consciousness* 397

W. E. B. Du Bois (American, 1868–1963), *The Talented Tenth* 401

Charlotte Perkins Gilman (American, 1860–1936), *The Economic Status of Women* 409

Dorothy E. Smith (Canadian, 1926–), *Feminist Standpoint Theory* 414

Patricia Hill Collins (American, 1948–), *Black Feminist Thought* 418

Judith Butler (American, 1956–), *Performative Theory of Gender Acts* 429

PART XI Systems and Networks 435

Niklas Luhmann (German, 1927–1998), *Autopoietic Systems* 437

Jürgen Habermas (German, 1929–), *Lifeworld and Social System* 442

Immanuel Wallerstein (American, 1930–), *World-Systems Analysis* 447

Manuel Castells (Spanish, 1942–), *The Network Society* 453

Bruno Latour (French, 1947–), *Actor-Network-Theory* 460

PART XII Late Modernity and Postmodernity 471

Alain Touraine (French, 1925–), *Sociological Intervention* 475

Anthony Giddens (British, 1938–), *Structuration Theory* 485

Anthony Giddens (British, 1938–), *Ontological Security, Existential Anxiety, and Self-Identity* 490

Pierre Bourdieu (French, 1930–2002), *Habitus* 495

Ulrich Beck (German, 1944–2015), *The Risk Society* 498

Zygmunt Bauman (Polish/British, 1925–), *Liquid Modernity* 502

Roland Robertson (British, 1938–), *Global Modernities* 510

Jean-François Lyotard (French, 1924–1998), *The Postmodern Condition* 520

Jean Baudrillard (French, 1929–2007), *Hyperreality* 529

About the Editor 535

PREFACE

The planet Solaria has a constant population of humans. Its population of robots—that outnumber the humans 20,000 to one—is highly specialized: There is one robot to serve every human need and want. All of Solaria's robots have been programmed to not injure a human being. Anselmo Quemot is the planet's only sociologist. He states that Solaria has solved the problem of ensuring a secure social order, with human masters perpetually at the top and their robot servants at the bottom. Contrary to Earth's history, throughout which potential rebellions by the dispossessed against the elites could only be prevented through harsh authoritarian measures, Solaria's human population has nothing to fear from its robots. Because of the software that prevents robots from harming humans, the robot servants cannot revolt against their human masters, who enjoy abundant leisure. Solarian society, Quemot states, is the first truly new society—a society where people are free of poverty and toil. It has achieved the greatest social invention since the creation of cities: a stable hierarchical social structure. So goes part of the story told in Isaac Asimov's science fiction novel, *The Naked Sun*.

Whatever Anselmo Quemot's deficiencies as a sociologist (and there are many, as revealed in the book), he nonetheless endeavors to *explain*—to give a convincing account of—why a leisure class can be maintained without militarizing society. In addition, he makes *comparisons* between Solarian society and Earth society. And he considers *history*: He points out that in ancient Sparta, the helots—the subservient group that formed the majority population—could not rise up against the considerably smaller number of free citizens because Sparta was a garrison state populated by soldiers. And while Quemot's inchoate observations about stratified society, on Solaria and on Earth, cannot be considered *sociological theory* proper, his attempt at explaining and at comparative and historical analysis get him closer to the theoretical enterprise. Quemot also employs the building blocks of theory: *concepts*—ideas about the social world articulated as terms—such as social revolution, social conflict, pyramidal social structure, leisure class, social invention, and so on.

Sociological Theory and Theorists

This anthology of sociological theory features the ideas of thinkers writing over a 200-year period—from the early 19th century to the early 21st century. Like their fictional counterpart, Anselmo Quemot, many of them sought to analyze social conditions of concern to them: the hierarchical structure of society, the rationalism of Western civilization, the civilizing process, and so on. Others wanted to *interpret*—to give a different meaning to—issues such as the definition of the situation, performances in everyday life, and the meaningfully produced social world. Still others engaged in *critique*; they gave a critical examination of oppressive social conditions—created by, for example, commodity fetishism, hegemony, and the culture industry—with the intent to emancipate.

Some theorists articulated their explanations, interpretations, and critiques in *general* terms, thus producing analytical frameworks, schemata, and theory in the "grand" style. This is particularly the case with thinkers like Karl Marx, Talcott Parsons, and Immanuel

Wallerstein. Others formulated their theories more *specifically*, as a collection of definitive concepts, as did Erving Goffman and Amitai Etzioni, or in the form of propositions, as did George C. Homans.

In addition, some thinkers took a *macro*approach in their sociological theorizing, thus focusing on larger social phenomena, such as culture, social structure, and social institutions. This is particularly true of Norbert Elias and Niklas Luhmann, for example. Other thinkers engaged in a *micro*analysis of social life, being principally concerned with the social self, social interaction, and social exchange. George Herbert Mead, Charles Horton Cooley, and Marcel Mauss excelled in this regard. Of particular note are those sociological theorists who attempted to bridge the macro–micro divide, like Alain Touraine, Anthony Giddens, and Pierre Bourdieu.

Relatedly, the micro-oriented theorists were likely to take a *subjectivist*, or "definitional," approach in accounting for how people construct social reality. Harold Garfinkle's analysis of the methods people use for understanding and producing their daily activities is in the subjectivist tradition. In contrast, the macro-oriented theorists take an *objectivist*, or "factist," approach, seeing social reality as being "out there" and exerting an influence on people. The exemplary thinker in this regard is Émile Durkheim, who advocated for the study of collective beliefs, tendencies, and practices that are permanent features of the social landscape.

Moreover, there were those thinkers, like Auguste Comte and Talcott Parsons, who were interested in accounting for how *social order* was maintained, whether through enduring institutions, socialization, or value consensus. Alternatively, there were those who preferred to examine *social conflict*—the various frictions and tensions prevalent in society and in social life. Included in this latter group were Ralf Dahrendorf, Theodor W. Adorno, and C. Wright Mills. The one theorist who explicitly considered both order and conflict was Lewis A. Coser.

The majority of sociological theorists, from Henri de Saint-Simon in the early 19th century to Zygmunt Bauman in the early 21st century, endeavored to analyze *modern* society, its culture and institutions. But in the second half of the 20th century, sociologists like Jean-François Lyotard and Jean Baudrillard wanted to understand a new, emerging era, which they called the *postmodern*.

Most of the theorists and their theories were products of Anglo-American and Western European culture. Thus, they were largely French, British, Italian, German, or American. Karl Mannheim and Georg Lukács were Hungarian, and Pitirim A. Sorokin was originally from Russia, but their most influential work was produced in the West or, in the case of Lukács, in relation to Western ideals.

Not all social thinkers had previously received the recognition they deserved for their theoretical contributions; this is particularly the case with those who were women and people of color, such as, for example, W. E. B. Du Bois and Charlotte Perkins Gilman. Nevertheless, their ideas about race and gender have contributed much to the development of sociological theory.

Regardless of whether the social thinkers considered in this anthology

- endeavored to explain, interpret, or critique;
- stated their theories in general or specific terms;
- took a macro or micro orientation;
- employed a subjectivist or objectivist approach;
- examined social order or social conflict; or
- considered modern or postmodern society,

one thing is certain: They, like Anselmo Quemot of Solaria, were all intently involved in theorizing the social.

The Book's Organization and Presentation

This anthology consists of 96 readings, grouped into 12 parts, that typically compose the catalog of writings on sociological theory. The readings are presented according to two orderings: (1) as a rough *chronology* that illustrates the historical development of theoretical knowledge in sociology and, relatedly, (2) as a *typology* of systems of sociological theorizing for more methodical consideration.

Most of the thinkers associated with these readings are generally considered to have made contributions to the *sociological* tradition, properly understood. The few exceptions are the philosophers Thomas Hobbes, Jean-Jacques Rousseau, and Charles de Montesquieu and, later, Sigmund Freud, a psychologist.

The selected readings have been revised in several ways. In most cases, they have been abridged and retitled. The former was done to help the reader focus on essential information; the latter was done to more accurately reflect the selections' contents. In addition, for purposes of readability, all annotations and references in the readings have been removed. While these revisions are acceptable in a compilation of this kind, there is no substitute for engaging with the original works in their complete textual presentation.

There are two unique features to this anthology. The first, designated as Part I, consists of an initial set of readings that pertain to *metatheory*—the investigation and analysis of sociological theory. These selections will assist the reader in better understanding the nature, structure, and types of the sociological theories that are presented throughout the volume. Immediately following this, in Part II, are readings associated with some core Enlightenment ideas—ideas that preceded and influenced the development of sociological thought.

Acknowledgments

I am grateful to the dozens of reviewers—instructors of courses in sociological theory—for their valuable suggestions for preparing this anthology. I am particularly thankful for encouragements and recommendations made by Horst J. Helle, Stephen Kalberg, and Natalia Ruiz-Junco.

PART I

THE NATURE, STRUCTURE, AND TYPES OF SOCIOLOGICAL THEORY

The five authors whose ideas compose Part I are largely engaged in some form of *metatheorizing*. They, in their own ways, theorize about the nature, structure, and types of sociological theory. More specifically, these writers tell what they believe sociological theory should be, what it should look like, and what it should do. The fact that there is little or no agreement concerning their views on sociological theory points to the unsettled condition of sociology as a knowledge field and to the complexity of its subject matter: social reality.

We begin with the essay, "On Intellectual Craftsmanship," where C. Wright Mills offers beginning students of sociology practical advice on how to stimulate the *sociological imagination*—the quality of mind that will help them use information and develop reason in order to achieve lucid summations of what is going on in the world and of what may be happening within themselves. While Mills is not typically considered a theorist, his recommendations for activating the sociological imagination can nonetheless be helpful in doing theoretical work.

Mills advocates an unbroken continuity between what students of sociology pursue intellectually and what they, as persons, observe and experience in their everyday lives. In other words, the intellectual's professional activities should always be fused with his or her personal life. Intellectual work may be properly described as a craft. Mills uses the phrase *intellectual craftsmanship* in referring to a style of work, as well as to the joyful experience of mastering the medium—language—used in that work. In order to engage in intellectual craftsmanship, Mills recommends that sociology students keep a "file," a journal of sorts, in which notes are habitually taken in an effort to join the personal with the professional, to record studies underway, as well as studies planned. The file should consist of a continually growing collection of facts and ideas, from the most vague to the most finished: personal notes, excerpts from books, bibliographical items, outlines of projects, and so forth. At a later point in time, the sociologist rearranges the file by playfully combining previously isolated ideas and notes on different topics and finding unsuspected connections between them. Rearranging the file releases the imagination, as the sociologist becomes receptive to unforeseen and unplanned linkages, all the while keeping in mind the several problems on which he or she is actively working. Then, through the use of ideal types, polar types, and cross-classification techniques, the sociologist attempts to systematically order the findings. On completing this, the findings are then pared down to essentials by relating them to one another in order to form a working model. Finally, the sociologist relates the working model to whatever he or she is endeavoring to explain.

While Mills was advocating the use of a pragmatic "working" model—a more-or-less systematic inventory of findings that can be used to understand something of social significance—Talcott Parsons was proposing the formulation of a universal conceptual scheme for the social sciences.

In 1949, Parsons promoted the formulation of a social theory that has the most *general* implications possible. In "The Importance of General Theory," Parsons maintains that the reason for engaging in general theorizing is that the cumulative development of knowledge is based on the degree of abstraction by which different findings and interpretations in the various social sciences can be systematically related to each other. At the time, Parsons was developing a master analytical scheme that would encompass the entire subject matter of anthropology, social psychology, and sociology. He would later articulate this comprehensive "system" theory in his landmark volumes *Toward a General Theory of Action* and *The Social System*.

In "Middle-Range Theories," Robert K. Merton proposes a distinctly different type of sociological theory from that of Parsons's general conceptual model, which is far removed from empirical confirmation. For Merton, sociological theorizing should be done at *midrange*—intermediate between an all-inclusive unified theory of social systems and minor and prosaic descriptions of observed data. Accordingly, middle-range theory involves neither broad abstractions nor trivial details; rather, it consists of logically interconnected propositions that can be empirically investigated. Examples of middle-range theories include a theory of reference groups, a theory of relative deprivation, and a theory of role sets. Merton argues that only by developing such specialized theories with limited conceptual ranges and gradually consolidating them will sociology advance its knowledge.

In "Theory as Explanation," George C. Homans asserts that any science, including sociology, has two main jobs to perform: discovery and explanation. Discovery involves stating and testing general relationships between properties of nature. A discovery takes the form of a *proposition*, or a statement of relationship between properties of nature. But in science, discovery alone isn't enough, there must also be *explanation*; there has to be a statement saying why, under given conditions, the relationship holds well. In other words, if there is some change in one of the properties—one of the variables—the proposition must specify what the change in the other variable will be, or if one of the variables increases in value, it must say how the other will too. In sum, then, a theory should be an explanation in the form of x varies as y. Thus, for Homans, an explanation of an empirical phenomenon can only be a *theory* of the phenomenon. But how does one arrive at a theory? Simply put, one does so through the method of *deduction*. The proposition to be explained is called the *explicandum*. The *explicandum* is explained in that it follows a logical conclusion, as a deduction, from more general propositions. For Homans, the purpose of sociological theory is to deduce a wide variety of empirical propositions under different given conditions.

In "The Oversocialized View of Human Nature," Dennis H. Wrong maintains that sociological theory should be an effort to find answers to eternal questions about human nature, such as the so-called Hobbesian problem of order: Why do people conform to institutionalized norms? Talcott Parsons gives the following answer: Because they have, through socialization, internalized the norms. Wrong critiques this implicit "oversocialized" view of human nature for dismissing other characteristics that are resistant to socialization—such as people's material interests, their sexual drives, and their quest for power—and characteristics that explain their motivations to conform (or, for that matter, not to conform). Sociological theory, says Wrong, must consider people as *social* beings, without treating them as entirely *socialized* beings.

Finally, in "The Theoretical Infrastructure," Alvin W. Gouldner introduces the notion of *domain assumptions*, by which he means those existential and normative *beliefs* that people have learned in their culture. Domain assumptions elicit certain *sentiments* that people have concerning their experience with the social world. Whether they realize it or not and admit it or not, Gouldner contends that the theories sociologists create reflect their domain assumptions and sentiments. What is more, these social theories also arouse certain sentiments in the students who study them. Whether students accept or reject a theory is based on the feeling—of satisfaction or discomfort, optimism or pessimism—that the theory evokes in them. Depending on which feeling it produces, the theory will also take on different political meanings. It will, for instance, be seen as progressive or conservative, as idealistic or practical. Gouldner refers to sociological theorists' domain assumptions and private sentiments as the "infrastructure" that determines the nature of the social theory they construct.

1

On Intellectual Craftsmanship*

C. Wright Mills

To the individual social scientist who feels himself a part of the classic tradition, social science is the practice of a craft. A man at work on problems of substance, he is among those who are quickly made impatient and weary by elaborate discussions of method-and-theory-in-general; so much of it interrupts his proper studies. It is much better, he believes, to have one account by a working student of how he is going about his work than a dozen 'codifications of procedure' by specialists who as often as not have never done much work of consequence. Only by conversations in which experienced thinkers exchange information about their actual ways of working can a useful sense of method and theory be imparted to the beginning student. I feel it useful, therefore, to report in some detail how I go about my craft. This is necessarily a personal statement, but it is written with the hope that others, especially those beginning independent work, will make it less personal by the facts of their own experience.

It is best to begin, I think, by reminding you, the beginning student, that the most admirable thinkers within the scholarly community you have chosen to join do not split their work from their lives. They seem to take both too seriously to allow such dissociation, and they want to use each for the enrichment of the other. Of course, such a split is the prevailing convention among men in general, deriving, I suppose, from the hollowness of the work which men in general now do. But you will have recognized that as a scholar you have the exceptional opportunity of designing a way of living which will encourage the habits of good workmanship. Scholarship is a choice of how to live as well as a choice of career; whether he knows it or not, the intellectual workman forms his own self as he works toward the perfection of his craft; to realize his own potentialities, and any opportunities that come his way, he constructs a character which has as its core the qualities of the good workman.

What this means is that you must learn to use your life experience in your intellectual work: continually to examine and interpret it. In this sense craftsmanship is the center of yourself and you are personally involved in every intellectual product upon which you may work. To say that you can 'have experience,' means, for one thing, that your past plays into and affects your present, and that it defines your capacity for future experience. As a social scientist, you have to control this rather elaborate interplay, to capture what you experience and sort it out; only in this way can you hope to use it to guide and test your reflection, and in the process shape yourself as an intellectual craftsman. But how can you do this? One answer is: you must set up a file, which is, I suppose, a sociologist's way of saying: keep a journal. Many creative writers keep journals; the sociologist's need for systematic reflection demands it.

In such a file as I am going to describe, there is joined personal experience and professional activities, studies under way and studies planned. In this file, you, as an intellectual craftsman, will try to get together what you are doing intellectually and what you are experiencing as a person. Here you will not be afraid to use your experience and relate it directly to various work in progress. By serving as a check on repititious work, your file also enables you to conserve your energy. It also encourages you to capture 'fringe-thoughts': various ideas which may be byproducts of everyday life, snatches of conversation overheard on the street, or, for that matter, dreams. Once noted, these may lead to more systematic thinking, as well as lend intellectual relevance to more directed experience.

You will have often noticed how carefully accomplished thinkers treat their own minds, how closely they observe their development and organize their experience. The reason they treasure their smallest experiences is that, in the course of a lifetime, modern man has so very little personal experience and yet experience is so important as a source of original intellectual work. To be able to trust yet to be skeptical of your own experience, I have come to believe, is one mark of the mature workman. This ambiguous confidence is indispensable to originality in any intellectual pursuit, and the file is one way by which you can develop and justify such confidence.

By keeping an adequate file and thus developing self-reflective habits, you learn how to keep your inner world awake. Whenever you feel strongly about events or ideas you must try not to let them pass from your mind, but instead to formulate them for your files and in so doing draw out their implications, show yourself either how foolish these feelings or ideas are, or how they might be articulated into productive shape. The file also helps you build up the habit of writing. You cannot 'keep your hand in' if you do not write something at least every week. In developing the file, you can experiment as a writer and thus, as they say, develop your powers of expression. To maintain a file is to engage in the controlled experience.

But, you may ask, how do ideas come? How is the imagination spurred to put all the images and facts together, to make images relevant and lend meaning to facts? I do not think I can really answer that; all I can do is talk about the general conditions and a few simple techniques which have seemed to increase my chances to come out with something.

The sociological imagination, I remind you, in considerable part consists of the capacity to shift from one perspective to another, and in the process to build up an adequate view of a total society and of its components. It is this imagination, of course, that sets off the social scientist from the mere technician. Adequate technicians can be trained in a few years. The sociological imagination can also be cultivated; certainly it seldom occurs without a great deal of often routine work. Yet there is an unexpected quality about it, perhaps because its essence is the combination of ideas that no one expected were combinable—say, a mess of ideas from German philosophy and British economics. There is a playfulness of mind back of such combining as well as a truly fierce drive to make sense of the world, which the technician as such usually lacks. Perhaps he is too well trained, too precisely trained. Since one can be trained only in what is already known, training sometimes incapacitates one from learning new ways; it makes one rebel against what is bound to be at first loose and even sloppy. But you must cling to such vague images and notions, if they are yours, and you must work them out. For it is in such forms that original ideas, if any, almost always first appear.

There are definite ways, I believe, of stimulating the sociological imagination:

(1) On the most concrete level, the re-arranging of the file, as I have already said, is one

way to invite imagination. You simply dump out heretofore disconnected folders, mixing up their contents, and then re-sort them. You try to do it in a more or less relaxed way. How often and how extensively you re-arrange the files will of course vary with different problems and with how well they are developing. But the mechanics of it are as simple as that. Of course, you will have in mind the several problems on which you are actively working, but you will also try to be passively receptive to unforeseen and unplanned linkages.

(2) An attitude of playfulness toward the phrases and words with which various issues are defined often loosens up the imagination. Look up synonyms for each of your key terms in dictionaries as well as in technical books, in order to know the full range of their connotations. This simple habit will prod you to elaborate the terms of the problem and hence to define them less wordily and more precisely. For only if you know the several meanings which might be given to terms or phrases can you select the exact ones with which you want to work. But such an interest in words goes further than that. In all work, but especially in examining theoretical statements, you will try to keep close watch on the level of generality of every key term, and you will often find it useful to break down a high-level statement into more concrete meanings. When that is done, the statement often falls into two or three components, each lying along different dimensions. You will also try to move up the level of generality: remove the specific qualifiers and examine the re-formed statement or inference more abstractly, to see if you can stretch it or elaborate it. So from above and from below, you will try to probe, in search of clarified meaning, into every aspect and implication of the idea.

(3) Many of the general notions you come upon, as you think about them, will be cast into types. A new classification is the usual beginning of fruitful developments. The skill to make up types and then to search for the conditions and consequences of each type will, in short, become an automatic procedure with you. Rather than rest content with existing classifications, in particular, common-sense ones, you will search for their common denominators and for differentiating factors within and between them. Good types require that the criteria of classification be explicit and systematic. To make them so you must develop the habit of cross-classification.

The technique of cross-classifying is not of course limited to quantitative materials; as a matter of fact, it is the best way to imagine and to get hold of new types as well as to criticize and clarify old ones. Charts, tables, and diagrams of a qualitative sort are not only ways to display work already done; they are very often genuine tools of production. They clarify the 'dimensions' of the types, which they also help you to imagine and build. As a matter of fact, in the past fifteen years, I do not believe I have written more than a dozen pages first-draft without some little cross-classification—although, of course, I do not always or even usually display such diagrams. Most of them flop, in which case you have still learned something. When they work, they help you to think more clearly and to write more explicitly. They enable you to discover the range and the full relationships of the very terms with which you are thinking and of the facts with which you are dealing.

For a working sociologist, cross-classification is what diagramming a sentence is for a diligent grammarian. In many ways, cross-classification is the very grammar of the sociological imagination. Like all grammar, it must be controlled and not allowed to run away from its purposes.

(4) Often you get the best insights by considering extremes—by thinking of the opposite of that with which you are directly concerned. If you think about despair, then also think about elation; if you study the miser, then also the spendthrift. The hardest thing in the world is to study one object; when you try to contrast objects, you get a better grip on the materials and you can then sort out the dimensions in terms of which the comparisons are made. You will find that shuttling between attention to these dimensions and to the concrete types is very illuminating. This technique is also logically sound, for without a sample, you can only guess about statistical frequencies anyway: what you can do is to give the range and the major types of some phenomenon, and for that it is more economical to begin by constructing 'polar types,' opposites along various dimensions. This does not mean, of course, that you will not strive to gain and to maintain a sense of proportion—to look for some lead to the frequencies of

given types. One continually tries, in fact, to combine this quest with the search for indices for which one might find or collect statistics.

The idea is to use a variety of viewpoints: you will, for instance, ask yourself how would a political scientist whom you have recently read approach this, and how would that experimental psychologist, or this historian? You try to think in terms of a variety of viewpoints and in this way to let your mind become a moving prism catching light from as many angles as possible. In this connection, the writing of dialogues is often very useful.

You will quite often find yourself thinking against something, and in trying to understand a new intellectual field, one of the first things you might well do is to lay out the major arguments. One of the things meant by 'being soaked in the literature' is being able to locate the opponents and the friends of every available viewpoint. By the way, it is not well to be too 'soaked in the literature'; you may drown in it, like Mortimer Adler. Perhaps the point is to know when you ought to read, and when you ought not to.

(5) The fact that, for the sake of simplicity, in cross-classification, you first work in terms of yes-or-no, encourages you to think of extreme opposites. That is generally good, for qualitative analysis cannot of course provide you with frequencies or magnitudes. Its technique and its end is to give you the range of types. For many purposes you need no more than that, although for some, of course, you do need to get a more precise idea of the proportions involved.

The release of imagination can sometimes be achieved by deliberately inverting your sense of proportion. If something seems very minute, imagine it to be simply enormous, and ask yourself: What difference might that make? And vice versa, for gigantic phenomena. What would pre-literate villages look like with populations of 30 millions? Nowadays at least, I should never think of actually counting or measuring anything, before I had played with each of its elements and conditions and consequences in an imagined world in which I control the scale of everything. This is one thing statisticians ought to mean, but never seem to, by that horrible little phrase about 'knowing the universe before you sample it.'

(6) Whatever the problem with which you are concerned, you will find it helpful to try to get a *comparative* grip on the materials. The search for comparable cases, either in one civilization and historical period or in several, gives you leads. You would never think of describing an institution in twentieth-century America without trying to bear in mind similar institutions in other types of structures and periods. That is so even if you do not make explicit comparisons. In time you will come almost automatically to orient your reflection historically. One reason for doing so is that often what you are examining is limited in number: to get a comparative grip on it, you have to place it inside an historical frame. To put it another way, the contrasting-type approach often requires the examination of historical materials. This sometimes results in points useful for a trend analysis, or it leads to a typology of phases. You will use historical materials, then, because of the desire for a fuller range, or for a more convenient range of some phenomenon—by which I mean a range that includes the variations along some known set of dimensions. Some knowledge of world history is indispensable to the sociologist; without such knowledge, no matter what else he knows, he is simply crippled.

(7) There is, finally, a point which has more to do with the craft of putting a book together than with the release of the imagination. Yet these two are often one: how you go about arranging materials for presentation always affects the content of your work. The idea I have in mind I learned from a great editor, Lambert Davis, who, I suppose, after seeing what I have done with it, would not want to acknowledge it as his child. It is the distinction between theme and topic.

A topic is a subject, like 'the careers of corporation executives' or 'the increased power of military officials' or 'the decline of society matrons.' Usually most of what you have to say about a topic can readily be put into one chapter or a section of a chapter. But the order in which all your topics are arranged often brings you into the realm of themes.

A theme is an idea, usually of some signal trend, some master conception, or a key distinction, like rationality and reason, for example. In working out the construction of a book, when you come to realize the two or three, or, as the case may be, the six or seven themes, then you will know that you are on top of the job. You will recognize these themes because they keep insisting upon being dragged into all sorts of topics and perhaps you will feel that they are mere repetitions. And sometimes that is all they are! Certainly very often they will be found in the more clotted and confused, the more badly written, sections of your manuscript.

What you must do is sort them out and state them in a general way as clearly and briefly as you can. Then, quite systematically, you must cross-classify them with the full range of your topics. This means that you will ask of each topic: Just how is it affected by each of these themes? And again: Just what is the meaning, if any, for each of these themes of each of the topics?

Sometimes a theme requires a chapter or a section for itself, perhaps when it is first introduced or perhaps in a summary statement toward the end. In general, I think most writers—as well as most systematic thinkers—would agree that at some point all the themes ought to appear together, in relation to one another. Often, although not always, it is possible to do this at the beginning of a book. Usually, in any well-constructed book, it must be done near the end. And, of course, all the way through you ought at least to try to relate the themes to each topic. It is easier to write about this than to do it, for it is usually not so mechanical a matter as it might appear. But sometimes it is—at least if the themes are properly sorted out and clarified. But that, of course, is the rub. For what I have here, in the context of literary craftsmanship, called themes, in the context of intellectual work are called ideas.

Sometimes, by the way, you may find that a book does not really have any themes. It is just a string of topics, surrounded, of course, by methodological introductions to methodology, and theoretical introductions to theory. These are indeed quite indispensable to the writing of books by men without ideas. And so is lack of intelligibility.

2

The Importance of General Theory*

Talcott Parsons

Two years ago at the annual meeting of this Society it was my privilege to act as chairman of the section on theory and thus to be responsible for a statement of its contemporary position, as part of the general stock-taking of the state of our discipline which was the keynote of that meeting. As that meeting was primarily concerned with taking stock of where we stood, the present one, with the keynote of frontiers of research, is primarily concerned with looking toward the future. It therefore seems appropriate to take advantage of the present occasion to speak of the future prospects of that aspect of sociological science on which more than any other I feel qualified to speak.

The history of science testifies eloquently to the fundamental importance of the state of its theory to any scientific field. Theory is only one of several ingredients which must go into the total brew, but for progress beyond certain levels it is an indispensable one. Social scientists are plagued by the problems of objectivity in the face of tendencies to value-bias to a much higher degree than is true of natural scientists. In addition, we have the problem of selection among an enormous number of possible variables. For both these reasons, it may be argued that perhaps theory is even more important in our field than in the natural sciences. At any rate, I hope I may presume to suggest that my own election to its presidency by the membership of this society may be interpreted as an act of recognition of this importance of theory, and a vote of confidence in its future development.

Though my primary concern this evening is with the future, perhaps just a word on where we stand at present is in order. Some fifteen years ago two young Americans, who, since they were my own children, I knew quite intimately, and who were aged approximately five and three respectively at the time, developed a little game of yelling at the top of their voices: "The sociology is about to begin, said the man with the loud speaker." However right they may have been about their father's professional achievements up to that time, as delivering a judgment of the state of the field as a whole I think they were a bit on the conservative side. It had already begun, but especially in the theoretical phase that beginning did not lie very far back. The historians of our

*"The Prospects of Sociological Theory," Talcott Parsons, *American Sociological Review* 15, 1 (1950): 3–16.

discipline will have to settle such questions at a future time, but I for one would not hesitate to label all the theoretical endeavors before the generation of Durkheim and Max Weber as proto-sociology. With these figures as the outstanding ones, but with several others including a number of Americans like Sumner, Park, Cooley, and Thomas, in a somewhat less prominent role, I feel that the real job of founding was done in the generation from about 1890 to 1920. We belong to the second generation, which already has foundations on which to build. But as for the building itself, a post here and there, and a few courses of bricks at the corners, are all that is yet visible above the ground. After all, two or, more correctly, one and a half generations, in the perspective of the development of a science, is a very short time.

When, roughly a quarter of a century ago, I attained some degree of the knowledge of good and evil in a professional sense, this founding phase was over. The speculative systems were still taken seriously. But the work of such writers as Sumner, Thomas, Simmel, Cooley, Park, and Mead, was beginning to enter into thinking in a much more particularized sense. In fact, a research tradition was already building up, in which a good deal of solid theory was embodied—as in Sumner's basic idea of the relativity of the mores, Thomas' four wishes, and many of Park's insights, as into the nature of competitive processes. This relatively particularized, attention focussing, problem selecting, use of theory in research, so different from the purely illustrative relation between theory and empirical fact in the Spencerian type of system, has continued to develop in the interim. Such fields as that of Industrial Sociology, starting from the Mayo-Roethlisberger work, and carried further at Chicago and Cornell, the study of Ethnic Relations and that of Social Stratification will serve to illustrate. At the same time controversies about total schools, which in my youth centered especially about Behaviorism, have greatly subsided.

Our own generation has seen at least the beginnings of a process of more general pulling together. Even when a good deal of theory was actually being used in research much of the *teaching* of theory was still in terms of the "systems" of the past, and was organized about names rather than working conceptual schemes. Graduate students frantically memorized the contents of Bogardus or Lichtenberger with little or no effect on their future research operations, and little guidance as to how it might be used. But this has gradually been changing. Theory has at least begun no longer to mean mainly a knowledge of "doctrines," but what matters far more, a set of patterns for habitual thinking. This change has, in my opinion, been considerably promoted by increased interest in more general theory, especially coming from study of the works of Weber and Durkheim and, though not so immediately sociological, of Freud. There has thus been the beginning at least, and to me a very encouraging beginning, of a process of coalescence of these types of more or less explicit theory which were really integrated importantly with research, into a more general theoretical tradition of some sophistication, really *the* tradition of a working professional group.

Compared to the natural sciences the amount of genuine empirical research done in our field is very modest indeed. Even so, it has been fairly substantial. But the most disappointing single thing about it has been the degree to which the results of this work have failed to be cumulative. The limitations of empirical research methods, limitations which are being overcome at a goodly rate, are in part responsible for this fact. But *probably the most crucial factor* has been precisely this lack of an adequate *working* theoretical tradition which is bred into the "bones" of empirical researchers themselves, so that "instinctively" the problems they work on, the hypotheses they frame and test, are such that the results, positive or negative, will have *significance* for a sufficiently generalized and integrated body of knowledge so that the mutual implications of many empirical studies will *play directly into each other.* There are, as I have noted, hopeful signs which point in this direction, but the responsibility on theory to promote this process is heavy indeed. So important is this point that I should like to have the view of the future role of theory in sociology, which I shall discuss in the remainder of this address, understood very largely in relation to it.

When, then, I turn to the discussion of the prospects of theory in our field I can hardly fail to express my own hope as well as a diagnosis. I hope to combine in my suggestions both a sense of the strategic significance of certain types of development, and a realistic sense of feasibility, if sufficient work by able people is done. I shall also be talking of the relatively near future, since the shape of our science two centuries hence, for instance, cannot, I fear, be realistically foreseen.

Here I should like to discuss five principal types or fields of theoretical development, which are by no means independent of one another; they actually overlap considerably as well as interact. They are:

(1) General theory, which I interpret primarily as the theory of the social system in its sociologically relevant aspects.

(2) The theory of motivation of social behavior and its bearing on the dynamic problems of social systems, its bearing both on the conditions of stability of social systems and the factors in their structural change. This of course involves the relations to the psychological level of analysis of personality and motivation.

(3) The theoretical bases of systematic comparative analysis of social structures on the various levels. This particularly involves the articulation with the anthropological analysis of culture.

(4) Special theories around particular empirical problem areas, the specific growing points of the field in empirical research. This involves their relations to general theory, and the bases of hypothesis construction in research.

(5) Last, but in no sense least, the "fitting" of theory to operational procedures of research and, vice versa, the adaption of the latter to theoretical needs.

The field of general theory presents peculiar difficulties of assessment in sociology. The era of what I have above called "proto-sociology" was, as I have noted, conspicuous for the prominence of speculative systems, of which that of Spencer is an adequate example. The strong and largely justified reaction against such systems combined with a general climate of opinion favorable to pragmatic empiricism, served to create in many quarters a very general scepticism of theory, particularly anything that called itself general or systematic theory, to say nothing of a *system* of theory. This wave of anti-theoretical empiricism has, I think fortunately, greatly subsided, but there is still marked reluctance to recognize the importance of high levels of generality. The most important recent expression of this latter sentiment, which in no sense should be confused with general opposition to theory, is that of my highly esteemed friend and former student, Robert Merton, first in his discussion paper directed to my own paper on the *Position of Sociological Theory,* two years ago, then repeated and amplified in the Introduction to his recent volume of essays.

The very first point must be the emphatic statement that what I mean by the place of general theory in the prospects of sociology is *not* the revival of speculative systems of the Spencerian type, and I feel that Merton's fears that this will be the result of the emphasis I have in mind are groundless. We have, I think, now progressed to a level of methodological sophistication adequate to protect ourselves against this pitfall.

The basic reason why general theory is so important is that the cumulative development of knowledge in a scientific field is a function of the degree of *generality of implications* by which it is possible to relate findings, interpretations, and hypotheses on different levels and in different specific empirical fields to each other. If there is to be a high degree of such generality there *must* on some level be a common conceptual scheme which makes the work of different investigators in a specific sub-field and those in different sub-fields commensurable.

The essential difficulty with the speculative systems has been their *premature closure* without the requisite theoretical clarification and integration, operational techniques or empirical evidence. This forced them to use empirical materials in a purely illustrative way without systematic verification of *general* propositions or the possibility of empirical evidence leading to modification of the theory. Put a little differently, they presumed to set up a theoretical system instead of a systematic conceptual scheme.

It seems quite clear, that in the sense of mechanics a *theoretical system* is *not* now or foreseeably possible in the sociological field. The difficulties Pareto's attempt encountered indicate that. But a *conceptual scheme* in a partially articulated form exists now and is for practical purposes in common use; its further refinement and development is imperative for the welfare of our field, and is entirely feasible.

In order to make clear what I mean, I would first like to note that there is a variety of ways in which what I am calling general theory can fruitfully influence research in the direction of making its results more cumulative. The first is what may be called a set of general categories of orientation to observation and problem choice in the field which defines its major problem areas and the directions in which to look for concealed factors and variables in explanation. Thus modern anthropology, by the "cultural point of view," heavily documented with comparative material, has clearly demonstrated the limits of purely biological explanations of human behavior and taught us to look to the processes by which culturally patterned modes are learned, transmitted and created. Similarly in our own field the reorientation particularly associated with the names of Durkheim and Weber showed the inadequacy of the "utilitarian" framework for the understanding of many social phenomena and made us look to "institutional" levels—a reorientation which is indeed the birthright of sociology. Finally, in the field of motivation, the influence of Freud's perspective has been immense.

Starting from such very broad orientation perspectives there are varying possible degrees of further specification. At any rate in a field like ours it seems impossible to stop there. The very basis on which the utilitarian framework was seen to be *theoretically* as well as empirically inadequate, required a clarification of the structure of systems of social action which went considerably farther than just indicating a new direction of interest or significance. It spelled out certain inherent relationships of the components of such systems which among many other things demonstrated the *need* for a theory of motivation on the psychological level of the general character of what Freud has provided.

This kind of structural "spelling out" narrows the range of theoretical arbitrariness. There are firmly specific points in the system of implications against which empirical results can be measured and evaluated. That is where a well-structured empirical problem is formulated. If the facts then, when properly stated and validated, turn out to be contrary to the theoretical expectation, something must be modified in the theory.

In the early stages these "islands" of theoretical implication may be scattered far apart on the sea of fact and so vaguely and generally seen that only relatively broad empirical statements are directly relevant to them. This is true of the interpretation of economic motivation which I will cite presently. But with refinement of general theoretical analysis, and the accumulation of empirical evidence directly relevant to it, the islands get closer and closer together, and their topography becomes more sharply defined. It becomes more and more difficult and unnecessary to navigate in the uncharted waters of unanalyzed fact without bumping into or at least orienting to several of them.

The development of general theory in this sense is a matter of degree. But in *proportion* as it develops, the generality of implication increases and the "degree of empiricism," to quote a phrase of President Conant's, is reduced. It is precisely the existence of such a general theoretical framework, the more so the further it has developed, which makes the kind of work at the middle theory level which Merton advocates maximally fruitful. For it is by virtue of their connections with these "islands" of general theoretical knowledge once demonstrated that their overlaps and their mutual implications for each other lead to their incorporation into a more general and consistent body of knowledge.

At the *end* of this road of increasing frequency and specificity of the islands of theoretical knowledge lies the ideal state, scientifically speaking, where *most* actual operational hypotheses of empirical research are directly derived from a general system of theory. On any broad front, to my knowledge, only in physics has this state been attained in any science. *We* cannot expect to be anywhere nearly in sight of it. But it does not follow that, distant as we are from that goal, steps in that *direction* are futile. Quite the contrary, any real step in that direction is an advance. Only at this *end* point do the islands merge into a continental land mass.

At the very least, then, general theory can provide a broadly orienting framework. It can also help to provide a common language to facilitate communication between workers in different branches of the field. It can serve to codify, interrelate and make available a vast amount of existing empirical knowledge. It also serves to call attention to gaps in our knowledge, and to provide canons for the criticism of theories and empirical generalizations. Finally, even if they cannot be systematically derived, it is indispensable to the systematic clarification of problems and the fruitful formulation of hypotheses. It is this organizing power of generalized theory even on its present levels which has made it possible for even a student like myself, who has done only a little actual empirical research, to illuminate a good many empirical problems and formulate suggestive hypotheses in several fields.

Though it is not possible to take time to discuss them adequately for those not already familiar with the fields, I should like to cite two examples from my own experience. The first is the reorientation of thinking about the field of the motivation of economic activity. The heritage of the classical economics and the utilitarian frame of reference, integrated with the central ideology of our society, had put the problem of the "incentives" involved in the "profit system" in a very particular way which had become the object of much controversy. Application of the emerging general theory of the institutionalization of motivation, specifically pointed up by the analysis of the contrast between the orientation of the professional groups and that of the business world, made it possible to work out a very fruitful reorientation to this range of problems. This new view eliminates the alleged absoluteness of the orientation to "self-interest" held to be inherent in "human nature." It emphasizes the crucial role of institutional definitions of the situation and the ways in which they channel many different components of a total motivation system into the path of conformity with institutionalized expectations. Without the general theoretical reorientation stemming mainly from Durkheim and Weber, this restructuring of the problem of economic motivation would not have been possible.

The second example illustrates the procedure by which it has become possible to make use of psychological knowledge in analyzing social phenomena without resort to certain kinds of "psychological interpretations" of the type which most sociologists have quite correctly repudiated. Such a phenomenon is the American "youth culture" with its rebellion against adult standards and control, its compulsive conformity within the peer group, its romanticism and its irresponsibility. Structural analysis of the American family system as the primary field of socialization of the child provides the primary setting. This in turn must be seen both in the perspective of the comparative variability of kinship structures and of the articulation of the family with other elements of our own social structure, notably the occupational role of the father. Only when this structural setting has been carefully analyzed in sociological terms does it become safe to bring in analysis of the operation of psychological mechanisms in terms derived particularly from psychoanalytic theory, and to make such statements as that the "revolt of youth" contains typically an element of reaction-formation against dependency needs with certain types of consequences. Again this type of analysis would not have been possible without the general reorientation of thinking about the relations between social structure and the psychological aspects of behavior which has resulted from the developments in general theory in the last generation or more; including explicit use of the contributions of Freud.

Perhaps I may pause in midpassage to apologize for inflicting on you on such an occasion, when your well-filled stomachs predispose you to relaxation rather than close attention, such an abstruse theoretical discourse. I feel the apology is necessary since what I am about to inflict on you is even more abstruse than what has gone before. Since I am emphasizing the integration of theory with empirical research, I might suggest that someone among you might want to undertake a little research project to determine the impact on a well-fed group of sociologists of such a discourse. I might suggest the following four categories for his classification.

(1) Those who have understood what I have said, whether they approve of it or not.

(2) Those who *think* they have understood it.

(3) Those who do not think they have but wish they had, and

(4) Those who didn't understand, know it and are glad of it.

I can only hope that the overwhelming majority will not be found to fall in the fourth category.

With relatively little alteration, everything I have said up to this point had been written, and has deliberately been left standing, when I underwent an important personal experience which produced what I hope will prove to be a significant theoretical advance precisely in the field of general theory. With the very able collaboration of several of my own Harvard colleagues and of Professors Tolman of California and Shils of Chicago, the present semester has been devoted to attempting to practice what I have preached, namely to press forward with systematic work in the field of general theory. Partly because of the intrinsic importance of the fields, partly because of its urgency in a department committed to the synthesis of sociology with parts of psychology and anthropology, we have been devoting our principal energies to the interrelations and common ground of the three branches of the larger field of social relations.

This new development, which is still too new for anything like adequate assessment, seems to consist essentially in a method of considerably increasing the number of theoretically known islands in the sea of social phenomena and thereby narrowing the stretches of uncharted water between them. The essential new insight, which unfortunately is not easy to state, concerns the most general aspects of the conception of the components of systems of social action and their relations to each other.

It seems to have been the previous assumption, largely implicit, for instance, in the thinking of Weber, of W. I. Thomas, and in my own, that there was, as it were, *one* "action-equation." The actor was placed on one side—"oriented to" a situation or a world of objects which constituted the other side. The difficulty concerned the status of "values" in action, not as the motivational *act* of "evaluation" of an object, but as the *standard* by which it was evaluated—in short, the concept "value-attitudes" which some of you will remember from my *Structure of Social Action.* I, following Weber, had tended to put value-standards or modes of value-orientation into the actor. Thomas and Znaniecki in their basic distinction between attitudes and values had put them into the object-system.

We have all long been aware that there were three main problem foci in the most general theory of human behavior which we may most generally call those of personality, of culture, and of social structure. But in spite of this awareness, I think we have tended to follow the biological model of thought—an organism and its environment, an actor and his situations. We have not *really* treated culture as independent, or if that has been done, as by some anthropologists, the tendency has been for them in turn to absorb either personality or social structure *into* culture, especially the latter, to the great discomfort of many sociologists. What we have done, which I wish to report is, I think, to take an important step toward drawing out for *working* theory the implications of the fundamental fact that *man is a culture-bearing animal.*

Our conclusion then is that value-standards or modes of value-orientation should be treated as a *distinct* range of components of action. In the older view the basic components could be set forth in a single "table" by classifying the modes of action or motivational orientation which we have found it convenient to distinguish as cognitive mapping (in Tolman's sense), cathectic (in the psychoanalytic sense) and evaluative, against a classification of the significant aspects or modalities of objects. These latter we have classified as quality complexes or attributes of persons and collectivities, action or performance complexes, and non-human environmental factors. By adding values as a fourth column to this classification, this had seemed to yield an adequate paradigm for the structural components of action-systems.

But something about this paradigm did not quite "click." It almost suddenly occurred to us to "pull" the value-element out and put it into a separate range, with a classification of its own into three modes of value-orientation: cognitive (in the *standard,* not content, sense), appreciative and moral. This gave us a paradigm of *three* "dimensions" in which *each* of the three ranges or sets of modes is classified against *each* of the other two.

This transformation opened up new possibilities of logical development and elaboration which are much too complex and technical to enter into here. Indeed the implications are as yet only very incompletely worked out or critically evaluated and it will be many months before they are in shape for publication. But certain of them are sufficiently clear to give *me* at any rate the conviction that they are of considerable importance, and taken together, will constitute a substantial further step in the direction of unifying our theoretical knowledge and broadening the range of generality of implication, with the probable consequence of contributing substantially to the cumulativeness of our empirical research.

Certain of these implications, which in broad outline already seem clear, touch two of the subjects on which I intended to speak anyway and can, I think, now speak much better. The first of these is the very fundamental one of the connection of the theories of motivation and personality structure on the psychological level with the sociological analysis of social structure. The vital importance of this connection is evident to all of us, and many sociologists have been working away at the field for a long time. Seen in the perspective of the years, I think great progress has been made. The kind of impasse where "psychology is psychology" and "sociology is sociology" and "never the twain shall meet," which was a far from uncommon feeling in the early stages of my career, has almost evaporated. There is a rapidly increasing and broadening area of mutual supplementation.

What has happened in our group opens up, I think, a way to eliminating the sources of some of the remaining theoretical difficulties in this field, and still more important, building the foundations for establishing more direct and specific connections than we have hitherto been able to attain. I should like to indicate some of these in two fields.

The first is the less radical. We have long suspected, indeed on some level, known, that the basic structure of the human personality was intimately involved with the social structure as well as vice versa. Indeed some have gone so far as to consider personality to be a direct "microcosm" of the society. Now, however, we have begun to achieve a considerable clarification of the bases on which this intimacy of involvement rests, and to bring personality, conceptually as well as genetically, into relation with social structure. It goes back essentially to the insight that the major axis around which the expectation-system of any personality becomes organized in the process of socialization is its *interlocking* with the expectation-systems of others, so that the mutuality of socially structured relationship patterns can no longer be thought of as a *resultant* of the motivation-systems of a plurality of actors, but becomes directly and fundamentally *constitutive* of those motivation systems. It has seemed to us possible in terms of this reoriented conception to bring large parts both of Tolman's type of behavior theory and the psychoanalytic type of theory of personality, including such related versions as that of Murray, together in a close relation to sociological theory. Perhaps the farthest we had dared to go before was to say something like that we considered social structure and personality were very closely related and intimately *interacting* systems of human action. Now I think it will probably prove safe to say that they are in a theoretical sense different phases or aspects of the *same* fundamental action-system. This does not in the least mean, I hasten to add, that personality is in danger of being "absorbed" into the social system, as one version of Durkheim's theory seemed to indicate. The distinction between the personality "level" of the organization of action and the social system level remains as vital as it ever was. But the *theoretical* continuity, and hence the possibility of using psychological theory in the motivation field for sociological explanation, have been greatly enhanced.

The second point I had in mind is essentially an extension of this one or an application of it. As those of you familiar with some of my own writing since the *Structure of Social Action* know, for some years I have been "playing" with a scheme of what I have found it convenient to call "pattern variables" in the field of social structure, which were originally derived by an analytical breakdown of Toennies' *Gemeinschaft-Gesellschaft* pair into what seemed to be more elementary components. This yielded such distinctions as that between universalism, as illustrated in technical competence or the "rule of law," and particularism as given in kinship or friendship relations, or to take another case, between the "functional specificity" of an economic exchange relationship and the "functional diffuseness" of marriage. Thus to take an illustration from my own work, the judgment of his technical competence on which the choice of a physician is supposed to rest is a universalistic criterion. Deviantly from the ideal pattern, however, some people choose a physician because he is Mary Smith's brother-in-law. This would be a particularistic criterion. Similarly the basis on which a physician may validate his claim to confidential information about his patient's private life is that it is necessary if he is to perform the specific function of caring for the patient's health. But the basis of a wife's claim to a truthful answer to the question "what were you doing last night that kept you out till three in the morning?" is the generally diffuse obligation of loyalty in the marriage relationship.

Again I cannot take time to go into the technicalities. But the theoretical development of which I have spoken has already indicated two significant results. First it has brought a scheme of five such pattern variables—the four I had been using, with the addition of the distinction of ascription and achievement which Linton first introduced into our conceptual armory—into a direct and fundamental relation to the structure of action systems themselves. These concepts can now be systematically derived from the basic frame of reference of action theory, which was not previously possible.

Secondly, however, it appears that the same basic distinctions, which were all worked out for the analysis of *social* structure, can, when rephrased in accord with psychological perspective, be identified as fundamental points of reference for the structuring of personality also. Thus what sociologically is called universalism in a social role definition can be psychologically interpreted as the impact of the mechanism of generalization in object-orientation and object choice. Correspondingly, what on the sociological level has been called the institutionalization of "affective neutrality" turns out to be essentially the same as the imposition of renunciation of immediate gratification in the interests of the disciplined organization and longer-run goals of the personality.

If this correspondence holds up, and I feel confident that it will, its implications for social science may be far reaching. For what these variables do on the personality level is to serve as foci for the structuring of the system of predispositions or needs. But it is precisely this aspect of psychological theory which is of most importance for the sociologist since it yields the *differentiations* of motivational orientation which are crucial to the understanding of socially structured behavior. *Empirically* we have known a good deal about these differentiations, but *theoretically* we have not been able to connect them up in a systematically generalized way. It looks as though an important step in this direction had now become possible. With regard to its potential importance, I may only mention the extent to which studies of the distribution of attitudes have come to occupy a central place in the empirical work both of sociologists and of social psychologists. The connection of these distribution data with the social structure on the one hand and the structure of motivational predispositions on the other has had to a high degree to be treated in empirically *ad hoc* terms. Any step in the direction of "reducing the degree of empiricism" in such an area will constitute a substantial scientific advance. I think it is probable that such an advance is in sight, which, if validated, will have developed from work in *general* theory.

Let us now turn to the other major theoretical field, the systematization of the bases for *comparative* analysis of social structures. First I should like to call attention to the acute embarrassment we have had to suffer in this field. On the level of what I have made bold to call "proto-sociology" it was thought that this problem was solved by the implications of the evolutionary formulae which arranged all possible structural types in a neat evolutionary series which *ipso facto* established both their comparability and their dynamic relationships. Unfortunately, from one point of view, this synthesis turned out to be premature; but from another this was fortunate, for in one sense the realization of this fact was the starting point of the transition from proto-sociology to real sociology. At any rate, in spite of the magnificence of Max Weber's attempt, the basic classificatory problem, the solution of which must underlie the achievement of high theoretical generality in much of our field, has remained basically unsolved.

As so often happens there has been a good deal of underground ferment going on in such a field before the results have begun to become widely visible. There are, I think, signs of important progress. One of these is the great step toward the systematization of the variability of kinship structure which our anthropological colleague, Professor Murdock, has reported in his recent book. For one critically important structural field we can now say that many of the basic problems have been solved. But this still leaves much to be worked out, particularly in the fields of more complex institutional variability in the literate societies, in such areas as occupation, religion, formal organization, social stratification and government.

Just as in the problem of the motivation of socially structured behavior our relations to psychology become peculiarly crucial and intimate, so in that of systematizing the structural variability of social systems, our relations to anthropology are correspondingly crucial. This, of course, is because of the ways in which the basic cultural orientations underlie and interpenetrate the structuring of social systems on the action level. Anything, therefore, which can help to clarify the most fundamental problems of the ways in which values and other cultural orientation elements are involved in action systems should sooner or later contribute to this sociological problem.

In general, anthropological theory in the culture field has in this respect been disappointing, not that it has not provided many empirical insights, which it certainly has, but precisely in terms of the present interest in systematization. I am happy to report that my colleague, Dr. Florence Kluckhohn has, in yet unpublished work, made some promising suggestions the implications of which will, I think, turn out to be of great importance. In what follows I wish gratefully to acknowledge my debt to her work.

In this connection it is important that the central new theoretical insight to which I have referred above came precisely in this field, in a new view of the way values are related to action. The essence of this is the *analytical* independence of value-orientation relative to the psychological aspects of motivation. It introduces an element of "play" into what had previously been a much more rigid relation, this rigidity having much to do with the unfortunate clash of sociological and anthropological "imperialisms."

The independence of value-orientation encourages the search for elements of structural focus in that area. The "problem areas" of value-choice seem to provide one set of such foci, that is, the evaluation of man's relation to the natural environment, to his biological nature and the like. But along with these there are foci differentiating the alternatives of the basic "directionality" of value-orientation itself. In this connection, it has become possible to see that a fundamental congruence exists between at least one part in the set of "pattern variables" mentioned above, that of universalism and particularism, and Max Weber's distinction, which runs throughout his sociology of religion, between transcendent and immanent orientations, the Western, especially Calvinistic orientation, illustrating the former, the Chinese the latter.

Bringing such a differentiation in relation to basic orientation-foci together with the problem foci seems to provide at least an initial and tentative basis for working out a systematic classification of some major possibilities of cultural orientation in their relevance to differentiations of social structure. Then through the congruence of these with the possible combinations of the values of pattern variables in the structuring of social roles themselves, it seems possible further to clarify some of the modes of articulation of the variability of cultural orientations with that of the structure of the social systems which are their bearers and, in the processes of culture change, their creators.

In this field even more than that of the relation between social structure and motivation, what I am in a position to give you now is not a report of theoretical work accomplished, but a vision of what *can* be accomplished if the requisite hard and competent work is done. This vision is not, however, I think, mere wishful thinking. I think we have gone far enough so that we can see real possibilities. We are in a position to organize a directed and concerted effort with definite goals, not merely to grope about in the hope that something will come out of it.

It seems to me that the importance of progress in this field of structural analysis which attempts to establish the bases of comparability of social structures can scarcely be exaggerated. I have indeed felt for some time that the fact that we had not been able to go farther in this direction was a more serious barrier to the all-important generality and cumulativeness of our knowledge than was the difficulty of adequately linking the analysis of social structure to psychological levels of the understanding of motivation.

The problem of the importance of structural variability and its analysis is most obvious when we are dealing with the broad structural contrasts between widely differing societies. It is, however, a serious error to suppose that its importance is confined to this level. Every society, seen close to, is to an important degree a *microcosm* of the various possibilities of the structuring of human relationships all over the world and throughout history. The variability *within* the same society, though subtler and less easy to analyze, is none the less authentic.

Of course in any one society *some* possibilities of structural variability are excluded altogether, or can appear only as radically deviant phenomena. But it must not be assumed that in spite of its conformity to a broad general type, the American middle-class family for instance is, *precisely in terms of social structure*, a uniform cut-and-dried thing. It is a complex of many importantly variant sub-types. For some sociological problems it may be precisely the structural differentiations between and distribution of these sub-types which constitute the most important data. To say merely that these are middle-class families will not solve such problems. But it is not necessary for the sociologist to stop there and resort to "purely psychological" considerations. He can and should push his distinctive type of structural analysis on down to these levels of "minor" variability.

In the present state of knowledge, or that of the foreseeable future, we are bound to a "structural-functional" level of theory. There will continue to be long stretches of open water between our islands of validated theory. In this situation we cannot achieve a high level of dynamic generalization for processes and interdependences even *within* the same society, unless our ranges of structural variability are really systematized so that when we get a shift from one to another we know *what* has changed, to *what* and *in what degree*. This order of systematization can, like all theoretical work, be verified only by empirical research. But experience shows that it cannot be worked out by sheer ad hoc empirical induction, letting the facts reveal their own pattern. It must be worked out by rigorous theoretical analysis, continually stimulating and being checked by empirical research. In sum I think this is one of the very few most vital areas for the development of sociological theory, and here as in the other I think the prospects are good.

The above two broad areas of prospective theoretical advance are so close to the most general of general theory that they would scarcely qualify as falling within the area of "special theories," which was the fourth area about which I wanted to talk. I have precisely taken so much time to discuss these because of their importance for more special theories. I am very far indeed from wishing to disparage the importance of this more special and in one sense more modest type of theoretical work; quite the contrary. It is here that the growing points of theory in their direct working interaction with empirical research are to be found. If the state of affairs at that level cannot be healthy we should indeed despair of our science.

I will go farther. It seems to me precisely that the fact that real working theory at the research levels did not exist and was not developed in connection with them was perhaps the most telling symptom that the "speculative systems" of which I have spoken were only pseudo-scientific, not genuinely so. Most emphatically I wish to say that the general theory on which I have placed such emphasis can *only* be justified in so far as it "spells out" on the research level, providing the more generalized conceptual basis for the frames of reference, problem statements and hypotheses, and many of the operating concepts of research. In these terms it underlies the problem-setting of research, it provides criteria of more generalized significance of the problem and its empirical solution, it provides the basis on which the results of one empirical study become fruitful, not merely in the particular empirical field itself, but beyond it for other fields; that is, for what above I have called its *generality of implication*. In my opinion it is precisely because of its orientation to a sound tradition of general theory, however incomplete and faulty, that the particular theories which are developing so rapidly in many branches of the field are so highly important and promising for the future. Let us, by all means, work most intensively on the middle theory level. That way lies real maturity as a science, and the ultimate test of whether the general theory is any good. And of course many of the most important contributions to general theory will come from this source.

This brings me finally to the fifth point on my agenda, the fitting in of theory with the operational procedures of research. Thus far I have been talking to you about theory, but I was careful to note at the outset that however important an ingredient of the scientific brew theory may be, it is only one of the ingredients. If it is to be *scientific* theory it must be tied in, in the closest possible manner, with the techniques of empirical research by which alone we can come to know whether our theoretical ideas are "really so" or just speculations of peculiar if not disordered minds.

Anyone who has observed the social science scene in this country over the past quarter century cannot fail to be impressed by the very great development of research technique in our field, in very many of its branches. Sampling has come in to make it possible for the social scientist to manufacture his own statistical data, instead of having to work only with the by-products of other interests. Techniques of statistical analysis themselves have undergone an immense amount of refinement, for example, in the development of scaling procedures. An altogether new level has already been attained in the collection and processing of raw data, as through questionnaire and interview, and the development of coding skills and the like. I used to think that the construction of a questionnaire was something any old dub could dream up if he only knew what information he wanted. I have learned better. The whole immense development of interviewing techniques with its range from psychoanalysis to Gallup and Roper lies almost within the time period we are talking about. The possibilities of the use of projective techniques in *sociological* research are definitely exciting. The Cross-Cultural Survey (now rechristened) and Mr. Watson of I.B.M. vie with each other to create more elaborate gadgets for the social scientist to play with. We have even, as in the communications and the small groups fields, begun to get somewhere with relatively rigorous experimental methods in sociology, no longer only in psychology among the sciences of human behavior.

This whole development is, in my opinion, in the larger picture *at least* as important as that of theory. It is, furthermore, exceedingly impressive, not merely for its accomplishments to date, important as these are, but *still more* for its promise for the future. There is a veritable ferment of invention going on in this area which is in the very best American tradition.

If I correctly assess the recipe for a really good brew of social science it is *absolutely imperative* that these two basic ingredients should get together and blend with each other. I do not think it fair to say that we are still in the stage of proto-science. But we are unquestionably in that of a distinctly *immature* science. If it is really to grow up and not regress into either of the two futilities of empiricist sterility or empirically irrelevant speculation, the synthesis must take place. In this as in other respects the beginning certainly has already been made but we must be quite clear that it is *only* a beginning.

This is a point where a division of labor is very much in order. It surely is not reasonable to suppose that all sociologists should become fully qualified specialists in theory and the most highly skilled research technicians at the same time. Some will, indeed must, have high orders of competence on both sides, but this will not be true of all. But the essential is that there should be a *genuine* division of labor. That means that all parties should directly contribute to the effectiveness of the whole. For the theoretical side this imposes an obligation to get together with the best research people and make every effort to make their theory researchable in the highest sense. For the research technician it implies the obligation to fit his operational procedures to the needs of theory as closely as he can.

It has been in the nature of the circumstances and processes of the historical development of theory that much of its empirical relevance has heretofore been made clear and explicit only on the level of "broad" observations of fact which were not checked and elaborated by really technical procedures. The value of this, as for instance it has appeared in the comparative institutional field, should not be minimized. But clearly this order of empirical validation is *only* a beginning. For opening the doors to much greater progress it is necessary to be able to put the relevant content of theory in terms which the empirical research operator can directly build into his technical operations. This is a major reason why the middle theories are so important, because it is on that level that theory will get *directly* into research techniques and vice versa. Again in this field the beginnings I happen to know about are sufficiently promising so that I think we can say that the prospects are good.

Theory has its justification *only* as part of the larger total of sociological science as a whole. Perhaps in closing I may be permitted a few general remarks about the prospects of sociology as a science. I have great confidence that they are good, a solider and stronger confidence than at any time in my own professional lifetime, provided of course that the social setting for its development remains reasonably stable and favorable.

These prospects are, however, bound up with the fulfillment of certain internal as well as external conditions. One of the most important of these on which I would like to say a word, is a proper balance between fundamental research, including its theoretical aspect, and applied or "engineering" work. This problem is of course of particular interest to our friends in the Conference on Family Welfare. Both the urgencies of the times and the nature of our American ethos make it unthinkable that social scientists as a professional group should shirk their social responsibilities. They, like the medical profession, must do what they can where they are needed. Indeed it is only on this assumption that they will do so that not only the very considerable financial investment of society in their work, but the interferences in other people's affairs which are inevitably bound up with our research, can be justified.

It is not a question of *whether* we try to live up to our social responsibilities, but of *how.* If we should put the overwhelming bulk of our resources, especially of trained talent, into immediately practical problems it would do some good, but I have no doubt that it would have to be at the expense of our greater usefulness to society in the future. For it is only by systematic work on problems where the probable *scientific* significance has priority over any immediate possibility of application that the greatest and most rapid scientific advance can be made. And it is in proportion as sociology attains stature as a science, with a highly generalized and integrated body of fundamental knowledge, that practical usefulness far beyond the present levels will become possible. This conclusion follows most directly from the role of theory, as I have tried to outline it above. If the prospects of sociological theory are good, so are, I am convinced, those of sociology as a science, but *only* if the scientifically fundamental work is done. Let us, by all means, not be stingy with the few golden eggs we now have. But let us also breed a flock of geese of the sort that we can hope will lay many more than we have yet dreamed of.

One final word. Like all branches of American culture, the roots of sociology as a science are deep in Europe. Yet I like to think of sociology as in some sense peculiarly an American discipline, or at least an American opportunity. There is no doubt that we have the leadership now. Our very lack of traditionalism perhaps makes it in some ways easier for us than for some others to delve deeply into the mysteries of how human action in society ticks. We certainly have all the makings for developing the technical know-how of research. We are good at organization which is coming to play an increasingly indispensable part in research.

It is my judgment that a great opportunity exists. Things have gone far enough so that it seems likely that sociology, in the closest connection with its sister-sciences of psychology and anthropology, stands near the beginning of one of those important configurations of culture growth which Professor Kroeber has so illuminatingly analyzed. Can American sociology seize this opportunity? One of our greatest national resources is the capacity to rise to a great challenge once it is put before us.

We can do it if we can put together the right *combination* of ingredients of the brew. Americans as scientists generally have been exceptionally strong on experimental work and empirical research. I have no doubt whatever of the capacity of American sociologists in this respect. But as *theorists* Americans have, relative to Europeans, not been so strong—hence the *special* challenge of the theoretical development of our field which justifies the theme of this address. If we American sociologists can rise to this part of the challenge the job will really get done. We are not in the habit of listening too carefully to the timid souls who say, why try, it can't be done. I think we have already taken up the challenge all along the line. "The sociology," as my children called it, is not *about* to begin. It has been gathering force for a generation and is now really under way.

3

Middle-Range Theories*

Robert K. Merton

Like so many words that are bandied about, the word theory threatens to become meaningless. Because its referents are so diverse—including everything from minor working hypotheses, through comprehensive but vague and unordered speculations, to axiomatic systems of thought—use of the word often obscures rather than creates understanding.

Throughout this book, the term *sociological theory* refers to logically interconnected sets of propositions from which empirical uniformities can be derived. Throughout we focus on what I have *called theories of the middle range:* theories that lie between the minor but necessary working hypotheses that evolve in abundance during day-to-day research and the all-inclusive systematic efforts to develop a unified theory that will explain all the observed uniformities of social behavior, social organization and social change.

Middle-range theory is principally used in sociology to guide empirical inquiry. It is intermediate to general theories of social systems which are too remote from particular classes of social behavior, organization and change to account for what is observed and to those detailed orderly descriptions of particulars that are not generalized at all. Middle-range theory involves abstractions, of course, but they are close enough to observed data to be incorporated in propositions that permit empirical testing. Middle-range theories deal with delimited aspects of social phenomena, as is indicated by their labels. One speaks of a theory of reference groups, of social mobility, or role-conflict and of the formation of social norms just as one speaks of a theory of prices, a germ theory of disease, or a kinetic theory of gases.

The seminal ideas in such theories are characteristically simple: consider Gilbert on magnetism, Boyle on atmospheric pressure, or Darwin on the formation of coral atolls. Gilbert *begins* with the relatively simple idea that the earth may be conceived as a magnet; Boyle, with the simple idea that the atmosphere may be conceived as a 'sea of air'; Darwin, with the idea that one can conceive of the atolls as upward and outward growths of coral over islands that had long since subsided into the sea. Each of these theories provides an image that gives rise to inferences. To take but one case: if the atmosphere is thought of as a sea of air, then, as Pascal inferred, there should be less air pressure on a mountain top than at its base. The initial idea thus suggests specific hypotheses which are tested by seeing whether the inferences from them are empirically confirmed. The idea itself is tested for its fruitfulness by noting the range

*Reprinted with the permission of The Free Press, a Division of Simon & Schuster, Inc., from *Social Theory and Social Structure,* Revised & Enlarged Edition by Robert K. Merton.

of theoretical problems and hypotheses that allow one to identify new characteristics of atmospheric pressure.

In much the same fashion, the theory of reference groups and relative deprivation starts with the simple idea, initiated by James, Baldwin, and Mead and developed by Hyman and Stouffer, that people take the standards of significant others as a basis for self-appraisal and evaluation. Some of the inferences drawn from this idea are at odds with common-sense expectations based upon an unexamined set of 'self-evident' assumptions. Common sense, for example, would suggest that the greater the actual loss experienced by a family in a mass disaster, the more acutely it will feel deprived. This belief is based on the unexamined assumption that the magnitude of objective loss is related linearly to the subjective appraisal of the loss and that this appraisal is confined to one's own experience. But the theory of relative deprivation leads to quite a different hypothesis—that self-appraisals depend upon people's comparisons of their own situation with that of other people perceived as being comparable to themselves. This theory therefore suggests that, under specifiable conditions, families suffering serious losses will feel less deprived than those suffering smaller losses if they are in situations leading them to compare themselves to people suffering even more severe losses. For example, it is people in the area of greatest impact of a disaster who, though substantially deprived themselves, are most apt to see others around them who are even more severely deprived. Empirical inquiry supports the theory of relative deprivation rather than the common-sense assumptions: "the feeling of being relatively *better off* than others *increases with objective loss up* to the category of highest loss" and only then declines. This pattern is reinforced by the tendency of public communications to focus on "the *most extreme sufferers* [which] tends to fix them as a reference group against which even other sufferers can compare themselves favorably." As the inquiry develops, it is found that these patterns of self-appraisal in turn affect the distribution of morale in the community of survivors and their motivation to help others. Within a particular *class* of behavior, therefore, the theory of relative deprivation directs us to a set of hypotheses that can be empirically tested. The confirmed conclusion can then be put simply enough: when few are hurt to much the same extent, the pain and loss of each seems great; where many are hurt in greatly varying degree, even fairly large losses seem small as they are compared with far larger ones. The probability that comparisons will be made is affected by the differing visibility of losses of greater and less extent.

The specificity of this example should not obscure the more general character of middle-range theory. Obviously, behavior of people confronted with a mass disaster is only one of an indefinitely large array of particular situations to which the theory of reference groups can be instructively applied, just as is the case with the theory of change in social stratification, the theory of authority, the theory of institutional interdependence, or the theory of anomie. But it is equally clear that such middle-range theories have not been logically *derived* from a single all-embracing theory of social systems, though once developed they may be consistent with one. Furthermore, each theory is more than a mere empirical generalization—an isolated proposition summarizing observed uniformities of relationships between two or more variables. A theory comprises a set of assumptions from which empirical generalizations have themselves been derived.

Another case of middle-range theory in sociology may help us to identify its character and uses. The theory of role-sets begins with an image of how social status is organized in the social structure. This image is as simple as Boyle's image of the atmosphere as a sea of air or Gilbert's image of the earth as a magnet. As with all middle-range theories, however, the proof is in the using not in the immediate response to the originating ideas as obvious or odd, as derived from more general theory or conceived of to deal with a particular class of problems.

Despite the very diverse meanings attached to the concept of *social status,* one sociological tradition consistently uses it to refer to a position in a social system, with its distinctive array of designated rights and obligations. In this tradition, as exemplified by Ralph Linton, the related concept of *social role* refers to the behavior of status-occupants that is oriented toward the patterned expectations of others (who accord the rights and exact the obligations). Linton, like others in this tradition, went on to state the long recognized and basic observation that each person in society inevitably occupies multiple statuses and that each of these statuses has its associated role.

It is at this point that the imagery of the role-set theory departs from this long-established tradition. The difference is initially a small one—some might say so small as to be insignificant—but the shift in the angle of vision leads to successively more fundamental theoretical differences. Role-set theory begins with the concept that each social status involves not a single associated role, but an array of roles. This feature of social structure gives rise to the concept of role-set: that complement of social relationships in which persons are involved simply because they occupy a particular social status. Thus, a person in the status of medical student plays not only the role of student *vis-à-vis* the correlative status of his teachers, but also an array of other roles relating him diversely to others in the system: other students, physicians, nurses, social workers, medical technicians, and the like. Again, the status of school teacher has its distinctive role-set which relates the teacher not only to the correlative status, pupil, but also to colleagues, the school principal and superintendent, the Board of Education, professional associations and, in the United States, local patriotic organizations.

Notice that the role-set differs from what sociologists have long described as 'multiple roles.' The latter term has traditionally referred not to the complex of roles associated with a single social status but to the various social statuses (often, in different institutional spheres) in which people find themselves—for example, one person might have the diverse statuses of physician, husband, father, professor, church elder, Conservative Party member and army captain. (This complement of distinct statuses of a person, each with its own role-set, is a status-set.)

Up to this point, the concept of role-set is *merely* an image for thinking about a component of the social structure. But this image is a beginning, not an end, for it leads directly to certain analytical problems. The notion of the role-set at once leads to the inference that social structures confront men with the task of articulating the components of countless role-sets—that is, the functional task of managing somehow to organize these so that an appreciable degree of social regularity obtains, sufficient to enable most people most of the time to go about their business without becoming paralyzed by extreme conflicts in their role-sets.

If this relatively simple idea of role-set has theoretical worth, it should generate distinctive problems for sociological inquiry. The concept of role-set does this. It raises the general but definite problem of identifying the social mechanisms—that is, the social processes having designated consequences for designated parts of the social structure—which articulate the expectations of those in the role-set sufficiently to reduce conflicts for the occupant of a status. It generates the further problem of discovering how these mechanisms come into being, so that we can also explain why the mechanisms do not operate effectively or fail to emerge at all in some social systems. Finally, like the theory of atmospheric pressure, the theory of role-set points directly to relevant empirical research. Monographs on the workings of diverse types of formal organization have developed empirically-based theoretical extensions of how role-sets operate in practice.

The theory of role-sets illustrates another aspect of sociological theories of the middle range. They are frequently consistent with a variety of so-called systems of sociological theory. So far as one can tell, the theory of role-sets is not inconsistent with such broad theoretical orientations as Marxist theory, functional analysis, social behaviorism, Sorokin's integral sociology, or Parsons' theory of action. This may be a horrendous observation for those of us who have been trained to believe that systems of sociological thought are logically close-knit and mutually exclusive sets of doctrine. But in fact, as we shall note later in this introduction, comprehensive sociological theories are sufficiently loose-knit, internally diversified, and mutually overlapping that *a given theory of the middle range*, which has a measure of empirical confirmation, can often be subsumed under comprehensive theories which are themselves discrepant in certain respects.

This reasonably unorthodox opinion can be illustrated by reexamining the theory of role-sets as a middle-range theory. We depart from the traditional concept by assuming that a single status in society involves, not a single role, but an array of associated roles, relating the status-occupant to diverse others. Second, we note that this concept of the role-set gives rise to distinctive theoretical problems, hypotheses, and so to empirical inquiry. One basic problem is that of identifying the social mechanisms which articulate the role-set and reduce conflicts among roles. Third, the concept of the role-set directs our attention to the structural problem of identifying the social arrangements which integrate as well as oppose the expectations of various members of the role-set. The concept of multiple roles, on the other hand, confines our attention to a different and no doubt important issue: how do *individual* occupants of statuses happen to deal with the many and sometimes conflicting demands made of them? Fourth, the concept of the role-set directs us to the further question of how these social mechanisms come into being; the answer to this question enables us to account for the many concrete instances in which the role-set operates ineffectively. (This no more assumes that all social mechanisms are functional than the theory of biological evolution involves the comparable assumption that no dysfunctional developments occur,) Finally, the logic of analysis exhibited in this sociological theory of the middle-range is developed wholly in terms of the elements of social structure rather than in terms of providing concrete *historical descriptions* of particular social systems. Thus, middle-range theory enables us to transcend the mock problem of a theoretical conflict between the nomothetic and the idiothetic, between the general and the altogether particular, between generalizing sociological theory and historicism.

From all this, it is evident that according to role-set theory there is always a *potential* for differing expectations among those in the role-set as to what is appropriate conduct for a status-occupant. The basic source of this potential for conflict—and it is important to note once again that on this point we are at one with such disparate general theorists as Marx and Spencer, Simmel, Sorokin and Parsons—is found in the structural fact that the other members of a role-set are apt to hold different social positions differing from that of the status-occupant in question. To the extent that members of a role-set are diversely located in the social structure, they are apt to have interests and sentiments, values and moral expectations, differing from those of the status-occupant himself. This, after all, is one of the principal assumptions of Marxist theory as it is of much other sociological theory: social differentiation generates distinct interests among those variously located in the structure of the society. For example, the members of a school board are often in social and economic strata that differ significantly from the stratum of the school teacher. The interests, values, and expectations of board members are consequently apt to differ from those of the teacher who may thus be subject to conflicting expectations from these and other members of his role-set: professional colleagues, influential members of the school board and, say, the Americanism Committee of the American Legion. An educational essential for one is apt to be judged as an educational frill by another, or as downright subversion, by the third. What holds conspicuously for this one status holds, in identifiable degree, for occupants of other statuses who are structurally related through their role-set to others who themselves occupy differing positions in society.

As a theory of the middle range, then, the theory of role-sets begins with a concept and its associated imagery and generates an array of theoretical problems. Thus, the assumed structural basis for potential disturbance of a role-set gives rise to a double question (which, the record shows, has not been raised in the absence of the theory): which social mechanisms, if any, operate to counteract the theoretically assumed instability of role-sets and, correlatively, under which circumstances do these social mechanisms fail to operate, with resulting inefficiency, confusion, and conflict? Like other questions that have historically stemmed from the general orientation of functional analysis, these do not assume that role-sets invariably operate with substantial efficiency. For this middle-range theory is not concerned with the historical generalization that a degree of social order or conflict prevails in society but with the analytical problem of identifying the social mechanisms which produce a greater degree of order or less conflict than would obtain if these mechanisms were not called into play.

Total Systems of Sociological Theory

The quest for theories of the middle range exacts a distinctly different commitment from the sociologist than does the quest for an all-embracing, unified theory. The pages that follow assume that this search for a total system of sociological theory, in which observations about every aspect of social behavior, organization, and change promptly find their preordained place, has the same exhilarating challenge and the same small promise as those many all-encompassing philosophical systems which have fallen into deserved disuse. The issue must he fairly joined. Some sociologists still write as though they expect, here and now, formulation of *the* general sociological theory broad enough to encompass the vast ranges of precisely observed details of social behavior, organization, and change and fruitful enough to direct the attention of research workers to a flow of problems for empirical research. This I take to be a premature and apocalyptic belief. We are not ready. Not enough preparatory work has been done.

An historical sense of the changing intellectual contexts of sociology should be sufficiently humbling to liberate these optimists from this extravagant hope. For one thing, certain aspects of our historical past are still too much with us. We must remember that early sociology grew up in an intellectual atmosphere in which vastly comprehensive systems of philosophy were being introduced on all sides. Any philosopher of the eighteenth and early nineteenth centuries worth his salt had to develop his own philosophical system—of these, Kant, Fichte, Schelling, Hegel were only the best known. Each system was a personal bid for the definitive overview of the universe of matter, nature and man.

These attempts of philosophers to create total systems became a model for the early sociologists, and so the nineteenth century was a century of sociological systems. Some of the founding fathers, like Comte and Spencer, were imbued with the *esprit de systeme,* which was expressed in their sociologies as in the rest of their wider-ranging philosophies. Others, such as Gumplowicz, Ward, and Giddings, later tried to provide intellectual legitimacy for this still "new science of a very ancient subject." This required that a general and definitive framework of sociological thought be built rather than developing special theories designed to guide the investigation of specific sociological problems within an evolving and provisional framework.

Within this context, almost all the pioneers in sociology tried to fashion his own system. The multiplicity of systems, each claiming to be the genuine sociology, led naturally enough to the formation of schools, each with its cluster of masters, disciples and epigoni. Sociology not only became differentiated with other disciples, but it became internally differentiated. This differentiation, however, was not in terms of specialization, as in the sciences, but rather, as in philosophy, in terms of total systems, typically held to be mutually exclusive and largely at odds. As Bertrand Russell noted about philosophy, this total sociology did not seize "the advantage, as compared with the [sociologies] of the system-builders, of being able to tackle its problems one at a time, instead of having to invent at one stroke a block theory of the whole [sociological] universe."

Another route has been followed by sociologists in their quest to establish the intellectual legitimacy of their discipline: they have taken as their prototype systems of scientific theory rather than systems of philosophy. This path too has sometimes led to the attempt to create total systems of sociology—a goal that is often based on one or more of three basic misconceptions about the sciences.

The first misinterpretation assumes that systems of thought can be effectively developed before a great mass of basic observations has been accumulated. According to this view, Einstein might follow hard on the heels of Kepler, without the intervening centuries of investigation and systematic thought about the results of investigation that were needed to prepare the terrain. The systems of sociology that stem from this tacit assumption are much like those introduced by the system-makers in medicine over a span of 150 years: the systems of Stahl, Boissier de Sauvages, Broussais, John Brown and Benjamin Hush. Until well into the nineteenth century eminent personages in medicine thought it necessary to develop a theoretical system of disease long before the antecedent empirical inquiry had been adequately developed. These garden-paths have since been closed off in medicine but this sort of effort still turns up in sociology. It is this tendency that led the biochemist and avocational sociologist, L. J. Henderson, to observe:

> A difference between most system-building in the social sciences and systems of thought and classification in the natural sciences is to be seen in their evolution. In the natural sciences both theories and descriptive systems grow by adaptation to the increasing knowledge and experience of the scientists. *In the social sciences,*

> *systems often issue fully formed from the mind of one man.* Then they may be much discussed if they attract attention, but *progressive adaptive modification as a result of the concerted efforts of great numbers of men is rare.*

The second misconception about the physical sciences rests on a mistaken assumption of historical contemporaneity—*that all cultural products existing at the same moment of history have the same degree of maturity.* In fact, to perceive differences here would be to achieve a sense of proportion. The fact that the discipline of physics and the discipline of sociology are both identifiable in the mid-twentieth century does not mean that the achievements of the one should be the measure of the other. True, social scientists today live at a time when physics has achieved comparatively great scope and precision of theory and experiment, a great aggregate of tools of investigation, and an abundance of technological by-products. Looking about them, many sociologists take the achievements of physics as the standard for self-appraisal. They want to compare biceps with their bigger brothers. They, too, want to count. And when it becomes evident that they neither have the rugged physique nor pack the murderous wallop of their big brothers, some sociologists despair. They begin to ask: is a science of society really possible unless we institute a total system of sociology? But this perspective ignores the fact that between twentieth-century physics and twentieth-century sociology stand billions of man-hours of sustained, disciplined, and cumulative research. Perhaps sociology is not yet ready for its Einstein because it has not yet found its Kepler—to say nothing of its Newton, Laplace, Gibbs, Maxwell or Planck.

Third, sociologists sometimes misread the actual state of theory in the physical sciences. This error is ironic, for physicists agree that they have not achieved an all-encompassing system of theory, and most see little prospect of it in the near future. What characterizes physics is an array of special theories of greater or less scope, coupled with the historically-grounded hope that these will continue to be brought together into families of theory. As one observer puts it: "though most of us hope, it is true, for an all embracive future theory which will unify the various postulates of physics, we do not wait for it before proceeding with the important business of science." More recently, the theoretical physicist, Richard Feynman, reported without dismay that "today our theories of physics, the laws of physics, are a multitude of different parts and pieces that do not fit together very well." But perhaps most telling is the observation by that most comprehensive of theoreticians who devoted the last years of his life to the unrelenting and unsuccessful search "for a unifying theoretical basis for all these single disciplines, consisting of a minimum of concepts and fundamental relationships, from which all the concepts and relationships of the single disciplines might be derived by logical process." Despite his own profound and lonely commitment to this quest, Einstein observed:

> The greater part of physical research is devoted to the development of the various branches in physics, in each of which the object is the theoretical understanding of more or less restricted fields of experience, and in each of which the laws and concepts remain as closely as possible related to experience.

These observations might be pondered by those sociologists who expect a sound general system of sociological theory in our time—or soon after. If the science of physics, with its centuries of enlarged theoretical generalizations, has not managed to develop an all-encompassing theoretical system, then *a fortiori* the science of sociology, which has only begun to accumulate empirically grounded theoretical generalizations of modest scope, would seem well advised to moderate its aspirations for such a system.

Utilitarian Pressures for Total Systems of Sociology

The conviction among some sociologists that we must, here and now, achieve a grand theoretical system not only results from a misplaced comparison with the physical sciences, it is also a response to the ambiguous position of sociology in contemporary society. The very uncertainty about whether the accumulated knowledge of sociology is adequate to meet the large demands now being made of it—by policymakers, reformers and reactionaries, by business-men and government-men, by college presidents and college sophomores—provokes an overly-zealous and defensive conviction on the part of some sociologists that they must somehow be equal to these demands, however premature and extravagant they may be.

This conviction erroneously assumes that a science must be adequate to meet *all* demands, intelligent or stupid, made of it. This conviction is implicitly based on the sacrilegious and masochistic assumption that one must be omniscient and omnicompetent—to admit to less than total knowledge is to admit to total ignorance. So it often happens that the exponents of a fledgling discipline make extravagant claims to total systems of theory, adequate to the entire range of problems encompassed by the discipline. It is this sort of attitude that Whitehead referred to in the epigraph to this book: "It is characteristic of a science in its earlier stages . . . to be both ambitiously profound in its aims and trivial in its handling of details."

Like the sociologists who thoughtlessly compared themselves with contemporary physical scientists because they both are alive at the same instant of history, the general public and its strategic decision-makers often err in making a definitive appraisal of social science on the basis of its ability to solve the urgent problems of society today. The misplaced masochism of the social scientist and the inadvertent sadism of the public both result from the failure to remember that social science, like all science, is continually developing and that there is no providential dispensation providing that at any given moment it will be adequate to the entire array of problems confronting men. In historical perspective this expectation would be equivalent to having forever prejudged the status and promise of medicine in the seventeenth century according to its ability to produce, then and there, a cure or even a preventative for cardiac diseases. If the problem had been widely acknowledged—look at the growing rate of death from coronary thrombosis!—its very importance would have obscured the *entirely independent question* of how adequate the medical knowledge of 1650 (or 1850 or 1950) was for solving a wide array of other health problems. Yet it is precisely this illogic that lies behind so many of the practical demands made on the social sciences. Because war and exploitation and poverty and racial discrimination and psychological insecurity plague modern societies, social science must justify itself by providing solutions for all of these problems. Yet social scientists may be no better equipped to solve these urgent problems today than were physicians, such as Harvey or Sydenham, to identify, study, and cure coronary thrombosis in 1655. Yet, as history testifies, the inadequacy of medicine to cope with this particular problem scarcely meant that it lacked powers of development.

If everyone backs only the sure thing, who will support the colt yet to come into its own?

My emphasis upon the gap between the practical problems assigned to the sociologist and the state of his accumulated knowledge and skills does not mean of course, that the sociologist should not seek to develop increasingly comprehensive theory or should not work on research directly relevant to urgent practical problems. Most of all, it does not mean that sociologists should deliberately seek out the pragmatically trivial problem. Different sectors in the spectrum of basic research and theory have different probabilities of being germane to particular practical problems; they have differing potentials of relevance. But it is important to re-establish an historical sense of proportion. The urgency or immensity of a practical social problem does not ensure its immediate solution. At any given moment, men of science are close to the solutions of some problems and remote from others. It must be remembered that necessity is only the mother of invention; socially accumulated knowledge is its father. Unless the two are brought together, necessity remains infertile. She may of course conceive at some future time when she is properly mated. But the mate requires time (and sustenance) if he is to attain the size and vigor needed to meet the demands that will be made upon him.

This book's orientation toward the relationship of current sociology and practical problems of society is much the same as its orientation toward the relationship of sociology and general sociological theory. It is a developmental orientation, rather than one that relies on the sudden mutations of one sociologist that suddenly bring solutions to major social problems or to a single encompassing theory. Though this orientation makes no marvellously dramatic claims, it offers a reasonably realistic assessment of the current condition of sociology and the ways in which it actually develops.

Total Systems of Theory and Theories of the Middle Range

From all this it would seem reasonable to suppose that sociology will advance insofar as its major (but not exclusive) concern is with developing theories of the middle range, and it will be retarded if its primary attention is focussed on developing total sociological systems. So it is that in his inaugural address at the London School of Economics, T. H. Marshall put in a plea for sociological "stepping-stones in the middle distance." Our major task today is to develop special theories applicable to limited conceptual ranges—theories, for example, of deviant behavior, the unanticipated consequences of purposive action, social perception, reference groups, social control, the interdependence of social institutions —rather than to seek immediately the total conceptual structure that is adequate to derive these and other theories of the middle range.

Sociological theory, if it is to advance significantly, must proceed on these interconnected planes: (1) by developing special theories from which to derive hypotheses that can be empirically investigated and (2) by evolving, not suddenly revealing, a progressively more general conceptual scheme that is adequate to consolidate groups of special theories.

To concentrate entirely on special theories is to risk emerging with specific hypotheses that account for limited aspects of social behavior, organization and change but that remain mutually inconsistent.

To concentrate entirely on a master conceptual scheme for deriving all subsidiary theories is to risk producing twentieth-century sociological equivalents of the large philosophical systems of the past, with all then-varied suggestiveness, their architectonic splendor, and their scientific sterility. The sociological theorist who is *exclusively* committed to the exploration of a total system with its utmost abstractions runs the risk that, as with modern decor, the furniture of his mind will be bare and uncomfortable.

The road to effective general schemes in sociology will only become clogged if, as in the early days of sociology, each charismatic sociologist tries to develop his own general system of theory. The persistence of this practice can only make for the balkanization of sociology, with each principality governed by its own theoretical system. Though this process has periodically marked the development of other sciences—conspicuously, chemistry, geology and medicine—it need not be reproduced in sociology if we learn from the history of science. We sociologists can look instead toward progressively comprehensive sociological theory which, instead of proceeding from the head of one man, gradually consolidates theories of the middle range, so that these become special cases of more general formulations.

Developments in sociological theory suggest that emphasis on this orientation is needed. Note how few, how scattered, and how unimpressive are the specific sociological hypotheses which are *derived* from a master conceptual scheme. The proposals for an all-embracing theory run so far ahead of confirmed special theories as to remain unrealized programs rather than *consolidations* of theories that at first seemed discrete. Of course, as Talcott Parsons and Pitirim Sorokin (in his *Sociological Theories of Today*) have indicated, significant progress has recently been made. The gradual convergence of streams of theory in sociology, social psychology and anthropology records large theoretical gains and promises even more. Nonetheless, a large part of what is now described as sociological theory consists of *general orientations toward data, suggesting types of variables which theories must somehow take into account, rather than clearly formulated, verifiable statements of relationships between specified variables.* We have many concepts but fewer confirmed theories; many points of view, but few theorems; many "approaches" but few arrivals. Perhaps some further changes in emphasis would be all to the good.

Consciously or unconsciously, men allocate their scant resources as much in the production of sociological theory as they do in the production of plumbing supplies, and their allocations reflect their underlying assumptions. Our discussion of middle range theory in sociology is intended to make explicit a policy decision faced by all sociological theorists. Which shall have the greater share of our collective energies and resources: the search for confirmed theories of the middle range or the search for an all-inclusive conceptual scheme? I believe—and beliefs are of course notoriously subject to error—that theories of the middle range hold the largest promise, *provided that* the search for them is coupled with a pervasive concern with consolidating special theories into more general sets of concepts and mutually consistent propositions. Even so, we must adopt the provisional outlook of our brothers and of Tennyson:

> Our little systems have their day;
> They have their day and cease to be.

4

Theory as Explanation*

George C. Homans

Any science has two main jobs to do: discovery and explanation. By the first we judge whether it is a science, by the second, how successful a science it is. Discovery is the job of stating and testing more or less general relationships between properties of nature. I call this discovery only because in many sciences the relationships were unknown before research revealed them: for instance, the discovery that bats navigate on the sonar principle. As we shall see, discovery in this sense, particularly discovery of the more general relationships, is much less characteristic of the social sciences than of the others, making one of the most striking differences between them.

A discovery takes the form of a statement of a relationship between properties of nature. Let us be sure we understand what this means. Take Boyle's familiar law: The volume of a gas in an enclosed space is inversely proportional to the pressure on it. A statement, a sentence like this, consists of two parts: first, a reference to what the relationship applies to—gas in an enclosed space—and second, a specification of the relationship between the properties, which must, of course, be at least two in number. Here the two properties are volume and pressure, and the relationship is inverse proportionality: if pressure goes up, volume will go down. Volume and pressure are continuous variables. In another variety of this kind of sentence, the properties, to speak loosely, can take only two values, as in the sentence: A man who loses his kidneys is dead. Here the variables are really classes: first, having kidneys or not having kidneys, and second, being alive or dead. And the relationship between the two is association: not having kidneys is definitely associated with being dead. Sentences of these two varieties I shall call "propositions." Propositions are the one essential product of any science.

In the words of Percy Bridgman, all propositions are accompanied, implicitly or explicitly, by a "text." In the case of Boyle's Law, the text would include answers to such questions as: What is a gas? What are pressure and temperature? How are they defined and measured? The text might also include a statement of the conditions within which the relationship held good. Boyle's Law holds good under the condition that the temperature of the gas is constant.

I have said that propositions, statements of relationships between properties of nature, were "more or less general." When I assert that the battle of Hastings was fought on October 14, 1066, I am certainly stating a relationship, but it is a relationship of association between a single event and a single time. If I asserted that all

*"Social Behavior as Exchange," George C. Homans, *American Journal of Sociology* 63, 6 (1958): 597–606. Reprinted with permission from the University of Chicago Press.

decisive battles were fought in October, the statement would, if true, begin to have some generality. And if I asserted that all battles whatsoever were fought in October, the generalization would be, in the terms used here, more general still. In the same way, Boyle's Law, which applies to all gases in an enclosed space and at constant temperature, is less general than a law applying to all gases at any temperature. But let us not worry much at the moment about the degree of generality of propositions. To have stated and tested a proposition of any degree of generality is no mean achievement. Let us remember Mr. Justice Holmes's dictum: "I always say that the chief end of man is to form general propositions," and let us not altogether forget what he added: "And no generalization is worth a damn."

Nonoperating Definitions

I suppose every professor has horrid moments of feeling that he is teaching his students everything but what they really need to know, everything what they really need to know, everything but the fundamentals. One reason why I have made the, after all, rather obvious points of the last few paragraphs is that I seldom teach my students how to recognize the different kinds of sentence that appear in the literature of social science, and I take the opportunity, belatedly and vicariously, of doing so now. Especially they need to be able to recognize a real proposition, or rather how to tell a real proposition from other kinds of sentence, for these nuggets are often few and far between. If, as Bridgman says, every proposition is accompanied by a text, the text in much of social science seems to take more room than it does in physical science. Indeed in some sociological writings no room is left for anything else.

Yet real propositions do appear in the literature of social science, and so do definitions of the terms that occur in them, the equivalents of the definition of pressure that accompanies Boyle's Law. These I call "operating definitions," because we actually work with them. An example might be a definition of the term "frequency" to accompany the proposition: The more valuable a man perceives the result of his action to be, the more frequently he will perform the action. I want my students to be able to distinguish operating definitions and real propositions from two other kinds of sentence, similar in form to definitions and propositions respectively, which appear very often in the literature of social science, particularly in introductory texts and in "general theory." These I call "nonoperating definitions" and "orienting statements."

Examples of nonoperating definitions include the definitions of some so-called central concepts in sociology and anthropology, concepts the workers in these fields take to be the glories of their sciences. Thus a "role" is the behavior expected of a man occupying a particular social position. And a "culture" is the inherited pattern of living of the members of a society. These are nonoperating definitions because they do not define variables that appear in the testable propositions of social science. Though "roles" and "cultures" could each perhaps be analyzed into clusters of variables, they certainly are not such themselves. It would be absurd to say: "The more the role, the more the something else." We might indeed say: "The more specific the role, the lower the social position in which the behavior is expected." But here the variable would be specificity and not role itself.

This example suggests that "role" may have the status in sociological propositions that "gas" has in Boyle's Law: we might speak of the specificity of the role as we speak of the pressure on the gas. But I am not sure that the parallel holds. Certainly the status of the two is not exactly alike. For some propositions, like Boyle's Law, that hold good of gases do not always hold good of non-gases—liquids and solids—but it is far from clear that there are propositions that hold good of roles but not of non-roles (whatever they may be). That is, the word "gas" makes a difference in meaning, and "role" may not.

I think the same sort of thing is true of "culture." But here I add a comment that gets me a little ahead of my argument. An anthropologist friend once said to me, in pointing out the usefulness of this concept: "If someone asks me, for instance, why the Chinese do not like milk, I can only say, 'Because of the culture.'"All I could say in turn was that, if that was all *he* could say, he was not saying much. All that the use of the word "culture" implied was that disliking milk had been characteristic of the behavior of some Chinese for some generations. But we knew that already; "culture" did not add anything. What we should have liked to know was why milk, specifically, rather than, say, tea was disliked. Talking about culture did not answer this question at all—not at all. More generally, "explanation by concept" is not explanation.

Yet I am loath to argue that the concepts "role" and "culture" are useless. What I want to be sure of is that we recognize the sort of usefulness they possess. They tell us roughly the kinds of thing we are going to talk about. They and their definitions tell us that we are going to talk about expected behavior and inherited patterns of behavior, and it may indeed be well for a new student to be forewarned. But sooner or later we must stop "being about to" talk about something and actually say something—that is, state propositions. Lingering over nonoperating definitions may actually get in the way of this primary job of science. This happens, I think, when nonoperating definitions are multiplied and elaborated into a nonoperating conceptual scheme (called a "general theory"), as in much—not all—of the work of Talcott Parsons. Some students get so much intellectual security out of such a scheme, because it allows them to give names to, and to pigeonhole, almost any social phenomenon, that they are hesitant to embark on the dangerous waters of actually saying something about the relations between the phenomena—because then they must actually take the risk of being found wrong. The failure to state real propositions leads in turn to a failure to create real theories, for, as we shall see, a real theory consists precisely of propositions. I sometimes think we need not be at such pains introducing our students to social science. Start them out at once with real propositions. They would find out soon enough what we were going to talk about: we should already be talking about it.

Orienting Statements

Just as "role" and "culture" are famous concepts, so what I call "orienting statements" include some of the most famous statements of social science. One is Marx's statement that the organization of the means of production determines the other features of a society. This is more than a definition and resembles a proposition in that it relates two phenomena to one another. But these phenomena—the means of production and the other features of a society—are not single variables. At best they are whole clusters of undefined variables. And the relationship between the phenomena is unspecified, except that the main direction of causation—determination—is from the former to the latter. Whereas Boyle's Law says that, if pressure goes up, volume will assuredly go down, what Marx's Law says is that, if there is some, any, change in the means of production, there will be some unspecified change or changes in the other features of society. Put the matter another way: Boyle will allow one to predict *what* will happen; Marx will only allow one to predict that *something* will happen. Accordingly I cannot grant his law the status of a real proposition.

In taking Marx's statement thus out of context, I do not in the least mean to imply that this is all he had to say about the relations between the infrastructure and the superstructure of society, or that his writings do not include other statements that are real propositions, or that this particular statement is unimportant. That is far from my view.

Another example of an orienting statement is the assertion by Parsons and Shils that, in social interaction between any two persons, the actions of each are sanctioned by the actions of the other. This is an important statement in that, in my view, the beginning of wisdom in the study of social behavior is to look at it as an exchange between at least two persons, in which the action of each rewards or punishes—that is, sanctions—the action of the other. But the statement in itself does not say what effect a change in the behavior of one will have on the behavior of another. Like Marx's Law, it implies that there will be *some* effect, but does not begin to say what. Only if Parsons and Shils had gone on to say, for instance, that the more rewarding (valuable) to one man is the action of the other, the more often will the first perform the action that gets him the reward—only then would they have stated a real proposition. Much of what they say suggests that they believe this proposition to be true, but they manage to avoid coming right out with it.

For my third example I do not take an isolated statement but a passage from a book, chosen for no better reason than that I read it recently. If it were a bad book, that fact would get in the way of my making the point that passages more or less like this one have been appearing for many years and in immense numbers in all the best literature of social science:

> An individual is born into a social system that possesses a culture. The socialization of that individual is a threefold process. It involves the inculcation of the culture upon the individual by the social system. The transmission of culture through socialization is never complete. The individual learns only a selected number of elements in the culture of his society. He introjects, or commits himself to, even fewer elements of that culture. In so doing he brings to bear the influence of his own personality upon the survival and growth of the culture. Also, the social system itself does not act upon the individual in his socialization. It is individual members of the system who act upon him. Their influence upon him reflects the uniformity of relationships that comprise the social system. Their influence also reflects their own idiosyncratic response to culture, based on the dynamics of their personalities. In this way, the individual is trained in the common bonds of society. But the pattern of his being taught and the lessons he learns are unique to him.

In a way, this is all sound as a bell. I suppose we could find out, for instance, what words like "culture" and "socialization" meant, and would even agree that culture was transmitted through socialization. But let us ask ourselves this question: Where in the passage do we find a single statement from which we could tell what specific change would occur, or even probably occur, along any one dimension of human behavior if there were a specific change along another? Yet it is the business of a science to make such statements. The passage tells us that things like culture, socialization, and the social system are all important and all somehow related to one another, but it tells us nothing *about* them. It is all true—and all powerless. After so many years of orientation, do we and our students really need so many weak truths?

Much writing in social science consists of orienting statements when it does not consist of nonoperating definitions. Orienting statements do not qualify as real propositions: they are of little use in prediction and of none at all, as we shall see, in explanation. Yet I should be slow to argue that they did no good in other ways. I must testify, perhaps complacently, that I personally have been greatly helped both by Marx and by Parsons and Shils. I claim that statements of this sort are really imperatives, telling us what we ought to look into further or how we ought to look at it. This is the reason why I call them orienting statements. Look at the relations between the means of production and the other features of society, for if you look, you will surely find! Look on social behavior as an exchange, for then you will begin to make progress! And, God knows, with the help of Marx at least, scholars have made progress. Looking where he pointed, they have discovered and tested statements that, if of smaller scope than Marx's, still have more of the character of real propositions.

Yet the very success of Marx's Law in being useful in its particular way teaches us that we should not mistake orienting statements for either the empirical or the theoretical results of science. A statement that tells us what to study or how to study it is an important statement. But it tells us little about the thing studied. In Merton's words, it gives us an approach, not an arrival. Let us not exhaust ourselves in the preliminaries, lest we fail at the consummation. We are always getting around to saying something we never actually come out with. But sooner or later a science must actually stick its neck out and say something definite. If there is a change in x, what sort of change will occur in y? Don't just tell me there will be *some* change. Tell me *what* change. Stand and deliver!

The Findings of Social Science

And the social sciences do this. Though nonoperating definitions and orienting statements are comparatively prevalent in them, especially in anthropology, sociology, and political science, and are comparatively often mistaken for real definitions and propositions, yet the social sciences now have a very large number of solid findings to their credit. At the turn of the century the mathematician Poincare could sneer that ". . . *sociology* is the science that possesses the most in the way of methods and the least in the way of results." He could not fairly say so now. Though we still talk endlessly about methodology, the other side of the balance has been redressed. Anyone, for instance, who reads the useful book by Bernard Berelson and Gary A. Steiner, *Human Behavior: An Inventory of Scientific Findings*, should be impressed with the number of generalizations (propositions) in this field that have now been pretty well tested against data.

Choosing almost at random, let us get an idea of their variety within some sub-field, such as social stratification. Every society, certainly every society of any size, is stratified by class or status. The rate of inter-generational mobility between classes is currently about the same in all highly industrialized nations. Family instability (divorce, separation, and abandonment) is greatest in the lower class, next in the upper, and least in the middle. The higher the class, the later the average age at marriage. And so forth. If the first job of a science is to establish generalizations, social science has established a great many.

But look at the characteristics of these propositions. Except for the first—that all societies are stratified—all of them state only central tendencies. It is not true of all members of an upper class that they marry late, but only of the average. And when the propositions state relationships between variables, the nature of the relationship, the function, is not very specific. We know that a rise in class position means a rise in the age of marriage; what we cannot say is, for instance, that one increases as the logarithm of the other. Sometimes a social science can get a little closer to specifying the shape of the function, as in the so-called law of diminishing marginal utility in economics: the curve relating the quantity of a good received by a man and the value to him of a unit of the good is concave downward. But few of our propositions ever state the exact function—which is one of the reasons why our science is not an exact science. Still, they are likely to say at least this much: that, for instance, as the value of one of the variables increases, the value of the other increases too which is enough, just enough, to make them real propositions and not simply orienting statements.

Even more important, our propositions, though they are generalizations all right, are seldom very general generalizations. They are known to hold good only within rather narrow limits, only within western industrial societies, for instance. Or if the limits are not known, they are still shrewdly suspected of being narrow. And finally, with one class of exceptions, which I shall speak of much later, even our apparently most general generalizations, like the proposition that all societies are stratified, do not possess much explanatory power. Thinking of these, I have sometimes entertained the hypothesis that in social science the greater the generalization, the less its explanatory power. But explanation brings in a new kind of consideration.

The Nature of Explanation

Most people interested in comparing the social sciences with the natural sciences, especially those interested in making sure that social science is a natural science, emphasize the greater difficulty the social sciences face in establishing, against data, the empirical truth of its propositions. It is certainly less easy in the social sciences than in some physical and biological sciences to manipulate variables experimentally and to control the other variables entering into a concrete phenomenon, so that the relationship between those the scientist is interested in at the moment shall be, beyond question, unmasked and stand out clearly. It is less easy to control the variables because it is less easy to control men than things. Indeed it is often immoral to try to control them: men are not to be submitted to the indignities to which we submit, as a matter of course, things and animals. Hence the relative prominence in some of the social sciences, even increasingly in history, of other methods of controlling variables, methods thought somehow to be less satisfactory, such as the use of statistical techniques.

I shall have no more to say about this difference between the social sciences and the others. Admittedly it is important, but it is also rather well understood, and much intelligence of a high order has been devoted to finding methods of dealing with the problem. Moreover, some of the biological sciences, such as medicine, suffer from difficulties of control almost as much as do the social sciences. Much less well understood are the differences between the social and the other sciences in the matter of explanation.

Though stating and testing relationships between properties of nature is what makes a science, it is certainly not the only thing a science tries to do. Indeed we judge not the existence, but the success, of a science by its capacity to explain. If there is one thing I should like my students to learn but seldom teach them is what an explanation is—not that it his hard to do. Again, no "big" word is more often used in social science than the word "theory." Yet how seldom do we ask our students—or, more significantly, ourselves—what a theory is. But a theory of a phenomenon is an explanation of the phenomenon, and nothing that is not an explanation is worthy of the name of theory.

I am, of course, using "explanation" in the special sense of explaining why under given conditions a particular phenomenon occurs and riot in one of the vaguer senses in which we use the word, as when we "explain" how to drive a car by telling a youngster what to do with the controls in various circumstances. In the special sense, the explanation of a finding, whether a generalization or a proposition about a single event, is the process of showing that the finding follows as a logical conclusion, as a deduction, from one or more general propositions under specified given conditions. Thus we explain the familiar finding that there are two low and two high tides a day (actually a little longer than twenty-four hours) by showing that it follows logically from the law of gravitation under the given conditions that the earth is largely covered with water, that it rotates on its axis, and that the moon moves in orbit around it.

But let me go into more detail, using a humble example but one that in the past had good reason to interest me. As a boy swimming in the fundamentally rather chilly waters of Massachusetts Bay in summer, I discovered, as others had done before me, that for comfort in swimming, the water near the shore was apt to be warmer when the wind was blowing onshore—towards the shore—than when it was blowing offshore. By thoroughly unsystematic statistical methods I tested the discovery and found it true. But why should it be true? I shall try to give the essentials of what I believe to be the correct, though obvious, explanation, without spelling it out in all its logical, but boring, rigor.

Warm water tends to rise. The sun warms the surface water more than the depths. For both reasons, surface water tends to be warmer than deeper water. The wind acts more on the surface water than it does on the depths, displacing it in the direction of the wind. Accordingly an onshore wind tends to pile up the wanner water along the shore, while an offshore wind tends to move it away from the shore, where, by the principle that "water seeks its own level," it is continuously replaced by other water, which, since it can only come from the depths, must be relatively cold. Therefore water along the shore tends to be wanner when the wind is blowing onshore than when it is blowing offshore. Q.E.D.

Simple though it is, the characteristics of this explanation are those of all explanations. Each step of the argument is itself a proposition stating a relationship between properties of nature: between, for instance, the temperature of water and the direction of its movement, up or down. That is why propositions are so important. Some of the propositions are more general than others. In the example, some of the more general propositions are that warm water tends to rise and that water seeks its own level. They are more general in that they apply to all water and not just water along a coast. Some of the propositions state the effect of the given conditions, such as that the wind sometimes blows onshore and sometimes offshore. By calling them given conditions we mean simply that we do not choose to explain them in turn—we do not choose to explain why the wind sometimes blows onshore—though no doubt we could do so. And the proposition to be explained, the *explicandurn*—in this case the difference in temperature of coastal water under onshore and offshore winds—is explained in the sense that it follows as a matter of logic from the general propositions under the specified given conditions. That is, the *explicandum* is deduced from, derived from, the other propositions, the whole set forming a "deductive system." The reason why orienting statements cannot play a part in explanation is that little in logic can be deduced from them.

Note that, if the *explicandum* can be deduced from the general propositions under the given conditions, the general propositions cannot be deduced in turn from the others in the set, any more than in the classic syllogism we can deduce that all men are mortal from the facts that Socrates is a man and that Socrates is mortal. That is, the process of deduction runs in one direction but not the other in the set of propositions. If it did both, the argument would be circular. On the other hand, the general propositions in our example can themselves be explained by, can themselves become the *explicanda* of, other deductive systems containing still more general propositions. That hot water rises is ultimately explained by propositions of thermodynamics relating the temperature of any substance to its volume and thus to its weight per unit volume. That water seeks its own level is ultimately explained by the law of gravitation. But as we move towards more and more general propositions, we reach, at any given time in the history of science, propositions that cannot themselves be explained. If we can judge from experience, this condition, for any particular proposition, is unlikely to last forever. Newton's law of gravitation stood unexplained for some two hundred years, but can now be shown to follow from Einstein's theory of relativity. Nevertheless at any given time there are always at least a few unexplainable propositions.

The explanation of the relation of water temperature to wind direction is also the theory of this phenomenon. But of course scientists generally use the word "theory" in a broader sense than this. They use it to refer, not just to an explanation of a single phenomenon, but to a cluster of explanations of related phenomena, when the explanations, the deductive systems, share some of the same general propositions. Thus someone might write a book called *The Theory of Water Temperatures*, which might explain the relations between variations in temperature and a number of other conditions besides the one chosen in our example, and which would apply, in doing so, a number of the same general propositions from thermodynamics and mechanics. Naturally any scholar is free to use the word "theory" in any way he likes, even for something different from what I call theory, provided he makes clear just how he is using it and does not, by slurring over the issue, claim for his kind of theory, by implication, virtues that belong to a different kind. All I submit here is that, normally in science, "theory" refers to the sort of thing I have described.

If we like, we can look on theory as a game. The winner is the man who can deduce the largest variety of empirical findings from the smallest number of general propositions, with the help of a variety of given conditions. Not everyone need get into the game. A man can be an admirable scientist and stick to empirical discovery, but most scientists do find themselves playing it sooner or later. It is fascinating in itself, and it has a useful ulterior result. A science whose practitioners have been good at playing it has achieved a great economy of thought. No longer does it face just one damn finding after another. It has acquired an organization, a structure. When Newtonian mechanics reached this sort of achievement it became the first thoroughly successful science, and other sciences have since become successful in the same way. But if theory is a game, it must like other games be played according to the rules, and the basic rules are that a player must state real propositions and make real deductions. Otherwise, no theory!

5

The Oversocialized View of Human Nature*

Dennis H. Wrong

Gertrude Stein, bed-ridden with a fatal illness, is reported to have suddenly muttered, "What, then, is the answer?" Pausing, she raised her head, murmured, "But what is the question?" and died. Miss Stein presumably was pondering the ultimate meaning of human life, but her brief final soliloquy has a broader and humbler relevance. Its point is that answers are meaningless apart from questions. If we forget the questions, even while remembering the answers, our knowledge of them will subtly deteriorate, becoming rigid, formal, and catechistic as the sense of indeterminacy, of rival possibilities, implied by the very putting of a question is lost.

Social theory must be seen primarily as a set of answers to questions we ask of social reality. If the initiating questions are forgotten, we readily misconstrue the task of theory and the answers previous thinkers have given become narrowly confining conceptual prisons, degenerating into little more than a special, professional vocabulary applied to situations and events that can be described with equal or greater precision in ordinary language. Forgetfulness of the questions that are the starting points of inquiry leads us to ignore the substantive assumptions "buried" in our concepts and commits us to a one-sided view of reality.

Perhaps this is simply an elaborate way of saying that sociological theory can never afford to lose what is usually called a "sense of significance;" or, as it is sometimes put, that sociological theory must be "problem-conscious." I choose instead to speak of theory as a set of answers to questions because reference to "problems" may seem to suggest too close a linkage with social criticism or reform. My primary reason for insisting on the necessity of holding constantly in mind the questions that our concepts and theories are designed to answer is to preclude defining the goal of sociological theory as the creation of a formal body of knowledge satisfying the logical criteria of scientific theory set up by philosophers and methodologists of natural science. Needless to say, this is the way theory is often defined by contemporary sociologists.

Yet to speak of theory as interrogatory may suggest too self-sufficiently intellectual an enterprise. Cannot questions be satisfactorily answered and then forgotten, the answers becoming the assumptions from which we start in framing new questions? It may convey my view of theory more

*"The Oversocialized Conception of Man in Modern Sociology," Dennis Wrong, *American Sociological Review* 26, 2 (1961): 183–93.

adequately to say that sociological theory concerns itself with questions arising out of problems that are inherent in the very existence of human societies and that cannot therefore be finally "solved" in the way that particular social problems perhaps can be. The "problems" theory concerns itself with are problems *for* human societies which, because of their universality, become intellectually problematic for sociological theorists.

Essentially, the historicist conception of sociological knowledge that is central to the thought of Max Weber and has recently been ably restated by Barrington Moore, Jr. and C. Wright Mills is a sound one. The most fruitful questions for sociology are always questions referring to the realities of a particular historical situation. Yet both of these writers, especially Mills, have a tendency to underemphasize the degree to which we genuinely wish and seek answers to trans-historical and universal questions about the nature of man and society. I do not, let it be clear, have in mind the formalistic quest for social "laws" or "universal propositions," nor the even more formalistic effort to construct all-encompassing "conceptual schemes." Moore and Mills are rightly critical of such efforts. I am thinking of such questions as, "How are men capable of uniting to form enduring societies in the first place?"; "Why and to what degree is change inherent in human societies and what are the sources of change?"; "How is man's animal nature domesticated by society?"

Such questions—and they are existential as well as intellectual questions—are the *raison d'être* of social theory. They were asked by men long before the rise of sociology. Sociology itself is an effort, under new and unprecedented historical conditions, to find novel answers to them. They are not questions which lend themselves to successively more precise answers as a result of cumulative empirical research, for they remain eternally problematic. Social theory is necessarily an interminable dialogue. "True understanding," Hannah Arendt has written, "does not tire of interminable dialogue and 'vicious circles' because it trusts that imagination will eventually catch at least a glimpse of the always frightening light of truth."

I wish briefly to review the answers modern sociological theory offers to one such question, or rather to one aspect of one question. The question may be variously phrased as, "What are the sources of social cohesion?"; or, "How is social order possible?"; or, stated in social-psychological terms, "How is it that man becomes tractable to social discipline?" I shall call this question in its social-psychological aspect the "Hobbesian question" and in its more strictly sociological aspect the "Marxist question." The Hobbesian question asks how men are capable of the guidance by social norms and goals that makes possible an enduring society, while the Marxist question asks how, assuming this capability, complex societies manage to regulate and restrain destructive conflicts between groups. Much of our current theory offers an oversocialized view of man in answering the Hobbesian question and an over-integrated view of society in answering the Marxist question.

A number of writers have recently challenged the overintegrated view of society in contemporary theory. In addition to Moore and Mills, the names of Bendix, Coser, Dahrendorf, and Lockwood come to mind. My intention, therefore, is to concentrate on the answers to the Hobbesian question in an effort to disclose the oversocialized view of man which they seem to imply.

Since my view of theory is obviously very different from that of Talcott Parsons and has, in fact, been developed in opposition to his, let me pay tribute to his recognition of the importance of the Hobbesian question—the "problem of order," as he calls it—at the very beginning of his first book, *The Structure of Social Action*. Parsons correctly credits Hobbes with being the first thinker to see the necessity of explaining why human society is not a "war of all against all;" why, if man is simply a gifted animal, men refrain from unlimited resort to fraud and violence in pursuit of their ends and maintain a stable society at all. There is even a sense in which, as Coser and Mills have both noted, Parsons' entire work represents an effort to solve the Hobbesian problem of order. His solution, however, has tended to become precisely the kind of elaboration of a set of answers in abstraction from questions that is so characteristic of contemporary sociological theory.

We need not be greatly concerned with Hobbes' own solution to the problem of order he saw with such unsurpassed clarity. Whatever interest his famous theory of the origin of the state may still hold for political scientists, it is clearly inadequate as an explanation of the origin of society. Yet the pattern as opposed to the details of Hobbes' thought bears closer examination.

The polar terms in Hobbes' theory are the state of nature, where the war of all against all prevails, and the authority of Leviathan, created by social contract. But the war of all against all is not simply effaced with the creation of political authority: it remains an ever-present potentiality in human society, at times quiescent, at times erupting into open violence. Whether Hobbes believed that the state of nature and the social contract were ever historical realities—and there is evidence that he was not that simple-minded and unsociological, even in the seventeenth century—is unimportant; the whole tenor of his thought is to see the war of all against all and Leviathan dialectically, as coexisting and interacting opposites. As R. G. Collingwood has observed, "According to Hobbes . . . *a body politic is a dialectical thing,* a Heraclitean world in which at any given time there is a negative element." The first secular social theorist in the history of Western thought, and one of the first clearly to discern and define the problem of order in human society long before Darwinism made awareness of it a commonplace, Hobbes was a dialectical thinker who refused to separate answers from questions, solutions to society's enduring problems from the conditions creating the problems.

What is the answer of contemporary sociological theory to the Hobbesian question? There are two main answers, each of which has come to be understood in a way that denies the reality and meaningfulness of the question. Together they constitute a model of human nature, sometimes clearly stated, more often implicit in accepted concepts, that pervades modern sociology. The first answer is summed up in the notion of the "internalization of social norms." The second, more commonly employed or assumed in empirical research, is the view that man is essentially motivated by the desire to achieve a positive image of self by winning acceptance or status in the eyes of others.

The following statement represents, briefly and broadly, what is probably the most influential contemporary sociological conception—and dismissal—of the Hobbesian problem: "To a modern sociologist imbued with the conception that action follows institutionalized patterns, opposition of individual and common interests has only a very limited relevance or is thoroughly unsound." From this writer's perspective, the problem is an unreal one: human conduct is totally shaped by common norms or "institutionalized patterns." Sheer ignorance must have led people who were unfortunate enough not to be modern sociologists to ask, "How is order possible?" A thoughtful bee or ant would never inquire, "How is the social order of the hive or ant-hill possible?" for the opposite of that order is unimaginable when the instinctive endowment of the insects ensures its stability and built-in harmony between "individual and common interests." Human society, we are assured, is not essentially different, although conformity and stability are there maintained by non-instinctive processes. Modern sociologists believe that they have understood these processes and that they have not merely answered but disposed of the Hobbesian question, showing that, far from expressing a valid intimation of the tensions and possibilities of social life, it can only be asked out of ignorance.

It would be hard to find a better illustration of what Collingwood, following Plato, calls *eristical* as opposed to dialectical thinking: the answer destroys the question, or rather destroys the awareness of rival possibilities suggested by the question which accounts for its having been asked in the first place. A reversal of perspective now takes place and we are moved to ask the opposite question: "How is it that violence, conflict, revolution, and the individual's sense of coercion by society manage to exist at all, if this view is correct?" Whenever a one-sided answer to a question compels us to raise the opposite question, we are caught up in a dialectic of concepts which reflects a dialectic in things. But let us examine the particular processes sociologists appeal to in order to account for the elimination from human society of the war of all against all.

The Changing Meaning of Internalization

A well-known section of *The Structure of Social Action,* devoted to the interpretation of Durkheim's thought, is entitled "The Changing Meaning of Constraint." Parsons argues that

Durkheim originally conceived of society as controlling the individual from the outside by imposing constraints on him through sanctions, best illustrated by codes of law. But in Durkheim's later work he began to see that social rules do not "merely regulate 'externally' . . . they enter directly into the constitution of the actors' ends themselves." Constraint, therefore, is more than an environmental obstacle which the actor must take into account in pursuit of his goals in the same way that he takes into account physical laws: it becomes internal, psychological, and self-imposed as well. Parsons developed this view that social norms are constitutive rather than merely regulative of human nature before he was influenced by psychoanalytic theory, but Freud's theory of the superego has become the source and model for the conception of the internalization of social norms that today plays so important a part in sociological thinking. The use some sociologists have made of Freud's idea, however, might well inspire an essay entitled, "The Changing Meaning of Internalization," although, in contrast to the shift in Durkheim's view of constraint, this change has been a change for the worse.

What has happened is that internalization has imperceptibly been equated with "learning," or even with "habit-formation" in the simplest sense. Thus when a norm is said to have been "internalized" by an individual, what is frequently meant is that he habitually both affirms it and conforms to it in his conduct. The whole stress on inner conflict, on the tension between powerful impulses and superego controls the behavioral outcome of which cannot be prejudged, drops out of the picture. And it is this that is central to Freud's view, for in psychoanalytic terms to say that a norm has been internalized, or introjected to become part of the superego, is to say no more than that a person will suffer guilt-feelings if he fails to live up to it, not that he will in fact live up to it in his behavior.

The relation between internalization and conformity assumed by most sociologists is suggested by the following passage from a recent, highly-praised advanced textbook: "Conformity to institutionalized norms is, of course, 'normal.' The actor, having internalized the norms, feels something like a need to conform. His conscience would bother him if he did not." What is overlooked here is that the person who conforms may be even more "bothered," that is, subject to guilt and neurosis, than the person who violates what are not only society's norms but his own as well. To Freud, it is precisely the man with the strictest superego, he who has most thoroughly internalized and conformed to the norms of his society, who is most wracked with guilt and anxiety.

Paul Kecskemeti, to whose discussion I owe initial recognition of the erroneous view of internalization held by sociologists, argues that the relations between social norms, the individual's selection from them, his conduct, and his feelings about his conduct are far from self-evident. "It is by no means true," he writes, "to say that acting counter to one's own norms always or almost always leads to neurosis. One might assume that neurosis develops even more easily in persons who *never* violate the moral code they recognize as valid but repress and frustrate some strong instinctual motive. A person who 'succumbs to temptation,' feels guilt, and then 'purges himself' of his guilt in some reliable way (e.g., by confession) may achieve in this way a better balance, and be less neurotic, than a person who never violates his 'norms' and never feels conscious guilt."

Recent discussions of "deviant behavior" have been compelled to recognize these distinctions between social demands, personal attitudes towards them, and actual conduct, although they have done so in a laboriously taxonomic fashion. They represent, however, largely the rediscovery of what was always central to the Freudian concept of the superego. The main explanatory function of the concept is to show how people repress themselves, imposing checks on their own desires and thus turning the inner life into a battlefield of conflicting motives, no matter which side "wins," by successfully dictating overt action. So far as behavior is concerned, the psychoanalytic view of man is less deterministic than the sociological. For psychoanalysis is primarily concerned with the inner life, not with overt behavior, and its most fundamental insight is that the wish, the emotion, and the fantasy are as important as the act in man's experience.

Sociologists have appropriated the superego concept, but have separated it from any equivalent of the Freudian id. So long as most individuals are "socialized," that is, internalize the norms and conform to them in conduct, the Hobbesian problem is not even perceived as a latent reality. Deviant behavior is accounted for by special circumstances: ambiguous norms, anomie, role conflict, or greater cultural stress on valued goals than on the approved means for attaining them. Tendencies to deviant behavior are not seen as dialectically related to conformity. The presence in man of motivational forces bucking against the hold social discipline has over him is denied.

Nor does the assumption that internalization of norms and roles is the essence of socialization allow for a sufficient range of motives underlying conformity. It fails to allow for variable "tonicity of the superego," in Kardiner's phrase. The degree to which conformity is frequently the result of coercion rather than conviction is minimized. Either someone has internalized the norms, or he is "unsocialized," a feral or socially isolated child, or a psychopath. Yet Freud recognized that many people, conceivably a majority, fail to acquire superegos. "Such people," he wrote, "habitually permit themselves to do any bad deed that procures them something they want, if only they are sure that no authority will discover it or make them suffer for it; their anxiety relates only to the possibility of detection. Present-day society has to take into account the prevalence of this state of mind." The last sentence suggests that Freud was aware of the decline of "inner-direction," of the Protestant conscience, about which we have heard so much lately. So let us turn to the other elements of human nature that sociologists appeal to in order to explain, or rather explain away, the Hobbesian problem.

Man the Acceptance-Seeker

The superego concept is too inflexible, too bound to the past and to individual biography, to be of service in relating conduct to the pressures of the immediate situation in which it takes place. Sociologists rely more heavily therefore on an alternative notion, here stated—or, to be fair, overstated—in its baldest form: "People are so profoundly sensitive to the expectations of others that all action is inevitably guided by these expectations."

Parsons' model of the "complementarity of expectations," the view that in social interaction men mutually seek approval from one another by conforming to shared norms, is a formalized version of what has tended to become a distinctive sociological perspective on human motivation. Ralph Linton states it in explicit psychological terms: "The need for eliciting favorable responses from others is an almost constant component of [personality]. Indeed, it is not too much to say that there is very little organized human behavior which is not directed toward its satisfaction in at least some degree."

The insistence of sociologists on the importance of "social factors" easily leads them to stress the priority of such socialized or socializing motives in human behavior. It is frequently the task of the sociologist to call attention to the intensity with which men desire and strive for the good opinion of their immediate associates in a variety of situations, particularly those where received theories or ideologies have unduly emphasized other motives such as financial gain, commitment to ideals, or the effects on energies and aspirations of arduous physical conditions. Thus sociologists have shown that factory workers are more sensitive to the attitudes of their fellow-workers than to purely economic incentives; that voters are more influenced by the preferences of their relatives and friends than by campaign debates on the "issues;" that soldiers, whatever their ideological commitment to their nation's cause, fight more bravely when their platoons are intact and they stand side by side with their "buddies."

It is certainly not my intention to criticize the findings of such studies. My objection is that their particular selective emphasis is generalized—explicitly or, more often, implicitly—to provide apparent empirical support for an extremely one-sided view of human nature. Although sociologists have criticized past efforts to single out one fundamental motive in human conduct, the desire to achieve a favorable self-image by winning approval from others frequently occupies such a position in their own thinking. The following "theorem" has been, in fact, openly put forward by Hans Zetterberg as "a strong contender for the position as the major Motivational Theorem in sociology":

> An actor's actions have a tendency to become dispositions that are related to the occurence [*sic*]

of favored uniform evaluations of the actor and-or his actions in his action system.

Now Zetterberg is not necessarily maintaining that this theorem is an accurate factual statement of the basic psychological roots of social behavior. He is, characteristically, far too self-conscious about the logic of theorizing and "concept formation" for that. He goes on to remark that "the maximization of favorable attitudes from others would thus be the counterpart in sociological theory to the maximization of profit in economic theory." If by this it is meant that the theorem is to be understood as a heuristic rather than an empirical assumption, that sociology has a selective point of view which is just as abstract and partial as that of economics and the other social sciences, and if his view of theory as a set of logically connected formal propositions is granted provisional acceptance, I am in agreement. (Actually, the view of theory suggested at the beginning of this paper is a quite different one.)

But there is a further point to be made. Ralf Dahrendorf has observed that structural-functional theorists do not "claim that order *is based on* a general consensus of values, but that it *can be conceived of in terms of* such consensus and that, if it is conceived of in these terms, certain propositions follow which are subject to the test of specific observations." The same may be said of the assumption that people seek to maximize favorable evaluations by others; indeed this assumption has already fathered such additional concepts as "reference group" and "circle of significant others." Yet the question must be raised as to whether we really wish to, in effect, define sociology by such partial perspectives. The assumption of the maximization of approval from others is the psychological complement to the sociological assumption of a general value consensus. And the former is as selective and one-sided a way of looking at motivation as Dahrendorf and others have argued the latter to be when it determines our way of looking at social structure. The oversocialized view of man of the one is a counterpart to the over-integrated view of society of the other.

Modern sociology, after all, originated as a protest against the partial views of man contained in such doctrines as utilitarianism, classical economics, social Darwinism, and vulgar Marxism. All of the great nineteenth and early twentieth century sociologists saw it as one of their major tasks to expose the unreality of such abstractions as economic man, the gain-seeker of the classical economists; political man, the power-seeker of the Machiavellian tradition in political science; self-preserving man, the security-seeker of Hobbes and Darwin; sexual or libidinal man, the pleasure-seeker of doctrinaire Freudianism; and even religious man, the God-seeker of the theologians. It would be ironical if it should turn out that they have merely contributed to the creation of yet another reified abstraction in socialized man, the status-seeker of our contemporary sociologists.

Of course, such an image of man is, like all the others mentioned, valuable for limited purposes so long as it is not taken for the whole truth. What are some of its deficiencies? To begin with, it neglects the other half of the model of human nature presupposed by current theory: moral man, guided by his built-in superego and beckoning ego-ideal. In recent years sociologists have been less interested than they once were in culture and national character as backgrounds to conduct, partly because stress on the concept of "role" as the crucial link between the individual and the social structure has directed their attention to the immediate situation in which social interaction takes place. Man is increasingly seen as a "role-playing" creature, responding eagerly or anxiously to the expectations of other role-players in the multiple group settings in which he finds himself. Such an approach, while valuable in helping us grasp the complexity of a highly differentiated social structure such as our own, is far too often generalized to serve as a kind of *ad hoc* social psychology, easily adaptable to particular sociological purposes.

But it is not enough to concede that men often pursue "internalized values" remaining indifferent to what others think of them, particularly when, as I have previously argued, the idea of internalization has been "hollowed out" to make it more useful as an explanation of conformity. What of desire for material and sensual satisfactions? Can we really dispense with the venerable notion of material "interests" and invariably replace it with the blander, more integrative "social values"? And what of striving for power, not necessarily for its own sake—that may be rare and pathological—but as a means by which men are able to *impose* a normative definition of reality on others? That material interests, sexual drives, and the quest for power have often been over-estimated as human motives is no reason to deny their reality. To do so is to suppress one term of the dialectic between conformity and rebellion, social norms and their violation, man and social order, as completely as the other term is suppressed by those who deny the reality of man's "normative orientation" or reduce it to the effect of coercion, rational calculation, or mechanical conditioning.

The view that man is invariably pushed by internalized norms or pulled by the lure of self-validation by others ignores—to speak archaically for a moment—both the highest and the lowest, both beast and angel, in his nature. Durkheim, from whom so much of the modern sociological point of view derives, recognized that the very existence of a social norm implies and even creates the possibility of its violation. This is the meaning of his famous dictum that crime is a "normal phenomenon." He maintained that "for the originality of the idealist whose dreams transcend his century to find expression, it is necessary that the originality of the criminal, who is below the level of his time, shall also be possible. One does not occur without the other." Yet Durkheim lacked an adequate psychology and formulated his insight in terms of the actor's cognitive awareness rather than in motivational terms. We do not have Durkheim's excuse for falling back on what Homans has called a "social mold theory" of human nature.

Social but Not Entirely Socialized

I have referred to forces in man that are resistant to socialization. It is not my purpose to explore the nature of these forces or to suggest how we ought best conceive of them as sociologists—that would be a most ambitious undertaking. A few remarks will have to suffice. I think we must start with the recognition that *in the beginning there is the body*. As soon as the body is mentioned the specter of "biological determinism" raises its head and sociologists draw back in fright. And certainly their view of man is sufficiently disembodied and non-materialistic to satisfy Bishop Berkeley, as well as being de-sexualized enough to please Mrs. Grundy.

Am I, then, urging us to return to the older view of a human nature divided between a "social man" and a "natural man" who is either benevolent, Rousseau's Noble Savage, or sinister and destructive, as Hobbes regarded him? Freud is usually represented, or misrepresented, as the chief modern proponent of this dualistic conception which assigns to the social order the purely negative role of blocking and re-directing man's "imperious biological drives." I say "misrepresented" because, although Freud often said things supporting such an interpretation, other and more fundamental strains in his thinking suggest a different conclusion. John Dollard, certainly not a writer who is oblivious to social and cultural "factors," saw this twenty-five years ago: "It is quite clear," he wrote, ". . . that he (Freud) does not regard the instincts as having a fixed social goal; rather, indeed, in the case of the sexual instinct he has stressed the vague but powerful and impulsive nature of the drive and has emphasized that its proper social object is not picked out in advance. His seems to be a drive concept which is not at variance with our knowledge from comparative cultural studies, since his theory does not demand that the 'instinct' work itself out with mechanical certainty alike in every varying culture."

So much for Freud's "imperious biological drives!" When Freud defined psychoanalysis as the study of the "vicissitudes of the instincts," he was confirming, not denying, the "plasticity" of human nature insisted on by social scientists. The drives or "instincts" of psychoanalysis, far from being fixed dispositions to behave in a particular way, are utterly subject to social channelling and transformation and could not even reveal themselves in behavior without social molding any more than our vocal chords can produce articulate speech if we have not learned a language. To psychoanalysis man is indeed a social animal; his social nature is profoundly reflected in his bodily structure.

But there is a difference between the Freudian view on the one hand and both sociological and neo-Freudian conceptions of man on the other. To Freud man is a *social* animal without being entirely a *socialized* animal. His very social nature is the source of conflicts and antagonisms that create resistance to socialization by the norms of any of the societies which have existed in the course of human history. "Socialization" may mean two quite distinct things; when they are confused an oversocialized view of man is the result. On the one hand socialization means the "transmission of the culture," the particular culture of the society an individual enters at birth; on the other hand the term is used to mean the "process of becoming human," of acquiring uniquely human attributes from interaction with others. All men are socialized in the latter sense, but this does not mean that they have been completely molded by the particular norms and values of their culture. All cultures, as Freud contended, do violence to man's socialized bodily drives, but this in no sense means that men could possibly exist without culture or independently of society. From such a standpoint, man may properly be called as Norman Brown has called him, the "neurotic" or the "discontented" animal and repression may be seen as the main characteristic of human nature as we have known it in history.

But isn't this psychology and haven't sociologists been taught to foreswear psychology, to look with suspicion on what are called "psychological variables" in contradistinction to the institutional and historical forces with which they are properly concerned? There is, indeed, as recent critics have complained, too much "psychologism" in contemporary sociology, largely, I think, because of the bias inherent in our favored research techniques. But I do not see how, at the level of theory, sociologists can fail to make assumptions about human nature. If our assumptions are left implicit, we will inevitably presuppose of a view of man that is tailor-made to our special needs; when our sociological theory over-stresses the stability and integration of society we will end up imagining that man is the disembodied, conscience-driven, status-seeking phantom of current theory. We must do better if we really wish to win credit outside of our ranks for special understanding of man, that plausible creature whose wagging tongue so often hides the despair and darkness in his heart.

6

The Theoretical Infrastructure*

Alvin W. Gouldner

One of the reasons that domain assumptions have importance as part of the entire sub-theoretical matrix on which theory rests is that they provide foci for feelings, affective states, and sentiments, although they are by no means the only structures around which sentiments come to be organized. To say, for example, that someone "believes" Negroes are lazy and also "believes" this is bad, is not entirely correct. For, those viewing this as "bad" do more than *believe* it; they *feel* it and may indeed feel it strongly. They may have sentiments of disgust and avoidance, or a wish to punish, associated with their assumptions about what the Negro is and with their devaluation of him. Sentiments entail a hormone-eliciting, muscle-tensing, tissue-embedded, fight-or-flight disposition of the total organism. While sentiments often may be organized around or elicited by domain assumptions, they are not the same thing. And they may, of course, be organized around or elicited by a great many things other than domain assumptions, for instance, individual persons or concrete situations.

Furthermore, people may have sentiments that are not conventionally called for by the domain assumptions that they have learned, but they are not for that reason any the less powerful and body-gripping. There may, in brief, be various forms of dissonance between the existential and normative beliefs that people learn in connection with domain-constituting categories, and the sentiments that they feel toward members of that category. Thus, for instance, a White woman may *feel* sexually aroused and attracted to a Black man, even though she also believes that Blacks are "dirty" and "disgusting." A man may *feel* pessimistic and despairing, resigned and quiescent, even though he also believes that men are good and that society progresses, simply because he himself is ill or aging. Correspondingly, a man may, when young, feel optimistic and energetically activistic, even though he may believe that the world is on a collision course with disaster and that there is little that can be done about it.

I am, of course, not suggesting that young men are invariably more optimistic than old ones, but what I am intimating, using age only as an example, is that people may feel things at variance with their domain assumptions, with their existential beliefs or normative values; feelings emerge from people's experience with the world, during which they often come to need and learn things that are somewhat different from what they are supposed to need or

*Excerpt from *The Coming Crisis in Western Sociology* by Alvin W. Gouldner.

were deliberately taught to learn. If Freud and other psychologists are right about the Oedipal Complex, many men in Western societies feel hostility toward their fathers even though they have never been taught to do so, and in fact have been taught to love and honor them. In short, men may have feelings at variance with those of their culturally prescribed "languages" that is, with the domain assumptions conventional to their group of society. Such sentiments may be idiosyncratic to an individual and derive from his unique experience, or they may be shared by large numbers and derive from an experience common to them, even if not culturally prescribed for them. Thus, at least since about the early nineteenth century, many young people in Western countries seem to be subjected to a common experience that induces them to be somewhat more anti-authoritarian, rebellious, or critical of the political and cultural status quo than were their elders.

The prescribed domain assumptions, then, are one thing; the sentiments men have may be quite another. When they diverge, when the things men feel are at variance with their domain assumptions, there is a dissonance or tension between the two levels. Sometimes this is dealt with simply by giving ritualistic "lip service" to the domain assumptions required and taught in the culture; sometimes men may openly rebel against them, adopting or seeking new domain assumptions more consonant with the feelings they actually have. But there is likely to be an intrinsic difficulty in such an open and active rebellion: first, unless there are already alternatives formulated, men may find it easier to live with the old uncomfortable assumptions than with none at all; second, men often experience their own deviant feelings as "wrong" and as perilous to their own security, and consequently may conceal their unprescribed feelings even from themselves; third, as a consequence of this, they may not openly communicate their deviant feelings to others who might share and therefore encourage and support them.

In consequence then, when a gap opens between the sentiments men feel and the domain assumptions they have been taught, their most immediate response may be to suppress or privatize the experienced dissonance. They may allow the tension to fester; or they may begin a kind of sporadic, cultural, guerrilla warfare against the prevailing domain assumptions, in which their dissatisfaction is intermittently expressed in squeaks of black humor or by an inertial apathy. This situation, very much like the attitude of some young radicals today toward academic sociology, begins to change importantly when domain categories and assumptions emerge that are more consonant with what people feel. When resistance to established assumptions lacks alternatives, it may at first be manifested socially among those who, while lacking a new language, do nonetheless recognize their common possession of deviant sentiments, and therefore may enter into informal solidarities with one another against those who they commonly feel share other sentiments. The current "generation gap" seems a case in point. When, however, the new sentiments begin to find or create their own appropriate language, the possibilities of larger solidarities and of rational public discussion are extended.

It is in part because social theories are shaped by and express domain assumptions that they are also sentiment-relevant: reactions to social theories involve the sentiments of the men who read and write them. Whether a theory is accepted or rejected, whether it undergoes change or remains essentially unchanged, is not simply a cerebral decision; it is in some part contingent upon the gratifications or tensions that it generates by dint of its relation to the sentiments of those involved. Social theories may be sentiment-relevant in various ways and to varying degrees may inhibit or arouse the expression of certain sentiments. As a limiting case, the degree to which they impinge upon sentiments may be so small that, for all practical purposes, they may be said to be "neutral" in their sentiment-relevance. Yet even this last case is consequential for reactions to the theory, for the sentiment-neutral theory may simply be eliciting apathetic or disinterested responses, the feeling that the theory is somehow "irrelevant," and thus induce avoidance of, if not active opposition to, it. Moreover, reactions to a social theory may also depend upon the *kinds* of sentiments that are aroused directly or by association. The activation of particular sentiments may at some times and for some people be enjoyable, or it may be discomfiting and painful.

Max Weber's theory of bureaucracy, for example, stressing, as it does, the inevitable proliferation of bureaucratic forms in the increasingly large and complex modern social organizations, tends to elicit and resonate sentiments of pessimism concerning the possibilities of large-scale social change that could successfully remedy human alienation, Those committed to efforts at such, change will experience such sentiments as dissonant and may therefore react critically to the theory, attempting to change it in ways that strip it of such consequences, or they may reject it altogether. Conversely, those who never had—or who once had but then relinquished—aspirations for social change, or whose inclination is to seek limited intra-system reforms, may for their part not experience the Weberian theory as inducing an unpleasant pessimism.

In one case, then, a theory may have a coherence-inducing or integrating effect, while in another it may have a tension- or conflict-inducing effect; each has different consequences for the individual's ability to pursue certain courses of *action* in the world and has different implications for different lines of political conduct. It is thus through its sentiment-relevance as well as through its domain assumptions that a social theory takes on political meanings and implications quite apart from whether these were knowingly intended or recognized either by those who formulated or those who accepted it. In the example mentioned above, concerning Weber's theory of bureaucracy, it is commonly understood that the theory has strongly antisocialist implications, for it implies that change toward socialism will not prevent bureaucratization and alienation.

Personal Reality and Social Theory

If every social theory is thus a tacit theory of politics, every theory is also a personal theory, inevitably expressing, coping, and infused with the personal experience of the individuals who author it.

Every social theory has both political and personal relevance, which, according to the technical canons of social theory, it is not supposed to have. Consequently, both the man and his politics are commonly screened out in what is deemed the proper presentation of presumably "autonomous" social theory.

Yet, however disguised, an appreciable part of any sociological enterprise devolves from the sociologist's effort to explore, to objectify, and to universalize some of his own most deeply personal experiences. Much of any man's effort to know the social world around him is prompted by an effort, more or less disguised or deliberate, to know things that are personally important to him; which is to say, he aims at knowing himself and the experiences he has had in his social world (his relationship to it), and at *changing* this relationship in some manner. Like it or not, and know it or not, in confronting the social world the theorist is also confronting himself. While this has no bearing on the validity of the resultant theory, it does bear on another legitimate interest: the sources, the motives, and the aims of the sociological quest.

Whatever their other differences, all sociologists seek to study something in the social world that they take to be real; and, whatever their philosophy of science, they seek to explain it in terms of something that they *feel* to be real. Like other men, sociologists impute reality to certain things in their social world. This is to say, they believe, sometimes with focal and sometimes only with subsidiary awareness, that certain things are truly attributable to the social world. In important part, their conception of what is "real" derives from the domain assumptions they have learned in their culture. These culturally standardized assumptions are, however, differentiated by personal experience in different parts of the social structure. Individually accented by particular sentiment-generating experiences, the common domain assumptions in time assume personal arrangements; they become part of a man's personal reality.

For simplicity's sake, I suggest that there are two kinds of "reality" with which sociologists must come to terms. One consists of "role realities," the things they learn as sociologists; these include what they believe to be the "facts" yielded by previous researches, whether conducted by themselves or others. The "facts," of course, entail imputations made by men about the world. To assign factuality to some imputation about the world is also to express a personal conviction about its truth, as well as about the propriety of the process by which it was made. To believe an imputation to be "factual" is to assign a high value to it, setting it above such things as "opinions" or "prejudices."

Inevitably, to assign factuality to an imputation is to make it an anchor point in the self's relation to the world, to make it or claim it should be central to the self. To assign factuality to an imputation is to invoke an obligation and duty upon the self: one must "take the facts into account" under certain conditions. There is the further obligation to inspect severely and to examine critically (in short to defend against) attacks on one's "factual" beliefs; a denial of beliefs previously thought to be factual is thus a self-mobilizing "challenge." Within scientific communities, therefore, men engage in committed personal efforts—through contest, conflict, struggle, and negotiation—to establish and maintain the facts. The facts are not automatically produced by the impersonal machinery of research. To assign factuality to a belief is a self-involving commitment; the person makes a claim upon the credence of another, or himself lends credence to the claim of another. In these and other ways, the factual becomes part of the sociologist's personal reality.

In particular those imputations that a sociologist makes about the factuality of beliefs based on research tend to become aspects of his reality, part of his *focal awareness as a sociologist.* Deemed relevant to his work as a sociologist and derived in accordance with methodological decorum, the sociologist commonly feels that he may with propriety publicly endorse such beliefs. Indeed, these *must* explicitly be attended to by him under certain conditions. In short, he must not ignore them, and he need not conceal his belief in them.

A second order of conceptions about reality held by sociologists consists of the "personally real." These are imputations about "realities" in the social world that sociologists make, not because of "evidence" or "research," but simply because of what they have seen, heard, been told, or read. While these beliefs differ from "facts" systematically gathered and scientifically evaluated, the sociologist nonetheless *experiences* them as no less real—and it is well for his sanity that he does. Still, while these are every bit as real to him as facts garnered through research, if not more so, the sociologist *qua* sociologist is not supposed to credit or attend to them in the same way that he treats "facts"; indeed, he may feel obliged as a sociologist to subject them to systematic doubt. Imputations about the world that are part of the sociologist's *personal* reality may therefore sink into his subsidiary awareness rather than remaining consciously available to him, when he acts as a conforming sociologist. But this, of course, is very far from saying that they thereby cease to have consequences for his work as a sociologist or social theorist. In practice, the sociologist's role realities and his personal realities interpenetrate and mutually influence one another.

During the 1940's and 1950's, largely under the influence of Talcott Parsons, many sociologists stressed the importance of theory in structuring research. Starting from the commonplace that sociologists did not view all parts of the social world as equally important, but rather focused their attention upon it selectively, they concluded that this perceptual organization was largely the result of the "theories," tacit or explicit, which were held. "Facts" were thus seen as the product of an effort to pursue the inferences of theories and, indeed, as being constituted by the conceptual schemes embedded in the theories. Facts were seen, at least primarily, as interacting with theories, confirming or disproving them, and thus as cumulatively shaping theoretical development; perceptual selectivity, and hence the focus of research, was largely accounted for in terms of the sociologist's theoretical commitment.

This emphasis tended to deprecate the earlier tradition of methodological empiricism, which had stressed the primary value of data and research. If the empiricists had stressed that sociologists are or should be guided by the facts yielded by properly conducted research, theory-stressing sociologists tended to reply that sociologists are or should be guided by articulate, explicit, and hence testable theory. From the standpoint presented here, however, both seem to have been at least partially mistaken.

Those who emphasized theory tended unduly to deprecate the self-implicating, perception-anchoring, and stabilizing role of "facts" (as distinct from their validity-testing function); the empiricists tended to miss the importance of previously held theoretical assumptions. Both, in addition, made a common error in limiting themselves to only one order of the imputably real, namely, the "factual." What both missed is that scientific factuality is only a special case of a larger set of beliefs, those imputing reality; both failed to see that whether an aspect of "role reality" or "personal reality," the imputably real has a special force in structuring the perception of the sociologist and shaping his subsequent theorizing and research. The theorists in particular failed to see the importance of the sub-theoretical level, including the "personally real," as consequential for theory and research. A situation defined as real is real in its consequences, for sociologists as for other men.

Whether part of his role reality or his personal reality, things to which the sociologist imputes reality play a role in his work in several ways. They may be elements that he is concerned to explain, in short, as "dependent variables" or effects; they may be part of his explanatory effort, serving as "independent variables" or possible "causes"; or, again, they may be used as explicit models or tacit paradigms that he employs to clarify the nature of what he wants to explain or the factors that explain it.

To amplify the latter point: the imputably real enters importantly into theory construction by being regarded as possessed of *generalizable* significance, by being treated as an example or case of, or a model or paradigm of, a larger set of things. Sociologists assume that things they have researched, or with which they have otherwise become personally acquainted and hence "know," are like (and may be used to understand) other things with which they are unacquainted at first hand or have not yet researched. Thus, while aiming to account for a set of events that extend beyond the sociologist's facts or personal realities, social theories are at the same time also influenced by his prior imputations about what is real in the world, whether these are his facts or personal realities. For example, Max Weber's general theory of bureaucracy was influenced both by his historical, scholarly researches and by his first-hand acquaintance with German bureaucracy and, in particular, with governmental rather than private bureaucracy. The German governmental bureaucracy, both as experienced social structure and as cultural ideal, constituted for Weber a personal reality that served as his central paradigm for all bureaucracies; it provided a framework for organizing and assimilating the facts yielded by his scholarly researches.

If personal reality shapes scholarly research, scholarly research is also a source of personal reality, not only of role reality. A man's research or work is commonly more than just a way he spends time; it is often a vital part of his life and a central part of the experience that shapes his personal reality. If this were not so, then all relevant research would be equally significant to a sociologist. But the truth is that researches and discoveries made by the scholar himself have a special importance for him; a man's own researches become a part of his personal reality in ways that the work of his colleagues usually does not. If nothing else, they become personal commitments that he wishes to defend.

The limited parts of the social world with which a sociologist's research bring him into contact are endowed with a compelling reality precisely because they are part of his personal experience. Limited though they are, they often come to be used as paradigms for other, unknown parts, and serve as the basis for generalizing about larger wholes. Thus, for example, *one* reason Malinowski's theory of magic differed from that of A. R. Radcliffe-Brown was because the different kinds of magic each had first closely studied came to stand for all other kinds of magic. Although Malinowski had focused on work- and subsistence-getting magic, and Radcliffe-Brown on childbirth magic, each treated his limited experience as a paradigm, exemplary of and essentially akin to other kinds of magic. Evidence incorporated into personal experience became part of a permeating personal reality to which the larger world was assimilated and by which it was shaped.

Sociologists, of course, are familiar with these dangers, at least *en principe*, and they seek to use systematic sampling as a way of obviating them. Nonetheless, systematic sampling cannot fully avoid the problem, for it provides a basis for testing a theory only subsequent to its formulation. Disciplined research entails the use of a systematic sample in order to test inferences from a theory, but, in the nature of the case, the theory must be formulated prior to the sample. Indeed, the more the sociologist stresses the importance of articulate theory, the more this is likely to be the case. The theory will therefore tend to devolve around, and consequently be shaped by, the limited facts and personal realities available to the theorist, *and in particular by those imputed realities that he treats as paradigms.*

Systematic sampling serves primarily as a restraint on unjustified generalization from "facts"; but it does not similarly restrain the influence of "personal realities." Since the latter commonly remains only at the fringes of subsidiary awareness, being deemed scientifically irrelevant, it is often (and mistakenly) assumed that it is scientifically inconsequential. In point of fact, the personally real and problematic often enough becomes the starting point for systematic inquiry—and, indeed, there is no scientific reason this should not be so.

What is personally real to men is real, frequently though not always, primarily because it is not unique to them—in the sense of idiosyncratic to, or uniquely different for, them—but rather is socially and collectively true. Since the sense of the reality of things often depends on mutual agreement or consensual validation, collectively held notions of reality are among the most firmly constituted components of an individual's personal reality. Yet the personally real does not entirely consist of or derive from collective definitions of social reality. It may also emerge from recurrent personal experience, whether unique to the person or shared with a few others. What becomes personally real to one individual, then, need not be personally real to others. But whether derived from collective definitions or from recurrent personal experiences, a man believes that some things are real; and these imputed realities are of special importance to the kinds of theories that he formulates, even if he happens to be a sociologist.

The Infrastructure of Social Theory

From this perspective all social theory is immersed in a sub-theoretical level of domain assumptions and sentiments which both liberate and constrain it. This sub-theoretical level is shaped by and shared with the larger culture and society, at least to some extent, as well as being individually organized, accented, differentiated, and changed by personal experience in the world. I call this sub-theoretical level the "infrastructure" of theory.

This infrastructure is important not because it is the ultimate determinant of the character of social theory, but because it is part of the most immediate, local surround from which the theory-work eventuates in theory-performances and theory-products. Theory-work is surely linked to, even if not solely determined by, the character of the theorist doing it. This infrastructure can never really be left behind, even in the most isolated and lonely moments of theory-work, when a man finally puts pen to paper in a room where there is no one but himself, The world is, of course, there in the room with him, in him; he has not escaped it. But it is not *the* world, not *the* society and *the* culture that is there with him, but *his* limited version and partial experience of it.

However individual a work of theory is, nonetheless, some (and perhaps much) of its individuality is conventional in character. The individuality of theory-work is, in part, a socially sanctioned illusion. For there are the assistants who have helped the theorist do his research and writing; there are the colleagues and the students, the friends and the lovers, on whom he has informally "tested" his ideas; there are those from whom he has learned and taken and those whom he opposes. All theory is not merely influenced but actually produced by a group. Behind each theory-product is not only the author whose name appears upon the work, but an entire shadow group for whom, we might say, the "author" is the emblem; in a way, the author's name serves as the name of an intellectual team.

Yet the "author" is not merely the puppet of these group forces, because to some extent he selects his team, recruits members to and eliminates them from his theory-working group, responds selectively to the things they suggest and the criticisms they make, accepting some and ignoring others, attending to some more closely than others. Thus, while authorship is always in some measure conventional, it is also in some measure the expression of the real activities and initiatives of an individual theorist whose "infrastructure" helps shape both the ideas and the shadow group whose tacit collaboration eventuates in theoretical performances.

A concern with sub-theory or the infrastructure of theory is not the expression of an inclination to psychologize theory and is certainly not a form of psychological reductionism. It is, rather, the outcome of a concern for empirical realism, an effort to come close to the human systems to which any theoretical work is most visibly and intimately linked. It is an effort that is peculiarly necessary for those working within a sociological tradition that tends to obscure and to cast doubt upon the importance and reality of persons, and to view them as the creatures of grander social structures. For those, such as myself, who have lived within a sociological tradition, the importance of the larger social structures and historical processes is not in doubt. What is intellectually in question, when the significance of theoretical infrastructure is raised, is the analytic means by which we may move between persons and social structures, between society and the local, more narrowly bounded environments from which social theory discernibly derives. My own view is that any sociological explanation or generalization implies (at least tacitly) certain psychological assumptions; correspondingly, any psychological generalization tacitly implies certain sociological conditions. In directing attention to the importance of the theoretical infrastructure, I have sought not to psychologize social theory and remove it from the larger social system, but rather to specify the analytic means by which I hope to *link it more firmly* with the larger social world.

PART II

The Enlightenment Roots of Sociological Theory

In a collection of readings in sociological theory as vast as this one, it is entirely reasonable to inquire as to where the *roots* of sociological theory lie. Who were the *forerunners* of such an enterprise? Arguments can be made that those roots reach all the way back to the Greek philosopher Plato, who, writing more than 2,400 years ago, made systematic inquiries about the good society. Or perhaps those roots lie in the ideas of the Renaissance thinker Niccolò Machiavelli, who advised "the prince," the wise ruler, to create stability and security between competing interests in society. But because sociology emerged as part of the *modernization* of Western society, it seems altogether proper to locate its more immediate roots in the Enlightenment, the guiding European intellectual movement of the 17th and 18th centuries. As such, we identify as its theoretical forerunners the Enlightenment philosophers—such as Thomas Hobbes, Jean-Jacques Rousseau, and Charles de Montesquieu—whose writings were informed by the principles of reason, science, and humanity. Though these thinkers were highly invested in the idea of human nature, they were just as interested in society—its origins, its workings, and its transformations. Indeed, they tended to be critical of existing social institutions (particularly the Church and the monarchy), urging that those that were contrary to human nature be altered or dismantled. Whatever their differences and similarities, the Enlightenment intellectuals were *reformers*, intent on bringing about social change through rational thought.

The first major Enlightenment thinker in England was Thomas Hobbes, and his most important work, *Leviathan*, appeared in 1651. In the selection titled "The Problem of Order," excerpted from *Leviathan*, Hobbes begins by stating that people are naturally equal in power. Even when there are differences in physical strength, the weaker can always overcome the stronger, either through plotting in secret or through colluding with others. And though there are differences in mental ability, people generally tend to see themselves as cleverer and more cunning than others. Due to this natural state of equality and the fact that people generally desire the same resources (food, shelter, land, etc.), which are limited, they will quarrel over them. This gives rise to a perpetual state of conflict—a continuous war of all against all—in which people, through force and fraud, endeavor to obtain what they want. All of this makes society impossible and causes people's lives to be "solitary, poor, nasty, brutish, and short." Without government making laws that forbid this social conflict, there is no sense of right or wrong, no notions of justice and injustice—in short, no *social order*. However, because people fear death, they seek peace. And what maintains peace, says Hobbes, are the laws of nature—the rules of self-preservation arrived at through reason.

Like Hobbes, the French philosophers Jean-Jacques Rousseau and Charles de Montesquieu also conceived of human nature in relation to society. Rousseau, in his most famous work, *The Social*

Contract, which was published in 1762, explained the creation of civil society. In "The Social Contract," Rousseau asserts that the social order is not a natural right but is instead based on convention—on people's agreements with each other. Indeed, the true origin of society is founded on a *social contract*. For their own self-preservation, rather than being in constant conflict, people unite and cooperate with each other. The social contract forms an association, a civil society, in which each member willingly concedes to surrender some freedoms to the general will—the common good—in return for protection and security. Social order is possible because people agree to follow the laws of society.

As for Montesquieu, in his major work of 1748, *The Spirit of the Laws*, he identified different types of politically organized societies and proposed the contemporary notion of the separation of powers, as well as the idea of a system of checks and balances in the political system. He was also one of the first to assert that laws, beliefs, and customs are relative: What one society considers right and proper, other societies may not. In "Laws, Mores, and Manners," Montesquieu maintains that human behavior is regulated by a variety of influences, including *laws* (formal rules), *mores* (beliefs), and *manners* (customs). These form the general spirit, or national character, of a particular country. It is important, however, that in any country, laws, which are established by a formal legislature, do not go contrary to mores and manners, which emerge spontaneously from social existence. Should mores and manners need to be changed, they should not be changed by laws but by other mores and manners. Indeed, mores and manners are of a different nature than law. While punishments deter violations of law, only behavioral examples can change manners.

7

The Problem of Order*

Thomas Hobbes

Nature hath made men so equal in the faculties of body and mind, as that, though there be found one man sometimes manifestly stronger in body or of quicker mind than another; yet when all is reckoned together, the difference between man and man is not so considerable as that one man can thereupon claim to himself any benefit to which another may not pretend as well as he. For as to the strength of body, the weakest has strength enough to kill the strongest, either by secret machination or by confederacy with others that are in the same danger with himself.

And as to the faculties of the mind, setting aside the arts grounded upon words, and especially that skill of proceeding upon general and infallible rules, called science, which very few have and but in few things, as being not a native faculty born with us, nor attained, as prudence, while we look after somewhat else, I find yet a greater equality amongst men than that of strength. For prudence is but experience, which equal time equally bestows on all men in those things they equally apply themselves unto. That which may perhaps make such equality incredible is but a vain conceit of one's own wisdom, which almost all men think they have in a greater degree than the vulgar, that is, than all men but themselves and a few others, whom by fame or for concurring with themselves, they approve. For such is the nature of men that howsoever they may acknowledge many others to be more witty or more eloquent or more learned, they will hardly believe there be many so wise as themselves; for they see their own wit at hand and other men's at a distance. But this proveth rather that men are in that point equal, than unequal. For there is not ordinarily a greater sign of the equal distribution of anything than that every man is contented with his share.

From this equality of ability ariseth equality of hope in the proceeds attaining of our ends. And therefore if any two men desire the diffidence, same thing, which nevertheless they cannot both enjoy, they become enemies; and in the way to their end (which is principally their own conservation, and sometimes their delectation only) endeavour to destroy or subdue one another. And from, hence it comes to pass that where an invader hath no more to fear than another man's single power, if one plant, sow, build, or possess a convenient seat, others may probably be expected to come prepared with forces united to dispossess and deprive him, not only of the fruit of his labour, but also of his life or liberty. And the invader again is in the like danger of another.

*Excerpts from *Leviathan*, by Thomas Hobbes, edited by A.P. Martinich. Broadview Press Ltd., 2005.

And from this diffidence of one another, there is no way for any man to secure himself so reasonable as anticipation, that is, by force or wiles, to master the persons of all men he can so long till he see no other power great enough to endanger him; and this is no more than his own conservation requireth, and is generally allowed. Also, because there be some that, taking pleasure in contemplating their own power in the acts of conquest, which they pursue farther than their security requires, if others, that otherwise would be glad to be at ease within modest bounds, should not by invasion increase their power, they would not be able, long time, by standing only on their defence, to subsist. And by consequence, such augmentation of dominion over men being necessary to a man's conservation, it ought to be allowed him.

Again, men have no pleasure (but on the contrary a great deal of grief) in keeping company where there is no power able to overawe them all. For every man looketh that his companion should value him at the same rate he sets upon himself, and upon all signs of contempt or undervaluing naturally endeavours, as far as he dares (which amongst them that have no common power to keep them in quiet is far enough to make them destroy each other), to extort a greater value from his contemners, by damage; and from others, by the example.

So that in the nature of man, we find three principal causes of quarrel. First, competition; secondly, diffidence; thirdly, glory.

The first maketh men invade for gain; the second, for safety; and the third, for reputation. The first use violence to make themselves masters of other men's persons, wives, children, and cattle; the second, to defend them; the third, for trifles, as a word, a smile, a different opinion, and any other sign of undervalue, either direct in their persons or by reflection in their kindred, their friends, their nation, their profession, or their name.

Hereby it is manifest that during the time men live without a common power to keep them all in awe, they are in that condition which is called war; and such a war as is of every man against every man. For WAR consisteth not in battle only, or the act of fighting, but in a tract of time, wherein the will to contend by battle is against every sufficiently known; and therefore the notion of *time* is to be considered in the nature of war, as it is in the nature of weather. For as the nature of foul weather lieth not in a shower or two of rain, but in an inclination thereto of many days together, so the nature of war consisteth not in actual fighting, but in the known disposition thereto during all the time there is no assurance to the contrary. All other time is Peace.

Whatsoever therefore is consequent to a time of war, where every man is enemy to every man, the same consequent to the time wherein men live without other security than what their own strength and their own invention shall furnish them withal. In such condition there is no place for industry, because the fruit thereof is uncertain; and consequendly no culture of the earth; no navigation, nor use of the commodities that may be imported by sea; no commodious building; no instruments of moving and removing such things as require much force; no knowledge of the face of the earth; no account of time; no arts; no letters; no society; and which is worst of all, continual fear, and danger of violent death; and the life of man, solitary, poor, nasty, brutish, and short.

It may seem strange to some man that has not well weighed these things that nature should thus dissociate and render men apt to invade and destroy one another; and he may therefore, not trusting to this inference, made from the passions, desire perhaps to have the same confirmed by experience. Let him therefore consider with himself; when taking a journey, he arms himself and seeks to go well accompanied; when going to sleep, he locks his doors; when even in his house he locks his chests; and this when he knows there be laws and public officers, armed to revenge all injuries shall be done him; what opinion he has of his fellow subjects, when he rides armed; of his fellow citizens, when he locks his doors; and of his children, and servants, when he locks his chests. Does he not there as much accuse mankind by his actions as I do by my words? But neither of us accuse man's nature in it. The desires and other passions of man are in themselves no sin. No more are the actions that proceed from those passions till they know a law that forbids them; which, till laws be made, they cannot know; nor can any law be made till they have agreed upon the person that shall make it.

It may peradventure be thought there was never such a time nor condition of war as this; and I believe it was never generally so, over all the world; but there are many places where they live so now. For the savage people in many places of America, except the government of small families, the concord whereof dependeth on natural lust, have no government at all, and live at this day in that brutish manner, as I said before. Howsoever, it may be perceived what manner of life there would be, where there were no common power to fear, by the manner of life which men that have formerly lived under a peaceful government use to degenerate into a civil war.

But though there had never been any time wherein particular men were in a condition of war one against another; yet in all times kings and persons of sovereign authority, because of their independency, are in continual jealousies, and in the state and posture of gladiators, having their weapons pointing and their eyes fixed on one another, that is, their forts, garrisons, and guns upon the frontiers of their kingdoms, and continual spies upon their neighbours, which is a posture of war. But because they uphold thereby the industry of their subjects, there does not follow from it that misery which accompanies the liberty of particular men.

To this war of every man against every man, this also is consequent; that nothing can be unjust. The notions of right and wrong, justice and injustice, have there no place. Where there is no common power, there is no law; where no law, no injustice. Force and fraud are in war the two cardinal virtues. Justice and injustice are none of the faculties neither of the body nor mind. If they were, they might be in a man that were alone in the world, as well as his senses and passions. They are qualities that relate to men in society, not in solitude. It is consequent also to the same condition that there be no propriety, no dominion, no *mine* and *thine* distinct; but only that to be every man's that he can get, and for so long as he can keep it. And thus much for the ill condition which man by mere nature is actually placed in; though with a possibility to come out of it, consisting partly in the passions, partly in his reason.

The passions that incline men to peace are fear of death, desire of such things as are necessary to commodious living, and a hope by their industry to obtain them. And reason suggesteth convenient articles of peace upon which men may be drawn to agreement. These articles are they which otherwise are called the laws of nature, whereof I shall speak more particularly in the two following chapters.

8

THE SOCIAL CONTRACT*

JEAN-JACQUES ROUSSEAU

Man is born free, and everywhere he is in chains. One believes himself the others' master, and yet is more a slave than they. How did this change come about? I do not know. What can make it legitimate? I believe I can solve this question.

If I considered only force, and the effect that follows from it, I would say; as long as a People is compelled to obey and does obey, it does well; as soon as it can shake off the yoke and does shake it off, it does even better; for in recovering its freedom by the same right as the right by which it was robbed of it, either the people is well founded to take it back, or it was deprived of it without foundation. But the social order is a sacred right, which provides the basis for all the others. Yet this right does not come from nature; it is therefore founded on conventions. The problem is to know what these conventions are.

That One Always Has to Go Back to a First Convention

There will always be a great difference between subjugating a multitude and ruling a society. When scattered men, regardless of their number, are successively enslaved to a single man, I see in this nothing but a master and slaves, I do not see in it a people and its chief; it is, if you will, an aggregation, but not an association; there is here neither public good, nor body politic. That man, even if he had enslaved half the world, still remains nothing but a private individual; his interest, separate from that of the others, still remains nothing but a private interest. When this same man dies, his empire is left behind scattered and without a bond, like an oak dissolves and collapses into a heap of ashes on being consumed by fire.

A people, says Grotius, can give itself to a king. So that according to Grotius a people is a people before giving itself to a king. That very gift is a civil act, it presupposes a public deliberation. Hence before examining the act by which a people elects a king, it would be well to examine the act by which a people is a people. For this act, being necessarily prior to the other, is the true foundation of society.

Indeed, if there were no prior convention, then, unless the election were unanimous, why would the minority be obliged to submit to the choice of the majority, and why would a hundred who want a master have the right to vote on behalf of ten who do not want one? The law of majority rule is itself something established by convention, and presupposes unanimity at least once.

Of the Social Pact

I assume men having reached the point where the obstacles that interfere with their preservation in the state of nature prevail by their resistance over the forces which each individual can muster to maintain himself in that state. Then that primitive state can no longer subsist, and humankind would perish if it did not change its way of being.

Now, since men cannot engender new forces, but only unite and direct those that exist, they are left with no other means of self-preservation than to form, by aggregation, a sum of forces that might prevail over those obstacles' resistance, to set them in motion by a single impetus, and make them act in concert.

This sum of forces can only arise from the cooperation of many: but since each man's force and freedom are his primary instruments of self-preservation, how can he commit them without harming himself, and without neglecting the cares he owes himself? This difficulty, in relation to my subject, can be stated in the following terms.

"To find a form of association that will defend and protect the person and goods of each associate with the full common force, and by means of which each, uniting with all, nevertheless obey only himself and remain as free as before." This is the fundamental problem to which the social contract provides the solution.

The clauses of this contract are so completely determined by the nature of the act that the slightest modification would render them null and void; so that although they may never have been formally stated, they are everywhere the same, everywhere tacitly admitted and recognized; until, the social compact having been violated, everyone is thereupon restored to his original rights and resumes his natural freedom while losing the conventional freedom for which he renounced it.

These clauses, rightly understood, all come down to just one, namely the total alienation of each associate with all of his rights to the whole community: For, in the first place, since each gives himself entirely, the condition is [361] equal for all, and since the condition is equal for all, no one has any interest in making it burdensome to the rest.

Moreover, since the alienation is made without reservation, the union is as perfect as it can be, and no associate has anything further to claim: For if individuals were left some rights, then, since there would be no common superior who might adjudicate between them and the public, each, being judge in his own case on some issue, would soon claim to be so on all, the state of nature would subsist and the association necessarily become tyrannical or empty.

Finally, each, by giving himself to all, gives himself to no one, and since there is no associate over whom one does not acquire the same right as one grants him over oneself, one gains the equivalent of all one loses, and more force to preserve what one has.

If, then, one sets aside everything that is not of the essence of the social compact, one finds that it can be reduced to the following terms: *Each of us puts his person and his full power in common under the supreme direction of the general will; and in a body we receive each member as an indivisible part of the whole.*

9

Laws, Mores, and Manners*

Charles de Montesquieu

Many things govern men: climate, religion, laws, the maxims of the government, examples of past things, mores, and manners; a general spirit is formed as a result.

To the extent that, in each nation, one of these causes acts more forcefully, the others yield to it. Nature and climate almost alone dominate savages; manners govern the Chinese; laws tyrannize Japan; in former times mores set the tone in Lacedaemonia; in Rome it was set by the maxims of government and the ancient mores.

If there were in the world a nation which had a sociable humor, an openness of heart; a joy in life, a taste, an ease in communicating its thoughts; which was lively, pleasant, playful, sometimes imprudent, often indiscreet; and which had with all that, courage, generosity, frankness, and a certain point of honor, one should avoid disturbing its manners by laws, in order not to disturb its virtues. If the character is generally good, what difference do a few faults make?

One could constrain its women, make laws to correct their mores, and limit their luxury, but who knows whether one would not lose a certain taste that would be the source of the nation's wealth and a politeness that attracts foreigners to it?

The legislator is to follow the spirit of the nation when doing so is not contrary to the principles of the government, for we do nothing better than what we do freely and by following our natural genius.

If one gives a pedantic spirit to a nation naturally full of gaiety, the state will gain nothing, either at home or abroad. Let it do frivolous things seriously and serious things gaily.

The more communicative peoples are, the more easily they change their manners, because each man is more a spectacle for another; one sees the singularities of individuals better. The climate that makes a nation like to communicate also makes it like to change, and what makes a nation like to change also makes its taste take form.

The society of women spoils mores and forms taste; the desire to please more than others establishes ornamentation, and the desire to please more than oneself establishes fashions. Fashions are an important subject; as one allows one's spirit to become frivolous, one constantly increases the branches of commerce.

Vanity is as good a spring for a government as arrogance is a dangerous one. To show this, one has only to imagine to oneself, on the one hand, the innumerable goods resulting from vanity: luxury, industry, the arts, fashions, politeness, and taste, and, on the other hand, the infinite evils born of the arrogance of certain nations: laziness, poverty, the abandonment of everything, and the destruction of the nations that chance has let fall

*Excerpts from *Montesquieu: The Spirit of the Laws* by Charles de Montesquieu, translated and edited by Anne M. Cohler, Basia Carolyn Miller, and Harold Samuel Stone.

into their hands as well as their own nation. Laziness is the effect of arrogance; work follows from vanity: the arrogance of a Spaniard will incline him not to work; the vanity of a Frenchman will incline him to try to work better than the others.

Every lazy nation is grave; for those who do not work regard themselves as sovereigns of those who work.

Examine all the nations and you will see that in most of them gravity, arrogance, and laziness go hand in hand.

The people of Achim are proud and lazy: those who have no slaves rent one, if only to walk a hundred steps and carry two pints of rice; they would believe themselves dishonored if they carried it themselves.

In many places on earth people let their fingernails grow in order to indicate that they do not work.

Women in the Indies believe it is shameful for them to learn to read; this is the business, they say, of the slaves who sing hymns in the pagodas. In one caste, they do not spin; in another they make only baskets and mats, and should not even mill the rice; in others, they must not fetch water. Arrogance there has established its rules and sees that they are followed. It is unnecessary to say that moral qualities have different effects according to the other qualities united with them; thus arrogance joined to a vast ambition, to the greatness of ideas, etc. produced among the Romans the effects which are known to all.

It is a maxim of capital importance that the mores and manners of a despotic state must never be changed; nothing would be more promptly followed by a revolution. For, in these states, there are no laws, so to speak; there are only mores and manners, and if you overturn them, you overturn everything.

Laws are established, mores are inspired; the latter depend more on the general spirit, the former depend more on a particular institution; now, it is as dangerous, if not more so, to overturn the general spirit as to change a particular institution.

One is less communicative in countries where each man, whether a superior or an inferior, exercises and suffers an arbitrary power, than in those in which liberty reigns in all conditions. Therefore, one changes manners and mores less in them; manners that are more fixed are closer to laws: thus, a prince or a legislator must run counter to mores there less than in any other country in the world.

Women are ordinarily enclosed there and have no tone to give. In other countries where they live with men, their desire to please and one's desire to please them too prompt one to change manners continually. The two sexes spoil each other; each loses its distinctive and essential quality; arbitrariness is put into what was absolute, and manners change every day.

What Are the Natural Means of Changing the Mores and Manners of a Nation

We have said that the laws were the particular and precise institutions of the legislator and the mores and manners, the institutions of the nation in general. From this it follows that when one wants to change the mores and manners, one must not change them by the laws, as this would appear to be too tyrannical; it would be better to change them by other mores and other manners.

Thus, when a prince wants to make great changes in his nation, he must reform by laws what is established by laws and change by manners what is established by manners, and it is a very bad policy to change by laws what should be changed by manners.

The law that obliged the Muscovites to shorten their beards and their clothing and the violence of Peter I in trimming up to the knees the long robes of those who entered the towns were both tyrannical. The means for preventing crimes are penalties; the means for changing manners are examples.

In general, peoples are very attached to their customs; taking their customs from them violently makes them unhappy: therefore, one must not change their customs, but engage the peoples to change them themselves.

Every penalty that does not derive from necessity is tyrannical. The law is not a pure act of power; things indifferent by their nature are not within its scope.

Mores and manners are usages that laws have not established, or that they have not been able, or have not wanted, to establish.

The difference between laws and mores is that, while laws regulate the actions of the citizen, mores regulate the actions of the man. The difference between mores and manners is that the first are more concerned with internal, and the latter external, conduct.

PART III

Protosociology

The five thinkers whose writings compose the readings in this part—Henri de Saint-Simon, Auguste Comte, Herbert Spencer, Harriet Martineau, and William Graham Sumner—never developed a coherent sociological theory. In fact, theirs was a *protosociological* effort at theorizing—one that was sociological in character but unsystematic and embryonic in form. Their sociological analysis was more speculative than proven; it was tentative and inchoate. It was, however, these thinkers' coinage of concepts and heuristics, which they proposed throughout the 19th century, that contributed greatly to the fundamentals of sociological theorizing in the 20th century.

We begin with Henri de Saint-Simon's essay of 1819, "An Unjust Social Order," in which he conducts a thought experiment. He does this in order to investigate the potential consequences for postrevolutionary French society if, all of a sudden, France lost a significant number of its very best workers in the sciences, fine arts, and industry. Now suppose that instead of losing these productive workers, Saint-Simon continues, France suddenly lost its royal household, nobility, diplomatic corps, and aristocracy. It is quite obvious that the former group of producers makes the real contributions to the country's social progress, and yet it is the latter group of idlers that is the more prized. This thought experiment, according to Saint-Simon, showed that France's social structure, as it then existed, was defective and unjust. Continuing with the theme that the working, or proletarian, class of scientists, artists, and industrialists contributes the most to national prosperity, Saint-Simon, in "The Hierarchical Structure of Society," argues that postrevolutionary French society must be completely reorganized. It is people from the proletarian class, with their knowledge of positive science—not the governors, judges, and clerks—who should now be the administrators of the national interests. It is they who will improve the moral and physical welfare of all. And while Saint-Simon agrees that French society should be hierarchically structured as a pyramid, with the monarch at the apex and the skilled workers at the base, it is the upper middle strata—of useless courtiers, nobles, the idle rich, and various government officials and functionaries—that must be eradicated.

In the first reading by Auguste Comte, "Order and Progress," he divides sociology and its theoretical development into two parts: the static and the dynamic. The *static*, which relates to social order, examines the *structures* of the major institutions; the *dynamic*, which concerns social progress, analyzes the *development* of those structures. Though the two principles of order and progress are separated (as statics and dynamics) for purposes of sociological theoretical analysis, in reality, they are complementary. Comte's theory of social dynamics is exemplified in the essay "Law of the Three Stages." Here, he examines the historical development of human ways of knowing, which, he claims, has implications for understanding social organization and experience. According to him, human thought progresses through three radically different stages: the theological, the metaphysical, and the positive. In the *theological stage*, people make sense of the entire physical and social world in reference to supernatural beings. In the *metaphysical stage*, everything is rationally understood in terms of the nature of things. In the final stage, the *positive*, all phenomena are scientifically explained through the observation, experimentation, and comparison of facts. It is on the basis of empirical facts that sociological theory is formed.

Herbert Spencer revisits the Comtean theme of societal development in his essay of 1857, "Social Progress." Here, Spencer explains social progress as a change that takes place through a process of successive steps, from *homogeneity to heterogeneity*. This process occurs at the level of *structure*, or organization, and at the level of *function*, or division of labor. Structurally, society gradually becomes differentiated into separate institutions (e.g., government, religion, and economy) and communities (classes of workers). Functionally, members of society increasingly take on specialized roles and tasks of production (e.g., butcher, baker, and candlestick maker). For Spencer, this transformation from simple to complex is the law of evolution of all societies. In "The Evolution of Society," Spencer further refines his conceptualization of the growth and development of societies, which he compares weakly and only by tentative analogy to an *organism*. Societies, like biological organisms (for example, living bodies), *grow* in two ways: (1) by the multiplication of cells or groups and (2) by the repetitive union of cells or groups. As societies increase in size, they also increase in the *complexity of their social structures* and in their *degree of integration*. Integration leads to the progressive *differentiation* of structures and functions. Differentiation of structures and functions leads to growing *interdependence*—cooperation—and this, in turn, leads back to greater integration. This, according to Spencer, is the process by which societies evolve from simple to complex.

In "The General Happiness," Harriet Martineau isn't as concerned with issues of social structure as she is with issues pertaining to *culture*, or way of life. As such, her focus is on *morals*, a society's ideas about right and wrong, and on *manners*, the customs or habitual practices of a society's members. Additionally, while Martineau's contributions are largely in the area of research methods—on collecting data about societies—and not in the development of sociological theory, her concept of *the general happiness* can make an important contribution to theoretical analysis. In her book, *How to Observe Morals and Manners*, published in 1838, she instructs the "traveler," or the observer of social life in cultures different from his or her own, not only to be alert to cultural differences but also to refrain from making prejudiced judgments on them. Indeed, there is only one neutral standard by which the observer can truly understand the morals and manners of another culture: by seeing how they contribute to the general happiness of the people in that culture.

In "Folkways and Mores," William Graham Sumner refines the concept of mores previously used by Montesquieu and Martineau by introducing the notion of *folkways*. For Sumner, people, in their efforts to live well, were first involved with actions that, through trial and error, were eventually selected as being the most expedient in satisfying their needs in life. These efforts were then carried out in groups, and as each group member profited by the others' experiences, there was agreement on those conventions that proved to be most conducive to social welfare. These conventions are *folkways*. *Mores*, by contrast, consist of those ways of doing things that are current in a society to satisfy human needs and desires but which include judgments about societal welfare. As such, mores contain philosophical and moral principles that guide attempts to live well and that also satisfy human needs under the current conditions. Finally, in "In-Groups, Out-Groups, and Ethnocentrism," Sumner introduces these indispensable concepts. He uses the term *in-group* to indicate a group whose members possess "we" feelings of loyalty, friendship, and peace toward each other. An in-group always exists in relation to an *out-group*: a group toward which members of the in-group feel hostility and contempt. People have a positive view toward members of their in-group and have a negative view toward members of the out-group. The basic in-group-versus-out-group dynamic is "us" versus "them." *Ethnocentrism* refers to the idea that the members of an in-group consider their group superior to other groups and thus look down on them.

10

An Unjust Social Order*

Henri de Saint-Simon

Suppose that France suddenly lost fifty of her best physicists, chemists, physiologists, mathematicians, poets, painters, sculptors, musicians, writers; fifty of her best mechanical engineers, civil and military engineers, artillery experts, architects, doctors, surgeons, apothecaries, seamen, clockmakers; fifty of her best bankers, two hundred of her best business men, two hundred of her best farmers, fifty of her best ironmasters, arms manufacturers, tanners, dyers, miners, cloth-makers, cotton manufacturers, silk-makers, linen-makers, manufacturers of hardware, of pottery and china, of crystal and glass, ship chandlers, carriers, printers, engravers, goldsmiths, and other metal-workers; her fifty best masons, carpenters, joiners, farriers, locksmiths, cutlers, smelters, and a hundred other persons of various unspecified occupations, eminent in the sciences, fine arts, and professions; making in all the three thousand leading scientists, artists, and artisans of France.

These men are the Frenchmen who are the most essential producers, those who make the most important products, those who direct the enterprises most useful to the nation, those who contribute to its achievements in the sciences, fine arts and professions. They are in the most real sense the flower of French society; they are, above all Frenchmen, the most useful to their country, contribute most to its glory, increasing its civilization and prosperity. The nation would become a lifeless corpse as soon as it lost them. It would immediately fall into a position of inferiority compared with the nations which it now rivals, and would continue to be inferior until this loss had been replaced, until it had grown another head. It would require at least a generation for France to repair this misfortune; for men who are distinguished in work of positive ability are exceptions, and nature is not prodigal of exceptions, particularly in this species.

Let us pass on to another assumption. Suppose that France preserves all the men of genius that she possesses in the sciences, fine arts and professions, but has the misfortune to lose in the same day Monsieur the King's brother, Monseigneur le due d'Angoulême, Monseigneur le duc de Berry, Monseigneur le duc d'Orléans, Monseigneur le duc de Bourbon, Madame la duchesse d'Angoulême, Madame la duchesse de Berry, Madame la duchesse d'Orléans, Madame la duchesse de Bourbon, and Mademoiselle de Condé. Suppose that France loses at the same time all the great officers of the royal household, all the ministers (with or without portfolio), all the councillors

*Excerpts from *Social Organization, The Science of Man and other Writings* by Henri De Saint-Simon. Edited and translated with an Introduction by Felix Markham. Harper Touchstone, 1964.

of state, all the chief magistrates, marshals, cardinals, archbishops, bishops, vicars-general, and canons, all the prefects and sub-prefects, all the civil servants, and judges, and, in addition, ten thousand of the richest proprietors who live in the style of nobles.

This mischance would certainly distress the French, because they are kind-hearted, and could not see with indifference the sudden disappearance of such a large number of their compatriots. But this loss of thirty-thousand individuals, considered to be the most important in the State, would only grieve them for purely sentimental reasons and would result in no political evil for the State.

In the first place, it would be very easy to fill the vacancies which would be made available. There are plenty of Frenchmen who could fill the function of the King's brother as well as can Monsieur; plenty who could take the place of a Prince as appropriately as Monseigneur le due d'Angoulême, or Monseigneur le due d'Orléans, or Monseigneur le duc de Bourbon. There are plenty of Frenchwomen who would be as good princesses as Madame la duchesse d'Angoulême, or Madame la duchesse de Berry, or Mesdames d'Orléans, de Bourbon, and de Condé.

The ante-chambers of the palace are full of courtiers ready to take the place of the great household officials. The army has plenty of soldiers who would be as good leaders as our present Marshals. How many clerks there are who are as good as our ministers? How many administrators who are capable of managing the affairs of the departments better than the existing prefects and sub-prefects? How many barristers who are as good lawyers as our judges? How many vicars as expert as our cardinals, archbishops, bishops, vicars-general, and canons? As for the ten thousand aristocratic landowners, their heirs could need no apprenticeship to do the honours of their drawing-rooms as well as they.

The prosperity of France can only exist through the effects of the progress of the sciences, fine arts and professions. The Princes, the great household officials, the Bishops, Marshals of France, prefects and idle landowners contribute nothing directly to the progress of the sciences, fine arts and professions. Far from contributing they only hinder, since they strive to prolong the supremacy existing to this day of conjectural ideas over positive science. They inevitably harm the prosperity of the nation by depriving, as they do, the scientists, artists, and artisans of the high esteem to which they are properly entitled. They are harmful because they expend their wealth in a way which is of no direct use to the sciences, fine arts, and professions: they are harmful because they are a charge on the national taxation, to the amount of three or four hundred millions under the heading of appointments, pensions, gifts, compensations, for the upkeep of their activities which are useless to the nation.

These suppositions underline the most important fact of present politics: they provide a point of view from which we can see this fact in a flash in all its extent; they show clearly, though indirectly, that our social organization is seriously defective: that men still allow themselves to be governed by violence and ruse, and that the human race (politically speaking) is still sunk in immorality.

The scientists, artists, and artisans, the only men whose work is of positive utility to society, and cost it practically nothing, are kept down by the princes and other rulers who are simply more or less incapable bureaucrats. Those who control honours and other national awards owe, in general, the supremacy they enjoy, to the accident of birth, to flattery, intrigue and other dubious methods.

Those who control public affairs share between them every year one half of the taxes, and they do not even use a third of what they do not pocket personally in a way which benefits the citizen.

These suppositions show that society is a world which is upside down.

The nation holds as a fundamental principle that the poor should be generous to the rich, and that therefore the poorer classes should daily deprive themselves of necessities in order to increase the superfluous luxury of the rich.

The most guilty men, the robbers on a grand scale, who oppress the mass of the citizens, and extract from them three or four hundred millions a year, are given the responsibility of punishing minor offences against society.

Ignorance, superstition, idleness and costly dissipation are the privilege of the leaders of society, and men of ability, hard-working and thrifty, are employed only as inferiors and instruments.

To sum up, in every sphere men of greater ability are subject to the control of men who are incapable. From the point of view of morality, the most immoral men have the responsibility of leading the citizens towards virtue; from the point of view of distributive justice, the most guilty men are appointed to punish minor delinquents.

11

The Hierarchical Structure of Society*

Henri de Saint-Simon

The mechanism of social organization was inevitably very complicated so long as the majority of individuals remained in a state of ignorance and improvidence which rendered them incapable of administering their own affairs. In this state of incomplete intellectual development they were swayed by brutal passions which urged them to revolt and every kind of anarchy.

In such a situation, which was the necessary prelude to a better social order, it was necessary for the minority to be organized on military lines, to obtain a monopoly of legislation, and so to keep all power to itself, in order to hold the majority in tutelage and subject the nation to strong discipline. Thus the main energies of the community have till now been directed to maintaining itself as a community, and any efforts directed to improving the moral and physical welfare of the nation have necessarily been regarded as secondary.

To-day this state of affairs can and should be completely altered. The main effort should be directed to the improvement of our moral and physical welfare; only a small amount of force is now required to maintain public order, since the majority have become used to work (which eliminates disorder) and now consists of men who have recently proved that they are capable of administering property, whether in land or money.

As the minority no longer has need of force to keep the proletarian class in subordination, the course which it should adopt is as follows:

1. A policy by which the proletariat will have the strongest interest in maintaining public order.
2. A policy which aims at making the inheritance of landed property as easy as possible.
3. A policy which aims at giving the highest political importance to the workers.

Such a policy is quite simple and obvious, if one takes the trouble to judge the situation by one's own intelligence, and to shake off the yoke enforced on our minds by the political principles of our ancestors—principles which were sound and useful in their own day, but are no longer applicable to present circumstances. The mass of the population is now composed of men (apart from exceptions which occur more or less equally in every class)

*Excerpts from *Social Organization, The Science of Man and Other Writings* by Henri De Saint-Simon. Edited and translated with an Introduction by Felix Markham. Harper Touchstone, 1964.

who are capable of administering property whether in land or in money, and therefore we can and must work directly for the improvement of the moral and physical welfare of the community.

The most direct method of improving the moral and physical welfare of the majority of the population is to give priority in State expenditure to ensuring work for all fit men, to secure their physical existence; spreading throughout the proletarian class a knowledge of positive science; ensuring for this class forms of recreation and interests which will develop their intelligence.

We must add to this the measures necessary to ensure that the national wealth is administered by men most fitted for it, and most concerned in its administration, that is to say the most important industrialists.

Thus the community, by means of these fundamental arrangements, will be organized in a way which will completely satisfy reasonable men of every class.

There will no longer be a fear of insurrection, and consequently no longer a need to maintain large standing armies to suppress it; no longer a need to spend enormous sums on a police force; no longer a fear of foreign danger, for a body of thirty millions of men who are a contented community would easily repel attack, even if the whole human race combined against them.

We might add that neither princes nor peoples would be so mad as to attack a nation of thirty millions who displayed no aggressive intentions against their neighbours, and were united internally by mutual interests.

Furthermore, there would no longer be a need for a system of police-spying in a community in which the vast majority had an interest in maintaining the established order.

The men who brought about the Revolution, the men who directed it, and the men who, since 1789 and up to the present day, have guided the nation, have committed a great political mistake. They have all sought to improve the governmental machine, whereas they should have subordinated it and put administration in the first place.

They should have begun by asking a question the solution of which is simple and obvious. They should have asked who, in the present state of morals and enlightenment, are the men most fitted to manage the affairs of the nation. They would have been forced to recognize the fact that the scientists, artists and industrialists, and the heads of industrial concerns are the men who possess the most eminent, varied, and most positively useful ability, for the guidance of men's minds at the present time. They would have recognized the fact that the work of the scientists, artists, and industrialists is that which, in discovery and application, contributes most to national prosperity.

They would have reached the conclusion that the scientists, artists and leaders of industrial enterprises are the men who should be entrusted with administrative power, that is to say, with the responsibility for managing the national interests; and that the functions of government should be limited to maintaining public order.

The reformers of 1789 should have said to themselves as follows.

The kings of England have given a good example to monarchy by agreeing to give no order without the approval and signature of a minister. The magnanimity of the kings of France demands that they shew still greater generosity to their people, and that they should agree to make no decision affecting the general interests of the nation without the approval of the men most fitted to judge their decisions—that is to say, without the approval of the scientists and the most eminent artists, without the approval of the most important industrialists.

The community has often been compared to a pyramid. I admit that the nation should be composed as a pyramid; I am profoundly convinced that the national pyramid should be crowned by the monarchy, but I assert that from the base of the pyramid to its summit the layers should be composed of more and more precious materials. If we consider the present pyramid, it appears that the base is made of granite, that up to a certain height the layers are composed of valuable materials, but that the upper part, supporting a magnificent diamond, is composed of nothing but plaster and gilt.

The base of the present national pyramid consists of workers in their routine occupations; the first layers above this base are the leaders of industrial enterprises, the scientists who improve the methods of manufacture and widen their application, the artists who give the stamp of good taste to all their products. The upper layers, which I assert to be composed of nothing but plaster, which is easily recognizable despite the gilding, are the courtiers, the mass of nobles whether or ancient or recent creation, the idle rich, the governing class from the prime minister to the humblest clerk. The monarchy is the magnificent diamond which crowns the pyramid.

12

Order and Progress*

Auguste Comte

It is necessary to resolve the positive study of humanity into two essential parts. The one, the static, will treat of the structural nature of this, the chief of organisms; the other, the dynamic, will treat of the laws of its actual development. Although in sociology these two classes of laws are even more intimately connected than they are in biology, yet the greater complexity that marks the highest of the sciences renders their separate treatment still more requisite in the former than it was in the latter science. This is, moreover, the method to which social speculation has naturally conformed during the long era of its growth, for the principles relating to order were sketched out much earlier than those relating to progress.

Again, this indispensable division of social philosophy into two parts is a further example of the universal principle upon which my positive scheme for the classification of the sciences is founded. For the study of social statics is at once more simple, more general, and more abstract than that of social dynamics. Moreover, social statics forms the direct link between the final science of society and the whole of the preceding sciences, and in a special manner between the final science and biology, of which sociology now becomes the natural complement. Unless based upon a sound theory of the laws of its *existence,* or fixed organic conditions, the study of the *movement,* or organic evolution, of human society would fall short of that scientific coherence needed for this study to attain to its full usefulness. Nor is this distinction of less importance in practice than it is in theory, for the dynamic laws find their chief application in politics, the static, in morals.

Between these two classes of social laws there reigns a sovereign spirit of harmony, by virtue of the general principle that here, as elsewhere, combines the study of movement with that of the existence. The value of this principle was first seen in the field of mere mathematics, but it is in sociology that its full importance and character will be finally displayed. Here its proper part is to picture progress as nothing but the gradual development of order. Conversely, it represents to us order as manifested forth by progress. Such is the intimate union of these two cardinal notions, equally valuable for purposes of theory as of practice, for the former defines the basis, the latter the end, of all social life, while it is animated throughout by the principle of universal affection. In biology we now regard all forms of life

*Excerpts from *Auguste Comte and Positivism: The Essential Writings* by Auguste Comte, edited and with an Introduction by Gertrud Lenzer. Harper & Row, 1975.

simply as an evolution, and we discard any notion of creation in the proper sense of that word. But this great axiom of science has especially its place in sociology, where, studying a course of development yet more complex, more extensive, and more gradual, we are forced to recognize the fundamental unity that runs through all the successive phases. In this science the static study and the dynamic study tend gradually to unite in one, as the essential spirit of each more and more distinctly comes out, to illustrate the intimate connection between them; and we explain alternately the laws of order by those of progress, and the laws of progress by those of order.

13

LAW OF THE THREE STAGES*

AUGUSTE COMTE

In order to understand the true value and character of the positive philosophy, we must take a brief general view of the progressive course of the human mind, regarded as a whole, for no conception can be understood otherwise than through its history.

From the study of the development of human intelligence, in all directions, and through all times, the discovery arises of a great fundamental law, to which it is necessarily subject, and which has a solid foundation of proof, both in the facts of our organization and in our historical experience. The law is this: that each of our leading conceptions—each branch of our knowledge—passes successively through three different theoretical conditions: the theological, or fictitious; the metaphysical, or abstract; and the scientific, or positive. In other words, the human mind, by its nature, employs in its progress three methods of philosophizing, the character of which is essentially different, and even radically opposed: namely, the theological method, the metaphysical, and the positive. Hence arise three philosophies, or general systems of conceptions on the aggregate of phenomena, each of which excludes the others. The first is the necessary point of departure of the human understanding, and the third is its fixed and definitive state. The second is merely a state of transition.

In the theological state, the human mind, seeking the essential nature of beings, the first and final causes (the origin and purpose) of all effects—in short, absolute knowledge—supposes all phenomena to be produced by the immediate action of supernatural beings.

In the metaphysical state, which is only a modification of the first, the mind supposes, instead of supernatural beings, abstract forces, veritable entities (that is, personified abstractions) inherent in all beings, and capable of producing all phenomena. What is called the explanation of phenomena is, in this stage, a mere reference of each to its proper entity.

In the final, the positive, state, the mind has given over the vain search after absolute notions, the origin and destination of the universe, and the causes of phenomena, and applies itself to the study of their laws—that is, their invariable relations of succession and resemblance. Reasoning and observation, duly combined, are the means of this knowledge. What is now understood when we speak of an explanation of facts is simply the establishment of a connection between single phenomena and some general facts, the

*Excerpts from *Auguste Comte and Positivism: The Essential Writings* by Auguste Comte, edited and with an Introduction by Gertrud Lenzer. Harper & Row, 1975.

number of which continually diminishes with the progress of science.

The theological system arrived at the highest perfection, of which it is capable when it substituted the providential action of a single Being for the varied operations of the numerous divinities that had been before imagined. In the same way, in the last stage of the metaphysical system, men substitute one great entity (Nature) as the cause of all phenomena, instead of the multitude of entities at first supposed. In the same way, again, the ultimate perfection of the positive system would be (if such perfection could be hoped for) to represent all phenomena as particular aspects of a single general fact—such as gravitation, for instance.

14

Social Progress*

Herbert Spencer

Leaving out of sight concomitants and beneficial consequences, let us ask what progress is in itself.

In respect to that progress which individual organisms display in the course of their evolution, this question has been answered by the Germans. The investigations of Wolff, Goethe, and von Baer, have established the truth that the series of changes gone through during the development of a seed into a tree, or an ovum into an animal, constitute an advance from homogeneity of structure to heterogeneity of structure. In its primary stage, every germ consists of a substance that is uniform throughout, both in texture and chemical composition. The first step is the appearance of a difference between two parts of this substance; or, as the phenomenon is called in physiological language, a differentiation. Each of these differentiated divisions presently begins itself to exhibit some contrast of parts: and by and by these secondary differentiations become as definite as the original one. This process is continuously repeated—is simultaneously going on in all parts of the growing embryo; and by endless such differentiations there is finally produced that complex combination of tissues and organs constituting the adult animal or plant. This is the history of all organisms whatever. It is settled beyond dispute that organic progress consists in a change from the homogeneous to the heterogeneous.

The change from the homogeneous to the heterogeneous is displayed in the progress of civilization as a whole, as well as in the progress of every nation; and is still going on with increasing rapidity. As we see in existing barbarous tribes, society in its first and lowest form is a homogeneous aggregation of individuals having like powers and like functions: the only marked difference of function being that which accompanies difference of sex. Every man is warrior, hunter, fisherman, tool-maker, builder; every woman performs the same drudgeries. Very early, however, in the course of social evolution, there arises an incipient differentiation between the governing and the governed. Some kind of chieftainship seems coeval with the first advance from the state of separate wandering families to that of a nomadic tribe. The authority of the strongest or the most cunning makes itself felt among a body of savages as in a herd of animals, or a posse of schoolboys. At first, however, it is indefinite, uncertain; is shared by others of scarcely inferior power; and is unaccompanied by any difference in occupation or style of living:

*Excerpts from *Essays: Scientific, Political and Speculative* by Herbert Spencer. Williams and Norgate, 1891.

the first ruler kills his own game, makes his own weapons, builds his own hut, and, economically considered, does not differ from others of his tribe. Gradually, as the tribe progresses, the contrast between the governing and the governed grows more decided. Supreme power becomes hereditary in one family; the head of that family, ceasing to provide for his own wants, is served by others; and he begins to assume the sole office of ruling. At the same time there has been arising a co-ordinate species of government—that of Religion. As all ancient records and traditions prove, the earliest rulers are regarded as divine personages. The maxims and commands they uttered during their lives are held sacred after their deaths, and are enforced, by their divinely-descended successors; who in their turns are promoted to the pantheon of the race, here to be worshipped and propitiated along with their predecessors : the most ancient of whom is the supreme god, and the rest subordinate gods. For a long time these connate forms of government—civil and religious—remain closely associated. For many generations the king continues to be the chief priest, and the priesthood to be members of the royal race. For many ages religious law continues to include more or less of civil regulation, and civil law to possess more or less of religious sanction ; and even among the most advanced nations these two controlling agencies are by no means completely separated from each other.

Simutlaneously there has been going on a second differentiation of a more familiar kind; that, namely, by which the mass of the community has been segregated into distinct classes and orders of workers. While the governing part has undergone the complex development above detailed, the governed part has undergone an equally complex development, which has resulted in that minute division of labour characterizing advanced nations. It is needless to trace out this progress from its first stages, up through the caste-divisions of the East and the incorporated guilds of Europe, to the elaborate producing and distributing organization existing among ourselves. It has been an evolution which, beginning with a tribe whose members severally perform the same actions each for himself, ends with a civilized community whose members severally perform different actions for each other; and an evolution which has transformed the solitary producer of any one commodity into a combination of producers who, united under a master, take separate parts in the manufacture of such commodity. But there are yet other and higher phases of this advance from the homogeneous to the heterogeneous in the industrial organization of society. Long after considerable progress has been made in the division of labour among different classes of workers, there is still little or no division of labour among the widely separated parts of the community : the nation continues comparatively homogeneous in the respect that in each district the same occupations are pursued. But when roads and other means of transit become numerous and good, the different districts begin to assume different functions, and to become mutually dependent. The calico manufacture locates itself in this county, the woollen-cloth manufacture in that; silks are produced here, lace there; stockings in one place, shoes in another; pottery, hardware, cutlery, come to have their special towns; and ultimately every locality becomes more or less distinguished from the rest by the leading occupation carried on in it. This subdivision of functions shows itself not only among the different parts of the same nation, but among different nations. That exchange of commodities which free-trade is increasing so largely, will ultimately have the effect of specializing, in a greater or less degree, the industry of each people. So that, beginning with, a barbarous tribe, almost if not quite homogeneous in the functions of its members, the progress has been, and still is, towards an economic aggregation of the whole human race; growing ever more heterogeneous in respect of the separate functions assumed by separate nations, the separate functions assumed by the local sections of each nation, the separate functions assumed by the many kinds of makers and traders in each town, and the separate functions assumed by the workers united in producing each commodity. But doubtless the reader is already weary of illustrations; and our promise has been amply fulfilled. Abundant proof has been given that the law of organic development formulated by von Baer, is the law of all development. The advance from, the simple to the complex, through a process of successive differentiations, is seen alike in the earliest changes of the Universe to which we can reason our way back, and in the earliest changes which we can inductively establish; it is seen in the geologic and climatic evolution of the Earth; it is seen in the unfolding of every single organism on its surface, and in the multiplication of kinds of organisms; it is seen in the evolution of Humanity, whether contemplated in the civilized individual, or in the aggregate of races; it is seen in the evolution of Society in respect alike of its political, its religious, and its economical organization; and it is seen in the evolution of all those endless concrete and abstract products of human activity which constitute the environment of our daily life. From, the remotest past which Science can fathom, up to the novelties of yesterday, that in which progress essentially consists, is the transformation of the homogeneous into the heterogeneous.

15

The Evolution of Society*

Herbert Spencer

When we say that growth is common to social aggregates and organic aggregates, we do not thus entirely exclude community with inorganic aggregates. Some of these, as crystals, grow in a risible manner; and all of them, on the hypothesis of evolution, have arisen by integration at some time or other. Nevertheless, compared with things we call inanimate, living bodies and societies so conspicuously exhibit augmentation of mass, that we may fairly regard this as characterizing them both. Many organisms grow throughout their lives; and the rest grow throughout considerable parts of their lives. Social growth usually continues either up to times when the societies divide, or up to times when they are overwhelmed.

Here, then, is the first trait by which societies ally themselves with the organic world and substantially distinguish themselves from the inorganic world.

It is also a character of social bodies, as of living bodies, that while they increase in size they increase in structure. Like a low animal, the embryo of a high one has few distinguishable parts; but while it is acquiring greater mass, its parts multiply and differentiate. It is thus with a society. At first the unlikenesses among its groups of units are inconspicuous in number and degree; but as population augments, divisions and sub-divisions become more numerous and more decided. Further, in the social organism as in the individual organism, differentiations cease only with that completion of the type which marks maturity and precedes decay.

Though in inorganic aggregates also, as in the entire Solar System and in each of its members, structural differentiations accompany the integrations; yet these are so relatively slow, and so relatively simple, that they may be disregarded. The multiplication of contrasted parts in bodies politic and in living bodies, is so great that it substantially constitutes another common character which marks them off from inorganic bodies.

This community will be more fully appreciated on observing that progressive differentiation of structures is accompanied by progressive differentiation of functions.

The divisions, primary, secondary, and tertiary, which arise in a developing animal, do not assume their major and minor unlikenesses to no purpose. Along with diversities in their shapes and compositions go diversities in the actions they perform: they grow into unlike organs having unlike duties. Assuming the entire function of absorbing nutriment at the same time that it takes on its structural characters, the alimentary system becomes gradually marked off into

*Excerpts from *The Principles of Sociology* Vol 1, by Herbert Spencer. D. Appleton and Company, 1900.

contrasted portions; each of which has a special function forming part of the general function. A limb, instrumental to locomotion or prehension, acquires divisions and sub-divisions which perform their leading and their subsidiary shares in this office. So is it with the parts into which a society divides. A dominant class arising does not simply become unlike the rest, but assumes control over the rest; and when this class separates into the more and the less dominant, these, again, begin to discharge distinct parts of the entire control. With the classes whose actions are controlled it is the same. The various groups into which they fall have various occupations: each of such groups also, within itself, acquiring minor contrasts of parts along with minor contrasts of duties.

And here we see more clearly how the two classes of things we are comparing, distinguish themselves from things of other classes; for such differences of structure as slowly arise in inorganic aggregates, are not accompanied by what we can fairly call differences of function.

Why in a body politic and in a living body, these unlike actions of unlike parts are properly regarded by us as functions, while we cannot so regard the unlike actions of unlike parts in an inorganic body, we shall perceive on turning to the next and most distinctive common trait.

Evolution establishes in them both, not differences simply, but definitely-connected differences—differences such that each makes the others possible. The parts of an inorganic aggregate are so related that one may change greatly without appreciably affecting the rest. It is otherwise with the parts of an organic aggregate or of a social aggregate. In either of these, the changes in the parts are mutually determined, and the changed actions of the parts are mutually dependent. In both, too, this mutuality increases as the evolution advances. The lowest type of animal is all stomach, all respiratory surface, all limb. Development of a type having appendages by which to move about or lay hold of food, can take place only if these appendages, losing power to absorb nutriment directly from surrounding bodies, are supplied with nutriment by parts which retain the power of absorption. A respiratory surface to which the circulating fluids are brought to be aerated, can be formed only on condition that the concomitant loss of ability to supply itself with materials for repair and growth, is made good by the development of a structure bringing these materials. Similarly in a society. What we call with perfect propriety its organization, necessarily implies traits of the same kind. While rudimentary, a society is all warrior, all hunter, all hut-builder, all tool-maker: every part fulfils for itself all needs. Progress to a stage characterized by a permanent army, can go on only as there arise arrangements for supplying that army with food, clothes, and munitions of war by the rest. If here the population occupies itself solely with agriculture and there with mining—if these manufacture goods while those distribute them, it must be on condition that in exchange for a special kind of service rendered by each part to other parts, these other parts severally give due proportions of their services.

Here let it once more be distinctly asserted that there exist no analogies between the body politic and a living body, save those necessitated by that mutual dependence of parts which they display in common. Though, in foregoing chapters, sundry comparisons of social structures and functions to structures and functions in the human body, have been made, they have been made only because structures and functions in the human body furnish familiar illustrations of structures and functions in general. The social organism, discrete instead of concrete, asymmetrical instead of symmetrical, sensitive in all its units instead of having a single sensitive centre, is not comparable to any particular type of individual organism, animal or vegetal. All kinds of creatures are alike in so far as each exhibits co-operation among its components for the benefit of the whole; and this trait, common to them, is a trait common also to societies. Further, among individual organisms, the degree of co-operation measures the degree of evolution; and this general truth, too, holds among social organisms. Once more, to effect increasing co-operation, creatures of every order show us increasingly-complex appliances for transfer and mutual influence; and to this general characteristic, societies of every order furnish a corresponding characteristic. These, then, are the analogies alleged: community in the fundamental principles of organization is the only community asserted.

16

The General Happiness*

Harriet Martineau

The traveller must have made up his mind as to what it is that he wants to know. In physical science, great results may be obtained by hap-hazard experiments; but this is not the case in Morals. A chemist can hardly fail of learning something by putting any substances together, under new circumstances, and seeing what will arise out of the combination; and some striking discoveries happened in this way, in the infancy of the science: though no one doubts that more knowledge may be gained by the chemist who has an aim in his mind, and who conducts his experiment on some principle. In Morals, the latter method is the only one which promises any useful results. In the workings of the social system, all the agents are known in the gross—all are determined. It is not their nature, but the proportions in which they are combined, which have to be ascertained.

What does the traveller want to know? He is aware that, wherever he goes, he will find men, women, and children; strong men, and weak men; just men and selfish men. He knows that he will every where find a necessity for food, clothing, and shelter; and every where some mode of general agreement how to live together. He knows that he will every where find birth, marriage and death; and therefore domestic affections. What results from all these elements of social life does he mean to look for?

For want of settling this question, one traveller sees nothing truly, because the state of things is not consistent with his speculations as to how human beings ought to live together; another views the whole with prejudice, because it is not like what he has been accustomed to see at home; yet each of these would shrink from the recognition of his folly, if it were fully placed before him. The first would be ashamed of having tried any existing community by an arbitrary standard of his own—an act much like going forth into the wilderness to see kings' houses full of men in soft raiment; and the other would perceive that different nations may go on judging one another by themselves till doomsday, without in any way improving the chance of self-advancement and mutual understanding. Going out with the disadvantage of a habit of mind uncounteracted by an intellectual aim, will never do. The traveller may as well stay at home, for any thing he will gain in the way of social knowledge.

The two considerations just mentioned must be subordinated to the grand one,—the only general one,—of the relative amount of human happiness. Every element of social life derives its

*Excerpts from *How to Observe Morals and Manners* by Harriet Martineau, with a new introduction, appendices, and index by Michael R. Hill. Transaction Publishers, 1989.

importance from this great consideration. The external conveniences of men, their internal emotions and affections, their social arrangements, graduate in importance precisely in proportion as they affect the general happiness of the section of the race among whom they exist. Here then is the wise traveller's aim,—to be kept in view to the exclusion of prejudice, both philosophical and national. He must not allow himself to be perplexed or disgusted by seeing the great ends of human association pursued by means which he could never have devised, and to the practice of which he could not reconcile himself. He is not to conclude unfavourably about the diet of the multitude because he sees them swallowing blubber, or scooping out water-melons, instead of regaling themselves with beef and beer. He is not to suppose their social meetings a failure because they eat with their fingers, instead of with silver forks, or touch foreheads instead of making a bow. He is not to conclude against domestic morals, on account of a diversity of methods of entering upon marriage. He might as well judge of the minute transactions of manners all over the world by what he sees in his native village. There, to leave the door open or to shut it bears no relation to morals, and but little to manners; whereas, to shut the door is as cruel an act in a Hindoo hut as to leave it open in a Greenland cabin. In short, he is to prepare himself to bring whatever he may observe to the test of some high and broad principle, and not to that of a low comparative practice. To test one people by another, is to argue within a very small segment of a circle; and the observer can only pass backwards and forwards at an equal distance from the point of truth. To test the morals and manners of a nation by a reference to the essentials of human happiness, is to strike at once to the centre, and to see things as they are.

17

Folkways and Mores*

William Graham Sumner

If we put together all that we have learned from anthropology and ethnography about primitive men and primitive society, we perceive that the first task of life is to live. Men begin with acts, not with thoughts. Every moment brings necessities which must be satisfied at once. Need was the first experience, and it was followed at once by a blundering effort to satisfy it. The method is that of trial and failure, which produces repeated pain, loss, and disappointments. Nevertheless, it is a method of rude experiment and selection. The earliest efforts of men were of this kind. Need was the impelling force. Pleasure and pain, on the one side and the other, were the rude constraints which defined the line on which efforts must proceed. The ability to distinguish between pleasure and pain is the only psychical power which is to be assumed. Thus ways of doing things were selected, which were expedient. They answered the purpose better than other ways, or with less toil and pain. Along the course on which efforts were compelled to go, habit, routine, and skill were developed. The struggle to maintain existence was carried on, not individually, but in groups. Each profited by the other's experience; hence there was concurrence towards that which proved to be most expedient. All at last adopted the same way for the same purpose; hence the ways turned into customs and became mass phenomena. Instincts were developed in connection with them. In this way folkways arise. The young learn them by tradition, imitation, and authority. The folkways, at a time, provide for all the needs of life then and there. They are uniform, universal in the group, imperative, and invariable. As time goes on, the folkways become more and more arbitrary, positive, and imperative.

The operation by which folkways are produced consists in the frequent repetition of petty acts, often by great numbers acting in concert or, at least, acting in the same way when face to face with the same need. The immediate motive is interest. It produces habit in the individual and custom in the group. It is, therefore, in the highest degree original and primitive. By habit and custom it exerts a strain on every individual within its range; therefore it rises to a societal force to which great classes of societal phenomena are due. Out of the unconscious experiment which every repetition of the ways includes, there issues pleasure or pain, and then, so far as the men are capable of reflection, convictions that the ways are conducive to societal welfare. When this conviction as to the relation to welfare is added to the folkways they are converted into

*Excerpt from *Folkways: A Study of the Sociological Importance of Usages, Manners, Customs, Mores, and Morals* by William Graham Sumner. Dover Publications, Inc., 1959.

mores, and, by virtue of the philosophical and ethical element added to them, they win utility and importance and become the source of the science and the art of living.

When the elements of truth and right are developed into doctrines of welfare, the folkways are raised to another plane. They then become capable of producing inferences, developing into new forms, and extending their constructive influence over men and society. Then we call them the mores. The mores are the folkways, including the philosophical and ethical generalizations as to societal welfare which are suggested by them, and inherent in them, as they grow.

The mores necessarily consist, in a large part of taboos, which indicate the things which must not be done. In part these are dictated by mystic dread of ghosts who might be offended by certain acts, but they also include such acts as have been found by experience to produce unwelcome results, especially in the food quest, in war, in health, or in increase on decrease of population.

We may now formulate a more complete definition of the mores. They are the ways of doing things which are current in a society to satisfy human needs and desires, together with the faiths, notions, codes, and standards of well living which inhere in those ways, having a genetic connection with them. By virtue of the latter element the mores are traits in the specific character (ethos) of a society or a period. They pervade and control the ways of thinking in all the exigencies of life, returning from the world of abstractions to the world of action, to give guidance and to win revivification.

A society is never conscious of its mores until it comes in contact with some other society which has different mores, or until, in higher civilization, it gets information by literature. The latter operation, however, affects only the literary classes, not the masses, and society never consciously sets about the task of making mores. In the early stages mores are elastic and plastic; later they become rigid and fixed. They seem to grow up, gain strength, become corrupt, decline, and die, as if they were organisms. The phases seem to follow each other by an inherent necessity, and as if independent of the reason and will of the men affected, but the changes are always produced by a strain towards better adjustment of the mores to conditions and interests of the society, or of the controlling elements in it. A society does not record its mores in its annals, because they are to it unnoticed and unconscious. When we try to learn the mores of any age or people we have to seek our information in incidental references, allusions, observations of travelers, etc. Generally works of fiction, drama, etc., give us more information about the mores than historical records. It is very difficult to construct from the Old Testament a description of the mores of the Jews before the captivity. It is also very difficult to make a complete and accurate picture of the mores of the English colonies in North America in the seventeenth century. The mores are not recorded for the same reason that meals, going to bed, sunrise, etc., are not recorded, unless the regular course of things is broken.

We see that we must conceive of the mores as a vast system of usages, covering the whole of life, and serving all its interests; also containing in themselves their own justification by tradition and use and wont, and approved by mystic sanctions until, by rational reflection, they develop their own philosophical and ethical generalizations, which are elevated into "principles" of truth and right. They coerce and restrict the newborn generation. They do not stimulate to thought, but the contrary. The thinking is already done and is embodied in the mores. They never contain any provision for their own amendment. They are not questions, but answers, to the problem of life. They present themselves as final and unchangeable, because they present answers which are offered as "the truth."

18

In-Groups, Out-Groups, and Ethnocentrism*

William Graham Sumner

The conception of "primitive society" which we ought to form is that of small groups scattered over a territory. The size of the groups is determined by the conditions of the struggle for existence. The internal organization of each group corresponds to its size. A group of groups may have some relation to each other (kin, neighborhood, alliance, connubium and commercium) which draws them together and differentiates them from others. Thus a differentiation arises between ourselves, the we-group, or in-group, and everybody else, or the others-groups, out-groups. The insiders in a we-group are in a relation of peace, order, law, government, and industry, to each other. Their relation to all outsiders, or others-groups, is one of war and plunder, except so far as agreements have modified it. If a group is exogamic, the women in it were born abroad somewhere. Other foreigners who might be found in it are adopted persons, guest friends, and slaves.

The relation of comradeship and peace in the we-group and that of hostility and war towards others-groups are correlative to each other. The exigencies of war with outsiders are what make peace inside, lest internal discord should weaken the we-group for war. These exigencies also make government and law in the in-group, in order to prevent quarrels and enforce discipline. Thus war and peace have reacted on each other and developed each other, one within the group, the other in the intergroup relation. The closer the neighbors, and the stronger they are, the intenser is the warfare, and then the intenser is the internal organization and discipline of each. Sentiments are produced to correspond. Loyalty to the group, sacrifice for it, hatred and contempt for outsiders, brotherhood within, warlikeness without,—all grow together, common products of the same situation. These relations and sentiments constitute a social philosophy. It is sanctified by connection with religion. Men of an others-group are outsiders with whose ancestors the ancestors of the we-group waged war. The ghosts of the latter will see with pleasure their descendants keep up the fight, and will help them. Virtue consists in killing, plundering, and enslaving outsiders.

*Excerpt from *Folkways: A Study of the Sociological Importance of Usages, Manners, Customs, Mores, and Morals* by William Graham Sumner. Dover Publications, Inc., 1959.

Ethnocentrism is the technical name for this view of things in which one's own group is the center of everything, and all others are scaled and rated with reference to it. Folkways correspond to it to cover both the inner and the outer relation. Each group nourishes its own pride and vanity, boasts itself superior, exalts its own divinities, and looks with contempt on outsiders. Each group thinks its own folkways the only right ones, and if it observes that other groups have other folkways, these excite its scorn. Opprobrious epithets are derived from these differences. "Pig-eater," "cow-eater," "uncircumcised," "jabberers," are epithets of contempt and abomination. The Tupis called the Portuguese by a derisive epithet descriptive of birds which have feathers around their feet, on account of trousers. For our present purpose the most important fact is that ethnocentrism leads a people to exaggerate and intensify everything in their own folkways which is peculiar and which differentiates them from others. It therefore strengthens the folkways.

PART IV

The Classical Tradition

The writings of the four social thinkers profiled in this part—Karl Marx, Émile Durkheim, Max Weber, and Georg Simmel—constitute what is regarded as "the canon" in sociological theory. Their ideas form the basis for much subsequent sociological theorizing. As such, sociological theory since Marx, Durkheim, Weber, and Simmel can be seen as an attempt to amplify, expand, and critique their ideas. Singly and collectively, these thinkers have a clear relation to the *classical tradition* in sociological theory—a tradition that endeavored to explain, interpret, and critique *modern society* through *systematic theorizing*. While Simmel's sociology did not achieve the high level of systemization as that of his three near contemporaries, he is nonetheless included as part of the classical tradition because of his early insights into the social life of modern individuals.

In "Commodity Fetishism," Karl Marx explains how a *commodity*—any object that satisfies human wants—takes on a mystical quality beyond its *use-value*, or intrinsic utility. This is because under capitalism, commodities are exchanged not on the basis of their inherent utility but on the basis of their *exchange-value* (price). Their exchange-value is determined by the amount of human *labor-power* (in the form of brains, nerves, and muscles) and *labor-time* (measured in hours, days, weeks, etc.) required to produce them. Accordingly, different commodities that were qualitatively unequal are now quantitatively equal if the same amount of labor-power and labor-time is expended in their production. The *fetishism of commodities* occurs when people forget that it is their labor that gives a product its value and existence. Instead, people begin to lose control over what they produce when they start to believe that the value of a commodity is a natural property of the thing itself. Commodity fetishism is a type of alienation because people see commodities has having an independent existence that then becomes coercive to the individual. Commodity fetishism distorts people's perception of their social world. Instead of seeing commodities as products of their own creation, they regard them as natural, permanent, and unchangeable.

In "Alienated Labor," Marx maintains that workers become commodities when, in relation to the capitalists, they exchange for wages their labor-power, which itself becomes an object of production. This introduces another important concept in Marxian thought: *alienation*, a state of estrangement that occurs when the consequences of people's actions are in contradiction to or removed from their creations, motives, needs, and goals. Under capitalism, alienation takes four general forms: (1) The worker is alienated from the product of his or her labor because he or she has no control over the product, (2) the worker is alienated from his or her labor because he or she has sold it for wages, (3) the worker is alienated from himself or herself as a human being because he or she is not fulfilling his or her true essence, and (4) the worker is alienated from others, with the relationship between capitalist and worker, for example, being one of mutual indifference, as human relations are reduced to mere commodity exchanges.

Marx's theory of the historical development of how things are produced, *the modes of production*, is articulated in "Historical Materialism." Here, Marx identifies three successive modes or stages of production in Western history. First, there is *tribal society*, where the means of production are simple—fishing, gathering, and hunting—and so is the division of labor. Next is *ancient communal property*, where the forces of production are beginning to develop (technology, raw materials, and labor-power) and the division of labor increases. In this stage, most of the production was done by slaves. Third, under *feudalism*, not slaves but serfs were motivated to produce on the estate, not only for the landowners but also for themselves. Marx then shifts the discussion from the modes of production to the *production of consciousness*—how ideas are developed. He famously states that ideas do not determine the material conditions of life, but rather, it is the material conditions of life that determine ideas. In other words, people's real-life experiences always influence their ways of thinking.

Émile Durkheim begins the selection "Mechanical and Organic Solidarity" with the concept of the *collective conscience*—a sort of group mind that consists of all of the beliefs and sentiments that are held in common by the majority of people in a society. The collective conscience arises from the fact that the members of that society share similar characteristics. As such, the collective conscience unites people; it contributes to *social solidarity*. The type of solidarity produced from the fact that individuals resemble each other, that they see themselves similarly, is what Durkheim calls *mechanical*. Here, the collective conscience is strong and controlling. The type of solidarity that arises from functional differences based on the division of labor is what Durkheim refers to as *organic*. In this case, people bond together in interdependence; they rely on each other's specialized capacities. Here, the collective conscience is weaker, and people have greater freedom to pursue their individual interests.

In "Types of Suicide," Durkheim treats suicide not as a personal act but as a social phenomenon. As such, he explains a group's suicide *rate* as being correlated with that group's degree of solidarity or *integration*, as well as with its degree of control or *regulation*. Durkheim defines suicide broadly as any circumstance that directly or indirectly leads to a victim's intention to die. In the case of a group with too little social integration, group members feel detached from others—from the collective conscience—and thus experience excessive individualism. This causes the type of suicide called *egoistic*. In a group with too much social integration, the group members experience intense altruism. This leads to *altruistic* suicide, in which they sacrifice their lives for the group. In the case of a group with too little social regulation, individuals' unlimited desires and unattainable goals are not properly satisfied, restricted, or restrained. This gives rise to the type of suicide called *anomic*. Finally, in the case of a group with too much social regulation, individuals' hopes and dreams and their freedoms and initiatives are excessively oppressed. This contributes to the *fatalistic* type of suicide.

In 1895, Durkheim published *The Rules of Sociological Method* with the aims of establishing precisely what sociology's subject matter is and distinguishing it from biological and psychological phenomena. In an excerpt from that book, the reading titled "Social Facts," Durkheim states that the proper study of sociology is the study of *social facts*—ways of acting, thinking, and feeling that are external to the individual and that have a constraining influence on the individual's behavior. The division of labor, social solidarity, and the suicide rate—as collective beliefs, tendencies, and practices—are social facts. Their source is not the individual but society.

In "The Rationalism of Western Civilization," Max Weber poses the question that was the cornerstone of his sociological thinking: What combination of cultural and historical factors led modern Western civilization to develop a high degree of rationalism in various arenas of social life—science, law, music, the state, the economy, and so forth? By *rationalism*, Weber is referring to a deliberate, systematic, and efficient way of organizing social actions in, above all, a society's legal, religious, economic, and political realms. He spends the balance of the essay analyzing the rational aspects of the type of capitalism that had its unique development only in the modern West: industrial capitalism. This type of capitalism, Weber explains, is characterized by, among other things, free labor, market rewards, bookkeeping, organization of labor efficiently administered, and a methodical work ethic.

In his most famous work of 1905, *The Protestant Ethic and the Spirit of Capitalism*, Weber argues that the "spirit" of modern capitalism—the way in which social life in the economy is organized—arises out of a particular religious "ethos": ascetic Protestantism, or Puritanism. In the reading, "The Spirit of Capitalism," Weber explains that under this ethos, punctuality, industry, and frugality are seen as virtues to be used for one reason only: the relentless accumulation of money and its reinvestment. This pursuit of wealth is seen as a vocational "calling" to which everyone has an ethical duty; in other words, everyone has an obligation to *work*. The dedication to work for profit in the manner of a calling, says Weber, originated from this religious rationalism—from a complex combination of ascetic Protestant values.

In "Types of Authority," Weber defines domination or authority as the probability that a specific group of people will obey a given command. For authority to be obeyed, it must be seen as credible or *legitimate*. Different types of legitimacy support various types of authority. Thus, legitimacy based on the belief in the abstract rules of an impersonal order, a bureaucracy, is *legal-rational authority*; legitimacy founded on long-standing sacred rules is *traditional authority*; and legitimacy grounded in the leader's extraordinary qualities of personality is *charismatic authority*.

"The Stranger" is an excursus written by Georg Simmel in 1908 where he treats the stranger not as an individual but as a *social type*, a sort of composite profile. But the stranger—or more precisely the quality of strangeness—is also to be understood as a specific *form of interaction* in relation to a particular group to which he or she does not originally belong. For Simmel, the stranger is, at the same time, *both near and far* in relation to the group. On the one hand, the stranger is close to group members because he or she shares certain *general* features with them, having to do, for example, with nationality or humanity. On the other hand, the stranger is also distant precisely because, not being fully part of the group, these features are not *specific* enough, and he or she does not share in the group's uniqueness. It is within this dialectic of nearness and remoteness that the stranger is freed from relational entanglements with group members; he or she possesses an objectivity that they do not. This objectivity endows the stranger with an unbiased viewpoint, thus making him or her a confidant to group members. Objectivity also frees the stranger from commitments to the group.

In addition to the social type, like the stranger, Simmel, in "Dyad and Triad," examines various *forms of sociation*, or patterns of interaction. The most fundamental of these is the *dyad*, a relationship that consists of only two social units—be they two people, two families, or two countries. There are specific characteristics that pertain only to dyadic relationships and no others. For example, two is the maximum number of individuals who can keep a secret relatively secure, largely because each of the individuals feels directly confronted by and responsible to the other. Contrary to larger associations, the dyad is not a group with a superpersonal structure. Indeed, it is a particularly fragile arrangement because it can quickly come to an end when one participant withdraws. In an association of three social units, the *triad*, the third member can, in the case of a conflict, serve as a mediator between the other two members and thus preserve the group. However, the third party, in an attempt at divide and conquer, may create and exploit the conflict between the other two participants to his or her advantage.

"The Metropolis and Mental Life" was originally a lecture that Simmel gave in 1903. Here, he describes how the urban dweller, or *metropolitan*, as a social type, is a product of life in the big city. The city creates a certain mental attitude through which people develop particular relationships with each other. This attitude arises from the fact that people in cities experience a high degree of sensory stimulation—an overstimulation, in fact—as they are constantly bombarded by an overwhelming variety of sensual stimuli: the fast pace of city life and the various sights, smells, sounds, and so on. As a kind of self-protection from this sensory overload, urban residents develop a heightened awareness of events, thus making them more reliant on intellect than on emotion. They thus relate to others impersonally, calculatingly, and pragmatically. Above all, people who live in cities develop a *blasé attitude* that makes them appear distant and aloof. In addition, they may adopt a defense mechanism, which Simmel characterized as a *blunting of discrimination*, seeing everything and everyone in flat colorless tones; nothing distracts, and nothing stands out. Finally, urbanites also exhibit *reserve*—they keep to themselves, thus seeming to be indifferent, cold, and heartless.

19

Commodity Fetishism*

Karl Marx

A commodity appears, at first sight, a very trivial thing, and easily understood. Its analysis shows that it is, in reality, a very queer thing, abounding in metaphysical subtleties and theological niceties. So far as it is a value in use, there is nothing mysterious about it, whether we consider it from the point of view that by its properties it is capable of satisfying human wants, or from the point that those properties are the product of human labour. It is as clear as noonday, that man, by his industry, changes the forms of the materials furnished by Nature, in such a way as to make them useful to him. The form of wood, for instance, is altered, by making a table out of it. Yet, for all that, the table continues to be that common, everyday thing, wood. But, so soon as it steps forth as a commodity, it is changed into something transcendent. It not only stands with its feet on the ground, but, in relation to all other commodities, it stands on its head, and evolves out of its wooden brain grotesque ideas, far more wonderful than "table-turning" ever was.

The mystical character of commodities does not originate, therefore, in their use value. Just as little does it proceed from the nature of the determining factors of value. For, in the first place, however varied the useful kinds of labour, or productive activities, may be, it is a physiological fact, that they are functions of the human organism, and that each such function, whatever may be its nature or form, is essentially the expenditure of human brain, nerves, muscles, &c. Secondly, with regard to that which forms the groundwork for the quantitative determination of value, namely, the duration of that expenditure, or the quantity of labour, it is quite clear that there is a palpable difference between its quantity and quality. In all states of society, the labour time that it costs to produce the means of subsistence, must necessarily be an object of interest to mankind, though not of equal interest in different stages of development. And lastly, from the moment that men in any way work for one another, their labour assumes a social form.

Whence, then, arises the enigmatical character of the product of labour, so soon as it assumes the form of commodities? Clearly from this form itself. The equality of all sorts of human labour is expressed objectively by their products all being equally values; the measure of the expenditure of labour-power by the duration of that expenditure, takes the form of the quantity of value of the products of labour; and finally the mutual relations of the producers, within which the social

*Excerpt from *Capital: A Critique of Political Economy* by Karl Marx, edited by Frederick Engels. Revised and amplified according to the Fourth German Edition by Ernest Untermann.

character of their labour affirms itself, take the form of a social relation between the products.

A commodity is therefore a mysterious thing, simply because in it the social character of men's labour appears to them as an objective character stamped upon the product of that labour; because the relation of the producers to the sum total of their own labour is presented to them as a social relation, existing not between themselves, but between the products of their labour. This is the reason why the products of labour become commodities, social things whose qualities are at the same time perceptible and imperceptible by the senses. In the same way the light from an object is perceived by us not as the subjective excitation of our optic nerve, but as the objective form of something outside the eye itself. But, in the act of seeing, there is at all events, an actual passage of light from one thing to another, from the external object to the eye. There is a physical relation between physical things. But it is different with commodities. There, the existence of the things quâ commodities, and the value relation between the products of labour which stamps them as commodities, have absolutely no connection with their physical properties and with the material relations arising therefrom. There it is a definite social relation between men, that assumes, in their eyes, the fantastic form of a relation between things. In order, therefore, to find an analogy, we must have recourse to the mist-enveloped regions of the religious world. In that world the productions of the human brain appear as independent beings endowed with life, and entering into relation both with one another and the human race. So it is in the world of commodities with the products of men's hands. This I call the Fetishism which attaches itself to the products of labour, so soon as they are produced as commodities, and which is therefore inseparable from the production of commodities.

This Fetishism of commodities has its origin, as the foregoing analysis has already shown, in the peculiar social character of the labour that produces them.

As a general rule, articles of utility become commodities, only because they are products of the labour of private individuals or groups of individuals who carry on their work independently of each other. The sum total of the labour of all these private individuals forms the aggregate labour of society. Since the producers do not come into social contact with each other until they exchange their products, the specific social character of each producer's labour does not show itself except in the act of exchange. In other words, the labour of the individual asserts itself as a part of the labour of society, only by means of the relations which the act of exchange establishes directly between the products, and indirectly, through them, between the producers. To the latter, therefore, the relations connecting the labour of one individual with that of the rest appear, not as direct social relations between individuals at work, but as what they really are, material relations between persons and social relations between things.

20

Alienated Labor*

Karl Marx

We have proceeded from the premises of political economy. We have accepted its language and its laws. We presupposed private property, the separation of labor, capital and land, and of wages, profit of capital and rent of land—likewise division of labor, competition, the concept of exchange-value, etc. On the basis of political economy itself, in its own words, we have shown that the worker sinks to the level of a commodity and becomes indeed the most wretched of commodities; that the wretchedness of the worker is in inverse proportion to the power and magnitude of his production; that the necessary result of competition is the accumulation of capital in a few hands, and thus the restoration of monopoly in a more terrible form; and that finally the distinction between capitalist and land-rentier, like that between the tiller of the soil and the factory-worker, disappears and that the whole of society must fall apart into the two classes—property-*owners* and propertyless *workers*.

Political economy proceeds from the fact of private property; but it does not explain it to us. It expresses in general, abstract formulas the *material* process through which private property actually passes, and these formulas it then takes for *laws*. It does not *comprehend* these laws—i.e., it does not demonstrate how they arise from the very nature of private property. Political economy does not disclose the source of the division between labor and capital, and between capital and land. When, for example, it defines the relationship of wages to profit, it takes the interest of the capitalists to be the ultimate cause; i.e., it takes for granted what it is supposed to evolve. Similarly, competition comes in everywhere. It is explained from external circumstances. As to how far these external and apparently fortuitous circumstances are but the expression of a necessary course of development, political economy teaches us nothing. We have seen how, to it, exchange itself appears to it be a fortuitous fact. The only wheels which political economy sets in motion are avarice, and the *war amongst the avaricious—competition*.

Precisely because political economy does not grasp the connections within the movement, it was possible to counterpoise, for instance, the doctrine of competition to the doctrine of monopoly, the doctrine of craft-liberty to the doctrine of the corporation, the doctrine of the division of landed property to the doctrine of the big estate—for competition, craft-liberty and the division of landed property were explained and comprehended only as fortuitous, premeditated and violent consequences of monopoly, the

*Excerpts from *Economic and Philosophic Manuscripts of 1844* by Karl Marx. Foreign Languages Publishing House, Moscow.

corporation, and feudal property, not as their necessary, inevitable and natural consequences.

Now, therefore, we have to grasp the essential connection between private property, avarice, and the separation of labour, capital and landed property; between exchange and competition, value and the devaluation of men, monopoly and competition, etc.; the connection between this whole estrangement and the *money*-system.

Do not let us go back to a fictitious primordial condition as the political economist does, when he tries to explain. Such a primordial condition explains nothing. He merely pushes the question away into a grey nebulous distance. He assumes in the form of fact, of an event, what he is supposed to deduce—namely, the necessary relationship between two things—between, for example, division of labour and exchange. Theology in the same way explains the origin of evil by the fall of man: that is, it assumes as a fact, in historical form, what has to be explained.

We proceed from an *actual* economic fact.

The worker becomes all the poorer the more wealth he produces, the more his production increases in power and range. The worker becomes an ever cheaper commodity the more commodities he creates. With the *increasing value* of the world of things proceeds in direct proportion the *devaluation* of the world of men. Labour produces not only commodities: it produces itself and the worker as a *commodity*—and does so in the proportion in which it produces commodities generally.

This fact expresses merely that the object which labour produces—labour's product—confronts it *as something alien*, as a *power independent* of the producer. The product of labour is labour which has been congealed in an object, which has become material: it is the *objectification* of labour. Labour's realization is its objectification. In the conditions dealt with by political economy this realization of labour appears as *loss of reality* for the workers; objectification as *loss of the object* and *object-bondage;* appropriation as *estrangement, as alienation.*

So much does labour's realization appear as loss of reality that the worker loses reality to the point of starving to death. So much does objectification appear as loss of the object that the worker is robbed of the objects most necessary not only for his life but for his work. Indeed, labour itself becomes an object which he can get hold of only with the greatest effort and with the most irregular interruptions. So much does the appropriation of the object appear as estrangement that the more objects the worker produces the fewer can he possess and the more he falls under the dominion of his product, capital.

All these consequences are contained in the definition that the worker is related to the *product of his labour* as to an *alien* object. For on this premise it is clear that the more the worker spends himself, the more powerful the alien objective world becomes which he creates over-against himself, the poorer he himself—his inner world—becomes, the less belongs to him as his own. It is the same in religion. The more man puts into God, the less he retains in himself. The worker puts his life into the object; but now his life no longer belongs to him but to the object. Hence, the greater this activity, the greater is the worker's lack of objects. Whatever the product of his labour is, he is not. Therefore the greater this product, the less is he himself. The *alienation* of the worker in his product means not only that his labour becomes an object, an *external* existence, but that it exists *outside him*, independently, as something alien to him, and that it becomes a power on its own confronting him; it means that the life which he has conferred on the object confronts him as something hostile and alien.

Let us now look more closely at the *objectification*, at the production of the worker; and therein at the *estrangement*, the *loss* of the object, his product.

The worker can create nothing without *nature*, without the *sensuous external world.* It is the material on which his labour is manifested, in which it is active, from which and by means of which it produces.

But just as nature provides labour with the *means of life* in the sense that labour cannot *live* without objects on which to operate, on the other hand, it also provides the *means of life* in the more restricted sense—i.e., the means for the physical subsistence of the *worker* himself.

Thus the more the worker by his labour *appropriates* the external world, sensuous nature, the more he deprives himself of *means of life* in the double respect: first, that the sensuous external world more and more ceases to be an object belonging to his labour—to be his labour's *means of life*: and secondly, that it more and more ceases to be *means of life* in the immediate sense, means for the physical subsistence of the worker.

Thus in this double respect the worker becomes a slave of his object, first, in that he receives an *object of labour*, i.e., in that he receives *work*; and secondly, in that he receives *means of subsistence*. Therefore, it enables him to exist, first, as a *worker*; and, second, as a *physical subject*. The extremity of this bondage is that it is only as a worker that he continues to maintain himself as a *physical subject*, and that it is only as a *physical subject* that he is a *worker*.

(The laws of political economy express the estrangement of the worker in his object thus: the more the worker produces, the less he has to consume; the more values he creates, the more valueless, the more unworthy he becomes; the better formed his product, the more deformed becomes the worker; the more civilized his object, the more barbarous becomes the worker; the mightier labour becomes, the more powerless becomes the worker; the more ingenious labour becomes, the duller becomes the worker and the more he becomes nature's bondsman.)

Political economy conceals the estrangement inherent in the nature of labour by not considering the direct relationship between the worker (labour) and production. It is true that labour produces for the rich wonderful things—but for the worker it produces privation. It produces palaces—but for the worker, hovels. It produces beauty—but for the worker, deformity. It replaces labour by machines—but some of the workers it throws hack to a barbarous type of labour, and the other workers it turns into machines. It produces intelligence—but for the worker idiocy, cretinism.

The direct relationship of labour to its produce is the relationship of the worker to the objects of his production. The relationship of the man of means to the objects of production and to production itself is only a *consequence* of this first relationship—and confirms it. We shall consider this other aspect later.

When we ask, then, what is the essential relationship of labour we are asking about the relationship of the *worker* to production.

Till now we have been considering the estrangement, the alienation of the worker only in one of its aspects, i.e., the worker's *relationship to the products of his labour.* But the estrangement is manifested not only in the result but in the *act of production*—within the *producing* activity itself. How would the worker come to face the product of his activity as a stranger, were it not that in the very act of production he was estranging himself from himself? The product is after all but the summary of the activity, of production. If then the product of labour is alienation, production itself must be active alienation, the alienation of activity, the activity of alienation. In the estrangement of the object of labour is merely summarized the estrangement, the alienation, in the activity of labour itself.

What, then, constitutes the alienation of labour?

First, the fact that labour is *external* to the worker, i.e., it does not belong to his essential being; that in his work, therefore, he does not affirm himself but denies himself, does not feel content but unhappy, does not develop freely his physical and mental energy but mortifies his body and ruins his mind. The worker therefore only feels himself outside his work, and in his work feels outside himself. He is at home when he is not working, and when he is working he is not at home. His labour is therefore not voluntary, but coerced; it is *forced labour*. It is therefore not the satisfaction of a need; it is merely a *means* to satisfy needs external to it. Its alien character emerges clearly in the fact that as soon as no physical or other compulsion exists, labour is shunned like the plague. External labour, in which man alienates himself, is a labour of self-sacrifice, of mortification. Lastly, the external character of labour for the worker appears in the fact that it is not his own, but someone else's, that it does not belong to him, that in it he belongs, not to himself, but to another. Just as in religion the spontaneous activity of the human imagination, of the human brain and the human heart, operates independently of the individual—that is, operates on him as an alien, divine or diabolical activity—in the same way the worker's activity is not his spontaneous activity. It belongs to another; it is the loss of his self.

As a result, therefore, man (the worker) no longer feels himself to be freely active in any but his animal functions—eating, drinking, procreating, or at most in his dwelling and in dressing-up, etc.; and in his human functions he no longer feels himself to be anything but an animal. What is animal becomes human and what is human becomes animal.

Certainly eating, drinking, procreating, etc., are also genuinely human functions. But in the abstraction which separates them from the sphere of all other human activity and turns them into sole and ultimate ends, they are animal.

We have considered the act of estranging practical human activity, labour, in two of its aspects. (1) The relation of the worker to the *product of labour* as an alien object exercising power over him. This relation is at the same time the relation to the sensuous external world, to the objects of nature as an alien world antagonistically opposed to him. (2) The relation of labour to the *act of production* within the *labour* process. This relation is the relation of the worker to his own activity as an alien activity not belonging to him; it is activity as suffering, strength as weakness, begetting as emasculating, the worker's *own* physical and mental energy, his personal life or what is life other than activity—as an activity which is turned against him, neither depends on nor belongs to him. Here we have *self-estrangement*, as we had previously the estrangement of the *thing*.

We have yet a third aspect of *estranged labour* to deduce from the two already considered.

Man is a species being, not only because in practice and in theory he adopts the species as his object (his own as well as those of other things), but—and this is only another way of expressing it—but also because he treats himself as the actual, living species; because he treats himself as a *universal* and therefore a free being.

The life of the species, both in man and in animals, consists physically in the fact that man (like the animal) lives on inorganic nature; and the more universal man is compared with an animal, the more universal is the sphere of inorganic nature on which he lives. Just as plants, animals, stones, the air, light, etc., constitute a part of human consciousness in the realm of theory, partly as objects of natural science, partly as objects of art—his spiritual inorganic nature, spiritual nourishment which he must first prepare to make it palatable and digestable—so too in the realm of practice they constitute a part of human life and human activity. Physically man lives only on these products of nature, whether they appear in the form of food, heating, clothes, a dwelling, or whatever it may be. The universality of man is in practice manifested precisely in the universality which makes all nature his *inorganic* body—both inasmuch as nature is (1) his direct means of life, and (2) the material, the object, and the instrument of his life-activity. Nature is man's *inorganic body*—nature, that is, in so far as it is not itself the human body. Man *lives* on nature—means that nature is his *body*, with which he must remain in continuous intercourse if he is not to die. That man's physical and spiritual life is linked to nature means simply that nature is linked to itself, for man is a part of nature.

In estranging from man (1) nature, and (2) himself, his own active functions, his life-activity, estranged labour estranges the *species* from man. It turns for him the *life of the species* into a means of individual life. First it estranges the life of the species and individual life, and secondly it makes individual life in its abstract form the purpose of the life of the species, likewise in its abstract and estranged form.

For in the first place labour, *life-activity*, productive *life* itself, appears to man merely as a *means* of satisfying a need—the need to maintain the physical existence. Yet the productive life is the life of the species. It is life-engendering life. The whole character of a species—its species character—is contained in the character of its life-activity; and free, conscious activity is man's species character. Life itself appears only as a *means to life*.

The animal is immediately identical with its life-activity. It does not distinguish itself from it. It is *its life-activity*. Man makes his life-activity itself the object of his will and of his consciousness. He has conscious life-activity. It is not a determination with which he directly merges. Conscious life-activity directly distinguishes man from animal life-activity. It is just because of this that he is a species being. Or it is only because he is a species being that he is a Conscious Being, i.e., that his own life is an object for him. Only because of that is his activity free activity. Estranged labour reverses this relationship, so that it is just because man is a conscious being that he makes his life-activity, his *essential* being, a mere means to his *existence*.

In creating an *objective world* by his practical activity, in *working-up* inorganic nature, man proves himself a conscious species being, i.e., as a being that treats the species as its own essential being, or that treats itself as a species being. Admittedly animals also produce. They build themselves nests, dwellings, like the bees, beavers, ants, etc. But an animal only produces what it immediately needs for itself or its young. It produces one-sidedly, whilst man produces universally. It produces only under the dominion of immediate physical need, whilst man produces even when he is free from physical need and only truly produces in freedom therefrom. An animal produces only itself, whilst man reproduces the whole of nature. An animal's product belongs immediately to its physical body, whilst man freely confronts his product. An animal forms things In accordance with the standard and the need of the species to which it belongs, whilst man knows how to produce in accordance with the standard of every species, and knows how to apply everywhere the inherent standard to the object. Man therefore also forms things in accordance with the laws of beauty.

It is just in the working-up of the objective world, therefore, that man first really proves himself to be a *species being*. This production is his active species life. Through and because of this production, nature appears as *his* work and his reality. The object of labour is, therefore, the *objectification of man's species life*: for he duplicates himself not only, as in consciousness, intellectually, but also actively, in reality, and therefore he contemplates himself In a world that he has created. In tearing away from man the object of his production, therefore, estranged labour tears from him his *species life*, his real species objectivity, and transforms his advantage over animals into the disadvantage that his inorganic body, nature, is taken from him.

Similarly, in degrading spontaneous activity, free activity, to a means, estranged labour makes man's species life a means to his physical existence.

The consciousness which man has of his species is thus transformed by estrangement in such a way that the species life becomes for him a means.

Estranged labour turns thus:

(3) *Man's species being*, both nature and his spiritual species property, into a being *alien* to him, into a *means* to his *individual* existence. It estranges man's own body from him, as it does external nature and his spiritual essence, his *human* being.

(4) An immediate consequence of the fact that man is estranged from the product of his labour, from his life-activity, from his species being is the *estrangement of man* from *man*. If a man is confronted by himself, he is confronted by the *other* man. What applies to a man's relation to his work, to the product of his labour and to himself, also holds of a man's relation to the other man, and to the other man's labour and object of labour.

In fact, the proposition that man's species nature is estranged from him means that one man is estranged from the other, as each of them is from man's essential nature.

The estrangement of man, and in fact every relationship in which man stands to himself, is first realized and expressed in the relationship in which a man stands to other men.

Hence within the relationship of estranged labour each man views the other in accordance with the standard and the position in which he finds himself as a worker.

We took our departure from a fact of political economy—the estrangement of the worker and his production. We have formulated the concept of this fact—*estranged, alienated* labour. We have analysed this concept—hence analysing merely a fact of political economy.

Let us now see, further, how in real life the concept of estranged, alienated labour must express and present itself.

If the product of labour is alien to me, if it confronts me as an alien power, to whom, then, does it belong?

If my own activity does not belong to me, if it is an alien, a coerced activity, to whom, then, does it belong?

To a being *other* than me.

Who is this being?

The *gods?* To be sure, in the earliest times the principal production (for example, the building of temples, etc., in Egypt, India and Mexico) appears to be in the service of the gods, and the product belongs to the gods. However, the gods on their own were never the lords of labour. No more was *nature*. And what a contradiction it would be if, the more man subjugated nature by his labour and the more the miracles of the gods were rendered superfluous by the miracles of industry, the more man were to renounce the joy of production and the enjoyment of the produce in favour of these powers.

The *alien* being, to whom labour and the produce of labour belongs, in whose service labour is done and for whose benefit the produce of labour is provided, can only be *man* himself.

If the product of labour does not belong to the worker, if it confronts him as an alien power, this can only be because it belongs to some *other man than the worker*. If the worker's activity is a torment to him, to another it must be *delight* and his life's joy. Not the gods, not nature, but only man himself can be this alien power over man.

We must bear in mind the above-stated proposition that man's relation to himself only becomes *objective* and *real* for him through his relation to the other man. Thus, if the product of his labour, his labour *objectified*, is for him an *alien*, hostile, powerful object independent of him, then his position towards it is such that someone else is master of this object, someone who is alien, hostile, powerful, and independent of him. If his own activity is to him an unfree activity, then he is treating it as activity performed in the service, under the dominion, the coercion and the yoke of another man.

Every self-estrangement of man from himself and from nature appears in the relation in which he places himself and nature to men other than and differentiated from himself. For this reason religious self-estrangement necessarily appears in the relationship of the layman to the priest, or again to a mediator, etc., since we are here dealing with the intellectual world. In the real practical world self-estrangement can only become manifest through the real practical relationship to other men. The medium through which estrangement takes place is itself *practical*. Thus through estranged labour man not only engenders his relationship to the object and to the act of production as to powers that are alien and hostile to him; he also engenders the relationship in which other men stand to his production and to his product, and the relationship in which he stands. to these other men. Just as he begets bis own production as the loss of his reality, as his punishment; just as he begets his own product as a loss, as a product not belonging to him; so he begets the dominion of the one who does not produce over production and over the product. Just as he estranges from himself his own activity, so he confers to the stranger activity which is not his own.

Till now we have only considered this relationship from the standpoint of the worker and later we shall be considering it also from the standpoint of the non-worker.

Through *estranged, alienated labour*, then, the worker produces the relationship to this labour of a man alien to labour and standing outside it. The relationship of the worker to labour engenders the relation to it of the capitalist, or whatever one chooses to call the master of labour. *Private property* is thus the product, the result, the necessary consequence, of *alienated labour*, of the external relation of the worker to nature and to himself.

Private property thus results by analysis from the concept of *alienated labour*—i.e., of *alienated man*, of estranged labour, of estranged life, of *estranged* man.

True, it is as a result of the *movement of private property that* we have obtained the concept of *alienated labour* (*of alienated life*) from political economy. But on analysis of this concept it becomes clear that though private property appears to be the source, the cause of alienated labour, it is really its consequence, just as the gods *in the beginning* are not the cause but the effect of man's intellectual confusion. Later this relationship becomes reciprocal.

Only at the very culmination of the development of private property does this, its secret, re-emerge, namely, that on the one hand it is the *product* of alienated labour, and that secondly it is the *means* by which labour alienates itself, the *realization of this alienation*.

This exposition immediately sheds light on various hitherto unsolved conflicts.

(1) Political economy starts from labour as the real soul of production; yet to labour it gives nothing, and to private property everything. From this contradiction Proudhon has concluded in favour of labour and against private property. We understand, however, that this apparent contradiction is the contradiction of *estranged labour* with itself, and that political economy has merely formulated the laws of estranged labour.

We also understand, therefore, that *wages* and *private property* are identical: where the product, the object of labour pays for labour itself, the wage is but a necessary consequence of labour's estrangement, for after all in the wage of labour, labour does not appear as an end in itself but as the servant of the wage. We shall develop this point later, and meanwhile will only deduce some conclusions.

A *forcing-up of wages* (disregarding all other difficulties, including the fact that it would only be by force, too, that the higher wages, being an anomaly, could be maintained) would therefore be nothing but *better payment for the slave*, and would not conquer either for the worker or for labour their human status and dignity.

Indeed, even the *equality of wages* demanded by Proudhon only transforms the relationship of the present-day worker to his labour into the relationship of all men to labour. Society is then conceived as an abstract capitalist.

Wages are a direct consequence of estranged labour, and estranged labour is the direct cause of private property. The downfall of the one aspect must therefore mean the downfall of the other.

(2) From the relationship of estranged labour to private property it further follows that the emancipation of society from private property, etc., from servitude, is expressed in the *political* form of the *emancipation of the workers*; not that *their* emancipation alone was at stake but because the emancipation of the workers contains universal human emancipation—and it contains this, because the whole of human servitude is involved in the relation of the worker to production, and every relation of servitude is but a modification and consequence of this relation.

Just as we have found the concept of *private property* from the concept of *estranged, alienated labour by analysis*, in the same way every category of political economy can be evolved with the help of these two factors; and we shall find again in each category, e.g., trade, competition, capital, money, only a *definite* and *developed expression* of the first foundations.

Before considering this configuration, however, let us try to solve two problems.

(1) To define the general *nature of private property*, as it has arisen as a result of estranged labour, in its relation to *truly human, social property*.

(2) We have accepted the *estrangement of labour*, its *alienation*, as a fact, and we have analysed this fact. How, we now ask, does *man* come to *alienate*, to estrange, *his labour?* How is this estrangement rooted in the nature of human development? We have already gone a long way to the solution of this problem by *transforming* the question as to the *origin of private property* into the question as to the relation of *alienated labour* to the course of humanity's development. For when one speaks of *private property*, one thinks of being concerned with something external to man. When one speaks of labour, one is directly concerned with man himself. This new formulation of the question already contains its solution.

As to (1): The general nature of private property and its relation to truly human property.

Alienated labour has resolved itself for us into two elements which mutually condition one another, or which are but different expressions of one and the same relationship. *Appropriation* appears as estrangement, as *alienation;* and *alienation* appears as *appropriation, estrangement* as true *enfranchisement*.

We have considered the one side—*alienated* labour in relation to the *worker* himself, i.e., the *relation of alienated labour to itself*. The *property-relation of the non-worker to the worker and to labour* we have found as the product, the necessary outcome of this relation of alienated labour *Private property*, as the material, summary expression of alienated labour, embraces both relations—the *relation of the worker to work, to the product of his labour and to the non-worker*, and the relation of the *non-worker to the worker and to the product of his labour*.

Having seen that in relation to the worker who *appropriates* nature by means of his labour, this appropriation appears as estrangement, his own spontaneous activity as activity for another and as activity of another, vitality as a sacrifice of life, production of the object as loss of the object to an alien power, to an *alien* person—we shall now consider the relation to the worker, to labour and its object of this person who is *alien* to labour and the worker.

First it has to be noticed, that everything which appears in the worker as an *activity of alienation, of estrangement*, appears in the non-worker as a *state of alienation, of estrangement*.

Secondly, that the worker's *real, practical attitude* in production and to the product (as a state of mind) appears in the non-worker confronting him as a *theoretical* attitude.

Thirdly, the non-worker does everything against the worker which the worker does against himself; but he does not do against himself what he does against the worker.

21

HISTORICAL MATERIALISM*

KARL MARX

The premises from which we begin are not arbitrary ones, not dogmas, but real premises from which abstraction can only be made in the imagination. They are the real individuals, their activity and the material conditions under which they live, both those which they find already existing and those produced by their activity. These premises can thus be verified in a purely empirical way.

The first premise of all human history is, of course, the existence of living human individuals. Thus the first fact to be established is the physical organisation of these individuals and their consequent relation to the rest of nature. Of course, we cannot here go either into the actual physical nature of man, or into the natural conditions in which man finds himself—geological, oreohydrographical, climatic and so on. The writing of history must always set out from these natural bases and their modification in the course of history through the action of men.

Men can be distinguished from animals by consciousness, by religion or anything else you like. They themselves begin to distinguish themselves from animals as soon as they begin to *produce* their means of subsistence, a step which is conditioned by their physical organisation. By producing their means of subsistence men are indirectly producing their actual material life.

The way in which men produce their means of subsistence depends first of all on the nature of the actual means of subsistence they find in existence and have to reproduce. This mode of production must not be considered simply as being the production of the physical existence of the individuals. Rather it is a definite form of activity of these individuals, a definite form of expressing their life, a definite *mode of life* on their part. As individuals express their life, so they are. What they are, therefore, coincides with their production, both with what they produce and with how they produce. The nature of individuals thus depends on the material conditions determining their production.

This production only makes its appearance with the *increase of population*. In its turn this presupposes the intercourse [*Verkehr*] of individuals with one another. The form of this intercourse is again determined by production.

The relations of different nations among themselves depend upon the extent to which each has developed its productive forces, the division of labour and internal intercourse. This statement is generally recognised. But not only the relation of one nation to others, but also the whole internal structure of the nation itself depends on the stage of development reached by its production and its internal and external intercourse. How far the productive forces of a

*Excerpt from *The German Ideology*, Part One, by Karl Marx and Frederick Engels, Edited and with an Introduction by C.J. Arthur. Laurence & Wishart, 1970. Reprinted with permission.

nation are developed is shown most manifestly by the degree to which the division of labour has been carried. Each new productive force, insofar as it is not merely a quantitative extension of productive forces already known (for instance the bringing into cultivation of fresh land), causes a further development of the division of labour.

The division of labour inside a nation leads at first to the separation of industrial and commercial from agricultural labour, and hence to the separation of *town* and *country* and to the conflict of their interests. Its further development leads to the separation of commerical from industrial labour. At the same time through the division of labour inside these various branches there develop various divisions among the individuals co-operating in definite kinds of labour. The relative position of these individual groups is determined by the methods employed in agriculture, industry and commerce (patriarchalism, slavery, estates, classes). These same conditions are to be seen (given a more developed intercourse) in the relations of different nations to one another.

The various stages of development in the division of labour are just so many different forms of ownership, i.e. the existing stage in the division of labour determines also the relations of individuals to one another with reference to the material, instrument, and product of labour.

The first form of ownership is tribal [*Stammeigentum*] ownership. It corresponds to the undeveloped stage of production, at which a people lives by *hunting and fishing*, by the rearing of beasts or, in the highest stage, agriculture. In the latter case it presupposes a great mass of uncultivated stretches of land. The division of labour is at this stage still very elementary and is confined to a further extension of the natural division of labour existing in the family. The social structure is, therefore, limited to an extension of the family; patriarchal family chieftains, below them the members of the tribe, finally slaves. The slavery latent in the family only develops gradually with the increase of population, the growth of wants, and with the extension of external relations, both of war and of barter.

The second form is the ancient communal and State ownership which proceeds especially from the union of several tribes into a *city* by agreement or by conquest, and which is still accompanied by slavery. Beside communal ownership we already find movable, and later also immovable, private property developing, but as an abnormal form subordinate to communal ownership. The citizens hold power over their labouring slaves only in their community, and on this account alone, therefore, they are bound to the form of communal ownership. It is the communal private property which compels the active citizens to remain in this spontaneously derived form of association over against their slaves. For this reason the whole structure of society based on this communal ownership, and with it the power of the people, decays in the same measure as, in particular, immovable private property evolves. The division of labour is already more developed. We already find the antagonism of town and country; later the antagonism between those states which represent town interests and those which represent country interests, and inside the towns themselves the antagonism between industry and maritime commerce. The class relation between citizens and slaves is now completely developed.

The third form of ownership is feudal or estate property. If antiquity started out from the *town* and its little territory, the Middle Ages started out from the *country*. This different starting-point was determined by the sparseness of the population at that time, which was scattered over a large area and which received no large increase from the conquerors. In contrast to Greece and Rome, feudal development at the outset, therefore, extends over a much wider territory, prepared by the Roman conquests and the spread of agriculture at first associated with it. The last centuries of the declining Roman Empire and its conquest by the barbarians destroyed a number of productive forces; agriculture had declined, industry had decayed for want of a market, trade had died out or been violently suspended, the rural and urban population had decreased. From these conditions and the mode of organisation of the conquest determined by them, feudal property developed under the influence of the Germanic military constitution. Like tribal and communal ownership, it is based again on a community; but the directly producing class standing over against it is not, as in the case of the ancient community, the slaves, but the enserfed small peasantry. As soon as feudalism is fully developed, there also arises antagonism to the towns. The hierarchical structure of landownership, and the armed bodies of retainers associated with it, gave the nobility power over the serfs. This feudal organisation was, just as much as the ancient communal ownership, an association against a subjected producing class; but the form of association and the relation to the direct producers were different because of the different conditions of production.

This feudal system of landownership had its counterpart in the *towns* in the shape of corporative property, the feudal organisation of trades. Here property consisted chiefly in the labour of each individual person. The necessity for association against the organised robbernobility, the need for communal covered markets in an age when the industrialist was at the same time a merchant, the growing competition of the escaped serfs swarming into the rising towns, the feudal structure of the whole country: these combined to bring about the *guilds*. The gradually accumulated small capital of individual craftsmen and their stable numbers, as against the growing population, evolved the relation of journeyman and apprentice, which brought into being in the towns a hierarchy similar to that in the country.

Thus the chief form of property during the feudal epoch consisted on the one hand of landed property with serf labour chained to it, and on the other of the labour of the individual with small capital commanding the labour of journeymen. The organisation of both was determined by the restricted conditions of production—the small-scale and primitive cultivation of the land, and the craft type of industry. There was little division of labour in the heyday of feudalism. Each country bore in itself the antithesis of town and country; the division into estates was certainly strongly marked; but apart from the differentiation of princes, nobility, clergy and peasants in the country, and masters, journeymen, apprentices and soon also the rabble of casual labourers in the towns, no division of importance took place. In agriculture it was rendered difficult by the strip-system, beside which the cottage industry of the peasants themselves emerged. In industry there was no division of labour at all in the individual trades themselves, and very little between them. The separation of industry and commerce was found already in existence in older towns; in the newer it only developed later, when the towns entered into mutual relations.

The grouping of larger territories into feudal kingdoms was a necessity for the landed nobility as for the towns. The organisation of the ruling class, the nobility, had, therefore, everywhere a monarch at its head.

The fact is, therefore, that definite individuals who are productively active in a definite way enter into these definite social and political relations. Empirical observation must in each separate instance bring out empirically, and without any mystification and speculation, the connection of the social and political structure with production. The social structure and the State are continually evolving out of the life-process of definite individuals, but of individuals, not as they may appear in their own or other people's imagination, but as they *really* are; i.e. as they operate, produce materially, and hence as they work under definite material limits, presuppositions and conditions independent of their will.

The production of ideas, of conceptions, of consciousness, is at first directly interwoven with the material activity and the material intercourse of men, the language of real life. Conceiving, thinking, the mental intercourse of men, appear at this stage as the direct efflux of their material behaviour. The same applies to mental production as expressed in the language of politics, laws, morality, religion, metaphysics, etc. of a people. Men are the producers of their conceptions, ideas, etc.—real, active men, as they are conditioned by a definite development of their productive forces and of the intercourse corresponding to these, up to its furthest forms. Consciousness can never be anything else than conscious existence, and the existence of men is their actual life-process. If in all ideology men and their circumstances appear upside-down as in a *camera obscura*, this phenomenon arises just as much from their historical life-process as the inversion of objects on the retina does from their physical life-process.

In direct contrast to German philosophy which descends from heaven to earth, here we ascend from earth to heaven. That is to say, we do not set out from what men say, imagine, conceive, nor from men as narrated, thought of, imagined, conceived, in order to arrive at men in the flesh. We set out from real, active men, and on the basis of their real life-process we demonstrate the development of the ideological reflexes and echoes of this life-process. The phantoms formed in the human brain are also, necessarily, sublimates of their material life-process, which is empirically verifiable and bound to material premises. Morality, religion, metaphysics, all the rest of ideology and their corresponding forms of consciousness, thus no longer retain the semblance of independence. They have no history, no development; but men, developing their material production and their material intercourse, alter, along with this their real existence, their thinking and the products of their thinking. Life is not determined by conciousness, but consciousness by life. In the first method of approach the starting-point is consciousness taken as the living individual; in the second method, which conforms to real life, it is the real living individuals themselves, and consciousness is considered solely as *their* consciousness.

This method of approach is not devoid of premises. It starts out from the real premises and does not abandon them for a moment. Its premises are men, not in any fantastic isolation and rigidity, but in their actual, empirically perceptible process of development under definite conditions. As soon as this active life-process is described, history ceases to be a collection of dead facts as it is with the empiricists (themselves still abstract), or an imagined activity of imagined subjects, as with the idealists.

Where speculation ends—in real life—there real, positive science begins: the representation of the practical activity, of the practical process of development of men. Empty talk about consciousness ceases, and real knowledge has to take its place. When reality is depicted, philosophy as an independent branch of knowledge loses its medium of existence. At the best its place can only be taken by a summing-up of the most general results, abstractions which arise from the observation of the historical development of men. Viewed apart from real history, these abstractions have in themselves no value whatsoever. They can only serve to facilitate the arrangement of historical material, to indicate the sequence of its separate strata. But they by no means afford a recipe or schema, as does philosophy, for neatly trimming the epochs of history. On the contrary, our difficulties begin only when we set about the observation and the arrangement—the real depiction—of our historical material, whether of a past epoch or of the present. The removal of these difficulties is governed by premises which it is quite impossible to state here, but which only the study of the actual life-process and the activity of the individuals of each epoch will make evident. We shall select here some of these abstractions, which we use in contradistinction to the ideologists, and shall illustrate them by historical examples.

Since we are dealing with the Germans, who are devoid of premium, we must begin by stating the first premise of all human existence and, therefore, of all history, the premise, namely, that men must be in a position to live in order to be able to "make history". But life involves before everything else eating and drinking, a habitation, clothing and many other things. The first historical act is thus the production of the means to satisfy these needs, the production of material life itself. And indeed this is an historical act, a fundamental condition of all history, which today, as thousands of years ago, must daily and hourly be fulfilled merely in order to sustain human life.

The second point is that the satisfaction of the first need (the action of satisfying, and the instrument of satisfaction which has been acquired) leads to new needs; and this production of new needs is the first historical act. Here we recognise immediately the spiritual ancestry of the great historical wisdom of the Germans who, when they run out of positive material and when they can serve up neither theological nor political nor literary rubbish, assert that this is not history at all, but the "prehistoric era". They do not, however, enlighten us as to how we proceed from this nonsensical "prehistory" to history proper; although, on the other hand, in their historical speculation they seize upon this "prehistory" with especial eagerness because they imagine themselves safe there from interference on the part of "crude facts," and, at the same time, because there they can give full rein to their speculative impulse and set up and knock down hypotheses by the thousand.

The third circumstance which, from the very outset, enters into historical development, is that men, who daily remake their own life, begin to make other men, to propagate their kind: the relation between man and woman, parents and children, the *family*. The family, which to begin with is the only social relationship, becomes later, when increased needs create a new social relations and the increased population new needs, a subordinate one (except in Germany), and must then be treated and analysed according to the existing empirical data, not according to "the concept of the family," as is the custom in Germany. These three aspects of social activity are not of course to be taken as three different stages, but just as three aspects or, to make it clear to the Germans, three "moments," which have existed simultaneously since the dawn of history and the first men, and which still assert themselves in history today.

The production of life, both of one's own in labour and of fresh life in procreation, now appears as a double relationship: on the one hand as a natural, on the other as a social relationship. By social we understand the co-operation of several individuals, no matter under what conditions, in what manner and to what end. It follows from this that a certain mode of production, or industrial stage, is always combined with a certain mode of co-operation, or social stage, and this mode of co-operation is itself a "productive force". Further, that the multitude of productive forces accessible to men determines the nature of society, hence, that the "history of humanity" must always be studied and treated in relation to the history of industry and exchange.

This conception of history depends on our ability to expound the real process of production, starting out from the material production of life itself, and to comprehend the form of intercourse connected with this and created by this mode of production (i.e. civil society in its various stages), as the basis of all history; and to show it in its action as State, to explain all the different theoretical products and forms of consciousness, religion, philosophy, ethics, etc. etc. and trace their origins and growth from that basis; by which means, of course, the whole thing can be depicted in its totality (and therefore, too, the reciprocal action of these various sides on one another). It has not, like the idealistic view of history, in every period to look for a category, but remains constantly on the real *ground* of history; it does not explain practice from the idea but explains the formation of ideas from material practice; and accordingly it comes to the conclusion that all forms and products of consciousness cannot be dissolved by mental criticism, by resolution into "self-consciousness" or transformation into "apparitions," "spectres," "fancies," etc. but only by the practical overthrow of the actual social relations which gave rise to this idealistic humbug; that not criticism but revolution is the driving force of history, also of religion, of philosophy and all other types of theory. It shows that history does not end by being resolved into "self-consciousness" as "spirit of the spirit," but that in it at each stage there is found a material result: a sum of productive forces, an historically created relation of individuals to nature and to one another, which is handed down to each generation from its predecessor; a mass of productive forces, capital funds and conditions, which, on the one hand, is indeed modified by the new generation, but also on the other prescribes for it its conditions of lifeand gives it a definite development, a special character. It shows that circumstances make men just as much as men make circumstances.

This sum of productive forces, capital funds and social forms of intercourse, which every individual and generation finds in existence as something given, is the real basis of what the philosophers have conceived as "substance" and "essence of man," and what they have deified and attacked; a real basis which is not in the least disturbed, in its effect and influence on the development of men, by the fact that these philosophers revolt against it as "self-consciousness" and the "Unique". These conditions of life, which different generations find in existence, decide also whether or not the periodically recurring revolutionary convulsion will be strong enough to overthrow the basis of the entire existing system. And if these material elements of a complete revolution are not present (namely, on the one hand the existing productive forces, on the other the formation of a revolutionary mass, which revolts not only against separate conditions of society up till then, but against the very "production of life" till then, the "total activity" on which it was based), then, as far as practical development is concerned, it is absolutely immaterial whether the *idea* of this revolution has been expressed a hundred times already, as the history of communism proves.

In the whole conception of history up to the present this real basis of history has either been totally neglected or else considered as a minor matter quite irrelevant to the course of history. History must, therefore, always be written according to an extraneous standard; the real production of life seems to be primeval history, while the truly historical appears to be separated from ordinary life, something extra-superterrestrial. With this the relation of man to nature is excluded from history and hence the antithesis of nature and history is created. The exponents of this conception of history have consequently only been able to see in history the political actions of princes and States, religious and all sorts of theoretical struggles, and in particular in each historical epoch have had to *share the illusion of that epoch*. For instance, if an epoch imagines itself to be actuated by purely "political" or "religious" motives, although "religion" and "politics" are only forms of its true motives, the historian accepts this opinion. The "idea," the "conception" of the people in question about their real practice, is transformed into the sole determining, active force, which controls and determines their practice. When the crude form in which the division of labour appears with the Indians and Egyptians calls forth the caste-system in their State and religion, the historian believes that the caste-system is the power which has produced this crude social form. While the French and the English at least hold by the political illusion, which is moderately close to reality, the Germans move in the realm of the "pure spirit," and make religious illusion the driving force of history.

22

Mechanical and Organic Solidarity*

Émile Durkheim

The totality of beliefs and sentiments common to average citizens of the same society forms a determinate system which has its own life; one may call it the *collective or common conscience.* No doubt, it has not a specific organ as a substratum; it is, by definition, diffuse in every reach of society. Nevertheless it has specific characteristics which make it a distinct reality. It is, in effect, independent of the particular conditions in which individuals are placed; they pass on and it remains. It is the same in the North and in the South, in great cities and in small, in different professions. Moreover, it does not change with each generation, but, on the contrary, it connects successive generations with one another. It is, thus, an entirely different thing from particular consciences, although it can be realized only through them. It is the psychical type of society, a type which has its properties, its conditions of existence, its mode of development, just as individual types, although in a different way.

There are in us two consciences: one contains states which are personal to each of us and which characterize us, while the states which comprehend the other are common to all society. The first represent only our individual personality and constitute it ; the second represent the collective type and, consequently, society, without which it would not exist. When it is one of the elements of this latter which determines our conduct, it is not in view of our personal interest that we act, but we pursue collective ends. Although distinct, these two consciences are linked one to the other, since, in sum, they are only one, having one and the same organic substratum. They are thus solidary. From this results a solidarity *sui generis,* which, born of resemblances, directly links the individual with society. We shall be better able to show in the next chapter why we propose to call it mechanical. This solidarity does not consist only in a general and indeterminate attachment of the individual to the group, but also makes the detail of his movements harmonious. In short, as these collective movements are always the same, they always produce the same effects. Consequently, each time that they are in play, wills move spontaneously and together in the same sense.

There are in each of us, as we have said, two consciences: one which is common to our group in its entirety, which consequently, is not ourself, but society living and acting within us ; the other, on the contrary, represents that in us which is personal and distinct, that which makes us an individual. Solidarity which comes from likenesses is at its maximum when the collective conscience completely envelops our whole conscience and coincides in all points with it. But, at that moment, our individuality is nil. It can be born only if the community takes smaller toll of us. There are, here, two contrary forces, one centripetal, the other centrifugal, which cannot flourish at the same time. We cannot, at one and the same time, develop ourselves in two opposite senses. If we have a lively desire to think and act for ourselves, we cannot be strongly inclined to think and act as others do. If our ideal is to present a singular and personal appearance, we do not want to resemble everybody else. Moreover, at the moment when this solidarity exercises its force, our personality vanishes, as our definition permits us to say, for we are no longer ourselves, but the collective life.

The social molecules which can be coherent in this way can act together only in the measure that they have no actions of their own, as the molecules of inorganic bodies. That is why we propose to call this type of solidarity mechanical. The term does not signify that it is produced by mechanical and artificial means. We call it that only by analogy to the cohesion which unites the elements of an inanimate body, as opposed to that which makes a unity out of the elements of a living body. What justifies this term is that the link which thus unites the individual to society is wholly analogous to that which attaches a thing to a person. The individual conscience, considered in this light, is a simple dependent upon the collective type and follows all of its movements, as the possessed object follows those of its owner. In societies where this type of solidarity is highly developed, the individual does not appear, as we shall see later. Individuality is something which the society possesses. Thus, in these social types, personal rights are not yet distinguished from real rights.

It is quite otherwise with the solidarity which the division of labor produces. Whereas the previous type implies that individuals resemble each other, this type presumes their difference. The first is possible only in so far as the individual personality is absorbed into the collective personality ; the second is possible only if each one has a sphere of action which is peculiar to him ; that is, a personality. It is necessary, then, that the collective conscience leave open a part of the individual conscience in order that special functions may be established there, functions which it cannot regulate. The more this region is extended, the stronger is the cohesion which results from this solidarity. In effect, on the one hand, each one depends as much more strictly on society as labor is more divided; and, on the other, the activity of each is as much more personal as it is more specialized. Doubtless, as circumscribed as it is, it is never completely original. Even in the exercise of our occupation, we conform to usages, to practices which are common to our whole professional brotherhood. But, even in this instance, the yoke that we submit to is much less heavy than when society completely controls us, and it leaves much more place open for the free play of our initiative. Here, then, the individuality of all grows at the same time as that of its parts. Society becomes more capable of collective movement, at the same time that each of its elements has more freedom of movement. This solidarity resembles that which we observe among the higher animals. Each organ, in effect, has its special physiognomy, its autonomy. And, moreover, the unity of the organism is as great as the individuation of the parts is more marked. Because of this analogy, we propose to call the solidarity which is due to the division of labor, organic.

23

Types of Suicide*

Émile Durkheim

So we reach the general conclusion: suicide varies inversely with the degree of integration of the social groups of which the individual forms a part.

But society cannot disintegrate without the individual simultaneously detaching himself from social life, without his own goals becoming preponderant over those of the community, in a word without his personality tending to surmount the collective personality. The more weakened the groups to which he belongs, the less he depends on them, the more he consequently depends only on himself and recognizes no other rules of conduct than what are founded on his private interests. If we agree to call this state egoism, in which the individual ego asserts itself to excess in the face of the social ego and at its expense, we may call egoistic the special type of suicide springing from excessive individualism.

Excessive individualism not only results in favoring the action of suicidogenic causes, but it is itself such a cause. It not only frees man's inclination to do away with himself from a protective obstacle, but creates this inclination out of whole cloth and thus gives birth to a special suicide which bears its mark. This must be clearly understood for this is what constitutes the special character of the type of suicide just distinguished and justifies the name we have given it. What is there then in individualism that explains this result?

It has been sometimes said that because of his psychological constitution, man cannot live without attachment to some object which transcends and survives him, and that the reason for this necessity is a need we must have not to perish entirely. Life is said to be intolerable unless some reason for existing is involved, some purpose justifying life's trials. The individual alone is not a sufficient end for his activity. He is too little. He is not only hemmed in spatially; he is also strictly limited temporally. When, therefore, we have no other object than ourselves we cannot avoid the thought that our efforts will finally end in nothingness, since we ourselves disappear. But annihilation terrifies us. Under these conditions one would lose courage to live, that is, to act and struggle, since nothing will remain of our exertions. The state of egoism, in other words, is supposed to be contradictory to human nature and, consequently, too uncertain to have chances of permanence.

But this is not all. This detachment occurs not only in single individuals. One of the constitutive elements of every national temperament consists of a certain way of estimating the value

*Reprinted with the permission of The Free Press, a Division of Simon & Schuster, Inc., from *Suicide: A Study in Sociology* by Emile Durkheim, translated by John A. Spaulding and George Simpson.

of existence. There is a collective as well as an individual humor inclining peoples to sadness or cheerfulness, making them see things in bright or sombre lights. In fact, only society can pass a collective opinion on the value of human life; for this the individual is incompetent. The latter knows nothing but himself and his own little horizon; thus his experience is too limited to serve as a basis for a general appraisal. He may indeed consider his own life to be aimless; he can say nothing applicable to others. On the contrary, without sophistry, society may generalize its own feeling as to itself, its state of health or lack of health. For individuals share too deeply in the life of society for it to be diseased without their suffering infection. What it suffers they necessarily suffer. Because it is the whole, its ills are communicated to its parts. Hence it cannot disintegrate without awareness that the regular conditions of general existence are equally disturbed. Because society is the end on which our better selves depend, it cannot feel us escaping it without a simultaneous realization that our activity is purposeless. Since we are its handiwork, society cannot be conscious of its own decadence without the feeling that henceforth this work is of no value. Thence are formed currents of depression and disillusionment emanating from no particular individual but expressing society's state of disintegration. They reflect the relaxation of social bonds, a sort of collective asthenia, or social malaise, just as individual sadness, when chronic, in its way reflects the poor organic state of the individual. Then metaphysical and religious systems spring up which, by reducing these obscure sentiments to formulae, attempt to prove to men the senselessness of life and that it is self-deception to believe that it has purpose. Then new moralities originate which, by elevating facts to ethics, commend suicide or at least tend in that direction by suggesting a minimal existence. On their appearance they seem to have been created out of whole cloth by their makers who are sometimes blamed for the pessimism of their doctrines. In reality they are an effect rather than a cause; they merely symbolize in abstract language and systematic form the physiological distress of the body social. As these currents are collective, they have, by virtue of their origin, an authority which they impose upon the individual and they drive him more vigorously on the way to which he is already inclined by the state of moral distress directly aroused in him by the disintegration of society. Thus, at the very moment that, with excessive zeal, he frees himself from the social environment, he still submits to its influence. However individualized a man may be, there is always something collective remaining—the very depression and melancholy resulting from this same exaggerated individualism. He effects communion through sadness when he no longer has anything else with which to achieve it.

Hence this type of suicide well deserves the name we have given it. Egoism is not merely a contributing factor in it; it is its generating cause. In this case the bond attaching man to life relaxes because that attaching him to society is itself slack. The incidents of private life which seem the direct inspiration of suicide and are considered its determining causes are in reality only incidental causes. The individual yields to the slightest shock of circumstance because the state of society has made him a ready prey to suicide.

If, as we have just seen, excessive individuation leads to suicide, insufficient individuation has the same effects. When man has become detached from society, he encounters less resistance to suicide in himself, and he does so likewise when social integration is too strong.

We thus confront a type of suicide differing by incisive qualities from the preceding one. Whereas the latter is due to excessive individuation, the former is caused by too rudimentary individuation. One occurs because society allows the individual to escape it, being insufficiently aggregated in some parts or even in the whole; the other, because society holds him in too strict tutelage. Having given the name of *egoism* to the state of the ego living its own life and obeying itself alone, that of *altruism* adequately expresses the opposite state, where the ego is not its own property, where it is blended with something not itself, where the goal of conduct is exterior to itself, that is, in one of the groups in which it participates. So we call the suicide caused by intense altruism *altruistic suicide*. But since it is also characteristically performed as a duty, the terminology adopted should express this fact. So we will call such a type *obligatory altruistic suicide*.

Under this head may notably be classified the death of some of the Christian martyrs. All those neophytes who without killing themselves, voluntarily allowed their own slaughter, are really suicides. Though they did not kill themselves, they sought death with all their power and behaved so as to make it inevitable. To be suicide, the act from which death must necessarily result need only have been performed by the victim with full knowledge of the facts. Besides, the passionate enthusiasm with which the believers in the new religion faced final torture shows that at this moment they had completely discarded their personalities for the idea of which they had become the servants. Probably the epidemics of suicide which devastated the monasteries on several occasions during the Middle Ages, apparently caused by excesses of religious fervor, were of this nature.

In our contemporary societies, as individual personality becomes increasingly free from the collective personality, such suicides could not be widespread. Some may doubtless be said to have yielded to altruistic motives, such as soldiers who preferred death to the humiliation of defeat, like Commandant Beaurepaire and Admiral Villeneuve, or unhappy persons who kill themselves to prevent disgrace befalling their family. For when such persons renounce life, it is for something they love better than themselves. But they are isolated and exceptional cases. Yet even today there exists among us a special environment where altruistic suicide is chronic: namely, the army.

It may now be better understood why we insisted on giving an objective definition of suicide and on sticking to it.

Because altruistic suicide, though showing the familiar suicidal traits, resembles especially in its most vivid manifestations some categories of action which we are used to honoring with our respect and even admiration, people have often refused to consider it as self-destruction. It is to be remembered that the deaths of Cato and of the Girondins were not suicides for Esquirol and Falret. But if suicides with the spirit of renunciation and abnegation as their immediate and visible cause do not deserve the name, it can be no more appropriate for those springing from the same moral disposition, though less apparently; for the second differ by only a few shades from the first. If the inhabitant of the Canary Islands who throws himself into an abyss to do honor to his god is not a suicide, how give this name to a Jain sectary who kills himself to obtain entry to oblivion; to the primitive who, under the influence of the same mental state, renounces life for a slight insult done him or merely to express his contempt for existence; to the bankrupt who prefers not to survive his disgrace; and finally to the many soldiers who every year increase the numbers of voluntary deaths? All these cases have for their root the same state of altruism.

But society is not only something attracting the sentiments and activities of individuals with unequal force. It is also a power controlling them. There is a relation between the way this regulative action is performed and the social suicide-rate.

No living being can be happy or even exist unless his needs are sufficiently proportioned to his means. In other words, if his needs require more than can be granted, or even merely something of a different sort, they will be under continual friction and can only function painfully. Movements incapable of production without pain tend not to be reproduced. Unsatisfied tendencies atrophy, and as the impulse to live is merely the result of all the rest, it is bound to weaken as the others relax.

But how determine the quantity of well-being, comfort or luxury legitimately to be craved by a human being? Nothing appears in man's organic nor in his psychological constitution which sets a limit to such tendencies. The functioning of individual life does not require them to cease at one point rather than at another; the proof being that they have constantly increased since the beginnings of history, receiving more and more complete satisfaction, yet with no weakening of average health. Above all, how establish their proper variation with different conditions of life, occupations, relative importance of services, etc.? In no society are they equally satisfied in the different stages of the social hierarchy. Yet human nature is substantially the same among all men, in its essential qualities. It is not human nature which can assign the variable limits necessary to our needs. They are thus unlimited so far as they depend on the individual alone. Irrespective of any external regulatory force, our capacity for feeling is in itself an insatiable and bottomless abyss.

But if nothing external can restrain this capacity, it can only be a source of torment to itself. Unlimited desires are insatiable by definition and insatiability is rightly considered a sign of morbidity. Being unlimited, they constantly and infinitely surpass the means at their command; they cannot be quenched. Inextinguishable thirst is constantly renewed torture. It has been claimed, indeed, that human activity naturally aspires beyond assignable limits and sets itself unattainable goals. But how can such an undetermined state be any more reconciled with the conditions of mental life than with the demands of physical life? All man's pleasure in acting, moving and exerting himself implies the sense that his efforts are not in vain and that by walking he has advanced. However, one does not advance when one walks toward no goal, or—which is the same thing—when his goal is infinity. Since the distance between us and it is always the same, whatever road we take, we might as well have made the motions without progress from the spot. Even our glances behind and our feeling of pride at the distance covered can cause only deceptive satisfaction, since the remaining distance is not proportionately reduced. To pursue a goal which is by definition unattainable is to condemn oneself to a state of perpetual unhappiness.

To achieve any other result, the passions first must be limited. Only then can they be harmonized with the faculties and satisfied. But since the individual has no way of limiting them, this must be done by some force exterior to him. A regulative force must play the same role for moral needs which the organism plays for physical needs. This means that the force can only be moral. The awakening of conscience interrupted the state of equilibrium of the animal's dormant existence; only conscience, therefore, can furnish the means to re-establish it. Physical restraint would be ineffective; hearts cannot be touched by physio-chemical forces. So far as the appetites are not automatically restrained by physiological mechanisms, they can be halted only by a limit that they recognize as just. Men would never consent to restrict their desires if they felt justified in passing the assigned limit. But, for reasons given above, they cannot assign themselves this law of justice. So they must receive it from an authority which they respect, to which they yield spontaneously. Either directly and as a whole, or through the agency of one of its organs, society alone can play this moderating role; for it is the only moral power superior to the individual, the authority of which he accepts. It alone has the power necessary to stipulate law and to set the point beyond which the passions must not go. Finally, it alone can estimate the reward to be prospectively offered to every class of human functionary, in the name of the common interest.

It is not true, then, that human activity can be released from all restraint. Nothing in the world can enjoy such a privilege. All existence being a part of the universe is relative to the remainder; its nature and method of manifestation accordingly depend not only on itself but on other beings, who consequently restrain and regulate it. Here there are only differences of degree and form between the mineral realm and the thinking person. Man's characteristic privilege is that the bond he accepts is not physical but moral; that is, social. He is governed not by a material environment brutally imposed on him, but by a conscience superior to his own, the superiority of which he feels. Because the greater, better part of his existence transcends the body, he escapes the body's yoke, but is subject to that of society.

But when society is disturbed by some painful crisis or by beneficent but abrupt transitions, it is momentarily incapable of exercising this influence; thence come the sudden rises in the curve of suicides which we have pointed out above.

In the case of economic disasters, indeed, something like a declassification occurs which suddenly casts certain individuals into a lower state than their previous one. Then they must reduce their requirements, restrain their needs, learn greater self-control. All the advantages of social influence are lost so far as they are concerned; their moral education has to be recommenced. But society cannot adjust them instantaneously to this new life and teach them to practice the increased self-repression to which they are unaccustomed. So they are not adjusted to the condition forced on them, and its very prospect is intolerable; hence the suffering which detaches them from a reduced existence even before they have made trial of it.

It is the same if the source of the crisis is an abrupt growth of power and wealth. Then, truly, as the conditions of life are changed, the standard according to which needs were regulated can no longer remain the same; for it varies with social resources, since it largely determines the share of each class of producers. The scale is upset; but a new scale cannot be immediately improvised. Time is required for the public conscience to reclassify men and things. So long as the social forces thus freed have not regained equilibrium, their respective values are unknown and so all regulation is lacking for a time. The limits are unknown between the possible and the impossible, what is just and what is unjust, legitimate claims and hopes and those which are immoderate. Consequently, there is no restraint upon aspirations. If the disturbance is profound, it affects even the principles controlling the distribution of men among various occupations. Since the relations between various parts of society are necessarily modified, the ideas expressing these relations must change. Some particular class especially favored by the crisis is no longer resigned to its former lot, and, on the other hand, the example of its greater good fortune arouses all sorts of jealousy below and about it. Appetites, not being controlled by a public opinion become disoriented, no longer recognize the limits proper to them. Besides, they are at the same time seized by a sort of natural erethism simply by the greater intensity of public life. With increased prosperity desires increase. At the very moment when traditional rules have lost their authority, the richer prize offered these appetites stimulates them and makes them more exigent and impatient of control. The state of de-regulation or anomy is thus further heightened by passions being less disciplined, precisely when they need more disciplining.

But then their very demands make fulfillment impossible. Over-weening ambition always exceeds the results obtained, great as they may be, since there is no warning to pause here. Nothing gives satisfaction and all this agitation is uninterruptedly maintained without appeasement. Above all, since this race for an unattainable goal can give no other pleasure but that of the race itself, if it is one, once it is interrupted the participants are left empty-handed. At the same time the struggle grows more violent and painful, both from being less controlled and because competition is greater. All classes contend among themselves because no established classification any longer exists. Effort grows, just when it becomes less productive. How could the desire to live not be weakened under such conditions?

This explanation is confirmed by the remarkable immunity of poor countries. Poverty protects against suicide because it is a restraint in itself. No matter how one acts, desires have to depend upon resources to some extent; actual possessions are partly the criterion of those aspired to. So the less one has the less he is tempted to extend the range of his needs indefinitely. Lack of power, compelling moderation, accustoms men to it, while nothing excites envy if no one has superfluity. Wealth, on the other hand, by the power it bestows, deceives us into believing that we depend on ourselves only. Reducing the resistance we encounter from objects, it suggests the possibility of unlimited success against them. The less limited one feels, the more intolerable all limitation appears.

Yet these dispositions are so inbred that society has grown to accept them and is accustomed to think them normal. It is everlastingly repeated that it is man's nature to be eternally dissatisfied, constantly to advance, without relief or rest, toward an indefinite goal. The longing for infinity is daily represented as a mark of moral distinction, whereas it can only appear within unregulated consciences which elevate to a rule the lack of rule from which they suffer. The doctrine of the most ruthless and swift progress has become an article of faith. But other theories appear parallel with those praising the advantages of instability, which, generalizing the situation that gives them birth, declare life evil, claim that it is richer in grief than in pleasure and that it attracts men only by false claims. Since this disorder is greatest in the economic world, it has most victims there.

Industrial and commercial functions are really among the occupations which furnish the greatest number of suicides. Almost on a level with the liberal professions, they sometimes surpass them; they are especially more afflicted than agriculture, where the old regulative forces still make their appearance felt most and where the fever of business has least penetrated. Here is best recalled what was once the general constitution of the economic order. And the divergence would be yet greater if, among the suicides of industry, employers were distinguished from workmen, for the former are probably most stricken by the state of anomy. The enormous rate of those with independent means (720 per million) sufficiently shows that the possessors of most comfort suffer most. Everything

that enforces subordination attenuates the effects of this state. At least the horizon of the lower classes is limited by those above them, and for this same reason their desires are more modest. Those who have only empty space above them are almost inevitably lost in it, if no force restrains them.

Anomy, therefore, is a regular and specific factor in suicide in our modern societies; one of the springs from which the annual contingent feeds. So we have here a new type to distinguish from the others. It differs from them in its dependence, not on the way in which individuals are attached to society, but on how it regulates them. Egoistic suicide results from man's no longer finding a basis for existence in life; altruistic suicide, because this basis for existence appears to man situated beyond life itself. The third sort of suicide, the existence of which has just been shown, results from man's activity's lacking regulation and his consequent sufferings. By virtue of its origin we shall assign this last variety the name of *anomic suicide.*

The above considerations show that there is a type of suicide the opposite of anomic suicide, just as egoistic and altruistic suicides are opposites. It is the suicide deriving from excessive regulation, that of persons with futures pitilessly blocked and passions violently choked by oppressive discipline. It is the suicide of very young husbands, of the married woman who is childless. So, for completeness' sake, we should set up a fourth suicidal type. But it has so little contemporary importance and examples are so hard to find aside from the cases just mentioned that it seems useless to dwell upon it. However it might be said to have historical interest. Do not the suicides of slaves, said to be frequent under certain conditions belong to this type, or all suicides attributable to excessive physical or moral despotism? To bring out the ineluctible and inflexible nature of a rule against which there is no appeal, and in contrast with the expression "anomy" which has just been used, we might call it fatalistic suicide.

24

Social Facts*

Émile Durkheim

Before inquiring into the method suited to the study of social facts, it is important to know which facts are commonly called "social." This information is all the more necessary since the designation "social" is used with little precision. It is currently employed for practically all phenomena generally diffused within society, however small their social interest. But on that basis, there are, as it were, no human events that may not be called social. Each individual drinks, sleeps, eats, reasons; and it is to society's interest that these functions be exercised in an orderly manner. If, then, all these facts are counted as "social" facts, sociology would have no subject matter exclusively its own, and its domain would be confused with that of biology and psychology.

But in reality there is in every society a certain group of phenomena which may be differentiated from those studied by the other natural sciences. When I fulfil my obligations as brother, husband, or citizen, when I execute my contracts, I perform duties which are defined, externally to myself and my acts, in law and in custom. Even if they conform to my own sentiments and I feel their reality subjectively, such reality is still objective, for I did not create them; I merely inherited them through my education. How many times it happens, moreover, that we are ignorant of the details of the obligations incumbent upon us, and that in order to acquaint ourselves with them we must consult the law and its authorized interpreters! Similarly, the church-member finds the beliefs and practices of his religious life ready-made at birth; their existence prior to his own implies their existence outside of himself. The system of signs I use to express my thought, the system of currency I employ to pay my debts, the instruments of credit I utilize in my commercial relations, the practices followed in my profession, etc., function independently of my own use of them. And these statements can be repeated for each member of society. Here, then, are ways of acting, thinking, and feeling that present the noteworthy property of existing outside the individual consciousness.

These types of conduct or thought are not only external to the individual but are, moreover, endowed with coercive power, by virtue of which they impose themselves upon him, independent of his individual will. Of course, when I fully consent and conform to them, this constraint is felt only slightly, if at all, and is therefore unnecessary. But it is, nonetheless, an intrinsic characteristic of these facts, the proof thereof being that it asserts itself as soon as I attempt to resist it. If I attempt to violate the law, it reacts against me so as to prevent my act before its accomplishment, or to nullify my violation by restoring the damage, if it is accomplished and reparable, or to make me expiate it if it cannot be compensated for otherwise.

In the case of purely moral maxims; the public conscience exercises a check on every act which offends it by means of the surveillance it exercises over the conduct of citizens, and the appropriate penalties at its disposal. In many cases the constraint is less violent, but nevertheless it always exists. If I do not submit to the conventions of society, if in my dress I do not conform to the customs observed in my country and in my class, the ridicule I provoke, the social isolation in which I am kept, produce, although in an attenuated form, the same effects as a punishment in the strict sense of the word. The constraint is nonetheless efficacious for being indirect. I am not obliged to speak French with my fellow-countrymen nor to use the legal currency, but I cannot possibly do otherwise. If I tried to escape this necessity, my attempt would fail miserably. As an industrialist, I am free to apply the technical methods of former centuries; but by doing so, I should invite certain ruin. Even when I free myself from these rules and violate them successfully, I am always compelled to struggle with them. When finally overcome, they make their constraining power sufficiently felt by the resistance they offer. The enterprises of all innovators, including successful ones, come up against resistance of this kind.

Here, then, is a category of facts with very distinctive characteristics: it consists of ways of acting, thinking, and feeling, external to the individual, and endowed with a power of coercion, by reason of which they control him. These ways of thinking could not be confused with biological phenomena, since they consist of representations and of actions; nor with psychological phenomena, which exist only in the individual consciousness and through it. They constitute, thus, a new variety of phenomena; and it is to them exclusively that the term "social" ought to be applied. And this term fits them quite well, for it is clear that, since their source is not in the individual, their substratum can be no other than society, either the political society as a whole or some one of the partial groups it includes, such as religious denominations, political, literary, and occupational associations, etc. On the other hand, this term "social" applies to them exclusively, for it has a distinct meaning only if it designates exclusively the phenomena which are not included in any of the categories of facts that have already been established and classified. These ways of thinking and acting therefore constitute the proper domain of sociology.

25

The Rationalism of Western Civilization*

Max Weber

Any heir of modern European culture will, unavoidably and justifiably, address universal-historical themes with a particular question in mind: What combination of circumstances led in the West, and only in the West, to the appearance of a variety of cultural phenomena that stand—at least as we like to imagine—in a historical line of development with *universal* significance and empirical validity?

Science, developed to the stage that we today recognize as "valid," exists only in the West. Empirical knowledge, reflection on the world and the problems of life, philosophical and theological wisdom of the deepest kind, extraordinarily refined knowledge and observation—all this has existed outside the West, above all in India, China, Babylon, and Egypt. Yet a fully developed systematic theology appeared only in Hellenic-influenced Christianity (even though some beginnings were apparent in Islam and a few sects in India). And despite empirical knowledge, Babylonian, and every other type of astronomy, lacked a mathematical foundation (rendering the development, in particular, of Babylonian astronomy all the more astonishing), which would be provided only later by the Greeks. A further product of the Hellenic mind, the idea of rational "proof," was absent from geometry in India. This mind also first created mechanics and physics. Moreover, although the natural sciences in India were quite well developed as concerns observation, they lacked the rational experiment, which was essentially a product of the Renaissance (although beginnings can be found in the ancient world). The modern laboratory was also missing in the natural sciences developed in India. For this reason, medicine in India, which was highly developed in terms of empirical technique, never acquired a biological and, especially, a biochemical foundation. A rational chemistry was absent from all regions outside the West.

The scholarly writing of history in China, which was very advanced, lacked the rigor of Thucydides [*ca.* 460–400 BCE]. Precursors of Machiavelli [1489–1527] existed in India, yet all Asian theorizing on the state omitted a systematic approach comparable to Aristotle's [384–322 BCE], as well as rational concepts in general. A rational jurisprudence based on rigorous juridical models and modes of thinking of the type found in Roman law and the Western law indebted to it was absent outside the West, despite all beginnings in India (School of Mimamsa) and the comprehensive codification of law in the Near East especially—and in spite of all the books on law written in India and elsewhere. A form of law similar to canon law cannot be found outside the West.

Similar conclusions must be drawn for art. The musical ear, apparently, was developed to a more refined degree among peoples outside the West than in the West to this day; or, at any rate, not less so. The most diverse sorts of polyphonic music have expanded across the globe, as did also the simultaneous playing of a number of instruments and singing in the higher pitches. All of the West's rational tone intervals were also widely calculated and known elsewhere. However, unique to the West were many musical innovations. Among them were rational, harmonic music (both counterpoint and harmony); formation of tone on the basis of three triads and the major third; and the understanding of chromatics and en-harmonics since the Renaissance harmonically and in rational form (rather than by reference to distance). Others were the orchestra with the string quartet as its core and the organization of ensembles of wind instruments; the bass accompaniment; and the system of musical notation (which made possible the composition and rehearsal of modern works of music and their very survival over time). Still other innovations were sonatas, symphonies, and operas (although organized music, onomatopoeia, chromatics, and alteration of tones have existed in the most diverse music as modes of expression). Finally, the West's basic instruments were the means for all this: the organ, piano, and violin.

[The situation is similar in architecture.] As a means of decoration, pointed arches existed outside the West, both in the ancient world and in Asia. Presumably, the juxtaposition of pointed arches and cross-arched vaults was not unknown in the Middle East. However, the rational utilization of the Gothic vault as a means to distribute thrust and to arch over variously formed spaces and, above all, as a principle of construction for large monumental buildings and as the foundation for a *style* that incorporated sculpture and painting, as was created in the Middle Ages—all this was missing outside the West. A solution to the weight problem introduced by domes was also lacking outside the West, even though the technical basis for its solution was taken from the Middle East. Every type of "classical" rationalization of the entire art world—as occurred in painting through the rational use of both linear and spatial perspective—was also lacking outside the West, where it began with the Renaissance.

Printing existed in China. Yet a printed literature intended *only* to be printed and made possible exclusively through printing—"daily newspapers" and "periodicals," mainly—originated only in the West.

Universities of all possible types existed also outside the West (China and the Islamic world), even universities that look externally similar to those in the West, especially to Western academics. A rational and systematic organization into scientific disciplines, however, with trained and specialized professionals (*Fachmenschentum*), existed only in the West. This becomes especially evident if these disciplines are viewed from the vantage point of whether they attained the culturally dominant significance they have achieved in the West today,

Above all, the cornerstone of the modern state and modern economy—specialized *civil servants*—arose only in the West. Only precursors of this stratum appeared outside the West. It never became, in any sense, as constitutive for the social order as occurred in the West. The "civil servant," of course, even the civil servant who performs specialized tasks, appeared in various societies, even in ancient times. However, only in the modern West is our entire existence—the foundational political, technical, and economic conditions of our being—absolutely and inescapably bound up in the casing (*Gehause*) of an *organization* of specially trained civil servants. No nation and no epoch has come to know state civil servants in the way that they are known in the modern West, namely, as persons trained in technical, commercial, and above all, legal areas of knowledge who are the social carriers of the most important everyday functions of social life.

[And what about the state?] The organization of political and social groups on the basis of *status* has existed historically on a broad scale. Yet the *Standestaat* in the Western sense—*rex et regnum*—has appeared only in the West. Moreover, parliaments of periodically elected "representatives," with demagogues and party leaders held responsible as "ministers" to parliamentary procedures, have come into existence only in the

West. This remains the case even though "political parties," of course, in the sense of organizations oriented to the acquisition of political power and the exercise of influence on political policy, can be found throughout the world. The "state," in fact, as a political institution (*Anstalt*) operated according to a rationally enacted "constitution" and rationally enacted laws, and administered by civil servants possessing *specialized* arenas of competence and oriented to rules and "laws," has existed with these distinguishing features only in the West, even though rudimentary developments in these directions have crystallized elsewhere.

The same may be said of that most fateful power of our modern life: *capitalism.*

A "drive to acquire goods" has actually nothing whatsoever to do with capitalism, as little as has the "pursuit of profit," money, and the greatest possible gain. Such striving has been found, and is to this day, among waiters, physicians, chauffeurs, artists, prostitutes, corrupt civil servants, soldiers, thieves, crusaders, gambling casino customers, and beggars. One can say that this pursuit of profit exists among "all sorts and conditions of men" [Sir Walter Besant], in all epochs and in all countries of the globe. It can be seen both in the past and in the present wherever the objective possibility for it somehow exists.

This naive manner of conceptualizing capitalism by reference to a "pursuit of gain" must be relegated to the kindergarten of cultural history methodology and abandoned once and for all. A fully unconstrained compulsion to acquire goods cannot be understood as synonymous with capitalism, and even less as its "*spirit*." On the contrary, capitalism *can* be identical with the *taming* of this irrational motivation, or at least with its rational tempering. Nonetheless, capitalism is distinguished by the striving for *profit*, indeed, profit is pursued in a rational, continuous manner in companies and firms, and then pursued *again and again*, as is *profitability*. There are no choices. If the entire economy is organized according to the rules of the open market, any company that fails to orient its activities toward the chance of attaining profit is condemned to bankruptcy.

Let us begin by *defining terms* in a manner more precise than often occurs. For us, a "*capitalist*" economic act involves first of all an expectation of profit based on the utilization of opportunities for *exchange*; that is, of (formally) *peaceful* opportunities for acquisition. Formal and actual acquisition through violence follows its own special laws and hence should best be placed, as much as one may recommend doing so, in a different category. Wherever capitalist acquisition is rationally pursued, action is oriented to *calculation* in terms of capital. What does this mean?

Such action is here oriented to a systematic utilization of skills or personal capacities on behalf of earnings in such a manner that, at the close of business transactions, the company's money *balances,* or "capital" (its earnings through transactions), exceed the estimated value of all production costs (and, in the case of a longer lasting company, *again and again* exceed costs). It is all the same whether goods entrusted to a traveling salesman are involved and he receives payment through barter, so that the closing calculation takes place in goods, or whether the assets of a large manufacturing corporation (such as buildings, machines, cash, basic materials, and partly or entirely manufactured goods) are weighed against its production costs. Decisive in both situations is that a *calculation* of earnings in money terms takes place, regardless of whether it is made on the basis of modern accounting methods or primitive, superficial procedures. Both at the beginning of the project and at the end there are specific calculations of balances. A starting balance is established and calculations are carried out before each separate transaction takes place; at every stage an instrumental assessment of the utility of potential transactions is calculated; and, finally, a concluding balance is calculated and the origin of "the profit" ascertained.

The beginning balance of the *commenda* transaction involves, for example, a designation of the amount of money agreed upon by both parties regarding what the relevant goods *should* be worth (assuming they have not already been given a monetary value). A final balance forms the estimate on the basis of which a distribution of profit and loss takes place. Calculation lies (as long as each case is rational) at the foundation of every single activity of the *commenda* partners. However, an actual exact accounting and appraisal may not exist, for on some occasions the transaction proceeds purely by reference to estimates or even on the basis of traditions and conventions. Indeed, such estimation appears in every form of capitalist enterprise even today wherever circumstances do not require more exact calculation. These points, however, relate only to the *degree* of rationality of capitalist acquisition.

Important for the formation of the *concept* of capitalism is only that economic action is decisively influenced by the *actual* orientation to a comparison of estimated monetary expenses with estimated monetary income, however primitive in form the comparison may be. Now in this sense we can see that, insofar as our documents on economies have reached into the distant past, "capitalism" and "capitalist" enterprises, at times with only a moderate degree of rationalization of capital accounting, have existed in all the world's civilizations, in other words, "capitalism" and "capitalist" enterprises have been found in China, India, Babylon, Egypt, the ancient Mediterranean, and medieval Europe, as well as in the modern West. Not only entirely isolated enterprises existed in these civilizations; rather, also businesses are found completely oriented to the continuous appearance of new companies and to a continuity of "operations." This remained the situation even though trade, over long periods, did not become perpetual, as it did in the West; instead, if assumed the character of a series of separate enterprises. A business context—the development of different "branches" for business—congealed only gradually and only slowly influenced the behavior of the *largescale* commercial traders. At any rate, the capitalist enterprise has been an enduring, highly universal, and ancient organization. Also capitalist businessmen, not only as occasional entrepreneurs but as persons oriented permanently to business, have been ancient, enduring, and highly universal figures.

The West, however, has given birth to types and forms of capitalism (as well as to directions for its unfolding) that have provided the foundation for the development of capitalism to an extent and significance unknown outside the West. Merchants have engaged in wholesale and retail trade, on a local as well as international scale, throughout the world. Businesses offering loans of every sort have existed widely, as have banks with the most diverse functions (although for the most part functions essentially similar to those of Western banks of the sixteenth century). Sea loans, *commenda*, and *kommandit* types of businesses and formal associations have been widespread. Wherever the financing of public institutions through *currency* has occurred, financiers have appeared—in Babylon, ancient Greece, India, China, and ancient Rome. They have financed above all wars, piracy, and all types of shipping and construction projects; as entrepreneurs in colonies they have served the international policy goals of nations. In addition, these *adventure* capitalists have acquired plantations and operated them using slaves or (directly or indirectly) forced labor; they have leased land and the rights to use honorific titles; they have financed both the leaders of political parties standing for re-election and mercenaries for civil wars; and, finally, as "speculators" they have been involved in all sorts of money-raising opportunities.

This type of entrepreneur—the adventure capitalist—has existed throughout the world. With the exception of trade, credit, and banking businesses, his money-making endeavors have been mainly either of a purely irrational and speculative nature or of a violent character, such as the capture of booty. This has taken place either through warfare or the continuous fiscal exploitation of subjugated populations.

Promoter, adventure, colonial, and, as it exists in the West, modern finance capitalism can be characterized often, even today, in terms of these features. This becomes especially apparent whenever capitalism is oriented to warfare, although it holds even in periods of peace. Single (and only single) components of large-scale international commerce today, as in the past, approximate adventure capitalism.

However, in the *modern* era the West came to know an entirely different type of capitalism. Absent from all other regions of the globe, or existing only in preliminary developmental stages, this capitalism appeared side-by-side with adventure capitalism and took as its foundation the rational-capitalist organization of (legally) *free labor*. With *coerced* labor, a certain degree of rational organization had been attained only on the plantations of antiquity and, to a very limited extent, on the ancient world's *ergasteria*. An even lesser degree of rationality was reached in agricultural forced-labor enterprises generally, the workshop-is of medieval manors, and in manor-based cottage industries utilizing the labor of serfs at the dawning of the modern era. Outside the West, free labor has been found only occasionally. Even the existence of actual "cottage industries" has been documented with certainty only rarely outside the West. And the use of day laborers, which naturally can be found everywhere, did not lead to manufacturing and not at all to a rational, apprenticeship-style organization of skilled labor of the type practiced in the West's Middle Ages. This must be said despite a very few, very unusual exceptions, and even these diverged significantly from the modern Western organization of industrial work in companies (especially from those companies that, through support from the state, held market monopolies).

However, the rational organization of industrial companies and their orientation to *market* opportunities, rather than to political violence or to irrational speculation, does not constitute the only distinguishing mark of Western capitalism. The modern, rational organization of the capitalist industrial firm would not have been possible without two prior important developments: (1) the *separation of the household from the industrial company*, which absolutely dominates economic life today, and, connected closely to this development, (2) the appearance of rational *accounting*.

The spatial separation of the place of labor or sales from the place of residence can be also found elsewhere (in the Oriental bazaar and in the *ergasteria* of other cultures). Capitalist associations with accounting procedures separate from personal accounts existed in East Asia as well as in the Middle East and the ancient world. Nonetheless, compared to the modern situation in which company operations are fully independent, these examples show only very limited beginnings. This remained the case above all because the *internal* preconditions for independent business operation—rational *accounting* methods and a *legal* separation of company wealth from personal wealth—were either entirely absent or developed only to preliminary stages. Instead, outside the West, industry-oriented endeavors tended to become simply one component of the feudal manor's *household* activities (the *oikos*). [Karl Johann] Rodbertus [1805–65] has already noted that all developments toward the *oikos* deviated distinctly from the route taken by capitalist activity in the West. Indeed, as he argues, and despite a number of apparent similarities, the *oikos* stood starkly in opposition to the Western pathway.

All these particular aspects of Western capitalism, however, in the end acquired their present-day significance as a result of their connection to the capitalist organization of *work*. Even what one is inclined to call "commercialization"—the development of stocks and bonds and the systematization, through stock markets, of speculation—must be seen as taking place in the context of a capitalist organization of labor. All this, even the development toward "commercialization," if it had been possible at all, would never have unfolded to anywhere near the same proportion and dimension if a capitalist-rational organization of work had been lacking. Hence, all of these new factors would never have significantly influenced the social structure and all those problems associated with it specific to the modern West. Exact calculation, the foundation for everything else, is possible only on the basis of *free* labor.

And as the world outside the modern West has not known the rational organization of work, it has also not known, and for this reason, rational *socialism*. Now, of course, just as history has experienced a full spectrum of types of economies, ranging from those, on the one hand, oriented to city development and city-organized food supply policies, mercantilism, the social welfare policies instituted by princes, the rationing of goods, a thorough regulation of the economy, and protectionism, and on the other hand to *laissez-faire* theories (also in China), the world has also known socialist and communist economies of the most diverse sorts. State socialist (in [ancient] Egypt) and cartel-monopolistic versions of socialism can be found, as can types of communism more rooted in (a) heterogeneous consumer organizations, (b) private sphere values of intimacy and the family, (c) religious values, and (d) military values. However (despite the existence everywhere at one time or another of guilds and brotherhood corporations, various legal distinctions between cities and provinces in the most diverse form, and cities that granted specific market advantages to particular groups), just as the concept of "citizen" is entirely missing except in the West and the concept of "bourgeoisie" is completely absent outside the modem West, so also the notion of a "proletariat" as a *class* is absent. Indeed, it could not appear outside the West precisely because a rational organization of *free labor* in *industrial enterprises* was lacking. "Class struggles" between strata of creditors and debtors, between those who owned land and those who did not (whether serfs or tenant sharecroppers), between persons with economic interests in commerce and consumers or owners of land—all these conflicts have existed for centuries in various constellations. Yet even the struggles typical in the West's medieval period between domestic industry entrepreneurs and their wage workers [the putting-out system] are found elsewhere only in a rudimentary form. The modern opposition between large-scale industrialists, as employers, and free workers paid a wage is completely lacking outside the West. And thus a situation of the type known to modern socialism also could not exist.

Hence, for us, as we investigate the universal history of civilizations, and even if we proceed by reference exclusively to issues directly related to the economy, the central problem in the end *cannot* be the unfolding of capitalist activity everywhere and the various forms it took. That is, our concern cannot be whether it appeared more as adventure capitalism, commercial capitalism, or a capitalism oriented to the opportunities for profit offered by war, politics, and state administration. Rather, the central problem must ultimately involve the origin of *middle class industrial* capitalism with its rational organization of *free labor*. Or, rendered in the terms of cultural history: The central problem must ultimately concern the origin of the Western middle class and its particular features. Of course, this theme is closely interwoven with the question of the origin of the capitalist organization of labor. Yet it is naturally not exactly the same—for the simple reason that a "middle class," in the sense of a stratum of people, existed before the development of this specifically Western capitalism anchored in the capitalist organization of labor. However, obviously this was the case *only* in the West.

Now evidently the capitalism specific to the modern West has been strongly influenced above all by advances in the realm of *technology*. The nature of the rationality of modern Western capitalism is today determined by the calculability of factors that are technically decisive. Indeed, these factors are the foundation for all more exact calculation. In turn this calculability is rooted fundamentally in the characteristic uniqueness of Western science, and especially in the natural sciences grounded in the exactness of mathematics and the controlled experiment.

The development of these sciences, and the technology that is based upon them, acquired—and continues to acquire—pivotal invigorating impulses from opportunities offered by capitalism. Market opportunities, that is, as rewards, are connected to the economic applications of these technologies. However, it must also be emphasized that the origin of Western science cannot be explained by the availability of such economic opportunities. Calculation, even with decimals, existed also in the algebra of India, where the decimal system was discovered. Yet in India it never led to modern calculation and accounting methods; this mode of calculation was first placed into *operation* only in the West's developing capitalism. Similarly, the origin of mathematics and physics was not determined by economic interests, yet the *technical* application of scientific knowledge was. Important for the quality of life of the broad population, this application was conditioned by economic rewards—and these crystallized precisely in the West. These rewards, however, flowed out of the particular character of the West's *social* order. It must then be asked: From *which* components of this unique social order did these rewards derive? Surely not all of its features have been of equal importance.

The rational structure of *law* and administration has undoubtedly been among the most central elements of this social order. This is the case for the simple reason that modern-rational industrial capitalism, just as it requires calculable technical means in order to organize work, also needs a calculable law and administration that function according to formal rules. Of course adventure capitalism and a trade-based capitalism oriented to speculation, as well as all types of capitalism determined by political considerations, can well exist without calculable law and administration. However, a rational industrial firm—with fixed capital and reliable *calculation*, and operating in a private economy—is not possible without this type of law and administration.

Yet this type of law and administration, in *this* degree of legal-technical and formal perfection, was placed at the disposal of the economy and its development *only* in the West. Hence, one must ask: What was the source of this type of law in the West? Undoubtedly, in addition to other circumstances, *also* economic interests paved the way for the rule of a stratum of jurists who were professionally trained in rational law and who, in a disciplined and regular manner, practiced and administered law. This is evident from every investigation. Yet these economic interests were not the exclusive, or even the primary, causal forces in the rise of this stratum to importance. Moreover, economic interests did not of themselves *create* this type of law. Rather, entirely different powers were active in respect to this development. And why then did capitalist interests not call forth this stratum of jurists and this type of law in China or India? How did it happen that scientific, artistic, and economic development, as well as state-building, were not directed in China and India into those tracks of *rationalization* specific to the West?

The issue in all of the cases mentioned above evidently involves a characteristic aspect of a specifically formed "rationalism" of Western civilization. Now this word can be understood as implying a vast spectrum of matters. There is, for example, "rationalization" of mystical contemplation, that is, of a type of behavior that is specifically "irrational" if viewed from the perspective of other realms of life. Similarly, there may be rationalization of the economy, technology, scientific work, education, warfare, administration, and the practice of law. One may further "rationalize" each one of these arenas from vantage points and goals of the most diverse sort and ultimate orientations. What may appear "rational" viewed from one angle may appear "irrational" when viewed from another.

Hence, we must note that rationalizations have occurred in the various arenas of life in highly varying ways and in all circles of cultural life. It is necessary, in order to identify the ways in which the multiple rationalization paths have characteristically varied according to cultural and historical factors, to assess *which* arenas have been rationalized and in what directions. Again, important here above all are the special *characteristic features* of Western rationalism and, within this particular type of rationalism, the characteristic features of modern Western rationalism. Our concern is to identify this uniqueness and to explain its origin.

Every such attempt at explanation, recognizing the fundamental significance of economic factors, must above all take account of these factors. However, the opposite line of causation should not be neglected if only because the origin of economic rationalism depends not only on an advanced development of technology and law but also on the capacity and disposition of persons to organize their lives in a practical-rational manner. Wherever magical and religious forces have inhibited the unfolding of this organized life, the development of an organized life oriented systematically toward *economic* activity has confronted broad-ranging internal resistance. Magical and religious powers, and the ethical notions of duty based on them, have been in the past among the most important formative influences upon the way life has been organized.

26

The Spirit of Capitalism*

Max Weber

Our focus at the beginning should be only to provide a provisional *illustration* of the activity implied here by the term *spirit of capitalism*. Indeed, such an illustration is indispensable in order to attain our aim now of simply understanding the object of our investigation. On behalf of this purpose we turn to a document that contains the spirit of concern to us in near classical purity, and simultaneously offers the advantage of being detached from *all* direct connection to religious belief—hence, for our theme, of being "free of presuppositions."

> Remember, that *time is money.* He that can earn ten shillings a day by his labour, and goes abroad, or sits idle one half of that day, though he spends but sixpence during his diversion or idleness, ought not to reckon that the only expense; he has really spent or rather thrown away five shillings besides.
>
> Remember, that *credit is money.* If a man lets his money lie in my hands after it is due, he gives me the interest, or so much as I can make of it during that time. This amounts to a considerable sum where a man has good and large credit, and makes good use of it.
>
> Remember, that money is of the *prolific, generating nature.* Money can beget money, and its offspring can beget more, and so on. Five shillings turned is six, turned again it is seven and threepence, and so on, till it becomes a hundred pounds. The more there is of it, the more it produces every turning, so that the profits rise quicker and quicker. He that kills a breeding-sow, destroys all her offspring to the thousandth generation. He that murders a crown, *destroys* all that it might have produced, even scores of pounds. . . .
>
> Remember this saying: The good *paymaster* is lord of another man's purse. He that is known to pay punctually and exactly to the time he promises, may at any time, and on any occasion, raise all the money his friends can spare.
>
> This is sometimes of great use. After industry and frugality, nothing contributes more to the *raising* of a young man in the world than punctuality and justice in all his dealings; therefore never keep borrowed money an hour beyond the time you promised, lest a disappointment shut up your friend's purse for ever.
>
> The most trifling actions that affect a man's *credit* are to be regarded. The sound of your hammer at five in the morning, or nine at night, heard by a creditor, makes him easy six months longer; but if he sees you at a billiard-table, or

*Excerpt from *The Protestant Ethic and the Spirit of Capitalism with Other Writings on the Rise of the West,* Fourth Edition, by Max Weber. Translated and Introduced by S. Kalberg.

> hears your voice at a tavern, when you should be at work, he sends for his money the next day;. . . [he] demands it before you are able to pay.
>
> It shows, besides, that you are mindful of what you owe; it makes you *appear* a careful as well as an *honest man,* and that still increases your credit.
>
> Beware of thinking that you own all that you possess, and of living accordingly. It is a mistake that many people who have credit fall into. To prevent this, keep an exact account both of your expenses and your income. If you make an effort to attend to particular expenses, it will have this good effect: you will discover how wonderfully small, trifling expenses mount up to large sums, and will discern what might have been, and may for the future be saved, without occasioning any great inconvenience.
>
> For six pounds a year you may have the use of one hundred pounds if you are a man of known prudence and honesty.
>
> He that spends a groat a day idly, spends idly above six pounds a year, which is the price of using one hundred pounds.
>
> He that wastes idly a groat's worth of his time per day, one day with another, wastes the privilege of using one hundred pounds each year.
>
> He that idly loses five shillings' worth of time, loses five shillings and might as prudently throw five shillings into the sea.
>
> He that loses five shillings not only loses that sum, but all the advantage that might be made by turning it in dealing, which by the time that a young man becomes old, amounts to a comfortable bag of money.

It is *Benjamin Franklin* [1706–90] who preaches to us in these sentences. As the supposed catechism of a Yankee, Ferdinand Kürnberger satirizes these axioms in his brilliantly clever and venomous *Picture of American Culture.* That the spirit of capitalism is here manifest in Franklin's words, even in a characteristic manner, no one will doubt. It will not be argued here, however, that *all aspects* of what can be understood by this spirit are contained in them.

Let us dwell a moment upon a passage, the worldly wisdom of which is summarized thusly by Kürnberger: "They make tallow for candles out of cattle and money out of men." Remarkably, the real peculiarity in the "philosophy of avarice" contained in this maxim is the ideal of the credit-worthy man of honor and, above all, the idea of the duty of the individual to increase his wealth, which is assumed to be a self-defined interest in itself. Indeed, rather than simply a common-sense approach to life, a peculiar "ethic" is preached here: its violation is treated not simply as foolishness but as a sort of forgetfulness *duty.* Above all, this distinction stands at the center of the matter. "Business savvy," which is found commonly enough, is here not *alone* taught; rather, an *ethos* is expressed in this maxim. Just this quality is of interest to us in this investigation.

A retired business partner of Jakob Fugger, [1459–1525, an extremely wealthy German financier, export merchant, and philanthropist], once sought to convince him to retire. Yet his colleague's argument—that he had accumulated enough wealth and should allow others their chance—was rebuked by Fugger as "contemptible timidity." He "viewed matters differently," Fugger answered, and "wanted simply to make money as long as he could."

Obviously, the spirit of this statement must be *distinguished* from Franklin's. Fugger's entrepreneurial daring and personal, morally indifferent proclivities now take on the character, in Franklin, of an *ethically*-oriented maxim for the **organization of life.** *The expression spirit of capitalism* will be used here in just this specific manner—naturally the spirit of **modern capitalism**. That is, in light of the formulation of our theme, it must be evident that the Western European and American capitalism of the last few centuries constitutes our concern rather than the "capitalism" that has appeared in China, India, Babylon, the ancient world, and the Middle Ages. As we will see, *just that peculiar ethic was missing in all these cases.*

Nevertheless, all of Franklin's moral admonishments are applied in a utilitarian fashion: Honesty is *useful* because it leads to the availability of credit. Punctuality, industry, and frugality are also useful, and are *therefore* virtues.

In truth, however, matters are not so simple. Benjamin Franklin's own character demonstrates that the issue is more complex: his character appears clearly, however seldom, in his autobiography as one of candor and truthfulness. It is also evident in Franklin's tracing of his realization—virtues can be "useful"—back to a revelation from God that was designed, he believed, to guide him onto the path of righteousness.

Something more is involved here than simply an embellishing of purely self-interested, egocentric maxims.

The complexity of this issue is above all apparent in the *summum bonum* ["supreme good"] of this "ethic": namely, the acquisition of money, and more and more money, takes place here simultaneously with the strictest avoidance of all spontaneous enjoyment of it. The pursuit of riches is fully stripped of all pleasurable (*eudämonistischen*), and surely all hedonistic, aspects. Accordingly, this striving becomes understood completely as an end in itself—to such an extent that it appears as fully outside the normal course of affairs and simply irrational, at least when viewed from the perspective of the "happiness" or "utility" of the single individual. Here, people are oriented to acquisition as the purpose of life; acquisition is no longer viewed as a means to the end of satisfying the substantive needs of life. Those people in possession of spontaneous, fun-loving dispositions experience this situation as an absolutely meaningless reversal of a "natural" condition (as we would say today). Yet this reversal constitutes just as surely a guiding principle of [modern] capitalism as incomprehension of this new situation characterizes all who remain untouched by [modern] capitalism's tentacles.

This reversal implies an internal line of development that comes into close contact with certain religious ideas. One can ask why then "money ought to be made out of persons." In his autobiography, and although he is himself a bland Deist, Franklin answers with a maxim from the Bible that, as he says, his strict Calvinist father again and again drilled into him in his youth: "Seest thou a man vigorous in his **vocational calling** (*Beruf*)? He shall stand before kings" (Prov. 22:29). As long as it is carried out in a legal manner, the acquisition of money in the modern economic order is the result and manifestation of competence and proficiency in a *vocational calling. This competence and proficiency* is the actual alpha and omega of Franklin's morality, as now can be easily recognized. It presents itself to us both in the passages cited above and, without exception, in all his writings.

In fact, this peculiar idea of a *duty to have a vocational calling*, so familiar to us today but actually not at all self-evident, is the idea that is characteristic of the "social ethic" of modern capitalist culture. In a certain sense, it is even of constitutive significance for it. It implies a notion of duty that individuals ought to experience, and do, vis-à-vis the content of their "vocational" activity. This notion appears regardless of the particular nature of the activity and regardless, especially, of whether this activity seems to involve (as it does for people with a spontaneous, fun-loving disposition) nothing more than a simple utilization of their capacity for labor or their treatment of it as only a material possession (as "capital").

Nevertheless, it is surely not the case that the idea of a duty in one's vocational calling could grow *only* on the soil of [modern] capitalism. Rather, our attempt later to trace its roots will take us to a period prior to [modern] capitalism. Naturally it will be argued here even less that, under *today's* capitalism, the subjective acquisition of these ethical maxims by capitalism's particular social carriers (such as businesspersons or workers in modern capitalist companies) constitutes a condition for capitalism's further existence. Rather, the capitalist economic order of today is a vast cosmos into which a person is born. It simply exists, to each person, as a factually unalterable casing (*unabänderliches Gehäuse*) in which he or she must live. To the extent that people are interwoven into the context of capitalism's market forces, the norms of its economic action are forced onto them. Every factory owner who operates in the long term against these norms will inevitably be eliminated from the economy. With the same degree of inevitability, every worker who cannot or will not adapt to the norms of the marketplace will become unemployed.

As a rule, the bold and unscrupulous speculators or the adventurous persons in pursuit of riches, such as are encountered in all epochs of economic development, have not created this transformation. It has been scarcely visible to all who investigate external changes only (such as a massive influx of new money), alterations in the forms of organizations, or changes in the organization of the economy. Nevertheless, these ethical qualities have been decisive for the infusion of economic life with this new spirit of capitalism. Nor were the "great financiers" pivotal. Rather, a different group proved central: men raised in the school of hard knocks, simultaneously calculating and daring but above all *dispassionate, steady,* shrewd, devoted fully to their cause, and in possession of strict, middle-class views and "principles."

One might be inclined to believe that not the slightest connection exists between these *personal* moral qualities and any ethical maxims, let alone any religious ideas as such. One might be further inclined to see here an essentially negative relationship: one could contend that leading an organized life oriented to business assumes a capacity to *withdraw* oneself from long-standing religious tradition. Hence, according to this line of reasoning, liberal "Enlightenment" views would constitute the adequate foundation for the life organized on behalf of business activity. In fact this argument is in general correct *today.* As a rule, a religious undergirding of the life oriented to business is absent.

Furthermore, wherever a relationship between business activity and religious belief exists, it turns out to be a negative one, at least in Germany. People who are saturated by the capitalist spirit *today* tend to be indifferent, if not openly hostile, to religion. The thought of pious boredom in paradise has little appeal for their activity-oriented natures, and religion appears to this group as a mechanism that pulls people away from the very foundation of existence—their work. If one were to question these people regarding the "meaning" of their restless hunt, which is never happy with possessions already owned—and for this reason alone must appear meaningless from the point of view of a completely this-worldly orientation of life—they would at times answer (if able to answer at all): "to care for the children and grandchildren." Nevertheless, because this motivation is apparently far from unique to them, and influences in the same manner all those with the approach to business of "economic traditionalism," they would more frequently offer the simple and more correct answer: With its stable work, the business is "indispensable to life." This answer is indeed the single actual motivation, and it immediately renders obvious the *irrationality,* from the point of view of one's personal happiness, of this organization of life: people live for their business rather than the reverse.

How then does it come about that activity which, in the most favorable case, is barely morally tolerable becomes a "calling" in the manner practiced by Benjamin Franklin? How is it to be explained historically that in Florence, the center of capitalist development in the fourteenth and fifteenth centuries and the marketplace for money and capital for all of the great political powers, striving for profit was viewed as either morally questionable or at best tolerated? Yet in the business relationships found in small companies in rural Pennsylvania, where scarcely a trace of large-scale commerce could be found, where only the beginning stages of a banking system were evident, and where the economy was continuously threatened with collapse into sheer barter (as a result of a simple lack of money), the same striving for profit became viewed as legitimate. Indeed, it became understood as the essence of a morally acceptable, even praiseworthy, way of organizing and directing life.

To speak *here* of a "reflection" of "material" conditions in the "ideal superstructure" would be complete nonsense. Hence, our question: What set of ideas gave birth to the ordering of activity oriented purely to profit under the category of a "calling," to which the person felt an *obligation*? Just this set of ideas provided the ethical substructure and backbone for the "new style" employer's organized life.

Some have depicted **economic rationalism** as the basic characteristic of the modern economy in general. Sombart in particular, often in successful and effective discussions, has done so. Surely he has done so correctly if "economic rationalism" refers to the increase in productivity that results from the organization of the production process according to *scientific* vantage points—hence the banishing of the situation in which gains were restricted owing to the naturally given "organic" limitations of people. This rationalization process in the arenas of technology and the economy undoubtedly also conditions an important part of the "ideals of life" in the modern, middle-class society in general

Work in the service of a rational production of material goods for the provision of humanity has without question always been hovering over the representatives of the capitalist spirit as a directing purpose of their life's labors. For example, one needs only to read about Franklin's efforts in Philadelphia in the service of community improvement to understand immediately this completely self-evident truth. Moreover, the joy and pride one feels in giving "work" to numerous people and in assisting the economic "flowering" (in the manner in which this term is associated, under capitalism, with population and trade figures) of one's hometown belongs obviously to the unique, and undoubtedly "idealistically" driven, satisfactions of the modern business establishment. And, likewise, the capitalist economy rationalizes on the basis of strictly *quantitative* calculations and is oriented to the sought-after economic success in a systematic and dispassionate manner.

These operating principles are inherent in and fundamental to capitalism. They contrast directly with the situation of the peasant who lives from hand to mouth, to the guild craftsmen in the medieval epoch who maintained market advantages rooted in old customs, and to the "adventure capitalist" who was oriented to political opportunities and irrational speculation. Thus it appears that the development of the "capitalist spirit" can be most easily understood as one component part in a larger and overarching development of rationalism as a whole. It appears further that this spirit should best be comprehended as derived from rationalism's basic position in respect to the ultimate problems of life. Hence, according to this interpretation, Protestantism would come into consideration historically only to the extent that it played a role as a "harbinger" of purely rationalistic views of life.

However, as soon as one seriously attempts to formulate the problem of the development of the spirit of capitalism in this way, it becomes clear that such a simple approach to this theme is inadequate. The reason is that the history of rationalism *by no means* charts out a progressive unfolding, according to which all the separate realms of life follow a *parallel* developmental line. The rationalization of private law, for example, if understood as the conceptual simplification and organization of the subject matter of the law, attained its heretofore highest form in the Roman law of later antiquity. It remained least rationalized, however, in some nations with the most highly rationalized economies. England offers an example. During the period of the development of [modern] capitalism in this nation, the power of large guilds of lawyers prevented the rebirth of Roman law. In contrast, rationalized Roman law has consistently remained dominant in the Catholic areas of southern Europe [where modern capitalism, compared to England, remained underdeveloped].

[Two more examples for the nonparallel development of the separate realms of life must suffice.] First, the purely secularized philosophy of the eighteenth century [the Enlightenment] surely was not based alone, or even primarily, in the highly developed capitalist nations. This philosophy of Voltaire [1694–1778] is even today the broad common inheritance of the upper and (what is more important practically) middle strata, especially in the Roman Catholic nations. Second, if one understands by the phrase *practical rationalism* that way of organizing life according to which the world's activities are consciously referred back to the practical interests of the particular person, and are judged from his or her specific vantage point, then this style of life was typically unique primarily to *liberum arbitrium* [easygoing] peoples. Even today practical rationalism permeates the flesh and blood of the Italians and the French. And we have already convinced ourselves this is not the soil that primarily nourishes persons who relate to their "calling" as a task, as [modern] capitalism needs.

A simple sentence should stand at the center of every study that delves into "rationalism." It must not be forgotten that one can in fact "rationalize" life from a vast variety of ultimate vantage points. Moreover, one can do so in very different directions. "Rationalism" is a historical concept that contains within itself a world of contradictions.

Our task now is to investigate from whose spiritual child this matter-of-fact form of "rational" thinking and living grew. The idea of a "calling," and of the giving over of one's self to work in a calling, originated here. As noted, the entire notion of a "calling" must appear fully irrational from the vantage point of the person's pure self-interest in happiness. Yet the dedication to work in the manner of a "calling" has in the past constituted one of the characteristic components of our capitalist economic culture. It remains so even today. What interests us here is precisely the ancestral lineage of that irrational element which lies in this, as in every, conception of a "calling."

27

Types of Authority*

Max Weber

Domination was defined above as the probability that certain specific commands (or all commands) will be obeyed by a given group of persons. It thus does not include every mode of exercising "power" or "influence" over other persons. Domination ("authority") in this sense may be based on the most diverse motives of compliance: all the way from simple habituation to the most purely rational calculation of advantage. Hence every genuine form of domination implies a minimum of voluntary compliance, that is, an *interest* (based on ulterior motives or genuine acceptance) in obedience.

Not every case of domination makes use of economic means; still less does it always have economic objectives. However, normally the rule over a considerable number of persons requires a staff, that is, a *special* group which can normally be trusted to execute the general policy as well as the specific commands. The members of the administrative staff may be bound to obedience to their superior (or superiors) by custom, by affectual ties, by a purely material complex of interests, or by ideal (*wertrationale*) motives. The quality of these motives largely determines the type of domination. *Purely* material interests and calculations of advantages as the basis of solidarity between the chief and his administrative staff result, in this as in other connexions, in a relatively unstable situation. Normally other elements, affectual and ideal, supplement such interests. In certain exceptional cases the former alone may be decisive. In everyday life these relationships, like others, are governed by custom and material calculation of advantage. But custom, personal advantage, purely affectual or ideal motives of solidarity, do not form a sufficiently reliable basis for a given domination. In addition there is normally a further element, the belief in *legitimacy.*

Experience shows that in no instance does domination voluntarily limit itself to the appeal to material or affectual or ideal motives as a basis for its continuance. In addition every such system attempts to establish and to cultivate the belief in its legitimacy. But according to the kind of legitimacy which is claimed, the type of obedience, the kind of administrative staff developed to guarantee it, and the mode of exercising authority, will all differ fundamentally. Equally fundamental is the variation in effect. Hence, it is useful to classify the types of domination according to the kind of claim to legitimacy typically made by each. In doing this, it is best to start from modem and therefore more familiar examples.

The Three Pure Types of Authority

There are three pure types of legitimate domination. The validity of the claims to legitimacy may be based on:

1. Rational grounds—resting on a belief in the legality of enacted rules and the right of those elevated to authority under such rules to issue commands (legal authority).

2. Traditional grounds—resting on an established belief in the sanctity of immemorial traditions and the legitimacy of those exercising authority under them (traditional authority); or finally,

3. Charismatic grounds—resting on devotion to the exceptional sanctity, heroism or exemplary character of an individual person, and of the normative patterns or order revealed or ordained by him (charismatic authority).

In the case of legal authority, obedience is owed to the legally established impersonal order. It extends to the persons exercising the authority of office under it by virtue of the formal legality of their commands and only within the scope of authority of the office. In the case of traditional authority, obedience is owed to the *person* of the chief who occupies the traditionally sanctioned position of authority and who is (within its sphere) hound by tradition. But here the obligation of obedience is a matter of personal loyalty within the area of accustomed obligations. In the case of charismatic authority, it is the charismatically qualified leader as such who is obeyed by virtue of personal trust in his revelation, his heroism or his exemplary qualities so far as they fall within the scope of the individual's belief in his charisma.

Legal Authority

Legal authority rests on the acceptance of the validity of the following mutually inter-dependent ideas.

1. That any given legal norm may be established by agreement or by imposition, on grounds of expediency or value-rationality or both, with a claim to obedience at least on the part of the members of the organization. This is, however, usually extended to include all persons within the sphere of power in question—which in the case of territorial bodies is the territorial area—who stand in certain social relationships or carry out forms of social action which in the order governing the organization have been declared to be relevant.

2. That every body of law consists essentially in a consistent system of abstract rules which have normally been intentionally established. Furthermore, administration of law is held to consist in the application of these rules to particular cases; the administrative process in the rational pursuit of the interests which are specified in the order governing the organization within the limits laid down by legal precepts and following principles which are capable of generalized formulation and are approved in the order governing the group, or at least not disapproved in it.

3. That thus the typical person in authority, the "superior," is himself subject to an impersonal order by orienting his actions to it in his own dispositions and commands. (This is true not only for persons exercising legal authority who are in the usual sense "officials," but, for instance, for the elected president of a state.)

4. That the person who obeys authority does so, as it is usually stated, only in his capacity as a "member" of the organization and what he obeys is only "the law." (He may in this connection be the member of an association, of a community, of a church, or a citizen of a state.)

5. In conformity with point 3, it is held that the members of the organization, insofar as they obey a person in authority, do not owe this obedience to him as an individual, but to the impersonal order. Hence, it follows that there is an obligation to obedience only within the sphere of the rationally delimited jurisdiction which, in terms of the order, has been given to him.

The following may thus be said to be the fundamental categories of rational legal authority:

1. A continuous rule-bound conduct of official business.

2. A specified sphere of competence (jurisdiction). This involves: (a) A sphere of obligations to perform functions which has been marked off as part of a systematic division of labor. (b) The provision of the incumbent with the necessary powers. (c) That the necessary means of compulsion are clearly defined and their use is subject to definite conditions. A unit exercising authority which is organized in this way will be called an "administrative organ" or "agency" (*Behörde*).

3. The organization of offices follows the principle of hierarchy; that is, each lower office is under the control and supervision of a higher one. There is a right of appeal and of statement of grievances from the lower to the higher. Hierarchies differ in respect to whether and in what cases complaints can lead to a "correct" ruling from a higher authority itself, or whether the responsibility for such changes is left to the lower office, the conduct of which was the subject of the complaint.

4. The rules which regulate the conduct of an office may be technical rules or norms. In both cases, if their application is to be fully rational, specialized training is necessary. It is thus normally true that only a person who has demonstrated an adequate technical training is qualified to be a member of the administrative staff of such an organized group, and hence only such persons are eligible for appointment to official positions. The administrative staff of a rational organization thus typically consists of "officials," whether the organization be devoted to political, hierocratic, economic—in particular, capitalistic—or other ends.

5. In the rational type it is a matter of principle that the members of the administrative staff should be completely separated from ownership of the means of production or administration. Officials, employees, and workers attached to the administrative staff do not themselves own the non-human means of production and administration. These are rather provided for their use, in kind or in money, and the official is obligated to render an accounting of their use. There exists, furthermore, in principle complete separation of the organization's property (respectively, capital), and the personal property (household) of the official. There is a corresponding separation of the place in which official functions are carried out—the "office" in the sense of premises—from the living quarters.

6. In the rational type case, there is also a complete absence of appropriation of his official position by the incumbent. Where "rights" to an office exist, as in the case of judges, and recently of an increasing proportion of officials and even of workers, they do not normally serve the purpose of appropriation by the official, but of securing the purely objective and independent character of the conduct of the office so that it is oriented only to the relevant norms.

7. Administrative acts, decisions, and rules are formulated and recorded in writing, even in cases where oral discussion is the rule or is even mandatory. This applies at least to preliminary discussions and proposals, to final decisions, and to all sorts of orders and rules. The combination of written documents and a continuous operation by officials constitutes the "office" (*Bureau*) which is the central focus of all types of modern organized action.

8. Legal authority can be exercised in a wide variety of different forms which will be distinguished and discussed later. The following ideal-typical analysis will be deliberately confined for the time being to the administrative staff that is most unambiguously a structure of domination: "officialdom" or "bureaucracy."

The purest type of exercise of legal authority is that which employs a bureaucratic administrative staff. Only the supreme chief of the organization occupies his position of dominance (*Herrenstellung*) by virtue of appropriation, of election, or of having been designated for the succession. But even *his* authority consists in a sphere of legal "competence." The whole administrative staff under the supreme authority then consists, in the purest type, of individual officials (constituting a "monocracy" as opposed to the "collegial" type, which will be discussed below) who are appointed and function according to the following criteria:

1. They are personally free and subject to authority only with respect to their impersonal official obligations.

2. They are organized in a clearly defined hierarchy of offices.

3. Each office has a clearly defined sphere of competence in the legal sense.

4. The office is filled by a free contractual relationship. Thus, in principle, there is free selection.

5. Candidates are selected on the basis of technical qualifications. In the most rational case, this is tested by examination or guaranteed by diplomas certifying technical training, or both. They are *appointed,* not elected.

6. They are remunerated by fixed salaries in money, for the most part with a right to pensions. Only under certain circumstances does the employing authority, especially in private organizations, have a right to terminate the appointment, but the official is always free to resign. The salary scale is graded according to rank in the hierarchy; but in addition to this criterion, the responsibility of the position and the requirements of the incumbent's social status may be taken into account.

7. The office is treated as the sole, or at least the primary, occupation of the incumbent.

8. It constitutes a career. There is a system of "promotion" according to seniority or to achievement, or both. Promotion is dependent on the judgment of superiors.

9. The official works entirely separated from ownership of the means of administration and without appropriation of his position.

10. He is subject to strict and systematic discipline and control in the conduct of the office.

This type of organization is in principle applicable with equal facility to a wide variety of different fields. It may be applied in profit-making business or in charitable organizations, or in any number of other types of private enterprises serving ideal or material ends. It is equally applicable to political and to hierocratic organizations. With the varying degrees of approximation to a pure type, its historical existence can be demonstrated in all these fields.

Traditional Authority

Authority will be called traditional if legitimacy is claimed for it and believed in by virtue of the sanctity of age-old rules and powers. The masters are designated according to traditional rules and are obeyed because of their traditional status (*Eigenwürde*). This type of organized rule is, in the simplest case, primarily based on personal loyalty which results from common upbringing. The person exercising authority is not a "superior," but a personal master, his administrative staff does not consist mainly of officials but of personal retainers, and the ruled are not "members" of an association but are either his traditional "comrades" or his "subjects." Personal loyalty, not the official's impersonal duty, determines the relations of the administrative staff to the master.

Obedience is owed not to enacted rules but to the person who occupies a position of authority by tradition or who has been chosen for it by the traditional master. The commands of such a person are legitimized in one of two ways:

(a) partly in terms of traditions which themselves directly determine the content of the command and are believed to be valid within certain limits that cannot be overstepped without endangering the master's traditional status;

(b) partly in terms of the master's discretion in that sphere which tradition leaves open to him; this traditional prerogative rests primarily on the fact that the obligations of personal obedience tend to be essentially unlimited.

Thus there is a double sphere:

(a) that of action which is bound to specific traditions;

(b) that of action which is free of specific rules.

In the latter sphere, the master is free to do good turns on the basis of his personal pleasure and likes, particularly in return for gifts—the historical sources of dues (*Gebühren*). So far as his action follows principles at all, these are governed by considerations of ethical common sense, of equity or of utilitarian expediency. They are not formal principles, as in the case of legal authority. The exercise of power is oriented toward the consideration of how far master and staff can go in view of the subjects' traditional compliance without arousing their resistance. When resistance occurs, it is directed against the master or his servant personally, the accusation being that he failed to observe the traditional limits of his power. Opposition is not directed against the system as such—it is a case of "traditionalist revolution."

In the pure type of traditional authority it is impossible for law or administrative rule to be deliberately created by legislation. Rules which in fact are innovations can be legitimized only by the claim that they have been "valid of yore," but have only now been recognized by means of "Wisdom" [the *Weistum* of ancient Germanic law]. Legal decisions as "finding of the law" (*Rechtsfindung*) can refer only to documents of tradition, namely to precedents and earlier decisions.

Charismatic Authority

The term "charisma" will be applied to a certain quality of an individual personality by virtue of which he is considered extraordinary and treated as endowed with supernatural, superhuman, or at least specifically exceptional powers or qualities. These are such as are not accessible to the ordinary person, but are regarded as of divine origin or as exemplary, and on the basis of them the individual concerned is treated as a "leader." In primitive circumstances this peculiar kind of quality is thought of as resting on magical powers, whether of prophets, persons with a reputation for therapeutic or legal wisdom, leaders in the hunt, or heroes in war. How the quality in question would be ultimately judged from any ethical, aesthetic, or other such point of view is naturally entirely indifferent for purposes of definition. What is alone important is how the individual is actually regarded by those subject to charismatic authority, by his "followers" or "disciples."

I. It is recognition on the part of those subject to authority which is decisive for the validity of charisma. This recognition is freely given and guaranteed by what is held to be a proof, originally always a miracle, and consists in devotion to the corresponding revelation, hero worship, or absolute trust in the leader. But where charisma is genuine, it is not this which is the basis of the claim to legitimacy. This basis lies rather in the conception that it is the duty of those subject to charismatic authority to recognize its genuineness and to act accordingly. Psychologically this recognition is a matter of complete personal devotion to the possessor of the quality, arising out of enthusiasm, or of despair and hope.

II. If proof and success elude the leader for long, if he appears deserted by his god or his magical or heroic powers, above all, if his leadership fails to benefit his followers, it is likely that his charismatic authority will disappear. This is the genuine meaning of the divine right of kings (*Gottesgnadentum*).

III. An organized group subject to charismatic authority will be called a charismatic community (*Gemeinde*). It is based on an emotional form of communal relationship (*Vergemeinschaftung*). The administrative staff of a charismatic leader does not consist of "officials"; least of all are its members technically trained. It is not chosen on the basis of social privilege nor from the point of view of domestic or personal dependency. It is rather chosen in terms of the charismatic qualities of its members. The prophet has his disciples; the warlord his bodyguard; the leader, generally, his agents (*Vertrauensmänner*). There is no such thing as appointment or dismissal, no career, no promotion. There is only a call at the instance of the leader on the basis of the charismatic qualification of those he summons. There is no hierarchy; the leader merely intervenes in general or in individual cases when he considers the members of his staff lacking in charismatic qualification for a given task. There is no such thing as a bailiwick or definite sphere of competence, and no appropriation of official powers on the basis of social privileges. There may, however, be territorial or functional limits to charismatic powers and to the individual's mission. There is no such thing as a salary or a benefice.

Disciples or followers tend to live primarily in a communistic relationship with their leader on means which have been provided by voluntary gift. There are no established administrative organs. In their place are agents who have been provided with charismatic authority by their chief or who possess charisma of their own. There is no system of formal rules, of abstract legal principles, and hence no process of rational judicial decision oriented to them. But equally there is no legal wisdom oriented to judicial precedent. Formally concrete judgments are newly created from case to case and are originally regarded as divine judgments and revelations. From a substantive point of view, every charismatic authority would have to subscribe to the proposition, "It is written . . . but I say unto you . . ." The genuine prophet, like the genuine military leader and every true leader in this sense, preaches, creates, or demands new obligations—most typically, by virtue of revelation, oracle, inspiration, or of his own will, which are recognized by the members of the religious, military, or party group because they come from such a source. Recognition is a duty. When such an authority comes into conflict with the competing authority of another who also claims charismatic sanction, the only recourse is to some kind of a contest, by magical means or an actual physical battle of the leaders. In principle, only one side can be right in such a conflict; the other must be guilty of a wrong which has to be expiated.

Since it is "extra-ordinary," charismatic authority is sharply opposed to rational, and particularly bureaucratic, authority, and to traditional authority, whether in its patriarchal, patrimonial, or estate variants, all of which are everyday forms of domination; while the charismatic type is the direct antithesis of this. Bureaucratic authority is specifically rational in the sense of being bound to intellectually analysable rules; while charismatic authority is specifically irrational in the sense of being foreign to all rules. Traditional authority is bound to the precedents handed down from the past and to this extent is also oriented to rules. Within the sphere of its claims, charismatic authority repudiates the past, and is in this sense a specifically revolutionary force. It recognizes no appropriation of positions of power by virtue of the possession of property, either on the part of a chief or of socially privileged groups. The only basis of legitimacy for it is personal charisma so long as it is proved; that is, as long as it receives recognition and as long as the followers and disciples prove their usefulness charismatically.

IV. Pure charisma is specifically foreign to economic considerations. Wherever it appears, it constitutes a "call" in the most emphatic sense of the word, a "mission" or a "spiritual duty." In the pure type, it disdains and repudiates economic exploitation of the gifts of grace as a source of income, though, to be sure, this often remains more an ideal than a fact. It is not that charisma always demands a renunciation of property or even of acquisition, as under certain circumstances prophets and their disciples do. The heroic warrior and his followers actively seek booty; the elective ruler or the charismatic party leader requires the material means of power. The former in addition requires a brilliant display of his authority to bolster his prestige. What is despised, so long as the genuinely charismatic type is adhered to, is traditional or rational everyday economizing, the attainment of a regular income by continuous economic activity devoted to this end. Support by gifts, either on a grand scale involving donation, endowment, bribery and honoraria, or by begging, constitute the voluntary type of support. On the other hand, "booty" and extortion, whether by force or by other means, is the typical form of charismatic provision for needs. From the point of view of rational economic activity, charismatic want satisfaction is a typical anti-economic force. It repudiates any sort of involvement in the everyday routine world. It can only tolerate, with an attitude of complete emotional indifference, irregular, unsystematic acquisitive acts. In that it relieves the recipient of economic concerns, dependence on property income can be the economic basis of a charismatic mode of life for some groups; but that is unusual for the normal charismatic "revolutionary."

V. In traditionalist periods, charisma is the great revolutionary force. The likewise revolutionary force of "reason" works from without: by altering the situations of life and hence its problems, finally in this way changing men's attitudes toward them; or it intellectualizes the individual. Charisma, on the other hand, may effect a subjective or internal reorientation born out of suffering, conflicts, or enthusiasm. It may then result in a radical alteration of the central attitudes and directions of action with a completely new orientation of all attitudes toward the different problems of the "world." In prerationalistic periods, tradition and charisma between them have almost exhausted the whole of the orientation of action.

28

The Stranger*

Georg Simmel

If wandering is the libration from every given point in space, and thus the conceptional opposite to fixation at such a point, the sociological form of the "stranger" presents the unity, as it were, of these two characteristics. This phenomenon too, however, reveals that spatial relations are only the condition, on the one hand, and the symbol, on the other, of human relations. The stranger is thus being discussed here, not in the sense often touched upon in the past, as the wanderer who comes today and goes tomorrow, but rather as the person who comes today and stays tomorrow. He is, so to speak, the *potential* wanderer: although he has not moved on, he has not quite overcome the freedom of coming and going. He is fixed within a particular spatial group, or within a group whose boundaries are similar to spatial boundaries. But his position in this group is determined, essentially, by the fact that he has not belonged to it from the beginning, that he imports qualities into it, which do not and cannot stem from the group itself.

The unity of nearness and remoteness involved in every human relation is organized, in the phenomenon of the stranger, in a way which may be most briefly formulated by saying that in the relationship to him, distance means that he, who is close by, is far, and strangeness means that he, who also is far, is actually near. For, to be a stranger is naturally a very positive relation; it is a specific form of interaction. The inhabitants of Sirius are not really strangers to us, at least not in any sociologically relevant sense: they do not exist for us at all; they are beyond far and near. The stranger, like the poor and like sundry "inner enemies," is an element of the group itself. His position as a full-fledged member involves both being outside it and confronting it. The following statements, which are by no means intended as exhaustive, indicate how elements which increase distance and repel, in the relations of and with the stranger produce a pattern of coordination and consistent interaction.

Throughout the history of economics the stranger everywhere appears as the trader, or the trader as stranger. As long as economy is essentially self-sufficient, or products are exchanged within a spatially narrow group, it needs no middleman: a trader is only required for products that originate outside the group. Insofar as members do not leave the circle in order to buy these necessities—in which case *they* are the "strange" merchants in that outside territory—the trader *must* be a stranger, since nobody else has a chance to make a living.

This position of the stranger stands out more sharply if he settles down in the place of his activity, instead of leaving it again: in innumerable cases even this is possible only if he can live by intermediate trade. Once an economy is somehow closed, the land is divided up, and handicrafts are established that satisfy the demand for them, the trader, too, can find his existence. For in trade, which alone makes possible unlimited combinations, intelligence always finds expansions and new territories, an achievement which is very difficult to attain for the original producer with his lesser mobility and his dependence upon a circle of customers that can be increased only slowly. Trade can always absorb more people than primary production; it is, therefore, the sphere indicated for the stranger, who intrudes as a supernumerary, so to speak, into a group in which the economic positions are actually occupied—the classical example is the history of European Jews. The stranger is by nature no "owner of soil"—soil not only in the physical, but also in the figurative sense of a life-substance which is fixed, if not in a point in space, at least in an ideal point of the social environment. Although in more intimate relations, he may develop all kinds of charm and significance, as long as he is considered a stranger in the eyes of the other, he is not an "owner of soil." Restriction to intermediary trade, and often (as though sublimated from it) to pure finance, gives him the specific character of *mobility*. If mobility takes place within a closed group, it embodies that synthesis of nearness and distance which constitutes the formal position of the stranger. For, the fundamentally mobile person comes in contact, at one time or another, with every individual, but is not organically connected, through established ties of kinship, locality, and occupation, with any single one.

Another expression of this constellation lies in the objectivity of the stranger. He is not radically committed to the unique ingredients and peculiar tendencies of the group, and therefore approaches them with the specific attitude of "objectivity." But objectivity does not simply involve passivity and detachment; it is a particular structure composed of distance and nearness, indifference and involvement. I refer to the discussion of the dominating positions of the person who is a stranger in the group; its most typical instance was the practice of those Italian cities to call their judges from the outside, because no native was free from entanglement in family and party interests.

With the objectivity of the stranger is connected the fact that he often receives the most surprising openness—confidences which sometimes have the character of a confessional and which would be carefully withheld from a more closely related person. Objectivity is by no means non-participation (which is altogether outside both subjective and objective interaction), but a positive and specific kind of participation—just as the objectivity of a theoretical observation does not refer to the mind as a passive *tabula rasa* on which things inscribe their qualities, but on the contrary, to its full activity that operates according to its own laws, and to the elimination, thereby, of accidental dislocations and emphases, whose individual and subjective differences would produce different pictures of the same object.

Objectivity may also be defined as freedom: the objective individual is bound by no commitments which could prejudice his perception, understanding, and evaluation of the given. The freedom, however, which allows the stranger to experience and treat even his close relationships as though from a bird's-eye view, contains many dangerous possibilities. In uprisings o£ all sorts, the party attacked has claimed, from the beginning of things, that provocation has come from the outside, through emissaries and instigators. Insofar as this is true, it is an exaggeration of the specific role of the stranger: he is freer, practically and theoretically; he surveys conditions with less prejudice; his criteria for them are more general and more objective ideals; he is not tied down in his action by habit, piety, and precedent.

Finally, the proportion of nearness and remoteness which gives the stranger the character of objectivity, also finds practical expression in the more *abstract nature* of the relation to him. That is, with the stranger one has only certain *more general* qualities in common, whereas the relation to more organically connected persons is based on the commonness of specific differences from merely general features. In fact, all somehow personal relations follow this scheme in various patterns. They are determined not only by the circumstance that certain common features exist among the individuals, along with individual differences, which either influence the relationship or remain outside of it. For, the common features themselves are basically determined in their effect upon the relation by the question whether they exist only between the participants in this particular relationship, and thus are quite general in regard to this relation, but are specific and incomparable in regard to everything outside of it—or whether the participants feel that these features are common to them because they are common to a group, a type, or mankind in general. In the case of the second alternative, the effectiveness of the common features becomes diluted in proportion to the size of the group composed of members who are similar in this sense. Although the commonness functions as their unifying basis, it does not make *these* particular persons interdependent on one another, because it could as easily connect everyone of them with all kinds of individuals other than the members of his group. This too, evidently, is a way in which a relationship includes both nearness and distance at the same time: to the extent to which the common features are general, they add, to the warmth of the relation founded on them, an element of coolness, a feeling of the contingency of precisely *this* relation—the connecting forces have lost their specific and centripetal character.

In the relation to the stranger, it seems to me, this constellation has an extraordinary and basic preponderance over the individual elements that are exclusive with the particular relationship. The stranger is close to us, insofar as we feel between him and ourselves common features of a national, social, occupational, or generally human, nature. He is far from us, insofar as these common features extend beyond him or us, and connect us only because they connect a great many people.

A trace of strangeness in this sense easily enters even the most intimate relationships. In the stage of first passion, erotic relations strongly reject any thought of generalization: the lovers think that there has never been a love like theirs; that nothing can be compared either to the person loved or to the feelings for that person. An estrangement—whether as cause or as consequence it is difficult to decide—usually comes at the moment when this feeling of uniqueness vanishes from the relationship. A certain skepticism in regard to its value, in itself and for them, attaches to the very thought that in their relation, after all, they carry out only a generally human destiny; that they experience an experience that has occurred a thousand times before; that, had they not accidentally met their particular partner, they would have found the same significance in another person.

Something of this feeling is probably not absent in any relation, however close, because what is common to two is never common to them alone, but is subsumed under a general idea which includes much else besides, many *possibilities* of commonness. No matter how little these possibilities become real and how often we forget them, here and there, nevertheless, they thrust themselves between us like shadows, like a mist which escapes every word noted, but which must coagulate into a solid bodily form before it can be called jealousy. In some cases, perhaps the more general, at least the more unsurmountable, strangeness is not due to different and ununderstandable matters. It is rather caused by the fact that similarity, harmony, and nearness are accompanied by the feeling that they are not really the unique property of this particular relationship: they are something more general, something which potentially prevails between the partners and an indeterminate number of others, and therefore gives the relation, which alone was realized, no inner and exclusive necessity.

On the other hand, there is a kind of "strangeness" that rejects the very commonness based on something more general which embraces the parties. The relation of the Greeks to the Barbarians is perhaps typical here, as are all cases in which it is precisely general attributes, felt to be specifically and purely human, that are disallowed to the other. But "stranger," here, has no positive meaning; the relation to him is a non-relation; he is not what is relevant here, a member of the group itself.

As a group member, rather, he is near and far *at the same time*, as is characteristic of relations founded only on generally human commonness. But between nearness and distance, there arises a specific tension when the consciousness that only the quite general is common, stresses that which is not common. In the case of the person who is a stranger to the country, the city, the race, etc., however, this non-common element is once more nothing individual, but merely the strangeness of origin, which is or could be common to many strangers. For this reason, strangers are not really conceived as individuals, but as strangers of a particular type: the element of distance is no less general in regard to them than the element of nearness.

This form is the basis of such a special case, for instance, as the tax levied in Frankfort and elsewhere upon medieval Jews. Whereas the *Beede* [tax] paid by the Christian citizen changed with the changes of his fortune, it was fixed once for all for every single Jew. This fixity rested on the fact that the Jew had his social position as a *Jew*, not as the individual bearer of certain objective contents. Every other citizen was the owner of a particular amount of property, and his tax followed its fluctuations. But the Jew as a taxpayer was, in the first place, a Jew, and thus his tax situation had an invariable element. This same position appears most strongly, of course, once even these individual characterizations (limited though they were by rigid invariance) are omitted, and all strangers pay an altogether equal head-tax.

In spite of being inorganically appended to it, the stranger is yet an organic member of the group. Its uniform life includes the specific conditions of this element. Only we do not know how to designate the peculiar unity of this position other than by saying that it is composed of certain measures of nearness and distance. Although some quantities of them characterize all relationships, a *special* proportion and reciprocal tension produce the particular, formal relation to the "stranger."

29

DYAD AND TRIAD*

GEORG SIMMEL

The simplest sociological formation, methodologically speaking, remains that which operates between two elements. It contains the scheme, germ, and material of innumerable more complex forms. Its sociological significance, however, by no means rests on its extensions and multiplications only. It itself is a sociation. Not only are many general forms of sociation realized in it in a very pure and characteristic fashion; what is more, the limitation to two members is a condition under which alone several forms of relationship exist. Their typically sociological nature is suggested by two facts. One is that the greatest variation of individualities and unifying motives does not alter the identity of these forms. The other is that occasionally these forms exist as much between two groups—families, states, and organizations of various kinds—as between two individuals.

Everyday experiences show the specific character that a relationship attains by the fact that only two elements participate in it. A common fate or enterprise, an agreement or secret between two persons, ties each of them in a very different manner than if even only three have a part in it. This is perhaps most characteristic of the secret. General experience seems to indicate that this minimum of two, with which the secret ceases to be the property of the one individual, is at the same time the maximum at which its preservation is relatively secure. A secret religious-political society which was formed in the beginning of the nineteenth century in France and Italy, had different degrees among its members. The real secrets of the society were known only to the higher degrees; but a discussion of these secrets could take place only between any two members of the high degrees. The limit of two was felt to be so decisive that, where it could not be preserved in regard to knowledge, it was kept at least in regard to the verbalization of this knowledge. More generally speaking, the difference between the dyad and larger groups consists in the fact that the dyad has a different relation to each of its two elements than have larger groups to *their* members. Although, for the outsider, the group consisting of two may function as an autonomous, super-individual unit, it usually does not do so for its participants. Rather, each of the two feels himself confronted only by the other, not by a collectivity above him. The social structure here rests immediately on the one and on the other of the two, and the secession of either would destroy the whole. The dyad, therefore, does not attain that super-personal life which the individual feels to be independent of himself. As soon, however, as there is a sociation of three, a group continues to exist even in case one of the members drops out.

This dependence of the dyad upon its two individual members causes the thought of its existence to be accompanied by the thought of its termination much more closely and impressively than in any other group, where every member knows that even after his retirement or death, the group can continue to exist. Ideally, any large group can be immortal. This fact gives each of its members, no matter what may be his personal reaction to death, a very specific sociological feeling. A dyad, however, depends on each of its two elements alone—in its death, though not in its life: for its life, it needs *both*, but for its death, only one. This fact is bound to influence the inner attitude of the individual toward the dyad, even though not always consciously nor in the same way. It makes the dyad into a group that feels itself both endangered and irreplaceable, and thus into the real locus not only of authentic sociological tragedy, but also of sentimentalism and elegiac problems.

The fact that from the beginning it is defined as one that will die gives it a peculiar stamp—which the dyad, because of the numerical condition of its structure, has always.

Characteristics of the Dyad

It is for the same structural reason that in reality dyads alone are susceptible to the peculiar coloration or discoloration which we call triviality. For only where there is a claim on the irreplaceable individuality of appearance or performance, does its failure to materialize produce a feeling of triviality. We have hardly paid sufficient attention to the way in which relationships of like content take on a different color, according to whether their members think that there are many, or only very few, similar ones. And it is by no means only erotic relations which attain a special, significant timbre, beyond their describable content and value, through the notion that an experience like theirs has never existed before. Quite generally in fact, there is perhaps hardly any object of external possession whose value—not only its economic value—is not co-determined, consciously or no, by its rarity or frequency. And so, perhaps no relation is independent, in its inner significance for the participants, of the factor of "how many other times, too"; and this factor may even refer to the repetition of the same contents, situations, excitations within the relationship. "Triviality" connotes a certain measure of frequency, of the consciousness that a content of life is repeated, while the value of this content depends on its very opposite—a certain measure of rarity. In regard to the life of a super-individual societal unit and the relation of the individual to such a unit, this question seems not to emerge. Here, where the content of the relation transcends individuality, individuality in the sense of uniqueness or rarity seems to play no role, and its non-existence, therefore, seems not to have the effect of triviality. But in dyadic relations—love, marriage, friendship—and in larger groupings (often, for instance, "social parties") which do *not* result in higher units, the tone of triviality frequently becomes desperate and fatal. This phenomenon indicates the sociological character of the dyad: the dyad is inseparable from the immediacy of interaction; for neither of its two elements is it the super-individual unit which elsewhere confronts the individual, while at the same time it makes him participate in it.

In the dyad, the sociological process remains, in principle, within personal interdependence and does not result in a structure that grows beyond its elements. This also is the basis of "intimacy." The "intimate" character of certain relations seems to me to derive from the individual's inclination to consider that which distinguishes him from others, that which is individual in a qualitative sense, as the core, value, and chief matter of his existence. The inclination is by no means always justifiable; in many people, the very opposite—that which is typical, which they share with many—is the essence and the substantial value of their personality. The same phenomenon can be noted in regard to groups. They, too, easily make their specific content, that is shared only by the members, not by outsiders, their center and real fulfillment. Here we have the form of intimacy.

In probably each relation, there is a mixture of ingredients that its participants contribute to it alone and to no other, and of other ingredients that are not characteristic of it exclusively, but in the same or similar fashion are shared by its members with other persons as well. The peculiar color of intimacy exists if the ingredients of the first type, or more briefly, if the "internal" side of the relation, is felt to be essential; if its whole affective structure is based on what each of the two participants gives or shows only to the one other person and to nobody else. In other words, intimacy is not based on the *content* of the relationship. Two relationships may have an identical mixture of the two types of ingredients, of individual-exclusive and expansive contents. But only that is intimate in which the former function as the vehicle or the axis of the relation itself. Inversely, certain external situations or moods may move us to make very personal statements and confessions, usually reserved for our closest friends only, to relatively strange people. But in such cases we nevertheless feel that this "intimate" *content* does not yet make the relation an intimate one. For in its basic significance, the whole relation to these people is based only on its general, un-individual ingredients. That "intimate" content, although we have perhaps never revealed it before and thus limit it entirely to this particular relationship, does nevertheless not become the basis of its form, and thus leaves it outside the sphere of intimacy.

It is this nature of intimacy which so often makes it a danger to close unions between two persons, most commonly perhaps to marriage. The spouses share the indifferent "intimacies" of the day, the amiable and the unpleasant features of every hour, and the weaknesses that remain carefully hidden from all others. This easily causes them to place the accent and the substance of their relationship upon these wholly individual but objectively irrelevant matters. It leads them to consider what they share with others and what perhaps is the most important part of their personalities—objective, intellectual, generally interesting, generous features—as lying outside the marital relation; and thus they gradually eliminate it from their marriage.

It is obvious that the intimacy of the dyad is closely tied up with its sociological specialty, not to form a unit transcending the two members. For, in spite of the fact that the two individuals would be its only participants, this unit would nevertheless constitute a third element which might interpose itself between them. The larger the group is, the more easily does it form an objective unit up and above its members, and the less intimate does it become: the two characteristics are intrinsically connected. The condition of intimacy consists in the fact that the participants in a given relationship see only one another, and do not see, at the same time, an objective, super-individual structure which they feel exists and operates on its own. Yet in all its purity, this condition is met only rarely even in groups of as few as three. Likewise, the third element in a relation between two individuals—the unit which has grown out of the interaction among the two—interferes with the most intimate nature of the dyad; and this is highly characteristic of its subtler structure. Indeed, it is so fundamental that even marriages occasionally succumb to it, namely, when the first child is born.

The Triad

The triad as such seems to me to result in three kinds of typical group formations. All of them are impossible if there are only two elements; and, on the other hand, if there are more than three, they are either equally impossible or only expand in quantity but do not change their formal type.

The Non-Partisan and the Mediator

In the most significant of all dyads, monogamous marriage, the child or children, as the third element, often has the function of holding the whole together. In general, the common preoccupations of a married couple with the child reveal that their union passes through the child, as it were; the union often consists of sympathies which could not exist without such a point of mediation.

When the third element functions as a non-partisan, we have a different variety of mediation. The non-partisan either produces the concord of two colliding parties, whereby he withdraws after making the effort of creating direct contact between the unconnected or quarreling elements; or he functions as an arbiter who balances, as it were, their contradictory claims against one another and eliminates what is incompatible in them. Differences between labor and management, especially in England, have developed both forms of unification. There are boards of conciliation where the parties negotiate their conflicts under the presidency of a non-partisan.

Here we have a phenomenon which is very significant for the development of purely psychological influences. A third mediating social element deprives conflicting claims of their affective qualities because it neutrally formulates and presents these claims to the two parties involved. Thus this circle that is fatal to all reconciliation is avoided: the vehemence of the one no longer provokes that of the other, which in turn intensifies that of the first, and so forth, until the whole relationship breaks down. Furthermore, because of the non-partisan, each party to the conflict not only listens to more objective matters but is also forced to put the issue in more objective terms than it would if it confronted the other without mediation.

It is important for the analysis of social life to realize clearly that the constellation thus characterized constantly emerges in all groups of more than two elements. To be sure, the mediator may not be specifically chosen, nor be known or designated as such. But the triad here serves merely as a type or scheme; ultimately all cases of mediation can be reduced to this form. From the conversation among three persons that lasts only an hour, to the permanent family of three, there is no triad in which a dissent between any two elements does not occur from time to time—a dissent of a more harmless or more pointed, more momentary or more lasting, more theoretical or more practical nature—and in which the third member does not play a mediating role.

After all that has been said, it is clear that from an over-all viewpoint, the existence of the impartial third element serves the perpetuation of the group. As the representative of the intellect, he confronts the two conflicting parties, which for the moment are guided more by will and feeling. He thus, so to speak, complements them in the production of that psychological unity which resides in group life. On the one hand, the nonpartisan tempers the passion of the others. On the other hand, he can carry and direct the very movement of the whole group if the antagonism of the other two tends to paralyze their forces.

The Third Who Benefits

In the combinations thus far considered, the impartiality of the third element either served or harmed the group as a whole. Both the mediator and the arbitrator wish to save the group unity from the danger of splitting up. But, evidently, the nonpartisan may also use his relatively superior position for purely egoistic interests. While in the cases discussed, he behaved as a means to the ends of the group, he may also, inversely, make the interaction that takes place between the parties and between himself and them, a means for his own purposes. In the social life of well consolidated groups, this may happen merely as one event among others. But often the relation between the parties and the non-partisan emerges as a new relationship: elements that have never before formed an interactional unit may come into conflict; a third non-partisan element, which before was equally unconnected with either, may spontaneously seize upon the chances that this quarrel gives him; and thus an entirely unstable interaction may result which can have an animation and wealth of forms, for each of the elements engaged in it, which are out of all proportion to its brief life.

I will only mention two forms of the *tertius gaudens* in which the interaction within the triad does not emerge very distinctly; and here we are interested in its more typical formations. In these two, the essential characteristic is rather a certain passivity, either of the two engaged in the conflict or of the *tertius* [third element, party, or person]. The advantage of the *tertius* may result from the fact that the remaining two hold each other in check, and he can make a gain which one of the two would otherwise deny him. The discord here only effectuates a paralyzation of forces which, if they only could, would strike against him. The situation thus really suspends interaction among the three elements, instead of fomenting it, although it is certainly, nonetheless, of the most distinct consequences for all of them. Meanwhile the second form appears when the *tertius* gains an advantage only because action by one of the two conflicting parties brings it about for its own purposes—the *tertius* does not need to take the initiative. A case in point are the benefits and promotions which a party bestows upon him, only in order to offend its adversary. Thus, the English laws for the protection of labor originally derived, in part at least, from the mere rancor of the Tories against liberal manufacturers. Various charitable actions that result from competition for popularity also belong here. Strangely enough, it is a particularly petty and mean attitude that befriends a third element for the sake of annoying a second: indifference to the moral autonomy of altruism cannot appear more sharply than in this exploitation of altruism. And it is doubly significant that the purpose of annoying one's adversary can be achieved by favoring either one's friend or one's enemy.

The formations that are more essential here emerge whenever the *tertius* makes his own indirect or direct gain by turning toward one of the two conflicting parties—but not intellectually and objectively, like the arbitrator, but practically, supporting or granting. This general type has two main variants: either two parties are hostile toward one another and therefore compete for the favor of a third element; or they compete for the favor of the third element and therefore are hostile toward one another.

Divide et Impera

The previously discussed combinations of three elements were characterized by an existing or emerging conflict between two, from which the third drew his advantage. One particular variety of this combination must now be considered separately, although in reality it is not always clearly delimited against other types. The distinguishing nuance consists in the fact that the third element intentionally produces the conflict in order to gain a dominating position. Its outline is that initially two elements are united or mutually dependent in regard to a third, and that this third element knows how to put the forces combined against *him* into action against *one another*. The outcome is that the two either keep each other balanced so that he, who is not interfered with by either, can pursue his advantages; or that they so weaken one another that neither of them can stand up against his superiority.

30

The Metropolis and Mental Life*

Georg Simmel

An inquiry into the inner meaning of specifically modern life and its products, into the soul of the cultural body, so to speak, must seek to solve the equation which structures like the metropolis set up between the individual and the super-individual contents of life. Such an inquiry must answer the question of how the personality accommodates itself in the adjustments to external forces. This will be my task today.

The psychological basis of the metropolitan type of individuality consists in the *intensification of nervous stimulation* which results from the swift and uninterrupted change of outer and inner stimuli. Man is a differentiating creature. His mind is stimulated by the difference between a momentary impression and the one which preceded it. Lasting impressions, impressions which differ only slightly from one another, impressions which take a regular and habitual course and show regular and habitual contrasts—all these use up, so to speak, less consciousness than does the rapid crowding of changing images, the sharp discontinuity in the grasp of a single glance, and the unexpectedness of onrushing impressions. These are the psychological conditions which the metropolis creates. With each crossing of the street, with the tempo and multiplicity of economic, occupational and social life, the city sets up a deep contrast with small town and rural life with reference to the sensory foundations of psychic life. The metropolis exacts from man as a discriminating creature a different amount of consciousness than does rural life. Here the rhythm of life and sensory mental imagery flows more slowly, more habitually, and more evenly. Precisely in this connection the sophisticated character of metropolitan psychic life becomes understandable—as over against small town life which rests more upon deeply felt and emotional relationships. These latter are rooted in the more unconscious layers of the psyche and grow most readily in the steady rhythm of uninterrupted habituations. The intellect, however, has its locus in the transparent, conscious, higher layers of the psyche; it is the most adaptable of our inner forces. In order to accommodate to change and to the contrast of phenomena, the intellect does not require any shocks and inner upheavals; it is only through such upheavals that the more conservative mind could accommodate to the metropolitan rhythm of events. Thus the metropolitan type

*Reprinted with the permission of Free Press, a Division of Simon & Schuster, Inc. from *The Sociology of Georg Simmel* by Georg Simmel, translated and edited by Kurt H. Wolff.

of man—which, of course, exists in a thousand individual variants—develops an organ protecting him against the threatening currents and discrepancies of his external environment which would uproot him. He reacts with his head instead of his heart. In this an increased awareness assumes the psychic prerogative. Metropolitan life, thus, underlies a heightened awareness and a predominance of intelligence in metropolitan man. The reaction to metropolitan phenomena is shifted to that organ which is least sensitive and quite remote from the depth of the personality. Intellectuality is thus seen to preserve subjective life against the overwhelming power of metropolitan life, and intellectuality branches out in many directions and is integrated with numerous discrete phenomena.

The metropolis has always been the seat of the money economy. Here the multiplicity and concentration of economic exchange gives an importance to the means of exchange which the scantiness of rural commerce would not have allowed. Money economy and the dominance of the intellect are intrinsically connected. They share a matter-of-fact attitude in dealing with men and with things; and, in this attitude, a formal justice is often coupled with an inconsiderate hardness. The intellectually sophisticated person is indifferent to all genuine individuality, because relationships and reactions result from it which cannot be exhausted with logical operations. In the same manner, the individuality of phenomena is not commensurate with the pecuniary principle. Money is concerned only with what is common to all: it asks for the exchange value, it reduces all quality and individuality to the question: How much? All intimate emotional relations between persons are founded in their individuality, whereas in rational relations man is reckoned with like a number, like an element which is in itself indifferent. Only the objective measurable achievement is of interest. Thus metropolitan man reckons with his merchants and customers, his domestic servants and often even with persons with whom he is obliged to have social intercourse. These features of intellectuality contrast with the nature of the small circle in which the inevitable knowledge of individuality as inevitably produces a warmer tone of behavior, a behavior which is beyond a mere objective balancing of service and return. In the sphere of the economic psychology of the small group it is of importance that under primitive conditions production serves the customer who orders the good, so that the producer and the consumer are acquainted. The modern metropolis, however, is supplied almost entirely by production for the market, that is, for entirely unknown purchasers who never personally enter the producer's actual field of vision. Through this anonymity the interests of each party acquire an unmerciful matter-of-factness; and the intellectually calculating economic egoisms of both parties need not fear any deflection because of the imponderables of personal relationships. The money economy dominates the metropolis; it has displaced the last survivals of domestic production and the direct barter of goods; it minimizes, from day to day, the amount of work ordered by customers. The matter-of-fact attitude is obviously so intimately interrelated with the money economy, which is dominant in the metropolis, that nobody can say whether the intellectualistic mentality first promoted the money economy or whether the latter determined the former. The metropolitan way of life is certainly the most fertile soil for this reciprocity, a point which I shall document merely by citing the dictum of the most eminent English constitutional historian: throughout the whole course of English history, London has never acted as England's heart but often as England's intellect and always as her moneybag!

In certain seemingly insignificant traits, which lie upon the surface of life, the same psychic currents characteristically unite. Modern mind has become more and more calculating. The calculative exactness of practical life which the money economy has brought about corresponds to the ideal of natural science: to transform the world into an arithmetic problem, to fix every part of the world by mathematical formulas. Only money economy has filled the days of so many people with weighing, calculating, with numerical determinations, with a reduction of qualitative values to quantitative ones. Through the calculative nature of money a new precision, a certainty in the definition of identities and differences, an unambiguousness in agreements and arrangements has been brought about in the relations of life-elements—just as externally this precision has been effected by the universal diffusion of pocket watches. However, the conditions of metropolitan life are at once cause and effect of this trait. The relationships and affairs of the typical metropolitan usually are so varied and complex that without the strictest punctuality in promises and services the whole structure would break down into an inextricable chaos. Above all, this necessity is brought about by the aggregation of so many people with such differentiated interests, who must integrate their relations and activities into a highly complex organism. If all clocks and watches in Berlin would suddenly go wrong in different ways, even if only by one hour, all economic life and communication of the city would he disrupted for a long time. In addition an apparently mere external factor: long distances, would make all waiting and broken appointments result in an ill-afforded waste of time. Thus, the technique of metropolitan life is unimaginable without the most punctual integration of all activities and mutual relations into a stable and impersonal time schedule. Here again the general conclusions of this entire task of reflection become obvious, namely, that from each point on the surface of existence—however closely attached to the surface alone—one may drop a sounding into the depth of the psyche so that all the most banal externalities of life finally are connected with the ultimate decisions concerning the meaning and style of life. Punctuality, calculability, exactness are forced upon life by the complexity and extension of metropolitan existence and are not only most intimately connected with its money economy and intellectualistic character.

The same factors which have thus coalesced into the exactness and minute precision of the form of life have coalesced into a structure of the highest impersonality; on the other hand, they have promoted a highly personal subjectivity. There is perhaps no psychic phenomenon which has been so unconditionally reserved to the metropolis as has the blasé attitude. The blasé attitude results first from the rapidly changing and closely compressed contrasting stimulations of the nerves. From this, the enhancement of metropolitan intellectuality, also, seems originally to stem. Therefore, stupid people who are not intellectually alive in the first place usually are not exactly blasé. A life in boundless pursuit of pleasure makes one blasé because it agitates the nerves to their strongest reactivity for such a long time that they finally cease to react at all. In the same way, through the rapidity and contradictoriness of their changes, more harmless impressions force such violent responses, tearing the nerves so brutally hither and thither that their last reserves of strength are spent; and if one remains in the same milieu they have no time to gather new strength. An incapacity thus emerges to react to new sensations with the appropriate energy. This constitutes that blasé attitude which, in fact, every metropolitan child shows when compared with children of quieter and less changeable milieus.

This physiological source of the metropolitan blasé attitude is joined by another source which flows from the money economy. The essence of the blasé attitude consists in the blunting of discrimination. This does not mean that the objects are not perceived, as is the case with the half-wit, but rather that the meaning and differing values of things, and thereby the things themselves, are experienced as insubstantial. They appear to the blasé person in an evenly flat and gray tone; no one object deserves preference over any other. This mood is the faithful subjective reflection of the completely internalized money economy. By being the equivalent to all the manifold things in one and the same way, money becomes the most frightful leveler. For money expresses all qualitative differences of things in terms of "how much?" Money, with all its colorlessness and indifference, becomes the common denominator of all values; irreparably it hollows out the core of things, their individuality, their specific value, and their incomparability. All things float with equal specific gravity in the constantly moving stream of money. All things lie on the same level and differ from one another only in the size of the area which they cover. In the individual case this coloration, or rather discoloration, of things through their money equivalence may be unnoticeably minute. However, through the relations of the rich to the objects to be had for money, perhaps even through the total character which the mentality of the contemporary public everywhere imparts to these objects, the exclusively pecuniary evaluation of objects has become quite considerable. The large cities, the main seats of the money exchange, bring the purchasability of things to the fore much more impressively than do smaller localities. That is why cities are also the genuine locale of the blasé attitude. In the blasé attitude the concentration of men and things stimulate the nervous system of the individual to its highest achievement so that it attains its peak. Through the mere quantitative intensification of the same conditioning factors this achievement is transformed into its opposite and appears in the peculiar adjustment of the blasé attitude. In this phenomenon the nerves find in the refusal to react to their stimulation the last possibility of accommodating to the contents and forms of metropolitan life. The self-preservation of certain personalities is brought at the price of devaluating the whole objective world, a devaluation which in the end unavoidably drags one's own personality down into a feeling of the same worthlessness.

Whereas the subject of this form of existence has to come to terms with it entirely for himself, his self-preservation in the face of the large city demands from him a no less negative behavior of a social nature. This mental attitude of metropolitans toward one another we may designate, from a formal point of view, as reserve. If so many inner reactions were responses to the continuous external contacts with innumerable people as are those in the small town, where one knows almost everybody one meets and where one has a positive relation to almost everyone, one would be completely atomized internally and come to an unimaginable psychic state. Partly this psychological fact, partly the right to distrust which men have in the face of the touch-and-go elements of metropolitan life, necessitates our reserve. As a result of this reserve we frequently do not even know by sight those who have been our neighbors for years. And it is this reserve which in the eyes of the small-town people makes us appear to be cold and heartless. Indeed, if I do not deceive myself, the inner aspect of this outer reserve is not only indifference but, more often than we are aware, it is a slight aversion, a mutual strangeness and repulsion, which will break into hatred and fight at the moment of a closer contact, however caused. The whole inner organization of such an extensive communicative life rests upon an extremely varied hierarchy of sympathies, indifferences, and aversions of the briefest as well as of the most permanent nature. The sphere of indifference in this hierarchy is not as large as might appear on the surface. Our psychic activity still responds to almost every impression of somebody else with a somewhat distinct feeling. The unconscious, fluid and changing character of this impression seems to result in a state of indifference. Actually this indifference would be just as unnatural as the diffusion of indiscriminate mutual suggestion would be unbearable. From both these typical dangers of the metropolis, indifference and indiscriminate suggestibility, antipathy protects us. A latent antipathy and the preparatory stage of practical antagonism effect the distances and aversions without which this mode of life could not at all be led. The extent and the mixture of this style of life, the rhythm of its emergence and disappearance, the forms in which it is satisfied—all these, with the unifying motives in the narrower sense, form the inseparable whole of the metropolitan style of life. What appears in the metropolitan style of life directly as dissociation is in reality only one of its elemental forms of socialization.

This reserve with its overtone of hidden aversion appears in turn as the form or the cloak of a more general mental phenomenon of the metropolis: it grants to the individual a kind and an amount of personal freedom which has no analogy whatsoever under other conditions. The metropolis goes back to one of the large developmental tendencies of social life as such, to one of the few tendencies for which an approximately universal formula can be discovered. The earliest phase of social formations found in historical as well as in contemporary social structures is this: a relatively small circle firmly closed against neighboring, strange, or in some way antagonistic circles. However, this circle is closely coherent and allows its individual members only a narrow field for the development of unique qualities and free, self-responsible movements. Political and kinship groups, parties and religious associations begin in this way. The self-preservation of very young associations requires the establishment of strict boundaries and a centripetal unity. Therefore they cannot allow the individual freedom and unique inner and outer development. From this stage social development proceeds at once in two different, yet corresponding, directions. To the extent to which the group grows—numerically, spatially, in significance and in content of life—to the same degree the group's direct, inner unity loosens, and the rigidity of the original demarcation against others is softened through mutual relations and connections. At the same time, the individual gains freedom of movement, far beyond the first jealous delimitation. The individual also gains a specific individuality to which the division of labor in the enlarged group gives both occasion and necessity. The state and Christianity, guilds and political parties, and innumerable other groups have developed according to this formula, however much, of course, the special conditions and forces of the respective groups have modified the general scheme. This scheme seems to me distinctly recognizable also in the evolution of individuality within urban life. The small-town life in Antiquity and in the Middle Ages set barriers against movement and relations of the individual toward the outside, and it set up barriers against individual independence and differentiation within the individual self. These barriers were such that under them modern man could not have breathed. Even today a metropolitan man who is placed in a small town feels a restriction similar, at least, in kind. The smaller the circle which forms our milieu is, and the more restricted those relations to others are which dissolve the boundaries of the individual, the more anxiously the circle guards the achievements, the conduct of life, and the outlook of the individual, and the more readily a quantitative and qualitative specialization would break up the framework of the whole little circle.

It is not only the immediate size of the area and the number of persons which, because of the universal historical correlation between the enlargement of the circle and the personal inner and outer freedom, has made the metropolis the locale of freedom. It is rather in transcending this visible expanse that any given city becomes the seat of cosmopolitanism. The horizon of the city expands in a manner comparable to the way in which wealth develops; a certain amount of property increases in a quasi-automatical way in ever more rapid progression. As soon as a certain limit has been passed, the economic, personal, and intellectual relations of the citizenry, the sphere of intellectual predominance of the city over its hinterland, grow as in geometrical progression. Every gain in dynamic extension becomes a step, not for an equal, but for a new and larger extension. From every thread spinning out of the city, ever new threads grow as if by themselves, just as within the city the unearned increment of ground rent, through the mere increase in communication, brings the owner automatically increasing profits. At this point, the quantitative aspect of life is transformed directly into qualitative traits of character. The sphere of life of the small town is, in the main, self-contained and autarchic. For it is the decisive nature of the metropolis that its inner life overflows by waves into a far-flung national or international area. Weimar is not an example to the contrary, since its significance was hinged upon individual personalities and died with them; whereas the metropolis is indeed characterized by its essential independence even from the most eminent individual personalities. This is the counterpart to the independence, and it is the price the individual pays for the independence, which he enjoys in the metropolis. The most significant characteristic of the metropolis is this functional extension beyond its physical boundaries. And this efficacy reacts in turn and gives weight, importance, and responsibility to metropolitan life. Man does not end with the limits of his body or the area comprising his immediate activity. Rather is the range of the person constituted by the sum of effects emanating from him temporally and spatially. In the same way, a city consists of its total effects which extend beyond its immediate confines.

PART V

THE INTERSTITIAL STATEMENTS

The readings featured in Part V were written during a time of extraordinary transition in sociology and in sociological theorizing: from the fin de siècle to the post–World War I period, between the classical tradition that produced the canonical writings and the second generation of sociologists that would bring the theoretical enterprise to full maturity (the subject of Part VI). These interstitial thinkers were largely European: Gaetano Mosca, Vilfredo Pareto, Robert Michels, Gustave Le Bon, Gabriel Tarde, and Sigmund Freud. Of these, only Freud is not typically considered a sociologist, but as the founder of psychoanalysis, he occasionally applied his clinical concepts to analyzing society. Increasingly, during this era of sociological development, more Americans were contributing to theoretical progress. Two of them were Thorstein Veblen and William F. Ogburn. Like the protosociologists, the interstitial thinkers did not produce a coherent theoretical program in sociology. And unlike the classical theorists, their work has not gained nearly as much recognition. Still, their ideas remain as important and relevant today as they were during the 30-year period of their appearance, from 1890 to 1920.

Gaetano Mosca, Vilfredo Pareto, and Robert Michels are the scholars most associated with the so-called Italian school of elitism. All three were concerned with the power structure of society—the rule of the few over the many—and as such, they contributed to elite theory.

In "The Ruling Class," Mosca contends that in all societies, there exist—and must exist—two classes: one that rules and the other that is ruled. The *ruling class* is an organized political community, made up of a relatively small number of people, that monopolizes power and manages public affairs to its advantage. The class that is ruled, by contrast, consists of an unorganized majority of people that defers to the ruling class and is governed by it. Members of the ruling class possess "superior" qualities and capacities—of a material, intellectual, and moral nature—that contribute to their leadership over the masses. But Mosca makes it clear that any major changes to a society's social structure or culture can make the ruling class irrelevant and drive it from power. Then, after the transformation, when society becomes more settled, a new ruling class arises and replaces the old one.

Vilfredo Pareto's "The Circulation of the Elites" is essentially an extension of Mosca's thesis. Pareto begins by pointing out two facts of particular importance to social stability: The first is that modern society consists of a great diversity of groups, and the second is that these groups are always in flux. In short, he explains the phenomenon of the "circulation" of the *elites*, or those groups that are composed of people with a high degree of intelligence, character, skill, and capacity. People may use these traits for moral or immoral purposes, but the important point for Pareto is that they make maximum use of them. In reference to political power, there are two types of elite groups: a *governing elite* that rules and a *nongoverning elite* that does not. Below this upper stratum of elite groups are the *nonelite*, who are the ruled. There is, however, a movement in quantity and quality—an upward and downward social mobility—between the members of the governing elite and the members of the nongoverning elite. According to Pareto, any impediment to the rotation of ruling abilities between the two elite groups will disrupt the equilibrium of society.

In "The Iron Law of Oligarchy," from the year 1915, Robert Michels maintains that democracy is a fragile form of government fraught with dangers. This is particularly the case given that democracy contains a dominant political party that will inevitably attempt to attain its own unique interests, which are often in opposition to those of the masses. This produces a conflict of interests. Michels believed that all bureaucratic organizations, including political parties, possess inherent oligarchical tendencies. Thus, given that political organizations always seek to protect their power, these organizations—even when based on democratic and socialist ideals—eventually turn into oligarchies. History shows that old oligarchies are continuously replaced by new ones. This sociological phenomenon of oligarchical successions is what Michels refers to as the *iron law of oligarchies*.

Gustave Le Bon, Gabriel Tarde, and Sigmund Freud made important theoretical contributions to the sociopsychological study of crowds and masses. These three men, each in their own way, emphasized the influence that the collectivity has over the individual's emotions, thoughts, and behavior.

According to Le Bon, in "The Crowd Mind," a *crowd* is a loose gathering of individuals who have come together for any purpose. But beyond this empirical fact, a crowd may possess a *collective mind*, with its own thoughts and feelings that are independent of the people making it up. When this collective mind forms, the crowd is said to have social organization. Thus, the individuals who compose an organized crowd feel, think, and act quite differently than if they were alone. People in a crowd are in a kind of hypnotic state, which means that they stop operating under their own wills. This gives them unique characteristics they would not otherwise possess. By being in a crowd with many others, crowd members acquire *anonymity*, which endows them with feelings of *invincibility* and makes them less *responsible* for their actions. In any crowd, feelings, thoughts, and actions are *contagious*—thus, every member is affected by every other member. Finally, crowd members, having entirely lost their own conscious personalities, are more *suggestible* to influences from others.

Gabriel Tarde extended the notion of suggestion to the realm of social relations in proposing the principle of *imitation*. Tarde begins "The Laws of Imitation," written in 1890, with the notion that all social phenomena—whether words, ideas, or inventions—are directly or indirectly diffused throughout society by a pattern of repetition: a process of imitation. Sometimes, people's attempts to imitate are based on logical or rational reasons, as when they imitate a phenomenon because they see it as useful or efficient. Most of the time, however, imitation is manifested nonlogically in three main ways: (1) Imitation starts with emotion, then becomes thought, and is only later put into practice; (2) innovations are usually introduced by social superiors and copied by social inferiors; and (3) sometimes, custom, which is old, is imitated, and sometimes, fashion, which is new, is imitated.

Like Le Bon and Tarde before him, Sigmund Freud also considers the social psychology of people as members of a group. He argues, in "The Herd Instinct," that people's experience of a group feeling—a *herd instinct*—emanates from the *libido*, the sexual energy that inclines people to seek *identification* with others and become like them. But in desiring the approval of a leader, such as a parent or a hero, people will compete with each other, which creates hostile feelings between them. They soon demand that everyone be treated equally so that no one member of the group is preferred over the others by the leader. Many equals identify with each other, and this creates a "we" feeling, an *esprit de corps*, among group members.

Freud applies psychoanalytic principles in understanding the workings of society in his most famous book, *Civilization and Its Discontents*, which appeared in 1930. In the reading, "The Conscience of Society," Freud maintains that *civilization*, or moral society, imposes great restrictions on people's freedom, thus causing their unhappiness. In short, civilization, because it demands conformity, causes people to be discontent. There exists a continuous tension between people wanting to satisfy their primitive instincts—having to do with uninhibited sexuality and aggression—and civilization's attempt to curb these impulses so that social order does not disintegrate into chaos. People are able to control their primitive inclinations and live in relative harmony because they have developed a *superego*, a conscience. More importantly, they subdue these desires of sexuality and aggression in the unconscious; they *repress* them. Repression produces a sense of guilt, which is experienced as a permanent internal unhappiness. However, it is not only the individual but also civilized society that develops a conscience, a *cultural superego*, which is articulated in ethical principles such as the commandment to love one's neighbor as oneself.

The two Americans whose writings are included in this section are frequently recalled on the basis of the singular terms they popularized: *conspicuous consumption*, in the case of Thorstein Veblen, and *cultural lag*, in the case of William F. Ogburn. They were both intensely interested in the changing culture of U.S. society and, accordingly, took a cultural approach in their sociological analyses.

Writing in the late 19th century, Veblen, in "Conspicuous Consumption," describes the lifestyle habits of the *leisure class*—the group that was exempt from work and that involved itself in making lavish expenditures. The leisure class engaged in *conspicuous consumption*, or the purchase of products for no other purpose than their ostentatious display, and in *conspicuous leisure*, or the pursuit of recreation and economically unproductive activities. Failure by the gentlemen of the upper class to consume in this way was seen as dishonorable. By contrast, in the lower middle class, because the male head of the household devoted himself to work, it fell to his wife to engage in conspicuous consumption and leisure. Above all, conspicuous consumption, in order to be effective in impressing others, must involve the purchase of luxuries, not basic necessities.

Finally, in the reading "Cultural Lag," William F. Ogburn proposes a theory that accounts for social change through causation and adaptation. *Cultural lag*, a concept that Ogburn coined in 1922, occurs when two interconnected parts of culture diverge from each other, thus creating maladjustment between them. In order to address the maladjustment, one part of culture, the dependent variable, must adapt to the independent variable, the part that changed initially. In this way, the discrepancy and the unequal time interval—the "lag"—between the two cultural parts are brought into accord. In modern society, the initiating part of culture is nearly always about the introduction of new technologies. In sum, cultural lag causes social change.

31

The Ruling Class*

Gaetano Mosca

In all societies—from societies that are very meagerly developed and have barely attained the dawnings of civilization, down to the most advanced and powerful societies—two classes of people appear—a class that rules and a class that is ruled. The first class, always the less numerous, performs all political functions, monopolizes power and enjoys the advantages that power brings, whereas the second, the more numerous class, is directed and controlled by the first, in a manner that is now more or less legal, now more or less arbitrary and violent, and supplies the first, in appearance at least, with material means of subsistence and with the instrumentalities that are essential to the vitality of the political organism.

In practical life we all recognize the existence of this ruling class (or political class, as we have elsewhere chosen to define it). We all know that, in our own country, whichever it may be, the management of public affairs is in the hands of a minority of influential persons, to which management, willingly or unwillingly, the majority defer. We know that the same thing goes on in neighboring countries, and in fact we should be put to it to conceive of a real world otherwise organized—a world in which all men would be directly subject to a single person without relationships of superiority or subordination, or in which all men would share equally in the direction of political affairs. If we reason otherwise in theory, that is due partly to inveterate habits that we follow in our thinking and partly to the exaggerated importance that we attach to two political facts that loom far larger in appearance than they are in reality.

The first of these facts—and one has only to open one's eyes to see it—is that in every political organism there is one individual who is chief among the leaders of the ruling class as a whole and stands, as we say, at the helm of the state. That person is not always the person who holds supreme power according to law. At times, alongside of the hereditary king or emperor there is a prime minister or a major-domo who wields an actual power that is greater than the sovereign's. At other times, in place of the elected president the influential politician who has procured the president's election will govern. Under special circumstances there may be, instead of a single person, two or three who discharge the functions of supreme control.

*Excerpt from *The Ruling Class* by Gaetano Mosca, Translation by Hannah D. Kahn. Edited and Revised, with an Introduction by Arthur Livingston.

The second fact, too, is readily discernible. Whatever the type of political organization, pressures arising from the discontent of the masses who are governed, from the passions by which they are swayed, exert a certain amount of influence on the policies of the ruling, the political, class.

But the man who is at the head of the state would certainly not be able to govern without the support of a numerous class to enforce respect for his orders and to have them carried out; and granting that he can make one individual, or indeed many individuals, in the ruling class feel the weight of his power, he certainly cannot be at odds with the class as a whole or do away with it. Even if that were possible, he would at once be forced to create another class, without the support of which action on his part would be completely paralyzed. On the other hand, granting that the discontent of the masses might succeed in deposing a ruling class, inevitably, as we shall later show, there would have to be another organized minority within the masses themselves to discharge the functions of a ruling class. Otherwise all organization, and the whole social structure, would be destroyed.

We think it may be desirable, nevertheless, to reply at this point to an objection which might very readily be made to our point of view. If it is easy to understand that a single individual cannot command a group without finding within the group a minority to support him, it is rather difficult to grant, as a constant and natural fact, that minorities rule majorities, rather than majorities minorities. But that is one of the points—so numerous in all the other sciences—where the first impression one has of things is contrary to what they are in reality. In reality the dominion of an organized minority, obeying a single impulse, over the unorganized majority is inevitable. The power of any minority is irresistible as against each single individual in the majority, who stands alone before the totality of the organized minority. At the same time, the minority is organized for the very reason that it is a minority. A hundred men acting uniformly in concert, with a common understanding, will triumph over a thousand men who are not in accord and can therefore be dealt with one by one. Meanwhile it will be easier for the former to act in concert and have a mutual understanding simply because they are a hundred and not a thousand. It follows that the larger the political community, the smaller will the proportion of the governing minority to the governed majority be, and the more difficult will it be for the majority to organize for reaction against the minority.

However, in addition to the great advantage accruing to them from the fact of being organized, ruling minorities are usually so constituted that the individuals who make them up are distinguished from the mass of the governed by qualities that give them a certain material, intellectual or even moral superiority; or else they are the heirs of individuals who possessed such qualities. In other words, members of a ruling minority regularly have some attribute, real or apparent, which is highly esteemed and very influential in the society in which they live.

What we see is that as soon as there is a shift in the balance of political forces—when, that is, a need is felt that capacities different from the old should assert themselves in the management of the state, when the old capacities, therefore, lose some of their importance or changes in their distribution occur—then the manner in which the ruling class is constituted changes also. If a new source of wealth develops in a society, if the practical importance of knowledge grows, if an old religion declines or a new one is born, if a new current of ideas spreads, then, simultaneously, far-reaching dislocations occur in the ruling class. One might say, indeed, that the whole history of civilized mankind comes down to a conflict between the tendency of dominant elements to monopolize political power and transmit possession of it by inheritance, and the tendency toward a dislocation of old forces and an insurgence of new forces; and this conflict produces an unending ferment of endosmosis and exosmosis between the upper classes and certain portions of the lower. Ruling classes decline inevitably when they cease to find scope for the capacities through which they rose to power, when they can no longer render the social services which they once rendered, or when their talents and the services they render lose in importance in the social environment in which they live. So the Roman aristocracy declined when it was no longer the exclusive source of higher officers for the army, of administrators for the commonwealth, of governors for the provinces. So the Venetian aristocracy declined when its nobles ceased to command the galleys and no longer passed the greater part of their lives in sailing the seas and in trading and fighting.

On the other hand it may happen in the history of a nation that commerce with foreign peoples, forced emigrations, discoveries, wars, create new poverty and new wealth, disseminate knowledge of things that were previously unknown or cause infiltrations of new moral, intellectual and religious currents. Or again—as a result of such infiltrations or through a slow process of inner growth, or from both causes—it may happen that a new learning arises, or that certain elements of an old, long forgotten learning return to favor so that new ideas and new beliefs come to the fore and upset the intellectual habits on which the obedience of the masses has been founded. The ruling class may also be vanquished and destroyed in whole or in part by foreign invasions, or, when the circumstances just mentioned arise, it may be driven from power by the advent of new social elements who are strong in fresh political forces. Then, naturally, there comes a period of renovation, or, if one prefer, of revolution, during which individual energies have free play and certain individuals, more passionate, more energetic, more intrepid or merely shrewder than others, force their way from the bottom of the social ladder to the topmost rungs.

Suppose now that a society gradually passes from its feverish state to calm. Since the human being's psychological tendencies are always the same, those who belong to the ruling class will begin to acquire a group spirit. They will become more and more exclusive and learn better and better the art of monopolizing to their advantage the qualities and capacities that are essential to acquiring power and holding it. Then, at last, the force that is essentially conservative appears—the force of habit. Many people become resigned to a lowly station, while the members of certain privileged families or classes grow convinced that they have almost an absolute right to high station and command.

32

The Circulation of the Elites*

Vilfredo Pareto

We have more than once found ourselves called upon to consider the heterogeneous character of society, and we shall have to consider it all the more closely now that we are coming to our investigation of the conditions that determine the social equilibrium. To have a clear road ahead of us, it would be wise to go into that matter somewhat thoroughly at this point.

Whether certain theorists like it or not, the fact is that human society is not a homogeneous thing, that individuals are physically, morally, and intellectually different. Here we are interested in things as they actually are. Of that fact, therefore, we have to take account. And we must also take account of another fact: that the social classes are not entirely distinct, even in countries where a caste system prevails; and that in modern civilized countries circulation among the various classes is exceedingly rapid. To consider at all exhaustively here this matter of the diversity of the vastly numerous social groups and the numberless ways in which they mix is out of the question. As usual, therefore, since we cannot have the more, we must rest content with the less and try to make the problem easier in order to have it the more manageable. That is a first step along a path that others may go on following. We shall consider the problem only in its bearing on the social equilibrium and try to reduce as far as possible the numbers of the groups and the modes of circulation, putting under one head phenomena that prove to be roughly and after a fashion similar.

Social élites and their circulation. Suppose we begin by giving a theoretical definition of the thing we are dealing with, making it as exact as possible, and then go on to see what practical considerations we can replace it with to get a first approximation. Let us for the moment completely disregard considerations as to the good or bad, useful or harmful, praiseworthy or reprehensible character of the various traits in individuals, and confine ourselves to degrees—to whether, in other words, the trait in a given case be slight, average, intense, or more exactly, to the index that may be assigned to each individual with reference to the degree, or intensity, in him of the trait in question.

*Excerpt from *The Mind and Society* by Vilfredo Pareto, edited by Arthur Livingston. Translated by Andrew Bongiorno and Arthur Livingston. Volume Three: Theory of Derivations. Copyright 1935 by Harcourt, Brace and Company, Inc.

Let us assume that in every branch of human activity each individual is given an index which stands as a sign of his capacity, very much the way grades are given in the various subjects in examinations in school. The highest type of lawyer, for instance, will be given 10. The man who does not get a client will be given 1—reserving zero for the man who is an out-and-out idiot. To the man who has made his millions—honestly or dishonestly as the case may be—we will give 10. To the man who has earned his thousands we will give 6; to such as just manage to keep out of the poor-house, 1, keeping zero for those who get in. To the woman "in politics," such as the Aspasia of Pericles, the Maintenon of Louis XIV, the Pompadour of Louis XV, who has managed to infatuate a man of power and play a part in the man's career, we shall give some higher number, such as 8 or 9; to the strumpet who merely satisfies the senses of such a man and exerts no influence on public affairs, we shall give zero. To a clever rascal who knows how to fool people and still keep clear of the penitentiary, we shall give 8, 9, or 10, according to the number of geese he has plucked and the amount of money he has been able to get out of them. To the sneak-thief who snatches a piece of silver from a restaurant table and runs away into the arms of a policeman, we shall give 1. To a poet like Carducci we shall give 8 or 9 according to our tastes; to a scribbler who puts people to rout with his sonnets we shall give zero. For chess-players we can get very precise indices, noting what matches, and how many, they have won. And so on for all the branches of human activity.

We are speaking, remember, of an actual, not a potential, state. If at an English examination a pupil says: "I could know English very well if I chose to; I do not know any because I have never seen fit to learn," the examiner replies: "I am not interested in your alibi. The grade for what you know is zero." If, similarly, someone says: "So-and-so does not steal, not because he couldn't, but because he is a gentleman," we reply: "Very well, we admire him for his self-control, but his grade as a thief is zero."

There are people who worship Napoleon Bonaparte as a god. There are people who hate him as the lowest of criminals. Which are right? We do not choose to solve that question in connexion with a quite different matter. Whether Napoleon was a good man or a bad man, he was certainly not an idiot, nor a man of little account, as millions of others are. He had exceptional qualities, and that is enough for us to give him a high ranking, though without prejudice of any sort to questions that might be raised as to the ethics of his qualities or their social utility.

In short, we are here as usual resorting to scientific analysis, which distinguishes one problem from another and studies each one separately. As usual, again, we are replacing imperceptible variations in absolutely exact numbers with the sharp variations corresponding to groupings by class, just as in examinations those who are passed are sharply and arbitrarily distinguished from those who are "failed," and just as in the matter of physical age we distinguish children from young people, the young from the aged.

So let us make a class of the people who have the highest indices in their branch of activity, and to that class give the name of *élite*.

For the particular investigation with which we are engaged, a study of the social equilibrium, it will help if we further divide that class into two classes: a *governing élite*, comprising individuals who directly or indirectly play some considerable part in government, and a *non-governing élite* comprising the rest.

A chess champion is certainly a member of the *élite*, but it is no less certain that his merits as a chess-player do not open the doors to political influence for him; and hence unless he has other qualities to win him that distinction, he is not a member of the governing *élite*. Mistresses of absolute monarchs have oftentimes been members of the *élite*, either because of their beauty or because of their intellectual endowments; but only a few of them, who have had, in addition, the particular talents required by politics, have played any part in government.

So we get two strata in a population: (1) A lower stratum, the *non-élite*, with whose possible influence on government we are not just here concerned; then (2) a higher stratum, *the élite*, which is divided into two: (*a*) a *governing élite;* (b) a non-governing *élite*.

In the concrete, there are no examinations whereby each person is assigned to his proper place in these various classes. That deficiency is made up for by other means, by various sorts of labels that serve the purpose after a fashion. Such labels are the rule even where there are examinations. The label "lawyer" is affixed to a man who is supposed to know something about the law and often does, though sometimes again he is an ignoramus. So, the governing *elite* contains individuals who wear labels appropriate to political offices of a certain altitude—ministers, Senators, Deputies, chief justices, generals, colonels, and so on—making the apposite exceptions for those who have found their way into that exalted company without possessing qualities corresponding to the labels they wear.

Such exceptions are much more numerous than the exceptions among lawyers, physicians, engineers, millionaires (who have made their own money), artists of distinction, and so on; for the reason, among others, that in these latter departments of human activity the labels are won directly by each individual, whereas in the *elite* some of the labels—the label of wealth, for instance—are hereditary. In former times there were hereditary labels in the governing *élite* also—in our day hardly more than the label of king remains in that status; but if direct inheritance has disappeared, inheritance is still powerful indirectly; and an individual who has inherited a sizable patrimony can easily be named Senator in certain countries, or can get himself elected to the parliament by buying votes or, on occasion, by wheedling voters with assurances that he is a democrat of democrats, a Socialist, an Anarchist. Wealth, family, or social connexions also help in many other cases to win the label of the *élite* in general, or of the governing *élite* in particular, for persons who otherwise hold no claim upon it.

In societies where the social unit is the family the label worn by the head of the family also benefits all other members. In Rome, the man who became Emperor generally raised his freedmen to the higher class, and oftentimes, in fact, to the governing *élite*. For that matter, now more, now fewer, of the freedmen taking part in the Roman government possessed qualities good or bad that justified their wearing the labels which they had won through imperial bounty. In our societies, the social unit is the individual; but the place that the individual occupies in society also benefits his wife, his children, his connexions, his friends.

If all these deviations from type were of little importance, they might be disregarded, as they are virtually disregarded in cases where a diploma is required for the practice of a profession. Everyone knows that there are persons who do not deserve their diplomas, but experience shows that on the whole such exceptions may be overlooked.

One might, further, from certain points of view at least, disregard deviations if they remained more or less constant quantitatively—if there were only a negligible variation in proportions between the total of a class and the people who wear its label without possessing the qualities corresponding.

As a matter of fact, the real cases that we have to consider in our societies differ from those two. The deviations are not so *few* that they can be disregarded. Then again, their number is variable, and the variations give rise to situations having an important bearing on the social equilibrium. We are therefore required to make a special study of them.

Furthermore, the manner in which the various groups in a population intermix has to be considered. In moving from one group to another an individual generally brings with him certain inclinations, sentiments, attitudes, that he has acquired in the group from which he comes, and that circumstance cannot be ignored.

To this mixing, in the particular case in which only two groups, the *élite* and the *non-élite*, are envisaged, the term "circulation of élites" has been applied—in French, *circulation des élites* [or in more general terms "class-circulation"].

In conclusion we must pay special attention (1), in the case of one single group, to the proportions between the total of the group and the number of individuals who are nominally members of it but do not possess the qualities requisite for effective membership; and then (2), in the case of various groups, to the ways in which transitions from one group to the other occur, and to the intensity of that movement—that is to say, to the velocity of the circulation.

Velocity in circulation has to be considered not only absolutely but also in relation to the supply of and the demand for certain social elements. A country that is always at peace does not require many soldiers in its governing class, and the production of generals may be overexuberant as compared with the demand. But when a country is in a state of continuous warfare many soldiers are necessary, and though production remains at the same level it may not meet the demand. That, we might note in passing, has been one of the causes for the collapse of many aristocracies.

Another example. In a country where there is little industry and little commerce, the supply of individuals possessing in high degree the qualities requisite for those types of activity exceeds the demand. Then industry and commerce develop and the supply, though remaining the same, no longer meets the demand.

We must not confuse the *state of law* with the state of fact. The latter alone, or almost alone, has a bearing on the social equilibrium. There are many examples of castes that are legally closed, but into which, in point of fact, new-comers make their way, and often in large numbers. On the other hand, what difference does it make if a caste is legally open, but conditions *de facto* prevent new accessions to it? If a person who acquires wealth thereby becomes a member of the governing class, but no one gets rich, it is as if the class were closed; and if only a few get rich, it is as if the law erected serious barriers against access to the caste. Something of that sort was observable towards the end of the Roman Empire. People who acquired wealth entered the order of the curials. But only a few individuals made any money. Theoretically we might examine any number of groups. Practically we have to confine ourselves to the more important. We shall proceed by successive approximations, starting with the simple and going on to the complex.

Higher class and lower class in general. The least we can do is to divide society into two strata: a higher stratum, which usually contains the rulers, and a lower stratum, which usually contains the ruled. That fact is so obvious that it has always forced itself even upon the most casual observation, and so for the circulation of individuals between the two strata. Even Plato had an inkling of class-circulation and tried to regulate it artificially. The "new man," the upstart, the *parvenu,* has always been a subject of interest, and literature has analyzed him unendingly. Here, then, we are merely giving a more exact form to things that have long been perceived more or less vaguely. Above, we noted a varying distribution of residues in the various social groupings, and chiefly in the higher and the lower class. Such heterogeneousness is a fact perceived by the most superficial glance.

The upper stratum of society, the *élite*, nominally contains certain groups of peoples, not always very sharply defined, that are called aristocracies. There are cases in which the majority of individuals belonging to such aristocracies actually possess the qualities requisite for remaining there; and then again there are cases where considerable numbers of the individuals making up the class do not possess those requisites. Such people may occupy more or less important places in the governing *élite* or they may be barred from it.

In the beginning, military, religious, and commercial aristocraries and plutocracies—with a few exceptions not worth considering—must have constituted parts of the governing *élite* and sometimes have made up the whole of it. The victorious warrior, the prosperous merchant, the opulent plutocrat, were men of such parts, each in his own field, as to be superior to the average individual. Under those circumstances the label corresponded to an actual capacity. But as time goes by, considerable, sometimes very considerable, differences arise between the capacity and the label; while on the other hand, certain aristocracies originally figuring prominently in the rising *élite* end by constituting an insignificant element in it. That has happened especially to military aristocracies.

Aristocracies do not last. Whatever the causes, it is an incontestable fact that after a certain length of time they pass away. History is a graveyard of aristocracies. The Athenian "People" was an aristocracy as compared with the remainder of a population of resident aliens and slaves. It vanished without leaving any descent. The various aristocracies of Rome vanished in their time. So did the aristocracies of the Barbarians. Where, in France, are the descendants of the Frankish conquerors? The genealogies of the English nobility have been very exactly kept; and they show that very few families still remain to claim descent from the comrades of William the Conqueror. The rest have vanished. In Germany the aristocracy of the present day is very largely made up of descendants of vassals of the lords of old. The populations of European countries have increased enormously during the past few centuries. It is as certain as certain can be that the aristocracies have not increased in proportion.

They decay not in numbers only. They decay also in quality, in the sense that they lose their vigour, that there is a decline in the proportions of the residues which enabled them to win their power and hold it. The governing class is restored not only in numbers, but—and that is the more important thing—in quality, by families rising from the lower classes and bringing with them the vigour and the proportions of residues necessary for keeping themselves in power. It is also restored by the loss of its more degenerate members.

If one of those movements comes to an end, or worse still, if they both come to an end, the governing class crashes to ruin and often sweeps the whole of a nation along with it. Potent cause of disturbance in the equilibrium is the accumulation of superior elements in the lower classes and, conversely, of inferior elements in the higher classes. If human aristocracies were like thorough-breds among animals, which reproduce themselves over long periods of time with approximately the same traits, the history of the human race would be something altogether different from the history we know.

In virtue of class-circulation, the governing *élite* is always in a state of slow and continuous transformation. It flows on like a river, never being today what it was yesterday. From time to time sudden and violent disturbances occur. There is a flood—the river overflows its banks. Afterwards, the new governing *élite* again resumes its slow transformation. The flood has subsided, the river is again flowing normally in its wonted bed.

Revolutions come about through accumulations in the higher strata of society—either because of a slowing-down in class-circulation, or from other causes—of decadent elements no longer possessing the residues suitable for keeping them in power, and shrinking from the use of force; while meantime in the lower strata of society elements of superior quality are coming to the fore, possessing residues suitable for exercising the functions of government and willing enough to use force.

In general, in revolutions the members of the lower strata are captained by leaders from the higher strata, because the latter possess the intellectual qualities required for outlining a tactic, while lacking the combative residues supplied by the individuals from the lower strata.

Violent movements take place by fits and starts, and effects therefore do not follow immediately on their causes. After a governing class, or a nation, has maintained itself for long periods of time on force and acquired great wealth, it may subsist for some time still without using force, buying off its adversaries and paying not only in gold, but also in terms of the dignity and respect that it had formerly enjoyed and which constitute, as it were, a capital. In the first stages of decline, power is maintained by bargainings and concessions, and people are so deceived into thinking that that policy can be carried on indefinitely. So the decadent Roman Empire bought peace of the Barbarians with money and honours. So Louis XVI, in France, squandering in a very short time an ancestral inheritance of love, respect, and almost religious reverence for the monarchy, managed, by making repeated concessions, to be the King of the Revolution. So the English aristocracy managed to prolong its term of power in the second half of the nineteenth century down to the dawn of its decadence, which was heralded by the "Parliament Bill" in the first years of the twentieth.

33

The Iron Law of Oligarchy*

Robert Michels

Socialists of the subsequent epoch, and above all revolutionary socialists, while not denying the possibility, in the remote future, of a democratic government by majority, absolutely denied that such a government could exist in the concrete present. Bakunin opposed any participation of the working class in elections. He was convinced that in a society where the people, the mass of the wage-earners, is under the economic dominion of a minority consisting of possessors, the freest of electoral systems could be nothing more than an illusion. Democracy is even regarded as the worst of all the bourgeois regimes. The republic, which is presented to us as the most elevated form of bourgeois democracy, was said by Proudhon to possess to an extreme degree that fanatical and petty authoritative spirit (*zèle gouvernemental*) which believes that it can dare everything with impunity, being always ready to justify its despotic acts under the convenient pretext that they are done for the good of the republic and in the general interest. Even the political revolution signifies merely "un dèplacement de l'autoritè."

The only scientific doctrine which can boast of ability to make an effective reply to all the theories, old or new, affirming the immanent necessity for the perennial existence of the "political class" is the Marxist doctrine. In this doctrine the state is identified with the ruling class—an identification from which Bakunin, Marx's pupil, drew the extreme consequences. The state is merely the executive committee of the ruling class.

The Marxist theory of the state, when conjoined with a faith in the revolutionary energy of the working class and in the democratic effects of the socialization of the means of production, leads logically to the idea of a new social order which to the school of Mosca appears utopian. According to the Marxists the capitalist mode of production transforms the great majority of the population into proletarians, and thus digs its own grave. As soon as it has attained maturity, the proletariat will seize political power, and will immediately transform private property into state property.

The constitution of a new dominant minority would, in addition, be especially facilitated by the manner in which, according to the Marxist conception of the revolution, the social transformation is to be effected. Marx held that the period between the destruction of capitalist society and the establishment of communist society would be

*Excerpts from *Political Parties: A Sociological Study of the Oliogarchical Tendencies of Modern Democracy* by Robert Michels, translated by Eden and Cedar Paul. First published in 1915. Glencoe, IL: The Free Press.

bridged by a period of revolutionary transition in the economic field, to which would correspond a period of political transition, "when the state could not be anything other than the revolutionary dictatorship of the proletariat." To put the matter less euphemistically, there will then exist a dictatorship in the hands of those leaders who have been sufficiently astute and sufficiently powerful to grasp the sceptre of dominion in the name of socialism, and to wrest it from the hands of the expiring bourgeois society.

There is little difference, as far as practical results are concerned, between individual dictatorship and the dictatorship of a group of oligarchs. Now it is manifest that the concept *dictatorship* is the direct antithesis of the concept *democracy*. The attempt to make dictatorship serve the ends of democracy is tantamount to the endeavour to utilize war as the most efficient means for the defence of peace, or to employ alcohol in the struggle against alcoholism. It is extremely probable that a social group which had secured control of the instruments of collective power would do all that was possible to retain that control. Theophrastus noted long ago that the strongest desire of men who have attained to leadership in a popularly governed state is not so much the acquirement of personal wealth as the gradual establishment of their own sovereignty at the expense of popular sovereignty. The danger is imminent lest the social revolution should replace the visible and tangible dominant classes which now exist and act openly, by a clandestine demagogic oligarchy, pursuing its ends under the cloak of equality.

In practice, the acceptance of the programme does not suffice to abolish the conflict of interests between capital and labour. Among the members belonging to higher social strata who have made their adhesion to the political organization of the working class, there will be some who will, when the occasion demands it, know how to sacrifice themselves, who will be able to unclass themselves. The majority of such persons, however, notwithstanding their outward community of ideas with the proletariat, will continue to pursue economic interests opposed to those of the proletariat. There is, in fact, a conflict of interests, and the decision in this conflict will be determined by the relationship which the respective interests bear towards the principal necessities of life. Consequently it is by no means impossible that an economic conflict may arise between the bourgeois members and the proletarian members of the party, and that as this conflict extends it will culminate in political dissensions. Economic antagonism stifles the ideological superstructure. The programme then becomes a dead letter, and beneath the banner of "socialism" and within the bosom of the party, a veritable class struggle goes on. We learn from actual experience that in their conduct towards persons in their employ the bourgeois socialists do not always subordinate personal interests to those of their adoptive class. When the party includes among its members the owners of factories and workshops, it may be noticed that these, notwithstanding personal goodwill and notwithstanding the pressure which is exercised on them by the party, have the same economic conflict with their employees as have those employers whose convictions harmonize with their economic status, and who think not as socialists but as bourgeois.

But there exists yet another danger. The leadership of the socialist party may fall into the hands of persons whose practical tendencies are in opposition with the programme of the working class, so that the labour movement will be utilized for the service of interests diametrically opposed to those of the proletariat. This danger is especially great in countries where the working-class party cannot dispense with the aid and guidance of capitalists who are not economically dependent upon the party; it is least conspicuous where the party has no need of such elements, or can at any rate avoid admitting them to leadership.

When the leaders, whether derived from the bourgeoisie or from the working class, are attached to the party organism as employees, their economic interest coincides as a rule with the interest of the party. This, however, serves to eliminate only one aspect of the danger. Another aspect, graver because more general, depends upon the opposition which inevitably arises between the leaders and the rank and file as the party grows in strength.

The party, regarded as an entity, as a piece of mechanism, is not necessarily identifiable with the totality of its members, and still less so with the class to which these belong. The party is created as a means to secure an end. Having, however, become an end in itself, endowed with aims and interests of its own, it undergoes detachment, from the teleological point of view, from the class which it represents. In a party, it is far from obvious that the interests of the masses which have combined to form the party will coincide with the interests of the bureaucracy in which the party becomes personified. The interests of the body of employees are always conservative, and in a given political situation these interests may dictate a defensive and even a reactionary policy when the interests of the working class demand a bold and aggressive policy; in other cases, although these are very rare, the roles may be reversed. By a universally applicable social law, every organ of the collectivity, brought into existence through the need for the division of labour, creates for itself, as soon as it becomes consolidated, interests peculiar to itself. The existence of these special interests involves a necessary conflict with the interests of the collectivity. Nay, more, social strata fulfilling peculiar functions tend to become isolated, to produce organs fitted for the defence of their own peculiar interests. In the long run they tend to undergo transformation into distinct classes.

The principle that one dominant class inevitably succeeds to another, and the law deduced from that principle that oligarchy is, as it were, a preordained form of the common life of great social aggregates, far from conflicting with or replacing the materialist conception of history, completes that conception and reinforces it. There is no essential contradiction between the doctrine that history is the record of a continued series of class struggles and the doctrine that class struggles invariably culminate in the creation of new oligarchies which undergo fusion with the old. The existence of a political class does not conflict with the essential content of Marxism, considered not as an economic dogma but as a philosophy of history ; for in each particular instance the dominance of a political class arises as the resultant of the relationships between the different social forces competing for supremacy, these forces being of course considered dynamically and not quantitatively.

34

The Crowd Mind*

Gustave Le Bon

In its ordinary sense the word "crowd" means a gathering of individuals of whatever nationality, profession, or sex, and whatever be the chances that have brought them together. From the psychological point of view the expression "crowd" assumes quite a different signification. Under certain given circumstances, and only under those circumstances, an agglomeration of men presents new characteristics very different from those of the individuals composing it. The sentiments and ideas of all the persons in the gathering take one and the same direction, and their conscious personality vanishes. A collective mind is formed, doubtless transitory, but presenting very clearly defined characteristics. The gathering has thus become what, in the absence of a better expression, I will call an organised crowd, or, if the term is considered preferable, a psychological crowd. It forms a single being, and is subjected to the *law of the mental unity of crowds.*

Among the psychological characteristics of crowds there are some that they may present in common with isolated individuals, and others, on the contrary, which are absolutely peculiar to them and are only to be met with in collectivities. It is these special characteristics that we shall study, first of all, in order to show their importance.

The most striking peculiarity presented by a psychological crowd is the following: Whoever be the individuals that compose it, however like or unlike be their mode of life, their occupations, their character, or their intelligence, the fact that they have been transformed into a crowd puts them in possession of a sort of collective mind which makes them feel, think, and act in a manner quite different from that in which each individual of them would feel, think, and act were he in a state of isolation.

Different causes determine the appearance of these characteristics peculiar to crowds, and not possessed by isolated individuals. The first is that the individual forming part of a crowd acquires, solely from numerical considerations, a sentiment of invincible power which allows him to yield to instincts which, had he been alone, he would perforce have kept under restraint. He will be the less disposed to check himself from the consideration that, a crowd being anonymous, and in consequence irresponsible, the sentiment of responsibility which always controls individuals disappears entirely.

*Excerpts from *The Crowd: A Study of the Popular Mind* by Gustave LeBon, With a new Introduction by Robert A. Nye. Originally published in 1895.

The second cause, which is contagion, also intervenes to determine the manifestation in crowds of their special characteristics, and at the same time the trend they are to take. Contagion is a phenomenon of which it is easy to establish the presence, but that it is not easy to explain. It must be classed among those phenomena of a hypnotic order, which we shall shortly study. In a crowd every sentiment and act is contagious, and contagious to such a degree that an individual readily sacrifices his personal interest to the collective interest. This is an aptitude very contrary to his nature, and of which a man is scarcely capable, except when he makes part of a crowd.

A third cause, and by far the most important, determines in the individuals of a crowd special characteristics which are quite contrary at times to those presented by the isolated individual. I allude to that suggestibility of which, moreover, the contagion mentioned above is neither more nor less than an effect.

To understand this phenomenon it is necessary to bear in mind certain recent physiological discoveries. We know to-day that by various processes an individual may be brought into such a condition that, having entirely lost his conscious personality, he obeys all the suggestions of the operator who has deprived him of it, and commits acts in utter contradiction with his character and habits. The most careful observations seem to prove that an individual immerged for some length of time in a crowd in action soon finds himself—either in consequence of the magnetic influence given out by the crowd, or from some other cause of which we are ignorant—in a special state, which much resembles the state of fascination in which the hypnotised individual finds himself in the hands of the hypnotiser. The activity of the brain being paralysed in the case of the hypnotised subject, the latter becomes the slave of all the unconscious activities of his spinal cord, which the hypnotiser directs at will. The conscious personality has entirely vanished; will and discernment are lost. All feelings and thoughts are bent in the direction determined by the hypnotiser.

Such also is approximately the state of the individual forming part of a psychological crowd. He is no longer conscious of his acts. In his case, as in the case of the hypnotised subject, at the same time that certain faculties are destroyed, others may be brought to a high degree of exaltation. Under the influence of a suggestion, he will undertake the accomplishment of certain acts with irresistible impetuosity. This impetuosity is the more irresistible in the case of crowds than in that of the hypnotised subject, from the fact that, the suggestion being the same for all the individuals of the crowd, it gains in strength by reciprocity. The individualities in the crowd who might possess a personality sufficiently strong to resist the suggestion are too few in number to struggle against the current. At the utmost, they may be able to attempt a diversion by means of different suggestions. It is in this way, for instance, that a happy expression, an image opportunely evoked, have occasionally deterred crowds from the most bloodthirsty acts.

We see, then, that the disappearance of the conscious personality, the predominance of the unconscious personality, the turning by means of suggestion and contagion of feelings and ideas in an identical direction, the tendency immediately to transform the suggested ideas into acts; these we see, are the principal characteristics of the individual forming part of a crowd. He is no longer himself, but has become an automaton who has ceased to be guided by his will.

35

The Laws of Imitation*

Gabriel Tarde

Our starting-point lies here in the re-inspiring initiatives which bring new wants, together with new satisfactions, into the world, and which then, through spontaneous and unconscious or artificial and deliberate imitation, propagate or tend to propagate, themselves, at a more or less rapid, but regular, rate, like a wave of light, or like a family of termites. The regularity to which I refer is not in the least apparent in social things until they are resolved into their several elements, when it is found to lie in the simplest of them, in combinations of distinct inventions, in flashes of genius which have been accumulated and changed into commonplace lights. I confess that this is an extremely difficult analysis. Socially, everything is either invention or imitation.

All resemblances of social origin in society are the direct or indirect fruit of the various forms of imitation,—custom-imitation or fashion-imitation, sympathy-imitation or obedience-imitation, precept-imitation or education-imitation, naive imitation, deliberate imitation, etc. In this lies the excellence of the contemporaneous method of explaining doctrines and institutions through their history.

Let me point out a new order of analogies. Imitations are modified in passing from one race or nation to another, like vibrations or living types in passing from one environment to another. We see this, for example, in the transition of certain words, or religious myths, or military secrets, or literary forms, from the Hindoos to the Germans, or from the Latins to the Gauls. In certain cases, the record of these modifications has been sufficiently full to suggest what their general and uniform trend has been. This is especially true of language; Grimm's, or, better still, Raynouard's, laws might well be called the laws of linguistic refraction.

Statistics gives us a sort of empirical law or graphical formula for the very complex causes of the particular spread of every kind of imitation. We must now consider those general laws, laws which are really worthy the name of science, which govern all imitations, and to this end we must study, one by one, the different categories of causes which we have heretofore merged together.

Our problem is to learn why, given one hundred different innovations conceived of at the same time—innovations in the forms of words, in mythological ideas, in industrial processes, etc.—ten will spread abroad, while ninety will be forgotten.

Now, social causes are of two kinds, the logical and the non-logical. This distinction is of

*Excerpts from *The Laws of Imitation* by Gabriel Tarde. Translated from the Second French Edition by Elsie Clews Parsons, with an Introduction by Franklin H. Giddings. New York: Henry Holt & Company, 1903.

the greatest importance. Logical causes operate whenever an individual prefers a given innovation to others because he thinks it is more useful or more true than others, that is, more in accord than they are with the aims or principles that have already found a place in his mind (through imitation, of course). In such instances, the old or new inventions or discoveries are themselves the only question; they are isolated from any prestige or discredit which may have attached to those circulating them or to the time and place of their origin. But logical action is very rarely untrammelled in this way. In general, the extra-logical influences to which I have referred interfere in the choice of the examples to be followed, and often, as we shall see further on, the poorest innovations, from the point of view of logic, are selected because of their place, or even date or birth.

Invention and imitation are, as we know, the elementary social acts. But what is the social substance or force through which this act is accomplished and of which it is merely the form? In other words, what is invented or imitated? The *thing* which is invented, the *thing* which is imitated, is always an idea or a volition, a judgment or a purpose, which embodies a certain amount of *belief and desire*. And here we have, in fact, the very soul of words, of religious prayers, of state administration, of the articles of a code, of moral duties, of industrial achievements or of artistic processes. Desire and belief: they are the substance and the force, they are the two psychological quantities which are found at the bottom of all the *sensational* qualities with which they combine; and when invention and then imitation takes possession of them in order to organise and use them, they also are the real social quantities. Societies are organised according to the agreement or opposition of beliefs which reinforce or limit one another. Social institutions depend entirely upon these conditions. Societies function according to the competition or co-operation of their desires or wants. Beliefs, principally religious and moral beliefs, but juristic and political beliefs as well, and even linguistic beliefs (for how many acts of faith are implied in the lightest talk and what an irresistible although unconscious power of persuasion our mother tongue, a true mother indeed, exerts over us), are the plastic forces of societies. Economic or aesthetic wants are their functional forces.

Suppose that a discovery, an invention, has appeared. There are straightway two facts for us to note about it: its gains in faith, as it spreads from one person to another, and the losses in faith to which it subjects the invention which had the same object or satisfied the same desire when it intervened. Such an encounter gives rise to a logical duel. For example, cuneiform writing spread for a long time undisturbed throughout Central Asia, while Phoenician writing had the same career in the Mediterranean basin. But one day these two alphabets came into conflict over the territory of the former; and cuneiform writing slowly receded, but did not disappear until about the first century of our era.

All imitations in which logic has no place fall into two great categories, namely, credulity and docility, imitation of belief and imitation of desires. It may see strange to call passive adherence to the idea of another, imitation; but if, as I have said, it matters little whether the reflection of one brain upon another be active or passive in character, the extension which I give to the usual meaning of this word is highly legitimate. If we say that the scholar imitates his master when he repeats his spoken words, why should we not say that the former has already imitated the latter as soon as he has adopted in thought the idea which he afterwards expresses in speech? It may also surprise the reader to find that I consider obedience a kind of imitation; but this assimilation, which can, at any rate, be easily justified, is necessary, and it alone permits, the full significance of the phenomenon of imitation to be recognised. When one person copies another, when one class begins to pattern its dress, its furniture, and its amusements after those of another, it means that it has already borrowed from, the latter the wants and sentiments of which these methods of life are the outward manifestations. Consequently it can and must have borrowed the latter's volitions, that is, have willed in accordance with its will.

In this way imitation passes on from one people to another, as well as from one class to another within the same people. Do we ever see one class which is in contact with, but which has never, hypothetically, been subject to the control of, another determine to copy its accent, its dress, its furniture, and its buildings, and end by embracing its principles and beliefs? This would invert the universal and necessary order of things. The strongest proof, indeed, that imitation spreads from within to without is to be found in the fact that in the relations between different classes, envy never precedes obedience and trust, but is always, on the contrary, the sign and the result of a previous state of obedience and trust. Blind and docile devotion to the Roman patricians, to the Athenian eupatrides, or to the French nobility of the old regime preceded the envy. *i. e.,* the desire to imitate them externally, which they came to inspire. Envy is the symptom of a social transformation which, in bringing classes together and in lessening the inequality of their resources, renders possible not only the transmission, as before, of their thoughts and aims, not only patriotic or religious communion and participation in the same worship, but the radiation of their luxury and well-being as well. Obedience, the cause, engenders envy, the effect. Consequently, when, for example, the ancient plebeians or the middle class Guelphs in the Italian cities of the Middle Ages, came into power, their manner of using it was an evidence and a continuation of their preceding bondage, since the oppressive laws which they enacted against the sometime reigning aristocracies were suggested by the need which they felt to copy their ancient masters.

It will be observed that obedience and trust, the subjective imitation of a recognised superior, is prompted by a devotion and, so to speak, loving admiration, just as the objective imitation of a questioned or disowned superior results from envious disparagement; and it is clear that communities pass from love to covert envy or from admiration to open contempt in respect to their old masters, but that they never pass back, as far as the latter are concerned, at any rate, from envy to love or from contempt to admiration. To satisfy their persistent need of loving and admiring, they must continue to raise up new idols for themselves, from time to time, only to shatter them later on.

The profoundly subjective character that is taken on from the earliest times by human imitation, the privilege which it has of binding souls together from their very centres, involves, as may be seen from what has preceded, the growth of human inequality and the formation of a social hierarchy. This was inevitable, since the relation of model to copy developed into that of apostle to neophyte, of master to subject. Consequently, from the very fact that imitation proceeded from the inside to the outside of the model, it had to consist in a *descent* of example, in a descent from the superior to the inferior. This is a second law that is partly implied in the first.

Whatever may be the organisation of a society, aristocratic or democratic, we may be sure, if we see imitation making rapid strides in it, that the inequality between its different levels is very great, besides being more or less apparent. And we have only to learn the set of its main current of examples, overlooking the unimportant *back eddies,* to discover the real social power. If the nation is on an aristocratic basis the thing is very simple. Given the opportunity, a nobility will always and everywhere imitate its leaders, its kings or suzerains, and the people, likewise, given the opportunity, its nobility.

In periods when custom is in the ascendant, men are more infatuated about their country than about their time; for it is the past which is pre-eminently praised. In ages when fashion rules, men are prouder, on the contrary, of their time than of their country.

The supreme law of imitation seems to be its tendency towards indefinite progression. But unless this tendency be backed up by the coming together of inventions which are logically and teleologically auxiliary, or by the help of the prestige which belongs to alleged superiorities, it is checked by the different obstacles which it has successively to overcome or to turn aside. These obstacles are the logical and teleological contradictions which are opposed to it by other inventions, or the barriers which have been raised up by a thousand causes, by racial pride and prejudice, for the most part, between different families and tribes and peoples and, within each people or tribe, between different classes.

But, at the same time, Tradition and Custom, the conservative forms of imitation, have been fixing and perpetuating its new acquisitions, and consolidating its increments in the heart of every class of people that has been raised up through the example of higher classes or of more civilised neighbours. At the same time, too, every germ of imitation which may have been secreted in the brain of any imitator in the form of a new belief or aspiration, of a new idea or faculty, has been steadily developing in outward signs, in words and acts which, according to the law of the march from within to without, have penetrated into his entire nervous and muscular systems.

36

THE HERD INSTINCT*

SIGMUND FREUD

It might be said that the intense emotional ties which we observe in groups are quite sufficient to explain one of their characteristics—the lack of independence and initiative in their members, the similarity in the reactions of all of them, their reduction, so to speak, to the level of group individuals. But if we look at it as a whole, a group shows us more than this. Some of its features—the weakness of intellectual ability, the lack of emotional restraint, the incapacity for moderation and delay, the inclination to exceed every limit in the expression of emotion and to work it off completely in the form of action—these and similar features, which we find so impressively described in Le Bon, show an unmistakable picture of a regression of mental activity to an earlier stage such as we are not surprised to find among savages or children. A regression of this sort is in particular an essential characteristic of common groups, while, as we have heard, in organized and artificial groups it can to a large extent be checked.

We thus have an impression of a state in which an individual's separate emotion and personal intellectual act are too weak to come to anything by themselves and are absolutely obliged to wait till they are reinforced through being repeated in a similar way in the other members of the group. We are reminded of how many of these phenomena of dependence are part of the normal constitution of human society, of how little originality and personal courage are to be found in it, of how much every individual is ruled by those attitudes of the group mind which exhibit themselves in such forms as racial characteristics, class prejudices, public opinion, etc. The influence of suggestion becomes a greater riddle for us when we admit that it is not exercised only by the leader, but by every individual upon every other individual; and we must reproach ourselves with having unfairly emphasized the relation to the leader and with having kept the other factor of mutual suggestion too much in the background.

After this encouragement to modesty, we shall be inclined to listen to another voice, which promises us an explanation based upon simpler grounds. Such a one is to be found in Trotter's thoughtful book upon the herd instinct, concerning which my only regret is that it does not

*Excerpts from *Group Psychology and the Analysis of the Ego* by Sigmund Freud, translation by James Strachey. New York: Boni and Liveright Publishers, 1922.

entirely escape the antipathies that were set loose by the recent great war.

Trotter derives the mental phenomena that are described as occurring in groups from a herd instinct ('gregariousness'), which is innate in human beings just as in other species of animals. Biologically this gregariousness is an analogy to multicellularity and as it were a continuation of it. From the standpoint of the libido theory it is a further manifestation of the inclination, which proceeds from the libido, and which is felt by all living beings of the same kind, to combine in more and more comprehensive units. The individual feels 'incomplete' if he is alone. The dread shown by small children would seem already to be an expression of this herd instinct. Opposition to the herd is as good as separation from it, and is therefore anxiously avoided. But the herd turns away from anything that is new or unusual. The herd instinct would appear to be something primary, something 'which cannot be split up'.

Trotter gives as the list of instincts which he considers as primary those of self-preservation, of nutrition, of sex, and of the herd. The last often comes into opposition with the others. The feelings of guilt and of duty are the peculiar possessions of a gregarious animal. Trotter also derives from the herd instinct the repressive forces which psycho-analysis has shown to exist in the ego, and from the same source accordingly the resistances which the physician comes up against in psycho-analytic treatment. Speech owes its importance to its aptitude for mutual understanding in the herd, and upon it the identification of the individuals with one another largely rests.

While Le Bon is principally concerned with typical transient group formations, and McDougall with stable associations, Trotter has chosen as the centre of his interest the most generalised form of assemblage in which man, that ζώονπολιτικόν, passes his life, and he gives us its psychological basis. But Trotter is under no necessity of tracing back the herd instinct, for he characterizes it as primary and not further reducible. Boris Sidis's attempt, to which he refers, at tracing the herd instinct back to suggestibility is fortunately superfluous as far as he is concerned; it is an explanation of a familiar and unsatisfactory type, and the converse proposition—that suggestibility is a derivative of the herd instinct—would seem to me to throw far more light on the subject.

But Trotter's exposition, with even more justice than the others', is open to the objection that it takes too little account of the leader's part in a group, while we incline rather to the opposite judgement, that it is impossible to grasp the nature of a group if the leader is disregarded. The herd instinct leaves no room at all for the leader; he is merely thrown in along with the herd, almost by chance; it follows, too, that no path leads from this instinct to the need for a God; the herd is without a herdsman. But besides this Trotter's exposition can be undermined psychologically; that is to say, it can be made at all events probable that the herd instinct is not irreducible, that it is not primary in the same sense as the instinct of self-preservation and the sexual instinct.

It is naturally no easy matter to trace the ontogenesis of the herd instinct. The dread which is shown by small children when they are left alone, and which Trotter claims as being already a manifestation of the instinct, nevertheless suggests more readily another interpretation. The dread relates to the child's mother, and later to other familiar persons, and it is the expression of an unfulfilled desire, which the child does not yet know, how to deal with in any way except by turning it into dread. Nor is the child's dread when it is alone pacified by the sight of any haphazard 'member of the herd', but on the contrary it is only brought into existence by the approach of a 'stranger' of this sort. Then for a long time nothing in the nature of herd instinct or group feeling is to be observed in children. Something like it grows up first of all, in a nursery containing many children, out of the children's relation to their parents, and it does so as a reaction to the initial envy with which the elder child receives the younger one. The elder child would certainly like to put its successor jealously aside, to keep it away from the parents, and to rob it of all its privileges; but in face of the fact that this child (like all that come later) is loved by the parents in just the same way, and in consequence of the impossibility of maintaining its hostile attitude without damaging itself, it is forced into identifying itself with the other children. So there grows up in the troop of children a communal or group feeling, which is then further developed at school.

The first demand made by this reaction-formation is for justice, for equal treatment for all. We all know how loudly and implacably this claim is put forward at school. If one cannot be the favourite oneself, at all events nobody else shall be the favourite. This transformation—the replacing of jealousy by a group feeling in the nursery and classroom—might be considered improbable, if the same process could not later on be observed again in other circumstances. We have only to think of the troop of women and girls, all of them in love in an enthusiastically sentimental way, who crowd round a singer or pianist after his performance. It would certainly be easy for each of them to be jealous of the rest; but, in face of their numbers and the consequent impossibility of their reaching the aim of their love, they renounce it, and, instead of pulling out one another's hair, they act as a united group, do homage to the hero of the occasion with their common actions, and would probably be glad to have a share of his flowing locks. Originally rivals, they have succeeded in identifying themselves with one another by means of a similar love for the same object. When, as is usual, a situation in the field of the instincts is capable of various outcomes, we need not be surprised if the actual outcome is one which involves the possibility of a certain amount of satisfaction, while another, even though in itself more obvious, is passed over because the circumstances of life prevent its attaining this aim.

What appears later on in society in the shape of *Gemeingeist, espirt de corps*, 'group spirit', etc., does not belie its derivation from what was originally envy. No one must want to put himself forward, every one must be the same and have the same. Social justice means that we deny ourselves many things so that others may have to do without them as well, or, what is the same thing, may not be able to ask for them. This demand for equality is the root of social conscience and the sense of duty. It reveals itself unexpectedly in the syphilitic's dread of infecting other people, which psycho-analysis has taught us to understand. The dread exhibited by these poor wretches corresponds to their violent struggles against the unconscious wish to spread their infection on to other people; for why should they alone be infected and cut off from so much? why not other people as well? And the same germ is to be found in the pretty anecdote of the judgement of Solomon. If one woman's child is dead, the other shall not have a live one either. The bereaved woman is recognized by this wish.

Thus social feeling is based upon the reversal of what was first a hostile feeling into a positively-toned tie of the nature of an identification. So far as we have hitherto been able to follow the course of events, this reversal appears to be effected under the influence of a common tender tie with a person outside the group. We do not ourselves regard our analysis of identification as exhaustive, but it is enough for our present purpose that we should revert to this one feature—its demand that equalization shall be consistently carried through. We have already heard in the discussion of the two artificial groups, church and army, that their preliminary condition is that all their members should be loved in the same way by one person, the leader. Do not let us forget, however, that the demand for equality in a group applies only to its members and not to the leader. All the members must be equal to one another, but they all want to be ruled by one person. Many equals, who can identify themselves with one another, and a single person superior to them all—that is the situation that we find realised in groups which are capable of subsisting. Let us venture, then, to correct Trotter's pronouncement that man is a herd animal and assert that he is rather a horde animal, an individual creature in a horde led by a chief.

37

The Conscience of Society*

Sigmund Freud

The liberty of the individual is no gift of civilization. It was greatest before there was any civilization, though then, it is true, it had for the most part no value, since the individual was scarcely in a position to defend it. The development of civilization imposes restrictions on it, and justice demands that no one shall escape those restrictions. What makes itself felt in a human community as a desire for freedom may be their revolt against some existing injustice, and so may prove favourable to a further development of civilization; it may remain compatible with civilization. But it may also spring from the remains of their original personality, which is still untamed by civilization and may thus become the basis in them of hostility to civilization. The urge for freedom, therefore, is directed against particular forms and demands of civilization or against civilization altogether. It does not seem as though any influence could induce a man to change his nature into a termite's. No doubt he will always defend his claim to individual liberty against the will of the group. A good part of the struggles of mankind centre round the single task of finding an expedient accommodation—one, that is, that will bring happiness—between this claim of the individual and the cultural claims of the group; and one of the problems that touches the fate of humanity is whether such an accommodation can be reached by means of some particular form of civilization or whether this conflict is irreconcilable.

Men are not gentle creatures who want to be loved, and who at the most can defend themselves if they are attacked; they are, on the contrary, creatures among whose instinctual endowments is to be reckoned a powerful share of aggressiveness. As a result, their neighbour is for them not only a potential helper or sexual object, but also someone who tempts them to satisfy their aggressiveness on him, to exploit his capacity for work without compensation, to use him sexually without his consent, to seize his possessions, to humiliate him, to cause him pain, to torture and to kill him.

The existence of this inclination to aggression, which we can detect in ourselves and justly assume to be present in others, is the factor which disturbs our relations with our neighbour and which forces civilization into such a high expenditure [of energy]. In consequence of this primary mutual hostility of human beings, civilized society is perpetually threatened with

*Excerpts from *Civilization and Its Discontents* by Sigmund Freud. Translated from the German and edited by James Strachey.

disintegration. The interest of work in common would not hold it together; instinctual passions are stronger than reasonable interests. Civilization has to use its utmost efforts in order to set limits to man's aggressive instincts and to hold the manifestations of them in check by psychical reaction-formations. Hence, therefore, the use of methods intended to incite people into identifications and aim-inhibited relationships of love, hence the restriction upon sexual life, and hence too the ideal's commandment to love one's neighbour as oneself—a commandment which is really justified by the fact that nothing else runs so strongly counter to the original nature of man.

If civilization imposes such great sacrifices not only on man's sexuality but on his aggressivity, we can understand better why it is hard for him to be happy in that civilization. In fact, primitive man was better off in knowing no restrictions of instinct. To counterbalance this, his prospects of enjoying this happiness for any length of time were very slender. Civilized man has exchanged a portion of his possibilities of happiness for a portion of security.

In all that follows I adopt the standpoint, therefore, that the inclination to aggression is an original, self-subsisting instinctual disposition in man, and I return to my view that it constitutes the greatest impediment to civilization. At one point in the course of this enquiry I was led to the idea that civilization was a special process which mankind undergoes, and I am still under the influence of that idea. I may now add that civilization is a process in the service of Eros, whose purpose is to combine single human individuals, and after that families, then races, peoples and nations, into one great unity, the unity of mankind. Why this has to happen, we do not know; the work of Eros is precisely this. These collections of men are to be libidinally bound to one another. Necessity alone, the advantages of work in common, will not hold them together. But man's natural aggressive instinct, the hostility of each against all and of all against each, opposes this programme of civilization. This aggressive instinct is the derivative and the main representative of the death instinct which we have found alongside of Eros and which shares world-dominion with it. And now, I think, the meaning of the evolution of civilization is no longer obscure to us. It must present the struggle between Eros and Death, between the instinct of life and the instinct of destruction, as it works itself out in the human species. This struggle is what all life essentially consists of, and the evolution of civilization may therefore be simply described as the struggle for life of the human species.

Another question concerns us more nearly. What means does civilization employ in order to inhibit the aggressiveness which opposes it, to make it harmless, to get rid of it, perhaps? We have already become acquainted with a few of these methods, but not yet with the one that appears to be the most important. This we can study in the history of the development of the individual. What happens in him to render his desire for aggression innocuous? Something very remarkable, which we should never have guessed and which is nevertheless quite obvious. His aggressiveness is introjected, internalized; it is, in point of fact, sent back to where it came from—that is, it is directed towards his own ego. There it is taken over by a portion of the ego, which sets itself over against the rest of the ego as super-ego, and which now, in the form of 'conscience', is ready to put into action against the ego the same harsh aggressiveness that the ego would have liked to satisfy upon other, extraneous individuals. The tension between the harsh super-ego and the ego that is subjected to it, is called by us the sense of guilt; it expresses itself as a need for punishment.

Thus we know of two origins of the sense of guilt: one arising from fear of an authority, and the other, later on, arising from fear of the super-ego. The first insists upon a renunciation of instinctual satisfactions; the second, as well as doing this, presses for punishment, since the continuance of the forbidden wishes cannot be concealed from the super-ego. We have also learned how the severity of the super-ego—the demands of conscience—is to be understood. It is simply a continuation of the severity of the external authority, to which it has succeeded and which it has in part replaced. We now see in what relationship the renunciation of instinct stands to the sense of guilt. Originally, renunciation of instinct was the result of fear of an external authority: one renounced one's satisfactions in order not to lose its love. If one has carried out this renunciation, one is, as it were, quits with the authority and no sense of guilt should remain. But with fear of the superego the case is different. Here, instinctual renunciation is not enough, for the wish persists and cannot be concealed from the super-ego. Thus, in spite of the renunciation that has been made, a sense of guilt comes about. This constitutes a great economic disadvantage in the erection of a super-ego, or, as we may put it, in the formation of a conscience. Instinctual renunciation now no longer has a completely liberating effect; virtuous continence is no longer rewarded with the assurance of love. A threatened external unhappiness—loss of love and punishment on the part of the external authority—has been exchanged for a permanent internal unhappiness, for the tension of the sense of guilt.

In the course of our analytic work we have discovered to our surprise that perhaps every neurosis conceals a quota of unconscious sense of guilt, which in its turn fortifies the symptoms by making use of them as a punishment. It now seems plausible to formulate the following proposition. When an instinctual trend undergoes repression, its libidinal elements are turned into symptoms, and its aggressive components into a sense of guilt. Even if this proposition is only an average approximation to the truth, it is worthy of our interest.

The analogy between the process of civilization and the path of individual development may be extended in an important respect. It can be asserted that the community, too, evolves a super-ego under whose influence cultural development proceeds.

The cultural super-ego has developed its ideals and set up its demands. Among the latter, those which deal with the relations of human beings to one another are comprised under the heading of ethics. People have at all times set the greatest value on ethics, as though they expected that it in particular would produce especially important results. And it does in fact deal with a subject which can easily be recognized as the sorest spot in every civilization. Ethics is thus to be regarded as a therapeutic attempt—as an endeavour to achieve, by means of a command of the super-ego, something which has so far not been achieved by means of any other cultural activities. As we already know, the problem before us is how to get rid of the greatest hindrance to civilization—namely, the constitutional inclination of human beings to be aggressive towards one another; and for that very reason we are especially interested in what is probably the most recent of the cultural commands of the super-ego, the commandment to love one's neighbour as oneself. The commandment is impossible to fulfil; such an enormous inflation of love can only lower its value, not get rid of the difficulty. Civilization pays no attention to all this; it merely admonishes us that the harder it is to obey the precept the more meritorious it is to do so. But, anyone who follows such a precept in present-day civilization only puts himself at a disadvantage *vis-à-vis* the person who disregards it. What a potent obstacle to civilization aggressiveness must be, if the defence against it can cause as much unhappiness as aggressiveness itself!

38

Conspicuous Consumption*

Thorstein Veblen

In what has been said of the evolution of the vicarious leisure class and its differentiation from the general body of the working classes, reference has been made to a further division of labour,— that between different servant classes. One portion of the servant class, chiefly those persons whose occupation is vicarious leisure, come to undertake a new, subsidiary range of duties—the vicarious consumption of goods. The most obvious form in which this consumption occurs is seen in the wearing of liveries and the occupation of spacious servants' quarters. Another, scarcely less obtrusive or less effective form of vicarious consumption, and a much more widely prevalent one, is the consumption of food, clothing, dwelling, and furniture by the lady and the rest of the domestic establishment.

The consumption of luxuries, in the true sense, is a consumption directed to the comfort of the consumer himself, and is, therefore, a mark of the master. Any such consumption by others can take place only on a basis of sufferance. In communities where the popular habits of thought have been profoundly shaped by the patriarchal tradition we may accordingly look for survivals of the tabu on luxuries at least to the extent of a conventional deprecation of their use by the unfree and dependent class. This is more particularly true as regards certain luxuries, the use of which by the dependent class would detract sensibly from the comfort or pleasure of their masters, or which are held to be of doubtful legitimacy on other grounds. In the apprehension of the great conservative middle class of Western civilisation the use of these various stimulants is obnoxious to at least one, if not both, of these objections; and it is a fact too significant to be passed over that it is precisely among these middle classes of the Germanic culture, with their strong surviving sense of the patriarchal proprieties, that the women are to the greatest extent subject to a qualified tabu on narcotics and alcoholic beverages. With many qualifications — with more qualifications as the patriarchal tradition has gradually weakened — the general rule is felt to be right and binding that women should consume only for the benefit of their masters.

With the disappearance of servitude, the number of vicarious consumers attached to any one gentleman tends, on the whole, to decrease. The like is of course true, and perhaps in a still higher degree, of the number of dependents who perform vicarious leisure for him. In a general way, though not wholly nor consistently, these two groups coincide. The dependent who was first delegated for these duties was the wife,

*Excerpts from *The Theory of the Leisure Class: An Economic Study of Institutions* by Thorstein Veblen. The Modern Library.

or the chief wife; and, as would be expected, in the later development of the institution, when the number of persons by whom these duties are customarily performed gradually narrows, the wife remains the last. In the higher grades of society a large volume of both these kinds of service is required; and here the wife is of course still assisted in the work by a more or less numerous corps of menials. But as we descend the social scale, the point is presently reached where the duties of vicarious leisure and consumption devolve upon the wife alone. In the communities of the Western culture this point is at present found among the lower middle class.

And here occurs a curious inversion. It is a fact of common observation that in this lower middle class there is no pretence of leisure on the part of the head of the household. Through force of circumstances it has fallen into disuse. But the middle-class wife still carries on the business of vicarious leisure, for the good name of the household and its master. In descending the social scale in any moder nindustrial community, the primary fact — the conspicuous leisure of the master of the household — disappears at a relatively high point. The head of the middle-class household has been reduced by economic circumstances to turn his hand to gaining a livelihood by occupations which often partake largely of the character of industry, as in the case of the ordinary business man of to-day. But the derivative fact — the vicarious leisure and consumption rendered by the wife, and the auxiliary vicarious performance of leisure by menials — remains in vogue as a conventionality which the demands of reputability will not suffer to be slighted. It is by no means an uncommon spectacle to find a man applying himself to work with the utmost assiduity, in order that his wife may in due form render for him that degree of vicarious leisure which the common sense of the time demands.

The requirement of vicarious consumption at the hands of the wife continues in force even at a lower point in the pecuniary scale than the requirement of vicarious leisure. At a point below which little if any pretence of wasted effort, in ceremonial cleanness and the like, is observable, and where there is assuredly no conscious attempt at ostensible leisure, decency still requires the wife to consume some goods conspicuosly for the reputability of the household and its head. So that, as the latter-day outcome of this evolution of an archaic institution, the wife, who was at the outset the drudge and chattel of the man, both in fact and in theory, — the producer of goods for him to consume — has become the ceremonial consumer of goods which he produces. But she still quite unmistakably remains his chattel in theory; for the habitual rendering of vicarious leisure and consumption is the abiding mark of the unfree servant.

This latter-day uneasy reaching-out for some form of purposeful activity that shall at the same time not be indecorously productive of either individual or collective gain marks a difference of attitude between the modern leisure class and that of the quasi-peaceable stage.

In the narrower sphere of vicarious leisure a similar change has gone forward. Instead of simply passing her time in visible idleness, as in the best days of the patriarchal régime, the housewife of the advanced peaceable stage applies herself assiduously to household cares. The salient features of this development of domestic service have already been indicated.

Throughout the entire evolution of conspicuous expenditure, whether of goods or of services or human life, runs the obvious implication that in order to effectually mend the consumer's good fame it must be an expenditure of superfluities. In order to be reputable it must be wasteful. No merit would accrue from the consumption of the bare necessaries of life, except by comparison with the abjectly poor who fall short even of the subsistence minimum; and no standard of expenditure could result from such a comparison, except the most prosaic and unattractive level of decency. A standard of life would still be possible which should admit of invidious comparison in other respects than that of opulence; as, for instance, a comparison in various directions in the manifestation of moral, physical, intellectual, or aesthetic force. Comparison in all these directions is in vogue to-day; and the comparison made in these respects is commonly so inextricably bound up with the pecuniary comparison as to be scarcely distinguishable from the latter. This is especially true as regards the current rating of expressions of intellectual and aesthetic force or proficiency; so that we frequently interpret as aesthetic or intellectual a difference which in substance is pecuniary only.

39

Cultural Lag*

William F. Ogburn

I shall begin with a definition. A cultural lag occurs when one of two parts of culture which are correlated changes before or in greater degree than the other part does, thereby causing less adjustment between the two parts than existed previously.

An illustration is the lag in the construction of highways for automobile traffic. The two parts in this illustration are the automobile and the highway. These two parts of culture were in good adjustment in, say, 1910, when the automobile was slow and the highways were narrow country roads with curves and bends over which had been laid a hard surface. The automobile traveled at not a great rate of speed and could take the turns without too much trouble or danger. It was essentially for local transportation. But as time went on, this first part, the automobile, which is called an independent variable, underwent many changes, particularly the engine, which developed speeds capable of 60, 70, 80 miles an hour, with brakes that could stop the car relatively quickly. But the narrow highways with sharp bends did not change as soon as did the automobile. On these roads the driver must slow up or have accidents. A decade or more later we are building a few broad highways with no sharp curves, which will make the automobile a vehicle for long-distance travel. The old highways, the dependent variable, are not adapted to the new automobiles, so that there is a maladjustment between the highways and the automobile. The adjustment, as measured by speeds, was better for local travel around 1910 than it is for long-distance travel in these roads at present. The adjustment will be better on the new express highways. Since the adjustment is made by the dependent variable, it is that part of culture which adapts and is called adaptive culture.

The concept of cultural lag, just defined and illustrated, was first published in 1922 in a chapter of a book on social change which carried this title, "The Hypothesis of Cultural Lag." Since I was not sure whether this term would be understood, I asked my colleague Lee McBain, then Dean of the Faculty of Political Science at Columbia University, whether he thought it was an appropriate title. He advised me not to use it, because, he said with a twinkle in his eye, it might be mistaken for a dance step. This was in the 1920's, when new types of dances in the night clubs of the prohibition era were very popular. However, I did use the term, and I note with interest that it now appears in the

*"Cultural Lag as Theory," William F. Ogburn, Sociology and Social Research 41, 3 (1957): 167–174.

dictionary and is in use in several countries in different parts of the world and has, in the United States, been found particularly useful by historians.

There is some interest always in the origin of an invention and how ideas develop. It therefore seems appropriate that I discuss briefly how this theory of "the cultural lag" was developed.

I am happy to discuss its origin, since I have been accused by some of taking the theory from Thorstein Veblen, and by others from Karl Marx. I am quite sure there was no direct taking over of the idea from Veblen because I had never read him on this point. I had read Marx, and his materialistic interpretation of history was well known to social scientists and historians in general. This idea was a base, however, from which the theory of cultural lag was developed, but certainly neither the materialistic interpretation of history nor economic determinism is the same as cultural lag.

I first used the term in 1914 when I was a professor of economics and sociology at Reed College. I had for a long time been impressed with the economic interpretation of history, though as a user of partial correlation techniques I was appreciative of its limitations. The economic interpretation of history may be illustrated by the claim that the Crusades in the Middle Ages for the recovery of the Holy Land from the possession of the infidels were not a product of religious motives but resulted from the search for trade routes to the East. This economic drive utilized the religious fervor for purposes of enlistment. I do not wish to discuss the validity of the economic interpretation in this particular instance but rather to note that there was an economic factor in the Crusades and that it was obscured or disguised.

This word, "disguised," was widely current in the early part of the twentieth century because of the influence of Freud, all of whose writings I had read at the time. In his book *The Interpretation of Dreams,* he called the dream, as first remembered, the manifest content; and the interpretation of the dream, the latent content. Thus, if a person dreamed that a steam roller was about to crush him, that would be the manifest content; but, if the interpretation showed that the steam roller was a symbol for a dominating father, that would be the latent content. The latent content was disguised. About this time, I read before the American Economic Association a paper stressing this point and entitled "The Psychological Basis for the Economic Interpretation of History," claiming that the economic factor was often disguised. But as I thought more about it, the disguise factor in social causation seemed less important than the time factor.

I noticed this time factor in unequal rates of change, particularly in the course I was giving on the family. I remarked that many changes were taking place in the family and that most of them seemed to be due to the economic factor which removed production activities such as spinning, weaving, soapmaking, tanning of leather from the household and put them in factories, thus taking away many household duties of the wife. Yet the ideology of the position of the housewife persisted. It was said that woman's place was in the home. Also at the beginning of the twentieth century there was serious discussion as to whether women should go to college or not, because their place was in the home. I was impressed with the fact that the transfer of production from the home to the factory was precipitating a new locale for women outside the home. But there was a great time interval, that is to say, there was a lag in changing the position of women; so I came to see great importance in this lag, and, being active at that time in various reform movements, I was disturbed about the maladjustment in the position of women who were kept at home. I was an ardent feminist. So both lag and maladjustment impressed me.

I should like to digress for a moment and say that I do not consider all delays in taking up a new idea as being a lag. For instance, I have been told that Queen Mary of England, who died in 1953, had never used a telephone. Well, she certainly delayed adopting a new invention; however, the failure to adopt a new invention is a delay—not a cultural lag. The theory of the cultural lag is somewhat more complex. It calls for the following steps: (1) the identification of at least two variables; (2) the demonstration that these two variables were in adjustment; (3) the determination by dates that one variable has changed while the other has not changed or one has changed in greater degree than the other; and (4) that when one variable has changed earlier or in greater degree than the other, there is a less satisfactory adjustment than existed before.

I call attention to this series of steps in the formulation of the theory of cultural lag because it has sometimes been commented that the cultural lag is merely a concept. It is surely a much more elaborate concept than that, for instance, of primary group. I think it better to say that, since it is a concept of a relationship, it is a theory. It is therefore more than merely a new term in the language.

This theory I had fully developed by 1915, but I hesitated to publish it, because I thought that theories should have some proof before publication. In order to prove a theory, one must set it up in a form that can be proved, with places for the relevant data. Thus, for proof, a theory evolves into a hypothesis. But the war came along, and it was only after the war that I took up the verification of this hypothesis by considering the adjustment of law to industrial accidents, which were increasing because of the introduction of whirling machinery with rapidly moving wheels. In this case, the independent variable was technology, the machinery of which, before the factory system, had been simple tools such as those on early farms to which the common law of accidents was very well suited. But after the coming of the factories in the United States around 1870, accidents continued to be dealt with by the old common law and with much maladjustment, for, where workers suffered loss of life or an injury to a limb, there was little compensation and long delay in paying for these disasters to the individual or his family. It was not until around 1910 that employers' liability and workmen's compensation were adopted in this country. So that there was a lag of about 30 or 40 years when the maladjustment could be measured by inadequate provision for several hundred thousand injuries and deaths to which there would have been a better adjustment if we had had laws of employers' liability or workmen's compensation.

I still considered it a hypothesis because we needed more proof than one particular case. I attempted, though, to cite many hypotheses of cultural lag, and in nearly all cases the independent variable proved to be a scientific discovery or mechanical invention. For instance, the invention of the steam engine led to the factory, and only afterwards to the change in the legal rights of women. Most of the illustrations given at this time were initiated by technological changes and scientific discoveries, and the lagging adaptive culture was generally some social organization or ideology. These illustrations led to a characterization, by some, of the theory of cultural lag as a technological interpretation of history. I stated, however, at the time the hypothesis of cultural lag was published that the independent variable could very well be an ideology or a nontechnological variable, For instance, changes in the law of primogeniture, an independent variable, constituted a change in the legal system and not in technology. Changes in the law of primogeniture were accompanied, after a lag, by a change in the economic system related to agriculture and household production. So the fact that the technological change came first was simple observation of a temporal nature, and not inherent in the theory as such. For instance, it is quite probable that religion and not technology was the cause of most social changes in India 2,500 years ago at about the time of Buddha. Also students of stone age techniques have pointed out the essential conservative nature of stone technology, that it was very resistant to change and that probably the causes of changes then were ideological or social. But in our times in the Western world, technology and science are the great prime movers of social change. That this is so is an almost universal observation.

I did attempt to generalize the theory. It is this: A cultural lag is independent of the nature of the initiating part or of the lagging part, provided that they are interconnected. The independent variable may be technological, economic, political, ideological, or anything else. But when the unequal time or degree of change produces a strain on the interconnected parts, or is expressed differently when the correlation is lessened, then it is called a cultural lag. The extent of the generalized applicability of the theory rests on how much interconnection exists among the parts of culture. That many connections exist is obvious. Religion is interrelated with science. Family is correlated with education. Education and industry have connections. Highways are necessary for automobiles. On the other hand, some interrelations are slight or do not exist at all between other parts. Painting is not related to the production of gasoline. And I was about to say that writing poetry is unrelated to aviation. But I recall seeing a sizable book of collected poems on aviation. To the extent that culture is like a machine with parts that fit, cultural lag is widespread. If, however, cultural parts are no more related than pebbles strewn on the beach, then cultural lags are rare. There must, of course, be change occurring at unequal time intervals. An indication that cultural lags are common phenomena is suggested by the incorporation of the theory in books on general sociology. There have been criticisms, however.

One in particular should be noted. It has been said that the hypothesis of cultural lag is not a scientific instrument, because, it is claimed, it cannot be scientifically demonstrated. The reason why, critics claim, maladjustments (and presumably adjustments) cannot be objectively determined is that there is a subjective factor which exists because of a value judgment, and value judgments are not subject to measurement.

Values are truly difficult to rank or to measure. We can measure the temperature by a thermometer, but it is said we cannot measure the goodness in morals. This observation does not invalidate the hypothesis of cultural lag. It only concerns the difficulty of determining degrees of maladjustment. But, of course, many maladjustments are quite demonstrable irrespective of the variation in value systems. Maladjustment was an essential factor in Darwin's theory of evolution and he had no difficulty in proving maladjustment. He used death as a test. But there are other tests. Sickness is another. So is insanity. Furthermore, maladjustment may be conceived as a deviation from a social norm. Certainly norms can be described and measured and hence deviations also. Even though maladjustment be difficult to demonstrate, and even though we fail to show it in some cases, it can be proved in many cases, and the hypothesis of cultural lag is not invalidated.

The application of the theory to modern times suggests a possible appendix to the theory which runs like this: The number of patents, discoveries in applied science, and inventions has been increasing in something like an exponential curve. Most of these are minor; but important ones have been coming very rapidly, as, for instance, the magnifying of light or the putting of vision on tape or the isotopes from nuclear fission. As these discoveries and inventions are adopted, we must adjust to them, we must adapt ourselves to this changing environment, but we do it with a certain amount of lag. So an addendum to the theory of cultural lags is that lags accumulate because of the great rapidity and volume of technological change.

However, there are certain events that tend to cause cultural lags to crumble. One of these, I pointed out in my book *Social Change,* is revolution; and the reports we get from the revolutionary movement in China in the 1950's indicate that there are many lags having to do with the family and rural life and Confucianism that have been toppled over by the revolution. For instance, women are less in bondage since the revolution. Also, feudalism has been overthrown. An observation closer to home is that war causes a decline in the pile of accumulated lags. For instance, the war has taken more women out of the home and put more of them into industry, offices, and stores, where they tend to remain after the war is over. Similarly, the position of Negroes has been changed by war. As Negroes have been differentiated into upper classes, middle classes, professional groups, it becomes obvious that the whites cannot treat these upper-class educated Negroes in the same way that they formerly treated Negro field hands or domestic servants. Yet many Negroes in the twentieth century cities with their middle and upper classes are being treated as they were in villages of the South when they emerged from slavery shortly after the Civil War. The war, however, broke some of the old lags down because it put Negroes into association on the basis of equality with the whites of the armed forces and the Negroes were drawn into the cities of the North. So war tends to break down cultural lags. It may preserve a few too. This is a matter for empirical observation.

Even though war and revolution are breaking down cultural lags, there are many that persist. For instance, one such lag that is clearly demonstrable regards our foreign policy. In the eighteenth century the advice of President Washington to avoid entangling alliances with foreign powers was very appropriate because of our isolation, because of the abundance of our natural resources, and because of slow transportation. But in the twentieth century there have come the airplane, the fast steamboat, the radio, telephone, and also the search for raw materials which are needed for our industries and which are widely but universally distributed over the world. The old foreign policy of isolationism is a maladjustment to the changed technological situation. Isolationism however is diminishing. How long it may persist is a question. In the 1950's nonisolationists are the most influential in guiding our foreign policy. Yet for a large part of the twentieth century, isolationism in foreign policy was a lag.

Another illustration which, I think, is clearly demonstrable has to do with the death rate and the birth rate in their relation to the increase in population, particularly in South East Asia. Throughout the great period of written history, the birth rate and the death rate have tended to be the same except for intermittent periods when the death rate fell and the birth rate stayed high. When that occurred, there was, of course, an increase in population. Such is occurring now in India, where the birth rate is probably around 35 per 1,000 and where the death rate is about 25 per 1,000. The result is the increase in the population of India of 4 million per year. Occurring in an agricultural country where the farms have an acreage of about 3 acres, this pressure of population upon the food supply will bring hardships and may result in great human tragedies and will certainly make it very difficult for the standard of living to be raised.

This imbalance of births and deaths produces a maladjustment in other countries also, as for instance in Egypt and probably, if we had the figures, in China. The adjustment could be restored by raising the death rate, which of course we do not wish to do, or by lowering the birth rate, which is resisted by some moral and religious groups and by customs. However, the imbalance in the birth and death rate represents a cultural lag in some densely populated countries.

A long-continuing lag is in the adjustment to cities which were produced in great numbers and in large sizes by the factory and the railroad. In many ways we were better adjusted to rural life. For instance, a greater death rate exists in cities than in the rural districts. There is also more crime in cities. Thus in several respects we have not adjusted well to this urban environment.

I have time to mention only one other lag, the lag in adjusting to the atomic bomb. The atomic bomb brought the possibility of great destruction to cities in a war. The atomic bomb was produced in 2½ years. And yet a decade later we have developed no defense against the atomic bomb, nor have we made an adjustment either in the dispersion of urban populations or in controlling atomic energy or in agreeing to ban the atomic bomb. Possibly many decades may pass before we will adjust to the atomic bomb—a lag of great danger.

If there were time, dozens of cultural lags causing very serious problems could be listed, lags which arise largely because inventions and technology have increased in volume and rapidity, faster than we are making adaptations to them. The great need of our time is to reduce this lag. Cultural lags are one characteristic of the process of social evolution which occurs in a closely integrated society in periods of rapid change. In the long perspective of history, though, lags are not visible because they have been caught up. They are visible phenomena largely at the present time.

PART VI

The Second Generation

Both the great thinkers of the classical tradition and, to a lesser extent, the interstitial scholars were responsible for laying the foundation on which the second generation of sociologists, whose major writings are featured in this part, were to build. The second-generation thinkers of the post–World War II period took sociological theory in more sophisticated directions—and if not always with optimism, they would at least do so with greater confidence. These theorists, most of whom were American, included the Harvard University sociologists Pitirim A. Sorokin and Talcott Parsons, who did much to further a systematic theorizing of social and cultural systems. Also included are Robert K. Merton, Hans H. Gerth, and C. Wright Mills, who conceptualized society not in terms of an all-inclusive comprehensive social system but in terms of the practical workings of social structure. And finally, David Riesman also considered the intricacies of social structure but always in relation to issues of social character.

In the selection titled "Ideational, Sensate, and Idealistic Cultures," Pitirim A. Sorokin examines three main types of *integrated* culture. As such, he creates three models, used for analytical purposes, that constitute logically and functionally comprehensible sociocultural *systems*. Each has its own *mentality*, or particular form of reality adaptation for satisfying needs and ends. All empirically existing sociocultural systems consist, to one degree or another, of combinations of each of these three conceptual types. The first, *ideational culture*, defines reality in terms of transcendence, and needs and ends are spiritual. In *sensate culture*, social reality is experienced through the senses, and needs and ends are physical. Finally, *idealistic culture* is a mixture of the ideational and the sensate; here, social reality, needs, and ends are both spiritual and physical in varying degrees.

In the second reading by Sorokin, "Imminent Sociocultural Change," he proposes a theory of sociocultural change. Sorokin establishes as a main principle that the major causes of a sociocultural system's transformation are located within it—in its inherent tendencies—rather than in factors external to it. In other words, it is a sociocultural system's *destiny*, not its external environment, that primarily determines the system's *normal career*—its future course of development. In addition, those systems that have the greatest determination over their own normal career are those that have the greatest degree of integration and that have the most power.

In 1937, Talcott Parsons proposed the *voluntaristic theory of social action*, in which he states that social actors are capable of voluntary action in relation to goals that they attempt to achieve through choices they make. In "The Pattern Variables," Parsons goes further and maintains that the ways in which social action is organized have to do with the choices actors make among a grouping of *pattern variables*—a set of five dichotomies that may be used to categorize actors' orientations. The actor must make all five dichotomous choices before a social situation can become meaningful and before the actor can act with respect to that situation. The first pattern variable involves the dilemma of *affectivity versus affective neutrality*, and it covers the emotion—or lack of it—that is appropriate in a given situation. *Self-orientation versus collectivity orientation* covers orientations of action either to individual interests or to group interests. The third pattern variable, *universalism versus particularism*, is generated by interactions where the type of evaluative standards to be applied are either general and consensual or ones that are unique to particular actors involved. The fourth pattern variable involves *ascription versus achievement* and covers the dilemma of whether to assess other actors in terms of general performance criteria (e.g., educational qualification, business success, etc.) or in terms of qualities that are ascribed on the basis of heredity or other forms of endowment (e.g., sex, age, race, ethnicity, etc.). Finally, the fifth pattern variable, involving the dilemma of *specificity versus diffuseness*, concerns the range or scope of orientations that an actor has toward a given interaction situation.

The pattern variables serve as the bridge between Parsons's comments on social action and his conceptualization of the *social system*. In the reading "The Social System," Parsons posits that a social system is made up of the actions of individual actors or, more accurately, their *roles* in the context of the choices that involve the pattern variables. This sets up the organized interaction, or *role expectations*, between two or more actors. Social life consists of a *double contingency of expectations*, which means that what ego (self) regards as his or her role expectations are viewed by "alter" (other) as his or her required responses (sanctions)—and vice versa. Parsons therefore defines a social system as a plurality of actors who are members of a collectivity and whose interactions are integrated by a reciprocity of role expectations and responses. A social system that is self-sufficient in meeting all of its essential requirements—in addressing all of its problems—over time is called a *society*. All other social systems of a society are its *subsystems*.

In "The AGIL Schema," Parsons explains how a social system addresses problems of its continued functioning over time. This is accomplished through a series of four phases (later called the *functional imperatives*). According to Parsons, all social systems can be analyzed in terms referable to the solution of four functional problems: adaptation, goal-attainment, integration, and latency. This has become known as the *AGIL schema*, in accordance with the acronym of the first letters of these four functional requirements. The "A" function, *adaptation*, refers to the processes through which the social system procures and distributes the resources it requires for its activities. The "G" function, *goal-attainment*, refers to the social system's formulation of goals and the motivation and mobilization of resources directed to achieve those goals. The "I" function, *integration*, is concerned with the coordination of the various relations that make up the social system for the purpose of establishing its boundaries. Lastly, the "L" function, *latency*, refers to the processes whereby the social system maintains cultural patterns. The AGIL phases operate at the level of a total social system (the macrocosm) and at the level of its subsystems (the microcosm).

In "Manifest and Latent Functions," Robert K. Merton also undertakes a functionalist analysis of society. Here, he distinguishes between those outcomes for social systems or individuals that are intended and those outcomes that are unintended. *Manifest functions* refer to the *intended and recognized consequences* that certain actions of individuals or structures of social systems contribute to their adjustment or adaptation. *Latent functions*, by contrast, are the *unintended and unrecognized consequences* of actions and structures that make a similar contribution. Because the consequences of a latent function are hidden, it is up to the sociologist to reveal what they are and whether or not they have been achieved.

Originally published in 1938, Merton's "Social Structure and Anomie" is an important paper that explains how the social structure's *malfunctioning* pressures certain individuals to engage in deviant behavior. He begins by stating that every social structure has certain *cultural goals* that it encourages its members to strive to attain. Additionally, every social structure defines the *institutional means* that are deemed appropriate in achieving those goals. As long as individuals are successful in their achievement of the goals and satisfied in their participation in the means, they are said to be in conformity, and the social structure is said to be in equilibrium. However, when there is a *dissociation* between the cultural goals and the institutionalized means, cultural chaos, or *anomie*, ensues, and antisocial behavior results. Merton then identifies five ways in which individuals can adapt to the means and goals phases of the social structure: conformity, innovation, ritualism, retreatism, and rebellion.

In "The Self-Fulfilling Prophecy," Merton points to a basic social process that is, in most instances, responsible for creating social reality. The *self-fulfilling prophecy* is a misleading prediction, rumor, or expectation that, once declared, affects actual outcomes; it leads to its own realization. Though it is initially a false conception, it evokes behavior that makes it come true. For example, stereotypes that members of an in-group have of members of an out-group are reinforced and actualized not on the basis of external facts but on the basis of the stereotype itself. The self-fulfilling prophecy is therefore established through circular reasoning: members of the out-group are believed to be inferior, and they are subsequently treated as inferior because they are members of the out-group. According to Merton, the way out of this circle of paradox is through deliberate institutional change.

In their 1953 book, *Character and Social Structure*, Hans H. Gerth and C. Wright Mills reject the conceptualization of society as a social system. Rather than taking as their unit of analysis a coordinated "whole" made up of interrelated parts, in the excerpt "Structural Integration and Change," they present a procedural scheme for explaining the integration of a social structure. Gerth and Mills begin with the most convenient "units" that prevail in a society, which they identify as the institutional order and their corresponding institutions, spheres, and roles. An *institutional order* consists of the five institutions that have similar ends or which serve similar objective functions. These are the political order, the economic order, the military order, the kinship order, and the religious order. Gerth and Mills are interested in tracing the *ramifications*, or those activities which are ends in one order but which are used as means of another institutional order, and in understanding how such ramifications may facilitate or limit activities and policies in other orders. They then propose that the institutional orders composing a social structure are integrated through four modes of integration, or principles of structural change: *correspondence*, *coincidence*, *coordination*, and *convergence*.

One of the most popular books of the mid-20th century was David Riesman's *The Lonely Crowd*, with Nathan Glazer and Reuel Denney, from which the reading "Character and Conformity" is taken. Published in 1950, it proposes a theory of *social character*, a shared cultural personality. Given that that the main function of character is to provide for compliance, Riesman et al. examine the relationship between three population phases, the historical character types associated with them, and how these are correlated with conformity. First, a society in the stage of high growth potential—one that is preindustrial—produces the *tradition-directed* character type that conforms on the basis of rigid tradition. Second, a society in a period of transitional population growth—one marked by economic and political expansion—produces the *inner-directed* type, with an internalized set of goals and standards. The metaphor of a *gyroscope* illustrates the inner-directed person, as he or she maintains a delicate balance between personal life orientations and the demands of the external environment. Finally, a society in an epoch of incipient population decline—the then-current industrialized, urbanized, and bureaucratized U.S. society—produces the *other-directed* type that conforms on the basis of extreme sensitivity to others' wishes and opinions. The *radar* is the metaphor that illustrates the other-directed person, as he or she is continually receptive to signals from others. The emotional experiences that ensure conformity for each of these three character types, respectively, are shame, guilt, and anxiety.

40

Ideational, Sensate, and Idealistic Cultures*

Pitirim A. Sorokin

Many systems of logically integrated culture are conceivable, each with a different set of major premises but consistent within itself. Not all those, however, are likely to be found in those cultural complexes which have been in actual existence; and still fewer will serve as fruitful instruments for ordering the chaos of the cultural worlds which we can perceive into a limited number of completely comprehensible unities.

We can begin by distinguishing two profoundly different types of the integrated culture. Each has its own mentality; its own system of truth and knowledge; its own philosophy and *Weltanschauung;* its own type of religion and standards of "holiness"; its own system of right and wrong; its own forms of art and literature; its own mores, laws, code of conduct; its own predominant forms of social relationships; its own economic and political organization ; and, finally, its own type of *human personality,* with a peculiar mentality and conduct. The values which correspond to one another throughout these cultures are irreconcilably at variance in their nature; but within each culture all the values fit closely together, belong to one another logically, often functionally.

Of these two systems one may be termed *Ideational* culture, the other *Sensate.* And as these names characterize the cultures as a whole, so do they indicate the nature of each of the component parts.

The probability is that neither the Ideational nor the Sensate type has ever existed in its pure form; but all integrated cultures have in fact been composed of divers combinations of these two pure logico-meaningful forms. In some the first type predominates; in others, the second; in still others both mingle in equal proportions and on an equal basis. Accordingly, some cultures have been nearer to the Ideational, others to the Sensate type; and some have contained a balanced synthesis of both pure types. This last I term the *Idealistic* type of culture. (It should not be confused with the Ideational.)

Let us now turn to a closer scrutiny of the culture types we have named. *What specifically is meant by the Ideational, the Sensate, the Idealistic,*

*Excerpts from *Social and Cultural Dynamics*, Volume One: Fluctuation of Forms of Art by Pitirim A. Sorokin. Copyright 1937 by The Bedminster Press.

and other intermediary categories? What are their major characteristics? How are these characteristics combined and how do they operate to give united or integrated systems of culture? And, finally, why should these types of culture be regarded as fundamental and capable of providing the best possible means of understanding how the millions of fragments of the perceptual sociocultural world have been integrated into ordered systems? Such are the problems with which we shall start our study.

Since the character of any culture is determined by its internal aspect—by its *mentality,* as we agreed to call it—the portraiture of the Ideational, Sensate, and Mixed types of culture begins properly with the delineation of the major premises of their mentality. As a starting point let us assume that these major premises concern the following four items: (1) *the nature of reality;* (2) *the nature of the needs and ends to be satisfied;* (3) *the extent to which these needs and ends are to be satisfied;* (4) *the methods of satisfaction.*

A. *The Nature of Reality.* The same complex of material objects which compose one's milieu is not perceived and interpreted identically by various human individuals. Without entering here into the psychological, biological, and other reasons for this, let us simply state the fact that the heterogeneity of individual experiences, together with other factors, leads to a multiplicity of the modes of perception of the same phenomenon by different persons. On one extreme is a mentality for which reality is that which can be perceived by the organs of sense; it does not see anything beyond the sensate being of the milieu (cosmic and social). Those who possess this sort of mentality try to adapt themselves to those conditions which appear to the sense organs, or more exactly, to the exterior receptors of the nervous system. On the other extreme are persons who perceive and apprehend the same sensate phenomena in a very different way. For them they are mere appearance, a dream, or an illusion. True reality is not to be found here; it is something beyond, hidden by the appearance, different from this material and sensate veil which conceals it. Such persons do not try to adapt themselves to what now seems superficial, illusory, unreal. They strive to adapt themselves to the true reality which is beyond appearances. Whether it be styled God, Nirvana, Brahma, Om, Self, Tao, Eternal Spirit, *l' élan vital,* Unnamed, the City of God, Ultimate Reality, *Ding für und an sich,* or what not, is of little importance. What is important is that such mentality exists; that here the ultimate or true reality is usually considered supersensate, immaterial, spiritual. Consequently, this difference in the perception and interpretation of reality, to which one has to adapt oneself, must be taken into account at the very starting point of any inquiry into the nature of a culture type. Otherwise, the inquiry will suffer at its very inception from a failure to recognize properly what are the "facts" in the situation and what are not. This has happened with most of the studies in the field.

It is evident that the mentality which accepts the milieu in its sensate and material reality will stress the satisfaction of the sensual bodily needs. Those who see it as a mere appearance will seek the satisfaction mainly of spiritual needs through an interaction with the ultimate reality. Those who occupy an intermediate position will be sensitive to needs partly sensate and partly spiritual.

B. *The Nature of the Needs and Ends to Be Satisfied.* Needs may be viewed as purely *carnal* or *sensual,* like hunger and thirst, sex, shelter, and comforts of the body generally; as purely *spiritual,* like salvation of one's soul, the performance of sacred duty, service to God, categoric moral obligations, and other spiritual demands which exist for their own sake, regardless of any social approval or disapproval; or as *mixed* or *carnal-spiritual,* like the striving for superiority in scientific, artistic, moral, social, and other creative achievements, partly for their own sake and partly for the sake of human fame, glory, popularity, money, physical security and comfort, and other "earthly values" of an empirical character. Of course, in reality one class of needs passes gradually and imperceptibly into another, but, as in any classification, this does not mean that the gradual scale may not be divided into a few main categories for purposes of reference.

C. *The Extent to Which These Needs and Ends Are to Be Satisfied.* Each need may be regarded as requiring satisfaction to a different extent or on a different level, from the widest and most luxurious maximum to the narrowest and poorest minimum. One's need for food may range from a small amount of coarse bread and water, barely sufficient to maintain the physiological expenditures of the body, to the most extravagant gluttony, where all means are employed not only to supply luxurious and fine foods but also to stimulate the satiated appetite by various devices. The same is to be said of clothing, shelter, sex, self-protection, recreation, and amusement. This also holds true for the purely spiritual and for the mixed or carnal-spiritual needs.

D. *The Methods of Satisfaction of Needs.* These may be, or appear to be, different with various individuals. We can divide them roughly into three main classes:

(1) Modification of one's milieu in that manner which will yield the means of satisfying a given need: for instance, one suffering from cold can start a furnace, build a fire, put on a warm fur coat, etc.

(2) Modification of self, one's body and mind, and their parts—organs, wishes, convictions, or the whole personality—in such a way as to become virtually free from a given need, or to sublimate it through this "readjustment of self." In the above illustration of suffering from cold one can train oneself to become less sensitive to cold or to endure it within considerably broad limits. The same can be said of other needs.

(3) Modification partly of milieu and partly of self. In the case of cold, to return to our example, we often resort to both methods—we may light a fire, but also engage in vigorous physical activity to warm ourselves.

I. Ideational Culture

In the terms of the above four items its major premises are these: (1) Reality is perceived as nonsensate and nonmaterial, everlasting Being (*Sein*); (2) the needs and ends are mainly spiritual; (3) the extent of their satisfaction is the largest, and the level, highest; (4) the method of their fulfillment or realization is self-imposed minimization or elimination of most of the physical needs, and to the greatest possible extent. These major premises are common to all branches of the Ideational culture mentality. But, on the basis of variations under (4), it is possible to distinguish two fundamental subclasses of the Ideational culture mentality and the related culture system:

A. *Ascetic Ideationalism.* This seeks the consummation of the needs and ends through an excessive elimination and minimization of the carnal needs, supplemented by a complete detachment from the sensate world and even from oneself, viewing both as mere illusion, nonreal, nonexisting. The whole sensate milieu, and even the individual "self," are dissolved in the supersensate, ultimate reality.

B. *Active Ideationalism.* Identical with general Ideationalism in its major premises, it seeks the realization of the needs and ends, not only through minimization of the carnal needs of individuals, but also through the transformation of the sensate world, and especially of the sociocultural world, in such a way as to reform it along the lines of the spiritual reality and of the ends chosen as the main value. Its bearers do not "flee from the world of illusion" and do not entirely dissolve it and their own souls in the ultimate reality, but strive to bring it nearer to God, to save not only their own souls but the souls of all other human beings. The great spiritual reformers, like the early Christian Apostles and such popes as Gregory the Great and Leo the Great, may serve as examples of the Active Ideational mentality.

Such, then, are two main varieties of the Ideational mentality and system of culture, as far as their major premises are concerned.

II. Sensate Culture

The Sensate mentality views reality as only that which is presented to the sense organs. It does not seek or believe in any supersensory reality; at the most, in its diluted form, it assumes an agnostic attitude toward the entire world beyond the senses. The Sensate reality is thought of as a Becoming, Process, Change, Flux, Evolution, Progress, Transformation. Its needs and aims are mainly physical, and maximum satisfaction is sought of these needs. The method of realizing them is not that of a modification within the human individuals composing the culture, but of a modification or exploitation of the external world. In brief, the Sensate culture is the opposite of the Ideational in its major premises.

These traits are common to all varieties of the Sensate culture mentality. But on the basis of the variation in the fourth item (*i.e.*, method of adjustment) it is possible to distinguish three main varieties of this type.

A. *Active Sensate Culture Mentality* (Active "Epicureans") Sharing with other forms of

Sensate mentality all the above four premises, it seeks the consummation of its needs and ends mainly through the most "efficient" modification, adjustment, readjustment, reconstruction, of the external milieu. The transformation of the inorganic, organic (technology, medicine, and the applied disciplines), and the sociocultural world, viewed mainly externally, is the method of this variety. The great executives of history, the great conquerors, builders of empire, are its incarnation.

B. *Passive Sensate Mentality* (Passive "Epicureans"). This is characterized by the attempt to fulfill physical needs and aims, neither through the inner modification of "self," nor through efficient reconstruction of the external world, but through a parasitic exploitation and utilization of the external reality as it is, viewed as the mere means for enjoying sensual pleasures. "Life is short"; "*Carpe diem*"; "Wine, women, and song"; "Eat, drink, and be merry"—these are the mottoes of this mentality.

C. *Cynical Sensate Mentality* (Cynical "Epicureans"). The civilization dominated by this type of mentality, in seeking to achieve the satisfaction of its needs, uses a specific technique of donning and doffing those Ideational masks which promise the greatest returns in physical profit. This mentality is exemplified by all the Tartufes of the world, those who are accustomed to change their psychosocial "colors" and to readjust their values in order to run along with the stream. They are enthusiastic monarchists under a monarchy; ardent communists when a communistic regime comes to power; and if, instead of communism, theocracy reigns supreme, they "adapt" themselves to this regime as well. In every case their main concern is bread and butter. In its premises the Cynical Sensate mentality clearly belongs to the Sensate class, resembling only superficially the Ideational type in its apparent modification of self rather than of environment.

III. The Mixed Types of Mentality and Culture

All the other culture mentalities represent in their major premises a mixture of the Ideational and Sensate forms in various combinations and proportions. With one conspicuous exception they are, therefore, eclectic, self-contradictory, poorly integrated logically. Their Ideational and Sensate elements remain adjacent and mechanically coexistent, without achieving genuine inner synthesis. Sometimes the coexistence is comparatively inconspicuous and does not lead to an active antagonism between opposites. Sometimes their latent antagonism flares up into open war; then we have a culture mentality divided against itself.

The Mixed culture type has many varieties, according to the mode of combination of the Ideational and Sensate elements, and the proportion of each in the mixture. Of these, two should be specifically mentioned.

A. *Idealistic Culture Mentality.* This is the only form of the Mixed class which is—or at least appears to be—logically integrated. Quantitatively it represents a more or less balanced unification of Ideational and Sensate, with, however, a predominance of the Ideational elements. Qualitatively it synthesizes the premises of both types into one inwardly consistent and harmonious unity. For it reality is many-sided, with the aspects of everlasting Being and ever-changing Becoming of the spiritual and the material. Its needs and ends are both spiritual and material, with the material, however, subordinated to the spiritual. The methods of their realization involve both the modification of self and the transformation of the external sensate world: in other words, it gives *suum cuique* to the Ideational and the Sensate. Each of them it views as real, as a mode or aspect of the supreme reality. Its face is simultaneously otherworldly and of this world. Recognizing the Ideational values as supreme, it does not declare the Sensate world a mere illusion or of negative value; on the contrary, as far as the Sensate is in harmony with the Ideational, it possesses positive value.

B. *Pseudo-Ideational Culture Mentality.* Another specific form of the Mixed type is the unintegrated, Pseudo-Ideational mentality. One might style it "subcultural" if the term culture were used to designate only a logically integrated system. This type has occupied a conspicuous place in the history of culture mentality. Its characteristics are as follows.

The nature of reality is not clearly defined, but is felt largely as Sensate. Here needs and ends are predominantly of a physical nature. They are only moderately satisfied, and the method of satisfaction is neither an active modification of the milieu to any appreciable degree, nor a free modification of self, nor a search for pleasure, nor successful hypocrisy. It is a dull and passive endurance of blows and privations, coming from the outside, as long as these can be borne physically. This minimization of spiritual and carnal needs is not freely sought, it is imposed by some external agency (*vis absoluta*). It is the result of helplessness to resist. The oppressive power is so overwhelming that, after several unsuccessful attempts to oppose it, there remains to those oppressed no energy to try to free themselves and to adapt themselves physically and spiritually to a better order. Given an opportunity, a Pseudo-Ideationalist may easily plunge into Passive, Cynical, or even Active "Epicureanism." The life processes of slaves under dire and cruel conditions, of many prisoners, of subjects under the cruel regime of their rulers, of some primitive people who live in a condition of misery and privation, of groups stricken by a great catastrophe bringing with it utter ruin, of sensate persons stricken by an incurable malady—these offer examples of this type of mentality. Life under such conditions is dull, painful, aimless; no physical comfort mitigates its long agony; nor does the inner light of the triumphant spirit brighten its unending darkness.

41

Imminent Sociocultural Change*

Pitirim A. Sorokin

A. *Principle of Immanent Generation of Consequences.* The first implication of the principle of immanent change may be formulated as follows: *As long as it exists and functions, any sociocultural system incessantly generates consequences which are not the results of the external factors to the system, but the consequences of the existence of the system and of its activities. As such, they must be imputed to it, regardless of whether they are good or bad, desirable or not, intended or not by the system. One of the specific forms of this immanent generation of consequences is an incessant change of the system itself, due to its existence and activity.*

B. *Principle of Immanent Self-Determination of the System's Destiny* (Existence Career). The second fundamental implication of the principle of immanent change is the principle of immanent self-determination of the potentially given course of the existence of a sociocultural system. It may be formulated as follows: *As soon as a sociocultural system emerges, its essential and "normal" course of existence, the forms, the phases, the activities of its life career or destiny are determined mainly by the system itself, by its potential nature and the totality of its properties. The totality of the external circumstances is relevant, but mainly in the way of retarding or accelerating the unfolding of the immanent destiny; weakening or reinforcing some of the traits of the system; hindering or facilitating a realization of the immanent potentialities of the system; finally, in catastrophic changes, destroying the system; but these external circumstances cannot force the system to manifest what it potentially does not have; to become what it immanently cannot become; to do what, it immanently is incapable of doing. Likewise, the external conditions can crush the system or terminate an unfolding of its immanent destiny at one of the earliest phases of its development (its immanent life career), depriving it of a realization of its complete life career; but they cannot fundamentally change the character and the quality of each phase of the development; nor can they, in many cases, reverse or fundamentally change the sequence of the phases of the immanent destiny of the system.*

This proposition is a mere result of the principle of immanent change and immanent generation of the consequences. With all the traits at a

*Excerpts from *Social and Cultural Dynamics*, Volume Four: Basic Problems, Principles and Methods by Pitirim A. Sorokin. Copyright 1941 by The Bedminster Press.

given moment (T^1), the system acts in the form of A; A introduces changes in the milieu and in the system itself. Therefore, for the next moment, T^1, the system's total situation is determined by the external and internal consequences of the act A. This situation at T^1 is thus determined by the system's properties and activities at the moment T^1. The same is true for the moment T^2, T^3 . . . T^n, up to the end of the existence of the system. This means that any sociocultural system, as soon as it emerges as a system, bears in itself its future destiny. To use Aristotle's example, an acorn as soon as it emerges bears in itself its destiny, namely the unfolding destiny of an oak and of nothing else. So with the initial system of any plant or animal organism. The same is still truer of a sociocultural system: a moronic family cannot unfold itself into the Great Christian Church or develop the properties of the Royal Scientific Society; from an emerged contractual business concern one cannot expect the properties, functions. and life career of the early Christian monastery; from a Sensate "Society of Connoisseurs of Wines and Women" the characteristics and destiny of an ascetic society; from the State, the functions and destiny of a sentimental philanthropic society; from a real university, the functions, behavior and life career of a criminal gang; and so on. As soon as a sociocultural system emerges, with all its properties and *modus vivendi* and *modus agendi,* it contains in itself its "normal" future. At any moment of its existence and activity it creates it, controls it, determines it, and molds it. In this sense, to use the proverb, any sociocultural system is the molder of its own future.

This does not deny the role of the external circumstances. But as mentioned, it specifies their functions. The external agencies may crush the system and in this way prevent it from a realization of its immanent destiny. Earthquake, fire, plague, inundation, war, and other agencies external to a given system—the family, the artistic society, the religious or political sect—can kill all or a part of its members; can destroy its property and other instrumentalities of its activities; can disperse the members; can destroy the scientific libraries and laboratories, art museums and churches, means of transportation and communication, food supply; and in hundreds of forms may put an end to the existence of the system. Still more frequently, the external circumstances may accelerate or retard, facilitate or hinder, reinforce or weaken a realization of the immanent potentialities of the system and therefore of its destiny. All this is granted as self-evident. And yet, all this does not determine fundamentally the "normal" career and phases of the development of the system. All this does not and cannot force the system A (oak, man, criminal gang), destined to have a life career B to have a life career fundamentally different, for which A does not have any potentiality: for instance, for a female to become a male; for a criminal gang to change into a society of the real saints; for the State to become a night club; and so on. This "normal" career or destiny is an unfolding of the immanent potentialities of the system given at the moment of its emergence.

C. *Immanent Self-Determinism as Synthesis of Determinism and Indeterminism. The preceding analysis raises the question: What is the relationship of the immanent principle to the problem of determinism-indeterminism?* Is the immanent principle of change a variety of determinism or is it that of indeterminism? The answer is: neither or both. So far as the immanent principle implies that the normal course and the essential trails of the system are greatly determined by the potentialities of the system at the moment of its emergence, it is deterministic. It is also deterministic so far as the influence of external factors is concerned, when it reaches beyond the margin of the system's autonomy. Considering, however, that the determining potentialities of the system are *the system itself* and are its immanent properties, *the determinism of the system turns into self-determinism. Self-determinism is the equivalent of freedom.* When we ourselves determine something, we feel ourselves free; and especially when this self-determination flows spontaneously from us as something quite natural to us and emanating from our very nature. The self-determination of a system is exactly this: it is rooted in the system; it expresses its very nature and its most essential potentialities; it flows spontaneously from the system and cannot do otherwise. For all these reasons the principle of immanent self-determination is equivalent to indeterminism. It is indeterministic also in the sense that the very notion of the potentialities of the system, as we shall see in the next paragraph, contains an element of indeterminacy on its fringes and in no way means a rigid necessity, as has been shown above. In all these aspects, the principle of immanent change of a system is indeterministic and implies a considerable margin of autonomy from all the agencies that are external to the system; and also some amount of indeterminacy within the system itself, so far as realization of its potentialities is concerned.

Such is the definite and precise answer to the question raised. The answer appears to be more adequate and sound than the half-truths of pure determinism and indeterminism. The stated principle organically and logically unites in itself the valid parts of either of these principles and is free from the fallacies of either, it clearly indicates in what sense and to what degree the sociocultural system is indeterministic or free, and in what respects it is deterministic. In application to man and man's sociocultural world it synthesizes the doctrine of "free will" with the doctrine of determinism and "predestination." The next paragraph will specify still more fully the conclusion reached.

D. *Principle, of Differential Degrees of Self-Determination and Dependence for Various Sociocultural Systems.* If any sociocultural system bears in itself the reason of its change and determination of its destiny, three questions arise:

1. In the unfolding of the potentialities of the system in its life career, is there only one quite rigid and definite course for the system, or are there several possibilities or routes to be traveled?
2. Is the margin of self-determination of the system and its dependence upon the external conditions the same for all sociocultural systems or is it different for different systems?
3. If so, upon what conditions does the relative portion of self-determination and dependence upon external agencies in the systems depend?

These are the three questions to be answered. Turn to the first problem.

Thus, the role of the external milieu and the nature of the immanent potentialities of any sociocultural system force us to admit a margin of indetermined possibilities in the development of the life career of the system. I say a "margin," not the complete indeterminacy. Such a margin means the rejection of a fatalistic and absolutely determined course of development of the system. Put in symbolic form, this thesis means that a given system A has an immanent potentiality B, which has to be unfolded in the course of its existence. But, granting even similar external circumstances, this B in one case will actualize into Ba, in another into Bb, in the third into Bc, and so on, up to Bn. In different external milieus, the difference between the actualizations of this B will be still greater.

Turn now to the second question: *Is the margin of self-determination of the future career of the system the same for all sociocultural systems?* Phrased in different form this question means: Are all the social and cultural systems equally dependent upon or independent of the external conditions in shaping their own destiny?

This destiny is shaped, as we have seen, by the immanent forces of the system itself and by the milieu in which it exists. Are the shares of both "molders" constant for any system?

Is it possible to indicate a few more or less general conditions upon which depends the amount of self-determination of its destiny by the system?

First of all, it depends upon the *kind of social or cultural system.*

Second, the amount of self-determination of various systems depend also upon the *kind of milieu.*

Third, we must distinguish farther between *the total and the specific immunity* of the system from its environment, in the molding of its own destiny.

Let us assume, first, that we have social and cultural systems *of the same kind:* say, the family, or the State, or the business firm; or a philosophical school or an art system.

E. *Other conditions being equal (including the milieu), in the social and cultural systems of the same kind, the greater and better is their integration, the greater is their self-determination (and autonomy from the environment) in molding their own destiny.*

Unfolded, the proposition implies:

(1) *Other conditions being equal, of the social and cultural complexes, the least amount of self-determination is found in unorganized social groups and in cultural congeries.*

(2) *Other conditions being equal, the highest amount of self-determination belongs to those social and cultural systems which are most perfectly integrated, causally and meaningfully,* where the causal interdependence of the components and elements of the system is the greatest; and their relationship is the most solidary (among human agents) and most consistent among the components, where, neither actually nor potentially, is there any contradiction, any *Spannung,* any inner tension, antagonism or conflict.

Finally, *between these types stand the intermediate systems, which are neither congeries nor perfectly integrated systems.* Such are the social systems where only the causal interdependence is found but where relationships are not quite solidary; or the cultural systems where relationships of the elements of the system are somewhat eclectic, not quite consistent, and actually or latently conflicting between and in each of its components. In such systems there always is found what Max Weber, M. Seheler and K. Barthel style *Spannung,* a kind of tension or latent antagonism; a hidden split or crack, which flares into an open split of the system as soon as the respective adverse interference of the external conditions takes place.

One word of caution: *integration and lack of it should not be mixed with fashionable terms like "plasticity," "capacity of adjustment to environment," "progressiveness" and the like.* These terms are not equivalent to good or poor integration.

Well-integrated systems may be both elastic and rigid in their structure and tactics, according to the conditions; the same is true of the poorly integrated systems.

Of other conditions relevant to the amount of self-direction of a system in molding its own destiny, the following ones can be mentioned:

(3) *Other conditions being equal (including the identical environment and the perfection of integration), the greater the power of the system, the greater its autonomy from the social, biological and cosmic environment, and the greater its self-control and self-direction.* Put in that form, the proposition is almost axiomatic. The more powerful system naturally has the greater chance to resist, overcome, and therefore to carry on its aims and potentialities, in its environment, than a less powerful system. The weakness of the proposition consists in the indeterminacy of the term "power." Left at that, it is valid, but fairly indefinite. What is the power of a sociocultural system? How can it be measured? And measured it must be, in order that we can say which system is more powerful.

I do not know any satisfactory device for a measurement as well as for a clear definition of the power of a social or cultural system. All that one can do is to indicate a few rough criteria which are somewhat measurable, and which can give at least a very rough, but nevertheless hardly misleading, "index" of the power of the system.

Other conditions being equal, *(a) the greater the membership of a social system; (b) the better their biological and mental and social qualities; (c) the greater the sum total of real knowledge, experience, and wisdom at its disposal; (d) the more efficient its organization in the sense of the distribution of rights-duties-functions among its members* (including the distribution to everybody according to his talent and ability); *(e) the greater the sum total of the means and instruments of influencing human conduct as well as of modifying biological and cosmic nature; and finally, (f) the better its solidary integration (discussed above); the greater is the power of the group—the more independent it is from the external conditions in the realization of its potentialities.*

With a slight modification, the same criteria are applicable to the comparative power of cultural systems. *The greater the number of the human agents of the system (of art, religion, philosophy, science, etc.); the better their biological, mental, moral, and social qualities; the greater the wisdom, knowledge, and value it incorporates* (value or system of meanings: religious, scientific, artistic, ethical, etc.); *the better it fits the social organization of its followers; the greater is its logico-causal integration* (within the system of meanings and between all its components); *the greater the sum total of means or vehicles for its unfolding, broadcasting, and maintenance at its disposal; the greater the power of the cultural system—the more independent it is from its environmental forces.*

Here, however, a greater emphasis is to be put upon the value (the system of meanings) the system incorporates and the consistency of the integration of its elements and components than in the social system.

Each of these conditions is unquestionably a basic constituent of the power of a social or cultural system. Taken separately, each condition cannot be an index of the power of the system. Taken together, they give a very approximate, but hardly misleading, indicator of that power.

This proposition then sums up, if not all, then probably the most essential uniform conditions of the comparative autonomy of the system (in building its destiny) from the external conditions, and explains the relative share of the system's self-control and self-regulation in molding its own destiny.

Summary

1. The reason or cause of a change of any sociocultural system is in the system itself, and need not be looked for anywhere else.

2. Additional reason for change of a system is its milieu, which is again composed mostly of the immanently changing systems.

3. Any sociocultural system changing immanently, incessantly generates a series of immanent consequences, which change not only the milieu of the system but also the system itself.

4. Bearing the seeds of its change in itself, any sociocultural system bears also in itself the power of molding its own destiny or life career. Beginning with the moment of emergence, each sociocultural system is the main factor of its own destiny. This destiny, or the system's subsequent life career, represents mainly an unfolding of the immanent potentialities of the system in the course of its existence.

5. The environmental forces are not negligible, but their role consists essentially in retardation or acceleration; facilitation or hindrance; reinforcement or weakening, of the realization of the immanent potentialities of the system. Sometimes they can crush the system and put an end to its existence; or stop the process of unfolding the immanent potentialities at one of the early phases. They cannot, however, change fundamentally the immanent potentialities of the system and its normal destiny in the sense of making the life career of an unfolding acorn that of a cow, or vice versa.

6. So far as the system, since the moment of its emergence, bears in itself its future career, it is a determinate system and in this sense deterministic. So far as the future of the system is determined mainly not by external agents, but by the system itself, such a determinism is indeterministic or free, as flowing spontaneously, in accordance with its nature, from the system itself.

7. The process of unfolding the immanent potentialities of the emerged system is somewhat predetermined by the system, but this predetermination leaves a considerable margin for variations. In this sense it is not absolutely and narrowly preconditioned. Only the main direction and the main phases of the unfolding are predetermined; the rest, including most of the details, are "free" and become an unforeseen and unpredictable matter of chance, environment, and free choice of the system.

8. Since the destiny or life career of any system is the result of the system's self-control and of the influence of the environmental forces, the relative share of each of these two factors in molding the system's career is not constant for all sociocultural systems. The share of the self-control of the system is the greater, the more perfectly the system is integrated and the more powerful it is.

9. As a rough indicator of the elusive concept of the power of a sociocultural system, the following less elusive combination of the criteria is offered: the greater the membership of the system; the better the members biologically, mentally, morally and socially; the greater the actual wisdom, knowledge and experience the system has at its disposal; the better it is organized; the greater the total sum of means of influencing human behavior and forces of nature at its disposal; the more solidarity (or consistently) the system is integrated; the more powerful it is; the more independent from the forces of the environment—the greater is the share of Its own control in molding its destiny.

42

The Pattern Variables*

Talcott Parsons

An actor in a situation is confronted by a series of major dilemmas of orientation, a series of choices that the actor must make before the situation has a determinate meaning for him. The objects of the situation do not interact with the cognizing and cathecting organism in such a fashion as to determine automatically the meaning of the situation. Rather, the actor must make a series of choices before the situation will have a determinate meaning. Specifically, we maintain, the actor must make five specific dichotomous choices before any situation will have a determinate meaning. The five dichotomies which formulate these choice alternatives are called the *pattern variables* because any specific orientation (and consequently any action) is characterized by a pattern of the five choices.

At the risk of being repititious, let us restate our definition: *a pattern variable* is a dichotomy, one side of which must be chosen by an actor before the meaning of a situation is determinate for him, and thus before he can act with respect to that situation. We maintain that there are only five *basic* pattern variables (i.e., pattern variables deriving directly from the frame of reference of the theory of action) and that, in the sense that they are all of the pattern variables which so derive, they constitute a system. Let us list them and give them names and numbers so that we can more easily refer to them in the future. They are:

1. Affectivity—Affective neutrality.
2. Self-orientation—Collectivity-orientation.
3. Universalism—Particularism.
4. Ascription—Achievement.
5. Specificity—Diffuseness.

The first concerns the problem of whether or not evaluation is to take place in a given situation. The second concerns the primacy of moral standards in an evaluative procedure. The third concerns the relative primacy of cognitive and cathectic standards. The fourth concerns the seeing of objects as quality or performance complexes. The fifth concerns the scope of significance of the object.

The Definitions of Pattern Variables

(1) *Affectvity:* the role-expectation that the incumbent of the role may freely express certain

*Excerpt reprinted with permission from *Toward a General Theory of Action* edited by Talcott Parsons and Edward A. Shils.

affective reactions to objects in the situation and need not attempt to control them in the interest of discipline. (2) *Affective neutrality*: the role-expectation that the incumbent of the role in question should restrain any impulses to certain affective expressions and subordinate them to considerations of discipline. In both cases the affect may be positive or negative, and the discipline (or permissiveness) may apply only to certain qualitative types of affective expression (e.g., sexual).

(1) *Self-orientation:* the role-expectation by the relevant actors that it is *permissible* for the incumbent of the role in question to give priority in the given situation to his own private interests, whatever their motivational content or quality, independently of their bearing on the interests or values of a given collectivity of which he is a member, or the interests of other actors. (2) *Collectivity-orientation:* the role-expectation by the relevant actors that the actor is *obliged*, as an incumbent of the role in question, to take directly into account the values and interests of the collectivity of which, in this role, he is a member. When there is a potential conflict with his private interests, he is expected in the particular choice to give priority to the collective interest. This also applies to his action in representative roles on behalf of the collectivity.

(1) *Universalism:* the role-expectation that, in qualifications for memberships and decisions for differential treatment, priority will be given to standards defined in completely generalized terms, independent of the particular relationship of the actor's own statuses (qualities or performances, classificatory or relational) to those of the object. (2) *Particularism:* the role-expectation that, in qualifications for memberships and decisions for differential treatment, priority will be given to standards which assert the primacy of the values attached to objects by their particular relations to the actor's properties (qualities or performances, classificatory or relational) as over against their general universally applicable class properties.

(1) *Ascription:* the role-expectation that the role incumbent, in orienting himself to social objects in the relevant choice situation, will accord priority to the objects' given attributes (whether universalistically or particularistically defined) over their actual or potential performances. (2) *Achievement:* the role-expectation that the role incumbent, in orienting to social objects in the relevant choice situation, will give priority to the objects' actual or expected performances, and to their attributes only as directly relevant to these performances, over attributes which are essentially independent of the specific performances in question.

(1) *Diffuseness*: the role-expectation that the role incumbent, at the relevant choice point, will accept any potential significance of a social object, including obligation to it, which is compatible with his other interests and obligations, and that he will give priority to this expectation over any disposition to confine the role-orientation to a specific range of significance of the object. (2) *Specificity:* the role-expectation that the role incumbent, at the relevant choice point, will be oriented to a social object only within a specific range of its relevance as a cathectic object or as an instrumental means or condition and that he will give priority to this expectation over any disposition to include potential aspects of significance of the object not specifically defined in the expectation pattern.

43

THE SOCIAL SYSTEM*

TALCOTT PARSONS

The social system is made up of the actions of individuals. The actions which constitute the social system are also the same actions which make up the personality systems of the individual actors. The two systems are, however, analytically discrete entitites, despite this identity of their basic components.

The difference lies in their *foci of organization* as systems and hence in the substantive functional problems of their operation as systems. The "individual" actor as a concrete system of action is not usually the most important unit of a social system. For most purposes *the conceptual unit of the social system is the role.* The role is a sector of the individual actor's total system of action. It is the point of contact between the system of action of the individual actor and the social system.

The primary ingredient of the role is the role-expectation. Role-expectations are patterns of evaluation; their primary constituents are analytically derivable from the pattern-variable combinations and from derivatives of the pattern variables when these are combined with the specific types of situations. Role-expectations organize (in accordance with general value-orientations) the reciprocities, expectations, and responses to those expectations in the specific interaction systems of ego and one or more alters. This reciprocal aspect must always be borne in mind since the expectations of an ego *always* imply the expectations of one or more alters. It is in this reciprocity or complementarity that sanctions enter and acquire their place in systems of action. What an actor is expected to do in a given situation both by himself and by others constitutes the expectations of that role. What the relevant alters are expected to do, contingent on ego's action, constitute the sanctions. Role expectations and sanctions are, therefore, in terms of the content of action, the *reciprocal of each other.* What are sanctions to ego are also role-expectations to alter, and vice versa. However, the content of ego's and alter's expectations concerning ego's action need not be identical with the content of the expectations of alter and ego regarding alter's action in response to ego's.

In a social system, roles vary in the degree of their institutionalization. By institutionalization we mean the integration of the complementary role-expectation and sanction patterns with a generalized value system *common* to the members of the more inclusive collectivity, of which the system of complementary role-actions may be a part. Insofar as ego's set of role-expectations is institutionalized, the sanctions which express the role-expectations of the other actors will tend to reinforce his own need-dispositions to

*Excerpt reprinted with permission from *Toward a General Theory of Action* edited by Talcott Parsons and Edward A. Shils.

conform with these expectations by rewarding it and by punishing deviance.

The sanctions will be rewards when they facilitate the realization of the goals which are part of his action or when they add further gratifications upon the completion of the action at certain levels of proficiency; they will be punishments when they hinder his realization of the goals which are part of his action or when they add further deprivations during or after the execution of the action. Conformity on the part of alter with ego's expectations is a condition of ego's goal realization. In addition to the conformity or divergence of alter's actions with respect to ego's expectations, alter's attitudes of approval or disapproval toward ego's behavior are also positive or negative sanctions. In addition to these two immediate types of reward and punishment, there should be mentioned alter's supplementary granting of gratifications for ego's conformity with expectations or transcendence of them and alter's supplementary infliction of deprivations for deficiencies.

Thus far we have been treating the social system only in its most elementary form; namely, as the interaction in which the actions of the incumbents of each role are regulated by the double contingency of expectations. Concrete social systems are, however, more than the simple interaction of two or more individual actors with a common system of values. Social systems give rise to, and often themselves constitute, collective actors in the sense that the individual members interact with one another and with members of other social systems for the achievement of shared collective goals. By collective goals we mean (1) those which are either prescribed by persons acting in a legitimate position of authority and in which the goal is expected to involve gratifications for members other than but including the particular actor, or (2) those goals which, without being specifically prescribed by authority, have the same content as regards the recipients of their gratifications. Shared collective goals are goals which, having the content described in the preceding sentence, have the further property of being simultaneously pursued by a plurality of persons in the same system of interaction.

A social system having the three properties of collective goals, shared goals, and of being a single system of interaction with boundaries defined by incumbency in the roles constituting the system, will be called a *collectivity.* The action of the collectivity may be viewed as the *action in concert* of a plurality of individual actors. Collectivities may act in concert toward their own members or toward objects outside themselves. In the latter case, complementarity of expectations and the associated shared value system exist among the actors within the collectivity but it will not exist *to the same extent* with the actors who are part of another social system. In the case of the former, complementarity of expectations and the shared value system might well exist among all the actors in the situation, with all reorganization of the action of the members being in accordance with shared general value-orientations and with specifically complementary expectations. Even in this case, there will always be involved some orientation toward social and/or nonsocial objects which are outside the collectivity.

The concept of boundary is of crucial significance in the definition of a collectivity. The boundary of a collectivity is that criterion whereby some persons are included as members and others are excluded as nonmembers. The inclusion or exclusion of a person depends on whether or not he has a membership role in the collectivity. Thus all persons who have such roles are members; they are within the boundary. Thus, the boundary is defined in terms of membership roles.

A collectivity is characterized by the *solidarity* of its members. Solidarity is characterized by the institutionalization of shared value-orientations; the values being, of course, oriented toward collective gratifications. Acceptance of common value patterns permits the more differentiated institutionalization of the action of the members of the collectivity in a wide range of specific situations. The range may be broad or narrow, but in each specific situation institutionalization exists when each actor in the situation does, and believes he should do, what the other actors whom he confronts believe he should do. Thus institutionalization is an articulation or integration of the actions of a plurality of actors in a specific type of situation in which the various actors accept jointly a set of harmonious rules regarding goals and procedures.

A social system, then, is a system of interaction of a plurality of actors, in which the action is oriented by rules which are complexes of complementary expectations concerning roles and sanctions. *As a system*, it has determinate internal organization and determinate patterns of structural change. It has, furthermore, as a system, a variety of mechanisms of adaptation to changes in the external environment. Those mechanisms function to create one of the important properties of a system; namely, the tendency to maintain boundaries. A total social system which, for practical purposes, may be treated as self-subsistent—which, in other words, contains within approximately the boundaries defined by membership all the functional mechanisms required for its maintenance as a system—is here called a *society*. Any other is a *subsystem* of a society. It is of the greatest importance in connection with any specific problem to place the subsystem in question explicitly in the context of those parts of the total society which are outside the subsystem for the purposes at hand.

44

The AGIL Schema*

Talcott Parsons

A "phase" may be regarded as the changing state of the system through some interval in time, when its movement in a given dimension is maximized relative to its movement in the other three dimensions. Phases are *technically* described by the specification of the direction and amount of movement taking place within the time interval on *each* of the four dimensions, but for purposes of convenience, are named in terms of the dimension of major movement. An act is conceived as exerting some kind of directing influence on the movement of the system, and may thus be described by the direction of movement of the system, which it signalizes. A series of "pure types" may be visualized, which coincide with the maximum point of the phases.

The system problems as described in earlier papers may be thought of as problems of maximizing the movement of the system in *each* of the four dimensions. Since preponderance of all phases cannot be achieved at one point in time, the system goes through phases or time cycles in which first one direction of movement and then another is preponderant. The overt acts are thus "addressed to" or are "associated with" the solution of system problems, and by the frequency of their occurrence hold the system within given phases, and move the system from one phase to the next.

A. Adaptation. Successful adaptation involves (a) an accommodation of the system to inflexible "reality demands," and (b) an active transformation of the situation external to the system.

G. Goal Gratification or Enjoyment of Goal-state. Goal attainment involves intrinsically gratifying activity, it is the culminating phase of a sequence of preparatory activities.

I. Integration. The attitude toward the object is *affectively* toned, and the relation to the object is *particularistic*. Successful integration involves a determinate set of relations among the member units of the system such that it retains and reinforces its boundary-maintaining character as a single entity.

L. Latency. A system is confronted by the necessity, as a precondition for its continued existence, of maintaining and renewing the motivational and cultural patterns which are integral to its interaction as a system. This involves both their maintenance in a condition of latency and under certain conditions their expression. The latter involves moreover the expression of the motivations and cultural patterns which are integral to the system and those which are integral to the units. These unit motivations and cultural patterns may be in themselves in conflict with

FIGURE 1 Phases in the Relationship of a System to Its Situation

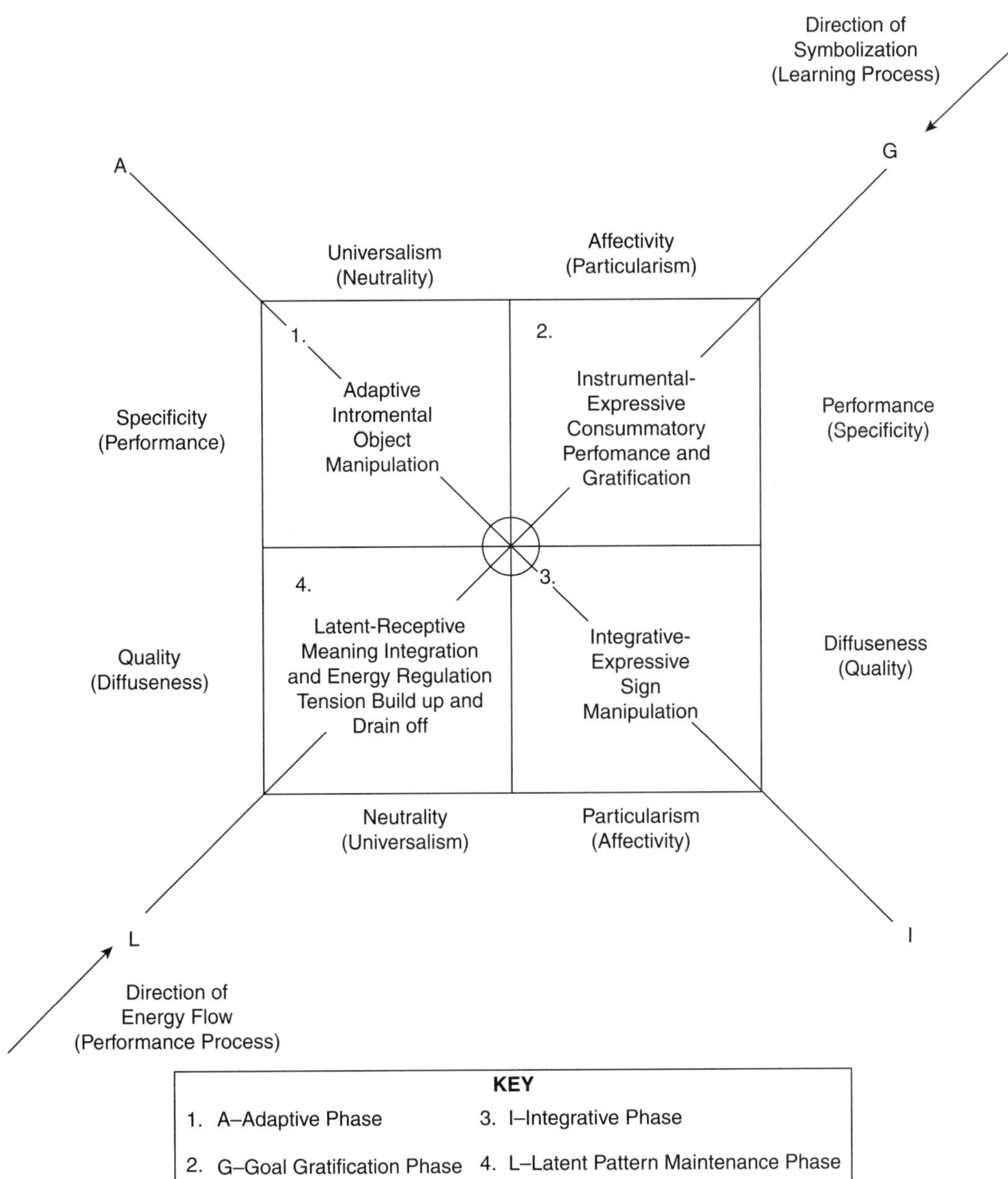

the motivations and patterns integral to the system but their expression periodically is usually a prerequisite of the system's continued or renewed functioning.

The phases which we have described are not merely descriptions of different possible states of systems. There are determinate dynamic relations among them, in consequence of the one way flow of motivational energy. There is a general tendency for systems to move towards the G (goal-attainment) phase through either the A (adaptive) phase or I (system-integrative) phase. The system-economy necessitates, after prolonged action in one phase, a shift to another phase to reestablish the balance of the system and to meet the system problems which had been disregarded while the system was in the former phase.

FIGURE 2 Microcosm to Macrocosm Relation

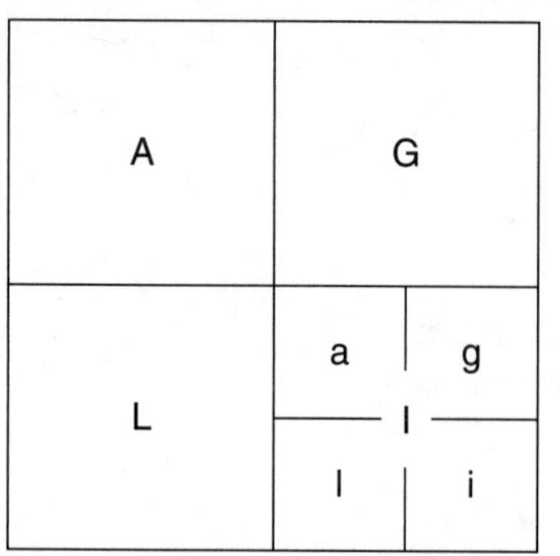

Let us call the macroscopic system of action and objects we are theorizing about a "world of events". Let the "world of events" be represented by the total figure. Let the phases of the total system or "world of events" be represented by the large quadrants, A, G, I, and L, with the phase meanings we have given them above. Let the "world of symbols" used in *interpersonal* communication within the system be represented by the small quadrants a, g, i, and 1. These are all to be found in the large quadrant I. Let "a" be a symbol or cluster of them which refers to "A," let "g" have a similar relation to "G," and so on, so that each large quadrant is represented by a small quadrant with the same letter designation.

Now we may say that I, as constituted by the quadrants a, g, i, and 1, is a *microcosm* of the *macrocosm* A, G, I, L. But at the same time, I, and so its constituent parts, is a *part* of the whole, A, G, I, L. This is the kind of relation we suppose interpersonal communication to bear to the more macroscopic systems of action in which it is embedded.

45

Manifest and Latent Functions*

Robert K. Merton

As has been implied in earlier sections, the distinction between manifest and latent functions was devised to preclude the inadvertent confusion, often found in the sociological literature, between conscious *motivations* for social behavior and its *objective consequences.* Our scrutiny of current vocabularies of functional analysis has shown how easily, and how unfortunately, the sociologist may identify *motives* with *functions.* It was further indicated that the motive and the function vary independently and that the failure to register this fact in an established terminology has contributed to the unwitting tendency among sociologists to confuse the subjective categories of motivation with the objective categories of function. This, then, is the central purpose of our succumbing to the not-always-commendable practice of introducing new terms into the rapidly growing technical vocabulary of sociology, a practice regarded by many laymen as an affront to their intelligence and an offense against common intelligibility.

As will be readily recognized, I have adapted the terms "manifest" and "latent" from their use in another context by Freud (although Francis Bacon had long ago spoken of "latent process" and "latent configuration" in connection with processes which are below the threshold of superficial observation).

The distinction itself has been repeatedly drawn by observers of human behavior at irregular intervals over a span of many centuries. Indeed, it would be disconcerting to find that a distinction which we have come to regard as central to functional analysis had not been made by any of that numerous company who have in effect adopted a functional orientation. We need mention only a few of those who have, in recent decades, found it necessary to distinguish in their specific interpretations of behavior between the end-in-view and the functional consequences of action.

> George H. Mead: ". . . that attitude of hostility toward the lawbreaker has the unique advantage [read: latent function] of uniting all members of the community in the emotional solidarity of aggression. While the most admirable of humanitarian efforts are sure to run counter to the

*Reprinted with the permission of The Free Press, a Division of Simon & Schuster, Inc., from *Social Theory and Social Structure,* Revised & Enlarged Edition by Robert K. Merton.

individual interests of very many in the community, or fail to touch the interest and imagination of the multitude and to leave the community divided or indifferent, the cry of thief or murderer is attuned to profound complexes, lying below the surface of competing individual efforts, and citizens who have [been] separated by divergent interests stand together against the common enemy."

Emile Durkheim's similar analysis of the social functions of punishment is also focused on its latent functions (consequences for the community) rather than confined to manifest functions (consequences for the criminal).

W. G. Sumner: ". . . from the first acts by which men try to satisfy needs, each act stands by itself, and looks no further than the immediate satisfaction. From recurrent needs arise habits for the individual and customs for the group, but these results are consequences which were never conscious, and never foreseen or intended. They are not noticed until they have long existed, and it is still longer before they are appreciated." Although this fails to locate the latent functions of standardized social actions for a designated social structure, it plainly makes the basic distinction between ends-in-view and objective consequences.

R. M. MacIver: In addition to the direct effects of institutions, "there are further effects by way of control which lie outside the direct purposes of men . . . this type of reactive form of control . . . may, though unintended, be of profound service to society."

W. I. Thomas and F. Znaniecki: "Although all the new [Polish peasant cooperative] institutions are thus formed with the definite purpose of satisfying certain specific needs, their social function is by no means limited to their explicit and conscious purpose . . . every one of these institutions—commune or agricultural circle, loan and savings bank, or theater—is not merely a mechanism for the management of certain values but also an association of people, each member of which is supposed to participate in the common activities as a living, concrete individual. Whatever is the predominant, official common interest upon which the institution is founded, the association as a concrete group of human personalities unofficially involves many other interests; the social contacts between its members are not limited to their common pursuit, though the latter, of course, constitutes both the main reason for which the association is formed and the most permanent bond which holds it together. Owing to this combination of an abstract political, economic, or rather rational mechanism for the satisfaction of specific needs with the concrete unity of a social group, the new institution is also the best intermediary link between the peasant primary-group and the secondary national system."

These and numerous other sociological observers have, then, from time to time distinguished between categories of subjective disposition ("needs, interests, purposes") and categories of generally unrecognized but objective functional consequences ("unique advantages," "never conscious" consequences, "unintended . . . service to society," "function not limited to conscious and explicit purpose").

Since the occasion for making the distinction arises with great frequency, and since the purpose of a conceptual scheme is to direct observations toward salient elements of a situation and to prevent the inadvertent oversight of these elements, it would seem justifiable to designate this distinction by an appropriate set of terms. This is the rationale for the distinction between manifest functions and latent functions; the first referring to those objective consequences for a specified unit (person, subgroup, social or cultural system) which contribute to its adjustment or adaptation and were so intended; the second referring to unintended and unrecognized consequences of the same order.

There are some indications that the christening of this distinction may serve a heuristic purpose by becoming incorporated into an explicit conceptual apparatus, thus aiding both systematic observation and later analysis. In recent years, for example, the distinction between manifest and latent functions has been utilized in analyses of racial intermarriage, social stratification, affective frustration, Veblen's sociological theories, prevailing American orientations toward Russia, propaganda as a means of social control, Malinowski's anthropological theory, Navajo witchcraft, problems in the sociology of knowledge, fashion, the dynamics of personality, national security measures, the internal social dynamics of bureaucracy, and a great variety of other sociological problems.

The very diversity of these subject-matters suggests that the theoretic distinction between manifest and latent functions is not bound up with a limited and particular range of human behavior. But there still remains the large task of ferreting out the specific uses to which this distinction can be put, and it is to this large task that we devote the remaining pages of this chapter.

Heuristic Purposes of the Distinction

Clarifies the analysis of seemingly irrational social patterns. In the first place, the distinction aids the sociological interpretation of many social practices which persist even though their manifest purpose is clearly not achieved. The time-worn procedure in such instances has been for diverse, particularly lay, observers to refer to these practices as "superstitions," "irrationalities," "mere inertia of tradition," *etc.* In other words, when group behavior does not—and, indeed, often cannot—attain its ostensible purpose there is an inclination to attribute its occurrence to lack of intelligence, sheer ignorance, survivals, or so-called inertia. Thus, the Hopi ceremonials designed to produce abundant rainfall may be labelled a superstitious practice of primitive folk and that is assumed to conclude the matter. It should be noted that this in no sense accounts for the group behavior. It is simply a case of name-calling; it substitutes the epithet "superstition" for an analysis of the actual role of this behavior in the life of the group. Given the concept of latent function, however, we are reminded that this behavior may perform a function for the group, although this function may be quite remote from the avowed purpose of the behavior.

The concept of latent function extends the observer's attention beyond the question of whether or not the behavior attains its avowed purpose. Temporarily ignoring these explicit purposes, it directs attention toward another range of consequences: those bearing, for example, upon the individual personalities of Hopi involved in the ceremony and upon the persistence and continuity of the larger group. Were one to confine himself to the problem of whether a manifest (purposed) function occurs, it becomes a problem, not for the sociologist, but for the meteorologist. And to be sure, our meteorologists agree that the rain ceremonial does not produce rain; but this is hardly to the point. It is merely to say that the ceremony does not have this technological use; that this purpose of the ceremony and its actual consequences do not coincide. But with the concept of latent function, we continue our inquiry, examining the consequences of the ceremony not for the rain gods or for meteorological phenomena, but for the groups which conduct the ceremony. And here it may be found, as many observers indicate, that the ceremonial does indeed have functions—but functions which are non-purposed or latent.

Ceremonials may fulfill the latent function of reinforcing the group identity by providing a periodic occasion on which the scattered members of a group assemble to engage in a common activity. As Durkheim among others long since indicated, such ceremonials are a means by which collective expression is afforded the sentiments which, in a further analysis, are found to be a basic source of group unity. Through the systematic application of the concept of latent function, therefore, apparently irrational behavior may at times be found to be positively functional for the group. Operating with the concept of latent function, we are not too quick to conclude that if an activity of a group does not achieve its nominal purpose, then its persistence can be described only as an instance of "inertia," "survival," or "manipulation by powerful subgroups in the society."

In point of fact, some conception like that of latent function has very often, almost invariably, been employed by social scientists observing *a standardized practice designed to achieve an objective which one knows from accredited physical science cannot be thus achieved.* This would plainly be the case, for example, with Pueblo rituals dealing with rain or fertility. *But with behavior which is not directed toward a clearly unattainable objective, sociological observers are less likely to examine the collateral or latent functions of the behavior.*

Directs attention to theoretically fruitful fields of inquiry. The distinction between manifest and latent functions serves further to direct the attention of the sociologist to precisely those realms of behavior, attitude and belief where he can most fruitfully apply his special skills. For what is his task if he confines himself to the study of manifest functions? He is then concerned very largely with determining whether a practice instituted for a particular purpose does, in fact, achieve this purpose. He will then inquire, for example, whether a new system of wage-payment achieves its avowed purpose of reducing labor turnover or of increasing output. He will ask whether a propaganda campaign has indeed gained its objective of increasing "willingness to fight" or "willingness to buy war bonds," or "tolerance toward other ethnic groups." Now, these are important, and complex, types of inquiry. But, so long as sociologists *confine* themselves to the study of manifest functions, their inquiry is set for them by practical men of affairs (whether a captain of industry, a trade union leader, or, conceivably, a Navaho chieftain, is for the moment immaterial), rather than by the theoretic problems which are at the core of the discipline. By dealing primarily with the realm of manifest functions, with the key problem of whether deliberately instituted practices or organizations succeed in achieving their objectives, the sociologist becomes converted into an industrious and skilled recorder of the altogether familiar pattern of behavior. *The terms of appraisal are fixed and limited by the question put to him by the non-theoretic men of affairs, e.g.*, has the new wage-payment program achieved such-and-such purposes?

But armed with the concept of latent function, the sociologist extends his inquiry in those very directions which promise most for the theoretic development of the discipline. He examines the familiar (or planned) social practice to ascertain the latent, and hence generally unrecognized, functions (as well, of course, as the manifest functions). He considers for example, the consequences of the new wage plan for, say, the trade union in which the workers are organized or the consequences of a propaganda program, not only for increasing its avowed purpose of stirring up patriotic fervor, but also for making large numbers of people reluctant to speak their minds when they differ with official policies, etc. In short, it is suggested that the *distinctive* intellectual contributions of the sociologist are found primarily in the study of unintended consequences (among which are latent functions) of social practices, as well as in the study of anticipated consequences (among which are manifest functions).

There is some evidence that it is precisely at the point where the research attention of sociologists has shifted from the plane of manifest to the plane of latent functions that they have made their *distinctive* and major contributions. This can be extensively documented but a few passing illustrations must suffice.

46

Social Structure and Anomie*

Robert K. Merton

There persists a notable tendency in sociological theory to attribute the malfunctioning of social structure primarily to those of man's imperious biological drives which are not adequately restrained by social control. In this view, the social order is solely a device for "impulse management" and the "social processing" of tensions. These impulses which break through social control, be it noted, are held to be biologically derived. Nonconformity is assumed to be rooted in original nature. Conformity is by implication the result of an utilitarian calculus or unreasoned conditioning. This point of view, whatever its other deficiences, clearly begs one question. It provides no basis for determining the nonbiological conditions which induce deviations from prescribed patterns of conduct. In this paper, it will be suggested that certain phases of social structure generate the circumstances in which infringement of social codes constitutes a "normal" response.

The conceptual scheme to be outlined is designed to provide a coherent, systematic approach to the study of socio-cultural sources of deviate behavior. Our primary aim lies in discovering how some social structures *exert a definite pressure* upon certain persons in the society to engage in nonconformist rather than conformist conduct. The many ramifications of the scheme cannot all be discussed; the problems mentioned outnumber those explicitly treated.

Among the elements of social and cultural structure, two are important for our purposes. These are analytically separable although they merge imperceptibly in concrete situations. The first consists of culturally defined goals, purposes, and interests. It comprises a frame of aspirational reference. These goals are more or less integrated and involve varying degrees of prestige and sentiment. They constitute a basic, but not the exclusive, component of what Linton aptly has called "designs for group living." Some of these cultural aspirations are related to the original drives of man, but they are not determined by them. The second phase of the social structure defines, regulates, and controls the acceptable modes of achieving these goals. Every social group invariably couples its scale of desired ends with moral or institutional regulation of permissible and required procedures for attaining these ends. These regulatory norms and

*"Social Structure and Anomie," by Robert K. Merton, American Sociological Review 8,2 (1938): 672–682.

moral imperatives do not necessarily coincide with technical or efficiency norms. Many procedures which from the standpoint of *particular individuals* would be most efficient in securing desired values, e.g., illicit oil-stock schemes, theft, fraud, are ruled out of the institutional area of permitted conduct. The choice of expedients is limited by the institutional norms.

To say that these two elements, culture goals and institutional norms, operate jointly is not to say that the ranges of alternative behaviors and aims bear some constant relation to one another. The emphasis upon certain goals may vary independently of the degree of emphasis upon institutional means. There may develop a disproportionate, at times, a virtually exclusive, stress upon the value of specific goals, involving relatively slight concern with the institutionally appropriate modes of attaining these goals. The limiting case in this direction is reached when the range of alternative procedures is limited only by technical rather than institutional considerations. Any and all devices which promise attainment of the all important goal would be permitted in this hypothetical polar case. This constitutes one type of cultural malintegration. A second polar type is found in groups where activities originally conceived as instrumental are transmuted into ends in themselves. The original purposes are forgotten and ritualistic adherence to institutionally prescribed conduct becomes virtually obsessive. Stability is largely ensured while change is flouted. The range of alternative behaviors is severely limited. There develops a tradition-bound, sacred society characterized by neophobia. The occupational psychosis of the bureaucrat may be cited as a case in point. Finally, there are the intermediate types of groups where a balance between culture goals and institutional means is maintained. These are the significantly integrated and relatively stable, though changing, groups.

An effective equilibrium between the two phases of the social structure is maintained as long as satisfactions accrue to individuals who conform to both constraints, viz., satisfactions from the achievement of the goals and satisfactions emerging directly from the institutionally canalized modes of striving to attain these ends. Success, in such equilibrated cases, is twofold. Success is reckoned in terms of the product and in terms of the process, in terms of the outcome and in terms of activities. Continuing satisfactions must derive from sheer *participation* in a competitive order as well as from eclipsing one's competitors if the order itself is to be sustained. The occasional sacrifices involved in institutionalized conduct must be compensated by socialized rewards. The distribution of statuses and roles through competition must be so organized that positive incentives for conformity to roles and adherence to status obligations are provided *for every position* within the distributive order. Aberrant conduct, therefore, may be viewed as a symptom of dissociation between culturally defined aspirations and socially structured means.

Of the types of groups which result from the independent variation of the two phases of the social structure, we shall be primarily concerned with the first, namely, that involving a disproportionate accent on goals. This statement must be recast in a proper perspective. In no group is there an absence of regulatory codes governing conduct, yet groups do vary in the degree to which these folkways, mores, and institutional controls are effectively integrated with the more diffuse goals which are part of the culture matrix. Emotional convictions may cluster about the complex of socially acclaimed ends, meanwhile shifting their support from the culturally defined implementation of these ends. As we shall see, certain aspects of the social structure may generate countermores and antisocial behavior precisely because of differential emphases on goals and regulations. In the extreme case, the latter may be so vitiated by the goal-emphasis that the range of behavior is limited only by considerations of technical expediency. The sole significant question then becomes, which available means is most efficient in netting the socially approved value? The technically most feasible procedure, whether legitimate or not, is preferred to the institutionally prescribed conduct. As this process continues, the integration of the society becomes tenuous and anomie ensues.

Thus, in competitive athletics, when the aim of victory is shorn of its institutional trappings and success in contests becomes construed as "winning the game" rather than "winning through circumscribed modes of activity," a premium is implicitly set upon the use of illegitimate but technically efficient means. The star of the opposing football team is surreptitiously slugged; the wrestler furtively incapacitates his opponent through ingenious but illicit techniques; university alumni covertly subsidize "students" whose talents are largely confined to the athletic field. The emphasis on the goal has so attenuated the satisfactions deriving from sheer participation in the competitive activity that these satisfactions are virtually confined to a successful outcome. Through the same process, tension generated by the desire to win in a poker game is relieved by successfully dealing oneself four aces, or, when the cult of success has become completely dominant, by sagaciously shuffling the cards in a game of solitaire. The faint twinge of uneasiness in the last instance and the surreptious nature of public delicts indicate clearly that the institutional rules of the game *are known* to those who evade them, but that the emotional supports of these rules are largely vitiated by cultural exaggeration of the success-goal. They are microcosmic images of the social macrocosm.

Of course, this process is not restricted to the realm of sport. The process whereby exaltation of the end generates a literal demoralization, i.e., a deinstitutionalization, of the means is one which characterizes many groups in which the two phases of the social structure are not highly integrated. The extreme emphasis upon the accumulation of wealth as a symbol of success in our own society militates against the completely effective control of institutionally regulated modes of acquiring a fortune. Fraud, corruption, vice, crime, in short, the entire catalogue of proscribed behavior, becomes increasingly common when the emphasis on the *culturally induced* success-goal becomes divorced from a coordinated institutional emphasis. This observation is of crucial theoretical importance in examining the doctrine that antisocial behavior most frequently derives from biological drives breaking through the restraints imposed by society. The difference is one between a strictly utilitarian interpretation which conceives man's ends as random and an analysis which finds these ends deriving from the basic values of the culture.

Our analysis can scarcely stop at this juncture. We must turn to other aspects of the social structure if we are to deal with the social genesis of the varying rates and types of deviate behavior characteristic of different societies. Thus far, we have sketched three ideal types of social orders constituted by distinctive patterns of relations between culture ends and means. Turning from these types of *culture patterning*, we find five logically possible, alternative modes of adjustment or adaptation by *individuals* within the culture-bearing society or group. These are schematically presented in the following table, where (+) signifies "acceptance," (–) signifies "elimination" and (±) signifies "rejection and substitution of new goals and standards."

Our discussion of the relation between these alternative responses and other phases of the social structure must be prefaced by the observation that persons may shift from one alternative to another as they engage in different social activities. These categories refer to role adjustments in specific situations, not to personality *in toto*. To treat the development of this process in various spheres of conduct would introduce a complexity unmanageable within the confines of this paper. For this reason, we shall be concerned primarily with economic activity in the broad sense, "the production, exchange, distribution and consumption of goods and services" in our competitive society, wherein wealth has taken on a highly symbolic cast. Our task is to search out some of the factors which exert pressure upon individuals to engage in certain of these logically possible alternative responses. This choice, as we shall see, is far from random.

In every society, Adaptation I (conformity to both culture goals and means) is the most common and widely diffused. Were this not so, the stability and continuity of the society could not

	Culture Goals	*Institutionalized Means*
I. Conformity	+	+
II. Innovation	+	–
III. Ritualism	–	+
IV. Retreatism	–	–
V. Rebellion	±	±

be maintained. The mesh of expectancies which constitutes every social order is sustained by the modal behavior of its members falling within the first category. Conventional role behavior oriented toward the basic values of the group is the rule rather than the exception. It is this fact alone which permits us to speak of a human aggregate as comprising a group or society.

Conversely, Adaptation IV (rejection of goals and means) is the least common. Persons who "adjust" (or maladjust) in this fashion are, strictly speaking, *in* the society but not *of* it. Sociologically, these constitute the true "aliens." Not sharing the common frame of orientation, they can be included within the societal population merely in a fictional sense. In this category are *some* of the activities of psychotics, psychoneurotics, chronic autists, pariahs, outcasts, vagrants, vagabonds, tramps, chronic drunkards and drug addicts. These have relinquished, in certain spheres of activity, the culturally defined goals, involving complete aim-inhibition in the polar case, and their adjustments are not in accord with institutional norms. This is not to say that in some cases the source of their behavioral adjustments is not in part the very social structure which they have in effect repudiated nor that their very existence within a social area does not constitute a problem for the socialized population.

This mode of "adjustment" occurs, as far as structural sources are concerned, when both the culture goals and institutionalized procedures have been assimilated thoroughly by the individual and imbued with affect and high positive value, but where those institutionalized procedures which promise a measure of successful attainment of the goals are not available to the individual. In such instances, there results a twofold mental conflict insofar as the moral obligation for adopting institutional means conflicts with the pressure to resort to illegitimate means (which may attain the goal) and inasmuch as the individual is shut off from means which are both legitimate *and* effective. The competitive order is maintained, but the frustrated and handicapped individual who cannot cope with this order drops out. Defeatism, quietism and resignation are manifested in escape mechanisms which ultimately lead the individual to "escape" from the requirements of the society. It is an expedient which arises from continued failure to attain the goal by legitimate measures and from an inability to adopt the illegitimate route because of internalized prohibitions and institutionalized compulsives, *during which process the supreme value of the success-goal has as yet not been renounced.* The conflict is resolved by eliminating both precipitating elements, the goals and means. The escape is complete, the conflict is eliminated and the individual is a socialized.

Be it noted that where frustration derives from the inaccessibility of effective institutional means for attaining economic or any other type of highly valued "success," that Adaptations II, III and V (innovation, ritualism and rebellion) are also possible. The result will be determined by the particular personality, and thus, the *particular* cultural background, involved. Inadequate socialization will result in the innovation response whereby the conflict and frustration are eliminated by relinquishing the institutional means and retaining the success-aspiration; an extreme assimilation of institutional demands will lead to ritualism wherein the goal is dropped as beyond one's reach but conformity to the mores persists; and rebellion occurs when emancipation from the reigning standards, due to frustration or to marginalist perspectives, leads to the attempt to introduce a "new social order."

Our major concern is with the illegitimacy adjustment. This involves the use of conventionally proscribed but frequently effective means of attaining at least the simulacrum of culturally defined success,—wealth, power, and the like. As we have seen, this adjustment occurs when the individual has assimilated the cultural emphasis on success without equally internalizing the morally prescribed norms governing means for its attainment. The question arises, Which phases of our social structure predispose toward this mode of adjustment? We may examine a concrete instance, effectively analyzed by Lohman, which provides a clue to the answer. Lohman has shown that specialized areas of vice in the near north side of Chicago constitute a "normal" response to a situation where the cultural emphasis upon pecuniary success has been absorbed, but where there is little access to conventional and legitimate means for attaining such success. The conventional occupational opportunities of persons in this area are almost completely limited to manual labor. Given our cultural stigmatization of manual labor, and its correlate, the prestige of white collar work, it is clear that the result is a strain toward innovational practices. The limitation of opportunity to unskilled labor and the resultant low income can not compete *in terms of conventional standards of achievement* with the high income from organized vice.

For our purposes, this situation involves two important features. First, such antisocial behavior is in a sense "called forth" by certain conventional values of the culture *and* by the class structure involving differential access to the approved opportunities for legitimate, prestige-bearing pursuit of the culture goals. The lack of high integration between the means-and-end elements of the cultural pattern and the particular class structure combine to favor a heightened frequency of antisocial conduct in such groups. The second consideration is of equal significance. Recourse to the first of the alternative responses, legitimate effort, is limited by the fact that actual advance toward desired success-symbols through conventional channels is, despite our persisting open-class ideology, relatively rare and difficult for those handicapped by little formal education and few economic resources. The dominant pressure of group standards of success is, therefore, on the gradual attenuation of legitimate, but by and large ineffective, strivings and the increasing use of illegitimate, but more or less effective, expedients of vice and crime. The cultural demands made on persons in this situation are incompatible. On the one hand, they are asked to orient their conduct toward the prospect of accumulating wealth and on the other, they are largely denied effective opportunities to do so institutionally. The consequences of such structural inconsistency are psycho-pathological personality, and/or antisocial conduct, and/or revolutionary activities. The equilibrium between culturally designated means and ends becomes highly unstable with the progressive emphasis on attaining the prestige-laden ends by any means whatsoever. Within this context, Capone represents the triumph of amoral intelligence over morally prescribed "failure," when the channels of vertical mobility are closed or narrowed *in a society which places a high premium on economic affluence and social ascent for all its members.*

This last qualification is of primary importance. It suggests that other phases of the social structure besides the extreme emphasis on pecuniary success, must be considered if we are to understand the social sources of antisocial behavior. A high frequency of deviate behavior is not generated simply by "lack of opportunity" or by this exaggerated pecuniary emphasis. A comparatively rigidified class structure, a feudalistic or caste order, may limit such opportunities far beyond the point which obtains in our society today. It is only when a system of cultural values extols, virtually above all else, certain *common* symbols of success *for the population at large* while its social structure rigorously restricts or completely eliminates access to approved modes of acquiring these symbols *for a considerable part of the same population,* that antisocial behavior ensues on a considerable scale. In other words, our egalitarian ideology denies by implication the existence of noncompeting groups and individuals in the pursuit of pecuniary success. The same body of success-symbols is held to be desirable for all. These goals are held to *transcend class lines,* not to be bounded by them, yet the actual social organization is such that there exist class differentials in the accessibility of these *common* success-symbols. Frustration and thwarted aspiration lead to the search for avenues of escape from a culturally induced intolerable situation; or unrelieved ambition may eventuate in illicit attempts to acquire the dominant values. The American stress on pecuniary success and ambitiousness for all thus invites exaggerated anxieties, hostilities, neuroses and antisocial behavior.

This theoretical analysis may go far toward explaining the varying correlations between crime and poverty. Poverty is not an isolated variable. It is one in a complex of interdependent social and cultural variables. When viewed in such a context, it represents quite different states of affairs. Poverty as such, and consequent limitation of opportunity, are not sufficient to induce a conspicuously high rate of criminal behavior. Even the often mentioned "poverty in the midst of plenty" will not necessarily lead to this result. Only insofar as poverty and associated disadvantages in competition for the culture values approved for *all* members of the society is linked with the assimilation of a cultural emphasis on monetary accumulation as a symbol of success is antisocial conduct a "normal" outcome. Thus, poverty is less highly correlated with crime in southeastern Europe than in the United States. The possibilities of vertical mobility in these European areas would seem to be fewer than in this country, so that neither poverty *per se* nor its association with limited opportunity is sufficient to account for the varying correlations. It is only when the full configuration is considered, poverty, limited opportunity and a commonly shared system of success symbols, that we can explain the higher association between poverty and crime in our society than in others where rigidified class structure is coupled with *differential class symbols of achievement.*

In societies such as our own, then, the pressure of prestige-bearing success tends to eliminate the effective social constraint over means employed to this end. "The-end-justifies-the-means" doctrine becomes a guiding tenet for action when the cultural structure unduly exalts the end and the social organization unduly limits possible recourse to approved means. Otherwise put, this notion and associated behavior reflect a lack of cultural coordination. In international relations, the effects of this lack of integration are notoriously apparent. An emphasis upon national power is not readily coordinated with an inept organization of legitimate, i.e., internationally defined and accepted, means for attaining this goal. The result is a tendency toward the abrogation of international law, treaties become scraps of paper, "undeclared warefare" serves as a technical evasion, the bombing of civilian populations is rationalized, just as the same societal situation induces the same sway of illegitimacy among individuals.

The social order we have described necessarily produces this "strain toward dissolution." The pressure of such an order is upon outdoing one's competitors. The choice of means within the ambit of institutional control will persist as long as the sentiments supporting a competitive system, i.e., deriving from the possibility of outranking competitors and hence enjoying the favorable response of others, are distributed throughout the entire system, of activities and are not confined merely to the final result. A stable social structure demands a balanced distribution of affect among its various segments. When there occurs a shift of emphasis from the satisfactions deriving from competition itself to almost exclusive concern with successful competition, the resultant stress leads to the breakdown of the regulatory structure. With the resulting attenuation of the institutional imperatives, there occurs an approximation of the situation erroneously held by utilitarians to be typical of society generally wherein calculations of advantage and fear of punishment are the sole regulating agencies. In such situations, as Hobbes observed, force and fraud come to constitute the sole virtues in view of their relative efficiency in attaining goals,—which were for him, of course, not culturally derived.

It should be apparent that the foregoing discussion is not pitched on a moralistic plane. Whatever the sentiments of the writer or reader concerning the ethical desirability of coordinating the means-and-goals phases of the social structure, one must agree that lack of such coordination leads to anomie. Insofar as one of the most general functions of social organization is to provide a basis for calculability and regularity of behavior, it is increasingly limited in effectiveness as these elements of the structure become dissociated. At the extreme, predictability virtually disappears and what may be properly termed cultural chaos or anomie intervenes.

This statement, being brief, is also incomplete. It has not included an exhaustive treatment of the various structural elements which predispose toward one rather than another of the alternative responses open to individuals; it has neglected, but not denied the relevance of, the factors determining the specific incidence of these responses; it has not enumerated the various concrete responses which are constituted by combinations of specific values of the analytical variables; it has omitted, or included only by implication, any consideration of the social functions performed by illicit responses; it has not tested the full explanatory power of the analytical scheme by examining a large number of group variations in the frequency of deviate and conformist behavior; it has not adequately dealt with rebellious conduct which seeks to refashion the social framework radically; it has not examined the relevance of cultural conflict for an analysis of culture-goal and institutional-means malintegration. It is suggested that these and related problems may be profitably analyzed by this scheme.

47

THE SELF-FULFILLING PROPHECY*

ROBERT K. MERTON

In a series of works seldom consulted outside the academic fraternity, W. I. Thomas, the dean of American sociologists, set forth a theorem basic to the social sciences: "If men define situations as real, they are real in their consequences." Were the Thomas theorem and its implications more widely known more men would understand more of the workings of our society. Though it lacks the sweep and precision of a Newtonian theorem, it possesses the same gift of relevance, being instructively applicable to many, if indeed not most, social processes.

"If men define situations as real, they are real in their consequences," wrote Professor Thomas. The suspicion that he was driving at a crucial point becomes all the more insistent when we note that essentially the same theorem had been repeatedly set forth by disciplined and observant minds long before Thomas.

When we find such otherwise discrepant minds as the redoubtable Bishop Bossuet in his passionate seventeenth-century defense of Catholic orthodoxy; the ironic Mandeville in his eighteenth-century allegory honeycombed with observations on the paradoxes of human society; the irascible genius Marx in his revision of Hegel's theory of historical change; the seminal Freud in works which have perhaps gone further than any others of his day toward modifying man's outlook on man; and the erudite, dogmatic, and occasionally sound Yale professor, William Graham Sumner, who lives on as the Karl Marx of the middle classes—when we find this mixed company (and I select from a longer if less distinguished list) agreeing on the truth and the pertinence of what is substantially the Thomas theorem, we may conclude that perhaps it's worth our attention as well.

To what, then, are Thomas and Bossuet, Mandeville, Marx, Freud and Sumner directing our attention?

The first part of the theorem provides an unceasing reminder that men respond not only to the objective features of a situation, but also, and at times primarily, to the meaning this situation has for them. And once they have assigned some meaning to the situation, their consequent behavior and some of the consequences of that behavior are determined by the ascribed meaning. But this is still rather abstract, and

---

*"The Self-Fulfilling Prophecy," by Robert K. Merton in *The Antioch Review* 8, 2 (Summer 1948): 193–210.

abstractions have a way of becoming unintelligible if they are not occasionally tied to concrete data. What is a case in point?

It is the year 1932. The Last National Bank is a flourishing institution. A large part of its resources is liquid without being watered. Cart-wright Millingville has ample reason to be proud of the banking institution over which he presides. Until Black Wednesday. As he enters his bank, he notices that business is unusually brisk. A little odd, that, since the men at the A.M.O.K. steel plant and the K.O.M.A. mattress factory are not usually paid until Saturday. Yet here are two dozen men, obviously from the factories, queued up in front of the tellers' cages. As he turns into his private office, the president muses rather compassionately: "Hope they haven't been laid off in midweek. They should be in the shop at this hour."

But speculations of this sort have never made for a thriving bank, and Millingville turns to the pile of documents upon his desk. His precise signature is affixed to fewer than a score of papers when he is disturbed by the absence of something familiar and the intrusion of something alien. The low discreet hum of bank business has given way to a strange and annoying stridency of many voices. A situation has been defined as real. And that is the beginning of what ends as Black Wednesday—the last Wednesday, it might be noted, of the Last National Bank.

Cartwright Millingville had never heard of the Thomas theorem. But he had no difficulty in recognizing its workings. He knew that, despite the comparative liquidity of the bank's assets, a rumor of insolvency, once believed by enough depositors, would result in the insolvency of the bank. And by the close of Black Wednesday—and Blacker Thursday—when the long lines of anxious depositors, each frantically seeking to salvage his own, grew to longer lines of even more anxious depositors, it turned out that he was right.

The stable financial structure of the bank had depended upon one set of definitions of the situation: belief in the validity of the interlocking system of economic promises men live by. Once depositors had defined the situation otherwise, once they questioned the possibility of having these promises fulfilled, the consequences of this unreal definition was real enough.

A familiar type-case, this, and one doesn't need the Thomas theorem to understand how it happened—not, at least, if one is old enough to have voted for Franklin Roosevelt in 1932. But with the aid of the theorem the tragic history of Millingville's bank can perhaps be converted into a sociological parable which may help us understand not only what happened to hundreds of banks in the '30's but also what happens to the relations between Negro and white, between Protestant and Catholic and Jew in these days.

The parable tells us that public definitions of a situation (prophecies or predictions) become an integral part of the situation and thus affect subsequent developments. This is peculiar to human affairs. It is not found in the world of nature. Predictions of the return of Halley's comet do not influence its orbit. But the rumored insolvency of Millingville's bank did affect the actual outcome. The prophecy of collapse led to its own fulfillment.

So common is the pattern of the self-fulfilling prophecy that each of us has his favored specimen. Consider the case of the examination neurosis. Convinced that he is destined to fail, the anxious student devotes more time to worry than to study and then turns in a poor examination. The initially fallacious anxiety is transformed into an entirely justified fear. Or it is believed that war between two nations is "inevitable." Actuated by this conviction, representatives of the two nations become progressively alienated, apprehensively countering each "offensive" move of the other with a "defensive" move of their own. Stockpiles of armaments, raw materials, and armed men grow larger and eventually the anticipation of war helps create the actuality.

The self-fulfilling prophecy is, in the beginning, a *false* definition of the situation evoking a new behavior which makes the originally false conception come *true*. The specious validity of the self-fulfilling prophecy perpetuates a reign of error. For the prophet will cite the actual course of events as proof that he was right from the very beginning. (Yet we know that Millingville's bank was solvent, that it would have survived for many years had not the misleading rumor *created* the very conditions of its own fulfillment.) Such are the perversities of social logic.

It is the self-fulfilling prophecy which goes far toward explaining the dynamics of ethnic and racial conflict in the America of today. That this is the case, at least for relations between Negroes and whites, may be gathered from the fifteen hundred pages which make up Gunnar Myrdal's

An American Dilemma. That the self-fulfilling prophecy may have even more general bearing upon the relations between ethnic groups than Myrdal has indicated is the thesis of the considerably briefer discussion which follows.

II

As a result of their failure to comprehend the operation of the self-fulfilling prophecy, many Americans of good will are (sometimes reluctantly) brought to retain enduring ethnic and racial prejudices. They experience these beliefs, not as prejudices, not as prejudgments, but as irresistible products of their own observation. "The facts of the case" permit them no other conclusion.

Thus our fair-minded white citizen strongly supports a policy of excluding Negroes from his labor union. His views are, of course, based not upon prejudice, but upon the cold hard facts. And the facts seem clear enough. Negroes, "lately from the nonindustrial South, are undisciplined in traditions of trade unionism and the art of collective bargaining." The Negro is a strikebreaker. The Negro, with his "low standard of living," rushes in to take jobs at less than prevailing wages. The Negro is, in short, "a traitor to the working class," and should manifestly be excluded from union organizations. So run the facts of the case as seen by our tolerant but hard-headed union member, innocent of any understanding of the self-fulfilling prophecy as a basic process of society.

Our unionist fails to see, of course, that he and his kind have produced the very "facts" which he observes. For by defining the situation as one in which Negroes are held to be incorrigibly at odds with principles of unionism and by excluding Negroes from unions, he invited a series of consequences which indeed made it difficult if not impossible for many Negroes to avoid the role of scab. Out of work after World War I, and kept out of unions, thousands of Negroes could not resist strikebound employers who held a door invitingly open upon a world of jobs from which they were otherwise excluded.

History creates its own test of the theory of self-fulfilling prophecies. That Negroes were strikebreakers because they were excluded from unions (and from a large range of jobs) rather than excluded because they were strikebreakers can be seen from the virtual disappearance of Negroes as scabs in industries where they have gained admission to unions in the last decades.

The application of the Thomas theorem also suggests how the tragic, often vicious, circle of self-fulfilling prophecies can be broken. The initial definition of the situation which has set the circle in motion must be abandoned. Only when the original assumption is questioned and a new definition of the situation introduced, does the consequent flow of events give the lie to the assumption. Only then does the belief no longer father the reality.

But to question these deep-rooted definitions of the situation is no simple act of the will. The will, or, for that matter, good will, cannot be turned on and off like a faucet. Social intelligence and good will are themselves *products* of distinct social forces. They are not brought into being by mass propaganda and mass education, in the usual sense of these terms so dear to the sociological panaceans. In the social realm, no more than in the psychological realm, do false ideas quietly vanish when confronted with the truth. One does not expect a paranoiac to abandon his hard-won distortions and delusions upon being informed that they are altogether groundless. If psychic ills could be cured merely by the dissemination of truth, the psychiatrists of this country would be suffering from technological unemployment rather than from overwork. Nor will a continuing "educational campaign" itself destroy racial prejudice and discrimination.

This is not a particularly popular position. The appeal to "education" as a cure-all for the most varied social problems is rooted deep in the mores of America. Yet it is nonetheless illusory for all that. For how would this program of racial education proceed? Who is to do the educating? The teachers in our communities? But, in some measure like many other Americans, the teachers share the very prejudices they are being urged to combat. And when they don't, aren't they being asked to serve as conscientious martyrs in the cause of educational utopianism? How long would be the tenure of an elementary school teacher in Alabama or Mississippi or Georgia who attempted meticulously to disabuse his young pupils of the racial beliefs they acquired at home? Education may serve as an operational adjunct but not as the chief basis for any but excruciatingly slow change in the prevailing patterns of race relations.

To understand further why educational campaigns cannot be counted on to eliminate prevailing ethnic hostilities, we must examine the operation of "in-groups" and "out-groups" in our society. Ethnic out-groups, to adopt Sumner's useful bit of sociological jargon, consist of all those who are believed to differ significantly from "ourselves" in terms of nationality, race, or religion. Counterpart of the ethnic out-group is of course the ethnic in-group, constituted by those who "belong." There is nothing fixed or eternal about the lines separating the in-group from out-groups. As situations change, the lines of separation change. For a large number of white Americans, Joe Louis is a member of an out-group— when the situation is defined in racial terms. On another occasion, when Louis defeated the nazified Schmeling, many of these same white Americans acclaimed him as a member of the (national) in-group. National loyalty took precedence over racial separatism. These abrupt shifts in group boundaries sometimes prove embarrassing. Thus, when Negro-Americans ran away with the honors in the Olympic games held in Berlin, the Nazis, pointing to the second-class citizenship assigned Negroes in various regions of this country, denied that the United States had really won the games, since the Negro athletes were by our own admission "not full-fledged" Americans. And what could Bilbo or Rankin say to that?

Under the benevolent guidance of the dominant in-group, ethnic out-groups are continuously subjected to a lively process of prejudice which, I think, goes far toward vitiating mass education and mass propaganda for ethnic tolerance. This is the process whereby "in-group virtues become out-group vices," to paraphrase a remark by the sociologist Donald Young. Or, more colloquially and perhaps more instructively, it may be called the "damned-if-you-do and damned-if-you-don't" process in ethnic and racial relations.

III

To discover that ethnic out-groups are damned if they do embrace the values of white Protestant society and damned if they don't, we have only to turn to one of the in-group culture heroes, examine the qualities with which he is endowed by biographers and popular belief, and thus distill the qualities of mind and action and character which are generally regarded as altogether admirable.

Periodic public opinion polls are not needed to justify the selection of Abe Lincoln as the culture hero who most fully embodies the cardinal American virtues. As the Lynds point out in *Middletown*, the people of that typical small city allow George Washington alone to join Lincoln as the greatest of Americans. He is claimed as their very own by almost as many well-to-do Republicans as by less well-to-do Democrats.

Even the inevitable schoolboy knows that Lincoln was thrifty, hardworking, eager for knowledge, ambitious, devoted to the rights of the average man, and eminently successful in climbing the ladder of opportunity from the lowermost rung of laborer to the respectable heights of merchant and lawyer. (We need follow his dizzying ascent no further.)

If one did not know that these attributes and achievements are numbered high among the values of middle-class America, one would soon discover it by glancing through the Lynds' account of "The Middletown Spirit." For there we find the image of the Great Emancipator fully reflected in the values in which Middletown believes. And since these are their values, it is not surprising to find the Middletowns of America condemning and disparaging those individuals and groups who fail, presumably, to exhibit these virtues. If it appears to the white in-group that Negroes are *not* educated in the same measure as themselves, that they have an "unduly" high proportion of unskilled workers and an "unduly" low proportion of successful business and professional men, that they are thriftless, and so on through the catalogue of middle-class virtue and sin, it is not difficult to understand the charge that the Negro is "inferior" to the white.

Sensitized to the workings of the self-fulfilling prophecy, we should be prepared to find that the anti-Negro charges which are not patently false are only speciously true. The allegations are "true" in the Pickwickian sense that we have found self-fulfilling prophecies in general to be true. Thus, if the dominant in-group believes that Negroes are inferior, and sees to it that funds for education are not "wasted on these incompetents" and then proclaims as final evidence of this inferiority that Negroes have proportionately "only" one-fifth as many college graduates as whites, one can scarcely be amazed by this transparent bit of social legerdemain. Having seen the rabbit carefully though not too adroitly placed in the hat, we can only look askance at the triumphant air with which it is finally produced. (In fact, it is a little embarrassing to note that a larger proportion of Negro than of white high school graduates go on to college; obviously, the Negroes who are hardy enough to scale the high walls of discrimination represent an even more highly selected group than the run-of-the-high-school white population.)

So, too, when the gentleman from Mississippi (a state which spends five times as much on the average white pupil as on the average Negro pupil) proclaims the essential inferiority of the Negro by pointing to the per capita ratio of physicians among Negroes as less than one-fourth that of whites, we are impressed more by his scrambled logic than by his profound prejudices. So plain is the mechanism of the self-fulfilling prophecy in these instances that only those forever devoted to the victory of sentiment over fact can take these specious evidences seriously. Yet the spurious evidence often creates a genuine belief. Self-hypnosis through one's own propaganda is a not infrequent phase of the self-fulfilling prophecy.

So much for out-groups being damned if they don't (apparently) manifest in-group virtues. It is a tasteless bit of ethnocentrism, seasoned with self-interest. But what of the second phase of this process? Can one seriously mean that out-groups are also damned if they *do* possess these virtues? Precisely.

Through a faultlessly bisymmetrical prejudice, ethnic and racial out-groups get it coming and going. The systematic condemnation of the out-grouper continues largely *irrespective of what he does.* More: through a freakish exercise of capricious judicial logic, the victim is punished for the crime. Superficial appearances notwithstanding, prejudice and discrimination aimed at the out-group are not a result of what the out-group does, but are rooted deep in the structure of our society and the social psychology of its members.

To understand how this happens, we must examine the moral alchemy through which the in-group readily transmutes virtue into vice and vice into virtue, as the occasion may demand. Our studies will proceed by the case-method.

We begin with the engagingly simple formula of moral alchemy: the same behaviour muse be differently evaluated according to the person who exhibitis it. For example, the proficient alchemist will at once know that the word "firm" is properly declined as follows:

> I am firm
> Thou art obstinate,
> He is pigheaded.

There are some, unversed in the skills of this science, who will tell you that one and the same term should be applied to all three instances of identical behavior. Such unalchemical nonsense should simply be ignored.

With this experiment in mind, we are prepared to observe how the very same behavior undergoes a complete change of evaluation in its transition from the in-group Abe lincoln to the out-group Abe Cohen or Abe Kurokawa. We proceed systematically. Did Lincoln work far into the night? This testifies that he was industrious, resolute, perseverant, and eager to realize his capacities to the full. Do the out-group Jews or Japanese keep these same hours? This only bears witness to their sweat-shop mentality, their ruthless undercutting of American standards, their unfair competitive practices. Is the in-group hero frugal, thrifty, and sparing? Then the out-group villain is stingy, miserly and penny-pinching. All honor is due the in-group Abe for his having been smart, shrewd and intelligent and, by the same token, all contempt is owing the out-group Abes for their being sharp, cunning, crafty, and too clever by far. Did the indomitable Lincoln refuse to remain content with a life of work with the hands? Did he prefer to make use of his brain? Then, all praise for his plucky climb up the shaky ladder of opportunity. But, of course, the eschewing of manual work for brain work among the merchants and lawyers of the out-group deserves nothing but censure for a parasitic way of life. Was Abe Lincoln eager to learn the accumulated wisdom of the ages by unending study? The trouble with the Jew is that he's a greasy grind, with his head always in a book, while decent people are going to a show or a ball game. Was the resolute Lincoln unwilling to limit his standards to those of his provincial community? That is what we should expect of a man of vision. And if the out-groupers criticize the vulnerable areas in our society, then send 'em back where they came from. Did Lincoln, rising high above his origins, never forget the rights of the common man and applaud the right of workers to strike? This testifies only that, like all real Americans, this greatest of Americans was deathlessly devoted to the cause of freedom. But, as you examine the recent statistics on strikes, remember that these un-American practices are the result of out-groupers pursuing their evil agitation among otherwise contented workers.

Once stated, the classical formula of moral alchemy is clear enough. Through the adroit use of these rich vocabularies of encomium and opprobrium, the in-group readily transmutes its own virtues into others' vices. But why do so many in-groupers qualify as moral alchemists? Why are so many in the dominant in-group so fully devoted to this continuing experiment in moral transmutation?

An explanation may be found by putting ourselves at some distance from this country and following the anthropologist Malinowski to the Trobriand Islands. For there we find an instructively similar pattern. Among the Trobrianders, to a degree which Americans, despite Hollywood and die confession magazines, have apparently not yet approximated, success with women confers honor and prestige on a man. Sexual prowess is a positive value, a moral virtue. But if a rank-and-file Trobriander has "too much" sexual success, if he achieves "too many" triumphs of the heart, an achievement which should of course be limited to the elite, the chiefs or men of power, then this glorious record becomes a scandal and an abomination. The chiefs are quick *to resent any personal achievement not warranted by social position.* The moral virtues remain virtues only so long as they are jealously confined to the proper in-group. The right activity by the wrong people becomes a thing of contempt, not of honor. For clearly, only in this way, by holding these virtues exclusively to themselves, can the men of power retain their distinction, their prestige, and their power. No wiser procedure could be devised to hold intact a system of social stratification and social power.

The Trobrianders can teach us more. For it seems clear that the chiefs have not calculatingly devised this program of entrenchment. Their behavior is spontaneous, unthinking, and immediate. Their resentment of "too much" ambition or "too much" success in the ordinary Trobriander is not contrived, it is genuine. It just happens that this prompt emotional response to the "misplaced" manifestation of in-group virtues also serves the useful expedient of reinforcing the chiefs' special claims to the good things of Trobriand life. Nothing could be more remote from the truth and more distorted a reading of the facts than to assume that this conversion of in-group virtues into out-group vices is part of a calculated, deliberate plot of Trobriand chiefs to keep Trobriand commoners in their place. It is merely that the chiefs have been indoctrinated with an appreciation of the proper order of things, and see it as their heavy burden to enforce the mediocrity of others.

Nor, in quick revulsion from the culpabilities of the moral alchemists, need we succumb to the equivalent error of simply upending the moral status of the in-group and the out-groups. It is not that Jews and Negroes are one and all angelic while Gentiles and whites are one and all fiendish. It is not that individual virtue will now be found exclusively on the wrong side of the ethnic-racial tracks and individual viciousness on the right side. It is conceivable even that there are as many corrupt and vicious men and women among Negroes and Jews as among Gentile whites. It is only that the ugly fence which encloses the in-group happens to exclude the people who make up the out-groups from being treated with the decency ordinarily accorded human beings.

IV

We have only to look at the consequences of this peculiar moral alchemy to see that there is no paradox at all in damning out-groupers if they do and if they don't exhibit in-group virtues. Condemnation on these two scores performs one and the same social function. Seeming opposites coalesce. When Negroes are tagged as incorrigibly inferior because they (apparently) don't manifest these virtues, this confirms the natural rightness of their being assigned an inferior status in society. And when Jews or Japanese are tagged as having too many of the in-group values, it becomes plain that they must be securely controlled by the high walls of discrimination. In both cases, the special status assigned the several out-groups can be seen to be eminently reasonable.

Yet this distinctly reasonable arrangement persists in having most unreasonable consequences, both logical and social. Consider only a few of these.

In some contexts, the limitations enforced upon the out-group—say, rationing the number of Jews permitted to enter colleges and professional schools—logically imply a fear of the alleged superiority of the out-group. Were it otherwise, no discrimination need be practiced. The unyielding, impersonal forces of academic competition would soon trim down the number of Jewish (or Japanese or Negro) students to an "appropriate" size.

This implied belief in the superiority of the out-group seems premature. There is simply not enough scientific evidence to demonstrate Jewish or Japanese or Negro superiority. The effort of the in-group discriminator to supplant the myth of Aryan superiority with the myth of non-Aryan superiority is condemned to failure by science. Moreover, such myths are ill-advised. Eventually, life in a world of myth must collide with fact in the world of reality. As a matter of simple self-interest and social therapy, therefore, it might be wise for the in-group to abandon the myth and cling to the reality.

The pattern of being damned-if-you-do and damned-if-you-don't has further consequences—among the out-groups themselves. The response to alleged deficiencies is as clear as it is predictable. If one is repeatedly told that one is inferior, that one lacks any positive accomplishments, it is all too human to seize upon every bit of evidence to the contrary. The in-group definitions force upon the allegedly inferior out-group a defensive tendency to magnify and exalt "race accomplishments." As the distinguished Negro sociologist, Franklin Frazier, has noted, the Negro newspapers are "intensely race conscious and exhibit considerable pride in the achievements of the Negro, most of which are meagre performances as measured by broader standards." Self-glorification, found in some measure among all groups, becomes a frequent counter-response to persistent belittlement from without.

It is the damnation of out-groups for "excessive achievement," however, which gives rise to truly bizarre behavior. For, after a time and often as a matter of self-defense, these out-groups become persuaded that their virtues really are vices. And this provides the final episode in a tragicomedy of inverted values.

Let us try to follow the plot through its intricate maze of self-contradictions. Respectful admiration for the arduous climb from office boy to president is rooted deep in American culture. This long and strenuous ascent carries with it a two-fold testimonial: it testifies that careers are abundantly open to genuine talent in American society and it testifies to the worth of the man who has distinguished himself by his heroic rise. It would be invidious to choose among the many stalwart figures who have fought their way up, against all odds, until they have reached the pinnacle, there to sit at the head of the long conference table in the longer conference room of The Board. Taken at random, the saga of Frederick H. Ecker, chairman of the board of one of the largest privately managed corporations in the world, the Metropolitan Life Insurance Company, will suffice as the prototype. From a menial and poorly paid job, he rose to a position of eminence. Appropriately enough, an unceasing flow of honors has come to this man of large power and large achievement. It so happens, though it is a matter personal to this eminent man of finance, that Mr. Ecker is a Presbyterian. Yet at last report, no elder of the Presbyterian church has risen publicly to announce that Mr. Ecker's successful career should not be taken too seriously, that, after all, relatively few Presbyterians have risen from rags to riches and that Presbyterians do not actually "control" the world of finance—or life insurance, or investment housing. Rather, one would suppose, Presbyterian elders join with other Americans imbued with middle-class standards of success to felicitate the eminently successful Mr. Ecker and to acclaim other sons of the faith who have risen to almost equal heights. Secure with their in-group status, they point the finger of pride rather than the finger of dismay at individual success.

Prompted by the practice of moral alchemy, noteworthy achievements by out-groupers elicit other responses. Patently, if achievement is a vice, the achievement must be disclaimed—or at least, discounted. Under these conditions, what is an occasion for Presbyterian pride must become an occasion for Jewish dismay. If the Jew is condemned for his educational or professional or scientific or economic success, then, understandably enough, many Jews will come to feel that these accomplishments must be minimized in simple self-defense. Thus is the circle of paradox closed by out-groupers busily engaged in assuring the powerful in-group that they have not, in fact, been guilty of inordinate contributions to science, the professions, the arts, the government, and the economy.

In a society which ordinarily looks upon wealth as a warrant of ability, an out-group is compelled by the inverted attitudes of the dominant in-group to deny that many men of wealth are among its members. "Among the 200 largest nonbanking corporations. . . only ten have a Jew as president or chairman of the board." Is this an observation of an anti-Semite, intent on proving the incapacity and inferiority of Jews who have done so little "to build the corporations which have built America"? No; it is a retort of the Anti-Defamation League of B'Nai Brith to anti-Semitic propaganda.

In a society where, as a recent survey by the National Opinion Research Center has shown, the profession of medicine ranks higher in social prestige than any other of ninety occupations (save that of United States Supreme Court Justice), we find some Jewish spokesmen manoeuvred by the attacking in-group into the fantastic position of announcing their "deep concern" over the number of Jews in medical practice, which is "disproportionate to the number of Jews in other occupations." In a nation suffering from a notorious undersupply of physicians, the Jewish doctor becomes a deplorable occasion for deep concern, rather than receiving applause for his hard-won acquisition of knowledge and skills and for his social utility. Only when the New York Yankees publicly announce deep concern over their eleven World Series titles, so disproportionate to the number of triumphs achieved by other major league teams, will this self-abnegation seem part of the normal order of things.

In a culture which consistently judges the professionals higher in social value than even the most skilled hewers of wood and drawers of water, the out-group finds itself in the anomalous position of pointing with defensive relief to the large number of Jewish painters and paper hangers, plasterers and electricians, plumbers and sheet-metal workers.

But the ultimate reversal of values is yet to be noted. Each succeeding census finds more and more Americans in the city and its suburbs. Americans have travelled the road to urbanization until less than one-fifth of the nation's population live on farms. Plainly, it is high time for the Methodist and the Catholic, the Baptist and the Episcopalian to recognize the iniquity of this trek of their coreligionists to the city. For, as is well known, one of the central accusations levelled against the Jew is his heinous tendency to live in cities. Jewish leaders, therefore, find themselves in the incredible position of defensively urging their people to move into the very farm areas being hastily vacated by city-bound hordes of Christians. Perhaps this is not altogether necessary. As the Jewish crime of urbanism becomes ever more popular among the in-group, it may be reshaped into transcendent virtue. But, admittedly, one can't be certain. For in this daft confusion of inverted values, it soon becomes impossible to determine when virtue is sin and sin, moral perfection.

Amid this confusion, one fact remains unambiguous. The Jews, like other peoples, have made distinguished contributions to world culture. Consider only an abbreviated catalogue. In the field of creative literature (and with acknowledgment of large variations in the calibre of achievement), Jewish authors include Heine, Karl Kraus, Börne, Hofmannsthal, Schnitzler, Kafka. In the realm of musical composition, there are Meyerbeer, Felix Mendelssohn, Offenbach, Mahler, and Schönberg. Among the musical virtuosi, consider only Rosenthal, Schnabel, Godowsky, Pachmann, Kreisler, Hubermann, Milstein, Elman, Heifetz, Joachim, and Menuhin. And among scientists of a stature sufficient to merit the Nobel prize, examine the familiar list which includes Beranyi, Mayerhof, Ehrlich, Michelson, Lippmann, Haber, Willstätter, and

Einstein. Or in the esoteric and imaginative universe of mathematical invention, take note only of Kronecker, the creator of the modern theory of numbers; Hermann Minkowski, who supplied the mathematical foundations of the special theory of relativity; or Jacobi, with his basic work in the theory of elliptical functions. And so through each special province of cultural achievement, we are supplied with a list of pre-eminent men and women who happened to be Jews.

And who is thus busily engaged in singing the praises of the Jews? Who has so assiduously compiled the list of many hundreds of distinguished Jews who contributed so notably to science, literature and the arts—a list from which these few cases were excerpted? A philo-Semite, eager to demonstrate that his people have contributed their due share to world culture? No, by now we should know better than that. The complete list will be found in the thirty-sixth edition of an anti-Semitic handbook by the racist Fritsch. In accord with the alchemical formula for transmuting in-group virtues into out-group vices, he presents this as a roll call of sinister spirits who have usurped the accomplishments properly owing the Aryan in-group.

Once we comprehend the predominant role of the in-group in defining the situation, the further paradox of the seemingly opposed behavior of the Negro out-group and the Jewish out-group falls away. The behavior of both minority groups is in response to the majority-group allegations.

If the Negroes are accused of inferiority, and their alleged failure to contribute to world culture is cited in support of this accusation, the human urge for self-respect and a concern for security leads them *defensively* often to magnify each and every achievement by members of the race. If Jews are accused of "excessive" achievements and "excessive" ambitions, and lists of pre-eminent Jews are compiled in support of this counter-accusation, then the urge for security leads them *defensively* to minimize the actual achievements of members of the group. Apparently opposed types of behavior have the same psychological and social functions. Self-assertion and self-effacement become the devices for seeking to cope with condemnation for alleged group deficiency and condemnation for alleged group excesses, respectively. And with a fine sense of moral superiority, the secure in-group looks on these curious performances by the out-groups with mingled derision and contempt.

V

Will this desolate tragicomedy run on and on, marked only by minor changes in the cast? Not necessarily.

Were moral scruples and a sense of decency the only bases for bringing the play to an end, one would indeed expect it to continue an indefinitely long run. In and of themselves, moral sentiments are not much more effective in curing social ills than in curing physical ills. Moral sentiments no doubt help to motivate efforts for change, but they are no substitute for hard-headed instrumentalities for achieving the objective, as the thickly populated graveyard of soft-headed Utopias bears witness.

There are ample indications that a deliberate and planned halt can be put to the workings of the self-fulfilling prophecy and the vicious circle in society. The sequel to our sociological parable of the Last National Bank provides one clue to the way in which this can be achieved. During the fabulous '20's, when Coolidge undoubtedly caused a Republican era of lush prosperity, an average of 635 banks a year quietly suspended operations. And during the four years immediately before and after The Crash, when Hoover undoubtedly did not cause a Republican era of sluggish depression, this zoomed to the more spectacular average of 2,276 bank suspensions annually. But, interestingly enough, in the twelve years following the establishment of the Federal Deposit Insurance Corporation and the enactment of other banking legislation while Roosevelt presided over Democratic depression and revival, recession and boom, bank suspensions dropped to a niggardly average of 28 a year. Perhaps money panics have not been institutionally exorcized by legislation. Nevertheless, millions of depositors no longer have occasion to give way to panic-motivated runs on banks simply because deliberate institutional change has removed the grounds for panic. Occasions for racial hostility are no more inborn psychological constants than are occasions for panic. Despite the teachings of amateur psychologists, blind panic and racial aggression are not rooted in "human nature."

These patterns of human behavior are largely a product of the modifiable structure of society.

For a further clue, return to our instance of widespread hostility of white unionists toward the Negro strikebreakers brought into industry by employers after the close of the very first World War. Once the initial definition of Negroes as not deserving of union membership had largely broken down, the Negro, with a wider range of work opportunities, no longer found it necessary to enter industry through the doors held open by strikebound employers. Again, appropriate institutional change broke through the tragic circle of the self-fulfilling prophecy. Deliberate social change gave the lie to the firm conviction that "it just ain't in the nature of the nigra" to join co-operatively with his white fellows in trade unions.

A final instance is drawn from a study of a biracial housing project which I have been conducting with Patricia J. Salter, under a grant from the Lavanburg Foundation. Located in Pittsburgh, this community of Hilltown is made up of fifty per cent Negro families and fifty per cent white. It is not a twentieth-century utopia. There is some interpersonal friction here, as elsewhere. But in a community made up of equal numbers of the two races, fewer than a fifth of the whites and less than a third of the Negroes report that this friction occurs between members of *different races.* By their own testimony, it is very largely confined to disagreements *within* each racial group. Yet only one in every twenty-five whites initially *expected* relations between the races in this community to run smoothly, whereas five times as many expected serious trouble, the remainder anticipating a tolerable, if not altogether pleasant, situation. So much for expectations. Upon reviewing their actual experience, three of every four of the most apprehensive whites subsequently found that the "races get along fairly well," after all. This is not the place to report the findings of the Lavanburg study in detail, but substantially these demonstrate anew that under *appropriate institutional and administrative conditions,* the experience of interracial amity can supplant the fear of interracial conflict.

These changes, and others of the same kind, do not occur automatically. *The self-fulfilling prophecy, whereby fears are translated into reality, operates only in the absence of deliberate institutional controls.* And it is only with the rejection of social fatalism implied in the notion of unchangeable human nature that the tragic circle of fear, social disaster, reinforced fear can be broken.

Ethnic prejudices do die—but slowly. They can be helped over the threshold of oblivion, not by insisting that it is unreasonable and unworthy of them to survive, but by cutting off their sustenance now provided by certain institutions of our society.

If we find ourselves doubting man's capacity to control man and his society, if we persist in our tendency to find in the patterns of the past the chart of the future, it is perhaps time to take up anew the wisdom of Tocqueville's 112-year-old apothegm: "What we call necessary institutions are often no more than institutions to which we have grown accustomed."

Nor can widespread, even typical, failures in planning human relations between ethnic groups be cited as evidence for pessimism. In the world laboratory of the sociologist, as in the more secluded laboratories of the physicist and chemist, it is the successful experiment which is decisive and not the thousand-and-one failures which preceded it. More is learned from the single success than from the multiple failures. A single success proves it can be done. Thereafter, it is necessary only to learn what made it work. This, at least, is what I take to be the sociological sense of those revealing words of Thomas Love Peacock: "Whatever is, is possible."

48

Structural Integration and Change*

Hans H. Gerth
C. Wright Mills

It is easy to believe that each section of a society is related to every other section, that society is in some manner a whole of busily interacting parts. But this assumption does not tell us very much. As a beginning point it is useful, but by itself it is an uninformative truism. For what it does, at best, is advise us to be on the lookout for specific connections between specific parts and their relations to the whole. Whatever models of integration we end up with, much less whatever theory, there is a descriptive task at hand for anyone who would intelligently describe social structures as "wholes." This task will be governed in the first instance by the units of social structure that are used. So our first question is:

I. *Units*: How shall we *articulate* a society—that is, what unit or units shall we seize upon or abstract as "parts" which we would relate to other "parts"? And, specifically, for any given society, how articulated or autonomous are these units?

Our unit, the institutional order (with its sub-units of specific institutions and finally of role), along with the idea of spheres, satisfies in a provisional way, we feel, these critieria.

II. *Relations:* The second question we face is of more immediate concern to the problem of integration: Precisely how are these units interrelated, that is, what is the "dimension," or what are the dimensions, in terms of which we would relate them with one another? The relations of our units are conveniently construed in terms of a means-ends *schema*, which involves the dimension of power. Thus we are interested in finding to what extent, if any, events in one institutional order may be considered preconditions of events in other orders. We are also interested in tracing the ramifications of trends in one order with other orders, and in understanding how such ramifications may facilitate or limit activities and policies in other orders. In short, our units—institutional orders—may be related with one

*Excerpts from *Character and Social Structure: The Psychology of Social Institutions* by Hans H. Gerth and C. Wright Mills.

INSTITUTIONAL ORDERS				SPHERES { EDUCATION, STATUS, SYMBOLS, TECHNOLOGY	
POLITICAL	1				
ECONOMIC	6	2			
MILITARY	7	10	3		
RELIGIOUS	8	11	13	4	
KINSHIP	9	12	14	15	5
	POLITICAL	ECONOMIC	MILITARY	RELIGIOUS	KINSHIP

another causally in a variety of ways and degrees. Given orders may be functionally independent or dependent of one another.

III. *Procedural Scheme*: Let us make our answers to both of these questions more concrete, and thus begin to illustrate why we feel that the scheme invites description of prevailing units and of the causal relations obtaining among them.

In examining a specific society our first decision has to do with whether we will use as our prime units institutional orders, institutions, or roles.

We thus have three levels of unit, as it were, to choose among as our first level of description. We say the *first* level of description because obviously in cases where institutions are the units we shall also handle the roles, and where institutional orders have been unfolded as articulate units, we shall also handle the institutions that prevail in each and the kinds of roles that in turn compose them.

Why do we always choose the "higher" of these three units that exist for our first description? Because the roles in which we are most interested are part of an institution and can be understood only with reference to its institutional context; and, institutions, if they are part of an institutional order, can most readily be understood as part of the order in which they occur. This contextual guide-line is important; for example, apparently identical institutions may be found in different orders, but qualitative differences may occur to what, in isolation, may appear to be identical.

The problem of the unity of a social structure, especially as it bears upon the unit chosen, obviously differs for differently articulated societies. The first empirical task, in approaching any given society, is to discover the most convenient units that prevail, in terms of which the problem of structural unity or integration may best be stated.

Having due regard to this, we will nevertheless assume institutional orders as our unit, and use that unit in presenting our procedural scheme, for this enables us to handle, at least formally, the salient problems of unity encountered in societies that are not articulated into orders. For a society in which all five orders are autonomous enough to permit separate delineation and thus relationships, one must "fill in" the following boxes:

First, the range and the basic characteristics of the institutions prevailing in each order are determined: 1 through 5. This first task includes a description of the spheres of each of these orders: education, status, symbols, technology.

Second, the relations between each of the orders with each of the others are described: 6 through 15. This second task consists of a detailed tracing of the ramifications and other relations of each order upon all others. So much is basic: Only when this is done on a purely descriptive level do we have (1) a basis for comparing different social structures and (2) a basis for causal imputations in explanation of various roles, institutions, or the shape of the social structure as a whole.

"Ramification" refers to the operation of one order within other orders: or, to the use of one order for the ends of the ramifying order. The "ramifications" of any order refer to its total range of such operations in all other orders.

Modes of Integration

From a somewhat formal standpoint, we can observe certain general ways in which the institutional orders composing a social structure are integrated. These modes of integration are, for us, analytic models which sensitize us to certain types of linkage of one order with another. They may also, of course, be viewed dynamically, as processes of social-historical change.

We have found some four principles of structural change useful in understanding the integration of a society:

I. By *correspondence* we mean that a social structure is unified by the working out in its several institutional orders of a common structural principle, which thus operates in a parallel way in each.

II. By *coincidence* we mean that different structural principles or developments in various orders result in their combined effects in the same, often unforeseen, outcome of unity for the whole society.

III. By *co-ordination* we refer to the integration of a society by means of one or more institutional orders which become ascendant over other orders and direct them; thus other orders are regulated and managed by the ascendant order or orders.

IV. By *convergence* we mean that two or more institutional orders coincide to the point of fusion; they become one institutional setup.

It is quite difficult to isolate concrete societies which fully and exclusively exemplify each of these types of integration because reality is usually mixed. The integrations of some areas of a society can often best be understood in terms of one mode of integration, while other parts can best be understood by application of another mode. Nevertheless, to make clear what is involved in each type of integration, we can, in a brief way, sketch cases in which each seems to predominate.

I. *Correspondence*. The handiest case of correspondence is perhaps the model of a classic liberal society, best exemplified by the society prevailing in the first half of the nineteenth century in the United States. The meaning of "laissez-faire" for the economic order is a demand on the part of economic agents for freedom from political dominance. It is paralleled by the religious demand for autonomy from political or state control or even sponsorship of any one type of religious institution; moreover, here too, one Protestant man faced his God, free of any hierarchy of interpreters. In the political area, as in the economic market, there is a free competition for the individual's vote. In the kinship order, also, marriage is a contract between the marriage partners into which they enter of their own free will; marriages are not to be arranged by parental collusion of economic or status sort. Just as free individuals compete economically, so do they in the status sphere: "the self-made man" stands in contrast to "the family-made man" of the kinship order's status sphere, just as a much as to the man who moves on his own across the autonomous economic markets. So status styles are often represented as conspicuous consumption of the self-made businessman.

On the highest level of abstraction, in the symbol sphere, the idea of human freedom, of the spontaneity of thinking, acting, and judging, is proclaimed and elaborated. In particular, the conception of human genius, of the prerogative of free creativity, becomes central, and even sets an ideal model for the nature of human nature. So educators attempt "to make the student think for himself."

The basic legitimation of instituted conduct in each of these orders is very much the same: the free initiative of the autonomous individual for rational and moral self-determination. Thus the symbol spheres of the various orders run in parallel or corresponding fashion. In each order free individuals could institute new organizations according to the principle—or at times even the expectation—of voluntary associations. Independent decision-making and organization thus unify what on the surface might appear as merely the unplanned complexity and enormous variety of nineteenth-century "causes."

The correspondence of diverse and relatively autonomous orders is the outcome of processes in which all significant orders develop in the direction of an integrative principle of competition or laissez faire. In all orders competition means that individuals act in a field of action which impersonally disciplines them for uniform strivings and motives, and in its terms free men find their places. This principle also secured a rather smooth and gradual transferal or shift in power within and between orders. The translation of economic into political power is particularly relevant.

II. *Coincidence*. We are not aware of any society that is integrated solely in terms of coincidence: different structural and psychological tendencies in each of the different orders bringing about a unified end product. But there are many instances at hand of the partial operation of coincidence as a mode of integration, which represents the unplanned, unforeseen, and "fortuitous" result of institutional dynamics. Every coincidence is of course causally determined, but insofar as causal ascription to material or ideal interests has to be made, such interests might well be heterogeneous, and, being anchored in different orders, perhaps even ultimately conflicting.

The most striking and detailed case of a coincidence of orders is provided by Max Weber's work on Protestant religion and capitalist economics, on the role of Puritanism in the character formation of the economic vanguard of modern capitalism.

The theology of Calvinism emphasizes the view that man is evil and that due to the inscrutable will of a stern and hidden God only few men are predestined for salvation. This interpretation of Christianity at once reinforces and resolves intense anxieties in the believer as to whether he is or is not among the elect. Out of this situation two possibilities derive: fatalism or intense activism. Puritanism interprets man's Christian conduct in everyday life as being an indicator though not a guarantee of his salvation chances, so a religious significance is attributed to everyday work. Whereas formerly only certain monastic orders had used work as a means of religious asceticism, now every believer has to prove his religious worth by self-denying work in this world. He must work not for profits, not out of enjoyment of his work, nor yet of its fruits. His work must be an ascetic exercise pursued methodically for the sake of the kingdom to come. His work becomes his "calling," and only those who have consistently proved themselves in their callings can claim to be "elected." Those who successfully claim to be among the elect associate themselves in sects, and admit new members, by adult baptism, only after a scrutiny of the applicant's total record of conduct. The earliest sects adopted anabaptism, meaning the rebaptism of qualified adults and their reception into an exclusive, voluntary association.

The economic consequence of such motivation is the emergence of a type of person who, in the economic order, will not readily consume the profits he makes—as an entrepreneur or middleman. Suspicious of ostentatious wealth and luxury, he considers his accumulation of wealth as Christian stewardship. He has only one course open: reinvestment in his business for extended production. This in turn gives the Puritan enterpriser the opportunity to employ additional men, in religious terms to extend opportunities to anguished souls who in an age of enclosures and vagrancy, crave to prove themselves as God-fearing Christians. Thus, the entrepreneur provides institutional opportunities under Puritan control to unemployed and dependent groups. From his perspective, wages increase the workers' opportunities to prove themselves as frugal and sober and hard working. High wages would only constitute temptations to wander from the ascetic path. The worker, in turn, knows that what counts is to prove himself in whatever workaday life God has placed him.

The importance of such a psychological type for modern capitalism is evidenced by the fact that even after the universal process of secularization and the disappearance of the specific theological symbols—voluntary associations and clubs, fraternal societies and the like—prestige premiums are still placed upon such character traits, which they justify in terms of conventional middle-class morality.

The ramifications of Puritanism, and hence of a primarily religious phenomenon, fed into the great economic transition from feudalism to modern industrial capitalism. The decline of the guild system and of its restraints on competition, the technological and organizational advances of the workshop, were reinforced by the migration of persecuted Protestant minorities who established themselves outside urban jurisdictions. The parceling up of markets by politically privileged monopolies was successfully fought by Puritan businessmen. Thus numerous technological, monetary, and organizational changes in the age of discoveries, and changes in trade routes from the Mediterranean to the Atlantic, found an area of coinciding changes in religion, in personality formation, and in new religiously motivated ways of playing the crucial roles instrumental in the emergence of modern industrial capitalism.

III. *Co-ordination.* In co-ordination unity is achieved by the subordination of several orders to the regulation or direct management of other orders. This in twentieth-century "totalitarian" societies unity is guaranteed by the rule of the one-party state over all other institutions and associations. But these societies also involve correspondence and coincidence.

The general schema—for the integration of Nazi Germany, for example—runs like this: during the 1920's the economic and political orders develop quite differently: within the economic order institutions are highly centralized; a few big units more or less control the operations and the results of the entire order; within the political order there is fragmentation, many parties competing to influence the state but no one of them powerful enough to control the results of economic concentration. So, there is a political movement which successfully exploits the mass despair of the great depression and brings the political, military, and economic orders into close correspondence; one party monopolizes and revamps the political order; it abolishes or amalgamates all other parties that would compete for power. To do this requires that the Nazi party find points of coincidence and/or correspondence with monopolies in the economic order and certain high agents of the military order. In these three orders there is a corresponding high concentration of power; then each of them coincides and co-operates in the taking of power. The army under President Hindenburg is not interested in defending the Weimar Republic by crushing the marching columns of a popular war party. Big business circles help finance the Nazi party, which, among other things, promised to smash the labor movement. And the three types of chieftains join in an often uneasy coalition to maintain power in their respective orders and to co-ordinate the rest of society. Rival political parties are either suppressed and outlawed, or they disband voluntarily. Kinship and religious institutions, as well as all organizations within and between all orders, are "politicized," infiltrated, and coordinated, or at least neutralized and subdued.

The immediate organization by means of which certain high agents in each of the three dominant orders coincide, and by which they co-ordinate their own and other orders and institutions, is the totalitarian party-state. It becomes the over-all frame organization which imposes and defines substantive policy goals for all institutional orders instead of merely guaranteeing government by law. The totalitarian party extends itself by prowling everywhere in "auxiliaries" and "affiliations" to other orders. It either breaks up or infiltrates, and so controls, every organization, even down to the family.

The legal order is reduced to an adjunct of the police state, with its terrorist organizations of elite guards and police forces. The individual has no "constitutional rights" which courts would or could enforce against arbitrary acts of men in high places. The individual does not count; the ruler abolishes "the rule of law" and proclaims "the rule of men." In the military order, the party leader establishes an autonomous bodyguard subject only to his personal command, and the army is duplicated by the elite guard of about half a million men who are sufficiently segregated in composition and command as to be a party-controlled army, existing alongside of the mass army of the nation. The kinship order and educational institutions are controlled through a compulsory organization of all youth in a "state youth," which in turn is controlled by a youth auxiliary of the party. A voluntary mass organization of women controlled through a party auxiliary guarantees control of the management of the household, which in turn steers the consumption of rationed *ersatz.* The state party acquires economic enterprises through expropriation (of Jews and politically disloyal owners). Outstanding examples are the Göring works, the Eher publishing house, the numerous party papers owned by the party, and numerous municipal enterprises and public utilities which either are directly appropriated by the party or are under the management of party members.

A system of state and hence party controlled "chambers" is organized, membership in which is compulsory for all entrepreneurs and corporations. Farming is organized into a compulsory cartel, the Reich's Food Estate. The labor market is controlled through the compulsory organization of all gainfully employed persons in the Labor Front. The free professions in addition to their traditional state control are organized in party controlled chambers of culture, seven of them, under the direction of a propaganda ministry. Thus, with the partial exception of the churches, the symbolic sphere of all orders is centrally managed.

There is more than one official hierarchy, and this fact, through the resultant competition and overlapping of ill-defined authority, allows for periodic purges, as well as quick changes of the official line. This fact also means that the *Führer*, and his inner circle, are relatively independent of the pressure of his own staffs. His personal decisions are ultimate and are enforceable by the effective use of his bodyguard, which reaches into the army and into the police. When most of the institutions in an order cannot be superseded by an organizational monopoly, the state party tries to occupy at least the strategic institutions or to co-ordinate the institutions under a superimposed party auxiliary.

The symbolic sphere of all orders, as we have said, is controlled by the party. With the partial exception of the religious order, no rival claims to autonomous legitimacy are permitted. There is of course a party monopoly of all formal communications, including the educational sphere; and all symbols are recast to form the basic legitimation of the co-ordinated society: the principle of absolute and magical leadership in a strict and unilateral hierarchy is widely and increasingly promulgated.

IV. *Convergence.* Two different orders may coincide, often in completely unplanned ways, to the point of fusion or convergence. In a rapidly expanding society, for example, the frontier zones of the nineteenth-century United States, the institutional articulation of different orders in the East may peter out on the vanguard edges. So, for lack of functional specification, certain Eastern institutional orders converge in the West. The frontier farmer is thus a military agent as well as an economic man, and the household becomes a small military outpost as well as a family abode. "Neighborliness"—or the relations between contiguous kinship units—fills in the gaps of institutions not yet organized. There is no church, there are no police, there are no schools—so, in this kinship-centered society, these functions converge in and are carried by the family. The roles of women as wife and mother come also to include the nurse, the midwife, and the teacher; the roles of men as husband and father, to include the lay religious leader and, if needed, of the vigilante and militiaman.

It should, of course, be understood that in any concrete social structure, we may well find mixtures of these four types of structural integration or structural change. The task is to search within and between institutional orders for points of correspondence and coincidence, for points of convergence and co-ordination, and to examine them in detail. The presence of one type does not exclude the possibility of others. We do not believe that there is any single or general rule governing the composition and unity of orders and spheres which holds for all societies. Reality is not often neat and orderly; it is the task of analysis to single out what is relevant to neat and orderly understanding.

49

Character and Conformity*

David Riesman

Since this study assumes that character is socially conditioned, it also takes for granted that there is some observable relation between a particular society and the kind of social character it produces. What is the best way to define this relation? Since the social function of character is to insure or permit conformity, it appears that the various types of social character can be defined most appropriately in terms of the modes of conformity that are developed in them. Finally, any prevalent mode of conformity may itself be used as an index to characterize a whole society.

As there are numberless ways of classifying people, none of them definitive, none of them more than approximations, none of them useful for more than a limited range of analytic purposes, so there exists in the social science literature an enormous number of different ways of classifying societies. I myself have chosen to emphasize some possible relationships between the population growth of a society and the historical sequence of character types. For I think it fruitful in developing a historical characterology to explore the correlations between the conformity demands put on people in a society and the broadest of the social indexes that connect men with their environment—the demographic indexes. A useful key to those indexes is the theory developed by modern students of population who see all societies as located in and moving along a *curve of population growth and distribution.*

Actually there is no single curve of population, but a variety. We are interested here in a particular kind of S-shaped curve that appears in the history of the long-industrialized countries, as well as in the projected populations of certain other countries as they are expected to take shape in the future. The S-shaped curve begins at a point where the number of births and deaths are fairly equal (both birth rates and death rates being high) and moves through a period of rapid population increase to a new plateau where births and deaths are again equal (both rates being low).

Population theorists distinguish three phases on the population S-curve. Societies of high birth rate and equally high death rate are said to be in the phase of "high growth potential": their population would increase with great rapidity if the death rate were lowered by, say, a sudden advance in hygiene. Societies which have passed into the phase of decreased death rate are said to be in the phase of "transitional growth." Finally, societies which have passed through both these earlier phases and are beginning to move toward a net decrease in population are said to be in the phase of "incipient population decline." (It should be noted that all references to the population phase of a society are to averages which do not take account of the very different rates that may characterize classes or ethnic groups within the society—our treatment is highly generalized.)

It would be very surprising if variations in the basic conditions of reproduction, livelihood, and survival chances, that is, in the supply of and demand for human beings, failed to influence character. My thesis is, in fact, that each of these three different phases on the population curve appears to be occupied by a society that enforces conformity and molds social character in a definably different way.

The society of high growth potential develops in its typical members a social character whose conformity is insured by their tendency to follow tradition; these I shall term *tradition-directed* people and the society in which they live a *society dependent on tradition-direction.*

The society of transitional population growth develops in its typical members a social character whose conformity is insured by their tendency to acquire early in life an internalized set of goals. These I shall term *inner-directed* people and the society in which they live *a society dependent on inner-direction.*

Finally, the society of incipient population decline develops in its typical members a social character whose conformity is insured by their tendency to be sensitized to the expectations and preferences of others. These I shall term *other-directed* people and the society in which they live one *dependent on other-direction.*

High Growth Potential: Tradition-Directed Types

It has already been stated that a society characterized by high birth rates and high death rates is in the stage of high growth potential. The mortality rates are so high that any decline in them permits a very rapid expansion of the population. This is the situation of more than half the world's population: in India, Egypt, and China (which have already grown immensely in recent generations), for most preliterate peoples in Central Africa, parts of Central and South America, in fact in most areas of the world relatively untouched by industrialization. Here death rates are so high that if birth rates were not also high the populations would die out.

As the precarious relation to the food supply is built into the going culture, it helps create a pattern of conventional conformity which is reflected in many, if not in all, societies in the stage of high growth potential. This is what we mean when we speak of tradition-direction.

A definition of tradition-direction. Since the type of social order we have been discussing is relatively unchanging, the conformity of the individual tends to be dictated to a very large degree by power relations among the various age and sex groups, the clans, castes, professions, and so forth—relations which have endured for centuries and are modified but slightly, if at all, by successive generations. The culture controls behavior minutely, and, while the rules are not so complicated that the young cannot learn them during the period of intensive socialization, careful and rigid etiquette governs the fundamentally influential sphere of kin relationships. Moreover, the culture, in addition to its economic tasks, or as part of them, provides ritual, routine, and religion to occupy and to orient everyone. Little energy is directed toward finding new solutions of the age-old problems, let us say, of agricultural technique or "medicine," the problems to which people are acculturated.

Transitional Growth: Inner-Directed Types

A change in the relatively stable ratio of births to deaths, which characterizes the period of high growth potential, is both the cause and consequence of other profound social changes. In most of the cases known to us a decline takes place in mortality prior to a decline in fertility; hence there is some period in which the population expands rapidly.

A definition of inner-direction. In western history the society that emerged with the Renaissance and Reformation and that is only now vanishing serves to illustrate the type of society in which inner-direction is the principal mode of securing conformity. Such a society is characterized by increased personal mobility, by a rapid accumulation of capital (teamed with devastating technological shifts), and by an almost constant *expansion:* intensive expansion in the production of goods and people, and extensive expansion in exploration, colonization, and imperialism. The greater choices this society gives—and the greater initiatives it demands in order to cope with its novel problems—are handled by character types who can manage to live socially without strict and self-evident tradition-direction. These are the inner-directed types.

Societies in which inner-direction becomes important, though they also are concerned with behavioral conformity, cannot be satisfied with behavioral conformity alone. Too many novel situations are presented, situations which a code cannot encompass in advance. Consequently the problem of personal choice, solved in the earlier period of high growth potential by channeling choice through rigid social organization, in the period of transitional growth is solved by channeling choice through a rigid though highly individualized character.

As the situational controls of the primary group are loosened—the group that both socializes the young and controls the adult in the earlier era—a new psychological mechanism appropriate to the more open society is "invented": it is a psychological gyroscope. This instrument, once it is set by the parents and other authorities, keeps the inner-directed person, as we shall see, "on course" even when tradition, as responded to by his character, no longer dictates his moves. The inner-directed person becomes capable of maintaining a delicate balance between the demands upon him of his life goal and the buffetings of his external environment.

Incipient Decline of Population: Other-Directed Types

As the birth rate begins to follow the death rate downward, societies move toward the epoch of incipient decline of population—the prelude to the time when the birth rate will plunge below the already lowered death rate, so that total population will decline.

Fewer and fewer people work on the land or in the extractive industries or even in manufacturing. Hours are short. People may have material abundance and leisure besides. They pay for these changes however—here, as always, the solution of old problems gives rise to new ones—by finding themselves in a centralized and bureaucratized society and a world shrunken and agitated by the contact—accelerated by industrialization—of races, nations, and cultures.

A definition of other-direction. The type of character I shall describe as other-directed seems to be emerging in very recent years in the upper middle class of our larger cities: more prominent in New York than in Boston, in Los Angeles than in Spokane, in Cincinnati than in Chillicothe. Yet in some respects this type is strikingly similar to *the* American, whom Tocqueville and other curious and astonished visitors from Europe, even before the Revolution, thought to be a new kind of man. Indeed, travelers' reports on America impress us with their unanimity. The American is said to be shallower, freer with his money, friendlier, more uncertain of himself and his values, more demanding of approval than the European. It all adds up to a pattern which, without stretching matters too far, resembles the kind of character that a number of social scientists have seen as developing in contemporary, highly industrialized, and bureaucratic America: Fromm's "marketer," Mills's "fixer," Arnold Green's "middle class male child."

Tentatively, I am inclined to think that the other-directed type does find itself most at home in America, due to certain constant elements in American society, such as its recruitment from Europe and its lack of any seriously feudal past. As against this, I am also inclined to put more weight on capitalism, industrialism, and urbanization—these being international tendencies—than on any character-forming peculiarities of the American scene.

Bearing these qualifications in mind, it seems appropriate to treat contemporary metropolitan America as our illustration of a society—so far, perhaps, the only illustration—in which other-direction is the dominant mode of insuring conformity. It would be premature, however, to say that it is already the dominant mode in America as a whole. But since the other-directed types are to be found among the young, in the larger cities, and among the upper income groups, we may assume that, unless present trends are reversed, the hegemony of other-direction lies not far off.

If we wanted to cast our social character types into social class molds, we could say that inner-direction is the typical character of the "old" middle class—the banker, the tradesman, the small entrepreneur, the technically oriented engineer, etc.—while other-direction is becoming the typical character of the "new" middle class—the bureaucrat, the salaried employee in business, etc.

What is common to all other-directeds is that their contemporaries are the source of direction for the individual—either those known to him or those with whom he is indirectly acquainted, through friends and through the mass media. This source is of course "internalized" in the sense that dependence on it for guidance in life is implanted early. The goals toward which the other-directed person strives shift with that guidance: it is only the process of striving itself and the process of paying close attention to the signals from others that remain unaltered throughout life. This mode of keeping in touch with others permits a close behavioral conformity, not through drill in behavior itself, as in the tradition-directed character, but rather through an exceptional sensitivity to the actions and wishes of others.

The three types compared. While for analytic purposes it is sound to visualize all these differences sharply, it would be a mistake to expect to find such a sharp separation in the world of living people. In one respect all human behavior is inner-directed, in the sense that it is motivated, and all human behavior is other-directed, in the sense that it results from the process of socialization by others. And, of course, neither the tradition-directed nor the inner-directed person is immune to the impact of the opinions and directions of others. Nevertheless, one way to see the structural differences between the three types is to see the differences—again, as a matter of degree only—in the emotional sanction, control, or "tuning" in each type.

The tradition-directed person feels the impact of his culture as a unit, but it is nevertheless mediated through the specific, small number of individuals with whom he is in daily contact. These expect of him not so much that he be a certain type of person but that he behave in the approved way. Consequently the sanction for behavior tends to be the fear of being *shamed.*

The inner-directed person has early incorporated a psychic gyroscope which is set going by his parents and can receive signals later on from other authorities who resemble his parents. He goes through life less independent than he seems, obeying this internal piloting. Getting off course, whether in response to inner impulses or to the fluctuating voices of contemporaries, may lead to the feeling of *guilt.*

Since the direction to be taken in life has been learned in the privacy of the home from a small number of guides and since principles, rather than details of behavior, are internalized, the inner-directed person is capable of great stability. Especially so when it turns out that his fellows have gyroscopes too, spinning at the same speed and set in the same direction. But many inner-directed individuals can remain stable even when the reinforcement of social approval is not available—as in the upright life of the stock Englishman in the tropics.

Contrasted with such a type as this, the other-directed person learns to respond to signals from a far wider circle than is constituted by his parents. The family is no longer a closely knit unit to which he belongs but merely part of a wider social environment to which he early becomes attentive. In these respects the other-directed person resembles the tradition-directed person: both live in a group milieu and lack the inner-directed person's capacity to go it alone. The nature of this group milieu, however, differs radically in the two cases. The other-directed person is cosmopolitan. For him the border between the familiar and the strange—a border clearly marked in the societies depending on tradition-direction—has broken down. As the family continuously absorbs the strange and so reshapes itself, so the strange becomes familiar. While the inner-directed person could be "at home abroad" by virtue of his relative insensitivity to others, the other-directed person is, in a sense, at home everywhere and nowhere, capable of a superficial intimacy with and response to everyone.

The tradition-directed person takes his signals from others, but they come in a cultural monotone; he needs no complex receiving equipment to pick them up. The other-directed person must be able to receive signals from far and near;

the sources are many, the changes rapid. What can be internalized, then, is not a code of behavior but the elaborate equipment needed to attend to such messages and occasionally to participate in their circulation. As against guilt-and-shame controls, though of course these survive, one prime psychological lever of the other-directed person is a diffuse *anxiety.* This control equipment, instead of being like a gyroscope, is like a radar.

PART VII

THE CRITICAL EDGE

The critical edge in sociological theorizing was a movement away from the exclusive focus on order, stability, and solidarity to an earnest consideration of the conflicts, tensions, and inequalities that are omnipresent in society. Influenced to one degree or another by the Marxian critique of capitalism, the critical theorists altered and extended that critique to account for the conditions that were quickly bringing into being a postindustrial mass society. Writing in the mid- to late 1950s, Lewis A. Coser and Ralf Dahrendorf adopted aspects of functionalist theory and Marxian theory to explain social conflicts that arise not only from socioeconomic conditions but from various kinds of social structures. Karl Mannheim, Antonio Gramsci, Georg Lukács, and Max Horkheimer developed further Marx's assertion that economic conditions determine forms of consciousness and explored its flip side: how ideology, through the intellectuals, could transform capitalism. Finally, Theodor W. Adorno and C. Wright Mills turn their attention to critiquing the commodification of culture in a capitalist economy.

Influenced more by Simmel's ideas of conflict as a form of sociation than by Marx's notion of class oppression, Lewis A. Coser, in "Social Structures, Social Conflicts, and Safety-Valve Institutions," examines the functions that conflict may have in maintaining social order. According to Coser, groups with different types of social structure experience different types of social conflict. In tightly structured groups, where members are completely involved with each other, the acting out of hostilities between them is usually suppressed. Conflicts build up, and when they finally break out, they are particularly intense and thus threaten the very core of the members' relationships. By contrast, in loosely structured groups, where members participate only tangentially, and conflicts are allowed to occur, hostilities do not accumulate and, when expressed, are not intense. However, no society, no matter how flexibly structured and open it is, always permits the total expression of aggressions. Thus, there is the need for *safety-valve institutions* that provide an outlet for the release of hostilities and that divert them away from unsatisfactory relationships so that they do not become disruptive.

In "Class Conflict and Structural Change," Ralf Dahrendorf extends Marx's notion of class beyond its exclusive focus on wealth and advocates for a theory of social structure that acknowledges relations of *authority*. Authority relations always involve superordinate elements that legitimately control the behavior of subordinates. Those who occupy positions of domination and those who occupy positions of subjugation have, by virtue of their positions, conflicting *interests*. Those in positions of domination have an interest in maintaining the authority structure; those in positions of subjugation have an interest in changing the authority structure. Dahrendorf calls organizations with this type of authority structure *imperatively coordinated associations*. Groups that arise out of imperatively coordinated associations are what he calls *classes*, and these engage in class conflicts in order to bring about structural change. For Dahrendorf, there are three ways of bringing about structural change in an association through class conflict: (1) by replacing all of the personnel in positions of domination, (2) by replacing some of the personnel in positions of domination, and (3) by incorporating the interests of the subjugated group into the association.

In "The Sociology of Knowledge," Karl Mannheim advocates for conducting a sociohistorical analysis in understanding the various styles of thought of a given society at a given period of time. Such an analysis must consider that society is stratified according to social classes. Understanding the patterns of thought of the social classes requires knowing about their various *world postulates*, or ideologies. Moreover, the social classes make up an *intellectual stratum*, or group of intellectuals who share the same ideology—whether conservative or progressive—to which they are committed. Because each ideology is different, they thus come into conflict. But as society changes, its intellectual strata also change and so too do their corresponding ideologies. Thus, when a *social* change produces a change of *meaning*, a new ideology is formed.

Antonio Gramsci, in "Hegemony," also takes up the notion of an intellectual stratum, but he sees the dominant social group as having its own intellectuals that act on its behalf. These intellectuals have relations with the *civil society* of trade unions, the church, schools, and other institutions. They also have relations with the *political society* that encompasses the state, the police, and the courts. In the case of civil society, the intellectuals extend the ruling class's *hegemony*, or dominant ideology, to the subordinate group. Because this ideology is presented as the dominant one, the subordinate group "spontaneously" consents to it. In the case of political society, the ruling class exercises coercive power over those subordinate groups that do not consent to its ideology. Thus, the ruling class "dominates" by political coercion and "leads" by social hegemony.

In the next reading, "The Reification of Consciousness," Georg Lukács advances Marx's concept of commodity fetishism from characterizing only the economy to characterizing the totality of society, in particular, its forms of thought. According to Lukács, because the fetishism, or *reification*, of commodities is pervasive in all aspects of modern capitalist society, people's consciousness becomes subjugated to the reification. They develop a *reified consciousness* that considers the commodification of all products and relationships as the true representations of social reality. This reification of consciousness takes its most extreme form with the workers who perceive themselves as nothing more than commodities in the process of production. But as workers are awakened to the fact that they, as *subjects*, are treated as *objects*, they begin to recognize the fetish character of capitalism. With this overcoming of reification, the workers become conscious—self-conscious—of their social existence and are then able to transform capitalist society.

In "Critical Theory," Max Horkheimer presents a critical way of thinking that questions the blind acceptance of the rules of conduct that are provided by the existing social order on the basis of the division of labor and class distinctions. Critical thinking endows people with self-awareness and emancipates them from the oppressive expectations of social structure. Critical thinkers experience a dialectical tension between their own world of will and reason and the alien world of capitalism. Those who accept a critical theory of society are the intellectuals. But unlike Gramsci, Horkheimer does not believe that there is an intellectual stratum connected to a particular social class. Rather, there exists a *suprasocial* stratum—an *intelligentsia*—made up of professors, civil servants, doctors, and lawyers, who are independent of economic and political affiliations, including the proletariat. The goal of critical-thinking intellectuals is to transform the whole of capitalist society by pointing out its social injustices.

Theodor W. Adorno, in "The Culture Industry," argues that there has arisen an organization of mass media, which he calls the *culture industry*, that spreads its influence throughout the masses. All those products of the culture industry—art, literature, film, and music—are mechanically churned out, produced and reproduced, for profit; they are commodified. Cultural products are standardized, commercialized, and subject to the advertising techniques of mass marketing. The culture industry distracts its consumers from questioning the quality, truth, and aesthetics of its products. As the culture industry spreads its ideology, which is supportive of the status quo, it makes social life vacuous, banal, and conformist. This makes the consumers of culture complacent and fetters their consciousness. It restricts their emancipation and inhibits independent thought—a crucial requirement in a democratic society.

In the final reading, "The Designer as Cultural Worker," C. Wright Mills maintains that the American designer, involved in artistic and intellectual endeavors, is a central figure in the cultural apparatus. By the *cultural apparatus*, Mills means all those settings—schools, theaters, newspapers, the census bureau, studios, laboratories, museums, little magazines, and radio networks—in which artistic, intellectual, and scientific work is being done. In the United States, the cultural apparatus is, however, very much a commercial enterprise that is part of the capitalist economy. Mills explains that since the end of World War II, the designer has become caught in the middle of two great trends. One is the shift in economic emphasis from production to distribution; the other is the subordination of culture to the capitalist economy. Designers, as cultural workers, occupy a contradictory place at the intersection of these trends. And because they are now involved in the commercialization of the culture they produce, they are experiencing guilt, insecurity, and frustration in their work.

50

Social Structures, Social Conflicts, and Safety-Valve Institutions*

Lewis A. Coser

Conflict within a group, we have seen, may help to establish unity or to re-establish unity and cohesion where it has been threatened by hostile and antagonistic feelings among the members. Yet, we noted that not *every* type of conflict is likely to benefit group structure, nor that conflict can subserve such functions for *all* groups. Whether social conflict is beneficial to internal adaptation or not depends on the type of issues over which it is fought as well as on the type of social structure within which it occurs. However, types of conflict and types of social structure are not independent variables.

Internal social conflicts which concern goals, values or interests that do not contradict the basic assumptions upon which the relationship is founded tend to be positively functional for the social structure. Such conflicts tend to make possible the readjustment of norms and power relations within groups in accordance with the felt needs of its individual members or subgroups.

Internal conflicts in which the contending parties no longer share the basic values upon which the legitimacy of the social system rests threaten to disrupt the structure.

One safeguard against conflict disrupting the consensual basis of the relationship, however, is contained in the social structure itself: it is provided by the institutionalization and tolerance of conflict. Whether internal conflict promises to be a means of equilibration of social relations or readjustment of rival claims, or whether it threatens to "tear apart," depends to a large extent on the social structure within which it occurs.

In every type of social structure there are occasions for conflict, since individuals and subgroups are likely to make from time to time rival claims to scarce resources, prestige or power positions. But social structures differ in the way in which they allow expression to antagonistic claims. Some show more tolerance of conflict than others.

Closely knit groups in which there exists a high frequency of interaction and high personality involvement of the members have a tendency to suppress conflict. While they provide frequent occasions for hostility (since both sentiments of love and hatred are intensified through frequency of interaction), the acting out of such feelings is sensed as a danger to such intimate relationships, and hence there is a tendency to suppress rather than to allow expression of hostile feelings. In close-knit groups, feelings of hostility tend, therefore, to accumulate and hence to intensify. If conflict breaks out in a group that has consistently tried to prevent expression of hostile feelings, it will be particularly intense for two reasons: First, because the conflict does not merely aim at resolving the immediate issue which led to its outbreak; all accumulated grievances which were denied expression previously are apt to emerge at this occasion. Second, because the total personality involvement of the group members makes for mobilization of all sentiments in the conduct of the struggle.

Hence, the closer the group, the more intense the conflict. Where members participate with their total personality and conflicts are suppressed, the conflict, if it breaks out nevertheless, is likely to threaten the very root of the relationship.

In groups comprising individuals who participate only segmentally, conflict is less likely to be disruptive. Such groups are likely to experience a multiplicity of conflicts. This in itself tends to constitute a check against the breakdown of consensus: the energies of group members are mobilized in many directions and hence will not concentrate on *one* conflict cutting through the group. Moreover, where occasions for hostility are not permitted to accumulate and conflict is allowed to occur wherever a resolution of tension seems to be indicated, such a conflict is likely to remain focused primarily on the condition which led to its outbreak and not to revive blocked hostility; in this way, the conflict is limited to "the facts of the case." One may venture to say that multiplicity of conflicts stands in inverse relation to their intensity.

So far we have been dealing with internal social conflict only. At this point we must turn to a consideration of external conflict, for the structure of the group is itself affected by conflicts with other groups in which it engages or which it prepares for. Groups which are engaged in continued struggle tend to lay claim on the total personality involvement of their members so that internal conflict would tend to mobilize all energies and affects of the members. Hence such groups are unlikely to tolerate more than limited departures from the group unity. In such groups there is a tendency to suppress conflict; where it occurs, it leads the group to break up through splits or through forced withdrawal of dissenters.

Groups which are not involved in continued struggle with the outside are less prone to make claims on total personality involvement of the membership and are more likely to exhibit flexibility of structure. The multiple internal conflicts which they tolerate may in turn have an equilibrating and stabilizing impact on the structure.

In flexible social structures, multiple conflicts crisscross each other and thereby prevent basic cleavages along one axis. The multiple group affiliations of individuals makes them participate in various group conflicts so that their total personalities are not involved in any single one of them. Thus segmental participation in a multiplicity of conflicts constitutes a balancing mechanism within the structure.

In loosely structured groups and open societies, conflict, which aims at a resolution of tension between antagonists, is likely to have stabilizing and integrative functions for the relationship. By permitting immediate and direct expression of rival claims, such social systems are able to readjust their structures by eliminating the sources of dissatisfaction. The multiple conflicts which they experience may serve to eliminate the causes for dissociation and to re-establish unity. These systems avail themselves, through the toleration and institutionalization of conflict, of an important stabilizing mechanism.

In addition, conflict within a group frequently helps to revitalize existent norms; or it contributes to the emergence of new norms. In this sense, social conflict is a mechanism for adjustment of norms adequate to new conditions. A flexible society benefits from conflict because such behavior, by helping to create and modify norms, assures its continuance under changed conditions. Such mechanism for readjustment of norms is hardly available to rigid systems: by suppressing conflict, the latter smother a useful warning signal, thereby maximizing the danger of catastrophic breakdown.

Internal conflict can also serve as a means for ascertaining the relative strength of antagonistic interests within the structure, and in this way constitute a mechanism for the maintenance or continual readjustment of the balance of power. Since the outbreak of the conflict indicates a rejection of a previous accommodation between parties, once the respective power of the contenders has been ascertained through conflict, a new equilibrium can be established and the relationship can proceed on this new basis. Consequently, a social structure in which there is room for conflict disposes of an important means for avoiding or redressing conditions of disequilibrium by modifying the terms of power relations.

Conflicts with some produce associations or coalitions with others. Conflicts through such associations or coalitions, by providing a bond between the members, help to reduce social isolation or to unite individuals and groups otherwise unrelated or antagonistic to each other. A social structure in which there can exist a multiplicity of conflicts contains a mechanism for bringing together otherwise isolated, apathetic or mutually hostile parties and for taking them into the field of public social activities. Moreover, such a structure fosters a multiplicity of associations and coalitions whose diverse purposes crisscross each other, we recall, thereby preventing alliances along one major line of cleavage.

Once groups and associations have been formed through conflict with other groups, such conflict may further serve to maintain boundary lines between them and the surrounding social environment. In this way, social conflict helps to structure the larger social environment by assigning position to the various subgroups within the system and by helping to define the power relations between them.

Not all social systems in which individuals participate segmentally allow the free expression of antagonistic claims. Social systems tolerate or institutionalize conflict to different degrees. There is no society in which any and every antagonistic claim is allowed immediate expression. Societies dispose of mechanisms to channel discontent and hostility while keeping intact the relationship within which antagonism arises. Such mechanisms frequently operate through "safety-valve" institutions which provide substitute objects upon which to displace hostile sentiments as well as means of abreaction of aggressive tendencies.

Safety-valve institutions may serve to maintain both the social structure and the individual's security system, but they are incompletely functional for both of them. They prevent modification of relationships to meet changing conditions and hence the satisfaction they afford the individual can be only partially or momentarily adjustive. The hypothesis has been suggested that the need for safety-valve institutions increases with the rigidity of the social structure, i.e., with the degree to which it disallows direct expression of antagonistic claims.

Safety-valve institutions lead to a displacement of goal in the actor: he need no longer aim at reaching a solution of the unsatisfactory situation, but merely at releasing the tension which arose from it. Where safety-valve institutions provide substitute objects for the displacement of hostility, the conflict itself is channeled away from the original unsatisfactory relationship into one in which the actor's goal is no longer the attainment of specific results, but the release of tension.

51

Class Conflict and Structural Change*

Ralf Dahrendorf

Generally speaking, it seems to me that two (meta-)theories can and must be distinguished in contemporary sociology. One of these, the *integration theory of society*, conceives of social structure in terms of a functionally integrated system held in equilibrium by certain patterned and recurrent processes. The other one, the *coercion theory of society*, views social structure as a form of organization held together by force and constraint and reaching continuously beyond itself in the sense of producing within itself the forces that maintain it in an unending process of change.

From the point of view of the integration theory of social structure, units of social analysis ("social systems") are essentially voluntary associations of people who share certain values and set up institutions in order to ensure the smooth functioning of cooperation. From the point of view of coercion theory, however, the units of social analysis present an altogether different picture. Here, it is not voluntary cooperation or general consensus but enforced constraint that makes social organizations cohere. In institutional terms, this means that in every social organization some positions are entrusted with a right to exercise control over other positions in order to ensure effective coercion; it means, in other words, that there is a differential distribution of power and authority. One of the central theses of this study consists in the assumption that this differential distribution of authority invariably becomes the determining factor of systematic social conflicts of a type that is germane to class conflicts in the traditional (Marxian) sense of this term. The structural origin of such group conflicts must be sought in the arrangement of social roles endowed with expectations of domination or subjection. Wherever there are such roles, group conflicts of the type in question are to be expected. Differentiation of groups engaged in such conflicts follows the lines of differentiation of roles that are relevant from the point of view of the exercise of authority. Identification of variously equipped authority roles is the first task of conflict analysis; conceptually and empirically all further steps of analysis follow from the investigation of distributions of power and authority.

*Excerpts from *Class and Class Conflict in Industrial Society* by Ralph Dahrendorf.

In the present study we are concerned exclusively with relations of authority, for these alone are part of social structure and therefore permit the systematic derivation of group conflicts from the organization of total societies and associations within them. The significance of such group conflicts rests with the fact that they are not the product of structurally fortuitous relations of power but come forth wherever authority is exercised—and that means in all societies under all historical conditions. (1) Authority relations are always relations of super-and subordination. (2) Where there are authority relations, the superordinate element is socially expected to control, by orders and commands, warnings and prohibitions, the behavior of the subordinate element. (3) Such expectations attach to relatively permanent social positions rather than to the character of individuals; they are in this sense legitimate. (4) By virtue of this fact, they always involve specification of the persons subject to control and of the spheres within which control is permissible. Authority, as distinct from power, is never a relation of generalized control over others. (5) Authority being a legitimate relation, noncompliance with authoritative commands can be sanctioned; it is indeed one of the functions of the legal system (and of course of quasi-legal customs and norms) to support the effective exercise of legitimate authority.

In conflict analysis we are concerned *inter alia* with the generation of conflict groups by the authority relations obtaining in imperatively coordinated associations. Since imperative coordination, or authority, is a type of social relation present in every conceivable social organization, it will be sufficient to describe such organizations simply as associations.

The analytical process of conflict group formation can be described in terms of a model. Throughout, the categories employed in this model will be used in terms of the coercion theory of social structure. With this restriction in mind, the thesis that conflict groups are based on the dichotomous distribution of authority in imperatively coordinated associations can be conceived of as the basic assumption of the model. To this assumption we now add the proposition that differentially equipped authority positions in associations involve, for their incumbents, conflicting interests. The occupants of positions of domination and the occupants of positions of subjection hold, by virtue of these positions, certain interests which are contradictory in substance and direction.

Our model of conflict group formation involves the proposition that of the two aggregates of authority positions to be distinguished in every association, one—that of domination—is characterized by an interest in the maintenance of a social structure that for them conveys authority, whereas the other—that of subjection—involves an interest in changing a social condition that deprives its incumbents of authority. The two interests are in conflict.

Empirically, group conflict is probably most easily accessible to analysis if it be understood as a conflict about the legitimacy of relations of authority. In every association, the interests of the ruling group are the values that constitute the ideology of the legitimacy of its rule, whereas the interests of the subjected group constitute a threat to this ideology and the social relations it covers.

Interest groups are groups in the strict sense of the sociological term; and they are the real agents of group conflict. They have a structure, a form of organization, a program or goal, and a personnel of members. If Ginsberg demands for such groups "regular contact or communication," however, this applies only in an indirect sense. Interest groups are always "secondary groups"; their members are in contact with each other only by virtue of their membership or by way of their elected or appointed representatives. One might emphasize the difference between interest groups and primary groupings such as family or friendship by calling them with MacIver "associations" or with Malinowski "institutions." However, it seems to me that the concept of interest group is sufficiently unambiguous if, apart from terminological considerations, we keep the modern political party in mind as an example of such organizations.

In terms of our model, the term "class" signifies conflict groups that are generated by the differential distribution of authority in imperatively coordinated associations.

Classes, understood as conflict groups arising out of the authority structure of imperatively coordinated associations, are in conflict. What are—so we must ask if we want to understand the lawfulness of this phenomenon—the social consequences, intended or unintended, of such conflicts?

In the present context, all structure changes will be understood as changes involving the personnel of positions of domination in imperatively coordinated associations.

The immediate effect of class conflicts is brought to bear on the incumbents of positions of domination, and changes are introduced by way of these positions.

This operational specification seems tenable in view of the role and definition of authority in the theory here proposed. Insofar as the distribution of authority in associations can be described as the formal object of class conflict, changes resulting from class conflict are in their formal aspect always changes in these authority structures or in their personnel. Moreover, authority is, from the point of view of sociological analysis, an instrumental value. In class theory, the possession of authority does not figure as a value sought for its own sake but as an opportunity to realize specific interests. This conception of authority is in keeping with our distinction of power and authority by the central category of legitimacy. It follows from it that, e.g., an exchange of the personnel of positions of domination has to be viewed not only as a process of rejuvenation of a basically constant "ruling class" or "elite," but above all as the instrumental aspect of a process which substantively represents structure change. In this sense, exchanges of personnel are not in themselves structure changes, but merely a condition for (from the point of view of the *status quo*) "new" interests becoming values or realities. Problems of changing patterns of recruitment to an upper stratum are meaningful only in the context of integration theory. For coercion theory, changes of the personnel of authority roles are merely the formal or instrumental aspect of changes of social structure on both the normative and the institutional levels.

The operational approach suggested permits the distinction of at least three modes of structure change, each of which requires some comment. A first mode of change, in this sense, consists in the total (or near-total) exchange of the personnel of positions of domination in an association. This is clearly the most sudden type of structure change. For purposes of illustration we might use the association of the state, and assume a specific state to be divided the opposition parties. In modern states, such sudden changes are a comparatively rare occurrence; the last outstanding example was probably provided by the Bolshevik revolution in Russia. Generally speaking, total exchange of ruling personnel might also be described as revolutionary change. It is at this point that the sociology of revolution ties in with the theory of group conflict.

Far more frequently we encounter in history, and especially in modern history, a second mode of structure change, namely, the partial exchange of the personnel of positions of domination. Such partial exchange signifies evolutionary rather than revolutionary change. In terms of our illustration, it would be present if the majority party chose to form a coalition with, say, the smaller one of the two opposition parties. In this case, some representatives of the hitherto subjected class penetrate the ruling class and influence the policies adopted and decisions made. Coalitions are of course not the only example of partial exchange if elections in democratic countries reverse the majority relations, they usually result in but partial exchanges of government personnel, so that, e.g., cabinet ministers are exchanged, but some of the judges, diplomats, and higher civil servants of the previous majority party remain in office.

But probably more important than either of these is a third mode of structure change by class conflict which does not involve any exchange of personnel. It is possible for structure changes in directions intended by subjected groups to be inaugurated without any members of these subjected groups penetrating into dominant positions. This seemingly accidental consequence of the process of social conflict occurs in democratic and totalitarian countries alike. In terms of our example, it would mean that majority and opposition remain stable and distinct over long periods of time, but the majority party incorporates proposals and interests of the opposition in its legislation and policies. Strange as it may initially appear that structure change should ever occur without an exchange of ruling personnel, there are nevertheless numerous illustrations in the history of states, enterprises, churches, and other associations. To be sure, this third mode of structure change marks the slowest type of evolution and requires particular skill on the part of the rulers to avoid such suppression of opposing interests as thereby to provoke revolts; it can nevertheless enable a dominant class to maintain the legitimacy of its authority over long periods of time.

Possibly, these three modes of structure change indicate the end points and center of a scale that measures the suddenness of change. Partial exchange of personnel is evidently a broad category that covers the whole field between total exchange and complete stability. However, while it may be said that structure change is more sudden in the extent to which more personnel is exchanged, this does not necessarily mean, that it is also more radical. Suddenness and radicalness of structure change are two dimensions of this phenomenon which can vary independently, much as the intensity and violence of class conflicts can vary independently. There are examples of relatively sudden changes that are accompanied by but slight modifications of values and institutions, and there are examples of extremely radical, although comparatively slow, evolutions. Majority shifts in democratic states illustrate the former case, while the latter is illustrated by such deep changes in class structure as we have analyzed earlier in this study.

The relation between the radicalness-suddenness dimension of structure change and the intensity-violence dimension of class conflict is more than merely logical. It may be argued that the suddenness of change varies directly with the violence of conflict. The more violent class conflicts are, the more sudden are the changes wrought by it likely to be. In this sense, effective conflict regulation serves to reduce the suddenness of change. Well-regulated conflict is likely to lead to very gradual change, often near the third mode distinguished above. Conflict regulation may, in fact, constitute a machinery for forcing on dominant groups recognition of the interests of subjected groups, which interests are then incorporated in policy. The example of a wage claim settled by conciliation is a case in point. Uncontrolled conflict, on the other hand, always threatens the incumbents of positions of domination in their very possession of authority; it aims at a total exchange of leading personnel, and, in this sense, at sudden change.

At least in theory, there is also a scale of the radicalness of structure change. However, an operational formulation of such a scale offers particular difficulties. In general, the radicalness of structure changes is evidently a function of what in particular historical situations represent the *status quo*. In eighteenth-century Europe, the peaceful utilization of nuclear energy would certainly have made for extremely radical changes, both technical and social. In twentieth-century Europe, the same process, although still involving some change, has no really radicals consequences but simply ties in with continuing trends of rationalization, automation, etc. Similarly—and more immediately to the point here—changes resulting from conflicts within the association of the Catholic church are, in most countries of today, far less radical than they were at earlier times. Thus, the radicalness of structure change is not merely a consequence of the intensity of class conflict. Within certain limits, however, this relation does obtain. The more strongly people are involved in given conflicts, the more far-reaching are their demands likely to be, and the more radical will be the changes resulting from this conflict, irrespective of the suddenness of such changes. Radicalness and suddenness of change, like intensity and violence of conflict, may coincide, but more often they diverge; and in any case their divergence presents more interesting problems of social analysis than their coincidence.

Apart from historical conditions, the co-variance of the intensity of conflict and radicalness of change as well as of the violence of conflict and suddenness of change is further restricted by the structural requisites of associations. This will become immediately apparent if we contrast industrial and political conflict. In political associations, exchange of leading personnel is a realistic possibility, so that the whole scale of suddenness of change can be applied here. In industrial associations, exchange of leading personnel is, except within certain very narrow limits, not possible. There are no elections (and there cannot be) as a result of which the members of management become workers, and representatives of labor become managers. Structure changes in industry will therefore almost invariably take the form of changes of policy unaccompanied by exchanges of personnel. To some extent, similar conditions obtain in most church organizations. Before investigating processes of structure change by class conflict in specific associations, we must therefore ascertain the range of possible modes of change in these associations.

In general, however, and without losing sight of additional intervening variables, we can propose that different modes of structure change co-vary with different modes of class conflict. The more intense class conflict is, the more radical are the changes likely to be which it brings about; the more violent class conflict is, the more sudden are structure changes resulting from it likely to be. Structure change is the final element of the theory of group conflict under discussion. Like all other elements of this theory, it represents but a segment of more inclusive phenomena of conflict and change. Possibly, the typology of change introduced in the preceding pages is applicable also to the consequences of kinds of conflict other than that between classes. As everywhere in this study, however, I have confined myself here to exploring the causes, forms, and consequences of conflicts generated by the authority structures of imperatively coordinated associations.

52

The Sociology of Knowledge*

Karl Mannheim

If we adopt a dynamic conception of truth and knowledge, then the central problem of a sociology of knowledge will be that of the existentially conditioned genesis of the various standpoints which encompass the patterns of thought available to any given epoch. The entire effort will be concentrated upon this one point, because the change and the inner growth of the various standpoints contains for us the whole substance of the history of thought. The sociological analysis of thought, undertaken thus far only in a fragmentary and casual fashion, now becomes the object of a comprehensive scientific programme which permits a division of labour once it has been decided to go through the intellectual output of each period and find out on what standpoints and systematic premises thought was based in each case. This, the first major problem of a sociology of knowledge can be tackled in conjunction with the work done in the field of the 'history of ideas', which has been extremely fruitful as regards both results and methods. In a number of fields (political, philosophical, economical, aesthetic, moral, etc.) the history of ideas shows us an extreme variety of changing elements of thought; but these labours will reach their culmination, the full realization of their meaning, only when we hear not only about changing contents of thought but also about the often merely implicit systematic premises on which a given idea was based in its original form—to be later modified so as to satisfy a different set of premises, and thus to survive under changed conditions. That is: the history of ideas can achieve its objective, that of accounting for the entire process of intellectual history in systematic fashion, only if it is supplemented by a historical structural analysis of the various centres of systematization that succeed each other in dynamic fashion. We do see beginnings of this kind of analysis (e.g. in works distinguishing 'romanticism' or 'Enlightenment' as different vital climates giving rise to different modes of thinking); and one would merely pursue these ideas to their ultimate logical consequences if one made a systematic effort to lay bare the ultimate axioms underlying 'romantic' and 'Enlightenment' thought respectively, and to define the type of system to which these patterns of thought belong with the greatest logical and

*Excerpts from *Essays on the Sociology of Knowledge* by Karl Mannheim, Edited by Paul Keoskemeti. First published in 1952 by Routledge and Kegan Paul Ltd. Reproduced by permission of Taylor & Francis Books UK.

methodological precision possible today. This would merely mean that one would utilize for historical analysis the logical precision which is characteristic of our time. At this point already, however, we have occasion to point out a limitation of the history of ideas—the fact that its analysis proceeds in terms of 'epochs'. From a sociological point of view, both 'nations' and 'epochs' are much too undifferentiated to serve as a basis of reference in describing the historical process. The historian knows that a certain epoch will appear as dominated by just one intellectual current only when we have a bird's eye view of it. Penetrating deeper into the historical detail, we shall see every epoch as divided among several currents; it may happen, at most, that one of these currents achieves dominance and relegates the others to the status of under-currents. No current is ever completely eliminated; even while one is victorious, all the others that belong to one or the other social sector will continue to exist as under-currents, ready to re-emerge and to reconstitute themselves on a higher level when the time is ripe. It is sufficient to think of the peculiar rhythm with which 'rationalistic' and 'romantic' phases constantly succeeded each other during the most recent period in European history to realize that we are dealing here with separate strands of evolution which nevertheless are related to each other by some higher law. However, it is not sufficient to recognize this evolution in separate strands; we also have to take into account the way in which the principal currents always adjust themselves to each other. Both these problems have to be worked out by a systematic history of ideas as the first chapter of a sociology of thought. For it cannot be overlooked, for instance, that whenever romanticism makes a new advance, it always takes into account the status of simultaneously existing and dominant rationalist thought; not only do the two schools learn from each other, but they even attempt to work out an ever broader synthesis, in order to master the new situation.

However, if we did not go any farther, we should never produce a *sociology* of knowledge. No matter how systematic it is, a purely immanent analysis of the genesis of intellectual standpoints is still nothing but a history of ideas. This preliminary systematic work in the history of ideas can lead to a sociology of knowledge only when we examine the problem of how the various intellectual standpoints and 'styles of thought' are rooted in an underlying historico-social reality. But in this connection, too, it would be a mistake, in our opinion, if one were to consider reality, social reality, as a unitary current. If within the history of ideas it is too undifferentiated a procedure to take epochs as units, then it is an equally great error to conceive the reality behind the ideological process as a homogeneous unit. After all, it cannot be doubted that any higher type of society is composed of several different strata, just as intellectual life shows a variety of currents; in our own society, stratification can best be described as class stratification. And the overall dynamic of society is a resultant of all the partial impulses emanating from these strata. The first task, then, will be to find out whether there is a correlation between the intellectual standpoints seen in immanence and the social currents (social standpoints). The finding of this correlation is the first task specific to the sociology of knowledge. The immanent description of the genesis of the intellectual standpoints may still be considered as the continuation of the work of the historian of ideas; the history of social stratification may still be seen as part of social history. But the combination of these two fields of inquiry introduces a specifically sociological approach. It is, however, important precisely at this point to eliminate naturalism, as well as those attitudes which are related to the original polemical intention of sociology. Although the problem outlined above has first been formulated in terms of the Marxian philosophy of history, we must, in studying it, be careful to renounce all materialist metaphysics and to exclude (or to reduce to the element of truth contained in them) all propagandistic considerations. First of all, even the most superficial glance at the historic data will show that it is quite impossible to identify any given intellectual standpoint with a given stratum or class—for example as if the proletariat had a science of its own, developed in a closed intellectual space, and the bourgeoisie another one, neatly separated from it. This crude propagandistic exaggeration can lead only to a faulty historical oversimplification; hence, we have to suspend belief until we have ascertained how much truth is contained in it (for it does have a certain element of truth).

Even the immanent examination of the various intellectual and cognitive standpoints, as it is carried out by a systematic history of ideas, shows that they do not float in thin air or develop and ramify purely from within, but must be put in correlation with certain tendencies embodied by social strata. At first, this 'putting in correlation' will present a certain difficulty for the sociologist. The naturalist epoch of Marxism recognized only one possible correlation between social reality and intellectual phenomena: namely, the correlation that an intellectual attitude is dictated by a material interest. It is because the initial phase of ideological research was solely motivated by 'unmasking' that being 'dictated by an interest' was the only form of social conditioning of ideas that was recognized. Not that we deny that certain intellectual positions can be adopted or promoted because this is useful either in propagating or in concealing group interests; and we admit that it can only be desirable to unmask such attitudes. However, this motivation by interest is not the only correlation that can exist between a social group and its intellectual positions. Socialist ideological research is one-sided, because it primarily concentrates attention upon that form of social conditioning of ideas which is represented by motivation by interest.

If, the category of interest is elevated to the rank of an absolute principle, the result can be only the reduction of the role of sociology to that of reconstructing the *homo economicus*, whereas sociology in fact has to examine man as a whole. Thus, we cannot assign a style of thought, a work of art, etc., to a group as its own on the basis of an analysis of interests. We can, however, show that a certain style of thought, an intellectual standpoint, is encompassed within a system of attitudes which in turn can be seen to be related to a certain economic and power system; we can then ask which social groups are 'interested' in the emergence and maintenance of this economic and social system and at the same time 'committed' to the corresponding world outlook.

Thus, the construction of a sociology of knowledge can be undertaken only by taking a circuitous route through the concept of the *total system* of a world outlook (through cultural sociology). We cannot relate an intellectual standpoint directly to a social class; what we can do is find out the correlation between the 'style of thought' underlying a given standpoint, and the 'intellectual motivation' of a certain social group.

If we examine the history of knowledge and thought with such questions in mind, seeking to understand how it is embedded in the history of the real, social process, then we shall find at each moment not only antagonistic groups combating each other, but also a conflict of opposed 'world postulates' (*Weltwollungen*). In the historical process, it is not only interests that combat interests, but world postulates compete with world postulates. And this fact is sociologically relevant, because these various 'world postulates' (of which the various 'styles of thought' are merely partial aspects) do not confront each other in a disembodied, arbitrary way; rather, each such postulate is linked to a certain group and develops within the thinking of that group. At each moment, it is just one stratum which is interested in maintaining the existing economic and social system and therefore clings to the corresponding style of thought; there are always other strata whose spiritual home is one or the other past stage of evolution, and yet others, just coming into being, which, being new, have not yet come into their own and therefore put their faith in the future. Since the different strata are 'interested in' and 'committed to' different world orders and world postulates, some of which are things of the past while others are just emerging, it is obvious that value conflicts permeate each stage of historical evolution.

That a 'style of thought' can be associated with the emergence of a certain social stratum is best demonstrated by the fact that modern rationalism (as was repeatedly pointed out) was linked to the world postulates and intellectual aspirations of the rising bourgeoisie, that later counter-currents allied themselves with irrationalism, and that a similar connection exists between romanticism and conservative aspirations. Starting from such insights, we can develop analyses of correlations between styles of thought and social strata—these, however, will be fruitful only if these attributions are not made in a static sense—e.g. by identifying rationalism with progressive and irrationalism with reactionary thought in every conceivable constellation. What we have to remember is that neither rationalism nor irrationalism (particularly in their present form) are eternal types of intellectual tendencies, and that a certain stratum is not always progressive or conservative respectively in the same sense. 'Conservative' and 'progressive' are *relative* attributes; whether a certain stratum is progressive, or conservative, or, worse still, reactionary, always depends on the direction, in which, the social process itself is moving. As the fundamental trend of economic and intellectual progress moves along, strata which began by being progressive may become conservative after they have achieved their ambition; strata which at a time played a leading role may suddenly feel impelled to go into opposition against the dominant trend.

It is thus important at this point already to avoid interpreting such relative concepts as eternal characteristics; but we must make still another distinction if we want to do justice to the enormous variety of historical reality. That is, in establishing correlations between products of the mind and social strata, we must distinguish between *intellectual* and *social* stratification. We can define social strata, in accordance with the Marxian concept of class, in terms of their role in the production process; but it is impossible, in our opinion, to establish a historical parallelism between intellectual standpoints and social strata defined in this fashion. Differentiation in the world of mind is much too great to permit the identification of each current, each standpoint, with a given class. Thus, we have to introduce an intermediary concept to effect the correlation between the concept of 'class', defined in terms of roles in the production process, and that of 'intellectual standpoint'. This intermediary concept is that of 'intellectual strata'. We mean by 'intellectual stratum' a group of people belonging to a certain social unit and sharing a certain 'world postulate' (as parts of which we may mention the economic system, the philosophical system, the artistic style 'postulated' by them), who at a given time are 'committed' to a certain style of economic activity and of theoretical thought.

We must first identify the various 'world postulates', systems of *Weltanschauung,* combating each other, and find the social groups that champion each; only when these 'intellectual strata' are specified, can we ask which 'social strata' correspond to them. Thus, it is possible to specify the groups of people who at a given moment are united in a 'conservative' outlook, and share in a common stock of ideas which are going through a ceaseless process of transformation; the sociologist of culture, however, should not be content with approaching this subject from this doctrinal point of view, but he should also ask himself which 'social classes' make up such an 'intellectual stratum'. We can understand the transformation of the various ideologies only on the basis of changes in the social composition of the intellectual stratum corresponding to them. The same applies obviously to the progressive types of *Weltanschauung*. The proletariat (to show the reverse side of the correlation we are dealing with) constitutes *one* class; but this one social class is divided as to the 'world postulates' of its members, as is clearly shown by the proletariat's following a number of different political parties. The only point of interest for the sociologist is this; what types of progressive world postulates exist at a given moment, what are the progressive intellectual strata adhering to them, and what social strata within the proletariat belong to these various intellectual strata?

The peculiar function of this intermediary concept, that of 'intellectual stratum', consists in making a co-ordination of intellectual configurations with social groups possible without blurring the inner differentiation either of the world of mind or of social reality. Further, we have to take the fact into account that at no moment in history does a social stratum produce its ideas, so to speak, out of thin air, as a matter of pure invention. Both conservative and progressive groups of various kinds inherit ideologies which somehow have existed in the past. Conservative groups fall back upon attitudes, methods of thought, ideas of remote epochs and adapt them to new situations; but newly emerging groups also take up at first already existing ideas and methods, so that a cross-section through the rival ideologies combating one another at a given moment also represents a cross-section through the historical past of the society in question. If, however, we focus our attention exclusively upon this 'inheritance' aspect of the; story, and try to reduce to it the entire relationship between social reality and the intellectual process, we obtain an entirely wrong kind of historicism. If we look at the process of intellectual evolution and the role of social strata in it solely from this point of view, then it will seem, in fact, as if nothing happened except the unfolding of potentialities given in advance. It is, however, merely a peculiarity of the conservative conception of historicism that the continuous nature of all historical processes is interpreted as implying that everything has its origin in something temporally preceding it. The progressive variant of historicism looks at the process of evolution from the angle of the *status nascendi.*

This perspective alone enables us to see that even motifs and aspects simply taken over from a predecessor always become something different owing to this very passage itself, merely because their sponsor is a different one, and relates them to a different situation. Or, to put it more succinctly: change of function of an idea always involves a change of meaning—this being one of the most essential arguments in favour of the proposition that history is a creative medium of meanings and not merely the passive medium in which pre-existent, self-contained meanings find their realization. Thus, we have to add to our list of categories this central concept of all sociology of culture and thought, that of 'change of function'; for without this, we could produce nothing but a mere history of ideas.

We shall, however, distinguish two types of change of function; an *immanent* and a *sociological*. We speak of an *immanent* change of function (in the realm of thought, to mention only one of the fields in which this phenomenon may occur), when a concept passes from one system of ideas into another. Terms like 'ego', 'money', 'romanticism', etc. mean something different, according to the system within which they are used. By a *sociological* change of function, however, we mean a change in the meaning of a concept which occurs when that concept is adopted by a group living in a different social environment, so that the vital significance of the concept becomes different. Each idea acquires a new meaning when it is applied to a new life situation. When new strata take over systems of ideas from other strata, it can always be shown that the same words mean something different to the new sponsors, because these latter think in terms of different aspirations and existential configurations. This *social* change of function, then, is, as stated above, also a change of meaning. And although it is true that different social strata cultivating the same cultural field share the same 'germinal' ideas (this being the reason why understanding is possible from one stratum to the other), developing social reality introduces something incalculable, creatively new into the intellectual process, because the unpredictable new situations emerging within reality constitute new existential bases of reference for familiar ideas. Social strata play a creative role precisely because they introduce new intentions, new directions of intentionality, new world postulates, into the already developed framework of ideas of older strata which then appropriate them, and thus subject their heritage to a productive change of function.

Different social strata, then, do not 'produce different systems of ideas' (*Weltanschauungen*) in a crude, materialistic sense—in the sense in which lying ideologies can be 'manufactured'—they 'produce' them, rather, in the sense that social groups emerging within the social process are always in a position to project new directions of that 'intentionality', that vital tension, which accompanies all life. The reason why it is so important in studying 'immanent' changes of function of a given idea (the passage of a unit of meaning into a new system), also to observe the tensions and vital aspirations operative behind theoretical thought, and introducing antagonisms into the life of the society as a whole—the reason why it is so important to study these real tensions is that it is extremely likely that an immanent change of function is preceded by a sociological one, i.e. that shifts in social reality are the underlying cause of shifts in theoretical systems.

If the task of a sociology of knowledge is approached with these premises in mind, it will present itself in the following form: the main task consists in specifying, for each temporal cross-section of the historical process, the various systematic intellectual standpoints on which the thinking of creative individuals and groups was based. Once this is done, however, these different trends of thought should not be confronted like positions in a mere theoretical debate, but we should explore their non-theoretical, vital roots. To do this, we first have to uncover the hidden metaphysical premises of the various systematic positions; then we must ask further which of the 'world postulates' coexisting in a given epoch are the correlates of a given style of thought. When these correspondences are established, we already have identified the intellectual strata combating each other. The sociological task proper, however, begins only after this 'immanent' analysis is done—it consists in finding the social strata making up the intellectual strata in question. It is only in terms of the role of these latter strata within the overall process, in terms of their attitudes toward the emerging new reality, that we can define the fundamental aspirations and world postulates existing at a given time which can absorb already existing ideas and methods and subject them to a change of function—not to speak of newly created forms. Such changes of function are in no way mysterious; it is possible to determine them with sufficient exactness by combining sociological methods with those of the history of ideas. We can, for instance, go back to the historical and sociological origin of an idea and then, following its evolution, determine, so to speak, the 'angle of refraction' each time it undergoes a change of function, by specifying the new systematic centre to which the idea becomes linked, and simultaneously asking what existential changes in the real background are mirrored by that change of meaning.

As a rather familiar example, we may mention the change of function of the dialectical method—the *leitmotiv* of the present discussion. Dialectics was clearly formulated for the first time by Hegel within the framework of a conservative world postulate (we shall not discuss the earlier history of the method). When Marx took it over, it became modified in various respects. We want to mention only two of these revisions. Firstly, dialectics was 'made to stand on its feet rather than on its head', i.e. it was lifted from its idealistic context and re-interpreted in terms of social reality. Secondly, the final term of historical dynamics became the future rather than the present. Both shifts, which represent a change of meaning in the method, may be explained by the 'change of function' brought about under the impact of the vital aspirations of the proletariat which Marx made his own. We can explain the new features of the system by recalling that the life of the proletariat revolves around economic problems, and that its vital tension is directed toward the future. On the other hand, Hegel's system, also may be shown to be sociologically determined. The fact that in this system the closing phase of the dynamism of history is the present mirrors the success achieved by a class which, having come into its own, merely wants to conserve what has already been accomplished.

If, then, we define the sociology of knowledge as a discipline which explores the functional dependence of each intellectual standpoint on the differentiated social group reality standing behind it, and which sets itself the task of retracing the evolution of the various standpoints, then it seems that the fruitful beginnings made by historicism may point in a direction in which further progress is possible. Having indicated the systematic premises characterizing historicism as a point of departure for a sociology of knowledge, we then went on to suggest a few methodological problems involved in this approach. At the same time, however, we also wanted to show the method in operation, and hence we described the principal 'standpoints' from which the elaboration of a sociology of knowledge may be undertaken in the present constellation. We thought that such an analysis of the present status of the problem in terms of the categories of the sociology of knowledge would contribute to give this discipline a clearer notion of itself.

53

Hegemony*

Antonio Gramsci

The relationship between the intellectuals and the world of production is not as direct as it is with the fundamental social groups but is, in varying degrees, "mediated" by the whole fabric of society and by the complex of superstructures, of which the intellectuals are, precisely, the "functionaries". It should be possible both to measure the "organic quality" [*organicità*] of the various intellectual strata and their degree of connection with a fundamental social group, and to establish a gradation of their functions and of the superstructures from the bottom to the top (from the structural base upwards). What we can do, for the moment, is to fix two major superstructural "levels": the one that can be called "civil society," that is the ensemble of organisms commonly called "private," and that of "political society" or "the State". These two levels correspond on the one hand to the function of "hegemony" which the dominant group exercises throughout society and on the other hand to that of "direct domination" or command exercised through the State and "juridical" government. The functions in question are precisely organisational and connective. The intellectuals are the dominant group's "deputies" exercising the subaltern functions of social hegemony and political government.

These comprise:

1. The "spontaneous" consent given by the great masses of the population to the general direction imposed on social life by the dominant fundamental group; this consent is "historically" caused by the prestige (and consequent confidence) which the dominant group enjoys because of its position and function in the world of production.

2. The apparatus of state coercive power which "legally" enforces discipline on those groups who do not "consent" either actively or passively. This apparatus is, however, constituted for the whole of society in anticipation of moments of crisis of command and direction when spontaneous consent has failed.

This way of posing the problem has as a result a considerable extension of the concept of intellectual, but it is the only way which enables one to reach a concrete approximation of reality. It also clashes with preconceptions of caste. The function of organising social hegemony and state domination certainly gives rise to a particular division of labour and therefore to a whole hierarchy of qualifications in some of which there is no apparent attribution of directive or

*Excerpts from *Selections from the Prison Notebooks of Antonio Gramsci.* Edited and Translated by Quintin Hoare and Geoffrey Nowell Smith.

organisational functions. For example, in the apparatus of social and state direction there exist a whole series of jobs of a manual and instrumental character (non-executive work, agents rather than officials or functionaries). It is obvious that such a distinction has to be made just as it is obvious that other distinctions have to be made as well. Indeed, intellectual activity must also be distinguished in terms of its intrinsic characteristics, according to levels which in moments of extreme opposition represent a real qualitative difference—at the highest level would be the creators of the various sciences, philosophy, art, etc., at the lowest the most humble "administrators" and divulgators of pre-existing, traditional, accumulated intellectual wealth.

The supremacy of a social group manifests itself in two ways, as "domination" and as "intellectual and moral leadership". A social group dominates antagonistic groups, which it tends to "liquidate," or to subjugate perhaps even by armed force; it leads kindred and allied groups. A social group can, and indeed must, already exercise "leadership" before winning governmental power (this indeed is one of the principal conditions for the winning of such power); it subsequently becomes dominant when it exercises power, but even if it holds it firmly in its grasp, it must continue to "lead" as well.

The function of Piedmont in the Italian Risorgimento is that of a "ruling class". In reality, what was involved was not that throughout the peninsula there existed nuclei of a homogeneous ruling class whose irresistible tendency to unite determined the formation of the new Italian national State. These nuclei existed, indubitably, but their tendency to unite was extremely problematic; also, more importantly, they—each in its own sphere—were not "leading". The "leader" presupposes the "led," and who was "led" by these nuclei? These nuclei did not wish to "lead" anybody, i.e. they did not wish to concord their interests and aspirations with the interests and aspirations of other groups. They wished to "dominate" and not to "lead". Furthermore, they wanted their interests to dominate, rather than their persons ; in other words, they wanted a new force, independent of every compromise and condition, to become the arbiter of the Nation : this force was Piedmont and hence the function of the monarchy. Thus Piedmont had a function which can, from certain aspects, be compared to that of a party, i.e. of the leading personnel of a social group (and in fact people always spoke of the "Piedmont party"): with the additional feature that it was in fact a State, with an army, a diplomatic service, etc.

This fact is of the greatest importance for the concept of "passive revolution"—the fact, that is, that what was involved was not a social group which "led" other groups, but a State which, even though it had limitations as a power, "led" the group which should have been "leading" and was able to put at the hitter's disposal an army and a politico-diplomatic strength. One may refer to what has been called the function of "Piedmont" in international politico-historical language. Serbia before the war posed as the "Piedmont" of the Balkans. (Moreover France after 1789 and for many years, up to the *coup d'état* of Louis Napoléon, was in this sense the Piedmont of Europe.) That Serbia did not succeed as Piedmont succeeded is due to the fact that after the war there occurred a political awakening of the peasantry such as did not exist after 1848. If one studies closely what is happening in the kingdom of Yugoslavia, one sees that within it the "Serbian" forces or those favourable to Serb hegemony are the forces which oppose agrarian reform. Both in Croatia and in the other non-Serb regions we find that there is an anti-Serb rural intellectual bloc, and that the conservative forces are favourable to Serbia. In this case, too, there do not exist local "hegemonic" groups—they are under the hegemony of Serbia; meanwhile the subversive forces do not have, as a social function, any great importance. Anybody who observes Serb affairs superficially might wonder what would have happened if so-called brigandage of the kind which occurred round Naples and in Sicily from 1860 to 1870 had occurred in Yugoslavia after 1919. Undoubtedly the phenomenon is the same, but the social weight and political experience of the peasant masses are quite different since 1919 from what they were after 1848. The important thing is to analyse more profoundly the significance of a "Piedmont"-type function in passive revolutions—i.e. the fact that a State replaces the local social groups in leading a struggle of renewal. It is one of the cases in which these groups have the function of "domination" without that of "leadership": dictatorship without hegemony. The hegemony will be exercised by a part of the social group over the entire group, and not by the latter over other forces in order to give power to the movement, radicalise it, etc.

The cast of theoretical syndicalism is different. Here we are dealing with a subaltern group, which is prevented by this theory from ever becoming dominant, or from developing beyond the economic-corporate stage and rising to the phase of ethical-political hegemony in civil society, and of domination in the State. In the case of *laissez-faire* liberalism, one is dealing with a fraction of the ruling class which wishes to modify not the structure of the State, but merely government policy ; which wishes to reform the laws controlling commerce, but only indirectly those controlling industry (since it is undeniable that protection, especially in countries with a poor and restricted market, limits freedom of industrial enterprise and favours unhealthily the creation of monopolies). What is at stake is a rotation in governmental office of the ruling-class parties, not the foundation and organisation of a new political society, and even less of a new type of civil society. In the case of the theoretical syndicalist movement the problem is more complex. It is undeniable that in it, the independence and autonomy of the subaltern group which it claims to represent are in fact sacrificed to the intellectual hegemony of the ruling class, since precisely theoretical syndicalism is merely an aspect of *laissez-faire* liberalism—justified with a few mutilated (and therefore banalised) theses from the philosophy of praxis. Why and how does this "sacrifice" come about? The transformation of the subordinate group into a dominant one is excluded, either because the problem is not even considered (Fabianism, De Man, an important part of the Labour Party), or because it is posed in an inappropriate and ineffective form (social-democratic tendencies in general), or because of a belief in the possibility of leaping from class society directly into a society of perfect equality with a syndical economy.

The attitude of economism towards expressions of political and intellectual will, action or initiative is to say the least strange—as if these did not emanate organically from economic necessity, and indeed were not the only effective expression of the economy. Thus it is incongruous that the concrete posing of the problem of hegemony should be interpreted as a fact subordinating the group seeking hegemony. Undoubtedly the fact of hegemony presupposes that account be taken of the interests and the tendencies of the groups over which hegemony is to be exercised, and that a certain compromise equilibrium should be formed—in other words, that the leading group should make sacrifices of an economic-corporate kind. But there is also no doubt that such sacrifices and such a compromise cannot touch, the essential ; for though hegemony is ethical-political, it must also be economic, must necessarily be based on the decisive function exercised by the, leading group in the decisive nucleus of economic activity.

54

The Reification of Consciousness*

Georg Lukács

The essence of commodity-structure has often been pointed out. Its basis is that a relation between people takes on the character of a thing and thus acquires a 'phantom objectivity', an autonomy that seems so strictly rational and all-embracing as to conceal every trace of its fundamental nature: the relation between people. It is beyond the scope of this essay to discuss the central importance of this problem for economics itself. Nor shall we consider its implications for the economic doctrines of the vulgar Marxists which follow from their abandonment of this starting-point.

Our intention here is to *base* ourselves on Marx's economic analyses and to proceed from there to a discussion of the problems growing out of the fetish character of commodities, both as an objective form and also as a subjective stance corresponding to it. Only by understanding this can we obtain a clear insight into the ideological problems of capitalism and its downfall.

Before tackling the problem itself we must be quite clear in our minds that commodity fetishism is a *specific* problem of our age, the age of modern capitalism. Commodity exchange and the corresponding subjective and objective commodity relations existed, as we know, when society was still very primitive. What is at issue *here*, however, is the question: how far is commodity exchange together with its structural consequences able to influence the *total* outer and inner life of society? Thus the extent to which such exchange is the dominant form of metabolic change in a society cannot simply be treated in quantitative terms—as would harmonise with the modern modes of thought already eroded by the reifying effects of the dominant commodity form. The distinction between a society where this form is dominant, permeating every expression of life, and a society where it only makes an episodic appearance is essentially one of quality. For depending on which is the case, all the subjective phenomena in the societies concerned are objectified in qualitatively different ways.

Marx lays great stress on the essentially episodic appearance of the commodity form in primitive societies.

We note that the observation about the disintegrating effect of a commodity exchange directed in upon itself clearly shows the qualitative change engendered by the dominance of commodities.

*Excerpt from *History and Class Consciousness: Studies in Marxist Dialectics* by Georg Lukacs, Translated by Rodney Livingstone.

However, even when commodities have this impact on the internal structure of a society, this does not suffice to make them constitutive of that society. To achieve that it would be necessary—as we emphasized above—for the commodity structure to penetrate society in all its aspects and to remould if in its own image. It is not enough merely to establish an external link with independent processes concerned with the production of exchange values. The qualitative difference between the commodity as one form among many regulating the metabolism of human society and the commodity as the universal structuring principle has effects over and above the fact that the commodity relation as an isolated phenomenon exerts a negative influence at best on the structure and organisation of society. The distinction also has repercussions upon the nature and validity of the category itself Where the commodity is universal it manifests itself differently from the commodity as a particular, isolated, non-dominant phenomenon.

And *this* development of the commodity to the point where it becomes the dominant form in society did not take place until the advent of modern capitalism. Hence if is not to be wondered at that the personal nature of economic relations was still understood clearly on occasion at the start of capitalist development, but that as the process advanced and forms became more complex and less direct, it became increasingly difficult and rare to find anyone penetrating the veil of reification.

The commodity can only be understood in its undistorted essence when it becomes the universal category of society as a whole. Only in this context does the reification produced by commodity relations assume decisive importance both for the objective evolution of society and for the stance adopted by men towards it. Only then does the commodity become crucial for the subjugation of men's consciousness to the forms in which this reification finds expression and for their attempts to comprehend the process or to rebel against its disastrous effects and liberate themselves from servitude to the 'second nature' so created.

Marx describes the basic phenomenon of reification as follows: "A commodity is therefore a mysterious thing, simply because in it the social character of men's labour appears to them as an objective character stamped upon the product of that labour; because the relation of the producers to the sum total of their own labour is presented to them as a social relation, existing not between themselves, but between the products of their labour. This is the reason why the products of labour become commodities, social things whose qualities are at the same time perceptible and imperceptible by the senses. . . . It is only a definite social relation between men that assumes, in their eyes, the fantastic form of a relation between things."

What is of central importance here is that because of this situation a man's own activity, his own labour becomes something objective and independent of him, something that controls him by virtue of an autonomy alien to man. There is both an objective and a subjective side to this phenomenon. *Objectively* a world of objects and relations between things springs into being (the world of commodities and their movements on the market). The laws governing these objects are indeed gradually discovered by man, but even so they confront him as invisible forces that generate their own power. The individual can use his knowledge of these laws to his own advantage, but he is not able to modify the process by his own activity. *Subjectively*—where the market economy has been fully developed—a man's activity becomes estranged from himself, it turns into a commodity which, subject to the non-human objectivity of the natural laws of society, must go its own way independently of man just like any consumer article. "What is characteristic of the capitalist age," says Marx, "is that in the eyes of the labourer himself labour-power assumes the form of a commodity belonging to him. On the other hand it is only at this moment that the commodity form ot the products of labour becomes general."

It must suffice to point out that modern capitalism does not content itself with transforming the relations of production in accordance with its own needs. It also integrates into its own system those forms of primitive capitalism that led an isolated existence in pre-capitalist times, divorced from production; it converts them into members of the henceforth unified process of radical capitalism. (*Cf.* merchant capital, the role of money as a hoard or as finance capital, etc)

These forms of capital are objectively subordinated, it is true, to the real life-process of capitalism, the extraction of surplus value in the course of production. They are, therefore, only to be explained in terms of the nature of industrial capitalism itself. But in the minds of people in bourgeois society they constitute the pure, authentic, unadulterated forms of capital. In them the relations between men that lie hidden in the immediate commodity relation, as well as the relations between men and the objects that should really gratify their needs, have faded to the point where they can be neither recognised nor even perceived.

For that very reason the reified mind has come to regard them as the true representatives of his societal existence. The commodity character of the commodity, the abstract, quantitative mode of calculability shows itself here in its purest form: the reified mind necessarily sees it as the form in which its own authentic immediacy becomes manifest and—as reified consciousness—does not even attempt to transcend it. On the contrary, it is concerned to make it permanent by 'scientifically deepening' the laws at work. Just as the capitalist system continuously produces and reproduces itself economically on higher and higher levels, the structure of reification progressively sinks more deeply, more fatefully and more definitively into the consciousness of man. Marx often describes this potentiation of reification in incisive fashion.

The distinction between a worker faced with a particular machine, the entrepreneur faced with a given type of mechanical development, the technologist faced with the state of science and the profitability of its application to technology, is purely quantitative; it does not directly entail *any qualitative difference in the structure of consciousness.*

Only in this context can the problem of modern bureaucracy be properly understood. Bureaucracy implies the adjustment of one's way of life, mode of work and hence of consciousness, to the general socio-economic premises of the capitalist economy, similar to that which we have observed in the case of the worker in particular business concerns. The formal standardisation of justice, the state, the civil service, etc., signifies objectively and factually a comparable reduction of all social functions to their elements, a comparable search for the rational formal laws of these carefully segregated partial systems. Subjectively, the divorce between work and the individual capacities and needs of the worker produces comparable effects upon consciousness. This results in an inhuman, standardised division of labour analogous to that which we have found in industry on the technological and mechanical plane.

It is not only a question of the completely mechanical, 'mind-less' work of the lower echelons of the bureaucracy which bears such an extraordinarily close resemblance to operating a machine and which indeed often surpasses it in sterility and uniformity. It is also a question, on the one hand, of the way in which objectively all issues are subjected to an increasingly *formal* and standardised treatment and in which there is an ever-increasing remoteness from the qualitative and material essence of the 'things' to which bureaucratic activity pertains.

The split between the worker's labour-power and his personality, its metamorphosis into a thing, an object that he sells on the market is repeated here too. But with the difference that not every mental faculty is suppressed by mechanisation; only one faculty (or complex of faculties) is detached from the whole personality and placed in opposition to it, becoming a thing, a commodity. But the basic phenomenon remains the same even though both the means by which society instills such abilities and their material and 'moral' exchange value are fundamentally different from labour-power (not forgetting of course, the many connecting links and nuances).

The specific type of bureaucratic 'conscientiousness' and impartiality, the individual bureaucrat's inevitable total subjection to a system of relations between the things to which he is exposed, the idea that it is precisely his 'honour' and his 'sense of responsibility' that exact this total submission, all this points to the fact that the division of labour which in the case of Taylorism invaded the psyche, here invades the realm of ethics. Far from weakening the reified structure of consciousness, this actually strengthens it. For as long as the fate of the worker still appears to be an individual fate (as in the case of the slave in antiquity), the life of the ruling classes is still free to assume quite different forms. Not until the rise of capitalism was a unified economic structure, and hence a—formally—unified structure of consciousness that embraced the whole society, brought into being. This unity expressed itself in the fact that the problems of consciousness arising from wage-labour were repeated in the ruling class in a refined and spiritualised, but, for that very reason, more intensified form. The specialised 'virtuoso', the vendor of his objectified and reified faculties does not just become the [passive] observer of society; he also lapses into a contemplative attitude *vis-à-vis* the workings of his own objectified and reified faculties.

The bourgeoisie always perceives the subject and object of the historical process and of social reality in a double form: in terms of his consciousness the single individual is a perceiving subject confronting the over-whelming objective necessities imposed by society of which only minute fragments can be comprehended. But in reality it is precisely the conscious activity of the individual that is to be found on the object-side of the process, while the subject (the class) cannot be awakened into consciousness and this activity must always remain beyond the consciousness of the—apparent—subject, the individual.

Thus we find the subject and object of the social process coexisting in a state of dialectical interaction. But as they always appear to exist in a rigidly twofold form, each external to the other, the dialectics remain unconscious and the objects retain their twofold and hence rigid character. This rigidity can only be broken by catastrophe and it then makes way for an equally rigid structure.

For the proletariat social reality does not exist in this double form. It appears in the first instance as the pure *object* of societal events. In every aspect of daily life in which the individual worker imagines himself to be the subject of his own life he finds this to be an illusion that is destroyed by the immediacy of his existence. This forces upon him the knowledge that the most elementary gratification of his needs, "his own individual consumption, whether it proceed within the workshop or outside it, whether it be part of the process of reproduction or not, forms therefore an aspect of the production and the reproduction of capital; just as cleaning machinery does, whether it be done while the machinery is working or while it is standing idle". The quantification of objects, their subordination to abstract mental categories makes its appearance in the life of the worker immediately as a process of abstraction of which he is the victim, and which cuts him off from his labour-power, forcing him to sell it on the market as a commodity, belonging to him. And by selling this, his only commodity, he integrates it (and himself: for his commodity is inseparable from his physical existence) into a specialised process that has been rationalised and mechanised, a process that he discovers already existing, complete and able to function without him and in which he is no more than a cipher reduced to an abstract quantity, a mechanised and rationalised tool.

Thus for the worker the reified character of the immediate manifestations of capitalist society receives the most extreme definition possible. It is true: for the capitalist also there is the same doubling of personality, the same splitting up of man into an element of the movement of commodities and an (objective and impotent) observer of that movement. But for his consciousness it necessarily appears as an activity (albeit this activity is objectively an illusion), in which effects emanate from himself. This illusion blinds him to the true state of affairs, whereas the worker, who is denied the scope for such illusory activity, perceives the split in his being preserved in the brutal form of what is in its whole tendency a slavery without limits. He is therefore forced into becoming the object of the process by which he is turned into a commodity and reduced to a mere quantity.

Above all the worker can only become conscious of his existence in society when he becomes aware of himself as a commodity. As we have seen, his immediate existence integrates him as a pure, naked object into the production process. Once this immediacy turns out to be the consequence of a multiplicity of mediations, once it becomes evident how much it presupposes, then the fetishistic forms of the commodity system begin to dissolve: in the commodity the worker recognises himself and his own relations with capital. Inasmuch as he is incapable in practice of raising himself above the role of object his consciousness is the *self-consciousness of the commodity;* or in other words it is the self-knowledge, the self-revelation of the capitalist society founded upon the production and exchange of commodities.

When the worker knows himself as a commodity his knowledge is practical. *That is to say, this knowledge brings about an objective structural change in the object of knowledge.* In this consciousness and through it the special objective character of labour as a commodity, its 'use-value' (i.e. its ability to yield surplus produce) which like every use-value is submerged without a trace in the quantitative exchange categories of capitalism, now awakens and becomes *social reality.* The special nature of labour as a commodity which in the absence of this consciousness acts as an unacknowledged driving wheel in the economic process now objectifies itself by means of this consciousness. The specific nature of this kind of commodity had consisted in the fact that beneath the cloak of the thing lay a relation between men, that beneath the quantifying crust there was a qualitative, living core. Now that this core is revealed it becomes possible to recognise the fetish character of *every commodity* based on the commodity character of labour power: in every case we find its core, the relation between men, entering into the evolution of society.

For the proletariat, however, this ability to go beyond the immediate in search of the 'remoter' factors means the *transformation of the objective nature of the objects of action.* At first sight it appears as if the more immediate objects are no less subject to this transformation than the remote ones. It soon becomes apparent, however, that in their case the transformation is even more visible and striking. For the change lies on the one hand in the practical interaction of the awakening consciousness and the objects from which it is born and of which it is the consciousness. And on the other hand, the change means that the objects that are viewed here as aspects of the development of society, i.e. of the dialectical totality become fluid: they become parts of a process. And as the innermost kernel of this movement is praxis, its point of departure is of necessity that of action; it holds the immediate objects of action firmly and decisively in its grip so as to bring about their total, structural transformation and thus the movement of the whole gets under way.

The category of totality begins to have an effect long before the whole multiplicity of objects can be illuminated by it. It operates by ensuring that actions which seem to confine themselves to particular objects, in both content and consciousness, yet preserve an aspiration towards the totality, that is to say: action is directed objectively towards a transformation of totality.

Reification is, then, the necessary, immediate reality of every person living in capitalist society. It can be overcome only by *constant and constantly renewed efforts to disrupt the reified structure of existence by concretely relating to the concretely manifested contradictions of the total development, by becoming conscious of the immanent meanings of these contradictions for the total development.* But it must be emphasided that (1) the structure can be disrupted only if the immanent contradictions of the process are made conscious. Only when the consciousness of the proletariat is able to point out the road along which the dialectics of history is objectively impelled, but which it cannot travel unaided, will the consciousness of the proletariat awaken to a consciousness of the process, and only then will the proletariat become the identical subject-object of history whose praxis will change reality.

(2) Inseparable from this is the fact that the relation to totality does not need to become explicit, the plenitude of the totality does not need to be consciously integrated into the motives and objects of action. What is crucial is that there should be an aspiration towards totality, that action should serve the purpose, described above, in the totality of the process.

Hence (3) when judging whether an action is right or wrong it is essential to relate it to its function in the total process. Proletarian thought is practical thought and as such is strongly pragmatic.

The eminently practical nature of this consciousness is to be seen (4) in that an adequate, correct consciousness means a change in its own objects, and in the first instance, in itself.

55

Critical Theory*

Max Horkheimer

There is a human activity which has society itself for its object. The aim of this activity is not simply to eliminate one or other abuse, for it regards such abuses as necessarily connected with the way in which the social structure is organized. Although it itself emerges from the social structure, its purpose is not, either in its conscious intention or in its objective significance, the better functioning of any element in the structure. On the contrary, it is suspicious of the very categories of better, useful, appropriate, productive, and valuable, as these are understood in the present order, and refuses to take them as nonscientific presuppositions about which one can do nothing. The individual as a rule must simply accept the basic conditions of his existence as given and strive to fulfill them; he finds his satisfaction and praise in accomplishing as well as he can the tasks connected with his place in society and in courageously doing his duty despite all the sharp criticism he may choose to exercise in particular matters. But the critical attitude of which we are speaking is wholly distrustful of the rules of conduct with which society as presently constituted provides each of its members. The separation between individual and society in virtue of which the individual accepts as natural the limits prescribed for his activity is relativized in critical theory. The latter considers the overall framework which is conditioned by the blind interaction of individual activities (that is, the existent division of labor and the class distinctions) to be a function which originates in human action and therefore is a possible object of planful decision and rational determination of goals.

The two-sided character of the social totality in its present form becomes, for men who adopt the critical attitude, a conscious opposition. In recognizing the present form of economy and the whole culture which it generates to be the product of human work as well as the organization which mankind was capable of and has provided for itself in the present era, these men identify themselves with this totality and conceive it as will and reason. It is their own world. At the same time, however, they experience the fact that society is comparable to nonhuman natural processes, to pure mechanisms, because cultural forms which are supported by war and oppression are not the creations of a unified, self-conscious will. That world is not their own but the world of capital.

Previous history thus cannot really be understood; only the individuals and specific groups in it are intelligible, and even these not totally,

*Excerpts from *Critical Theory: Selected Essays* by Max Horkheimer, translated by Matthew J. O. Connell and others.

since their internal dependence on an inhuman society means that even in their conscious action such individuals and groups are still in good measure mechanical functions. The identification, then, of men of critical mind with their society is marked by tension, and the tension characterizes all the concepts of the critical way of thinking. Thus, such thinkers interpret the economic categories of work, value, and productivity exactly as they are interpreted in the existing order, and they regard any other interpretation as pure idealism. But at the same time they consider it rank dishonesty simply to accept the interpretation; the critical acceptance of the categories which rule social life contains simultaneously their condemnation. This dialectical character of the self-interpretation of contemporary man is what, in the last analysis, also causes the obscurity of the Kantian critique of reason. Reason cannot become transparent to itself as long as men act as members of an organism which lacks reason. Organism as a naturally developing and declining unity cannot be a sort of model for society, but only a form of deadened existence from which society must emancipate itself. An attitude which aims at such an emancipation and at an alteration of society as a whole might well be of service in theoretical work carried on within reality as presently ordered.

Critical thinking is the function neither of the isolated individual nor of a sum-total of individuals. Its subject is rather a definite individual in his real relation to other individuals and groups, in his conflict with a particular class, and, finally, in the resultant web of relationships with the social totality and with nature. The subject is no mathematical point like the ego of bourgeois philosophy; his activity is the construction of the social present. Furthermore, the thinking subject is not the place where knowledge and object coincide, nor consequently the starting-point for attaining absolute knowledge. Such an illusion about the thinking subject, under which idealism has lived since Descartes, is ideology in the strict sense, for in it the limited freedom of the bourgeois individual puts on the illusory form of perfect freedom and autonomy. As a matter of fact, however, in a society which is untransparent and without self-awareness the ego, whether active simply as thinker or active in other ways as well, is unsure of itself too. In reflection on man, subject and object are sundered; their identity lies in the future, not in the present. The method leading to such an identification may be called explanation in Cartesian language, but in genuinely critical thought explanation signifies not only a logical process but a concrete historical one as well. In the course of it both the social structure as a whole and the relation of the theoretician to society are altered, that is both the subject and the role of thought are changed. The acceptance of an essential unchangeableness between subject, theory, and object thus distinguishes the Cartesian conception from every kind of dialectical logic.

Above all, however, critical theory has no material accomplishments to show for itself. The change which it seeks to bring about is not effected gradually, so that success even if slow might be steady. The growth in numbers of more or less clear-minded disciples, the influence of some among them on governments, the power position of parties which have a positive attitude towards this theory or at least do not outlaw it—all these are among the vicissitudes encountered in the struggle for a higher stage of man's life in community and are not found at the beginnings of the struggle. Such successes as these may even prove, later on, to have been only apparent victories and really blunders. Again: fertilization in agriculture, for example, or the application of a medical therapy may be far removed from ideal reality and yet accomplish something. Perhaps the theories underlying such technology may have to be refined, revised, or abolished in connection with specialized activity and with discoveries in other areas. Through such techniques, nonetheless, a certain amount of labor is saved in achieving results, and many an illness is healed or alleviated. But the first consequence of the theory which urges a transformation of society as a whole is only an intensification of the struggle with which the theory is connected.

Furthermore, although material improvements, originating in the increased powers of resistance of certain groups, are indirectly due to the critical theory, the groups in question are not sectors of society whose steady spread would finally bring the new society to pass. Such ideas mistake the fundamental difference between a fragmented society in which material and ideological power operates to maintain privileges and an association of free men in which each has the same possibility of self-development. Such an association is not an abstract Utopia, for the possibility in question can be shown to be real even at the present stage of productive forces. But how many tendencies will actually lead to this association, how many transitional phases have been reached, how desirable and intrinsically valuable individual preliminary stages may be, and what their historical importance is in relation to the idea—all this will be made clear only when the idea is brought to realization.

One thing which this way of thinking has in common with fantasy is that an image of the future which springs indeed from a deep understanding of the present determines men's thoughts and actions even in periods when the course of events seems to be leading far away from such a future and seems to justify every reaction except belief in fulfillment. It is not the arbitrariness and supposed independence of fantasy that is the common bond here, but its obstinacy. Within the most advanced group it is the theoretician who must have this obstinacy. The theoretician of the ruling class, perhaps after difficult beginnings, may reach a relatively assured position, but, on the other hand, the theoretician is also at times an enemy and criminal, at times a solitary Utopian; even after his death the question of what he really was is not decided. The historical significance of his work is not self-evident; it rather depends on men speaking and acting in such a way as to justify it. It is not a finished and fixed historical creation.

The capacity for such acts of thought as are required in everyday action, social or scientific, has been developed in men by a realistic training over many centuries. Failure here leads to affliction, failure, and punishment. The intellectual modality to which we refer consists essentially in this, that the conditions for bringing about an effect which has always appeared in the same circumstances before are known and in the appropriate context are supplied. There is an object-lesson kind of instruction through good and bad experiences and through organized experiment. The issue here is direct individual self-preservation, and in bourgeois society men have the opportunity of developing a sense of this. Knowledge in this traditional sense, including every type of experience, is preserved in critical theory and practice. But in regard to the essential kind of change at which the critical theory aims, there can be no corresponding concrete perception of it until it actually comes about. If the proof of the pudding is in the eating, the eating here is still in the future. Comparison with similar historical events can be drawn only in a limited degree.

Constructive thinking, then, plays a more important role than empirical verification in this theory as a whole, in comparison with what goes on in the activity of common sense. This is one of the reasons why men who in particular scientific areas or in other professional activity are able to do extremely competent work, can show themselves quite limited and incompetent, despite good will, when it comes to questions concerning society as a whole. In all past periods when social change was on the agenda, people who thought "too much" were regarded as dangerous. This brings us to the problem of the general relation of the intelligentsia to society.

The theoretician whose business it is to hasten developments which will lead to a society without injustice can find himself in opposition to views prevailing even among the proletariat, as we said above. If such a conflict were not possible, there would be no need of a theory; those who need it would come upon it without help. The conflict does not necessarily have anything to do with the class to which the theoretician belongs; nor does it depend on the kind of income he has. Engels was a businessman. In professional sociology, which derives its concept of class not from a critique of the economy but from its own observations, the theoretician's social position is determined neither by the source of his income nor by the concrete content of his theory but by the formal element of education. The possibility of a wider vision, not the kind possessed by industrial magnates who know the world market and direct whole states from behind the scenes, but the kind possessed by university professors, middle-level civil servants, doctors, lawyers, and so forth, is what constitutes the "intelligentsia," that is, a special social or even suprasocial stratum.

It is the task of the critical theoretician to reduce the tension between his own insight and oppressed humanity in whose service he thinks. But in the sociological concept of which we speak detachment from all classes is an essential mark of the intelligentsia, a sort of sign of superiority of which it is proud. Such a neutral category corresponds to the abstract self-awareness typical of the savant. To the bourgeois consumer under liberalism knowledge meant knowledge that was useful in some circumstances or other, no matter what kind of knowledge might be in question; the sociology we speak of approaches knowledge in the same way at the theoretical level. Marx and Mises, Lenin and Liefmann, Jaurès and Jevons all come under the same sociological heading, unless the politicians are left out of the list and put down as potential students of the political scientists, sociologists, and philosophers who are the real men of knowledge. From them the politician is to learn to use "such and such a means" when he takes "such and such a stand"; he must learn whether the practical position he adopts can be implemented with logical consistency. A division of labor is established between men who in social conflicts affect the course of history and the social theoreticians who assign them their standpoint.

Critical theory is in contradiction to the formalistic concept of mind which underlies such an idea of the intelligentsia. According to this concept there is only one truth, and the positive attributes of honesty, internal consistency, reasonableness, and striving for peace, freedom, and happiness may not be attributed in the same sense to any other theory and practice. There is likewise no theory of society, even that of the sociologists concerned with general laws, that does not contain political motivations, and the truth of these must be decided not in supposedly neutral reflection but in personal thought and action, in concrete historical activity. Now, it is disconcerting that the intellectual should represent himself in this way, as though a difficult labor of thought, which he alone could accomplish, were the prime requirement if men were accurately to choose between revolutionary, liberal, and fascist ends and means. The situation has not been like that for many decades. The avant-garde in the political struggle need prudence, but not academic instruction on their so-called standpoint. Especially at a time when the forces of freedom in Europe are themselves disoriented and seeking to regroup themselves anew, when everything depends on nuances of position within their own movement, when indifference to substantive content, created by defeat, despair, and corrupt bureaucracy, threatens to overwhelm all the spontaneity, experience, and knowledge of the masses despite the heroic efforts of a few, a conception of the intelligentsia which claims to transcend party lines and is therefore abstract represents a view of problems that only hides the decisive questions.

The critical theory of society also begins with abstract determinations; in dealing with the present era it begins with the characterization of an economy based on exchange. The concepts Marx uses, such as commodity, value, and money, can function as genera when, for example, concrete social relations are judged to be relations of exchange and when there is question of the commodity character of goods. But the theory is not satisfied to relate concepts of reality by way of hypotheses. The theory begins with an outline of the mechanism by which bourgeois society, after dismantling feudal regulations, the guild system, and vassalage, did not immediately fall apart under the pressure of its own anarchic principle but managed to survive. The regulatory effects of exchange are brought out on which bourgeois economy is founded. The conception of the interaction of society and nature, which is already exercising its influence here, as well as the idea of a unified period of society, of its self-preservation, and so on, spring from a radical analysis, guided by concern for the future, of the historical process. The relation of the primary conceptual interconnections to the world of facts is not essentially a relation of classes to instances. It is because of its inner dynamism that the exchange relationship, which the theory outlines, dominates social reality, as, for example, the assimilation of food largely dominates the organic life of plant and brute beast.

In critical theory, as in traditional theory, more specific elements must be introduced in order to move from fundamental structure to concrete reality. But such an intercalation of more detailed factors—for example the existence of large money reserves, the diffusion of these in sectors of society that are still precapitalist, foreign trade—is not accomplished by simple deduction as in theory that has been simplified for specialized use. Instead, every step rests on knowledge of man and nature which is stored up in the sciences and in historical experience. This is obvious, of course, for the theory of industrial technology. But in other areas too a detailed knowledge of how men react is applied throughout the doctrinal developments to which we have been referring. For example, the statement that under certain conditions the lowest strata of society have the most children plays an important role in explaining how the bourgeois society built on exchange necessarily leads to capitalism with its army of industrial reserves and its crises. To give the psychological reasons behind the observed fact about the lower classes is left to traditional science.

The hostility to theory as such which prevails in contemporary public life is really directed against the transformative activity associated with critical thinking. Opposition starts as soon as theorists fail to limit themselves to verification and classification by means of categories which are as neutral as possible, that is, categories which are indispensable to inherited ways of life. Among the vast majority of the ruled there is the unconscious fear that theoretical thinking might show their painfully won adaptation to reality to be perverse and unnecessary. Those who profit from the status quo entertain a general suspicion of any intellectual independence. The tendency to conceive theory as the opposite of a positive outlook is so strong that even the inoffensive traditional type of theory suffers from it at times. Since the most advanced form of thought at present is the critical theory of society and every consistent intellectual movement that cares about man converges upon it by its own inner logic, theory in general falls into disrepute. Every other kind of scientific statement which does not offer a deposit of facts in the most familiar categories and, if possible, in the most neutral form, the mathematical, is already accused of being theoretical.

There are no general criteria for judging the critical theory as a whole, for it is always based on the recurrence of events and thus on a self-reproducing totality. Nor is there a social class by whose acceptance of the theory one could be guided. It is possible for the consciousness of every social stratum today to be limited and corrupted by ideology, however much, for its circumstances, it may be bent on truth. For all its insight into the individual steps in social change and for all the agreement of its elements with the most advanced traditional theories, the critical theory has no specific influence on its side, except concern for the abolition of social injustice. This negative formulation, if we wish to express it abstractly, is the materialist content of the idealist concept of reason.

56

The Culture Industry*

Theodor W. Adorno

The term culture industry was perhaps used for the first time in the book *Dialectic of Enlightenment*, which Horkheimer and I published in Amsterdam in 1947. In our drafts we spoke of "mass culture." We replaced that expression with "culture industry" in order to exclude from the outset the interpretation agreeable to its advocates: that it is a matter of something like a culture that arises spontaneously from the masses themselves, the contemporary form of popular art. From the latter the culture industry must be distinguished in the extreme. The culture industry fuses the old and familiar into a new quality. In all its branches, products which are tailored for consumption by masses, and which to a great extent determine the nature of that consumption, are manufactured more or less according to plan. The individual branches are similar in structure or at least fit into each other, ordering themselves into a system almost without a gap. This is made possible by contemporary technical capabilities as well as by economic and administrative concentration. The culture industry intentionally integrates its consumers from above. To the detriment of both it forces together the spheres of high and low art, separated for thousands of years. The seriousness of high art is destroyed in speculation about its efficacy; the seriousness of the lower perishes with the civilizational constraints imposed on the rebellious resistance inherent within it as long as social control was not yet total. Thus, although the culture industry undeniably speculates on the conscious and unconscious state of the millions towards which it is directed, the masses are not primary, but secondary, they are an object of calculation; an appendage of the machinery. The customer is not king, as the culture industry would like to have us believe, not its subject but its object. The very word mass-media, specially honed for the culture industry, already shifts the accent onto harmless terrain. Neither is it a question of primary concern for the masses, nor of the techniques of communication as such, but of the spirit which sufflates them, their master's voice. The culture industry misuses its concern for the masses in order to duplicate, reinforce and strengthen their mentality, which it presumes is given and unchangeable. How this mentality might be changed is excluded throughout. The masses are not the measure but the ideology of the culture industry, even though the culture industry itself could scarcely exist without adapting to the masses.

The cultural commodities of the industry are governed, as Brecht and Suhrkamp expressed it thirty years ago, by the principle of their realization as value, and not by their own specific content and harmonious formation. The entire

* "The Culture Industry Reconsidered" Theodore Adorno, *New German Critique*, 6, Fall 1975, pp. 12–19.

practice of the culture industry transfers the profit motive naked onto cultural forms. Ever since these cultural forms first began to earn a living for their creators as commodities in the marketplace they had already possessed something of this quality. But then they sought after profit only indirectly, over and above their autonomous essence. New on the part of the culture industry is the direct and undisguised primacy of a precisely and thoroughly calculated efficacy in its most typical products. The autonomy of works of art, which of course rarely ever predominated in an entirely pure form, and was always permeated by a constellation of effects, is tendentially eliminated by the culture industry, with or without the conscious will of those in control. The latter include both those who carry out directives as well as those who hold the power. In economic terms they are or were in search of new opportunities for the realization of capital in the most economically developed countries. The old opportunities became increasingly more precarious as a result of the same concentration process which alone makes the culture industry possible as an omnipresent phenomenon. Culture, in the true sense, did not simply accomodate itself to human beings; but it always simultaneously raised a protest against the petrified relations under which they lived, thereby honoring them. Insofar as culture becomes wholly assimilated to and integrated in those petrified relations, human beings are once more debased. Cultural entities typical of the culture industry are no longer *also* commodities, they are commodities through and through. This quantitative shift is so great that it calls forth entirely new phenomena. Ultimately, the culture industry no longer even needs to directly pursue everywhere the profit interests from which it originated. These interests have become objectified in its ideology and have even made themselves independent of the compulsion to sell the cultural commodities which must be swallowed anyway. The culture industry turns into public relations, the manufacturing of "good will" per se, without regard for particular firms or saleable objects. Brought to bear is a general uncritical consensus, advertisements produced for the world, so that each product of the culture industry becomes its own advertisement.

Nevertheless, those characteristics which originally stamped the transformation of literature into a commodity are maintained in this process. More than anything in the world, the culture industry has its ontology, a scaffolding of rigidly conservative basic categories which can be gleaned, for example, from the commercial English novels of the late 17th and early 18th centuries. What parades as progress in the culture industry, as the incessantly new which it offers up, remains the disguise for an eternal sameness; everywhere the changes mask a skeleton which has changed just as little as the profit motive itself since the time it first gained its predominance over culture.

Thus, the expression "industry" is not to be taken literally. It refers to the standardization of the thing itself—such as that of the Western, familiar to every movie-goer—and to the rationalization of distribution techniques, but not strictly to the production process. Although in film, the central sector of the culture industry, the production process resembles technical modes of operation in the extensive division of labor, the employment of machines and the separation of the laborers from the means of production—expressed in the perennial conflict between artists active in the culture industry and those who control it—individual forms of production are nevertheless maintained. Each product affects an individual air; individuality itself serves to reinforce ideology, insofar as the illusion is conjured up that the completely reified and mediated is a sanctuary from immediacy and life. Now, as ever, the culture industry exists in the "service" of third persons, maintaining its affinity to the declining circulation process of capital, to the commerce from which it came into being. Its ideology above all makes use of the star system, borrowed from individualistic art and its commercial exploitation. The more dehumanized its methods of operation and content, the more diligently and successfully the culture industry propagates supposedly great personalities and operates with heart-throbs. It is industrial more in a sociological sense, in the incorporation of industrial forms of organization even where nothing is manufactured—as in the rationalization of office work—rather than in the sense of anything really and actually produced by technological rationality. Accordingly, the misinvestments of the culture industry are considerable, throwing those branches rendered obsolete by new techniques into crises, which seldom lead to changes for the better.

The concept of technique in the culture industry is only in name identical with technique in works of art. In the latter, technique is concerned with the internal organization of the object itself, with its inner logic. In contrast, the technique of the culture industry is, from the beginning, one of distribution and mechanical reproduction, and therefore always remains external to its object. The culture industry finds ideological support precisely insofar as it carefully shields itself from the full potential of the techniques contained in its products. It lives parasitically from the extra-artistic technique of the material production of goods, without regard for the obligation to the internal artistic whole implied by its functionality (*Sachlichkeit*), but also without concern for the laws of form demanded by aesthetic autonomy. The result for the physiognomy of the culture industry is essentially a mixture of streamlining, photographic hardness and precision on the one hand, and individualistic residues, sentimentality and an already rationally disposed and adapted romanticism on the other. Adopting Benjamin's designation of the traditional work of art by the concept of aura, the presence of that which is not present, the culture industry is defined by the fact that it does not strictly counterpose another principle to that of aura, but rather by the fact that it conserves the decaying aura as a foggy mist. By this means the culture industry betrays its own ideological abuses.

It has recently become customary among cultural officials as well as sociologists to warn against underestimating the culture industry while pointing to its great importance for the development of the consciousness of its consumers. It is to be taken seriously, without cultured snobbism. In actuality the culture industry is important as a moment of the spirit which dominates today. Whoever ignores its influence out of skepticism for what it stuffs into people would be naive. Yet there is a deceptive glitter about the admonition to take it seriously. Because of its social role, disturbing questions about its quality, about truth or untruth, and about the aesthetic niveau of the culture industry's emissions are repressed, or at least excluded from the so-called sociology of communications. The critic is accused of taking refuge in arrogant esoterica. It would be advisable first to indicate the double meaning of importance that slowly worms its way in unnoticed. Even if it touches the lives of innumerable people, the function of something is no guarantee of its particular quality. The blending of aesthetics with its residual communicative aspects leads art, as a social phenomenon, not to its rightful position in opposition to alleged artistic snobbism, but rather in a variety of ways to the defense of its baneful social consequences. The importance of the culture industry in the spiritual constitution of the masses is no dispensation for reflection on its objective legitimation, its essential being, least of all by a science which thinks itself pragmatic. On the contrary: such reflection becomes necessary precisely for this reason. To take the culture industry as seriously as its unquestioned role demands, means to take it seriously critically, and not to cower in the face of its monopolistic character.

Among those intellectuals anxious to reconcile themselves with the phenomenon and eager to find a common formula to express both their reservations against it and their respect for its power, a tone of ironic toleration prevails unless they have already created a new mythos of the 20th century from the imposed regression. After all, those intellectuals maintain, everyone knows what pocket novels, films off the rack, family television shows rolled out into serials and hit parades, advice to the lovelorn and horoscope columns are all about. All of this, however, is harmless and, according to them, even democratic since it responds to a demand, albeit a stimulated one. It also bestows all kinds of blessings, they point out, for example, through the dissemination of information, advice and stress reducing patterns of behavior. Of course, as every sociological study measuring something as elementary as how politically informed the public is has proven, the information is meager or indifferent. Moreover, the advice to be gained from manifestations of the culture industry is vacuous, banal or worse, and the behavior patterns are shamelessly conformist.

The two-faced irony in the relationship of servile intellectuals to the culture industry is not restricted to them alone. It may also be supposed that the consciousness of the consumers themselves is split between the prescribed fun which is supplied to them by the culture industry and a not particularly well-hidden doubt about its blessings. The phrase, the world wants to be deceived, has become truer than had ever been intended. People are not only, as the saying goes, falling for the swindle; if it guarantees them even the most fleeting gratification they desire a deception which is nonetheless transparent to them. They force their eyes shut and voice approval, in a kind of self-loathing, for what is meted out to them, knowing fully the purpose for which it is manufactured. Without admitting it they sense that their lives would be completely intolerable as soon as they no longer clung to satisfactions which are none at all.

The most ambitious defense of the culture industry today celebrates its spirit, which might safely be called ideology, as an ordering factor. In a supposedly chaotic world it provides human beings with something like standards for orientation, and that alone seems worthy of approval. However, what its defenders imagine is preserved by the culture industry is in fact all the more thoroughly destroyed by it. The color film demolishes the genial old tavern to a greater extent than bombs ever could: the film exterminates its *imago*. No homeland can survive being processed by the films which celebrate it, and which thereby turn the unique character on which it thrives into an interchangeable sameness.

That which legitimately could be called culture attempted, as an expression of suffering and contradiction, to maintain a grasp on the idea of the good life. Culture cannot represent either that which merely exists or the conventional and no longer binding categories of order which the culture industry drapes over the idea of the good life as if existing reality were the good life, and as if those categories were its true measure. If the response of the culture industry's representatives is that it does not deliver art at all, this is itself the ideology with which they evade responsibility for that from which the business lives. No misdeed is ever righted by explaining it as such.

The appeal to order alone, without concrete specificity, is futile; the appeal to the dissemination of norms, without these ever proving themselves in reality or before consciousness, is equally futile. The idea of an objectively binding order, huckstered to people because it is so lacking for them, has no claims if it does not prove itself internally and in confrontation with human beings. But this is precisely what no product of the culture industry would engage in. The concepts of order which it hammers into human beings are always those of the status quo. They remain unquestioned, unanalyzed and undialectically presupposed, even if they no longer have any substance for those who accept them. In contrast to the Kantian, the categorical imperative of the culture industry no longer has anything in common with freedom. It proclaims: you shall conform, without instruction as to what; conform to that which exists anyway, and to that which everyone thinks anyway as a reflex of its power and omnipresence. The power of the culture industry's ideology is such that conformity has replaced consciousness. The order that springs from it is never confronted with what it claims to be or with the real interests of human beings. Order, however, is not good in itself. It would be so only as a good order. The fact that the culture industry is oblivious to this and extols order *in abstracto*, bears witness to the impotence and untruth of the messages it conveys. While it claims to lead the perplexed, it deludes them with false conflicts which they are to exchange for their own. It solves conflicts for them only in appearance, in a way that they can hardly be solved in their real lives. In the products of the culture industry human beings get into trouble only so that they can be rescued unharmed, usually by representatives of a benevolent collective; and then in empty harmony, they are reconciled with the general, whose demands they had experienced at the outset as irreconcilable with their interests. For this purpose the culture industry has developed formulas which even reach into such non-conceptual areas as light musical entertainment. Here too one gets into a 'jam', into rhythmic problems, which can be instantly disentangled by the triumph of the basic beat.

Even its defenders, however, would hardly contradict Plato openly who maintained that what is objectively and intrinsically untrue cannot also be subjectively good and true for human beings. The concoctions of the culture industry are neither guides for a blissful life, nor a new art of moral responsibility, but rather exhortations to toe the line, behind which stand the most powerful interests. The consensus which it propagates strengthens blind, opaque authority. If the culture industry is measured not by its own substance and logic, but by its efficacy, by its position in reality and its explicit pretentions; if the focus of serious concern is with the efficacy to which it always appeals, the potential of its effect becomes twice as weighty. This potential, however, lies in the promotion and exploitation of the ego-weakness to which the powerless members of contemporary society, with its concentration of power, are condemned. Their consciousness is further developed retrogressively. It is no coincidence that cynical American film producers are heard to say that their pictures must take into consideration the level of eleven year olds. In doing so they would very much like to make adults into eleven year olds.

It is true that thorough research has not, for the time being, produced an airtight case proving the regressive effects of particular products of the culture industry. No doubt an imaginatively designed experiment could achieve this more successfully than the powerful financial interests concerned would find comfortable. In any case, it can be assumed without hesitation that steady drops hollow the stone, especially since the system of the culture industry that surrounds the masses tolerates hardly any deviation and incessantly drills the same formulas of behavior. Only their deep unconscious mistrust, the last residue of the difference between art and empirical reality in the spiritual makeup of the masses explains why they have not, to a person, long since perceived and accepted the world as it is constructed for them by the culture industry. Even if its messages were as harmless as they are made out to be—on countless occasions they are obviously not harmless, like the movies which chime in with currently popular hate campaigns against intellectuals by portraying them with the usual stereotypes—the attitudes which the culture industry calls forth are anything but harmless. If an astrologer urges his readers to drive carefully on a particular day, that certainly hurts no one; they will, however, be harmed indeed by the stupefication which lies in the claim that advice which is valid every day and which is therefore idiotic, needs the approval of the stars.

Human dependence and servitude, the vanishing point of the culture industry, could scarcely be more faithfully described than by the American interviewee who was of the opinion that the dilemmas of the contemporary epoch would end if people would simply follow the lead of prominent personalities. Insofar as the culture industry arouses a feeling of well-being that the world is precisely in that order suggested by the culture industry, the substitute gratification which it prepares for human beings cheats them out of the same happiness which it deceitfully projects. The total effect of the culture industry is one of anti-enlightenment, in which, as Horkheimer and I have noted, enlightenment, that is the progressive technical domination of nature, becomes mass deception and is turned into a means for fettering consciousness. It impedes the development of autonomous, independent individuals who judge and decide consciously for themselves. These, however, would be the precondition for a democratic society which needs adults who have come of age in order to sustain itself and develop. If the masses have been unjustly reviled from above as masses, the culture industry is not among the least responsible for making them into masses and then despising them, while obstructing the emancipation for which human beings are as ripe as the productive forces of the epoch permit.

57

THE DESIGNER AS CULTURAL WORKER*

C. WRIGHT MILLS

The American designer is at once a central figure in what I am going to call the cultural apparatus and an important adjunct of a very peculiar kind of economy. His art is a business, but his business is art and curious things have been happening both to the art and to the business—and so to him. He is caught up in two great developments of 20th-century America: One is the shift in economic emphasis from production to distribution, and along with it, the joining of the struggle for existence with the panic for status. The other is the bringing of art, science and learning into subordinate relation with the dominant institutions of the capitalist economy and the nationalist state.

Designers work at the intersection of these trends; their problems are among the key problems of the overdeveloped society. It is their dual involvement in them that explains the big split among designers and their frequent guilt; the enriched muddle of ideals they variously profess and the insecurity they often feel about the practice of their craft; their often great disgust and their crippling frustration. They cannot consider well their position or formulate their credo without considering both cultural and economic trends, and the shaping of the total society in which these are occurring.

I want briefly (1) to define certain meanings and functions of the cultural apparatus, and (2) to indicate the economic context in which the designer now does his work. It may then be useful (3) to invite you to reconsider certain ideals for which the designer might stand in the kind of world in which Americans are coming to live.

OUR WORLDS ARE SECOND-HAND

Our images of this world and of ourselves are given to us by crowds of witnesses we have never met and never shall meet. Yet for each of us these images—provided by strangers and dead men—are the very basis of our life as a human being. None of us stands alone directly confronting a world of solid fact. No such world is available: the closest we come to it is when we are infants or when we become insane: then, in a terrifying scene of meaningless events and senseless confusion, we are often seized with the panic of near-total insecurity. But in our everyday life we experience not

*Reprinted by permission of the estate of C. Wright Mills.

solid and immediate facts but stereotypes of meaning. We are aware of much more than what we have ourselves experienced, and our experience itself is always indirect and always guided. The first rule for understanding the human condition is that men live in second-hand worlds.

The consciousness of men does not determine their existence; nor does their existence determine their consciousness. Between the human consciousness and material existence stand communications and designs, patterns and values which influence decisively such consciousness as they have.

The mass arts, the public arts, the design arts are major vehicles of this consciousness. Between these arts and the everyday life, between their symbols and the level of human sensibility, there is now continual and persistent interplay. So closely do they reflect one another that it is often impossible to distinguish the image from its source. Visions whispered long before the age of consent, images received in the relaxation of darkness, slogans reiterated in home and in classroom, determine the perspective in which we see and fail to see the worlds in which we live; meanings about which we have never thought explicitly determine our judgments of how well and of how badly we are living in these worlds. So decisive to experience itself are the results of these communications that often men do not really believe what they "see before their very eyes" until they have been "informed" about it by the official announcement, the radio, the camera, the hand-out. Communications not only limit experience; often they expropriate the chances to have experience that can rightly be called "our own." For our standards of credibility, and of reality itself, as well as our judgments and discernments, are determined much less by any pristine experience we may have than by our exposure to the output of the cultural apparatus.

For most of what we call solid fact, sound interpretation, suitable presentation, we are increasingly dependent upon the observation posts, the interpretation centers, the presentation depots of the cultural apparatus. In this apparatus, standing between men and events, the meanings and images, the values and slogans that define all the worlds men know are organized and compared, maintained and revised, lost and found, celebrated and debunked.

By the cultural apparatus I mean all those organizations and milieux in which artistic, intellectual and scientific work goes on. I also mean all the means by which such work is made available to small circles, wider publics, and to great masses.

The most embracive and the most specialized domain of modern society, the cultural apparatus of art, science and learning fulfills the most functions: it conquers nature and remakes the environment; it defines the changing nature of man, and grasps the drift of world affairs; it revivifies old aspirations and shapes new ones. It creates models of character and styles of feeling, nuances of mood and vocabularies of motive. It serves decision-makers, revealing and obscuring the consequences of their decisions. It turns power into authority and debunks authority as mere coercion. It modifies the work men do and provides the tools with which they do it; it fills up their leisure, with nonsense and with pleasure. It changes the nature of war; it amuses and persuades and manipulates; it orders and forbids; it frightens and reassures; it makes men weep and it makes men laugh, go numb all over, then become altogether alive. It prolongs the life-span and provides the violent means to end it suddenly. It predicts what is going to happen and it explains what has occurred; it helps to shape and to pace an epoch, and without it there would be no consciousness of any epoch.

The world men are going to believe they understand is their often fraudulent packaging. He lays out the interiors and decorates the exteriors of corporate businesses as monuments to advertising. And then, along with his colleagues, he takes the history of commercial fraud one step further. With him, advertising is not one specialized activity, however central; with his capitalist advent, the arts and skills and crafts of the cultural apparatus itself become not only adjuncts of advertising but in due course themselves advertisements. He designs the product itself as if it were an advertisement, for his aim and his task—acknowledged by the more forthright—is less to make better products than to make products sell better. By brand and trademark, by slogan and package, by color and form, he gives the commodity a fictitious individuality, turning a little lanolin and water into an emulsified way to become erotically blessed; concealing the weight and quality of what is for sale; confusing the consumer's choice and banalizing her sensibilities.

The silly needs of salesmanship are thus met by the silly designing and redesigning of things.

The waste of human labor and material become irrationally central to the performance of the capitalist mechanism. Society itself becomes a great sales room, a network of public rackets, and a continuous fashion show. The gimmick of success becomes the yearly change of model as fashion is made universal. And in the mass society, the image of beauty itself becomes identified with the designer's speed-up and debasement of imagination, taste and sensibility.

The Growth of the Star System

The cultural workman himself, in particular the designer, tends to become part of the means of distribution, over which he tends to lose control. Having "established a market," and monopolized access to it, the distributor—along with his market researcher—claims to "know what they want." So his orders—even to the free-lance—become more explicit and detailed. The price he offers may be quite high; perhaps too high, he comes to think, and perhaps he is right. So he begins to hire and to manage in varying degree a stable of cultural workmen. Those who allow themselves to be managed by the mass distributor are selected and in time formed in such a way as to be altogether proficient, but perhaps not quite first-rate. So the search goes on for "fresh ideas," for exciting notions, for more alluring models; in brief, for the innovator. But in the meantime, back at the studio, the laboratory, the research bureau, the writers' factory—the distributor is ascendant over many producers who become the rank-and-file workmen of the commercially established cultural apparatus.

In this situation of increasing bureaucratization and yet of the continual need for innovation, the cultural workman tends to become a commercial hack or a commercial star. By a star, I mean a producer whose productions are so much in demand that he is able, to some extent at least, to make distributors serve as his adjuncts. This role has its own conditions and its own perils: The star tends to be trapped by his own success. He has painted this sort of thing and he gets $20,000 a throw for it. This man, however affluent, may become culturally bored by this style and wants to explore another. But often he cannot: he is used to the $20,000 a throw and there is demand for it. As a leader of fashions, accordingly, he is himself subject to fashion. Moreover, his success as a star depends upon his playing the market: he is not in educative interplay with a public that supports him as he develops and which he in turn develops. He too, by virtue of his success, becomes a marketeer.

The star system of American culture—along with the commercial hacks—tend to kill off the chance of the cultural workman to be a worthy craftsman. One is a smash hit or one is among the failures who are not produced; one is a best seller or one is among the hacks and failures; one is either absolutely tops or one is just nothing at all.

As an entrepreneur, you may value as you wish these several developments; but as a member of the cultural apparatus, you surely must realize that whatever else you may be doing, you are also creating and shaping the cultural sensibilities of men and women, and indeed the very quality of their everyday lives.

The Big Lie: "We Only Give Them What They Want"

The mere prevalence of the advertiser's skills and the designer's craft makes evident the falseness of the major dogma of the distributor's culture. That dogma is that "we only give them what they want." This is the Big Lie of mass culture and of debased art, and also it is the weak excuse for the cultural default of many designers.

The determination of "consumer wants and tastes" is one characterizing mark of the current phase of capitalism in America—and as well as what is called mass culture. And it is precisely in the areas in which wants are determined and changed that designers tend to do their work.

The merchandising apparatus, of which many designers are now members, operates more to create wants than to satisfy wants that are already active. Consumers are trained to "want" that to which they are most continually exposed. Wants do not originate in some vague realms of the consumer's personality; they are formed by an elaborate apparatus of jingle and fashion, of persuasion and fraud. now, in this cultural apparatus, being defined and built, made into a slogan, a story, a diagram, a release, a dream, a fact, a blue-print, a tune, a sketch, a formula; and presented to them. Such part as reason may have in human affairs, this apparatus, this put-together contraption, fulfills; such role as sensibility may play in the human drama, it enacts; such use as technique may have in history and in biography, it provides. It is the sect of civilization, which—in Matthew Arnold's phrase—is "the humanization of man in society." The only truths are the truths defined by the cultural apparatus. The only beauty is experiences and objects created and indicated by cultural workmen. The only goods are the cultural values with which men are made morally comfortable or morally uneasy.

From Production to Distribution to "Merchandising"

As an institutional fact, the cultural apparatus has assumed many forms. In some societies—notably that of Russia—it is established by an authority that post-dates capitalism: it is thus part of an official apparatus of psychic domination. In some—notably the nations of Western Europe—it is established out of a tradition that pre-dates capitalism; it is thus part of an Establishment in which social authority and cultural prestige overlap. Both cultural tradition and political authority are involved in any cultural Establishment, but in the USA the cultural apparatus is established commercially: it is part of an ascendant capitalist economy. This fact is the major key to understanding both the quality of everyday life and the situation of culture in America today.

The virtual dominance of commercial culture is the key to America's cultural scope, confusion, canalization, excitement, sterility. To understand the case of America today, one must understand the economic trends and the selling mechanics of a capitalist world in which the mass production and the mass sale of goods has become The Fetish of human life, the pivot both of work and of leisure. One must understand how the pervasive mechanisms of the market have penetrated every feature of life—including art, science and learning—and made them subject to the pecuniary evaluation. One must understand that what has happened to work in general in the last two centuries has in the 20th century been happening to the sphere of artistic and intellectual endeavor; these too have now become part of society as a salesroom. To understand the ambiguous position of the cultural workman in America one must see how he stands in the overlap of these two worlds: the world of such an overdeveloped society with its ethos of advertisement, and the world of culture as men have known it and as they might know it.

However harsh its effects upon the nature of work, the industrialization of underdeveloped countries must be seen as an enormous blessing: it is man conquering nature, and so freeing himself from dire want. But as the social and physical machineries of industrialization develop, new purposes and interests come into play. The economic emphasis moves from production to distribution and, in the overdeveloped society, to what is called "merchandising." The pivotal decade for this shift in the USA was the Twenties, but it is in the era since the ending of World War II that the new economy has flowered like a noxious weed. In this phase of capitalism, the distributor becomes ascendant over both the consumer and the producer.

As the capacity to produce goes far beyond existing demand, as monopoly replaces competition, as surpluses accumulate, the need is for the creation and maintenance of the national market and for its monopolistic closure. Then the salesman becomes paramount. Instead of cultivating and servicing a variety of publics, the distributor's aim is to create a mass volume of continuing sales. Continuous and expanding production requires continuous and expanding consumption, so consumption must be speeded up by all the techniques and frauds of marketing. Moreover, existing commodities must be worn out more quickly for as the market is saturated, the economy becomes increasingly dependent upon what is called replacement. It is then that obsolescence comes to be planned and its cycle deliberately shortened.

Silly Designs for Silly Needs

There are, I suppose, three kinds of obsolescence: (1) technological, as when something wears out or something better is produced; (2) artificial, as when something is deliberately designed so that it will wear out; and (3) status obsolescence, as when fashions are created in such ways that consumption brings disgrace or prestige in accordance with last year's or with this year's model, and alongside the old struggle for existence, there is added the panic for status.

It is in this economic situation that the designer gets his Main Chance. Whatever his esthetic pretension and his engineering ability, his economic task is to sell. In this he joins the advertising fraternity, the public relations counsel, and the market researched. These types have developed their skills and pretensions in order to serve men whose God is the Big Sell. And now the designer joins them.

Craftsmanship as a Value

I have of course been describing the role of the designer at what I hope is its worst. And I am aware that it is not only in the field of design that the American ambiguity of cultural endeavor is revealed, that it is not only the designer who commits the cultural default. In varying degrees all cultural workmen are part of a world dominated by the pecuniary ethos of the crackpot business man and also of a world unified only vaguely by the ideals of cultural sensibilility and human reason. The autonomy of all types of cultural workmen has in our time been declining. I also want to make it clear that I am aware of the great diversity among designers and the enormous difficulty any designer now faces in trying to escape the trap of the maniacs of production and distribution.

The problem of the designer can be solved only by radical consideration of fundamental values. But like most fundamental considerations his can begin very simply.

The idea of the cultural apparatus is an attempt to understand human affairs from the standpoint of the role within them of reason, technique and sensibility. As members of this cultural apparatus, it is important that designers realize fully what their membership means. It means, is brief, that you represent the sensibilities of man as a maker of material objects, of man as a creature related to nature itself and to changing it by humanly considered plan. The designer is a creator and a critic of the physical frame of private and public life. He represents man as a maker of his own milieu. He stands for the kind of sensibility which enables men to contrive a world of objects before which they stand delighted and which they are delighted to use. The designer is part of the unity of art, science and learning. That, in turn, means that he shares one cardinal value, that is the common denominator of art, science and learning and also the very root of human development. That value, I believe, is craftsmanship.

From craftsmanship, as ideal and as practice, it is possible to derive all that the designer ought to represent as an individual and all that he ought to stand for socially and politically and economically. As ideal, craftsmanship stands for the creative nature of work, and for the central place of such work in human development as a whole. As practice, craftsmanship stands for the classic role of the independent artisan who does his work in close interplay with the public, which in turn participates in it.

The most fundamental splits in contemporary life occur because of the break-up of the old unity of design, production and enjoyment. Between the image and the object, between the design and the work, between production and consumption, between work and leisure, there is a great cultural vacuum, and it is this vacuum that the mass distributor, and his artistic and intellectual satraps, have filled up with frenzy and trash and fraud. In one sentence, what has been lost is the fact and the ethos of man as craftsman.

By craftsmanship I refer to a style of work and a way of life having the following characteristics:

(1) In craftsmanship there is no ulterior motive for work other than the product being made and the processes of its creation. The craftsman imagines the completed product, often even as he creates it; and even if he does not make it, he sees and understands the meaning of his own exertion in terms of the total process of its production. Accordingly, the details of the craftsman's daily work are meaningful because they are not detached in his mind from the product of the work. The satisfaction he has in the results infuses the means of achieving it. This is the root connection between work and art: as esthetic experiences, both involve the power "to catch the enjoyment that belongs to the consummation, the outcome, an undertaking and to give to the implements, the objects that are instrumental in the undertaking, and to the acts that compose it

something of the joy and satisfaction that suffuse its successful accomplishment."

To quite small circles the appeal of modern art—notably painting and sculpture, but also of the crafts—lies in the fact that in an impersonal, a scheduled, a machined world, they represent the personal and the spontaneous. They are the opposite of the stereotyped and the banalized.

(2) In craftsmanship, plan and performance are unified, in both, the craftsman is master of the activity and of himself in the process. The craftsman is free to begin his working according to his own plan, and during the work he is free to modify its shape and the manner of its shaping. The continual joining of plan and performance brings even more firmly together the consummation of work and its instrumental activities, infusing the latter with the joy of the former. Work is a rational sphere of independent action.

(3) Since he works freely, the craftsman is able to learn from his work, to develop as well as use his capacities. His work is thus a means of developing himself as a man as well as developing his skill. This self-development is not an ulterior goal, but a cumulative result of devotion to and practice of his craft. As he gives to work the quality of his own mind and skill, he is also further developing his own nature; in this simple sense, he lives in and through his work, which confesses and reveals him to the world.

(4) The craftsman's way of livelihood determines and infuses his entire mode of living. For him there is no split of work and play, of work and culture. His work is the mainspring of his life; he does not flee from work into a separate sphere of leisure; he brings to his non-working hours the values and qualities developed and employed in his working time. He expresses himself in the very act of creating economic value; he is at work and at play in the same act; his work is a poem in action. In order to give his work the freshes of creativity, he must at times open himself to those influences that only affect us when our attentions are relaxed. Thus for the craftsman, apart from mere animal rest, leisure may occur in such intermittent periods as are necessary for individuality in his work.

(5) Such an independent stratum of craftsman cannot flourish unless there are publics who support individuals who may not turn out to be first-rate. Craftsmanship requires that such cultural workmen and such publics define what is first-rate. In the Communist bloc because of official bureaucracies, and in the capitalist because of the commercial ethos, standards are now not in the hands of such cultural producers and cultural publics. In both the mere distributor is the key to both consumption and production.

Some cultural workmen in America do of course remain independent. Perhaps three or four men actually earn a living here just by composing serious music; perhaps fifty or so by the writing of serious novels. But I am concerned now less with economic than with cultural requirements. The role of the serious craftsman requires that the cultural workman remain a cultural workman, and that he produce for other cultural producers and for circles and publics composed of people who have some grasp of what is involved in his production. For you cannot "possess" art merely by buying it; you cannot support art merely by feeding artists—although that does help. To possess it you must earn it by participating to some extent in what it takes to design it and to create it. To support it you must catch in your consumption of it something of what is involved in the production of it.

It is, I think, the absence of such a stratum of cultural workmen, in close interplay with such a participating public, that is the signal fault of the American cultural scene today. So long as it does not develop, the position of the designer will contain all the ambiguities and invite all the defaults I have indicated. Designers will tend to be commercial stars or commercial hacks. And human development will continue to be trivialized, human sensibilities blunted, and the quality of life distorted and impoverished.

As practice, craftsmanship in America has largely been trivialized into pitiful hobbies: it is part of leisure, not of work. As ethic, it is largely confined to small groups of privileged professionals and intellectuals. What I am suggesting to you is that designers ought to take the value of craftsmanship as the central value for which they stand; that in accordance with it they ought to do their work; and that they ought to use its norms in their social and economic and political visions of what society ought to become.

Craftsmanship cannot prevail without a properly developing society; such a society I believe would be one in which the fact and the ethos of craftsmanship would be pervasive. In terms of its norms, men and women ought to be formed and selected as ascendant models of character. In terms of its ethos, institutions ought to be constructed and judged. Human society, in brief, ought to be built around craftsmanship as the central experience of the unalienated human being and the very root of free human development. The most fruitful way to define the social problem is to ask how such a society can be built. For the highest human ideal is: to become a good craftsman.

PART VIII

The Self, Interactions, and Exchanges

The thinkers featured in this part were some of the first to formulate theories for the *microlevel of social analysis*—that aspect of sociology that examines the interactions and exchanges that characterize the everyday lives of people. The first four of these thinkers—W. I. Thomas, George Herbert Mead, Charles Horton Cooley, and Erving Goffman—were largely interested in how the social self is developed, experienced, and presented in relation to the subjective meanings that people give to social situations and social encounters. Alfred Schütz, Peter L. Berger, Thomas Luckmann, and Harold Garfinkel also theorize about the subjective dynamics of interpersonal relationships but go further in accounting, more generally, for how people meaningfully create social reality. The last four thinkers—Marcel Mauss, George C. Homans, Peter M. Blau, and James S. Coleman—also theorize about social associations but do so on the basis of reciprocal exchanges between individuals. While all of these theorists focused on the procedural dynamics of interactions and exchanges, they also endeavored to determine the *macrolevel*, or structural and institutional, conditions that are produced by these dynamics.

In "The Definition of the Situation," first published in 1923, W. I. Thomas begins with the premise that before people decide on how to act or react to their environment—and for that matter, on how they see themselves in relation to that environment—they first confront a process that he calls the *definition of the situation*. By this, he means the *shared collective meaning* that is given to particular social circumstances and to which individuals are expected to conform. The definition of the situation is created by those entities greater than the individual—the family and the community—and determines what social reality is. Later, in 1928, Thomas extended the concept in a declaration now known as the *Thomas theorem*, stating that the subjective meaning that people give to a situation will have objective consequences.

In "Self and Society," George Herbert Mead describes the *self* as a process by which people see themselves as objects. Because people can think of themselves as objects, the self is reflective, which means that people can have a conversation with themselves. This inner conversation with oneself is what Mead calls *mind*. The self becomes social when the person communicates with others. The *social self* develops fully through children's involvement in two stages of activities: their participation in play and their participation in organized games. When children *play* at something—at being mother, teacher, police officer, and so on—they *take the role of the other* and learn to become both subject and object. When playing in an organized *game*, the child takes the perspective of all of the other players involved in that game. The child must know what everyone else is going to do in order to know how to respond to them. This involves taking the role of the *generalized other*, the organized social group to which the child belongs, be that a family or a sports team. Mead then turns his attention to the two aspects of the self: the *I* and the *me*. According to him, the *I* is the subject part of the self that is present before people are aware of themselves as objects. It is not social. By contrast, the *me* is the object part of the self that arises when people become self-reflective and assume the collective point of view of others. Because it involves cooperation and communication with others, the *me* is social.

Another theorist who analyzed the self was Charles Horton Cooley. In the reading titled "The Looking-Glass Self," Cooley identifies the self as a *feeling*, a person's sensation of that which is peculiar to him or her. Further, the self is also an *idea* that the mind considers its own but always in relation to other persons. Cooley coined the term *looking-glass self* to refer to the idea that people have of who they are, which is based on how they think others perceive them. This self-image gives rise to some sort of self-feeling, of either pride or shame, depending on what people presume to be others' judgment of them.

In the next reading, "Primary Groups," Cooley proposes the concept of *primary groups*; these are intimate associations characterized by a "we" feeling that gives rise to cooperation among group members. Primary groups include a variety of associations, from the family to the neighborhood and many others in between, such as playgroups, social clubs, and fraternities. These groups are primary because they give their members their earliest and most complete experiences of belongingness.

Erving Goffman considers the ways that people present their selves in ordinary social interactions. In "Performances in Everyday Life," he contends that the performances that people give in face-to-face encounters must be seen as credible by those observing the performance, the *audience*. Giving a convincing performance before an audience involves putting on a *front*, by which Goffman means that expressive part of the performance that defines the situation for the audience. Bolstering the definition of the situation is the *setting* or background scenery in which the front is enacted. When a performance is offered to an audience, not only must the impression of sincerity be given, it must also be an *idealized* one. In an effort to foster an idealized impression, a person typically conceals information about himself or herself that may be seen as incompatible with the performance in question—that may *discredit* him or her. When a performer does not properly manage an idealized impression before an audience or when discrediting information is disclosed, *embarrassment* may ensue.

In "Managing Stigma," Goffman explores further the idea that idealized impressions must be managed but does so in the case of individuals whose social identities possess an attribute that is deeply discrediting—a *stigma*. Individuals with a stigma may be of two types. The *discredited* assume that their stigma, their undesired differentness, is already known or is immediately apparent to others. The *discreditable* are those people who assume that their stigma is neither known about by those present nor immediately perceivable by them. Goffman then identifies three types of stigma: (1) abominations of the body, (2) blemishes of individual character, and (3) tribal stigma. The prime sociological consideration for Goffman is the point at which the stigmatized come into face-to-face contact with "normals," those not similarly stigmatized. Because these mixed social situations evoke anxiety, discomfort, heightened awareness, and uneasiness, discredited individuals tend to become adept at managing them. However, those who are potentially discreditable must manage discrediting information about their self. They can do so by employing various *techniques of information control*, such as "passing" for normal and "covering" the defect.

Like Goffman, Alfred Schütz, in "The Meaningfully Produced Social World," is also concerned with face-to-face interaction but explicitly in reference to social orientation. According to Schütz, the face-to-face situation becomes a *We-relationship* when the interacting persons possess a *Thou-orientation* toward each other. In other words, they are Thou-oriented when they have a mutual awareness of each other's presence and of the other's existence as a real, living person. It is on the basis of the We-relationship that reciprocating partners can apprehend each other's subjective meanings of communication—that there can be an *intersubjective understanding*. This intersubjective understanding makes it possible for interactants to experience the world as a *social* world. For Schütz, social interactions involve a We-relationship, but they also go further: They consist of a mutuality of meanings that are grasped *reflectively* by the interacting partners, which is to say that the participants are sensitively aware of each other's stream of consciousness. In contrast, in *they-relationships*, people experience others indirectly because they are not copresent in the immediate face-to-face encounter. These anonymous others or impersonal "contemporaries" are known only in the abstract as *ideal types*. Their conscious experiences cannot be understood intersubjectively but only by inference from objective contexts of meaning.

Peter L. Berger and Thomas Luckmann were greatly influenced by Schütz's ideas about the meaningful construction of society. Given that society is a collection of institutions, in "Society as Objective Reality," Berger and Luckmann begin by explaining the origins of institutions, or what they call the process of *institutionalization*. For them, institutionalization occurs whenever specific patterns of conduct—*typifications*—are repeatedly shared by interacting individuals. In addition to this reciprocity of typifications, institutions have a shared history and act as mechanisms of social control. Institutions are thus experienced as possessing a reality of their own, a historical and *objective reality* that confronts the individual as an external and coercive fact. In time, people explain and justify—that is to say, they *legitimate*—institutions through language. It is through language that people communicate the social stock of knowledge, what is generally known about the social world. This commonsense knowledge, which is articulated in maxims, morals, values, and beliefs, serves to legitimize institutions. Society, then, is an objective reality that is humanly produced.

Also taking up the theme of commonsense knowledge is Harold Garfinkel, who, in "Ethnomethodology," introduces the concept of *indexicality*. This refers to the meaning that is given to talk and conduct based on assumptions made in accordance with the taken-for-granted context of everyday activities, which is to say, the commonsense knowledge of social structures. Because all symbolic communications are subject to the indexicality of meaning, their organization and rationality—their documentary interpretation—must be an ongoing accomplishment of interacting individuals. Garfinkel calls the sociological investigation of the methods that people use in making sense of their everyday life *ethnomethodology*.

Marcel Mauss examines social interaction that is rooted not on definitional processes of meaning but on commensurate *reciprocity*. In "Obligatory Exchange," Mauss considers the system of *gift giving*, which is found in traditional societies around the world, and identifies three obligations that it involves: to give presents, to receive them, and, most important, to repay gifts received. This compulsory giving, receiving, and repaying of gifts, which characterizes all institutional aspects of society, has a function beyond the perpetual circulation of objects: It contributes to amicable social relations.

While Mauss considered institutionalized exchanges as they occur in total societies, George C. Homans examines the transactions that characterize the *elementary* forms of social behavior as they occur in small groups. In "Social Behavior as Exchange," Homans maintains that all interactions between two or three persons involve an exchange of material and nonmaterial goods. (The latter include approval and prestige.) Further, social exchange involves a mutual reciprocity of *rewards and costs* between persons. Thus, for persons engaged in exchange, what they give may be a cost to them, just as what they receive may be a reward. The cost and the value of what they give and of what they receive vary with the quantity of what they give and receive. But persons involved in an exchange relationship also expect to receive as much as they give. That is to say, they seek *distributive justice*, or a fairly equitable exchange of rewards and costs between persons. For Homans, these dynamics of social exchange create the "structure" of the group in which its members are interacting.

Despite the fact that people expect reciprocal relationships to be equal in terms of rewards and costs, in the reading "Reciprocity, Power Imbalance, and Dialectical Change," Peter M. Blau contends that because a perfect balance of mutual rewards is rare, social associations are also characterized by an *imbalance* in the exchange. In a social association, a unilateral offering of rewards—whether these are affections or services—produces unilateral *power*. In other words, the party with the most to give has the most power—and this gives rise to differences in power in the association. But because those subject to the exercise of power tend to resist domination, they seek to bring about *change* in the social structure of the association. According to Blau, this structural change assumes a *dialectical* pattern because while, on one level, reciprocity generates *equilibrium* in the association, on another level, power differences generate *disequilibrium*.

Finally, in "Individual Interests and Systems of Exchange," James S. Coleman begins with the notion that actors are motivated to pursue their own *interests*. However, they do not always have control over the resources and events that can help them to satisfy those interests. When actors seek resources that they do not control but which other actors do control, they engage in various transactions; that is to say, they give up their right to control a resource that is of little interest to them in exchange for control of a resource that is of greater interest to them. At minimum, a social system involves two actors, each having control over *resources* (e.g., goods, events, actions, and information) of interest to the other. The simplest social system involves two actors engaged in the mutual exchange of resources. When there are no further exchanges that can increase the expected realization of interests for both actors, the system is said to be in equilibrium. At this point, each actor achieves his or her optimal satisfaction of interests under the circumstances but does not necessarily have equal control over resources and events. This is because systems of exchange satisfy interests not at the level of the individual but *in the aggregate*—they possess what Coleman sees as an inherent, or *constitutional*, distribution of control.

58

THE DEFINITION OF THE SITUATION*

W. I. THOMAS

One of the most important powers gained during the evolution of animal life is the ability to make decisions from within instead of having them imposed from without. Very low forms of life do not make decisions, as we understand this term, but are pushed and pulled by chemical substances, heat, light, etc., much as iron filings are attracted or repelled by a magnet. They do tend to behave properly in given conditions—a group of small crustaceans will flee as in a panic if a bit of strychnia is placed in the basin containing them and will rush toward a drop of beef juice like hogs crowding around swill—but they do this as an expression of organic affinity for the one substance and repugnance for the other, and not as an expression of choice or "free will." There are, so to speak, rules of behavior but these represent a sort of fortunate mechanistic adjustment of the organism to typically recurring situations, and the organism cannot change the rule.

On the other hand, the higher animals, and above all man, have the power of refusing to obey a stimulation which they followed at an earlier time. Response to the earlier stimulation may have had painful consequences and so the rule or habit in this situation is changed. We call this ability the power of inhibition, and it is dependent on the fact that the nervous system carries memories or records of past experiences. At this point the determination of action no longer comes exclusively from outside sources but is located within the organism itself.

Preliminary to any self-determined act of behavior there is always a stage of examination and deliberation which we may call *the definition of the situation*. And actually not only concrete acts are dependent on the definition of the situation, but gradually a whole life-policy and the personality of the individual himself follow from a series of such definitions.

But the child is always born into a group of people among whom all the general types of situation which may arise have already been defined and corresponding rules of conduct developed, and where he has not the slightest chance of making his definitions and following his wishes without interference. Men have always lived together in groups. Whether mankind has a true herd instinct or whether groups are held together

*From *The Unadjusted Girl: With Cases and Standpoint for Behavior Analysis* by William I. Thomas. Originally published in 1923 by Little Brown and Company.

because this has worked out to advantage is of no importance. Certainly the wishes in general are such that they can be satisfied only in a society. But we have only to refer to the criminal code to appreciate the variety of ways in which the wishes of the individual may conflict with the wishes of society. And the criminal code takes no account of the many unsanctioned expressions of the wishes which society attempts to regulate by persuasion and gossip.

There is therefore always a rivalry between the spontaneous definitions of the situation made by the member of an organized society and the definitions which his society has provided for him. The individual tends to a hedonistic selection of activity, pleasure first; and society to a utilitarian selection, safety first. Society wishes its member to be laborious, dependable, regular, sober, orderly, self-sacrificing; while the individual wishes less of this and more of new experience. And organized society seeks also to regulate the conflict and competition inevitable between its members in the pursuit of their wishes. The desire to have wealth, for example, or any other socially sanctioned wish, may not be accomplished at the expense of another member of the society,—by murder, theft, lying, swindling, blackmail, etc.

It is in this connection that a moral code arises, which is a set of rules or behavior norms, regulating the expression of the wishes, and which is built up by successive definitions of the situation. In practice the abuse arises first and the rule is made to prevent its recurrence. Morality is thus the generally accepted definition of the situation, whether expressed in public opinion and the unwritten law, in a formal legal code, or in religious commandments and prohibitions.

The family is the smallest social unit and the primary defining agency. As soon as the child has free motion and begins to pull, tear, pry, meddle, and prowl, the parents begin to define the situation through speech and other signs and pressures: "Be quiet," "Sit up straight," "Blow your nose," "Wash your face," "Mind your mother," "Be kind to sister," etc. This is the real significance of Wordsworth's phrase, "Shades of the prison house begin to close upon the growing child." His wishes and activities begin to be inhibited, and gradually, by definitions within the family, by playmates, in the school; in the Sunday school, in the community, through reading, by formal instruction, by informal signs of approval and disapproval, the growing member learns the code of his society.

In addition to the family we have the community as a defining agency. At present the community is so weak and vague that it gives us no idea of the former power of the local group in regulating behavior. Originally the community was practically the whole world of its members. It was composed of families related by blood and marriage and was not so large that all the members could not come together; it was a face-to-face group. I asked a Polish peasant what was the extent of an "*okolica*" or neighborhood—how far it reached. "It reaches," he said, "as far as the report of a man reaches—as far as a man is talked about." And it was in communities of this kind that the moral code which we now recognize as valid originated. The customs of the community are "folkways," and both state and church have in their more formal codes mainly recognized and incorporated these folkways.

The typical community is vanishing and it would be neither possible nor desirable to restore it in its old form. It does not correspond with the present direction of social evolution and it would now be a distressing condition in which to live. But in the immediacy of relationships and the participation of everybody in everything, it represents an element which we have lost and which we shall probably have to restore in some form of coöperation in order to secure a balanced and normal society,—some arrangement corresponding with human nature.

Very elemental examples of the definition of the situation by the community as a whole, corresponding to mob action as we know it and to our trial by jury, are found among European peasants. The three documents following, all relating to the Russian community or *mir*, give some idea of the conditions under which a whole community, a public, formerly defined a situation.

59

Self and Society*

George Herbert Mead

The self, as that which can be an object to itself, is essentially a social structure, and it arises in social experience. After a self has arisen, it in a certain sense provides for itself its social experiences, and so we can conceive of an absolutely solitary self. But it is impossible to conceive of a self arising outside of social experience. When it has arisen we can think of a person in solitary confinement for the rest of his life, but who still has himself as a companion, and is able to think and to converse with himself as he had communicated with others. That process to which I have just referred, of responding to one's self as another responds to it, taking part in one's own conversation with others, being aware of what one is saying and using that awareness of what one is saying to determine what one is going to say thereafter—that is a process with which we are all familiar. We are continually following up our own address to other persons by an understanding of what we are saying, and using that understanding in the direction of our continued speech. We are finding out what we are going to say, what we are going to do, by saying and doing, and in the process we are continually controlling the process itself. In the conversation of gestures what we say calls out a certain response in another and that in turn changes our own action, so that we shift from what we started to do because of the reply the other makes. The conversation of gestures is the beginning of communication. The individual comes to carry on a conversation of gestures with himself. He says something, and that calls out a certain reply in himself which makes him change what he was going to say. One starts to say something, we will presume an unpleasant something, but when he starts to say it he realizes it is cruel. The effect on himself of what he is saying checks him; there is here a conversation of gestures between the individual and himself. We mean by significant speech that the action is one that affects the individual himself, and that the effect upon the individual himself is part of the intelligent carrying-out of the conversation with others. Now we, so to speak, amputate that social phase and dispense with it for the time being, so that one is talking to one's self as one would talk to another person.

This process of abstraction cannot be carried on indefinitely. One inevitably seeks an audience, has to pour himself out to somebody. In reflective intelligence one thinks to act, and to act solely so that this action remains a part of a social process. Thinking becomes preparatory to social action. The very process of thinking is, of course, simply an inner conversation that goes on, but it is a conversation of gestures which in its completion implies the expression of that which one thinks to an audience. One separates the significance of what he is saying to others from the actual speech and gets it ready before saying it. He thinks it out, and perhaps writes it in the form of a book; but it is still a part of social intercourse in which one is addressing other persons and at the same time addressing one's self, and in which one controls the address to other persons by the response made to one's own gesture. That the person should be responding to himself is necessary to the self, and it is this sort of social conduct which provides behavior within which that self appears. I know of no other form of behavior than the linguistic in which the individual is an object to himself, and, so far as I can see, the individual is not a self in the reflexive sense unless he is an object to himself. It is this fact that gives a critical importance to communication, since this is a type of behavior in which the individual does so respond to himself.

Another set of background factors in the genesis of the self is represented in the activities of play and the game.

Among primitive people, as I have said, the necessity of distinguishing the self and the organism was recognized in what we term the "double": the individual has a thing-like self that is affected by the individual as it affects other people and which is distinguished from the immediate organism in that it can leave the body and come back to it. This is the basis for the concept of the soul as a separate entity.

We find in children something that answers to this double, namely, the invisible, imaginary companions which a good many children produce in their own experience. They organize in this way the responses which they call out in other persons and call out also in themselves. Of course, this playing with an imaginary companion is only a peculiarly interesting phase of ordinary play. Play in this sense, especially the stage which precedes the organized games, is a play at something. A child plays at being a mother, at being a teacher, at being a policeman; that is, it is taking different rôles, as we say. We have something that suggests this in what we call the play of animals: a cat will play with her kittens, and dogs play with each other. Two dogs playing with each other will attack and defend, in a process which if carried through would amount to an actual fight. There is a combination of responses which checks the depth of the bite. But we do not have in such a situation the dogs taking a definite rôle in the sense that a child deliberately takes the rôle of another. This tendency on the part of the children is what we are working with in the kindergarten where the rôles which the children assume are made the basis for training. When a child does assume a rôle he has in himself the stimuli which call out that particular response or group of responses. He may, of course, run away when he is chased, as the dog does, or he may turn around and strike back just as the dog does in his play. But that is not the same as playing at something. Children get together to "play Indian". This means that the child has a certain set of stimuli which call out in itself the responses that they would call out in others, and which answer to an Indian. In the play period the child utilizes his own responses to these stimuli which he makes use of in building a self. The response which he has a tendency to make to these stimuli organizes them. He plays that he is, for instance, offering himself something, and he buys it; he gives a letter to himself and takes it away; he addresses himself as a parent, as a teacher; he arrests himself as a policeman. He has a set of stimuli which call out in himself the sort of responses they call out in others. He takes this group of responses and organizes them into a certain whole. Such is the simplest form of being another to one's self. It involves a temporal situation. The child says something in one character and responds in another character, and then his responding in another character is a stimulus to himself in the first character, and so the conversation goes on. A certain organized structure arises in him and in his other which replies to it, and these carry on the conversation of gestures between themselves.

If we contrast play with the situation in an organized game, we note the essential difference that the child who plays in a game must be ready to take the attitude of everyone else involved in that game, and that these different rôles must have a definite relationship to each other. Taking a very simple game such as hide-and-seek, everyone with the exception of the one who is hiding is a person who is hunting. A child does not require more than the person who is hunted and the one who is hunting. If a child is playing in the first sense he just goes on playing, but there is no basic organization gained. In that early stage, he passes from one rôle to another just as a whim takes him. But in a game where a number of individuals are involved, then the child taking one rôle must be ready to take the rôle of everyone else. If he gets in a ball nine he must have the responses of each position involved in his own position. He must know what everyone else is going to do in order to carry out his own play. He has to take all of these rôles. They do not all have to be present in consciousness at the same time, but at some moments he has to have three or four individuals present in his own attitude, such as the one who is going to throw the ball, the one who is going to catch it, and so on. These responses must be, in some degree, present in his own make-up. In the game, then, there is a set of responses of such others so organized that, the attitude of one calls out the appropriate attitudes of the other.

The fundamental difference between the game and play is that in the latter the child must have the attitude of all the others involved in that game. The attitudes of the other players which the participant assumes organize into a sort of unit, and it is that organization which controls the response of the individual. The illustration used was of a person playing baseball. Each one of his own acts is determined by his assumption of the action of the others who are playing the game. What he does is controlled by his being everyone else on that team, at least in so far as those attitudes affect his own particular response. We get then an "other" which is an organization of the attitudes of those involved in the same process.

The organized community or social group which gives to the individual his unity of self may be called "the generalized other". The attitude of the generalized other is the attitude of the whole community. Thus, for example, in the case of such a social group as a ball team, the team is the generalized other in so far as it enters—as an organized process or social activity—into the experience of any one of the individual members of it.

I have pointed out, then, that there are two general stages in the full development of the self. At the first of these stages, the individual's self is constituted simply by an organization of the particular attitudes of other individuals toward himself and toward one another in the specific social acts in which he participates with them. But at the second stage in the full development of the individual's self that self is constituted not only by an organization of these particular individual attitudes, but also by an organization of the social attitudes of the generalized other or the social group as a whole to which he belongs. These social or group attitudes are brought within the individual's field of direct experience, and are included as elements in the structure or constitution of his self, in the same way that the attitudes of particular other individuals are; and the individual arrives at them, or succeeds in taking them, by means of further organizing, and then generalizing, the attitudes of particular other individuals in terms of their organized social bearings and implications. So the self reaches its full development by organizing these individual attitudes of others into the organized social or group attitudes, and by thus becoming an individual reflection of the general systematic pattern of social or group behavior in which it and the others are all involved—a pattern which enters as a whole into the individual's experience in terms of these organized group attitudes which, through the mechanism of his central nervous system, he takes toward himself, just as he takes the individual attitudes of others.

The "I" and the "Me"

We have discussed at length the social foundations of the self, and hinted that the self does not consist simply in the bare organization of social attitudes. We may now explicitly raise the question as to the nature of the "I" which is aware of the social "me."

The simplest way of handling the problem would be in terms of memory. I talk to myself, and I remember what I said and perhaps the emotional content that went with it. The "I" of this moment is present in the "me" of the next moment. There again I cannot turn around quick enough to catch myself. I become a "me" in so far as I remember what I said. The "I" can be given, however, this functional relationship. It is because of the "I" that we say that we are never fully aware of what we are, that we surprise ourselves by our own action. It is as we act that we surprise ourselves by our own action. It is in memory that the "I" is constantly present in experience. We can go back directly a few moments in our experience, and then we are dependent upon memory images for the rest. So that the "I" in memory is there as the spokesman of the self of the second, or minute, or day ago. As given, it is a "me," but it is a "me" which was the "I" at the earlier time. If you ask, then, where directly in your own experience the "I" comes in, the answer is that it comes in as a historical figure. It is what you were a second ago that is the "I" of the "me." It is another "me" that has to take that rôle. You cannot get the immediate response of the "I" the process. The "I" is in a certain sense that with which we do identify ourselves. The getting of it into experience constitutes one of the problems of most of our conscious experience; it is not directly given in experience.

There is neither "I" nor "me" in the conversation of gestures; the whole act is not yet carried out, but the preparation takes place in this field of gesture. Now, in so far as the individual arouses in himself the attitudes of the others, there arises an organized group of responses. And it is due to the individual's ability to take the attitudes of these others in so far as they can be organized that he gets self-consciousness. The taking of all of those organized sets of attitudes gives him his "me"; that is the self he is aware of. He can throw the ball to some other member because of the demand made upon him from other members of the team. That is the self that immediately exists for him in his consciousness. He has their attitudes, knows what they want and what the consequence of any act of his will be, and he has assumed responsibility for the situation. Now, it is the presence of those organized sets of attitudes that constitutes that "me" to which he as an "I" is responding. But what that response will be he does not know and nobody else knows. Perhaps he will make a brilliant play or an error. The response to that situation as it appears in his immediate experience is uncertain, and it is that which constitutes the "I."

We have discussed the self from the point of view of the "I" and the "me," the "me" representing that group of attitudes which stands for others in the community, especially that organized group of responses which we have detailed in discussing the game on the one hand and social institutions on the other. In these situations there is a certain organized group of attitudes which answer to any social act on the part of the individual organism. In any co-operative process, such as the family, the individual calls out a response from the other members of the group. Now, to the extent that those responses can be called out in the individual so that he can answer to them, we have both those contents which go to make up the self, the "other" and the "I." The distinction expresses itself in our experience in what we call the recognition of others and the recognition of ourselves in the others. We cannot realize ourselves except in so far as we can recognize the other in his relationship to us. It is as he takes the attitude of the other that the individual is able to realize himself as a self.

The person who communicates assumes the attitude of the other individual as well as calling it out in the other. He himself is in the rôle of the other person whom he is so exciting and influencing. It is through taking this rôle of the other that he is able to come back on himself and so direct his own process of communication. This taking the rôle of the other, an expression I have so often used, is not simply of passing importance. It is not something that just happens as an incidental result of the gesture, but it is of importance in the development of cooperative activity. The immediate effect of such rôle-taking lies in the control which the individual is able to exercise over his own response. The control of the action of the individual in a co-operative process can take place in the conduct of the individual himself if he can take the rôle of the other, It is this control of the response of the individual himself through taking the rôle of the other that leads to the value of this type of communication from the point of view of the organization of the conduct in the group. It carries the process of co-operative activity farther than it can be carried in the herd as such, or in the insect society.

60

THE LOOKING-GLASS SELF*

CHARLES HORTON COOLEY

It is well to say at the outset that by the word "self" in this discussion is meant simply that which is designated in common speech by the pronouns of the first person singular, "I," "me," "my," "mine," and "myself." "Self" and "ego" are used by metaphysicians and moralists in many other senses, more or less remote from the "I" of daily speech and thought, and with these I wish to have as little to do as possible. What is here discussed is what psychologists call the empirical self, the self that can be apprehended or verified by ordinary observation. I qualify it by the word social not as implying the existence of a self that is not social—for I think that the "I" of common language always has more or less distinct reference to other people as well as the speaker—but because I wish to emphasize and dwell upon the social aspect of it.

The distinctive thing in the idea for which the pronouns of the first person are names is apparently a characteristic kind of feeling which may be called the my-feeling or sense of appropriation. Almost any sort of ideas may be associated with this feeling, and so come to be named "I" or "mine," but the feeling, and that alone it would seem, is the determining factor in the matter.

The social self is simply any idea, or system of ideas, drawn from the *communicative* life, that the mind cherishes as its own. Self-feeling has its chief scope *within* the general life, not outside of it, the special endeavor or tendency of which it is the emotional aspect finding its principal field of exercise in a world of personal forces, reflected in the mind by a world of personal impressions.

That the "I" of common speech has a meaning which includes some sort of reference to other persons is involved in the very fact that the word and the ideas it stands for are phenomena of language and the communicative life. It is doubtful whether it is possible to use language at all without thinking more or less distinctly of someone else, and certainly the things to which we give names and which have a large place in reflective thought are almost always those which are impressed upon us by our contact with other people. Where there is no communication there can be no nomenclature and no developed thought. What we call "me," "mine," or "myself" is, then, not something separate from the general life, but the most interesting part of it, a part whose interest arises from the very fact that it is both general and individual. That is, we care for it just because it is that phase of the mind that is living and striving in the common life, trying to impress itself upon the minds of others. "I" is a

*Excerpt from *Human Nature and the Social Order* by Charles Horton Cooley. Copyright 1902 by Charles Scribner's Sons.

militant social tendency, working to hold and enlarge its place in the general current of tendencies. So far as it can it waxes, as all life does. To think of it as apart from society is a palpable absurdity of which no one could be guilty who really *saw* it as a fact of life.

The reference to other persons involved in the sense of self may be distinct and particular, as when a boy is ashamed to have his mother catch him at something she has forbidden, or it may be vague and general, as when one is ashamed to do something which only his conscience, expressing his sense of social responsibility, detects and disapproves; but it is always there. There is no sense of "I," as in pride or shame, without its correlative sense of you, or he, or they.

In a very large and interesting class of cases the social reference takes the form of a somewhat definite imagination of how one's self—that is any idea he appropriates—appears in a particular mind, and the kind of self-feeling one has is determined by the attitude toward this attributed to that other mind. A social self of this sort might be called the reflected or looking-glass self:

> "Each to each a looking-glass
> Reflects the other that doth pass."

As we see our face, figure, and dress in the glass, and are interested in them because they are ours, and pleased or otherwise with them according as they do or do not answer to what we should like them to be; so in imagination we perceive in another's mind some thought of our appearance, manners, aims, deeds, character, friends, and so on, and are variously affected by it.

A self-idea of this sort seems to have three principal elements: the imagination of our appearance to the other person; the imagination of his judgment of that appearance, and some sort of self-feeling, such as pride or mortification. The comparison with a looking-glass hardly suggests the second element, the imagined judgment, which is quite essential. The thing that moves us to pride or shame is not the mere mechanical reflection of ourselves, but an imputed sentiment, the imagined effect of this reflection upon another's mind. This is evident from the fact that the character and weight of that other, in whose mind we see ourselves, makes all the difference with our feeling. We are ashamed to seem evasive in the presence of a straightforward man, cowardly in the presence of a brave one, gross in the eyes of a refined one, and so on. We always imagine, and in imagining share, the judgments of the other mind. A man will boast to one person of an action—say some sharp transaction in trade—which he would be ashamed to own to another.

61

Primary Groups*

Charles Horton Cooley

By primary groups I mean those characterized by intimate face-to-face association and cooperation. They are primary in several senses, but chiefly in that they are fundamental in forming the social nature and ideals of the individual. The result of intimate association, psychologically, is a certain fusion of individualities in a common whole, so that one's very self, for many purposes at least, is the common life and purpose of the group. Perhaps the simplest way of describing this wholeness is by saying that it is a "we"; it involves the sort of sympathy and mutual identification for which "we" is the natural expression. One lives in the feeling of the whole and finds the chief aims of his will in that feeling.

It is not to be supposed that the unity of the primary group is one of mere harmony and love. It is always a differentiated and usually a competitive unity, admitting of self-assertion and various appropriative passions; but these passions are socialized by sympathy, and come, or tend to come, under the discipline of a common spirit. The individual will be ambitious, but the chief object of his ambition will be some desired place in the thought of the others, and he will feel allegiance to common standards of service and fair play. So the boy will dispute with his fellows a place on the team, but above such disputes will place the common glory of his class and school.

The most important spheres of this intimate association and coöperation—though by no means the only ones—are the family, the play-group of children, and the neighborhood or community group of elders. These are practically universal, belonging to all times and all stages of development; and are accordingly a chief basis of what is universal in human nature and human ideals. The best comparative studies of the family, such as those of Westermarck or Howard, show it to us as not only a universal institution, but as more alike the world over than the exaggeration of exceptional customs by an earlier school had led us to suppose. Nor can any one doubt the general prevalence of play-groups among children or of informal assemblies of various kinds among their elders. Such association is clearly the nursery of human nature in the world about us, and there is no apparent reason to suppose that the case has anywhere or at any time been essentially different.

As regards play, I might, were it not a matter of common observation, multiply illustrations of the universality and spontaneity of the group discussion and coöperation to which it gives rise. The general fact is that children, especially boys

*Excerpt from *Social Organization: A Study of the Larger Mind* by Charles Horton Cooley. Copyright 1909 by Charles Scribner's Sons

after about their twelfth year, live in fellowships in which their sympathy, ambition and honor are engaged even more, often, than they are in the family. Most of us can recall examples of the endurance by boys of injustice and even cruelty, rather than appeal from their fellows to parents or teachers—as, for instance, in the hazing so prevalent at schools, and so difficult, for this very reason, to repress. And how elaborate the discussion, how cogent the public opinion, how hot the ambitions in these fellowships.

Nor is this facility of juvenile association, as is sometimes supposed, a trait peculiar to English and American boys; since experience among our immigrant population seems to show that the offspring of the more restrictive civilizations of the continent of Europe form self-governing play-groups with almost equal readiness. Thus Miss Jane Addams, after pointing out that the "gang" is almost universal, speaks of the interminable discussion which every detail of the gang's activity receives, remarking that "in these social folk-motes, so to speak, the young citizen learns to act upon his own determination."

Of the neighborhood group it may be said, in general, that from the time men formed permanent settlements upon the land, down, at least, to the rise of modern industrial cities, it has played a main part in the primary, heart-to-heart life of the people. Among our Teutonic forefathers the village community was apparently the chief sphere of sympathy and mutual aid for the commons all through, the "dark" and middle ages, and for many purposes it remains so in rural districts at the present day. In some countries we still find it with all its ancient vitality notably in Russia, where the mir, or self-governing village group, is the main theatre of life, along with the family, for perhaps fifty millions of peasants.

In our own life the intimacy of the neighborhood has been broken up by the growth of an intricate mesh of wider contacts which leaves us strangers to people who live in the same house. And even in the country the same principle is at work, though less obviously, diminishing our economic and spiritual community with our neighbors. How far this change is a healthy development, and how far a disease, is perhaps still uncertain.

Besides these almost universal kinds of primary association, there are many others whose form depends upon the particular state of civilization; the only essential thing, as I have said, being a certain intimacy and fusion of personalities. In our own society, being little bound by place, people easily form clubs, fraternal societies and the like, based on congeniality, which may give rise to real intimacy. Many such relations are formed at school and college, and among men and women brought together in the first instance by their occupations—as workmen in the same trade, or the like. Where there is a little common interest and activity, kindness grows like weeds by the roadside.

But the fact that the family and neighborhood groups are ascendant in the open and plastic time of childhood makes them even now incomparably more influential than all the rest.

Primary groups are primary in the sense that they give the individual his earliest and completest experience of social unity, and also in the sense that they do not change in the same degree as more elaborate relations, but form a comparatively permanent source out of which the latter are ever springing. Of course they are not independent of the larger society, but to some extent reflect its spirit; as the German family and the German school bear somewhat distinctly the print of German militarism. But this, after all, is like the tide setting back into creeks, and does not commonly go very far. Among the German, and still more among the Russian, peasantry are found habits of free coöperation and discussion almost uninfluenced by the character of the state; and it is a familiar and well-supported view that the village commune, self-governing as regards local affairs and habituated to discussion, is a very widespread institution in settled communities, and the continuator of a similar autonomy previously existing in the clan. "It is man who makes monarchies and establishes republics, but the commune seems to come directly from the hand of God."

In our own cities the crowded tenements and the general economic and social confusion have sorely wounded the family and the neighborhood, but it is remarkable, in view of these conditions, what vitality they show; and there is nothing upon which the conscience of the time is more determined than upon restoring them to health.

These groups, then, are springs of life, not only for the individual but for social institutions. They are only in part moulded by special traditions, and, in larger degree, express a universal nature. The religion or government of other civilizations may seem alien to us, but the children or the family group wear the common life, and with them we can always make ourselves at home.

62

PERFORMANCES IN EVERYDAY LIFE*

ERVING GOFFMAN

When an individual plays a part he implicitly requests his observers to take seriously the impression that is fostered before them. They are asked to believe that the character they see actually possesses the attributes he appears to possess, that the task he performs will have the consequences that are implicitly claimed for it, and that, in general, matters are what they appear to be. In line with this, there is the popular view that the individual offers his performance and puts on his show "for the benefit of other people." It will be convenient to begin a consideration of performances by turning the question around and looking at the individual's own belief in the impression of reality that he attempts to engender in those among whom he finds himself.

At one extreme, one finds that the performer can be fully taken in by his own act; he can be sincerely convinced that the impression of reality which he stages is the real reality. When his audience is also convinced in this way about the show he puts on—and this seems to be the typical case—then for the moment at least, only the sociologist or the socially disgruntled will have any doubts about the "realness" of what is presented.

At the other extreme, we find that the performer may not be taken in at all by his own routine. This possibility is understandable, since no one is in quite as good an observational position to see through the act as the person who puts it on. Coupled with this, the performer may be moved to guide the conviction of his audience only as a means to other ends, having no ultimate concern in the conception that they have of him or of the situation. When the individual has no belief in his own act and no ultimate concern with the beliefs of his audience, we may call him cynical, reserving the term "sincere" for individuals who believe in the impression fostered by their own performance. It should be understood that the cynic, with all his professional disinvolvement, may obtain unprofessional pleasures from his masquerade, experiencing a kind of gleeful spiritual aggression from the fact that he can toy at will with something his audience must take seriously.

Front

I have been using the term "performance" to refer to all the activity of an individual which occurs during a period marked by his continuous presence before a particular set of observers and which has some influence on the observers. It will be convenient to label as "front" that part of the individual's performance which regularly functions in a general and fixed fashion to define the situation for those who observe the performance. Front, then, is the expressive equipment of a standard kind intentionally or unwittingly employed by the individual during his performance. For preliminary purposes, it will be convenient to distinguish and label what seem to be the standard parts of front.

First, there is the "setting," involving furniture, décor, physical layout, and other background items which supply the scenery and stage props for the spate of human action played out before, within, or upon it.

If we take the term "setting" to refer to the scenic parts of expressive equipment, one may take the term "personal front" to refer to the other items of expressive equipment, the items that we most intimately identify with the performer himself and that we naturally expect will follow the performer wherever he goes. As part of personal front we may include: insignia of office or rank; clothing; sex, age, and racial characteristics; size and looks; posture; speech patterns; facial expressions; bodily gestures; and the like. Some of these vehicles for conveying signs, such as racial characteristics, are relatively fixed and over a span of time do not vary for the individual from one situation to another. On the other hand, some of these sign vehicles are relatively mobile or transitory, such as facial expression, and can vary during a performance from one moment to the next.

It is sometimes convenient to divide the stimuli which make up personal front into "appearance" and "manner," according to the function performed by the information that these stimuli convey. "Appearance" may be taken to refer to those stimuli which function at the time to tell us of the performer's social statuses. These stimuli also tell us of the individual's temporary ritual state, that is, whether he is engaging in formal social activity, work, or informal recreation, whether or not he is celebrating a new phase in the season cycle or in his life-cycle. "Manner" may be taken to refer to those stimuli which function at the time to warn us of the interaction role the performer will expect to play in the oncoming situation. Thus a haughty, aggressive manner may give the impression that the performer expects to be the one who will initiate the verbal interaction and direct its course. A meek, apologetic manner may give the impression that the performer expects to follow the lead of others, or at least that he can be led to do so.

We often expect, of course, a confirming consistency between appearance and manner; we expect that the differences in social statuses among the interactants will be expressed in some way by congruent differences in the indications that are made of an expected interaction role. This type of coherence of front may be illustrated by the following description of the procession of a mandarin through a Chinese city:

> Coming closely behind . . . the luxurious chair of the mandarin, carried by eight bearers, fills the vacant space in the street. He is mayor of the town, and for all practical purposes the supreme power in it. He is an ideal-looking official, for he is large and massive in appearance, whilst he has that stern and uncompromising look that is supposed to be necessary in any magistrate who would hope to keep his subjects in order. He has a stern and forbidding aspect, as though he were on his way to the execution ground to have some criminal decapitated. This is the kind of air that the mandarins put on when they appear in public. In the course of many years' experience, I have never once seen any of them, from the highest to the lowest, with a smile on his face or a look of sympathy for the people whilst he was being carried officially through the streets.

But, of course, appearance and manner may tend to contradict each other, as when a performer who appears to be of higher estate than his audience acts in a manner that is unexpectedly equalitarian, or intimate, or apologetic, or when a performer dressed in the garments of a high position presents himself to an individual of even higher status.

Idealization

It was suggested earlier that a performance of a routine presents through its front some rather abstract claims upon the audience, claims that are likely to be presented to them during the performance of other routines. This constitutes one way in which a performance is "socialized," molded, and modified to fit into the understanding and expectations of the society in which it is presented. I want to consider here another important aspect of this socialization process—the tendency for performers to offer their observers an impression that is idealized in several different ways.

It is important to note that when an individual offers a performance he typically conceals something more than inappropriate pleasures and economies. Some of these matters for concealment may be suggested here.

First, in addition to secret pleasures and economies, the performer may be engaged in a profitable form of activity that is concealed from his audience and that is incompatible with the view of his activity which he hopes they will obtain. The model here is to be found with hilarious clarity in the cigar-store-bookie-joint, but something of the spirit of these establishments can be found in many places. A surprising number of workers seem to justify their jobs to themselves by the tools that can be stolen, or the food supplies that can be resold, or the traveling that can be enjoyed on company time, or the propaganda that can be distributed, or the contacts that can be made and properly influenced, etc. In all such cases, place of work and official activity come to be a kind of shell which conceals the spirited life of the performer.

Secondly, we find that errors and mistakes are often corrected before the performance takes place, while telltale signs that errors have been made and corrected are themselves concealed. In this way an impression of infallibility, so important in many presentations, is maintained. There is a famous remark that doctors bury their mistakes. Another example is found in a recent dissertation on social interaction in three government offices, which suggests that officers disliked dictating reports to a stenographer because they liked to go back over their reports and correct the flaws before a stenographer, let alone a superior, saw the reports.

Thirdly, in those interactions where the individual presents a product to others, he will tend to show them only the end product, and they will be led into judging him on the basis of something that has been finished, polished, and packaged. In some cases, if very little effort was actually required to complete the object, this fact will be concealed. In other cases, it will be the long, tedious hours of lonely labor that will be hidden. For example, the urbane style affected in some scholarly books can be instructively compared with the feverish drudgery the author may have endured in order to complete the index on time, or with the squabbles he may have had with his publisher in order to increase the size of the first letter of his last name as it appears on the cover of his book.

A fourth discrepancy between appearances and over-all reality may be cited. We find that there are many performances which could not have been given had not tasks been done which were physically unclean, semi-illegal, cruel, and degrading in other ways; but these disturbing facts are seldom expressed during a performance. In Hughes's terms, we tend to conceal from our audience all evidence of "dirty work," whether we do this work in private or allocate it to a servant, to the impersonal market, to a legitimate specialist, or to an illegitimate one.

Closely connected with the notion of dirty work is a fifth discrepancy between appearance and actual activity. If the activity of an individual is to embody several ideal standards, and if a good showing is to be made, it is likely then that some of these standards will be sustained in public by the private sacrifice of some of the others. Often, of course, the performer will sacrifice those standards whose loss can be concealed and will make this sacrifice in order to maintain standards whose inadequate application cannot be concealed. Thus, during times of rationing, if a *restaurateur*, grocer, or butcher is to maintain his customary show of variety, and affirm his customers' image of him, then concealable sources of illegal supply may be his solution. So, too, if a service is judged on the basis of speed and quality, quality is likely to fall before speed because poor quality can be concealed but not slow service. Similarly, if attendants in a mental ward are to maintain order and at the same time not hit patients, and if this combination of standards is difficult to maintain, then the unruly patient may be "necked" with a wet towel and choked into submission in a way that leaves no visible evidence of mistreatment. Absence of mistreatment can be faked, not order:

> Those rules, regulations, and orders which are most easily enforced are those which leave tangible evidence of having been either obeyed or

disobeyed, such as rules pertaining to the cleaning of the ward, locking doors, the use of intoxicating liquors while on duty, the use of restraints, etc.

Here it would be incorrect to be too cynical. Often we find that if the principal ideal aims of an organization are to be achieved, then it will be necessary at times to by-pass momentarily other ideals of the organization, while maintaining the impression that these other ideals are still in force. In such cases, a sacrifice is made not for the most visible ideal but rather for the most legitimately important one. An illustration is provided in a paper on naval bureaucracy:

> This characteristic [group-imposed secrecy] is not entirely attributable, by any means, to the fear of the members that unsavory elements will be brought to light. While this fear always plays some role in keeping off the record the "inside picture" of any bureaucracy, it is to one of the features of the informal structure itself that more importance must be assigned. For the informal structure serves the very significant role of providing a *channel of circumvention* of the formally prescribed rules and methods of procedure. No organization feels that it can afford to publicize those methods (by which certain problems are solved, it is important to note) which are antithetical to the officially sanctioned and, in this case, strongly sanctioned methods dear to the traditions of the group.

Finally, we find performers often foster the impression that they had ideal motives for acquiring the role in which they are performing, that they have ideal qualifications for the role, and that it was not necessary for them to suffer any indignities, insults, and humiliations, or make any tacitly understood "deals," in order to acquire the role. (While this general impression of sacred compatability between the man and his job is perhaps most commonly fostered by members of the higher professions, a similar element is found in many of the lesser ones.) Reinforcing these ideal impressions there is a kind of "rhetoric of training," whereby labor unions, universities, trade associations, and other licensing bodies require practitioners to absorb a mystical range and period of training, in part to maintain a monopoly, but in part to foster the impression that the licensed practitioner is someone who has been reconstituted by his learning experience and is now set apart from other men. Thus, one student suggests about pharmacists that they feel that the four-year university course required for license is "good for the profession" but that some admit that a few months' training is all that is really needed.

Maintenance of Expressive Control

When the audience is known to be secretly skeptical of the reality that is being impressed upon them, we have been ready to appreciate their tendency to pounce on trifling flaws as a sign that the whole show is false; but as students of social life we have been less ready to appreciate that even sympathetic audiences can be momentarily disturbed, shocked, and weakened in their faith by the discovery of a picayune discrepancy in the impressions presented to them. Some of these minor accidents and "unmeant gestures" happen to be so aptly designed to give an impression that contradiets the one fostered by the performer that the audience cannot help but be startled from a proper degree of involvement in the interaction, even though the audience may realize that in the last analysis the discordant event is really meaningless and ought to be completely overlooked. The crucial point is not that the fleeting definition of the situation caused by an unmeant gesture is itself so blameworthy but rather merely that it is *different* from the definition officially projected. This difference forces an acutely embarrassing wedge between the official projection and reality, for it is part of the official projection that it is the only possible one under the circumstances. Perhaps, then, we should not analyze performances in terms of mechanical standards, by which a large gain can offset a small loss, or a large weight a smaller one. Artistic imagery would be more accurate, for it prepares us for the fact that a single note off key can disrupt the tone of an entire performance.

In our society, some unmeant gestures occur in such a wide variety of performances and convey impressions that are in general so incompatible with the ones being fostered that these inopportune events have acquired collective symbolic status. Three rough groupings of these events may be mentioned. First, a performer may accidentally convey incapacity, impropriety, or disrespect by momentarily losing muscular control of himself. He may trip, stumble, fall; he may belch, yawn, make a slip of the tongue, scratch himself, or be flatulent; he may accidentally impinge upon the body of another participant. Secondly, the performer may act in such a way as to give the impression that he is too much or too little concerned with the interaction. He may stutter, forget his lines, appear nervous, or guilty, or self-conscious; he may give way to inappropriate outbursts of laughter, anger, or other kinds of affect which momentarily incapacitate him as an interactant; he may show too much serious involvement and interest, or too little. Thirdly, the performer may allow his presentation to suffer from inadequate dramaturgical direction. The setting may not have been put in order, or may have become readied for the wrong performance, or may become deranged during the performance; unforeseen contingencies may cause improper timing of the performer's arrival or departure or may cause embarrassing lulls to occur during the interaction.

Misrepresentation

Sometimes when we ask whether a fostered impression is true or false we really mean to ask whether or not the performer is authorized to give the performance in question, and are not primarily concerned with the actual performance itself. When we discover that someone with whom we have dealings is an impostor and out-and-out fraud, we are discovering that he did not have the right to play the part he played, that he was not an accredited incumbent of the relevant status. We assume that the impostor's performance, in addition to the fact that it misrepresents him, will be at fault in other ways, but often his masquerade is discovered before we can detect any other difference between the false performance and the legitimate one which it simulates. Paradoxically, the more closely the impostor's performance approximates to the real thing, the more intensely we may be threatened, for a competent performance by someone who proves to be an impostor may weaken in our minds the moral connection between legitimate authorization to play a part and the capacity to play it. (Skilled mimics, who admit all along that their intentions are unserious, seem to provide one way in which we can "work through" some of these anxieties.)

Further, while we may take a harsh view of performers such as confidence men who knowingly misrepresent every fact about their lives, we may have some sympathy for those who have but one fatal flaw and who attempt to conceal the fact that they are, for example, ex-convicts, deflowered, epileptic, or racially impure, instead of admitting their fault and making an honorable attempt to live it down. Also, we distinguish between impersonation of a specific, concrete individual, which we usually feel is quite inexcusable, and impersonation of category membership, which we may feel less strongly about. So, too, we often feel differently about those who misrepresent themselves to forward what they feel are the just claims of a collectivity, or those who misrepresent themselves accidentally or for a lark, than about those who misrepresent themselves for private psychological or material gain.

Perhaps most important of all, we must note that a false impression maintained by an individual in any one of his routines may be a threat to the whole relationship or role of which the routine is only one part, for a discreditable disclosure in one area of an individual's activity will throw doubt on the many areas of activity in which he may have nothing to conceal. Similarly, if the individual has only one thing to conceal during a performance, and even if the likelihood of disclosure occurs only at a particular turn or phase in, the performance, the performer's anxiety may well extend to the whole performance.

In previous sections of this chapter some general characteristic of performance were suggested: activity oriented towards work-tasks tends to be converted into activity oriented towards communication; the front behind which the routine is presented is also likely to be suitable for other, somewhat different routines and so is likely not to fit completely any particular routine; sufficient self-control is exerted so as to maintain a working consensus; an idealized impression is offered by accentuating certain facts and concealing others; expressive coherence is maintained by the performer taking more care to guard against minor disharmonies than the stated purpose of the performance might lead the audience to think was warranted. All of these general characteristics of performances can be seen as interaction constraints which play upon the individual and transform his activities into performances. Instead of merely doing his task and giving vent to his feelings, he will express the doing of his task and acceptably convey his feelings. In general, then, the representation of an activity will vary in some degree from the activity itself and therefore inevitably misrepresent it. And since the individual will be required to rely on signs in order to construct a representation of his activity, the image he constructs, however faithful to the facts, will be subject to all the disruptions that impressions are subject to.

While we could retain the common-sense notion that fostered appearances can be discredited by a discrepant reality, there is often no reason for claiming that the facts discrepant with the fostered impression are any more the real reality than is the fostered reality they embarrass. A cynical view of everyday performances can be as one-sided as the one that is sponsored by the performer. For many sociological issues it may not even be necessary to decide which is the more real, the fostered impression or the one the performer attempts to prevent the audience from receiving. The crucial sociological consideration, for this report at least, is merely that impressions fostered in everyday performances are subject to disruption. We will want to know what kind of impression of reality can shatter the fostered impression of reality, and what reality really is can be left to other students. We will want to ask, "What are the ways in which a given impression can be discredited?" and this is not quite the same as asking, "What are the ways in which the given impression is false?"

We come back, then, to a realization that while the performance offered by impostors and liars is quite flagrantly false and differs in this respect from ordinary performances, both are similar in the care their performers must exert in order to maintain the impression that is fostered. Thus, for example, we know that the formal code of British civil servants and of American baseball umpires obliges them not only to desist from making improper "deals" but also to desist from innocent action which might possibly give the (wrong) impression that they are making deals. Whether an honest performer wishes to convey the truth or whether a dishonest performer wishes to convey a falsehood, both must take care to enliven their performances with appropriate expressions, exclude from their performances expressions that might discredit the impression being fostered, and take care lest the audience impute unintended meanings. Because of these shared dramatic contingencies, we can profitably study performances that are quite false in order to learn about ones that are quite honest.

Reality and Contrivance

In our own Anglo-American culture there seems to be two common-sense models according to which we formulate our conceptions of behavior: the real, sincere, or honest performance; and the false one that thorough fabricators assemble for us, whether meant to be taken unseriously, as in the work of stage actors, or seriously, as in the work of confidence men. We tend to see real performances as something not purposely put together at all, being an unintentional product of the individual's unself-conscious response to the facts in his situation. And contrived performances we tend to see as something painstakingly pasted together, one false item on another, since there is no reality to which the items of behavior could be a direct response. It will be necessary to see now that these dichotomous conceptions are by way of being the ideology of honest performers, providing strength to the show they put on, but a poor analysis of it.

First, let it be said that there are many individuals who sincerely believe that the definition of the situation they habitually project is the real reality. In this report I do not mean to question their proportion in the population but rather the structural relation of their sincerity to the performances they offer. If a performance is to come off, the witnesses by and large must be able to believe that the performers are sincere. This is the structural place of sincerity in the drama of events. Performers may be sincere—or be insincere but sincerely convinced of their own sincerity—but this land of affection for one's part is not necessary for its convincing performance. There are not many French cooks who are really Russian spies, and perhaps there are not many women who play the part of wife to one man and mistress to another but these duplicities do occur, often being sustained successfully for long periods of time. This suggests that while persons usually are what they appear to be, such appearances could still have been managed. There is, then, a statistical relation between appearances and reality, not an intrinsic or necessary one. In fact, given the unanticipated threats that play upon a performance, and given the need (later to be discussed) to maintain solidarity with one's fellow performers and some distance from the witnesses, we find that a rigid incapacity to depart from one's inward view of reality may at times endanger one's performance. Some performances are carried off successfully with complete dishonesty, others with complete honesty; but for performances in general neither of these extremes is essential and neither, perhaps, is dramaturgically advisable.

The implication here is that an honest, sincere, serious performance is less firmly connected with the solid world than one might first assume. And this implication will be strengthened if we look again at the distance usually placed between quite honest performances and quite contrived ones. In this connection take, for example, the remarkable phenomenon of stage acting. It does take deep skill, long training, and psychological capacity to become a good stage actor. But this fact should not blind us to another one: that almost anyone can quickly learn a script well enough to give a charitable audience some sense of realness in what is being contrived before them. And it seems this is so because ordinary social intercourse is itself put together as a scene is put together, by the exchange of dramatically inflated actions, counteractions, and terminating replies. Scripts even in the hands of unpracticed players can come to life because life itself is a dramatically enacted thing. All the world is not, of course, a stage, but the crucial ways in which it isn't are not easy to specify.

63

MANAGING STIGMA*

ERVING GOFFMAN

The Greeks, who were apparently strong on visual aids, originated the term *stigma* to refer to bodily signs designed to expose something unusual and bad about the moral status of the signifier. The signs were cut or burnt into the body and advertised that the bearer was a slave, a criminal, or a traitor—a blemished person, ritually polluted, to be avoided, especially in public places. Later, in Christian times, two layers of metaphor were added to the term: the first referred to bodily signs of holy grace that took the form of eruptive blossoms on the skin; the second, a medical allusion to this religious allusion, referred to bodily signs of physical disorder. Today the term is widely used in something like the original literal sense, but is applied more to the disgrace itself than to the bodily evidence of it. Furthermore, shifts have occurred in the kinds of disgrace that arouse concern. Students, however, have made little effort to describe the structural preconditions of stigma, or even to provide a definition of the concept itself. It seems necessary, therefore, to try at the beginning to sketch in some very general assumptions and definitions.

PRELIMINARY CONCEPTIONS

Society establishes the means of categorizing persons and the complement of attributes felt to be ordinary and natural for members of each of these categories. Social settings establish the categories of persons likely to be encountered there. The routines of social intercourse in established settings allow us to deal with anticipated others without special attention or thought. When a stranger comes into our presence, then, first appearances are likely to enable us to anticipate his category and attributes, his "social identity"—to use a term that is better than "social status" because personal attributes such as "honesty" are involved, as well as structural ones, like "occupation."

We lean on these anticipations that we have, transforming them into normative expectations, into righteously presented demands.

Typically, we do not become aware that we have made these demands or aware of what they are until an active question arises as to whether or not they will be fulfilled. It is then that we are likely to realize that all along we had been making certain assumptions as to what the individual before us ought to be. Thus, the demands we make might better be called demands made "in effect," and the character we impute to the individual might better be seen as an imputation made in potential retrospect—a characterization "in effect," a *virtual social identity.* The category and attributes he could in fact be proved to possess will be called his *actual social identity.*

---

*Reprinted with the permission of Simon & Schuster, Inc. from *Stigma: Notes on the Management of Spoiled Identity* by Erving Goffman.

While the stranger is present before us, evidence can arise of his possessing an attribute that makes him different from others in the category of persons available for him to be, and of a less desirable kind—in the extreme, a person who is quite thoroughly bad, or dangerous, or weak. He is thus reduced in our minds from a whole and usual person to a tainted, discounted one. Such an attribute is a stigma, especially when its discrediting effect is very extensive; sometimes it is also called a failing, a shortcoming, a handicap. It constitutes a special discrepancy between virtual and actual social identity. Note that there are other types of discrepancy between virtual and actual social identity, for example the kind that causes us to reclassify an individual from one socially anticipated category to a different but equally well-anticipated one, and the kind that causes us to alter our estimation of the individual upward. Note, too, that not all undesirable attributes are at issue, but only those which are incongruous with our stereotype of what a given type of individual should be.

The term stigma, then, will be used to refer to an attribute that is deeply discrediting, but it should be seen that a language of relationships, not attributes, is really needed. An attribute that stigmatizes one type of possessor can confirm the usualness of another, and therefore is neither creditable nor discreditable as a thing in itself. For example, some jobs in America cause holders without the expected college education to conceal this fact; other jobs, however, can lead the few of their holders who have a higher education to keep this a secret, lest they be marked as failures and outsiders. Similarly, a middle class boy may feel no compunction in being seen going to the library; a professional criminal, however, writes:

> I can remember before now on more than one occasion, for instance, going into a public library near where I was living, and looking over my shoulder a couple of times before I actually went in just to make sure no one who knew me was standing about and seeing me do it.

So, too, an individual who desires to fight for his country may conceal a physical defect, lest his claimed physical status be discredited; later, the same individual, embittered and trying to get out of the army, may succeed in gaining admission to the army hospital, where he would be discredited if discovered in not really having an acute sickness. A stigma, then, is really a special kind of relationship between attribute and stereotype, although I don't propose to continue to say so, in part because there are important attributes that almost everywhere in our society are discrediting.

The term stigma and its synonyms conceal a double perspective: does the stigmatized individual assume his differentness is known about already or is evident on the spot, or does he assume it is neither known about by those present nor immediately perceivable by them? In the first case one deals with the plight of the *discredited,* in the second with that of the *discreditable.* This is an important difference, even though a particular stigmatized individual is likely to have experience with both situations. I will begin with the situation of the discredited and move on to the discreditable but not always separate the two.

Three grossly different types of stigma may be mentioned. First there are abominations of the body—the various physical deformities. Next there are blemishes of individual character perceived as weak will, domineering or unnatural passions, treacherous and rigid beliefs, and dishonesty, these being inferred from a known record of, for example, mental disorder, imprisonment, addiction, alcoholism, homosexuality, unemployment, suicidal attempts, and radical political behavior. Finally there are the tribal stigma of race, nation, and religion, these being stigma that can be transmitted through lineages and equally contaminate all members of a family. In all of these various instances of stigma, however, including those the Greeks had in mind, the same sociological features are found: an individual who might have been received easily in ordinary social intercourse possesses a trait that can obtrude itself upon attention and turn those of us whom he meets away from him, breaking the claim that his other attributes have on us. He possesses a stigma, an undesired differentness from what we had anticipated. We and those who do not depart negatively from the particular expectations at issue I shall call the *normals.*

When normals and stigmatized do in fact enter one another's immediate presence, especially when they there attempt to sustain a joint conversational encounter, there occurs one of the primal scenes of sociology; for, in many cases, these moments will be the ones when the causes and effects of stigma must be directly confronted by both sides.

The stigmatized individual may find that he feels unsure of how we normals will identify him and receive him. An illustration may be cited from a student of physical disability:

> Uncertainty of status for the disabled person obtains over a wide range of social interactions in addition to that of employment. The blind, the ill, the deaf, the crippled can never be sure what the attitude of a new acquaintance will be, whether it will be rejective or accepting, until the contact has been made. This is exactly the position of the adolescent, the light-skinned Negro, the second generation immigrant, the socially mobile person and the woman who has entered a predominantly masculine occupation.

This uncertainty arises not merely from the stigmatized individual's not knowing which of several categories he will be placed in, but also, where the placement is favorable, from his knowing that in their hearts the others may be defining him in terms of his stigma:

> And I always feel this with straight people—that whenever they're being nice to me, pleasant to me, all the time really, underneath they're only assessing me as a criminal and nothing else. It's too late for me to be any different now to what I am, but I still feel this keenly, that that's their only approach, and they're quite incapable of accepting me as anything else.

Thus in the stigmatized arises the sense of not knowing what the others present are "really" thinking about him.

Further, during mixed contacts, the stigmatized individual is likely to feel that he is "on," having to be self-conscious and calculating about the impression he is making, to a degree and in areas of conduct which he assumes others are not.

I am suggesting, then, that the stigmatized individual—at least the "visibly" stigmatized one—will have special reasons for feeling that mixed social situations make for anxious unanchored interaction. But if this is so, then it is to be suspected that we normals will find these situations shaky too. We will feel that the stigmatized individual is either too aggressive or too shamefaced, and in either case too ready to read unintended meanings into our actions. We ourselves may feel that if we show direct sympathetic concern for his condition, we may be overstepping ourselves; and yet if we actually forget that he has a failing we are likely to make impossible demands of him or unthinkingly slight his fellow-sufferers. Each potential source of discomfort for him when we are with him can become something we sense he is aware of, aware that we are aware of, and even aware of our state of awareness about his awareness; the stage is then set for the infinite regress of mutual consideration that Meadian social psychology tells us how to begin but not how to terminate.

Given what both the stigmatized and we normals introduce into mixed social situations, it is understandable that all will not go smoothly. We are likely to attempt to carry on as though in fact he wholly fitted one of the types of person naturally available to us in the situation, whether this means treating him as someone better than we feel he might be or someone worse than we feel he probably is. If neither of these tacks is possible, then we may try to act as if he were a "non-person," and not present at all as someone of whom ritual notice is to be taken. He, in turn, is likely to go along with these strategies, at least initially.

In consequence, attention is furtively withdrawn from its obligatory targets, and self-consciousness and "other-consciousness" occurs, expressed in the pathology of interaction—uneasiness. As described in the case of the physically handicapped:

> Whether the handicap is overtly and tactlessly responded to as such or, as is more commonly the case, no explicit reference is made to it, the underlying condition of heightened, narrowed, awareness causes the interaction to be articulated too exclusively in terms of it.This, as my informants described it, is usually accompanied by one or more of the familiar signs of discomfort and stickiness: the guarded references, the common everyday words suddenly made taboo, the fixed stare elsewhere, the artificial levity, the compulsive loquaciousness, the awkward solemnity.

In social situations with an individual known or perceived to have a stigma, we are likely, then, to employ categorizations that do not fit, and we and he are likely to experience uneasiness. Of course, there is often significant movement from this starting point. And since the stigmatized person is likely to be more often faced with these situations than are we, he is likely to become the more adept at managing them.

The Discredited and the Discreditable

When there is a discrepancy between an individual's actual social identity and his virtual one, it is possible for this fact to be known to us before we normals contact him, or to be quite evident when he presents himself before us. He is a discredited person, and it is mainly he I have been dealing with until now. As suggested, we are likely to give no open recognition to what is discrediting of him, and while this work of careful disattention is being done, the situation can become tense, uncertain, and ambiguous for all participants, especially the stigmatized one.

The cooperation of a stigmatized person with normals in acting as if his known differentness were irrelevant and not attended to is one main possibility in the life of such a person. However, when his differentness is not immediately apparent, and is not known beforehand (or at least known by him to be known to the others), when in fact his is a discreditable, not a discredited, person, then the second main possibility in his life is to be found. The issue is not that of managing tension generated during social contacts, but rather that of managing information about his failing. To display or not to display; to tell or not to tell; to let on or not to let on; to lie or not to lie; and in each case, to whom, how, when, and where. For example, while the mental patient is in the hospital, and when he is with adult members of his own family, he is faced with being treated tactfully as if he were sane when there is known to be some doubt, even though he may not have any; or he is treated as insane, when he knows this is not just. But for the ex-mental patient the problem can be quite different; it is not that he must face prejudice against himself, but rather that he must face unwitting acceptance of himself by individuals who are prejudiced against persons of the kind he can be revealed to be. Wherever he goes his behavior will falsely confirm for the other that they are in the company of what in effect they demand but may discover they haven't obtained, namely, a mentally untainted person like themselves. By intention or in effect the ex-mental patient conceals information about his real social identity, receiving and accepting treatment based on false suppositions concerning himself. It is this second general issue, the management of undisclosed discrediting information about self, that I am focusing on in these notes, in brief, "passing." The concealment of creditable facts—reverse passing—of course occurs, but is not relevant here.

Passing

It is apparent that if a stigmatizing affliction possessed by an individual is known to no one, including himself, as in the case, say, of someone with undiagnosed leprosy or unrecognized *petit-mal* seizures, then the sociologist has no interest in it, except as a control device for learning about the "primary" or objective implications of the stigma. Where the stigma is nicely invisible and known only to the person who possesses it, who tells no one, then here again is a matter of minor concern in the study of passing. The extent to which either of these two possibilities exists is of course hard to assess.

In a similar way, it should be clear that if a stigma were always immediately apparent to any and all persons with whom an individual had contact, then one's interest would be limited, too, although there would be some interest in the question of how much an individual can cut himself off from contact and still be allowed to function freely in society, in the question of tact and its breakdown, and in the question of self-derogation.

It is apparent, however, that these two extremes, where no one knows about the stigma and where everyone knows, fail to cover a great range of cases. First, there are important stigmas, such as the ones that prostitutes, thieves, homosexuals, beggars, and drug addicts have, which require the individual to be carefully secret about his failing to one class of persons, the police, while systematically exposing himself to other classes of persons, namely, clients, fellow-members, connections, fences, and the like. Thus, no matter what role tramps assume in the presence of the police, they often have to declare themselves to housewives in order to obtain a free meal, and may even have to expose their status to passers-by because of being served on back porches what they understandably call "exhibition meals." Secondly, even where an individual could keep an unapparent stigma secret, he will find that intimate relations with others, ratified in our society by mutual confession of invisible failings, cause him either to admit his situation to the intimate or to feel guilty for not doing so. In any case, nearly all matters which are very secret are still known to someone, and hence cast a shadow.

Similarly, there are many cases where it appears that an individual's stigma will always be apparent, but where this proves to be not quite the case; for on examination one finds that the individual will occasionally be in a position to elect to conceal crucial information about himself. For example, while a lame boy may seem always to present himself as such, strangers can momentarily assume that he has been in a temporarily incapacitating accident, just as a blind person led into a dark cab by a friend may find for a moment that sight has been imputed to her, or a blind man wearing dark glasses sitting in a dark bar may be taken as a seeing person by a newcomer, or a double hand-amputee with hooks watching a movie may cause a sexually forward female sitting next to him to scream in terror over what her hand has suddenly found. Similarly, black skinned Negroes who have never passed publicly may nonetheless find themselves, in writing letters or making telephone calls, projecting an image of self that is subject to later discrediting.

Given these several possibilities that fall between the extremes of complete secrecy on one hand and complete information on the other, it would seem that the problems people face who make a concerted and well-organized effort to pass are problems that wide ranges of persons face at some time or other. Because of the great rewards in being considered normal, almost all persons who are in a position to pass will do so on some occasion by intent. Further, the individual's stigma may relate to matters which cannot be appropriately divulged to strangers. An ex-convict, for example, can only disclose his stigma widely by improperly presuming on mere acquaintances, orally disclosing to them personal facts about himself which are more personal than the relationship really warrants. A conflict between candor and seemliness will often be resolved in favor of the latter. Finally, when the stigma relates to parts of the body that the normally qualified must themselves conceal in public places, then passing is inevitable, whether desired or not. A woman who has had a mastectomy or a Norwegian male sex offender who has been penalized by castration are forced to present themselves falsely in almost all situations, having to conceal their unconventional secrets because of everyone's having to conceal the conventional ones.

When an individual in effect or by intent passes, it is possible for a discrediting to occur because of what becomes apparent about him, apparent even to those who socially identify him solely on the basis of what is available to any stranger in the social situation. (Thus arises one variety of what is called "an embarrassing incident.") But this kind of threat to virtual social identity is certainly not the only kind. Apart from the fact that the individual's current actions can discredit his current pretensions, a basic contingency in passing is that he will be discovered by those who can personally identify him and who include in their biographical record of him unapparent facts that are incompatible with present claims. It is then, incidentally, that personal identification bears strongly on social identity.

Techniques of Information Control

Some of the common techniques the individual with a secret defect employs in managing crucial information about himself can now be considered.

Obviously, one strategy is to conceal or obliterate signs that have come to be stigma symbols. Name-changing is a well-known example. Drug addicts provide another example:

> [Re a New Orleans anti-drug drive:] The cops began stopping addicts on the street and examining their arms for needle marks. If they found marks, they pressured the addict to sign a statement admitting his condition so he could be charged under the "drug addicts law." The addicts were promised a suspended sentence if they would plead guilty and get the new law started. Addicts ransacked their persons looking for veins to shoot in outside the arm area. If the law could find no marks on a man they usually let him go. If they found marks they would hold him for seventy-two hours and try to make him sign a statement.

It should be noted that since the physical equipment employed to mitigate the "primary" impairment of some handicaps understandably becomes a stigma symbol, there will be a desire to reject using it. An example is the individual with declining eye sight who avoids wearing bifocal glasses because these might suggest old age. But of course this strategy can interfere with compensatory measures. Hence the making of this corrective equipment invisible will have a double function. The hard of hearing provide an illustration of the using of these unapparent correctives:

> Aunt Mary [a hard of hearing relative] knew all about early sound receptors, innumerable variations of the ear trumpet. She had pictures showing how such receptors had been built into hats, ornamental combs, canteens, walking sticks; hidden in arm chairs, in flower vases for the dining-room table; even hidden in men's beards.

A more current illustration is "inviso-blended lenses"—bifocals which do not show a "dividing line."

The concealment of stigma symbols sometimes occurs along with a related process, the use of disidentifiers, as can be illustrated from the practices of James Berry, England's first fully professionalized hangman:

> It is doubtful whether violence on Berry was ever really planned, but his reception in the streets was such that he took good care whenever possible to avoid being recognized. He told one interviewer that on a number of occasions when travelling to Ireland he concealed his rope and straps about his person so that he was not given away by the Gladstone bag, which was almost as much a mark of his trade as the little black bag was of the Victorian doctor. His sense of isolation and being disliked by everyone he met probably explained the extraordinary episode when his wife and small son accompanied him to Ireland for an execution, although the explanation he offered was that it was to conceal his identity, since—he rightly guessed—no one would suppose that a man walking along holding the hand of a ten-year-old boy would be the executioner on his way to hang a murderer.

One deals here with what espionage literature calls a "cover," and with what another literature describes as a conjugal service possible when a male homosexual and a female homosexual suppress their inclinations and marry one another.

When the individual's stigma is established in him during his stay in an institution, and when the institution retains a discrediting hold upon him for a period after his release, one may expect a special cycle of passing. For example, in one mental hospital it was found that patients re-entering the community often planned to pass in some degree. Patients who were forced to rely on the rehabilitation officer, the social service worker, or the employment agencies for a job, often discussed among their fellows the contingencies they faced and the standard strategy for dealing with them. For the first job, official entree would necessitate the employer knowing about their stigma, and perhaps the personnel officer, but always the lower levels of the organization and workmates could be kept in some ignorance. As suggested, it was felt that this could involve a certain amount of insecurity because it would not be known for sure who "knew" and who didn't, and how long-lasting would be the ignorance of those who didn't know. Patients expressed the feeling that after staying in a placement job of this kind for six months, long enough to save some money and get loose from hospital agencies, they would quit work and, on the basis of the six-month work record, get a job someplace else, this time trusting that everyone at work could be kept ignorant of the stay in a mental hospital.

Another strategy of those who pass is to present the signs of their stigmatized failing as signs of another attribute, one that is less significantly a stigma. Mental defectives, for example, apparently sometimes try to pass as mental patients, the latter being the lesser of the two social evils. Similarly, a hard of hearing person may intentionally style her conduct to give others the impression that she is a daydreamer, an absent-minded person, an indifferent, easily bored person—even someone who is feeling faint, or snores and therefore is unable to answer quiet questions since she is obviously asleep. These character traits account for failure to hear without requiring the imputation of deafness.

Covering

A sharp distinction has been drawn between the situation of the discredited with tension to manage and the situation of the discreditable with information to manage. The stigmatized employ an adaptive technique, however, which requires the student to bring together these two possibilities. The difference between visibility and obtrusiveness is involved.

It is a fact that persons who are ready to admit possession of a stigma (in many cases because it is known about or immediately apparent) may nonetheless make a great effort to keep the stigma from looming large. The individual's object is to reduce tension, that is, to make it easier for himself and the others to withdraw covert attention from the stigma, and to sustain spontaneous involvement in the official content of the interaction. However, the means employed for this task are quite similar to those employed in passing—and in some cases identical, since what will conceal a stigma from unknowing persons may also ease matters for those in the know. It is thus that a girl who gets around best on her wooden peg employs crutches or an artful but patently artificial limb when in company. This process will be referred to as *covering.* Many of those who rarely try to pass, routinely try to cover.

One type of covering involves the individual in a concern over the standards incidentally associated with his stigma. Thus the blind, who sometimes have a facial disfigurement in the region of the eyes, distinguish among themselves according to whether this is the case or not. Dark glasses sometimes worn to give voluntary evidence of blindness may at the same time be worn to cover evidence of defacement—a case of revealing unsightedness while concealing unsightliness:

> The blind, in all conscience, have enough advertisement of their condition without adding a cosmetic factor to it. I can think of nothing that would add so much to the tragedy of a blind man's position as the feeling that, in the fight to regain his vision, he had lost not only the fight but the wholesomeness of his appearance as well.

Similarly, since blindness can lead to the appearance of clumsiness, there may occur a special effort to re-learn motor propriety, an "ease and grace and adeptness at all those motions which the sighted world looks upon as 'normal.'"

A related type of covering involves an effort to restrict the display of those failings most centrally identified with the stigma. For example, a near-blind person who knows that the persons present know about his differentness may yet hesitate to read, because to do this he would have to bring the book up to a few inches of his eyes, and this he may feel expresses too glaringly the qualities of blindness. This type of covering, it should be noted, is an important aspect of the "assimilative" techniques employed by members of minority ethnic groups; the intent behind devices such as change in name and change in nose shape is not solely to pass, but also to restrict the way in which a known-about attribute obtrudes itself into the center of attention, for obtrusiveness increases the difficulty of maintaining easeful inattention regarding the stigma.

The most interesting expression of covering, perhaps, is that associated with the organization of social situations. As already suggested, anything which interferes directly with the etiquette and mechanics of communication obtrudes itself constantly into the interaction and is difficult to disattend genuinely. Hence individuals with a stigma, especially those with a physical handicap, may have to learn about the structure of interaction in order to learn about the lines along which they must reconstitute their conduct if they are to minimize the obtrusiveness of their stigma. From their efforts, then, one can learn about features of interaction that might otherwise be too much taken for granted to be noted.

For example, the hard of hearing learn to talk with the degree of loudness that listeners feel is appropriate for the situation, and also to be ready to deal with those junctures during interaction that specifically require good hearing if the proprieties are to be maintained:

> Frances figured out elaborate techniques to cope with "dinner lulls," intermissions at concerts, football game, dances, and so on, in order to protect her secret. But they served only to make her more uncertain, and in turn more cautious, and in turn more uncertain. Thus, Frances had it down pat that at a dinner party she should (1) sit next to someone with a strong voice; (2) choke, cough, or get hiccups, if someone asked her a direct question; (3) take hold of the conversation herself, ask someone to tell a story she had already heard, ask questions the answers to which she already knew.

Similarly, the blind sometimes learn to look directly at the speaker even though this looking accomplishes no seeing, for it prevents the blind from staring off into space or hanging the head or otherwise unknowingly violating the code regarding attention cues through which spoken interaction is organized.

64

The Meaningfully Produced Social World*

Alfred Schütz

I speak of another person as within reach of my direct experience when he shares with me a community of space and a community of time. He shares a community of space with me when he is present in person and I am aware of him as such, and, moreover, when I am aware of him as this person *himself*, this *particular* individual, and of his body as the field upon which play the symptoms of his inner consciousness. He shares a community of time with me when his experience is flowing side by side with mine, when I can at any moment look over and grasp his thoughts as they come into being, in other words, when we are growing older together. Persons thus in reach of each other's direct experience I speak of as being in the "face-to-face" situation. The face-to-face situation presupposes, then, an actual simultaneity with each other of two separate streams of consciousness.

This spatial and temporal immediacy is essential to the face-to-face situation. All acts of Other-orientation and of affecting-the-other, and therefore all orientations and relationships within the face-to-face situation, derive their own specific flavor and style from this immediacy.

Let us first look at the way in which the face-to-face situation is constituted from the point of view of a participant in that situation. In order to become aware of such a situation, the participant must become intentionally conscious of the person confronting him. He must assume a face-to-face Other-orientation toward the partner. We shall term this attitude "Thou-orientation," and shall now proceed to describe its main features.

First of all, the Thou-orientation is the pure mode in which I am aware of another human being as a person. I am already Thou-oriented from the moment that I recognize an entity which I directly experience as a fellow man (as a Thou), attributing life and consciousness to him. However, we must be quite clear that we are not here dealing with a conscious *judgment*. This is a prepredicative experience in which I become aware of a fellow human being as a *person*. The Thou-orientation can thus be defined as the intentionality of those Acts whereby the Ego grasps the existence of the other person in the mode of the original self. Every such external experience in the mode of the original self presupposes the actual presence of the other person and my perception of him as there.

Now, we wish to emphasize that it is precisely the being there (*Dasein*) of the Other toward which the Thou-orientation is directed, not necessarily the Other's specific characteristics. The concept of the Thou-orientation does not imply awareness of what is going on in the Other's mind. In its "pure" form the Thou-orientation consists merely of being intentionally directed toward the pure being-there of another alive and conscious human being. To be sure, the "pure" Thou-orientation is a formal concept, an intellectual construct, or, in Husserl's terminology, an "ideal limit." In real life we never experience the "pure existence" of others; instead we meet real people with their own personal characteristics and traits. The Thou-orientation as it occurs in everyday life is therefore not the "pure" Thou-orientation but the latter *actualized and rendered determinate* to some degree or other.

Now the fact that I look upon you as a fellow man does not mean that I am also a fellow man for you, unless you are aware of me. And, of course, it is quite possible that you may not be paying any attention to me at all. The Thou-orientation can, therefore, be either one-sided or reciprocal. It is one-sided if only one of us notices the presence of the other. It is reciprocal if we are mutually aware of each other, that is, if each of us is Thou-oriented toward the other. In this way there is constituted out of the Thou-orientation the face-to-face relationship (or directly experienced social relationship). The face-to-face relationship in which the partners are aware of each other and sympathetically participate in each other's lives for however short a time we shall call the "pure We-relationship." But the "pure We-relationship" is likewise only a limiting concept. The directly experienced social relationship of real life is the pure We-relationship concretized and actualized to a greater or lesser degree and filled with content.

To explain how our experiences of the Thou are rooted in the We-relationship, let us take conversation as an example. Suppose you are speaking to me and I am understanding what you are saying. As we have already seen, there are two senses of this understanding. First of all I grasp the "objective meaning" of your words, the meaning which they would have had, had they been spoken by you or anyone else. But second, of course, there is the subjective meaning, namely, what is going on in your mind as you speak. In order to get to your subjective meaning, I must picture to myself your stream of consciousness as flowing side by side with my own. Within this picture I must interpret and construct your intentional Acts as you choose your words. To the extent that you and I can mutually experience this simultaneity, growing older together for a time, to the extent that we can live in it together, to that extent we can live in each other's subjective contexts of meaning. However, our ability to apprehend each other's subjective contexts of meaning should not be confused with the We-relationship itself. For I get to your subjective meaning in the first place only by starting out with your spoken words as given and then by asking how you came to use those words. But this question of mine would make no sense if I did not already assume an actual or at least potential We-relationship between us. For it is only within the We-relationship that I can concretely experience you at a particular moment of your life. To put the point in terms of a formula: I can live in your subjective meaning-contexts only to the extent that I directly experience you within an actualized content-filled We-relationship.

The pure We-relationship is merely the reciprocal form of the pure Thou-orientation, that is, the pure awareness of the *presence* of another person. His presence, it should be emphasized, not his specific traits. The pure We-relationship involves our awareness of each other's presence and also the knowledge of each that the other is aware of him. But, if we are to have a social relationship, we must go beyond this. What is required is that the Other-orientation of each partner become colored by a specific knowledge of the specific manner in which he is being regarded by the other partner. This in turn is possible only within directly experienced social reality. Only here do our glances actually meet; only here can one actually note how the other is looking at him.

But one cannot become aware of this basic connection between the pure We-relationship and the face-to-face relationship while still a participant in the We-relationship. *One must step out of it and examine it.* The person who is still a participant in the We-relationship does not experience it in its pure form, namely, as an awareness that the other person is there. Instead, he simply lives within the We-relationship in the fullness of its concrete content. In other words, the pure We-relationship is a mere limiting concept which one uses in the attempt to get a theoretical grasp of the face-to-face situation. But there are no specific concrete experiences which correspond to it. For the concrete experiences which do occur within the We-relationship in real life grasp their object—the We—as something unique and unrepeatable. And they do this in *one* undivided intentional Act.

Concrete We-relationships exhibit many differences among themselves. The partner, for instance, may be experienced with different degrees of immediacy, different degrees of intensity, or different degrees of intimacy. Or he may be experienced from different points of view. He may appear within the center of attention or at its periphery.

These distinctions apply equally to orientation relationships and to social interactions, determining in each of them the directness with which the partners "know" each other. Compare, for instance, the knowledge two people have of each other in conversation with the knowledge they have of each other in sexual intercourse. What different degrees of intimacy occur here, what different levels of consciousness are involved! Not only do the partners experience the We more deeply in the one case than in the other, but each experiences himself more deeply and his partner more deeply. It is not only the *object*, therefore, that is experienced with greater or lesser directness; it is the *relationship* itself, the being turned toward the object, the relatedness.

These are only two *types* of relationship. But now consider the different ways in which they can actually take place! The conversation, for instance, can be animated or offhand, eager or casual, serious or light, superficial or quite personal.

The fact that we may experience others with such different degrees of directness is very important. It is, as a matter of fact, the key to understanding the transition from the direct experience of others to the indirect which is characteristic of the world of mere contemporaries. We shall be coming to this transition very shortly, but meanwhile let us continue our examination of direct social experience by describing the different types of face-to-face relationship.

First of all, let us remember that in the face-to-face situation I literally see my partner in front of me. As I watch his face and his gestures and listen to the tone of his voice, I become aware of much more than what he is deliberately trying to communicate to me. My observations keep pace with each moment of his stream of consciousness as it transpires. The result is that I am incomparably better attuned to him than I am to myself. I may indeed be more aware of my own past (to the extent that the latter can he captured in retrospect) than I am of my partner's. Yet I have never been face to face with myself as I am with him now; hence I have never caught myself in the act of actually living through an experience.

To this encounter with the other person I bring a whole stock of previously constituted knowledge. This includes both general knowledge of what another person is as such and any specific knowledge I may have of the person in question. It includes knowledge of other people's interpretive schemes, their habits, and their language. It includes knowledge of the taken-for-granted in-order-to and because-motives of others as such and of this person in particular. And when I am face to face with someone, my knowledge of him is increasing from moment to moment. My ideas of him undergo continuous revision as the concrete experience unfolds. For no direct social relationship is one isolated intentional Act. Rather it consists of a continuous series of such Acts. The orientation relationship, for instance, consists of a continuous series of intentional Acts of Other-orientation, while social interaction consists in a continuous series of Acts of meaning-establishment and meaning-interpretation. All these different encounters with my fellow man will be ordered in multiple meaning-contexts: they are encounters with a human being as such, with this particular human being, and with this particular human being at this particular moment of time. And these meaning-contexts of mine will be "subjective" to the extent that I am attending to your actual conscious experiences themselves and not merely to my own lived experiences of you. Furthermore, as I watch you, I shall see that you are oriented to me, that you are seeking the subjective meaning of my words, my actions, and what I have in mind insofar as you are concerned. And I will in turn take account of the fact that you are thus oriented to me, and this will influence both my intentions with respect to you and how I act toward you. This again you will see, I will see that you have seen it, and so on. This interlocking of glances, this thousand-faceted mirroring of each other, is one of the unique features of the face-to-face situation. We may say that it is a constitutive characteristic of this particular social relationship. However, we must remember that the pure We-relationship, which is the very form of every encounter with another person, is not itself grasped *reflectively* within the face-to-face situation. Instead of being observed, it is lived through. The many different mirror images of Self within Self are not therefore caught sight of one by one but are experienced as a continuum within a single experience. Within the unity of this experience I can be aware simultaneously of what is going on in my mind and in yours, *living through* the two series of experiences as one series—what we are experiencing together.

This fact is of special significance for the face-to-face situation. Within the face-to-face situation I can be a witness of your projects and also of their fulfillment or frustration as you proceed to action. Of course, once I know what you are planning to do, I may momentarily *suspend* the We-relationship in order to estimate *objectively* your chances of success. But it is only within the intimacy of the We-relationship itself that one can actually *live through* a course of action from its birth as a project to its ultimate outcome.

It is further essential to the face-to-face situation that you and I have the same environment. First of all I ascribe to you an environment corresponding to my own. Here, in the face-to-face situation, but only here, does this presupposition prove correct, to the extent that I can assume with more or less certainty within the directly experienced social realm that the table I see is identical (and identical in all its perspective variations) with the table you see, to the extent that I can assume this even if you are only my contemporary or my predecessor. Therefore, when I am in a face-to-face situation with you, I can *point* to something in our common environment, uttering the words "this table here" and, by means of the identification of lived experiences in the environmental object, I can assure the adequacy of my interpretive scheme to your expressive scheme. For practical social life it is of the greatest significance that I consider myself justified in equating my own interpretation of my lived experiences with your interpretation of yours on those occasions when we are experiencing one and the same object.

We have, then, the same undivided and common environment, which we may call "our environment." The world of the We is not private to either of us, but is our world, the one common intersubjective world which is right there in front of us. It is only from the face-to-face relationship, from the common lived experience of the world in the We, that the intersubjective world can be constituted. This alone is the point from which it can be deduced.

I can constantly check my interpretations of what is going on in other people's minds, due to the fact that, in the We-relationship, I share a common environment with them. In principle, it is only in the face-to-face situation that I can address a question to you. But I can ask you not only about the interpretive schemes which you are applying to our common environment. I can also ask you how you are interpreting your lived experiences, and, in the process, I can correct, expand, and enrich my own understanding of you. This becoming-aware of the correctness or incorrectness of my understanding of you is a higher level of the We-experience. On this level I enrich not only my experience of you but of other people generally.

If I know that you and I are in a face-to-face relationship, I also know something about the manner in which each of us is attuned to his conscious experiences, in other words, the "attentional modifications" of each of us. This means that the way we attend to our conscious experiences is actually modified by our relationship to each other. This holds for both of us. For there is a true social relationship only if you reciprocate my awareness of you in some manner or other. As soon as this happens, as soon as we enter the face-to-face situation, each of us begins to attend to his own experiences in a new way. This particular attentional modification in which the two partners of a directly experienced social relationship are mutually aware of each other has special implications for the social interaction which occurs in that situation. *Whenever I am interacting-with anyone, I take for granted as a constant in that person a set of genuine because- or in-order-to motives.* I do this on the ground of my own past experience of that particular person as well as of people generally. My own behavior toward that person is based in the first instance upon this taken-for-granted constellation of motives, regardless of whether they are his real motives or not. And here emerges the peculiarity of face-to-face interaction. It consists not in a specific structure of the reciprocal motivation context itself but in a specific *disclosure* of the motives of the other person. Even in face-to-face interactions I only project in phantasy the behavior of the other person as I plan my own action. This phantasy is, of course, merely the other's *expected* behavior, without the details as yet filled in and without, as yet, any confirmation. I have yet to see what my partner will actually do. But because he and I continually undergo modifications of attention with respect to each other in the We-relationship, I can actually live through and participate in the constitution of his motivational context. I interpret the present lived experiences which I impute to you as the in-order-to motives of the behavior I expect from you or as the consequences of your past experiences, which I then regard as their because-motives. I "orient" my action to these motivational contexts of yours, as you "orient" yours to mine. However, this "orienting oneself" takes place within the directly experienced social realm in the particular mode of "witnessing." When interacting with you within this realm, I *witness* how you react to my behavior, how you interpret my meaning, how my in-order-to motives trigger corresponding because-motives of your behavior. In between my expectation of your reaction and that reaction itself I have "grown older" and perhaps wiser, taking into account the realities of the situation, as well as my own hopes of what you would do. But in the face-to-face situation you and I grow older together, and I can add to my expectation of what you are going to do the actual sight of you making up your mind, and then of your action itself in all its constituent phases. During all this time we are aware of each other's stream of consciousness as contemporaneous with our own; we share a rich, concrete We-relationship without any need to reflect on it. In a flash I see your whole plan and its execution in action. This episode of my biography is full of continuous lived experiences of you grasped within the We-relationship; meanwhile, you are experiencing me in the same way, and I am aware of the fact.

The Transition From Direct to Indirect Social Experience: Continuous Social Relationships

We have already noted that the We-relationship can occur with varying degrees of concreteness. We have seen that in the relationship we may experience our fellow men with greater or lesser directness, intimacy, or intensity. However, in the face-to-face situation, directness of experience is essential, regardless of whether our apprehension of the Other is central or peripheral and regardless of how adequate our grasp of him is. I am still "Thou-oriented" even to the man standing next to me in the subway. When we speak of "pure" Thou-orientation or "pure" We-relationship, we are ordinarily using these as limiting concepts referring to the simple givenness of the Other in abstraction from any specification of the degree of concreteness involved. But we can also use these terms for the lower limits of experience obtainable in the face-to-face relationship, in other words, for the most peripheral and fleeting kind of awareness of the other person.

We make the transition from direct to indirect social experience simply by following this spectrum of decreasing vividness. The first steps beyond the realm of immediacy are marked by a decrease in the number of perceptions I have of the other person and a narrowing of the perspectives within which I view him. At one moment I am exchanging smiles with my friend, shaking hands with him, and bidding him farewell. At the next moment he is walking away. Then from the far distance I hear a faint good-by, a moment later I see a vanishing figure give a last wave, and then he is gone. It is quite impossible to fix the exact instant at which my friend left the world of my direct experience and entered the shadowy realm of those who are merely my contemporaries. As another example, imagine a face-to-face conversation, followed by a telephone call, followed by an exchange of letters, and finally messages exchanged through a third party. Here too we have a gradual progression from the world of immediately experienced social reality to the world of contemporaries. In both examples the total number of the other person's reactions open to my observation is progressively diminished until it reaches a minimum point. It is clear, then, that the world of contemporaries is itself a variant function of the face-to-face situation. They may even be spoken of as two poles between which stretches a continuous series of experiences.

The Contemporary as an Ideal Type: The Nature of the They-Relationship

My mere contemporary (or "contemporary"), then, is one whom I know coexists with me in time but whom I do not experience immediately. This kind of knowledge is, accordingly, always indirect and impersonal. I cannot call my contemporary "Thou" in the rich sense that this term has within the We-relationship. Of course, my contemporary may once have been my consociate or may yet become one, but this in no way alters his present status.

Let us now examine the ways in which the world of contemporaries is constituted and the modifications which the concepts "Other-orientation" and "social relationship" undergo in that world. These modifications are necessitated by the fact that the contemporary is only indirectly accessible and that his subjective experiences can only be known in the form of *general types* of subjective experience.

That this should be the case is easy to understand if we consider the difference between the two modes of social experience. When I encounter you face to face I know you as a person in one unique moment of experience. While this We-relationship remains unbroken, we are open and accessible to each other's intentional Acts. For a little while we grow older together, experiencing each other's flow of consciousness in a kind of intimate mutual possession.

It is quite otherwise when I experience you as my contemporary. Here you are not prepredicatively given to me at all. I do not even directly apprehend your existence (*Dasein*). My whole knowledge of you is mediate and descriptive. In this kind of knowledge your "characteristics" are established for me by inference. From such knowledge results the indirect We-relationship.

To become clear about this concept of "mediacy," let us examine two different ways in which I come to know a contemporary. The first way we have already mentioned: my knowledge is derived from a previous face-to-face encounter with the person in question. But this knowledge has since become mediate or indirect because he has moved outside the range of my direct observation. For I make inferences as to what is going on in his mind under the assumption that he remains much the same since I saw him last, although, in another sense, I know very well that he must have changed through absorbing new experiences or merely by virtue of having grown older. But, as to how he has changed, my knowledge is either indirect or nonexistent.

A second way in which I come to know a contemporary is to construct a picture of him from the past direct experience of someone with whom I am now speaking (for example, when my friend describes his brother, whom I do not know). This is a variant of the first case. Here too I apprehend the contemporary by means of a fixed concept, or type, derived ultimately from direct experience but now held invariant. But there are differences. First, I have no concrete vivid picture of my own with which to start: I must depend on what my friend tells me. Second, I have to depend on my friend's assumption, not my own, that the contemporary he is describing has not changed.

These are the modes of constitution of all the knowledge we have of our contemporaries derived from our own past experience, direct or indirect, and of all the knowledge we have acquired from others, whether through conversation or through reading. It is clear, then, that indirect social experiences derive their original validity from the direct mode of apprehension. But the instances cited above do not exhaust all the ways by which I can come to know my contemporaries. There is the whole world of cultural objects, for instance, including everything from artifacts to institutions and conventional ways of doing things. These, too, contain within themselves implicit references to my contemporaries. I can "read" in these cultural objects the subjective experiences of others whom I do not know. Even here, however, I am making inferences on the basis of my previous direct experience of others.

Now this is real Other-orientation, however indirect it may be. And under this indirect Other-orientation we will find the usual forms of simple Other-orientation, social behavior and social interaction. Let us call all such intentional Acts directed toward contemporaries cases of "They-orientation," in contrast to the

"Thou-orientation" of the intentional Acts of direct social experience.

The term "They-orientation" serves to call attention to the peculiar way in which I apprehend the conscious experiences of my contemporaries. For I apprehend them as anonymous processes. Consider the contrast to the Thou-orientation. When I am Thou-oriented, I apprehend the other person's experiences within their setting in his stream of consciousness. I apprehend them as existing within a subjective context of meaning, as being the unique experiences of a particular person. All this is absent in the indirect social experience of the They-orientation. Here I am not aware of the ongoing flow of the Other's consciousness. My orientation is not toward the existence (*Dasein*) of a concrete individual Thou. It is not toward any subjective experiences now being constituted in all their uniqueness in another's mind nor toward the subjective configuration of meaning in which they are taking place. Rather, the object of my They-orientation is my own experience (*Erfahrung*) of social reality in general, of human beings and their conscious processes as such, in abstraction from any individual setting in which they may occur. My knowledge of my contemporaries is, therefore, inferential and discursive. It stands, by its essential nature, in an objective context of meaning and only in such. It has within it no intrinsic reference to persons nor to the subjective matrix within which the experiences in question were constituted. However, it is due to this very abstraction from subjective context of meaning that they exhibit the property which we have called their "again and again" character. They are treated as typical conscious experiences of "someone" and, as such, as basically homogeneous and repeatable. The unity of the contemporary is not constituted originally in his own stream of consciousness. (Indeed, whether the contemporary has any stream of consciousness at all is a difficult question and one which we shall deal with later.) Rather, the contemporary's unity is constituted in my own stream of consciousness, being built up out of a synthesis of my own interpretations of his experiences. This synthesis is a synthesis of recognition in which I monothetically bring within one view my own conscious experiences of someone else. Indeed, these experiences of mine may have been of more than one person. And they may have been of definite individuals or of anonymous "people." It is in this synthesis of recognition that the *personal ideal type* is constituted.

We must be quite clear as to what is happening here. The subjective meaning-context has been abandoned as a tool of interpretation. It has been replaced by a series of highly complex and systematically interrelated objective meaning-contexts. The result is that the contemporary is anonymized in direct proportion to the number and complexity of these meaning-contexts. Furthermore, the synthesis of recognition does not apprehend the unique person as he exists within his living present. Instead it pictures him as always the same and homogeneous, leaving out of account all the changes and rough edges that go along with individuality. Therefore, no matter how many people are subsumed under the ideal type, it corresponds to no one in particular. It is just this fact that justified Weber in calling it "ideal."

Let us give a few examples to clarify this point. When I mail a letter, I assume that certain contemporaries of mine, namely, postal employees, will read the address and speed the letter on its way. I am not thinking of these postal employees as individuals. I do not know them personally and never expect to. Again, as Max Weber pointed out, whenever I accept money I do so without any doubt that others, who remain quite anonymous, will accept it in turn from me. To use yet another Weberian example, if I behave in such a way as to avoid the sudden arrival of certain gentlemen with uniforms and badges, in other words, to the extent that I orient myself to the laws and to the apparatus which enforces them, here, too, I am relating myself socially to my contemporaries conceived under ideal types.

On occasions like these I am always expecting others to behave in a definite way, whether it be postal employees, someone I am paying, or the police. My social relationship to them consists in the fact that I interact with them, or perhaps merely that, in planning my actions, I keep them in mind. But they, on their part, never turn up as real people, merely as anonymous entities defined exhaustively by their functions. Only as bearers of these functions do they have any relevance for my social behavior. How they happen to feel as they cancel my letter, process my check, or examine my income-tax return—these are considerations that never even enter my mind. I just assume that there are "some people" who "do these things." Their behavior in the conduct of their duty is from my point of view defined purely through an objective context of meaning. In other words, when I am They-oriented, I have "types" for partners.

The Constitution of the Ideal-Typical Interpretive Scheme

The concept "ideal type of human behavior" can be taken in two ways. It can mean first of all the ideal type of another person who is expressing himself or has expressed himself in a certain way. Or it may mean, second, the ideal type of the expressive process itself, or even of the outward results which we interpret as the signs of the expressive process. Let us call the first the "personal ideal type" and the second the "material" or "course-of-action *type*." Certainly an inner relation exists between these two. I cannot, for instance, define the ideal type of a postal clerk without first having in mind a definition of his job. The latter is a course-of-action type, which is, of course, an objective context of meaning. Once I am clear as to the course-of-action type, I can construct the personal ideal type, that is "the person who performs this job." And, in doing so, I imagine the corresponding subjective meaning-contexts which would be in his mind, the subjective contexts that would have to be adequate to the objective contexts already defined. The personal ideal type is therefore *derivative*, and the course-of-action type can be considered quite independently as a purely objective context of meaning.

Social Relationships Between Contemporaries and Indirect Social Observation

As social relationships in the face-to-face situation are based on the pure Thou-orientation, so social relationships between contemporaries are based on the pure They-orientation. But the situation has now changed. In the face-to-face situation the partners look into each other and are mutually sensitive to each other's responses. This is not the case in relationships between contemporaries. Here each partner has to be content with the probability that the other, to whom he is oriented by means of an anonymous type, will respond with the same kind of orientation. And so an element of doubt enters into every such relationship.

When I board a train, for instance, I orient myself to the fact that the engineer in charge can be trusted to get me to my destination. My relationship to him is a They-relationship at this time, merely because my ideal type "railroad engineer" means by definition "one who gets passengers like myself to their destination." It is therefore characteristic of my social relationships with my contemporaries that the orientation by means of ideal types is mutual. Corresponding to my ideal type "engineer" there is the engineer's ideal type "passenger." Taking up mutual They-orientations, we think of each other as "one of them."

I am not therefore apprehended by my partner in the They-relationship as a real living person. From this it follows that I can expect from him only a typical understanding of my behavior.

A social relationship between contemporaries, therefore, consists in this: Each of the partners apprehends the other by means of an ideal type; each of the partners is aware of this mutual apprehension; and each expects that the other's interpretive scheme will be congruent with his own. The They-relationship here stands in sharp contrast to the face-to-face situation. In the face-to-face situation my partner and I are sensitively aware of the nuances of each other's subjective experiences. But in the They-relationship this is replaced by the assumption of a shared interpretive scheme. Now, even though I, on my side, make this assumption, I cannot verify it. I do, however, have more reason to expect an adequate response from my partner, the more standardized is the scheme which I impute to him. This is the case with schemes derived from law, state, tradition, and systems of order of all kinds, and especially with schemes based on the means-end relation, in short, with what Weber calls "rational" interpretive schemes.

65

Society as Objective Reality*

Peter L. Berger
Thomas Luckmann

All human activity is subject to habitualization. Any action that is repeated frequently becomes cast into a pattern, which can then be reproduced with an economy of effort and which, *ipso facto*, is apprehended by its performer *as* that pattern. Habitualization further implies that the action in question may be performed again in the future in the same manner and with the same economical effort. This is true of non-social as well as of social activity. Even the solitary individual on the proverbial desert island habitualizes his activity. When he wakes up in the morning and resumes his attempts to construct a canoe out of matchsticks, he may mumble to himself, "There I go again," as he starts on step one of an operating procedure consisting of, say, ten steps. In other words, even solitary man has at least the company of his operating procedures.

Habitualized actions, of course, retain their meaningful character for the individual although the meanings involved become embedded as routines in his general stock of knowledge, taken for granted by him and at hand for his projects into the future. Habitualization carries with it the important psychological gain that choices are narrowed. While in theory there may be a hundred ways to go about the project of building a canoe out of matchsticks, habitualization narrows these down to one. This frees the individual from the burden of "all those decisions," providing a psychological relief that has its basis in man's undirected instinctual structure. Habitualization provides the direction and the specialization of activity that is lacking in man's biological equipment, thus relieving the accumulation of tensions that result from undirected drives. And by providing a stable background in which human activity may proceed with a minimum of decision-making most of the time, it frees energy for such decisions as may be necessary on certain occasions. In other words, the background of habitualized activity opens up a foreground for deliberation and innovation.

In terms of the meanings bestowed by man upon his activity, habitualization makes it unnecessary for each situation to be defined anew, step by step. A large variety of situations may be subsumed under its predefinitions. The activity to be undertaken in these situations can then be anticipated. Even alternatives of conduct can be assigned standard weights.

These processes of habitualization precede any institutionalization, indeed can be made to apply to a hypothetical solitary individual detached from any social interaction. The fact that even such a solitary individual, assuming that he has been formed as a self (as we would have to assume in the case of our matchstick-canoe builder), will habitualize his activity in accordance with biographical experience of a world of social institutions preceding his solitude need not concern us at the moment. Empirically, the more important part of the habitualization of human activity is coextensive with the latter's institutionalization. The question then becomes how do institutions arise.

Institutionalization occurs whenever there is a reciprocal typification of habitualized actions by types of actors. Put differently, any such typification is an institution. What must be stressed is the reciprocity of institutional typifications and the typicality of not only the actions but also the actors in institutions. The typifications of habitualized actions that constitute institutions are always shared ones. They are *available* to all the members of the particular social group in question, and the institution itself typifies individual actors as well as individual actions. The institution posits that actions of type X will be performed by actors of type X. For example, the institution of the law posits that heads shall be chopped off in specific ways under specific circumstances, and that specific types of individuals shall do the chopping (executioners, say, or members of an impure caste, or virgins under a certain age, or those who have been designated by an oracle).

Institutions further imply historicity and control. Reciprocal typifications of actions are built up in the course of a shared history. They cannot be created instantaneously. Institutions always have a history, of which they are the products. It is impossible to understand an institution adequately without an understanding of the historical process in which it was produced. Institutions also, by the very fact of their existence, control human conduct by setting up predefined patterns of conduct, which channel it in one direction as against the many other directions that would theoretically be possible. It is important to stress that this controlling character is inherent in institutionalization as such, prior to or apart from any mechanisms of sanctions specifically set up to support an institution. These mechanisms (the sum of which constitute what is generally called a system of social control) do, of course, exist in many institutions and in all the agglomerations of institutions that we call societies. Their controlling efficacy, however, is of a secondary or supplementary kind. As we shall see again later, the primary social control is given in the existence of an institution as such. To say that a segment of human activity has been institutionalized is already to say that this segment of human activity has been subsumed under social control. Additional control mechanisms are required only insofar as the processes of institutionalization are less than completely successful. Thus, for instance, the law may provide that anyone who breaks the incest taboo will have his head chopped off. This provision may be necessary because there have been cases when individuals offended against the taboo. It is unlikely that this sanction will have to be invoked continuously (unless the institution delineated by the incest taboo is itself in the course of disintegration, a special case that we need not elaborate here). It makes little sense, therefore, to say that human sexuality is socially controlled by beheading certain individuals. Rather, human sexuality is socially controlled by its institutionalization in the course of the particular history in question. One may add, of course, that the incest taboo itself is nothing but the negative side of an assemblage of typifications, which define in the first place which sexual conduct is incestuous and which is not.

In actual experience institutions generally manifest themselves in collectivities containing considerable numbers of people. It is theoretically important, however, to emphasize that the institutionalizing process of reciprocal typification would occur even if two individuals began to interact *de novo*. Institutionalization is incipient in every social situation continuing in time. Let us assume that two persons from entirely different social worlds begin to interact. By saying "persons" we presuppose that the two individuals have formed selves, something that could, of course, have occurred only in a social process. We are thus for the moment excluding the cases of Adam and Eve, or of two "feral" children meeting in a clearing of a primeval jungle. But we are assuming that the two individuals arrive at their meeting place from social worlds that have been historically produced in segregation from each other, and that the interaction therefore takes place in a situation that has not been institutionally defined for either of the participants. It may be possible to imagine a Man Friday joining our matchstick-canoe builder on his desert island, and to imagine the former as a Papuan and the latter as an American. In that case, however, it is likely that the American will have read or at least have heard about the story of Robinson Crusoe, which will introduce a measure of predefinition of the situation at least for him. Let us, then, simply call our two persons *A* and *B*.

As *A* and *B* interact, in whatever manner, typifications will be produced quite quickly. *A* watches *B* perform. He attributes motives to *B*'s actions and, seeing the actions recur, typifies the motives as recurrent. As *B* goes on performing, *A* is soon able to say to himself, "Aha, there he goes again." At the same time, *A* may assume that *B* is doing the same thing with regard to him. From the beginning, both *A* and *B* assume this reciprocity of typification. In the course of their interaction these typifications will be expressed in specific patterns of conduct. That is, *A* and *B* will begin to play roles *vis-à-vis* each other. This will occur even if each continues to perform actions different from those of the other. The possibility of taking the role of the other will appear with regard to the same actions performed by both. That is, *A* will inwardly appropriate *B*'s reiterated roles and make them the models for his own role-playing. For example, *B*'s role in the activity of preparing food is not only typified as such by *A*, but enters as a constitutive element into *A*'s own food-preparation role. Thus a collection of reciprocally typified actions will emerge, habitualized for each in roles, some of which will be performed separately and some in common. While this reciprocal typification is not yet institutionalization (since, there only being two individuals, there is no possibility of a typology of actors), it is clear that institutionalization is already present *in nucleo*.

At this stage one may ask what gains accrue to the two individuals from this development. The most important gain is that each will be able to predict the other's actions. Concomitantly, the interaction of both becomes predictable. The "There he goes again" becomes a "There *we* go again." This relieves both individuals of a considerable amount of tension. They save time and effort, not only in whatever external tasks they might be engaged in separately or jointly, but in terms of their respective psychological economies. Their life together is now defined by a widening sphere of taken-for-granted routines. Many actions are possible on a low level of attention. Each action of one is no longer a source of astonishment and potential danger to the other. Instead, much of what goes on takes on the triviality of what, to both, will be everyday life. This means that the two individuals are constructing a background, in the sense discussed before, which will serve to stabilize both their separate actions and their interaction. The construction of this background of routine in turn makes possible a division of labor between them, opening the way for innovations, which demand a higher level of attention. The division of labor and the innovations will lead to new habitualizations, further widening the background common to both individuals. In other words, a social world will be in process of construction, containing within it the roots of an expanding institutional order.

Generally, all actions repeated once or more tend to be habitualized to some degree, just as all actions observed by another necessarily involve some typification on his part. However, for the kind of reciprocal typification just described to occur there must be a continuing social situation in which the habitualized actions of two or more individuals interlock. Which actions are likely to be reciprocally typified in this manner?

The general answer is, those actions that are relevant to both *A* and B within their common situation. The areas likely to be relevant in this way will, of course, vary in different situations. Some will be those facing *A* and *B* in terms of their previous biographies, others may be the result of the natural, presocial circumstances of the situation. What will in all cases have to be habitualized is the communication process between *A* and *B*. Labor, sexuality and territoriality are other likely foci of typification and habitualization. In these various areas the situation of *A* and *B* is paradigmatic of the institutionalization occurring in larger societies.

Let us push our paradigm one step further and imagine that *A* and *B* have children. At this point the situation changes qualitatively. The appearance of a third party changes the character of the ongoing social interaction between *A* and *B*, and it will change even further as additional individuals continue to be added. The institutional world, which existed *in statu nascendi* in the original situation of *A* and *B*, is now passed on to others. In this process institutionalization perfects itself. The habitualizations and typifications undertaken in the common life of *A* and *B*, formations that until this point still had the quality of *ad hoc* conceptions of two individuals, now become historical institutions. With the acquisition of historicity, these formations also acquire another crucial quality, or, more accurately, perfect a quality that was incipient as soon as *A* and *B* began the reciprocal typification of their conduct: this quality is objectivity. This means that the institutions that have now been crystallized (for instance, the institution of paternity as it is encountered by the children) are experienced as existing over and beyond the individuals who "happen to" embody them at the moment. In other words, the institutions are now experienced as possessing a reality of their own, a reality that confronts the individual as an external and coercive fact.

As long as the nascent institutions are constructed and maintained only in the interaction of *A* and *B*, their objectivity remains tenuous, easily changeable, almost playful, even while they attain a measure of objectivity by the mere fact of their formation. To put this a little differently, the routinized background of *A*'s and *B*'s activity remains fairly accessible to deliberate intervention by *A* and *B*. Although the routines, once established, carry within them a tendency to persist, the possibility of changing them or even abolishing them remains at hand in consciousness. *A* and *B* alone are responsible for having constructed this world. *A* and *B* remain capable of changing or abolishing it. What is more, since they themselves have shaped this world in the course of a shared biography which they can remember, the world thus shaped appears fully transparent to them. They understand the world that they themselves have made. All this changes in the process of transmission to the new generation. The objectivity of the institutional world "thickens" and "hardens," not only for the children, but (by a mirror effect) for the parents as well. The "There we go again" now becomes "This is how these things are done." A world so regarded attains a firmness in consciousness; it becomes real in an ever more massive way and it can no longer be changed so readily. For the children, especially in the early phase of their socialization into it, it becomes *the* world. For the parents, it loses its playful quality and becomes "serious." For the children, the parentally transmitted world is not fully transparent. Since they had no part in shaping it, it confronts them as a given reality that, like nature, is opaque in places at least.

Only at this point does it become possible to speak of a social world at all, in the sense of a comprehensive and given reality confronting the individual in a manner analogous to the reality of the natural world. Only in this way, *as* an objective world, can the social formations be transmitted to a new generation. In the early phases of socialization the child is quite incapable of distinguishing between the objectivity of natural phenomena and the objectivity of the social formations. To take the most important item of socialization, language appears to the child as inherent in the nature of things, and he cannot grasp the notion of its conventionality. A thing *is* what it is called, and it could not be called anything else. All institutions appear in the same way, as given, unalterable and self-evident. Even in our empirically unlikely example of parents having constructed an institutional world *de novo*, the objectivity of this world would be increased for them by the socialization of their children, because the objectivity experienced by the children would reflect back upon their own experience of this world. Empirically, of course, the institutional world transmitted by most parents already has the character of historical and objective reality. The process of transmission simply strengthens the parents' sense of reality, if only because, to put it crudely, if one says, "This is how these things are done," often enough one believes it oneself.

An institutional world, then, is experienced as an objective reality. It has a history that antedates the individual's birth and is not accessible to his biographical recollection. It was there before he was born, and it will be there after his death. This history itself, as the tradition of the existing institutions, has the character of objectivity. The individual's biography is apprehended as an episode located within the objective history of the society. The institutions, as historical and objective facticities, confront the individual as undeniable facts. The institutions are *there*, external to him, persistent in their reality, whether he likes it or not. He cannot wish them away. They resist his attempts to change or evade them. They have coercive power over him, both in themselves, by the sheer force of their facticity, and through the control mechanisms that are usually attached to the most important of them. The objective reality of institutions is not diminished if the individual does not understand their purpose or their mode of operation. He may experience large sectors of the social world as incomprehensible, perhaps oppressive in their opaqueness, but real nonetheless. Since institutions exist as external reality, the individual cannot understand them by introspection. He must "go out" and learn about them, just as he must to learn about nature. This remains true even though the social world, as a humanly produced reality, is potentially understandable in a way not possible in the case of the natural world.

It is important to keep in mind that the objectivity of the institutional world, however massive it may appear to the individual, is a humanly produced, constructed objectivity. The process by which the externalized products of human activity attain the character of objectivity is objectivation. The institutional world is objectivated human activity, and so is every single institution. In other words, despite the objectivity that marks the social world in human experience, it does not thereby acquire an ontological status apart from the human activity that produced it The paradox that man is capable of producing a world that he then experiences as something other than a human product will concern us later on. At the moment, it is important to emphasize that the relationship between man, the producer, and the social world, his product, is and remains a dialectical one. That is, man (not, of course, in isolation but in his collectivities) and his social world interact with each other. The product acts back upon the producer. Externalization and objectivation are moments in a continuing dialectical process. The third moment in this process, which is internalization (by which the objectivated social world is retrojected into consciousness in the course of socialization), will occupy us in considerable detail later on. It is already possible, however, to see the fundamental relationship of these three dialectical moments in social reality. Each of them corresponds to an essential characterization of the social world. *Society is a human product. Society is an objective reality. Man is a social product.* It may also already be evident than an analysis of the social world that leaves out any one of these three moments will be distortive. One may further add that only with the transmission of the social world to a new generation (that is, internalization as effectuated in socialization) does the fundamental social dialectic appear in its totality. To repeat, only with the appearance of a new generation can one properly speak of a social world.

At the same point, the institutional world requires legitimation, that is, ways by which it can be "explained" and justified. This is not because it appears less real. As we have seen, the reality of the social world gains in massivity in the course of its transmission. This reality, however, is a historical one, which comes to the new generation as a tradition rather than as a biographical memory. In our paradigmatic example, *A* and *B*, the original creators of the social world, can always reconstruct the circumstances under which their world and any part of it was established. That is, they can arrive at the meaning of an institution by exercising their powers of recollection. *A*'s and *B*'s children are in an altogether different situation. Their knowledge of the institutional history is by way of "hearsay." The original meaning of the institutions is inaccessible to them in terms of memory. It, therefore, becomes necessary to interpret this meaning to them in various legitimating formulas. These will have to be consistent and comprehensive in terms of the institutional order, if they are to carry conviction to the new generation. The same story, so to speak, must be told to all the children. It follows that the expanding institutional order develops a corresponding canopy of legitimations, stretching over it a protective cover of both cognitive and normative interpretation. These legitimations are learned by the new generation during the same process that socializes them into the institutional order. This, again, will occupy us in greater detail further on.

The development of specific mechanisms of social controls also becomes necessary with the historicization and objectivation of institutions. Deviance from the institutionally "programmed" courses of action becomes likely once the institutions have become realities divorced from their original relevance in the concrete social processes from which they arose. To put this more simply, it is more likely that one will deviate from programs set up for one by others than from programs that one has helped establish oneself. The new generation posits a problem of compliance, and its socialization into the institutional order requires the establishment of sanctions. The institutions must and do claim authority over the individual, independently of the subjective meanings he may attach to any particular situation. The priority of the institutional definitions of situations must be consistently maintained over individual temptations at redefinition. The children must be "taught to behave" and, once taught, must be "kept in line." So, of course, must the adults. The more conduct is institutionalized, the more predictable and thus the more controlled it becomes. If socialization into the institutions has been effective, outright coercive measures can be applied economically and selectively. Most of the time, conduct will occur "spontaneously" within the institutionally set channels. The more, on the level of meaning, conduct is taken for granted, the more possible alternatives to the institutional "programs" will recede, and the more predictable and controlled conduct will be.

Language provides the fundamental superimposition of logic on the objectivated social world. The edifice of legitimations is built upon language and uses language as its principal instrumentality. The "logic" thus attributed to the institutional order is part of the socially available stock of knowledge and taken for granted as such. Since the well-socialized individual "knows" that his social world is a consistent whole, he will be constrained to explain both its functioning and malfunctioning in terms of this "knowledge." It is very easy, as a result, for the observer of any society to assume that its institutions do indeed function and integrate as they are "supposed to."

De facto, then, institutions *are* integrated. But their integration is not a functional imperative for the social processes that produce them; it is rather brought about in a derivative fashion. Individuals perform discrete institutionalized actions within the context of their biography. This biography is a reflected-upon whole in which the discrete actions are thought of not as isolated events, but as related parts in a subjectively meaningful universe whose meanings are not specific to the individual, but socially articulated and shared. Only by way of this detour of socially shared universes of meaning do we arrive at the need for institutional integration.

This has far-reaching implications for any analysis of social phenomena. If the integration of an institutional order can be understood only in terms of the "knowledge" that its members have of it, it follows that the analysis of such "knowledge" will be essential for an analysis of the institutional order in question. It is important to stress that this does not exclusively or even primarily involve a preoccupation with complex theoretical systems serving as legitimations for the institutional order. Theories also have to be taken into account, of course. But theoretical knowledge is only a small and by no means the most important part of what passes for knowledge in a society. Theoretically sophisticated legitimations appear at particular moments of an institutional history. The primary knowledge about the institutional order is knowledge on the pretheoretical level. It is the sum total of "what everybody knows" about a social world, an assemblage of maxims, morals, proverbial nuggets of wisdom, values and beliefs, myths, and so forth, the theoretical integration of which requires considerable intellectual fortitude in itself, as the long line of heroic integrators from Homer to the latest sociological system-builders testifies. On the pretheoretical level, however, every institution has a body of transmitted recipe knowledge, that is, knowledge that supplies the institutionally appropriate rules of conduct.

Such knowledge constitutes the motivating dynamics of institutionalized conduct. It defines the institutionalized areas of conduct and designates all situations falling within them. It defines and constructs the roles to be played in the context of the institutions in question. *Ipso facto,* it controls and predicts all such conduct. Since this knowledge is socially objectivated *as* knowledge, that is, as a body of generally valid truths about reality, any radical deviance from the institutional order appears as a departure from reality. Such deviance may be designated as moral depravity, mental disease, or just plain ignorance. While these fine distinctions will have obvious consequences for the treatment of the deviant, they all share an inferior cognitive status within the particular social world. In this way, the particular social world becomes the world *tout court.* What is taken for granted as knowledge in the society comes to be coextensive with the knowable, or at any rate provides the framework within which anything not yet known will come to be known in the future. This is the knowledge that is learned in the course of socialization and that mediates the internalization within individual consciousness of the objectivated structures of the social world. Knowledge, in this sense, is at the heart of the fundamental dialectic of society. It "programs" the channels in which externalization produces an objective world. It objectifies this world through language and the cognitive apparatus based on language, that is, it orders it into objects to be apprehended as reality. It is internalized again *as* objectively valid truth in the course of socialization. Knowledge about society is thus a *realization* in the double sense of the word, in the sense of apprehending the objectivated social reality, and in the sense of ongoingly producing this reality.

For example, in the course of the division of labor a body of knowledge is developed that refers to the particular activities involved. In its linguistic basis, this knowledge is already indispensable to the institutional "programming" of these economic activities. There will be, say, a vocabulary designating the various modes of hunting, the weapons to be employed, the animals that serve as prey, and so on. There will further be a collection of recipes that must be learned if one is to hunt correctly. This knowledge serves as a channeling, controlling force in itself, an indispensable ingredient of the institutionalization of this area of conduct. As the institution of hunting is crystallized and persists in time, the same body of knowledge serves as an objective (and, incidentally, empirically verifiable) description of it. A whole segment of the social world is objectified by this knowledge. There will be an objective "science" of hunting, corresponding to the objective reality of the hunting economy. The point need not be belabored that here "empirical verification" and "science" are not understood in the sense of modern scientific canons, but rather in the sense of knowledge that may be borne out in experience and that can subsequently become systematically organized as a body of knowledge.

Again, the same body of knowledge is transmitted to the next generation. It is learned as objective truth in the course of socialization and thus internalized as subjective reality. This reality in turn has power to shape the individual. It will produce a specific type of person, namely the hunter, whose identity and biography *as* a hunter have meaning only in a universe constituted by the aforementioned body of knowledge as a whole (say, in a hunters' society) or in part (say, in our own society, in which hunters come together in a subuniverse of their own). In other words, no part of the institutionalization of hunting can exist without the particular knowledge that has been socially produced and objectivated with reference to this activity. To hunt and to be a hunter implies existence in a social world defined and controlled by this body of knowledge. *Mutatis mutandis,* the same applies to any area of institutionalized conduct.

66

ETHNOMETHODOLOGY

HAROLD GARFINKEL

Properties that are exhibited by accounts (by reason of their being features of the socially organized occasions of their use) are available from studies by logicians as the properties of indexical expressions and indexical sentences. Husserl spoke of expressions whose sense cannot be decided by an auditor without his necessarily knowing or assuming something about the biography and the purposes of the user of the expression, the circumstances of the utterance, the previous course of the conversation, or the particular relationship of actual or potential interaction that exists between the expressor and the auditor.

WHAT IS ETHNOMETHODOLOGY?

The earmark of practical sociological reasoning, wherever it occurs, is that it seeks to remedy the indexical properties of members' talk and conduct. Endless methodological studies are directed to the tasks of providing members a remedy for indexical expressions in members' abiding attempts, with rigorous uses of ideals to demonstrate the observability of organized activities in actual occasions with situated particulars of talk and conduct.

The properties of indexical expressions and indexical actions are ordered properties. These consist of organizationally demonstrable sense, or facticity, or methodic use, or agreement among "cultural colleagues." Their ordered properties consist of organizationally demonstrable rational properties of indexical expressions and indexical actions. Those ordered properties are ongoing achievements of the concerted commonplace activities of investigators. The demonstrable rationality of indexical expressions and indexical actions retains over the course of its managed production by members the character of ordinary, familiar, routinized practical circumstances. As process and attainment the produced rationality of indexical expressions consists of practical tasks subject to every exigency of organizationally situated conduct.

I use the term "ethnomethodology" to refer to the investigation of the rational properties of indexical expressions and other practical actions as contingent ongoing accomplishments of organized artful practices of everyday life.

MAKING COMMONPLACE SCENES VISIBLE

In accounting for the stable features of everyday activities sociologists commonly select familiar settings such as familial households or work places and ask for the variables that contribute to their stable features. Just as commonly, one set of considerations are unexamined: the socially standardized and standardizing, "seen but unnoticed," expected, background features of everyday scenes. The member of the society uses background expectancies as a scheme of interpretation. With their use actual appearances are for him recognizable and intelligible as the appearances-of-familiar-events. Demonstrably he is responsive to this background, while at the same time he is at a loss to tell us specifically of what the expectancies consist. When we ask him about them he has little or nothing to say.

For these background expectancies to come into view one must either be a stranger to the "life as usual" character of everyday scenes, or become estranged from them. As Alfred Schutz pointed out, a "special motive" is required to make them problematic. In the sociologists' case this "special motive" consists in the programmatic task of treating a societal member's practical circumstances, which include from the member's point of view the morally necessary character of many of its background features, as matters of theoretic interest. The seen but unnoticed backgrounds of everyday activities are made visible and are described from a perspective in which persons live out the lives they do, have the children they do, feel the feelings, think the thoughts, enter the relationships they do, all in order to permit the sociologist to solve his theoretical problems.

Almost alone among sociological theorists, the late Alfred Schutz, in a series of classical studies of the constitutive phenomenology of the world of everyday life, described many of these seen but unnoticed background expectancies. He called them the "attitude of daily life." He referred to their scenic attributions as the "world known in common and taken for granted." Schutz' fundamental work makes it possible to pursue further the tasks of clarifying their nature and operation, of relating them to the processes of concerted actions, and assigning them their place in an empirically imaginable society.

Some Essential Features of Common Understandings

Various considerations dictate that common understandings cannot possibly consist of a measured amount of shared agreement among persons on certain topics. Even if the topics are limited in number and scope and every practical difficulty of assessment is forgiven, the notion that we are dealing with an amount of shared agreement remains essentially incorrect. This may be demonstrated as follows.

Students were asked to report common conversations by writing on the left side of a sheet what the parties actually said and on the right side what they and their partners understood that they were talking about. A student reported the following colloquy between himself and his wife. [See the next page.]

An examination of the colloquy reveals the following. (a) There were many matters that the partners understood they were talking about that they did not mention. (b) Many matters that the partners understood were understood on the basis not only of what was actually said but what was left unspoken. (c) Many matters were understood through a process of attending to the temporal series of utterances as documentary evidences of a developing conversation rather than as a string of terms. (d) Matters that the two understood in common were understood only in and through a course of understanding work that consisted of treating an actual linguistic event as "the document of," as "pointing to," as standing on behalf of an underlying pattern of matters that each already supposed to be the matters that the person, by his speaking, could be telling the other about. The underlying pattern was not only derived from a course of individual documentary evidences but the documentary evidences in their turn were interpreted on the basis of "what was known" and anticipatorily knowable about the underlying patterns. Each was used to elaborate the other. (e) In attending to the utterances as events-in-the-conversation each party made references to the biography and prospects of the present interaction which each used and attributed to the other as a common scheme of interpretation and expression. (f) Each waited for something more to be said in order to hear what had previously been talked about, and each seemed willing to wait.

For the purposes of *conducting their everyday affairs* persons refuse to permit each other to understand "what they are really talking about" in this way. The anticipation that persons *will* understand, the occasionality of expressions, the specific vagueness of references, the retrospective-prospective sense of a present occurrence, waiting for something later in order to see what

HUSBAND:	Dana succeeded in putting a penny in a parking meter today without being picked up.	This afternoon as I was bringing Dana, our four-year-old son, home from the nursery school, he succeeded in reaching high enough to put a penny in a parking meter when we parked in a meter parking zone, whereas before he has always had to be picked up to reach that high.
WIFE:	Did you take him to the record store?	Since he put a penny in a meter that means that you stopped while he was with you. I know that you stopped at the record store either on the way to get him or on the way back. Was it on the way back, so that he was with you or did you stop there on the way to get him and somewhere else on the way back?
HUSBAND:	No, to the shoe repair shop.	No, I stopped at the record store on the way to get him and stopped at the shoe repair shop on the way home when he was with me.
WIFE:	What for?	I know of one reason why you might have stopped at the shoe repair shop. Why did you in fact?
HUSBAND:	I got some new shoe laces for my shoes.	As you will remember I broke a shoe lace on one of my brown oxfords the other day so I stopped to get some new laces.
WIFE:	Your loafers need new heels badly.	Something else you could have gotten that I was thinking of. You could have taken in your black loafers which need heels badly. You'd better get them taken care of pretty soon.

was meant before, are sanctioned properties of common discourse. They furnish a background of seen but unnoticed features of common discourse whereby actual utterances are recognized as events of common, reasonable, understandable, plain talk. Persons require these properties of discourse as conditions under which they are themselves entitled and entitle others to claim that they know what they are talking about, and that what they are saying is understandable and ought to be understood. In short, their seen but unnoticed presence is used to entitle persons to conduct their common conversational affairs without interference.

Common Sense Knowledge of Social Structures: The Documentary Method of Interpretation in Lay and Professional Fact Finding

Sociologically speaking, "common culture" refers to the socially sanctioned grounds of inference and action that people use in their everyday affairs and which they assume that others use in the same way. Socially-sanctioned-facts-of-life-in-society-that-any-bona-fide-member-of-the-society-knows depict such matters as the conduct of family life, market organization, distributions of honor, competence, responsibility, goodwill, income, motives among members, frequency, causes of, and remedies for trouble, and the presence of good and evil purposes behind the apparent workings of things. Such socially sanctioned, facts of social life consist of descriptions from the point of view of the collectivity member's interests in the management of his practical affairs. Basing our usage upon the work of Alfred Schutz, we shall call such knowledge of socially organized environments of concerted actions "common sense knowledge of social structures."

The discovery of common culture consists of the discovery *from within* the society by social scientists of the existence of common sense knowledge of social structures. In that discovery the social scientist treats knowledge, and the procedures that societal members use for its assembly, test, management, and transmission, as objects of theoretical sociological interest.

This paper is concerned with common sense knowledge of social structures as an object of theoretical sociological interest. It is concerned with descriptions of a society that its members, *professional sociologists included*, as a condition of their enforceable rights to manage and communicate decisions of meaning, fact, method, and causal texture without interference—*i.e.*, as a condition of their "competence"—use and treat as known in common with other members, and with other members take for granted. Specifically the paper is directed to a description of the work whereby decisions of meaning and fact are managed, and how a body of factual knowledge of social structures is assembled in common sense situations of choice.

The Documentary Method of Interpretation

There are innumerable situations of sociological inquiry in which the investigator—whether he be a professional sociologist or a person undertaking an inquiry about social structures in the interests of managing his practical everyday affairs—can assign witnessed actual appearances to the status of an event of conduct only by imputing biography and prospects to the appearances. This he does by embedding the appearances in his presupposed knowledge of social structures. Thus it frequently happens that in order for the investigator to decide what he is now looking at he must wait for future developments, only to find that these futures in turn are informed by *their* history and future. By waiting to see what will have happened he learns what it was that he previously saw. Either that, or he takes imputed history and prospects for granted. Motivated actions, for example, have exactly these troublesome properties.

It therefore occurs that the investigator frequently must elect among alternative courses of interpretation and inquiry to the end of deciding matters of fact, hypothesis, conjecture, fancy, and the rest, despite the fact that in the calculable sense of the term "know," he does not and even cannot "know" what he is doing *prior to or while he is doing it*. Field workers, most particularly those doing ethnographic and linguistic studies in settings where they cannot presuppose a knowledge of social structures, are perhaps best acquainted with such situations, but other types of professional sociological inquiry are not exempt.

Nevertheless, a body of knowledge of social structures is somehow assembled. Somehow, decisions of meaning, facts, method, and causal texture are made. How, in the course of the inquiry during which such decisions must be made, does this occur?

In his concern for the sociologist's problem of achieving an adequate description of cultural events, an important case of which would be Weber's familiar "behaviors with a subjective meaning attached and governed thereby in their course," Karl Mannheim furnished an approximate description of one process. Mannheim called it "the documentary method of interpretation." It contrasts with the methods of literal observation, yet it has a recognizable fit with what many sociological researchers, lay and professional, actually do.

According to Mannheim, the documentary method involves the search for ". . . an identical homologous pattern underlying a vast variety of totally different realizations of meaning."

The method consists of treating an actual appearance as "the document of," as "pointing to," as "standing on behalf of" a presupposed underlying pattern. Not only is the underlying pattern derived from its individual documentary evidences, but the individual documentary evidences, in their turn, are interpreted on the basis of "what is known" about the underlying pattern. Each is used to elaborate the other.

The method is recognizable for the everyday necessities of recognizing what a person is "talking about" given that he does not say exactly what he means, or in recognizing such common occurrences and objects as mailmen, friendly gestures, and promises. It is recognizable as well in deciding such sociologically analyzed occurrence of events as Goffman's strategies for the management of impressions, Erickson's identity crises, Riesman's types of conformity, Parsons' value systems, Malinowski's magical practices, Bale's interaction counts, Merton's types of deviance, Lazarsfeld's latent structure of attitudes, and the U.S. Census' occupational categories.

How is it done by an investigator that from replies to a questionnaire he finds the respondent's "attitude"; that via interviews with office personnel he reports their "bureaucratically organized activities"; that by consulting crimes known to the police, he estimates the parameters of "real crime"? What is the work whereby the investigator sets the observed occurrence and the intended occurrence into a correspondence of meaning, such that the investigator finds it reasonable to treat witnessed actual appearances as evidences of the event he means to be studying?

Examples in Sociological Inquiry

Examples of the use of the documentary method can be cited from every area of sociological investigation. Its obvious application occurs in community studies where warrant is assigned to statements by the criteria of "comprehensive description" and "ring of truth." Its use is found also on the many occasions of survey research when the researcher, in reviewing his interview notes or in editing the answers to a questionnaire, has to decide "what the respondent had in mind." When a researcher is addressed to the "motivated character" of an action, or a theory, or a person's compliance to a legitimate order and the like, he will use what he has actually observed to "document" an "underlying pattern." The documentary method is used to epitomize the object. For example, just as the lay person may say of something that "Harry" says, "Isn't that just like Harry?" the investigator may use some observed feature of the thing he is referring to as a characterizing indicator of the intended matter. Complex scenes like industrial establishments, communities, or social movements are frequently described with the aid of "excerpts" from protocols and numerical tables which are used to epitomize the intended events. The documentary method is used whenever the investigator constructs a life history or a "natural history." The task of historicizing the person's biography consists of using the documentary method to select and order past occurrences so as to furnish the present state of affairs its relevant past and prospects.

67

Obligatory Exchange*

Marcel Mauss

To appreciate fully the institutions of total prestation and the potlatch we must seek to explain two complementary factors. Total prestation not only carries with it the obligation to repay gifts received, but it implies two others equally important: the obligation to give presents and the obligation to receive them. A complete theory of the three obligations would include a satisfactory fundamental explanation of this form of contract among Polynesian clans. For the moment we simply indicate the manner in which the subject might be treated.

It is easy to find a large number of facts on the obligation to receive. A clan, household, association or guest are constrained to demand hospitality, to receive presents, to barter or to make blood and marriage alliances. The Dayaks have even developed a whole set of customs based on the obligation to partake of any meal at which one is present or which one has seen in preparation.

The obligation to give is no less important. If we understood this, we should also know how men came to exchange things with each other. We merely point out a few facts. To refuse to give, or to fail to invite, is—like refusing to accept — the equivalent of a declaration of war; it is a refusal of friendship and intercourse. Again, one gives because one is forced to do so, because the recipient has a sort of proprietary right over everything which belongs to the donor. This right is expressed and conceived as a sort of spiritual bond. Thus in Australia the man who owes all the game he kills to his father-and mother-in-law may eat nothing in their presence for fear that their very breath should poison his food. We have seen above that the *taonga* sister's son has customs of this kind in Samoa, which are comparable with those of the sister's son (*vasu*) in Fiji.

In all these instances there is a series of rights and duties about consuming and repaying existing side by side with rights and duties about giving and receiving. The pattern of symmetrical and reciprocal rights is not difficult to understand if we realize that it is first and foremost a pattern of spiritual bonds between things which are to some extent parts of persons, and persons and groups that behave in some measure as if they were things.

All these institutions reveal the same kind of social and psychological pattern. Food, women, children, possessions, charms, land, labour, services, religious offices, rank—everything is stuff to be given away and repaid. In perpetual interchange of what we may call spiritual matter, comprising men and things, these elements pass and repass between clans and individuals, ranks, sexes and generations.

*Excerpts from *The Gift: Forms and Functions of Exchange in Archaic Societies* by Marcel Mauss, translated by Ian Cunnison. First published in the Norton Library 1967 by arrangement with Routledge and Kegan Paul Ltd. Reproduced by permission of Taylor & Francis Books UK.

Rules of Generosity (Andaman Islands)

Customs of the kind we are discussing are found with the pygmies who, according to Pater Schmidt, are the most primitive of men. In 1906 Radcliffe-Brown observed facts of this order in North Andaman, and described them admirably with reference to inter-group hospitality, visits, festivals and fairs, which present the opportunity for voluntary-obligatory exchanges — in this case of ochre and maritime produce against the produce of the chase. Despite the importance of these exchanges, 'as each local group and indeed each family was able to provide itself with everything that it needed in the way of weapons and utensils . . . the exchange of presents did not serve the same purpose as trade or barter in more developed communities. The purpose that it did serve was a moral one. The object of the exchange was to produce a friendly feeling between the two persons concerned, and unless it did this it failed of its purpose. . . No one was free to refuse a present offered to him. Each man and woman tried to outdo the others in generosity. There was a sort of amiable rivalry as to who could give away the greatest number of most valuable presents.' The gifts put a seal to marriage, forming a friendly relationship between the two sets of relatives. They give the two sides an identity which is revealed in the taboo which from then on prevents them from visiting or addressing each other, and in the obligation upon them thereafter to make perpetual gift-exchange. The taboo expresses both the intimacy and the fear which arise from this reciprocal creditor-debtor relationship. This is clearly the principle involved since the same taboo, implying simultaneous intimacy and distance, exists between young people of both sexes who have passed through the turtle- and pig-eating ceremonies together, and who are likewise obliged to exchange presents for the rest of their lives. Australia also provides facts of this kind. Radcliffe-Brown mentions rites of reunion—embracing and weeping—and shows how the exchange of presents is the equivalent of this, and how sentiments and persons are mingled. This confusion of personalities and things is precisely the mark of exchange contracts.

The *kula* is a kind of grand potlatch; it is the vehicle of a great inter-tribal trade extending over all the Trobriands, part of the d'Entrecasteaux group and part of the Amphletts. It has indirect influence on all the tribes and immediate influence on some: Dobu in the Amphletts; Kiriwina, Sinaketa and Kitava in the Trobriands; and Vakuta on Woodlark Island. Malinowski does not translate the word, which probably, however, means 'ring'; and in fact it seems as if all these tribes, the sea journeys, the precious objects, the food and feasts, the economic, ritual and sexual services, the men and the women, were caught in a ring around which they kept up a regular movement in time and space.

Kula trade is aristocratic. It seems to be reserved for the chiefs, who are chiefs of the *kula* fleet and canoes, traders for their vassals (children and brothers-in-law) and, apparently, chiefs over a number of vassal villages. The trade is carried out in noble fashion, disinterestedly and modestly. It is distinguished from the straightforward exchange of useful goods known as the *gimwali*. This is carried on as well as the *kula* in the great primitive fairs which mark inter-tribal *kula* gatherings and in the little *kula* markets of the interior; *gimwali*, however, is distinguished by most tenacious bargaining on both sides, a procedure unworthy of the *kula*. It is said of the individual who does not behave in his *kula* with proper magnanimity that he is conducting it 'as a *gimwali*'. In appearance at any rate, the *kula*, like the American potlatch, consists in giving and receiving, the donors on one occasion being the recipients on the next. Even in the largest, most solemn and highly competitive form of *kula*, that of the great maritime expeditions (*uvalaku*), the rule is to set out with nothing to exchange or even to give in return for food (for which of course it is improper to ask). On these visits one is recipient only, and it is when the visiting tribes the following year become the hosts that gifts are repaid with interest.

With the lesser *kula*, however, the sea voyage also serves as an opportunity for exchange of cargoes; the nobles themselves do business; numerous objects are solicited, demanded and exchanged, and many relationships are established in addition to *kula* ones; but the kula remains the most important reason for the expeditions and the relationships set up.

The ceremony of transfer is done with solemnity. The object given is disdained or suspect; it is not accepted until it is thrown on the ground. The donor affects an exaggerated modesty. Solemnly bearing his gift, accompanied by the blowing of a conch-shell, he apologizes for bringing only his leavings and throws the object at his partner's feet. Meanwhile the conch and the herald proclaim to one and all the dignity of the occasion. Pains are taken to show one's freedom and autonomy as well as one's magnanimity, yet all the time one is actuated by the mechanisms of obligation which are resident in the gifts themselves.

The most important things exchanged are *vaygu'a*, a kind of currency. These are of two sorts: *mwali*, the finely cut and polished armshells worn on great occasions by their owners or relatives, and the *soulava*, necklaces worked by the skilful turners of Sinaketa in handsome red spondylus shell. These are worn by women, and only rarely by men, for example, during sickness. Normally they are hoarded and kept for the joy of having. The manufacture of the one, and the gathering of the other, and the trading of these objects of prestige and exchange form, along with other more common and vulgar pursuits, the source of Trobriand wealth.

According to Malinowski these *vaygu'a* go in a sort of circular movement, the armshells passing regularly from west to east, and the necklaces from east to west. These two opposite movements take place between the d'Entrecasteaux group, the Amphletts, and the isolated islands of Woodlark, Marshall Bennett and Tubetube, and finally the extreme south-east coast of New Guinea, where the unpolished armshells come from. There this trade meets the great expeditions of the same nature from South Massim described by Seligman.

In theory these valuables never stop circulating. It is wrong to keep them too long or to be 'slow' and 'hard' with them; they are passed on only to predetermined partners in the arm-shell or necklace direction. They may be kept from one *kula* to the next while the community gloats over the *vaygu'a* which its chief has obtained. Although there are occasions, such as the preparation of funeral feasts, when it is permitted to receive and to pay nothing, these are no more than a prelude to the feast at which everything is repaid.

The gift received is in fact owned, but the ownership is of a particular kind. One might say that it includes many legal principles which we moderns have isolated from one another. It is at the same time property and a possession, a pledge and a loan, an object sold and an object bought, a deposit, a mandate, a trust; for it is given only on condition that it will be used on behalf of, or transmitted to, a third person, the remote partner (*murimuri*). Such is the economic, legal and moral complex, of quite a typical kind, that Malinowski discovered and described.

The Three Obligations: Giving, Receiving, Repaying

The Obligation to Give

This is the essence of potlatch. A chief must give a potlatch for himself, his son, his son-in-law or daughter and for the dead. He can keep his authority in his tribe, village and family, and maintain his position with the chiefs inside and outside his nation, only if he can prove that he is favourably regarded by the spirits, that he possesses fortune and that he is possessed by it. The only way to demonstrate his fortune is by expending it to the humiliation of others, by putting them 'in the shadow of his name'. Kwakiutl and Haida noblemen have the same notion of 'face' as the Chinese mandarin or officer. It is said of one of the great mythical chiefs who gave no feast that he had a 'rotten face'. The expression is more apt than it is even in China; for to lose one's face is to lose one's spirit, which is truly the 'face', the dancing mask, the right to incarnate a spirit and wear an emblem or totem. It is the veritable *persona* which is at stake, and it can be lost in the potlatch just as it can be lost in the game of gift-giving, in war, or through some error in ritual. In all these societies one is anxious to give; there is no occasion of importance (even outside the solemn winter gatherings) when one is *not* obliged to invite friends to share the produce of the chase or the forest which the gods or totems have sent; to redistribute everything received at a potlatch; or to recognize services from chiefs, vassals or relatives by means of gifts. Failing these obligations—at least for the nobles—etiquette is violated and rank is lost.

The Obligation to Receive

This is no less constraining. One does not have the right to refuse a gift or a potlatch. To do so would show fear of having to repay, and of being abased in default. One would 'lose the weight' of one's name by admitting defeat in advance. In certain circumstances, however, a refusal can be an assertion of victory and invincibility. It appears at least with the Kwakiutl that a recognized position in the hierarchy, or a victory through previous potlatches, allows one to refuse an invitation or even a gift without war ensuing. If this is so, then a potlatch must be carried out by the man who refuses to accept the invitation. More particularly, he has to contribute to the 'fat festival' in which a ritual of refusal may be observed. The chief who considers himself superior refuses the spoonful of fat offered him: he fetches his copper and returns with it to 'extinguish the fire' (of the fat). A series of formalities follow which mark the challenge and oblige the chief who has refused to give another potlatch or fat festival. In principle, however, gifts are always accepted and praised. You must speak your appreciation of food prepared for you. But you accept a challenge at the same time. You receive a gift 'on the back'. You accept the food and you do so because you mean to take up the challenge and prove that you are not unworthy. When chiefs confront each other in this manner they may find themselves in odd situations and probably they experience them as such. In like manner in ancient Gaul and Germany, as well as nowadays in gatherings of French farmers and students, one is pledged to swallow quantities of liquid to 'do honour' in grotesque fashion to the host. The obligation stands even although one is only heir to the man who bears the challenge. Failure to give or receive, like failure to make return gifts, means a loss of dignity.

The Obligation to Repay

Outside pure destruction the obligation to repay is the essence of potlatch. Destruction is very often sacrificial, directed towards the spirits, and apparently does not require a return unconditionally, especially when it is the work of a superior clan chief or of the chief of a clan already recognized as superior. But normally the potlatch must be returned with interest like all other gifts. The interest is generally between 30 and 100 per cent, a year. If a subject receives a blanket from his chief for a service rendered he will return two on the occasion of a marriage in the chief's family or on the initiation of the chief's son. But then the chief in his turn redistributes to him whatever he gets from the next potlatch at which rival clans repay the chief's generosity.

The obligation of worthy return is imperative. Face is lost for ever if it is not made or if equivalent value is not destroyed.

Sociological and Ethical Conclusions

We may be permitted another note about the method we have used. We do not set this work up as a model; it simply proffers one or two suggestions. It is incomplete: the analysis could be pushed farther. We are really posing questions for historians and anthropologists and offering possible lines of research for them rather than resolving a problem and laying down definite answers. It is enough for us to be sure for the moment that we have given sufficient data for such an end.

This being the case, we would point out that there is a heuristic element in our manner of treatment. The facts we have studied are all 'total' social phenomena. The word 'general' may be preferred although we like it less. Some of the facts presented concern the whole of society and its institutions (as with potlatch, opposing clans, tribes on visit, etc.); others, in which exchanges and contracts are the concern of individuals, embrace a large number of institutions.

These phenomena are at once legal, economic, religious, aesthetic, morphological and so on. They are legal in that they concern individual and collective rights, organized and diffuse morality; they may be entirely obligatory, or subject simply to praise or disapproval. They are at once political and domestic, being of interest both to classes and to clans and families. They are religious; they concern true religion, animism, magic and diffuse religious mentality. They are economic, for the notions of value, utility, interest, luxury, wealth, acquisition, accumulation, consumption and liberal and sumptuous expenditure are all present, although not perhaps in their modern senses. Moreover, these institutions have an important aesthetic side which we have left unstudied; but the dances performed, the songs and shows, the dramatic representations given between camps or partners, the objects made, used, decorated, polished, amassed and transmitted with affection, received with joy, given away in triumph, the feasts in which everyone participates—all these, the food, objects and services, are the source of aesthetic emotions as well as emotions aroused by interest. This is true not only of Melanesia but also, and particularly, of the potlatch of North-West America and still more true of the market-festival of the Indo-European world. Lastly, our phenomena are clearly morphological. Everything that happens in the course of gatherings, fairs and markets or in the feasts that replace them, presupposes groups whose duration exceeds the season of social concentration, like the winter potlatch of the Kwakiutl or the few weeks of the Melanesian maritime expeditions. Moreover, in order that these meetings may be carried out in peace, there must be roads or water for transport and tribal, intertribal or international alliances—*commercium* and *connubium*.

We are dealing then with something more than a set of themes, more than institutional elements, more than institutions, more even than systems of institutions divisible into legal, economic, religious and other parts. We are concerned with 'wholes', with systems in their entirety. We have not described them as if they were fixed, in a static or skeletal condition, and still less have we dissected them into the rules and myths and values and so on of which they are composed. It is only by considering them as wholes that we have been able to see their essence, their operation and their living aspect, and to catch the fleeting moment when the society and its members take emotional stock of themselves and their situation as regards others. Only by making such concrete observation of social life is it possible to come upon facts such as those which our study is beginning to reveal. Nothing in our opinion is more urgent or promising than research into 'total' social phenomena.

68

Social Behavior as Exchange*

George C. Homans

This essay will hope to honor the memory of Georg Simmel in two different ways. So far as it pretends to be suggestive rather than conclusive, its tone will be Simmel's; and its subject, too, will be one of his. Because Simmel, in essays such as those on sociability, games, coquetry, and conversation, was an analyst of elementary social behavior, we call him an ancestor of what is known today as small-group research. For what we are really studying in small groups is elementary social behavior: what happens when two or three persons are in a position to influence one another, the sort of thing of which those massive structures called "classes," "firms," "communities," and "societies" must ultimately be composed.

As I survey small-group research today, I feel that, apart from just keeping on with it, three sorts of things need to be done. The first is to show the relation between the results of experimental work done under laboratory conditions and the results of *quasi*-anthropological field research on what those of us who do it are pleased to call "real-life" groups in industry and elsewhere. If the experimental work has anything to do with real life—and I am persuaded that it has everything to do—its propositions cannot be inconsistent with those discovered through the field work. But the consistency has not yet been demonstrated in any systematic way.

The second job is to pull together in some set of general propositions the actual results, from the laboratory and from the field, of work on small groups—propositions that at least sum up, to an approximation, what happens in elementary social behavior, even though we may not be able to explain why the propositions should take the form they do. A great amount of work has been done, and more appears every day, but what it all amounts to in the shape of a set of propositions from which, under specified conditions, many of the observational results might be derived, is not at all clear—and yet to state such a set is the first aim of science.

The third job is to begin to show how the propositions that empirically hold good in small groups may be derived from some set of still more general propositions. "Still more general" means only that empirical propositions other than ours may also be derived from the set. This derivation would constitute the explanatory stage in the science of elementary social behavior, for explanation *is* derivation. (I myself suspect that the more general set will turn out to contain the propositions of behavioral psychology. I hold myself to be an "ultimate psychological reductionist," but I cannot know that I am right so long as the reduction has not been carried out.)

I have come to think that all three of these jobs would be furthered by our adopting the view that interaction between persons is an exchange of goods, material and non-material. This is one of the oldest theories of social behavior, and one that we still use every day to interpret our own behavior, as when we say, "I found so-and-so rewarding"; or "I got a great deal out of him"; or, even, "Talking with him took a great deal out of me." But, perhaps just because it is so obvious, this view has been much neglected by social scientists. So far as I know, the only theoretical work that makes explicit use of it is Marcel Mauss's *Essai sur le don,* published in 1925, which is ancient as social science goes. It may be that the tradition of neglect is now changing and that, for instance, the psychologists who interpret behavior in terms of transactions may be coming back to something of the sort I have in mind.

An incidental advantage of an exchange theory is that it might bring sociology closer to economics—that science of man most advanced, most capable of application, and, intellectually, most isolated. Economics studies exchange carried out under special circumstances and with a most useful built-in numerical measure of value. What are the laws of the general phenomenon of which economic behavior is one class?

In what follows I shall suggest some reasons for the usefulness of a theory of social behavior as exchange and suggest the nature of the propositions such a theory might contain.

An Exchange Paradigm

I start with the link to behavioral psychology and the kind of statement it makes about the behavior of an experimental animal such as the pigeon. As a pigeon explores its cage in the laboratory, it happens to peck a target, whereupon the psychologist feeds it corn. The evidence is that it will peck the target again; it has learned the behavior, or, as my friend Skinner says, the behavior has been reinforced, and the pigeon has undergone *operant conditioning.* This kind of psychologist is not interested in how the behavior was learned: "learning theory" is a poor name for his field. Instead, he is interested in what determines changes in the rate of emission of learned behavior, whether pecks at a target or something else.

The more hungry the pigeon, the less corn or other food it has gotten in the recent past, the more often it will peck. By the same token, if the behavior is often reinforced, if the pigeon is given much corn every time it pecks, the rate of emission will fall off as the pigeon gets *satiated.* If, on the other hand, the behavior is not reinforced at all, then, too, its rate of emission will tend to fall off, though a long time may pass before it stops altogether, before it is *extinguished.* In the emission of many kinds of behavior the pigeon incurs *aversive stimulation,* or what I shall call "cost" for short, and this, too, will lead in time to a decrease in the emission rate. Fatigue is an example of a "cost." Extinction, satiation, and cost, by decreasing the rate of emission of a particular kind of behavior, render more probable the emission of some other kind of behavior, including doing nothing. I shall only add that even a hard-boiled psychologist puts "emotional" behavior, as well as such things as pecking, among the unconditioned responses that may be reinforced in operant conditioning. As a statement of the propositions of behavioral psychology, the foregoing is, of course, inadequate for any purpose except my present one.

We may look on the pigeon as engaged in an exchange—pecks for corn—with the psychologist, but let us not dwell upon that, for the behavior of the pigeon hardly determines the behavior of the psychologist at all. Let us turn to a situation where the exchange is real, that is, where the determination is mutual. Suppose we are dealing with two men. Each is emitting behavior reinforced to some degree by the behavior of the other. How it was in the past that each learned the behavior he emits and how he learned to find the other's behavior reinforcing we are not concerned with. It is enough that each does find the other's behavior reinforcing, and I shall call the reinforcers—the equivalent of the pigeon's corn—*values,* for this, I think, is what we mean by this term. As he emits behavior, each man may incur costs, and each man has more than one course of behavior open to him.

This seems to me the paradigm of elementary social behavior, and the problem of the elementary sociologist is to state propositions relating the variations in the values and costs of each man to his frequency distribution of behavior among alternatives, where the values (in the mathematical sense) taken by these variable for one man determine in part their values for the other.

I see no reason to believe that the propositions of behavioral psychology do not apply to this situation, though the complexity of their implications in the concrete case may be great indeed. In particular, we must suppose that, with men as with pigeons, an increase in extinction, satiation, or aversive stimulation of any one kind of behavior will increase the probability of emission of some other kind. The problem is not, as it is often stated, merely, what a man's values are, what he has learned in the past to find reinforcing, but how much of any one value his behavior is getting him now. The more he gets, the less valuable any further unit of that value is to him, and the less often he will emit behavior reinforced by it.

The Influence Process

We do not, I think, possess the kind of studies of two-person interaction that would either bear out these propositions or fail to do so. But we do have studies of larger numbers of persons that suggest that they may apply, notably the studies by Festinger, Schachter, Back, and their associates on the dynamics of influence. One of the variables they work with they call *cohesiveness*, defined as anything that attracts people to take part in a group. Cohesiveness is a value variable; it refers to the degree of reinforcement people find in the activities of the group. Festinger and his colleagues consider two kinds of reinforcing activity: the symbolic behavior we call "social approval" (sentiment) and activity valuable in other ways, such as doing something interesting.

The other variable they work with they call *communication* and others call *interaction*. This is a frequency variable; it is a measure of the frequency of emission of valuable and costly verbal behavior. We must bear in mind that, in general, the one kind of variable is a function of the other.

Festinger and his co-workers show that the more cohesive a group is, that is, the more valuable the sentiment or activity the members exchange with one another, the greater the average frequency of interaction of the members. With men, as with pigeons, the greater the reinforcement, the more often is the reinforced behavior emitted. The more cohesive a group, too, the greater the change that members can produce in the behavior of other members in the direction of rendering these activities more valuable. That is, the more valuable the activities that members get, the more valuable those that they must give. For if a person is emitting behavior of a certain kind, and other people do not find it particularly rewarding, these others will suffer their own production of sentiment and activity, in time, to fall off. But perhaps the first person has found their sentiment and activity rewarding, and, if he is to keep on getting them, he must make his own behavior more valuable to the others. In short, the propositions of behavioral psychology imply a tendency toward a certain proportionality between the value to others of the behavior a man gives them and the value to him of the behavior they give him.

Schachter also studied the behavior of members of a group toward two kinds of other members, "conformers" and "deviates." I assume that conformers are people whose activity the other members find valuable. For conformity is behavior that coincides to a degree with some group standard or norm, and the only meaning I can assign to *norm* is "a verbal description of behavior that many members find it valuable for the actual behavior of themselves and others to conform to." By the same token, a deviate is a member whose behavior is not particularly valuable. Now Schachter shows that, as the members of a group come to see another member as a deviate, their interaction with him—communication addressed to getting him to change his behavior—goes up, the faster the more cohesive the group. The members need not talk to the other conformers so much; they are relatively satiated by the conformers' behavior: they have gotten what they want out of them. But if the deviate, by failing to change his behavior, fails to reinforce the members, they start to withhold social approval from him: the deviate gets low sociometric choice at the end of the experiment. And in the most cohesive groups—those Schachter calls "high cohesive-relevant"—interaction with the deviate also falls off in the end and is lowest among those members that rejected him most strongly, as if they had given him up as a bad job. But how plonking can we get? These findings are utterly in line with everyday experience.

PRACTICAL EQUILIBRIUM

At the beginning of this paper I suggested that one of the tasks of small-group research was to show the relation between the results of experimental work done under laboratory conditions and the results of field research on real-life small groups. Now the latter often appear to be in practical equilibrium, and by this I mean nothing fancy. I do not mean that all real-life groups are in equilibrium. I certainly do not mean that all groups must tend to equilibrium. I do not mean that groups have built-in antidotes to change: there is no homeostasis here. I do not mean that we assume equilibrium. I mean only that we sometimes *observe* it, that for the time we are with a group—and it is often short—there is no great change in the values of the variables we choose to measure. If, for instance, person A is interacting with B more than with C both at the beginning and at the end of the study, then at least by this crude measure the group is in equilibrium.

Many of the Festinger-Schachter studies are experimental, and their propositions about the process of influence seem to me to imply the kind of proposition that empirically holds good of real-life groups in practical equilibrium. For instance, Festinger *et al.* find that, the more cohesive a group is, the greater the change that members can produce in the behavior of other members. If the influence is exerted in the direction of conformity to group norms, then, when the process of influence has accomplished all the change of which it is capable, the proposition should hold good that, the more cohesive a group is, the larger the number of members that conform to its norms. And it does hold good.

Again, Schachter found, in the experiment I summarized above, that in the most cohesive groups and at the end, when the effort to influence the deviate had failed, members interacted little with the deviate and gave him little in the way of sociometric choice. Now two of the propositions that hold good most often of real-life groups in practical equilibrium are precisely that the more closely a member's activity conforms to the norms the more interaction he receives from other members and the more liking choices he gets from them too. From these main propositions a number of others may be derived that also hold good.

Yet we must ever remember that the truth of the proposition linking conformity to liking may on occasion be masked by the truth of other propositions. If, for instance, the man that conforms to the norms most closely also exerts some authority over the group, this may render liking for him somewhat less than it might otherwise have been.

Be that as it may, I suggest that the laboratory experiments on influence imply propositions about the behavior of members of small groups, when the process of influence has worked itself out, that are identical with propositions that hold good of real-life groups in equilibrium. This is hardly surprising if all we mean by equilibrium is that all the change of which the system is, under present conditions, capable has been effected, so that no further change occurs. Nor would this be the first time that statics has turned out to be a special case of dynamics.

PROFIT AND SOCIAL CONTROL

Though I have treated equilibrium as an observed fact, it is a fact that cries for explanation. I shall not, as structural-functional sociologists do, use an assumed equilibrium as a means of explaining, or trying to explain, why the other features of a social system should be what they are. Rather, I shall take practical equilibrium as something that is itself to be explained by the other features of the system.

If every member of a group emits at the end of, and during, a period of time much the same kinds of behavior and in much the same frequencies as he did at the beginning, the group is for that period in equilibrium. Let us then ask why any one member's behavior should persist. Suppose he is emitting behavior of value A_1. Why does he not let his behavior get worse (less valuable or reinforcing to the others) until it stands at A_1—ΔA? True, the sentiments expressed by others toward him are apt to decline in value (become less reinforcing to him), so that what he gets from them may be S_1— ΔS. But it is conceivable that, since most activity carries cost, a decline in the value of what he emits will mean a reduction in cost to him that more than offsets his losses in sentiment. Where, then, does he stabilize his behavior? This is the problem of social control.

Mankind has always assumed that a person stabilizes his behavior, at least in the short run, at the point where he is doing the best he can for himself under the circumstances, though his best may not be a "rational" best, and what he can do may not be at all easy to specify, except that he is not apt to think like one of the theoretical antagonists in the *Theory of Games*. Before a sociologist rejects this answer out of hand for its horrid profit-seeking implications, he will do well to ask himself if he can offer any other answer to the question posed. I think he will find that he cannot. Yet experiments designed to test the truth of the answer are extraordinarily rare.

I shall review one that seems to me to provide a little support for the theory, though it was not meant to do so. The experiment is reported by H. B. Gerard, a member of the Festinger-Schachter team, under the title "The Anchorage of Opinions in Face-to-Face Groups." The experimenter formed artificial groups whose members met to discuss a case in industrial relations and to express their opinions about its probable outcome. The groups were of two kinds: high-attraction groups, whose members were told that they would like one another very much, and low-attraction groups, whose members were told that they would not find one another particularly likable.

At a later time the experimenter called the members in separately, asked them again to express their opinions on the outcome of the case, and counted the number that had changed their opinions to bring them into accord with those of other members of their groups. At the same time, a paid participant entered into a further discussion of the case with each member, always taking, on the probable outcome of the case, a position opposed to that taken by the bulk of the other members of the group to which the person belonged. The experimenter counted the number of persons shifting toward the opinion of the paid participant.

The experiment had many interesting results, from which I choose only those summed up in Tables 1 and 2. The three different agreement classes are made up of people who, at the original sessions, expressed different degrees of agreement with the opinions of other members of their groups. And the figure 44, for instance, means that, of all members of high-attraction groups whose initial opinions were strongly in disagreement with those of other members, 44 per cent shifted their opinion later toward that of others.

In these results the experimenter seems to have been interested only in the differences in the sums of the rows, which show that there is more shifting toward the group, and less shifting toward the paid participant, in the high-attraction than in the low-attraction condition. This is in line with a proposition suggested earlier. If you think that the members of a group can give you much—in this case, liking—you are apt to give them much—in this case, a change to an opinion in accordance with their views—or you will not get the liking. And, by the same token, if the group can give you little of value, you will not be ready to give it much of value. Indeed, you may change your opinion so as to depart from agreement even further, to move, that is, toward the view held by the paid participant.

So far so good, but, when I first scanned these tables, I was less struck by the difference between them than by their similarity. The same classes of people in both tables showed much the same relative propensities to change their opinions, no matter whether the change was toward the group or toward the paid participant. We see, for instance, that those who change least are the high-attraction, agreement people and the low-attraction, strong-disagreement ones. And those who change most are the high-attraction, strong-disagreement people and the low-attraction, mild-disagreement ones.

How am I to interpret these particular results? Since the experimenter did not discuss them, I am free to offer my own explanation. The behavior emitted by the subjects is opinion and changes in opinion. For this behavior they have learned to expect two possible kinds of reinforcement. Agreement with the group gets the subject favorable sentiment (acceptance) from it, and the experiment was designed to give this reinforcement a higher value in the high-attraction condition than in the low-attraction one. The second kind of possible reinforcement is what I shall call the "maintenance of one's personal integrity," which a subject gets by sticking to his own opinion in the face of disagreement with the group. The experimenter does not mention this reward, but I cannot make sense of the results without something much like it. In different degrees for different subjects, depending on their initial positions, these rewards are in

Table 1 Percentage of Subjects Changing toward Someone in the Group

	Aggreement	*Mild Disagreement*	*Strong Disagreement*
High attraction. . . .	0	12	44
Low attraction. . . .	0	15	9

Table 2 Percentage of Subjects Changing toward the Paid Participant

	Aggreement	*Mild Disagreement*	*Strong Disagreement*
High attraction. . . .	7	13	25
Low attraction. . . .	20	38	8

competition with one another: they are alternatives. They are not absolutely scarce goods, but some persons cannot get both at once.

Since the rewards are alternatives, let me introduce a familiar assumption from economics—that the cost of a particular course of action is the equivalent of the foregone value of an alternative—and then add the definition: Profit = Reward - Cost.

Now consider the persons in the corresponding cells of the two tables. The behavior of the high-attraction, agreement people gets them much in the way of acceptance by the group, and for it they must give up little in the way of personal integrity, for their views are from the start in accord with those of the group. Their profit is high, and they are not prone to change their behavior. The low-attraction, strong-disagreement people are getting much in integrity, and they are not giving up for it much in valuable acceptance, for they are members of low-attraction groups. Reward less cost is high for them, too, and they change little. The high-attraction, strong-disagreement people are getting much in the way of integrity, but their costs in doing so are high, too, for they are in high-attraction groups and thus foregoing much valuable acceptance by the group. Their profit is low, and they are very apt to change, either toward the group or toward the paid participant, from whom they think, perhaps, they will get some acceptance while maintaining some integrity. The low-attraction, mild-disagreement people do not get much in the way of integrity, for they are only in mild disagreement with the group, but neither are they giving up much in acceptance, for they are members of low-attraction groups. Their rewards are low; their costs are low too, and their profit—the difference between the two—is also low. In their low profit they resemble the high-attraction, strong-disagreement people, and, like them, they are prone to change their opinions, in this case, more toward the paid participant. The subjects in the other two cells, who have medium profits, display medium propensities to change.

If we define profit as reward less cost, and if cost is value foregone, I suggest that we have here some evidence for the proposition that change in behavior is greatest when perceived profit is least. This constitutes no direct demonstration that change in behavior is least when profit is greatest, but if, whenever a man's behavior brought him a balance of reward and cost, he changed his behavior away from what got him, under the circumstances, the less profit, there might well come a time when his behavior would not change further. That is, his behavior would be stabilized, at least for the time being. And, so far as this were true for every member of a group, the group would have a social organization in equilibrium.

I do not say that a member would stabilize his behavior at the point of greatest conceivable profit to himself, because his profit is partly at the mercy of the behavior of others. It is a commonplace that the short-run pursuit of profit by several persons often lands them in positions where all are worse off than they might conceivably be. I do not say that the paths of behavioral change in which a member pursues his profit under the condition that others are pursuing theirs too are easy to describe or predict; and we can readily conceive that in jockeying for position they might never arrive at any equilibrium at all.

Distributive Justice

Yet practical equilibrium is often observed, and thus some further condition may make its attainment, under some circumstance, more probable than would the individual pursuit of profit left to itself. I can offer evidence for this further condition only in the behavior of subgroups and not in that of individuals. Suppose that there are two subgroups, working close together in a factory, the job of one being somewhat different from that of the other. And suppose that the members of the first complain and say: "We are getting the same pay as they are. We ought to get just a couple of dollars a week more to show that our work is more responsible." When you ask them what they mean by "more responsible," they say that, if they do their work wrong, more damage can result, and so they are under more pressure to take care. Something like this is a common feature of industrial behavior. It is at the heart of disputes not over absolute wages but over wage differentials—indeed, at the heart of disputes over rewards other than wages.

In what kind of propostion may we express observations like these? We may say that wages and responsibility give status in the group, in the sense that a man who takes high responsibility and gets high wages is admired, other things equal. Then, if the members of one group score higher on responsibility than do the members of another, there is a felt need on the part of the first to score higher on pay too. There is a pressure, which shows itself in complaints, to bring the *status factors,* as I have called them, into line with one another. If they are in line, a condition of *status congruence* is said to exist. In this condition the workers may find their jobs dull or irksome, but they will not complain about the relative position of groups.

But there may be a more illuminating way of looking at the matter. In my example I have considered only responsibility and pay, but these may be enough, for they represent the two kinds of thing that come into the problem. Pay is clearly a reward; responsibility may be looked on, less clearly, as a cost. It means constraint and worry—or peace of mind foregone. Then the proposition about status congruence becomes this: If the costs of the members of one group are higher than those of another, distributive justice requires that their rewards should be higher too. But the thing works both ways: If the rewards are higher, the costs should be higher too. This last is the theory of *noblesse oblige,* which we all subscribe to, though we all laugh at it, perhaps because the *noblesse* often fails to *oblige.* To put the matter in terms of profit: though the rewards and costs of two persons or the members of two groups may be different, yet the profits of the two—the excess of reward over cost—should tend to equality. And more than "should." The less-advantaged group will at least try to attain greater equality, as, in the example I have used, the first group tried to increase its profit by increasing its pay.

I have talked of distributive justice. Clearly, this is not the only condition determining the actual distribution of rewards and costs. At the same time, never tell me that notions of justice are not a strong influence on behavior, though we sociologists often neglect them. Distributive justice may be one of the conditions of group equilibrium.

Exchange and Social Structure

I shall end by reviewing almost the only study I am aware of that begins to show in detail how a stable and differentiated social structure in a real-life group might arise out of a process of exchange between members. This is Peter Blau's description of the behavior of sixteen agents in a federal law-enforcement agency.

The agents had the duty of investigating firms and preparing reports on the firms' compliance with the law. Since the reports might lead to legal action against the firms, the agents had to prepare them carefully, in the proper form, and take strict account of the many regulations that might apply. The agents were often in doubt what they should do, and then they were supposed to take the question to their supervisor. This they were reluctant to do, for they naturally believed that thus confessing to him their inability to solve a problem would reflect on their competence, affect the official ratings he made of their work, and so hurt their chances for promotion. So agents often asked other agents for help and advice, and, though this was nominally forbidden, the supervisor usually let it pass.

Blau ascertained the ratings the supervisor made of the agents, and he also asked the agents to rate one another. The two opinions agreed closely. Fewer agents were regarded as highly competent than were regarded as of middle or low competence; competence, or the ability to solve technical problems, was a fairly scarce good. One or two of the more competent agents would not give help and advice when asked, and so received few interactions and little liking. A man that will not exchange, that will not give you what he has when you need it, will not get from you the only thing you are, in this case, able to give him in return, your regard.

But most of the more competent agents were willing to give help, and of them Blau says:

> A consultation can be considered an exchange of values: both participants gain something, and both have to pay a price. The questioning agent is enabled to perform better than he could otherwise have done, without exposing his difficulties to his supervisor. By asking for advice, he implicitly pays his respect to the superior proficiency of his colleague. This acknowledgment of inferiority is the cost of receiving assistance. The consultant gains prestige, in return for which he is willing to devote some time to the consultation and permit it to disrupt his own work. The following remark of an agent illustrates this: "I like giving advice. It's flattering, I suppose, if you feel that others come to you for advice.

Blau goes on to say: "All agents liked being consulted, but the value of any one of very many consultations became deflated for experts, and the price they paid in frequent interruptions became inflated." This implies that, the more prestige an agent received, the less was the increment of value of that prestige; the more advice an agent gave, the greater was the increment of cost of that advice, the cost lying precisely in the foregone value of time to do his own work. Blau suggests that something of the same sort was true of an agent who went to a more competent colleague for advice: the more often he went, the more costly to him, in feelings of inferiority, became any further request. "The repeated admission of his inability to solve his own problems . . . undermined the self-confidence of the worker and his standing in the group."

The result was that the less competent agents went to the more competent ones for help less often than they might have done if the costs of repeated admissions of inferiority had been less high and that, while many agents sought out the few highly competent ones, no single agent sought out the latter much. Had they done so (to look at the exchange from the other side), the costs to the highly competent in interruptions to their own work would have become exorbitant. Yet the need of the less competent for help was still not fully satisfied. Under these circumstances they tended to turn for help to agents more nearly like themselves in competence. Though the help they got was not the most valuable, it was of a kind they could themselves return on occasion. With such agents they could exchange help and liking, without the exchange becoming on either side too great a confession of inferiority.

The highly competent agents tended to enter into exchanges, that is, to interact with many others. But, in the more equal exchanges I have just spoken of, less competent agents tended to pair off as partners. That is, they interacted with a smaller number of people, but interacted often with these few. I think I could show why pair relations in these more equal exchanges would be more economical for an agent than a wider distribution of favors. But perhaps I have gone far enough. The final pattern of this social structure was one in which a small number of highly competent agents exchanged advice for prestige with a large number of others less competent and in which the less competent agents exchanged, in pairs and in trios, both help and liking on more nearly equal terms.

Blau shows, then, that a social structure in equilibrium might be the result of a process of exchanging behavior rewarding and costly in different degrees, in which the increment of reward and cost varied with the frequency of the behavior, that is, with the frequency of interaction. Note that the behavior of the agents seems also to have satisfied my second condition of equilibrium: the more competent agents took more responsibility for the work, either their own or others', than did the less competent ones, but they also got more for it in the way of prestige. I suspect that the same kind of explanation could be given for the structure of many "informal" groups.

Summary

The current job of theory in small-group research is to make the connection between experimental and real-life studies, to consolidate the propositions that empirically hold good in the two fields, and to show how these propositions might be derived from a still more general set. One way of doing this job would be to revive and make more rigorous the oldest of theories of social behavior—social behavior as exchange.

Some of the statements of such a theory might be the following. Social behavior is an exchange of goods, material goods but also non-material ones, such as the symbols of approval or prestige. Persons that give much to others try to get much from them, and persons that get much from others are under pressure to give much to them. This process of influence tends to work out at equilibrium to a balance in the exchanges. For a person engaged in exchange, what he gives may be a cost to him, just as what he gets may be a reward, and his behavior changes less as profit, that is, reward less cost, tends to a maximum. Not only does he seek a maximum for himself, but he tries to see to it that no one in his group makes more profit than he does. The cost and the value of what he gives and of what he gets vary with the quantity of what he gives and gets. It is surprising how familiar these propositions are; it is surprising, too, how propositions about the dynamics of exchange can begin to generate the static thing we call "group structure" and, in so doing, generate also some of the propositions about group structure that students of real-life groups have stated.

In our unguarded moments we sociologists find words like "reward" and "cost" slipping into what we say. Human nature will break in upon even our most elaborate theories. But we seldom let it have its way with us and follow up systematically what these words imply. Of all our many "approaches" to social behavior, the one that sees it as an economy is the most neglected, and yet it is the one we use every moment of our lives—except when we write sociology.

69

Reciprocity, Power Imbalance, and Dialectical Change*

Peter M. Blau

There is a strain toward imbalance as well as toward reciprocity in social associations. The term "balance" itself is ambiguous inasmuch as we speak not only of balancing our books but also of a balance in our favor, which refers, of course, to a lack of equality between inputs and outputs. As a matter of fact, the balance of the accounting sheet merely rests, in the typical case, on an underlying imbalance between income and outlays, and so do apparent balances in social life. Individuals and groups are interested in, at least, maintaining a balance between inputs and outputs and staying out of debt in their social transactions; hence the strain toward reciprocity. Their aspirations, however, are to achieve a balance in their favor and accumulate credit that makes their status superior to that of others; hence the strain toward imbalance.

Arguments about equilibrium—that all scientific theories must be conceived in terms of equilibrium models or that any equilibrium model neglects the dynamics of real life—ignore the important point that the forces sustaining equilibrium on one level of social life constitute disequilibrating forces on other levels. For supply and demand to remain in equilibrium in a market, for example, forces must exist that continually disturb the established patterns of exchange. Similarly, the circulation of the elite, an equilibrium model, rests on the operation of forces that create imbalances and disturbances in the various segments of society. The principle suggested is that balanced social states depend on imbalances in other social states; forces that restore equilibrium in one respect do so by creating disequilibrium in others. The processes of association described illustrate this principle.

A person who is attracted to another will seek to prove himself attractive to the other. Thus a boy who is very much attracted to a girl, more so than she is to him, is anxious to make himself more attractive to her. To do so, he will try to impress her and, particularly, go out of his way to make associating with him an especially rewarding experience for her. He may devote a lot of thought to finding ways to please her, spend

*Excerpts from *Exchange and Power in Social Life* by Peter M. Blau. Copyright 1964 by John Wiley & Sons. Reprinted with permission from Transaction Publishers.

much money on her, and do the things she likes on their dates rather than those he would prefer. Let us assume that he is successful and she becomes as attracted to him as he is to her, that is, she finds associating with him as rewarding as he finds associating with her, as indicated by the fact that both are equally eager to spend time together.

Attraction is now reciprocal, but the reciprocity has been established by an imbalance in the exchange. To be sure, both obtain satisfactory rewards from the association at this stage, the boy as the result of her willingness to spend as much time with him as he wants, and the girl as the result of his readiness to make their dates enjoyable for her. These reciprocal rewards are the sources of their mutual attraction. The contributions made, however, are in imbalance. Both devote time to the association, which involves giving up alternative opportunities, but the boy contributes in addition special efforts to please her. Her company is sufficient reward by itself, while his is not, which makes her "the more useful or otherwise superior" in terms of their own evaluations, and he must furnish supplementary rewards to produce "equality in a sense between the parties." Although two lovers may, of course, be equally anxious to spend time together and to please one another, it is rare for a perfect balance of mutual affection to develop spontaneously. The reciprocal attraction in most intimate relations—marriages and lasting friendships as well as more temporary attachments—is the result of some imbalance of contributions that compensates for inequalities in spontaneous affection, notably in the form of one partner's greater willingness to defer to the other's wishes.

The theoretical principle that has been advanced is that a given balance in social associations is produced by imbalances in the same associations in other respects. This principle, which has been illustrated with the imbalances that underlie reciprocal attraction, also applies to the process of social differentiation. A person who supplies services in demand to others obligates them to reciprocate. If some fail to reciprocate, he has strong inducements to withhold the needed assistance from them in order to supply it to others who do repay him for his troubles in some form. Those who have nothing else to offer him that would be a satisfactory return for his services, therefore, are under pressure to defer to his wishes and comply with his requests in repayment for his assistance. Their compliance with his demands gives him the power to utilize their resources at his discretion to further his own ends. By providing unilateral benefits to others, a person accumulates a capital of willing compliance on which he can draw whenever it is to his interest to impose his will upon others, within the limits of the significance the continuing supply of his benefits has for them. The general advantages of power enable men who cannot otherwise repay for services they need to obtain them in return for their compliance; although in the extreme case of the person who has much power and whose benefits are in great demand, even an offer of compliance may not suffice to obtain them.

Here, an imbalance of power establishes reciprocity in the exchange. Unilateral services give rise to a differentiation of power that equilibrates the exchange. The exchange balance, in fact, rests on two imbalances: unilateral services and unilateral power. Although these two imbalances make up a balance or equilibrium in terms of one perspective, in terms of another, which is equally valid, the exchange equilibrium reinforces and perpetuates the imbalances of dependence and power that sustain it. Power differences not only are an imbalance by definition but also are actually experienced as such, as indicated by the tendency of men to escape from domination if they can. Indeed, a major impetus for the eagerness of individuals to discharge their obligations and reciprocate for services they receive, by providing services in return, is the threat of becoming otherwise subject to the power of the supplier of the services. While reciprocal services create an interdependence that balances power, unilateral dependence on services maintains an imbalance of power.

Differentiation of power evidently constitutes an imbalance in the sense of an inequality of power; but the question must be raised whether differentiation of power also necessarily constitutes an imbalance in the sense of a strain toward change in the structure of social relations. Power differences as such, analytically conceived and abstracted from other considerations, create such a pressure toward change, because it can be assumed that men experience having to submit to power as a hardship from which they would prefer to escape. The advantages men derive from their ruler or government, however, may outweigh the hardships entailed in submitting to his or its power, with the result that the analytical imbalance or disturbance introduced by power differences is neutralized. The significance of power imbalances for social change depends, therefore, on the reactions of the governed to the exercise of power.

Social reactions to the exercise of power reflect once more the principle of reciprocity and imbalance, although in a new form. Power over others makes it possible to direct and organize their activities. Sufficient resources to command power over large numbers enable a person or group to establish a large organization. The members recruited to the organization receive benefits, such as financial remuneration, in exchange for complying with the directives of superiors and making various contributions to the organization. The leadership exercises power within the organization, and it derives power from the organization for use in relation with other organizations or groups. The clearest illustration of this double power of organizational leadership is the army commander's power over his own soldiers and, through the force of their arms, over the enemy. Another example is the power business management exercises over its own employees and, through the strength of the concern, in the market. The greater the external power of an organization, the greater are its chances of accumulating resources that put rewards at the disposal of the leadership for possible distribution among the members.

The normative expectations of those subject to the exercise of power, which are rooted in their social experience, govern their reactions to it. In terms of these standards, the benefits derived from being part of an organization or political society may outweigh the investments required to obtain them, or the demands made on members may exceed the returns they receive for fulfilling these demands. The exercise of power, therefore, may produce two different kinds of imbalance, a positive imbalance of benefits for subordinates or a negative imbalance of exploitation and oppression.

If the members of an organization, or generally those subject to a governing leadership, commonly agree that the demands made on them are only fair and just in view of the ample rewards the leadership delivers, joint feelings of obligation and loyalty to superiors will arise and bestow legitimating approval on their authority. A positive imbalance of benefits generates legitimate authority for the leadership and thereby strengthens and extends its controlling influence. By expressing legitimating approval of, and loyalty to, those who govern them subordinates reciprocate for the benefits their leadership provides, but they simultaneously fortify the imbalance of power in the social structure.

If the demands of the men who exercise power are experienced by those subject to it as exploitative and oppressive, and particularly if these subordinates have been unsuccessful in obtaining redress for their grievances, their frustrations tend to promote disapproval of existing powers and antagonism toward them. As the oppressed communicate their anger and aggression to each other, provided there are opportunities for doing so, their mutual support and approval socially justify and reinforce the negative orientation toward the oppressors, and their collective hostility may inspire them to organize an opposition. The exploitative use of coercive power that arouses active opposition is more prevalent in the relations between organizations and groups than within organizations. Two reasons for this are that the advantages of legitimating approval restrain organizational superiors and that the effectiveness of legitimate authority, once established, obviates the need for coercive measures. But the exploitative use of power also occurs within organizations, as unions organized in opposition to exploitative employers show. A negative imbalance for the subjects of power stimulates opposition. The opposition negatively reciprocates, or retaliates, for excessive demands in an attempt to even the score, but it simultaneously creates conflict, disequilibrium, and imbalance in the social structure.

Even in the relatively simple structures of social association considered here, balances in one respect entail imbalances in others. The interplay between equilibrating and disequilibrating forces is still more evident, if less easy to unravel, in complex macrostructures with their cross-cutting substructures, where forces that sustain reciprocity and balance have disequilibrating and imbalancing repercussions not only on other levels of the same substructure but also on other substructures. As we shall see, disequilibrating and re-equilibrating forces generate a dialectical pattern of change in social structures.

Dialectic

There is a dialectic in social life, for it is governed by many contradictory forces. The dilemmas of social associations reflect this dialectic, and so does the character of social change. To conceive of change in social structures as dialectical implies that it involves neither evolutionary progress in a straight line nor recurring cycles but alternating patterns of intermittent social reorganization along different lines. The analysis of the relationship between reciprocity and imbalance illustrates the underlying conception.

Reciprocity is an equilibrating force, the assumption being that every social action is balanced by some appropriate counteraction. Individuals who receive needed benefits from others are obligated, lest the supply of benefits cease, to reciprocate in some form, whether through expressions of gratitude, approval, material rewards, services, or compliance. Reciprocity on one level, however, entails imbalances on others. If persons are obligated to accede to another's wishes because he renders essential services to them for which they cannot otherwise compensate him, their compliance reciprocates for the unilateral services they obtain and in this sense restores balance, but it also creates an imbalance of power. The reactions to the exercise of power superimpose a secondary exchange upon the primary one. The exercise of power with fairness and moderation earns a man social approval, whereas the oppressive use of power evokes disapproval. The social approval that rewards rulers for not taking full advantage of their power and the social disapproval that penalizes them for taking excessive advantage of it equilibrate the scales, so to speak. Simultaneously, however, the collective approval of subordinates legitimates the governing group's authority over them and thus reinforces the imbalance of power, and the collective disapproval of the oppressed tends to give rise to opposition forces that disturb social equilibrium and stimulate reorganizations in the social structure. Every social process restoring equilibrium engenders some new imbalances.

Social forces often have contradictory implications. One reason for this is that the conditions produced by a social force may provoke the emergence of another force in the opposite direction. Processes of social integration, in which group members impress each other with their outstanding qualities, give rise to differentiation of status, and social differentiation reinforces the need for processes that effect social integration. Inelastic supply of advice that is in high demand in a work group intensifies status differences, since experts gain much status in exchange for their counsel, but the high price of advice encourages the formation of mutual partnerships of consultation, which lessen the status differences in the group. The very increase in rewards intended to elicit greater contributions depreciates the value of these rewards as incentives for making contributions. By increasing the number of promotions in a company, for example, the level of expectations is raised, with the result that the same promotion no longer creates the same satisfaction as before. The deprivation of the underprivileged prompts them to organize unions and leftist opposition parries in order to improve their conditions, and the relative deprivation of the lower-middle class consequent to success in these endeavors fosters the development of rightist opposition movements.

The multiple consequences of a social force are another reason it may have contradictory repercussions in the social structure. The forces set in motion to restore equilibrium in one respect, or in one segment of the social structure, are typically disequilibrating forces in other respects, or in other segments. For supply and demand to reach an equilibrium, established exchange relations must be upset. The equilibrium in an organization is disturbed by membership turnover and promoted by a stable membership committed to the organization and their occupational careers in it, but these organizational attachments impede the mobility of individuals that is necessary for occupational investments and the returns received for them to attain a state of equilibrium. The success of some organized collectivities in competition, which produces optimum conditions for meeting internal requirements, spells the failure of others, with consequent internal disruptions and possible failure to survive altogether. Conditions established to further centralized planning and coordination in an organization interfere with the departmental autonomy required for effective operations. Many incompatible requirements exist in complex social structures, and given the interdependence between substructures, social processes that meet some requirements frequently create impediments for meeting others, stimulating the emergence of different social processes to meet these other requirements.

There is much resistance to social change in societies. Vested interests and powers, established practices and organizations, traditional values and institutions, and other kinds of social investments are forces of stability and resistance to basic social innovations and reorganizations. New problems and social needs continually arise, but they often persist for long periods of time before the adjustments necessary to meet them occur, since due to these forces of resistance considerable pressure toward change must build up before it is realized. Changes in major social institutions supported by interested powers as well as traditional values, in particular, require strenuous and prolonged struggles by strong opposition movements. Oppression and hardships must be severe and widespread for men to be likely to make social investments in a radical opposition movement and for the movement to have the wide appeal required for its ultimate success. The lesser opposition forces that crisscross complex social structures, overlapping and going in diverse directions, must also gather some momentum before they can produce readjustments. The existence of conflicting forces that pull in different directions itself would be reflected in social change in the direction of the resultant force, but in combination with the need for a latency period before opposition forces can realize their potential, it leads to structural change characterized not so much by continuous adjustments as by intermittent reorganizations.

Structural change, therefore, assumes a dialectical pattern. While social structures are governed by equilibrating forces, given the complex interdependence and incompatible requirements of intersecting substructures in a society, virtually every equilibrating force generates disequilibrium on other levels. In the process of creating readjustments in one respect, other dislocations are typically produced that necessitate further readjustments. Social imbalances may persist for prolonged periods, and social equilibrium is not constantly maintained, because a latency period intervenes before opposition forces have mobilized sufficient strength to effect adjustments. The recurrent disequilibrating and re-equilibrating forces on many levels of social structure are reflected in the dialectical nature of structural change.

70

Individual Interests and Systems of Exchange*

James S. Coleman

I have presented a general orientation to social theory. This involved explaining behavior of a social system by means of three components: the effects of properties of the system on the constraints or orientations of actors; the actions of actors who are within the system; and the combination or interaction of those actions, bringing about the systemic behavior.

This general metatheoretical structure can be described as a conceptual framework for social theory. A framework of this sort can serve a useful purpose in evaluating and guiding research. It would be possible to stop here, before explicit theory construction, and devote the remainder to examining the implications of this conceptual framework for research on various social phenomena. To do so, however, would be to stop short of theory itself. This would provide a less useful basis for the development of knowledge about social systems than will the explicit development of social theory within this conceptual framework.

An indication of the way the conceptual framework was laid out will be carried toward a more explicit theory is provided by considering the functioning of an economic market through a system of tentative contracts, as described by Walras. Here the idea of system behavior is something of a reification, because each actor's actions have direct effects only on those with whom that actor has discussed contracts, and each actor's changes of contracts might depend only on comparison of exchange rates with those in the immediate vicinity, unless an institution exists to ensure full communication of information about all tentative contracts. Yet, in this case of a market, the reification becomes more and more a reality as the spread of information leads various contracts to converge toward a single set of exchange rates for each pair of goods. The market price is an emergent property of the system that arises from the pairwise interactions.

As this example indicates, it may be more useful in the emergence of at least some system behavior to conceptualize the feedback processes that produce that behavior not as explicit micro-to-macro and macro-to-micro relations but as interdependencies among the actions of different actors. In the various developments of the theory I will sometimes conceptualize these processes in one of these two ways and sometimes in the other, depending on which appears more useful.

I will develop the conceptual base for interdependence among actions of individual actors. With this conceptual structure the only *action* takes place at the level of individual actors, and the "system level" exists solely as emergent properties characterizing the system of action as a whole. It is only in this sense that there is behavior of the system. Nevertheless, system-level properties will result, so propositions may be generated at the level of the system.

The Elements

There are two kinds of elements in the minimal system and two ways in which they are related. The elements are actors and things over which they have control and in which they have some interest. I will call these things resources or events, depending on their character. The relations between actors and resources are, as just implied, control and interest.

It is useful to consider briefly the concept of interest, for it has an extensive history in social thought. Hirschman locates its conceptual origins: "The term was originally pressed into service as a euphemism serving, already in the late Middle Ages, to make respectable an activity, the taking of interest on loans, that had long been considered contrary to divine law and known as the sin of usury". As Hirschman points out, the concept of interest, or self-interest, had an extraordinary growth in the sixteenth, seventeenth, and eighteenth centuries. It encouraged, beginning with Machiavelli's counsel to the prince, the emergence of the practice of statecraft unfettered by moral constraint; it aided the insights of the emerging discipline of economics in the work of Adam Smith and others; and it played a role in the conceptual revolution in ideas about the relation of self to society that was part of the French Revolution.

In the eighteenth century some saw interest as *the* central concept for the social world. The French philosopher Helvetius expressed this view; "As the physical world is ruled by the laws of movement so is the moral universe ruled by the laws of interest" (quoted by Hirschman, 1986, p. 45). The concept has had a checkered history since that time, both in its social-scientific role and in the regard in which it is held in society at large. Interest will play a central role in the theory presented here. The role it plays is close to that envisioned by Helvetius in the eighteenth century. However, I will examine the possibility of dissolving this concept through analysis of the internal structure of the actor.

If actors control all those resources that interest them, then their actions are straightforward: They merely exercise their control in a way that satisfies their interests (for example, if the resources are food, control is exercised by consuming the food). What makes a social system, in contrast to a set of individuals independently exercising their control over activities to satisfy their interests, is a simple structural fact: Actors are not fully in control of the activities that can satisfy their interests, but find some of those activities partially or wholly under the control of other actors. Thus pursuit of one's interests in such a structure necessarily requires that one engage in transactions of some type with other actors. Those transactions include not only what is normally thought of as exchange, but also a variety of other actions which fit under a broader conception of exchange. These include bribes, threats, promises, and resource investments. It is through these transactions, or social interactions, that persons are able to use the resources they control that have little interest for them to realize their interests that lie in resources controlled by other actors.

A minimal basis for a social system of action is two actors, each having control over resources of interest to the other. It is each one's interest in resources under the other's control that leads the two, as purposive actors, to engage in actions that involve each other. A diagram of that minimal basis, shown in Figure 1.1, gives a sense of why it

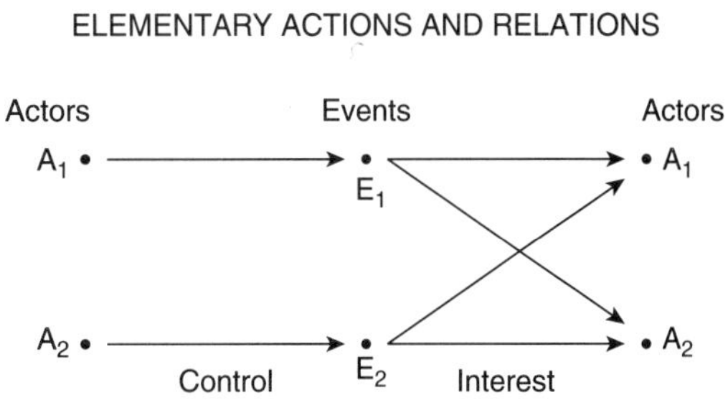

Figure 1.1 A Minimal System of Actors in Control of and Affected by Events

can be regarded as a system of action, rather than merely a pair of independent actors. It is this structure, together with the fact that the actors are purposive, each having the goal of maximizing the realization of his interests, that gives the interdependence, or systemic character, to their actions.

Forms of Interdependence

Friedman characterizes three kinds of interdependence among actors. The first he terms structural interdependence, in which each actor assumes the others' actions are independent of his own. In this form of interdependence each actor, in deciding on a course of action, can take the environment as fixed rather than reactive. A buyer's action in a market where prices can be regarded as fixed (that is, if that buyer is sufficiently small relative to others in the market that his actions do not affect prices) exemplifies structural interdependence. When a system involves only structural interdependence, rationality is well defined. Since the social environment is noncontingent, either rationality under certainty (when the outcome follows the action with certainty) or rationality under risk (when the outcome follows only with a certain probability less than 1.0) provides the appropriate model for rational action.

The second form of interdependence Friedman terms behavioral interdependence. In behavioral interdependence the actions of each actor are conditional on those of others at an earlier point in time. This implies that an actor must base his action on more complex considerations than apply in structural interdependence. He must recognize that his action may have consequences for him not only directly but indirectly through another whose action may be affected by his own. Furthermore, because of this effect on the other's action, his own subsequent action may be affected, which can lead to an effect on him that constitutes a second-order indirect effect of the current action. This sequence of indirect effects can continue into the indefinite future. In such a setting, the question of what is rational for the actor depends on his information, both about the number and character of future choices and about the kinds of strategies that will be pursued by others. In this form of interdependence the definition of what strategy is rational for an actor is not independent of the strategies used by others with whom he is interdependent.

An example of behavioral interdependence is bargaining between two or more actors, a process in which one's strategy depends on knowing not only the other's interests but also the other's strategy (which ordinarily will include assumptions about one's own strategy). Another example is the development of expectations and obligations between two persons over time, a process which depends on what each assumes about (or learns about) not only the other's interests but also the other's strategies.

A third form of interdependence identified by Friedman is evolutionary interdependence. In evolutionary interdependence there is behavioral interdependence over a sufficiently long period of time that, through selective survival, the mix of strategies in a population changes toward some "equilibrium of strategies"—which need not be a unique equilibrium point. Ideas of evolutionary biology, in particular the concept of evolutionarily stable strategies as developed by Maynard Smith, have been introduced to aid in the analysis of evolutionary interdependence.

A Note About Self-Interests of Purposive Actors

For some social scientists (depending in part on the norms and assumptions of their discipline) my insistence on beginning a theory of action using as elements persons who are assumed to be not only rational but also unconstrained by norms and purely self-interested may appear to be a serious error. Certainly norms do exist, persons do obey them (though not uniformly), and persons do often act in the interests of others or of a collectivity, "unselfishly" as we would say.

Because of all this, it is useful to clarify the sense in which I begin with norm-free, self-interested persons as elements of the theory. My intent is not to suggest that everywhere and always persons act without regard to norms and with purely selfish interests. It is, rather, to indicate that at some point in the theory I take as problematic genesis and maintenance of norms, adherence of persons to norms, development of a moral code, identification of one's own interest with the fortunes of others, and identification with collectivities. To begin with normative systems would preclude the construction of theory about how normative systems develop and are maintained. To assume adherence to norms would impose a determinism that would reduce the theory to a description of automata, not persons engaged in voluntary action. To assume that persons come equipped with a moral code would exclude all processes of socialization from theoretical examination. And to assume altruism or unselfishness would prevent the construction of theory about how persons come to act on behalf of others or on behalf of a collectivity when it goes against their private interests.

To begin with persons not endowed with altruism or unselfishness and lacking a shared normative system does not mean that in every part of the theory the persons who are actors are assumed to be without these added components of the self. To the contrary, most parts of the theory will assume that actors possess some of these components, although the assumptions are largely implicit. In general, the more universally held a norm or the more widespread a moral precept, the more likely I will be to overlook it, to take it always and everywhere as given, thus necessarily diminishing the scope of the theory. Some norms are not so widely shared and are therefore more readily recognized.

Actions and Transactions

In the parsimonious conception of a system of action that I want to establish, the types of action available to the actor are severely limited. All are carried out with a single purpose—to increase the actor's realization of interests. There are, of course, different types of action, which depend on the situational constraints. It is useful to describe these types here.

The first type of action is the simple one of exercising control over those resources one is interested in and has control over, in order to satisfy one's interest. This action, however, is socially trivial (unless it has effects on others) and can be ignored, since it involves no other actors.

The second type of action is the major action that accounts for much of social behavior—an actor's gaining control of those things that are of greatest interest to him. This is ordinarily accomplished by using those resources he has, by exchanging control over resources that are of little interest to him in return for control over those that are of greater interest. This process follows the overall purpose of increasing one's realization of interests under the assumption that those interests can be better realized if one controls something than if one does not. Ordinarily, it may be assumed that control of a resource by an actor makes it possible to realize whatever interests that actor has in it.

A third type of action that can be and is widely carried out in social systems is unilateral transfer of control over resources one is interested in. Such transfer is carried out when the assumption on which the second type of action is predicated (that one can best satisfy one's interests by gaining control of resources one is interested in) no longer holds. That is, an actor transfers control over resources unilaterally when he believes that another's exercise of control over those resources will better satisfy his interests than will his own exercise of control.

Types of Resources

The resources each actor has which are of interest to others include a wide variety of things. The most obvious of these are what economists call private goods. Neoclassical economic theory describes the functioning of systems in which each actor has control of certain private divisible goods that are of interest to other actors in the system. But private divisible goods are only one of several kinds of things over which actors have control and in which they are interested.

Actors may have control over events that have consequences for a number of other actors (that is, events in which other actors are interested). In the case in which control over such an event is partitioned among two or more actors, as when a collective decision is made by taking a vote, each actor has only partial control over the event.

Actors may have control over their own actions, and if the actors have certain attributes, such as skills or beauty, in which others are interested, they may give up rights to control certain of their own actions. Note that in this case I have used the phrase "give up rights to control" rather than "give up control." The reason is that direct control over one's own actions cannot be given up; it is inalienable. What can, however, be given up is a *right* to control the action. Physical inalienability from one's self is not the only kind of inalienability. Legal rules may also dictate inalienability of rights of control over physically alienable things. For example, for many collective decisions votes are made inalienable by rules of the system, but in some systems votes are alienable through the use of proxies.

Actors may also have control over resources which are not of direct interest to others but are effective in determining, or partially determining, the outcomes of events in which others are interested. There are further variations in the resources that actors control. For example, some resources, as part of a transaction with another actor, can be delivered only in the future or over a period of time in the future, whereas others can be delivered in the present. Another variation is that some resources exhibit the property of conservation; there is a fixed quantity of the resource. If one individual controls (or consumes) one portion of the resource, the total available for others to control (or consume) is diminished by just this portion. The property of conservation is usually possessed by those things we think of as goods, but the general class of resources that individuals control include many without this property. For example, information, as a resource over which actors have control, ordinarily does not exhibit conservation. Information which is passed on to another continues to be held by the original possessor as well. Still another property of certain resources is that their consumption or use has no consequences for actors other than the actor who consumes or uses them. Resources that are not like this but instead have inseparable consequences for more than the one actor are said to have external effects, or externalities.

That there is this wide variety of resources over which actors may have control and in which actors are interested (or which affect events or resources in which actors are interested) creates a terminological difficulty. I will ordinarily refer to the general class as resources, using the term to include what I have referred to above as goods, resources, and events.

As is evident in the above, there are several properties that distinguish types of resources, properties that have important consequences for the kinds of systems of action that emerge. These properties are divisibility, alienability, conservation, time of delivery, and absence of externalities. Economists, who ordinarily conceive of economic systems as involving goods, have employed a distinction between private goods and public goods. In terms of these properties a private good has no externalities and exhibits conservation. A public good does not exhibit conservation and is at the extreme of possessing externalities in that it has consequences for all (or, to use economists' terminology, is a good that cannot be supplied to one without being supplied to all). The prototypical private good also is divisible, alienable, and currently deliverable; that is, it has each of the properties described.

Social Exchange

One property of the theoretical system developed here is parsimony. Actors are connected to resources (and thus indirectly to one another) through only two relations: their control over resources and their interest in resources. Actors have a single principle of action, that of acting so as to maximize their realization of interests. Such action can be simply consummatory, to realize the actor's interest; if it is not, the maximization principle leads most often to a single kind of action—exchange of control (or rights to control) over resources or events. Under some circumstances, however, it may lead to unilateral transfer of control (or right to control) to another.

The simplest system of action using the concepts described is a pairwise exchange of resources that have all the properties of private goods. Although such exchanges may occur in competition with others, as they do in a barter market, they need not. Social exchange is pervasive throughout social life. Indeed, some social theorists, such as Homans and Blau, have constructed social theories based principally on exchange processes of this sort. In social exchanges of resources other than economic goods, the resources exchanged may not have all the properties of private goods, but this will not matter for certain qualitative deductions. In this section I will discuss the behavior of such systems and point to some of the qualitative deductions that can be made.

Exchange in social life can become complicated, for in many areas of social life institutions to facilitate exchanges of control (especially those exchanges that require more than two parties) are not as well developed as are institutions for the exchange of economic resources. Nevertheless, in this first and simplest system of action that I will outline, I make the assumption that such exchanges can be made.

The restriction to an exchange process is not as constraining as it initially appears, once the exchanges are no longer limited to economic goods. In an exchange of economic goods, each actor, in offering an exchange, can only improve the lot of the other actor, which is why we usually think of such exchanges as both voluntary and mutually beneficial. But when events of other types are included, exchange can also be used to characterize phenomena that are ordinarily conceived of as coercion; threats are included along with promises. When a parent threatens a child with a spanking if the child disobeys, the parent is giving up temporarily the right to strike the child (which the parent continuously holds by virtue of the parent's physical and legal control of the child) in return for the child's satisfying the parent's interest.

In addition, many phenomena that are ordinarily viewed not as exchange but as deployment of resources are predictable by a rather simple form of the theory. For example, Dahl notes in his study of New Haven, and other political scientists have noted elsewhere, that many potentially powerful actors in a community do not exercise their power in community decision making. The end result is often that decisions are made without the influence of the most powerful actors in the community, a somewhat puzzling phenomenon. But because political resources are often capable of being used on any of a number of events and are partially consumed in use (for example, popular support for a corporation having a plant in a town will be reduced if the corporation uses its power in opposition to a popular policy), selective deployment may be the way for an actor to maximize realization of interests.

The idea of a system within which exchanges arise spontaneously can be illustrated by Figure 1.1. In the system represented there, actor A_2 is interested in resource E_1 but has no control over it. The action principle for each actor in the system is one which leads him to gain control over the resources that interest him by giving up resources he has. The resource held by A_2 is control over E_2. Actor A_1 is interested in E_2, so A_2 should be able to gain some control over E_1 by giving up some control over E_2.

Social Equilibrium

Through exchanges such as those described above, there is a reduction in the discrepancy between interest and control, to the point where an equilibrium occurs—a point at which there are no exchanges that can increase the expected realization of interests for both actors. At this point each actor will have maximized his expected realization of interests to the degree allowed by the resources with which he began.

Under certain conditions, such as in a system with a small number of actors, there may not be a *single* equilibrium point. For example, in the case of two actors, each with control over a set of things of some interest to himself and of some interest to the other, there will be a whole set of equilibrium points, each of which would be better for both actors than the initial point (and better than any point outside this set) but none of which would be better for both actors than any other point in the set. There are a number of different exchange rates that would make both parties better off than before the exchange, and in the absence of a market it is indeterminate which of these will occur. The equilibrium point that is achieved in such a small system of exchange can be described as a property of the system, that is, a macro-level property, just as price is in market exchange. For example, Blau's study of the exchange of deference for advice in a government agency suggests that the amount of deference paid for a particular quantity and quality of advice constituted a property of the social system of the agency.

The end result of the exchange process is a redistribution of control over events, a redistribution that will give outcomes which are in a certain sense optimal. After an exchange each actor is in control of those events that most interest him, subject to the power of his initial resources, and since he will exercise that control toward achieving the outcome he prefers, there is no way that greater satisfaction can be achieved, given the initial distribution of control and of interests. In this sense the outcome is optimal.

To make such a statement as the last one appears to engage in a fallacy that has dogged welfare economics since the utilitarians, the fallacy of assuming some common metric which allows interpersonal comparison of utility. That is, making a statement about aggregate satisfaction, as is done above, implies a comparison which balances different persons' satisfactions so that satisfaction can be aggregated over those persons. As has been shown over and over again in the economic literature, such a comparison, carried out by an analyst, is meaningless. What is not meaningless, however, is the comparison that is carried out by social processes themselves. It is this kind of comparison that is intrinsic to social systems and to the model described above. The comparison which gives a common metric to the satisfactions of different persons is that which derives from the resources with which they begin. Thus, considering a patriarchal family as a system, what is meant by maximum aggregate satisfaction is an aggregate that weights the satisfactions of the male head of the household more heavily than those of his wife, because of his greater control over resources. In a matriarchal household the wife's satisfactions are weighted more heavily than the husband's in arriving at the maximum aggregate satisfaction, because of her greater power. Such maximizations cannot be normatively justified, except *within the set of values implied by the initial distribution of control among the actors in the system.*

A first implication of the theory to be developed then, is that systems of exchange mirrored by the theory do achieve a maximum overall satisfaction, but one that is specific to the initial control. I will call this control the constitutional control regardless of whether there is a formal constitution among the actors. This control expresses the constitution of the social system, whether implicit or explicit, through its expression of the rights and resources held by each of the actors. Such an aggregation of the various actors' interests might be a very different one from that which an outside observer would wish to see. For example, the aggregate satisfaction that is being maximized in a patriarchal household might not accord with that judged desirable by an outside observer. But it is the only aggregation that will be maximized in that system, because the aggregation is given by the distribution of constitutional control among the different actors in the system.

In fact, a confusion between the values that the observer would wish to place on each person's interests (for example, equality), on the one hand, and the internal functioning of the system (which because of constitutional control sets values on different persons' interests), on the other hand, has led to confusion about interpersonal comparisons of utility in welfare economics. There is no meaning to interpersonal comparisons carried out by an observer (except that they satisfy the observer), but there is a meaning to those carried out internally in a system of action. Those comparisons occur in the actual transactions that take place.

PART IX

COMMUNITY AND CIVIL SOCIETY

In the late 19th century, as urbanization became a worldwide phenomenon and as social ties in the family, neighborhood, and village seemed to be on the decline, sociologists began thinking about the loss of community and later, in the 20th century, about the search for community. It was important not only to adequately define the concept of community but also to relate it to other similar entities, such as *civil society*, which involves citizen participation in a democracy, and the *nation-state*, which involves the political workings and cultural identity of a country. In addition, the social thinkers whose writings are featured in Part IX—Ferdinand Tönnies, Robert A. Nisbet, Robert N. Bellah, Philip Selznick, Amitai Etzioni, and Norbert Elias—were concerned with the moral issues of national community and civil society, such as national solidarity, community well-being, the common good, and the autonomy of the individual.

In the reading "Gemeinschaft and Gesellschaft," first published in 1887, the German sociologist Ferdinand Tönnies examines two kinds of social associations. The first, *Gemeinschaft*, or community, is experienced by people as original and authentic. It refers to all social life that is lived in private and in intimate realms. In a Gemeinschaft, people form relationships of their own free will and mutually affirm and cooperate with each other. It is typically characterized by shared folkways, mores, and beliefs. Tönnies identifies three general types of Gemeinshaft: those formed by *kinship*, which he describes as communities by *blood*; (2) those defined by *neighborhood*, which are communities of *locality*; and (3) those that arise on the basis of *friendship*, which are communities of *mind*. The second type of association, *Gesellschaft*, or society, is experienced by people as an impersonal abstraction, a tightly organized collectivity. As an aggregate of individuals independent from each other, the Gesellschaft is characteristic of urban, public life. People in a Gesellschaft are isolated, uncooperative, and exist in tense relation with each other. Transactions between them are transitory, pragmatic, and self-serving. It is through the contractual exchange of objects and services that there exist *conventions* or utilitarian agreements that, in a Gesellschaft, act as a binding force on all.

By the mid-20th century, people had become preoccupied with regaining an impression of community that had been lost. In "The Quest for Community," published in 1953, Robert A. Nisbet argues that interpersonal relationships in family, neighborhood, and church had become socially irrelevant and morally meaningless. As a result, people were experiencing a growing sense of isolation, anxiety, and alienation. These social groups had, until recently, interceded between the concrete lives of individuals and the larger political and economic goals of society. But now that family, neighborhood, and church had weakened and declined in importance, they were unable to perform their function of conveying social integration and psychological purpose. Nisbet proposes that these traditional local groups be augmented with other *intermediate associations* of civil society—labor unions, charities, voluntary groups, and sports clubs—that provide purpose, membership, and status. It is in intermediate associations that community is available.

In his seminal article of 1967, "Civil Religion in America," Robert N. Bellah contends that there is a religious dimension in U.S. society that dates back to the earliest years of the American republic that he calls *civil religion*. It is rooted in a religious orientation that the majority of Americans share—namely, the obligation to carry out God's will. This national cult is a generic and nonsectarian religion and reference to "God," whether on solemn occasions or in the pledge to the flag, is not related to any particular theological doctrine or institution (e.g., the Trinity, Christ, salvation, the Church). Instead, it concerns the more secular notions of law, order, and right. It is a genuinely *American* religious nationalism with a special concern for and specific application to the United States. The American civil religion is expressed in a set of institutionalized *beliefs*, such as those values pertaining to freedom and democracy; in *symbols*, including the iconic images of Washington and Lincoln; and in the cultic celebration of civil *rituals*, as in the pageantry of presidential inaugurations and in Memorial Day observances. It is through these shared—and sacred—beliefs, symbols, and rituals that the civil religion fosters national solidarity. But more than that, it also functions to mobilize support for the attainment of national goals, both moral and political, such as, for example, granting equal rights to African Americans with the passage of the Voting Rights Act of 1965.

Philip Selznick begins the reading "A Normative Theory of Moral Community" by stating that due to a lack of consensus on a definition of community, it has been difficult to distinguish community from other forms of social organization, such as state, nation, and society. According to Selznick, community, at minimum, involves shared beliefs, interests, and commitments around concerted activity. But whatever definition of community is used, a coherent *theory* of community should be descriptive; that is to say, it must consider an accurate sociological account of people's actual experience of living in community. More important, it should be a theory that is *normative*, or morally informed, with the capacity to evaluate communities on the basis of a standard of general well-being. Such a theory is both *affirmative*, in that it considers the positive contributions of community to human flourishing, and *critical*, in that it assesses the extent to which community departs from the established moral standard. Moreover, a normative theory must take into account a *balanced* mixture of seven main elements involved in the formation and development of a moral community: (1) historicity, (2) identity, (3) mutuality, (4) plurality, (5) autonomy, (6) participation, and (7) integration.

In "Communitarianism," Amitai Etzioni highlights the tension in democratic societies between, on the one hand, the desire for *liberty*, in the sense of individual rights and freedom, and, on the other hand, the need for *order*, as articulated in the social virtues that lead to community life and the common good. Etzioni advances a paradigm that he calls *communitarianism* in an attempt to strengthen community and enhance civil society by balancing individual rights and social responsibilities. This requires a different way of approaching community life, one that can be articulated in a *new golden rule*, which should read as follows: Respect and uphold society's moral order as you would have society respect and uphold your autonomy. The new golden rule balances the two fundamental virtues of a good society: social order and individual autonomy.

Finally, in "The Civilizing Process," Norbert Elias explains how individuals become more *civilized*—how their personal habits, manners, and feelings become more structured and controlled. A full understanding of the civilizing process, Elias argues, requires a different image of the individual than that traditionally accepted by social theorists. This new image depicts the individual as being both relatively autonomous from other people but also oriented toward and dependent on other people. As such, the individual's personality structure is said to be less self-centered and more "open." In addition, the individual must be considered in relation to the social structure that Elias calls a *figuration*, a dynamic network of mutually oriented and interdependent people. The concept of figuration—rather than that of group, community, or society—allows for a better understanding of how personality structures and social structures change concurrently in the course of the civilizing process.

71

Gemeinschaft and Gesellschaft*

Ferdinand Tönnies

Human wills stand in manifold relations to one another. Every such relationship is a mutual action, inasmuch as one party is active, or gives, while the other party is passive, or receives. These actions are of such a nature that they tend either toward preservation or destruction of the other will or life; that is, they are either positive or negative. This study will consider as its subject of investigation only the relationships of mutual affirmation. Every such relationship represents unity in plurality or plurality in unity. It consists of assistance, relief, services, which are transmitted back and forth from one party to another and are to be considered as expressions of wills and their forces. The group which is formed through this positive type of relationship is called an association (*Verbindung*) when conceived of as a thing or being which acts as a unit inwardly and outwardly. The relationship itself, and also the resulting association, is conceived of either as real and organic life—this is the essential characteristic of the Gemeinschaft (community); or as imaginary and mechanical structure—this is the concept of Gesellschaft (society).

Through the application of these two terms we shall see that the chosen expressions are rooted in their synonymous use in the German language. But to date in scientific terminology they have been customarily confused and used at random without any distinction. For this reason, a few introductory remarks may explain the inherent contrast between these two concepts.

All intimate, private, and exclusive living together, so we discover, is understood as life in Gemeinschaft (community). Gesellschaft (society) is public life—it is the world itself. In Gemeinschaft with one's family, one lives from birth on, bound to it in weal and woe. One goes into Gesellschaft as one goes into a strange country. A young man is warned against bad Gesellschaft, but the expression bad Gemeinschaft violates the meaning of the word. Lawyers may speak of domestic (*häusliche*) Gesellschaft, thinking only of the legalistic concept of social association; but the domestic Gemeinschaft, or home life with its immeasurable influence upon the human soul, has been felt by everyone who ever shared it. Likewise, a bride or groom knows that he or she goes into marriage as a complete Gemeinschaft of life *(communio totius vitae)*. A Gesellschaft of life would be a contradiction in and of itself. One keeps or enjoys another's Gesellschaft, but not his Gemeinschaft in this sense. One becomes

*Excerpts from *Community and Society* (*Gemeinschaft and Gesellschaft*) by Ferdinand Tonnies, Translated and edited by Charles P. Loomis.

a part of a religious Gemeinschaft; religious Gesellschaften (associations or societies), like any other groups formed for given purposes, exist only in so far as they, viewed from without, take their places among the institutions of a political body or as they represent conceptual elements of a theory; they do not touch upon the religious Gemeinschaft as such. There exists a Gemeinschaft of language, of folkways or mores, or of beliefs; but, by way of contrast, Gesellschaft exists in the realm of business, travel, or sciences. So of special importance are the commercial Gesellschaften; whereas, even though a certain familiarity and Gemeinschaft may exist among business partners, one could indeed hardly speak of commercial Gemeinschaft. To make the word combination "joint-stock Gemeinschaft" would be abominable. On the other hand, there exists a Gemeinschaft of ownership in fields, forest, and pasture. The Gemeinschaft of property between man and wife cannot be called Gesellschaft of property. Thus many differences become apparent.

In the most general way, one could speak of a Gemeinschaft comprising the whole of mankind, such as the Church wishes to be regarded. But human Gesellschaft is conceived as mere coexistence of people independent of each other. Recently, the concept of Gesellschaft as opposed to and distinct from the state has been developed. This term will also be used, but can only derive its adequate explanation from the underlying contrast to the Gemeinschaft of the people.

Gemeinschaft is old; Gesellschaft is new as a name as well as a phenomenon. This has been recognized by an author who otherwise taught political science in all its aspects without penetrating to its fundamentals. "The entire concept of Gesellschaft (society) in a social and political sense," says Bluntschli *(Staatswörterbuch IV)*, "finds its natural foundation in the folkways, mores, and ideas of the third estate. It is not really the concept of a people *(Volks-Begriff)* but the concept of the third estate ... Its Gesellschaft has become the origin and expression of common opinion and tendencies ... Wherever urban culture blossoms and bears fruits, Gesellschaft appears as its indispensable organ. The rural people know little of it." On the other hand, all praise of rural life has pointed out that the Gemeinschaft among people is stronger there and more alive; it is the lasting and genuine form of living together. In contrast to Gemeinschaft, Gesellschaft is transitory and superficial. Accordingly, Gemeinschaft should be understood as a living organism, Gesellschaft as a mechanical aggregate and artifact.

In accordance with the preliminary explanations, the theory of Gemeinschaft starts from the assumption of perfect unity of human wills as an original or natural condition which is preserved in spite of actual separation. This natural condition is found in manifold forms because of dependence on the nature of the relationship between individuals who are differently conditioned. The common root of this natural condition is the coherence of vegetative life through birth and the fact that the human wills, in so far as each one of these wills is related to a definite physical body, are and remain linked to each other by parental descent and by sex, or by necessity become so linked. This close interrelation as a direct and mutual affirmation is represented in its most intense form by three types of relationships, namely: (1) the relation between a mother and her child; (2) the relation between husband and wife in its natural or general biological meaning; (3) the relation among brothers and sisters, that is, at least among those who know each other as being the offspring of the same mother. If in the relations of kindred individuals one may assume the embryo of Gemeinschaft or the tendency and force thereto, rooted in the individual wills, specific significance must be attributed to the three above-mentioned relationships, which are the strongest and most capable of development. Each, however, is important in a special way.

The Gemeinschaft by blood, denoting unity of being, is developed and differentiated into Gemeinschaft of locality, which is based on a common habitat. A further differentiation leads to the Gemeinschaft of mind, which implies only co-operation and co-ordinated action for a common goal. Gemeinschaft of locality may be conceived as a community of physical life, just as Gemeinschaft of mind expresses the community of mental life. In conjunction with the others, this last type of Gemeinschaft represents the truly human and supreme form of community. Kinship Gemeinschaft signifies a common relation to, and share in, human beings themselves, while in Gemeinschaft of locality such a common relation is established through collective ownership of land; and, in Gemeinschaft of mind, the common bond is represented by sacred places and worshiped deities. All three types of Gemeinschaft are closely interrelated in space as well as in time. They are, therefore, also related in all such single phenomena and in their development, as well as in general human culture and its history. Wherever human beings are related through their wills in an organic manner and affirm each other, we find one or another of the three types of Gemeinschaft. Either the earlier type involves the later one, or the later type has developed to relative independence from some earlier one. It is, therefore, possible to deal with (1) kinship, (2) neighborhood, and (3) friendship as definite and meaningful derivations of these original categories.

The house constitutes the realm and, as it were, the body of kinship. Here people live together under one protecting roof. Here they share their possessions and their pleasures; they feed from the same supply, they sit at the same table. The dead are venerated here as invisible spirits, as if they were still powerful and held a protecting hand over their family. Thus, common fear and common honor ensure peaceful living and co-operation with greater certainty. The will and spirit of kinship is not confined within the walls of the house nor bound up with physical proximity; but, where it is strong and alive in the closest and most intimate relationship, it can live on itself, thrive on memory alone, and overcome any distance by its feeling and its imagination of nearness and common activity. Nevertheless, it seeks all the more for physical proximity and is loath to give it up, because such nearness alone will fulfill the desire for love. The ordinary human being, therefore—in the long run and for the average of cases—feels best and most cheerful if he is surrounded by his family and relatives. He is among his own *(chez soi)*.

Neighborhood describes the general character of living together in the rural village. The proximity of dwellings, the communal fields, and even the mere contiguity of holdings necessitate many contacts of human beings and cause inurement to and intimate knowledge of one another. They also necessitate co-operation in labor, order, and management, and lead to common supplication for grace and mercy to the gods and spirits of land and water who bring blessing or menace with disaster. Although essentially based upon proximity of habitation, this neighborhood type of Gemeinschaft can nevertheless persist during separation from the locality, but it then needs to be supported still more than ever by well-defined habits of reunion and sacred customs.

Friendship is independent of kinship and neighborhood, being conditioned by and resulting from similarity of work and intellectual attitude. It comes most easily into existence when crafts or callings are the same or of similar nature. Such a tie, however, must be made and maintained through easy and frequent meetings, which are most likely to take place in a town. A worshiped deity, created out of common mentality, has an immediate significance for the preservation of such a bond, since only, or at least mainly, this deity is able to give it living and lasting form. Such good spirit, therefore, is not bound to any place but lives in the conscience of its worshipers and accompanies them on their travels to foreign countries. Thus, those who are brethren of such a common faith feel, like members of the same craft or rank, everywhere united by a spiritual bond and the co-operation in a common task. Urban community of life may be classified as neighborhood, as is also the case with a community of domestic life in which nonrelated members or servants participate. In contradistinction, spiritual friendship forms a kind of invisible scene or meeting which has to be kept alive by artistic intuition and creative will. The relations between human beings themselves as friends and comrades have the least organic and intrinsically necessary character. They are the least instinctive and are based less upon habit than are the relationships of neighborhood. They are of a mental nature and seem to be founded, therefore, as compared with the earlier relationships, upon chance or free choice. But a similar differentiation has been pointed out already for the relations of pure kinship and leads to the following statements.

The neighborhood may be compared with the kinship type in the same way as the husband-wife relationship; therefore, affinity in general may be compared with the mother-child relationship. What is achieved only by mutual liking in the mother-child relationship must be made up for by habit in the neighborhood type. As the relation among brothers and sisters—therefore, also all cousins and other relations of similar consanguinity—are comparable to the other organically conditioned relationships, so in the same manner friendship is comparable to neighborhood and kinship. Memory creates gratitude and faithfulness. The specific truth of such relationships must manifest itself in mutual trust and belief. As the foundations of these relationships are no longer spontaneous and so self-evident and as the individuals know and determine their own will and ability more definitely, these relationships are the most difficult to preserve and the most susceptible to disturbances—such as disputes and quarrels, which will happen in almost all group life. Not only does constant proximity and frequency of contacts mean mutual furtherance and affirmation, but inhibition and negation also become real possibilities or probabilities of a certain degree. Only as long as mutual furtherance and affirmation predominate can a relation really be considered Gemeinschaft. Thus, it is explained that, in conformity with many experiences, such purely mental or psychological brotherhoods can stand only to a certain limit the frequency and narrowness of physical proximity of real joint life. They have to find their counterpoise in a high degree of individual freedom.

The theory of the Gesellschaft deals with the artificial construction of an aggregate of human beings which superficially resembles the Gemeinschaft in so far as the individuals live and dwell together peacefully. However, in the Gemeinschaft they remain essentially united in spite of all separating factors, whereas in the Gesellschaft they are essentially separated in spite of all uniting factors. In the Gesellschaft, as contrasted with the Gemeinschaft, we find no actions that can be derived from an a priori and necessarily existing unity; no actions, therefore, which manifest the will and the spirit of the unity even if performed by the individual; no actions which, in so far as they are performed by the individual, take place on behalf of those united with him. In the Gesellschaft such actions do not exist. On the contrary, here everybody is by himself and isolated, and there exists a condition of tension against all others. Their spheres of activity and power are sharply separated, so that everybody refuses to everyone else contact with and admittance to his sphere; i.e., intrusions are regarded as hostile acts. Such a negative attitude toward one another becomes the normal and always underlying relation of these power-endowed individuals, and it characterizes the Gesellschaft in the condition of rest; nobody wants to grant and produce anything for another individual, nor will he be inclined to give ungrudgingly to another individual, if it be not in exchange for a gift or labor equivalent that he considers at least equal to what he has given. It is even necessary that it be more desirable to him than what he could have kept himself; because he will be moved to give away a good only for the sake of receiving something that seems better to him. Inasmuch as each and every one is possessed of such will it is self-evident that for the individual "B" the object "a" may possibly be better than the object "b," and correspondingly, for the individual "A" the object "b" better than the object "a"; it is, however, only with reference to these relations that "a" is better than "b" and at the same time "b" is better than "a." This leads us to the question: with what meaning may one speak of the worth or of the value of things, independently of such relationships?

The answer runs as follows: in the concept presented here, all goods are conceived to be separate, as also are their owners. What somebody has and enjoys, he has and enjoys to the exclusion of all others. So, in reality, something that has a common value does not exist. Its existence may, however, be brought about through fiction on the part of the individuals, which means that they have to invent a common personality and his will, to whom this common value has to bear reference. Now, a manipulation of this kind must be warranted by a sufficient occasion. Such an occasion is given when we consider the simple action of the delivery of an object by one individual and its acceptance by another one. For then a contact takes place and there is brought into existence a common sphere which is desired by both individuals and lasts through the same length of time as does the "transaction." This period of time may be so small as to be negligible, but, on the other hand, it may also be extended indefinitely. At any rate, during this period the piece which is getting separated from the sphere of, for example, individual "A" has ceased to be under the exclusive dominion of "A" and has not yet begun to be entirely under the dominion of "B." It is still under the partial dominion of "A" and already under the partial dominion of "B." It is still dependent upon both individuals, provided that their wills with reference to it are in accord. This is, however, the case as long as the act of giving and receiving continues. During this time it is a common good and represents a social value. Now the will that is directed to this common good is combined and mutual and *can* also be regarded as homogeneous in that it keeps demanding from either individual the execution of the twofold act until it is entirely completed. This will *must,* however, be regarded as a unity inasmuch as it is conceived as a personality or inasmuch as a personality is assigned to it; for to conceive something as existing or as a thing is the same as conceiving it as a unity. There, however, we must be careful to discern whether and to what extent such an artificial being *(ens fictivum)* exists only in the theory, i.e., in scientific thinking, or whether and under which conditions it is also implanted in the thinking of the individuals who are its thinking agents. This last-mentioned possibility presupposes, of course, that the individuals are already capable of common willing and acting. For, again, it is quite a different proposition if they are imagined to be only participants in the authorship of something that is conceived as objective in the scientific sense because it is that which under given conditions "each and every one" is compelled to think.

Now, it is to be admitted that each act of giving and receiving implicitly includes a social will, in the way just indicated. These acts are, furthermore, not conceivable except in connection with their purpose or end, i.e., the receipt of the compensating gift. As, however, this latter act is conditioned in like manner, neither act can precede the other; they must concur. Or, expressing the same thought in other words, the acceptance equals the delivery of an accepted compensation. Thus, the exchange itself, considered as a united and single act, represents the content of the assumed social will. With regard to this will the exchanged goods are of equal value. This equality is the judgment of the will and is valid for both individuals, since they have passed it when their wills were in concord; hence it is binding only for the moment in which the act of exchange takes place or for the space of time during which it continues. In order that the judgment may even with this qualification become objective and universally valid, it must appear as a judgment passed by "each and every one." Hence, each and every one must have this single will; in other words, the will of the exchange becomes universal, i.e., each and every one becomes a participant in the single act and he confirms it; thus it becomes an absolute and public act. On the contrary, the Gesellschaft may deny this act and declare "a" is not equal to "b," but smaller than "b" or greater than "b," i.e., the objects are not being exchanged according to their true values. The true value is explained as that value which each and every one attributes to a thing that we thus regard as a general Gesellschaft-conditioned good. Hence, the true value is ascertained if there is nobody who estimates either object as higher or lower in terms of the other. Now, a general consensus of each and every one that is not accidental, but necessary, will be effected only with reference to what is sensible, right, and true. Since all individuals are thus of one mind we may imagine them as concentrated in the person of a measuring, weighing, and knowing judge who passes the objective judgment. This judgment must be recognizable by each and every one, and each and every one must conform to it inasmuch as they themselves are endowed with judgment and objective thinking, or, figuratively speaking, as they use the same yardstick or weigh with the same scales.

The concord of will at each exchange, inasmuch as the exchange is regarded as taking place in the Gesellschaft, we call a contract. The contract is the resultant of two divergent individual wills, intersecting in one point. The contract lasts until the exchange has been completed, and it wills and demands the execution of the two acts of which it consists, each of which acts may be subdivided into a number of partial acts. Since the contract always deals with possible actions, it becomes meaningless and ceases to exist when such transactions either have been realized, or, on the other hand, have become impossible. We speak of the fulfillment or of a breach of the contract according to which of these two contingencies takes place. The individual will which enters into the contract refers either to a present and actual transaction, as, for example, the delivery of commodity or money, or to a future and possible transaction. This future transaction may appear in the form of a remaining part of a transaction which is regarded as present in its totality and which thus may consist in the delivery of the remainder of commodities or money. As a further alternative, the future transaction, inclusive of its beginning date, may be conceived as falling entirely within a period previous to a distant date (the due-date).

Under these conditions, the mere will *(der blosse Wille)* is being given and accepted either for the whole or for a part of the content of the contract. The mere will, it is true, may become evident also in other ways, but really perceptible only when transformed into the word. Thus, the word instead of an object is being given. For the recipient the word has the value of an object inasmuch as the connection of the word and the object is a necessary one, so that he is certain to obtain the object. The word is of no value as a "security," for it cannot be consumed nor can it be sold as a thing in itself. But it is equivalent to the surrender of the thing itself; i.e., the recipient has acquired the absolute right to the object, and this is all he can have by means of his own will, the actual power of which would form the natural basis of actual property. At the same time the recipient's right to the object is an outgrowth of the general will, i.e., of the will of the Gesellschaft. For the Gesellschaft is incapable of examining each case separately and, therefore, presumes that the delivery of a thing is a result of an exchange and in particular an exchange of equivalents. And this means that in the Gesellschaft, as rightly conceived, apart from the *de facto* condition of each individual, any exchange and any promise therewith is considered to be valid, that is, valid according to the will of each and every one. This means that any such promise is considered as rightful and therefore binding. However, the promise requires the consent of the receiver, for an object that belongs to him as a result of an exchange, an exchange being the only conceivable cause for this state of affairs, may only with his consent remain in the hands of the other individual. His consent may be interpreted as a promise not to tear away the object from the other, but to leave it to him until the day agreed upon.

In every exchange, the place of a perceivable object can be taken by an activity. The activity itself is given and received. It must be useful or agreeable to the receiver as a commodity. This activity is thought of as a commodity, the production and consumption of which coincide in time. Although the performance which is not given but only promised may be contrasted with the thing which is not given and only promised, the result in both cases is similar. It belongs to the receiver legally; after the term expires he can force the promising party legally to perform the activity promised, just as he could legally force the debtor to give that which is owed or have it taken with force. A performance which is owed can be acquired only by force. The promise of a performance can as well be mutual as one-sided; therefore, resulting rights to coercion can also be mutual or one-sided, as the case may be. In this respect, several people can bind themselves for a certain equal activity in such a manner that everyone uses the performance of the other as an aid to himself. Finally, several people can agree to regard their association as an existing and independent being of the same individual nature as they are themselves, and to grant this fictitious person a special will and the capacity to act and therefore to make contracts and to incur obligations. Like all other things related to contracts, this so-called person is to be conceived as objective and real only in so far as the Gesellschaft seems to co-operate with it and to confirm its existence. Only in this way is this so-called person a thinking agent of the legal order of the Gesellschaft, and it is called a society, an association or special-interest group, a corporation, or any such name. The natural content of such an order can be comprised in the one formula: *"Pacta esse observanda"*—contracts must be executed. This includes the presupposition of a condition of separate realms or spheres of will so that an accepted and consequently legal change of each sphere can take place by contract in favor or in disfavor of spheres which are outside the system, or within the system. This means that the agreement of all is involved. Such concurrence of wills is according to its nature momentarily punctual so that the change, as creation of a new situation, does not have to have a duration in time. This necessitates no modification of the most important rule, that everyone can do legally within his realm that which he wishes, but nothing outside. If, however, a common realm originates, as might be the case in a lasting obligation and in an organization, freedom itself, as the total of rights to act freely, must be divided and altered or a new artificial or fictitious form of freedom created. The simple form of the general will of the Gesellschaft, in so far as it postulates this law of nature, I call *convention*. Positive definitions and regulations of all kinds, which according to their origin are of a very different style, can be recognized as conventional, so that convention is often understood as a synonym for tradition and custom. But what springs from tradition and custom or the folkways and mores is conventional only in so far as it is wanted and maintained for its general use, and in so far as the general use is maintained by the individual for his use. Convention is not, as in the case of tradition, kept as sacred inheritance of the ancestors. Consequently, the words tradition, customs, or folkways and mores are not adequate to convey the meaning of "convention."

Gesellschaft, an aggregate by convention and law of nature, is to be understood as a multitude of natural and artificial individuals, the wills, and spheres of whom are in many relations with and to one another, and remain nevertheless independent of one another and devoid of mutual familiar relationships.

72

The Quest for Community*

Robert A. Nisbet

This is an age of economic interdependence and welfare States, but it is also an age of spiritual insecurity and preoccupation with moral certainty. Why is this? Why has the quest for community become the dominant social tendency of the twentieth century?

The ominous preoccupation with community revealed by modem thought and mass behavior is a manifestation of certain profound dislocations in the primary associative areas of society, dislocations that have been created to a great extent by the structure of the Western political State. As it is treated here, the problem is social—social in that it pertains to the statuses and social memberships which men hold, or seek to hold. But the problem is also political—political in that it is a reflection of the present location and distribution of power in society.

The two aspects, the social and the political, are inseparable. For, the allegiances and memberships of men, even the least significant, cannot be isolated from the larger systems of authority that prevail in a society or in any of its large social structures. Whether the dominant system of power is primarily religious, economic, or political in the usual sense is of less importance sociologically than the *way* in which the power reveals itself in practical operation and determines the smaller contexts of culture and association. Here we have reference to the degree of centralization, the remoteness, the impersonality of power, and to the concrete ways in which it becomes involved in human life.

We must begin with the role of the social group in present-day Western society, for it is in the basic associations of men that the real consequences of political power reveal themselves.

Where, then, are the dislocations and the deprivations that have driven so many men, in this age of economic abundance and political welfare, to the quest for community, to narcotic relief from the sense of isolation and anxiety? They lie in the realm of the small, primary, personal relationships of society—the relationships that mediate directly between man and his larger world of economic, moral, and political and religious values. Our problem may be ultimately concerned with all of these values and their greater or lesser accessibility to man, but it is, I think, primarily social: social in the exact sense of pertaining to the small areas of membership and association in which these values are ordinarily made meaningful and directive to men.

*Excerpts from The *Quest for Community: A Study in the Ethics of Order and Freedom* by Robert A. Nisbet. Copyright 1953. Reprinted by permission of the Estate of Robert A. Nisbet.

Behind the growing sense of isolation in society, behind the whole quest for community which infuses so many theoretical and practical areas of contemporary life and thought, lies the growing realization that the traditional primary relationships of men have become functionally irrelevant to our State and economy and meaningless to the moral aspirations of individuals. We are forced to the conclusion that a great deal of the peculiar character of contemporary social action comes from the efforts of men to find in large-scale organizations the values of status and security which were formerly gained in the primary associations of family, neighborhood, and church. This is the fact, I believe, that is as revealing of the source of many of our contemporary discontents as it is ominous when the related problems of political freedom and order are considered.

Historically, our problem must be seen in terms of the decline in functional and psychological significance of such groups as the family, the small local community, and the various other traditional relationships that have immemorially mediated between the individual and his society. These are the groups that have been morally decisive in the concrete lives of individuals. Other and more powerful forms of association have existed, but the major moral and psychological influences on the individual's life have emanated from the family and local community and the church. Within such groups have been engendered the primary types of identification: affection, friendship, prestige, recognition. And within them also have been engendered or intensified the principal incentives of work, love, prayer, and devotion to freedom and order.

This is the area of association from which the individual commonly gains his concept of the outer world and his sense of position in it. His concrete feelings of status and role, of protection and freedom, his differentiation between good and bad, between order and disorder and guilt and innocence, arise and are shaped largely by his relations within this realm of primary association. What was once called instinct or the social nature of man is but the product of this sphere of interpersonal relationships. It contains and cherishes not only the formal moral precept but what Whitehead has called 'our vast system of inherited symbolism.'

It can be seen that most contemporary themes of alienation have as their referents disruptions of attachment and states of mind which derive from this area of interpersonal relations. Feelings of moral estrangement, of the hostility of the world, the fear of freedom, of irrational aggressiveness, and of helplessness before the simplest of problems have to do commonly —as both the novelist and the psychiatrist testify—with the individual's sense of the inaccessibility of this area of relationship. In the child, or in the adult, the roots of a coherent, logical sense of the outer world are sunk deeply in the soil of close, meaningful interpersonal relations.

It is to this area of relations that the adjective 'disorganized' is most often flung by contemporary social scientists and moralists, and it is unquestionably in this area that most contemporary sensations of cultural dissolution arise.

But in any intelligible sense of the word it is not disorganization that is crucial to the problem of the family or of any other significant social group in our society. The most fundamental problem has to do with the *organized* associations of men. It has to do with the role of the primary social group in an economy and political order whose principal ends have come to be structured in such a way that the primary social relationships are increasingly functionless, almost irrelevant, with respect to these ends. What is involved most deeply in our problem is the diminishing capacity of organized, traditional relationships for holding a position of moral and psychological centrality in the individual's life.

Interpersonal relationships doubtless exist as abundantly in our age as in any other. But it is becoming apparent that for more and more people such relationships are morally empty and psychologically baffling. It is not simply that old relationships have waned in psychological influence; it is that new forms of primary relationships show, with rare exceptions, little evidence of offering even as much psychological and moral meaning for the individual as do the old ones. For more and more individuals the primary social relationships have lost much of their historic function of mediation between man and the larger ends of our civilization.

But the decline of effective meaning is itself a part of a more fundamental change in the role of such groups as the family and local community. At bottom social organization is a pattern of institutional functions into which are woven numerous psychological threads of meaning, loyalty, and interdependence. The contemporary sense of alienation is most directly perhaps a problem in symbols and meanings, but it is also a problem in the institutional functions of the relationships that ordinarily communicate integration and purpose to individuals.

In any society the concrete loyalties and devotions of individuals tend to become directed toward the associations and patterns of leadership that in the long run have the greatest perceptible significance in the maintenance of life. It is never a crude relationship; intervening strata of ritual and other forms of crystallized meaning will exert a distinguishable influence on human thought. But, at bottom, there is a close and vital connection between the effectiveness of the symbols that provide meaning in the individual's life and the institutional value of the social structures that are the immediate source of the symbols. The immediacy of the integrative meaning of the basic values contained in and communicated by the kinship or religious group will vary with the greater or less institutional value of the group to the individual *and to the other institutions in society.*

In earlier times, and even today in diminishing localities, there was an intimate relation between the local, kinship, and religious groups within which individuals consciously lived and the major economic, charitable, and protective functions which are indispensable to human existence. There was an intimate conjunction of larger institutional goals and the social groups small enough to infuse the individual's life with a sense of membership in society and the meaning of the basic moral values. For the overwhelming majority of people, until quite recently the structure of economic and political life rested upon, and even presupposed, the existence of the small social and local groups within which the cravings for psychological security and identification could be satisfied.

Family, church, local community drew and held the allegiances of individuals in earlier times not because of any superior impulses to love and protect, or because of any greater natural harmony of intellectual and spiritual values, or even because of any superior internal organization, but because these groups possessed a virtually indispensable relation to the economic and political order. The social problems of birth and death, courtship and marriage, employment and unemployment, infirmity and old age were met, however inadequately at times, through the associative means of these social groups. In consequence, a whole ideology, reflected in popular literature, custom, and morality, testified to the centrality of kinship and localism.

Our present crisis lies in the fact that whereas the small traditional associations, founded upon kinship, faith, or locality, are still expected to communicate to individuals the principal moral ends and psychological gratifications of society, they have manifestly become detached from positions of functional relevance to the larger economic and political decisions of our society. Family, local community, church, and the whole network of informal interpersonal relationships have ceased to play a determining role in our institutional systems of mutual aid, welfare, education, recreation, and economic production and distribution. Yet despite the loss of these manifest institutional functions, and the failure of most of these groups to develop any new institutional functions, we continue to expect them to perform adequately the implicit psychological or symbolic functions in the life of the individual.

Nowhere is the concern with the problem of community in Western society more intense than with respect to the family. The contemporary family, as countless books, articles, college courses, and marital clinics make plain, has become an obsessive problem. The family inspires a curious dualism of thought. We tend to regard it uneasily as a final manifestation of tribal society, somehow inappropriate to a democratic, industrial age, but, at the same time, we have become ever more aware of its possibilities as an instrument of social reconstruction.

The intensity of theoretical interest in the family has curiously enough risen in direct proportion to the decline of the family's basic institutional importance to our culture. The present 'problem' of the family is dramatized by the fact that its abstract importance to the moralist or psychologist has grown all the while that its tangible institutional significance to the layman and its functional importance to economy and State have diminished.

It is doubtless one more manifestation of the contemporary quest for security that students of the family increasingly see its main 'function' to be that of conferring 'adjustment' upon the individual, and, for the most part, they find no difficulty at all in supposing that this psychological function can be carried on by the family in what is otherwise a functional vacuum. Contemporary social psychology has become so single-mindedly aware of the psychological gratification provided by the group for individual needs of security and recognition that there is an increasing tendency to suppose that such a function is primary and can maintain itself autonomously, impervious to changes in *institutional* functions which normally give a group importance in culture. For many reasons the contemporary family is made to carry a conscious symbolic importance that is greater than ever, but it must do this with a structure much smaller in size and of manifestly diminishing relevance to the larger economic, religious, and political ends of contemporary society.

The current problem of the family, like the problem of any social group, cannot be reduced to simple sets of psychological complexes which exist universally in man's nature, or to an ignorance of sexual techniques, or to a lack of Christian morality. The family is a major problem in our culture simply because we are attempting to make it perform psychological and symbolic functions with a structure that has become fragile and an institutional importance that is almost totally unrelated to the economic and political realities of our society. Moreover, the growing impersonality and the accumulating demands of ever larger sections of our world of business and government tend to throw an extraordinary psychological strain upon the family. In this now small and fragile group we seek the security and affection denied everywhere else. It is hardly strange that timeless incompatibilities and emotion strains should, in the present age, assume an unwonted importance—their *meaning* has changed with respect to the larger context of men's lives. We thus find ourselves increasingly in the position of attempting to correct, through psychiatric or spiritual techniques, problems which, although assuredly emotional, derive basically from a set of historically given institutional circumstances.

Personal crises, underlying emotional dissatisfactions, individual deviations from strict rectitude—these have presumably been constant in all ages of history. Only our own age tends to blow up these tensions into reasons for a clinical approach to happiness. Such tensions appear more critical and painful, more intolerable to contemporary man, simply because the containing social structures of such tensions have become less vital to his existence. The social structures are expendable so far as the broad economic and political processes of our society are concerned and, consequently, they offer less support for particular emotional states. Not a few of the problems that give special concern to our present society—sex role, courtship and marriage, old age, the position of the child—do so because of the modified functional and psychological position of the family in our culture.

What has happened to the family has happened also to neighborhood and local community. As Robert S. Lynd has written: 'Neighborhood and community ties are not only optional but generally growing less strong; and along with them is disappearing the important network of intimate, informal, social controls traditionally associated with living closely with others.' Within all of these lay not merely controls but the incentives that supplied the motive force for such pursuits as education and religion and recreation.

The point is that with the decline in the significance of kinship and locality, and the failure of new social relationships to assume influences of equivalent evocative intensity, a profound change has occurred in the very psychological structure of society. And this is a change that has produced a great deal of the present problem of incentives in so many areas of our society. Most of our ideas and practices in the major institutional areas of society developed during an age when the residual psychological elements of social organization seemed imperishable. No less imperishable seemed the structure of personality itself. Educational goals and political objectives were fashioned accordingly, as were theories of economic behavior and population increase.

But we are learning that many of the motivations and incentives which an older generation of rationalists believed were inherent in the individual are actually supplied by social groups—social groups with both functional and moral relevance to the lives of individuals.

Modern planners thus frequently find themselves dealing, not simply with the upper stratum of decisions, which their forebears assumed would be the sole demand of a planned society, but with often baffling problems which reach down into the very recesses of human personality.

Basically, however, it is not the position of the family or of any other single group, old or new, that is crucial to the welfare of a social order. Associations may come and go under the impact of historical changes and cultural needs. There is no single type of family, anymore than there is a single type of religion, that is essential to personal security and collective prosperity. It would be wrong to assume that the present problem of community in Western society arises inexorably from the modifications which have taken place in old groups, however cherished these may be. But irrespective of particular groups, there must be in any stable culture, in any civilization that prizes its integrity, functionally significant and psychologically meaningful groups and associations lying intermediate to the individual and the larger values and purposes of his society. For these are the small areas of association within which alone such values and purposes can take on clear meaning in personal life and become the vital roots of the large culture. It is, I believe, the problem of intermediate association that is fundamental at the present time.

Under the lulling influence of the idea of Progress we have generally assumed until recently that history automatically provides its own solution to the basic problems of organization in society. We have further assumed that man is ineradicably gregarious and that from this gregariousness must come ever new and relevant forms of intermediate association.

It is tempting to believe this as we survey the innumerable formal organizations of modern life, the proliferation of which has been one of the signal facts in American history, or as we observe the incredible number of personal contacts which take place daily in the congested areas of modern urban life.

But there is a profound difference between the casual, informal relationships which abound in such areas and the kind of social groups which create a sense of belonging, which supply incentive, and which confer upon the individual a sense of status. Moreover, from some highly suggestive evidence supplied by such sociologists as Warner, Lazarsfeld, and especially Mirra Komarovsky, we can justly doubt that all sections of modern populations are as rich in identifiable social groups and associations as we have heretofore taken for granted.

The common assumption that, as the older associations of kinship and neighborhood have become weakened, they are replaced by new voluntary associations filling the same role is not above sharp question. That traditional groups have weakened in significance is apparently true enough but, on the evidence, their place has not been taken to any appreciable extent by new forms of association. Despite the appeal of the older sociological stereotype of the urban dweller who belongs to various voluntary associations, all of which have progressively replaced the older social unities, the facts so far gathered suggest the contrary: that a rising number of individuals belong to no organized association at all, and that, in the large cities, the unaffiliated persons may even constitute a majority of the population.

As for the psychological functions of the great formal associations in modern life—industrial corporations, governmental agencies, large-scale labor and charitable organizations—it is plain that not many of these answer adequately the contemporary quest for community. Such organizations, as Max Weber pointed out, are generally organized not around personal loyalties but around loyalty to an office or machine. The administration of charity, hospitalization, unemployment assistance, like the administration of the huge manufacturing corporation, may be more efficient and less given to material inequities, but the possible gains in technical efficiency do not minimize their underlying impersonality in the life of the individual.

Much of the contemporary sense of the impersonality of society comes from the rational impersonality of these great organizations. The widespread reaction against technology, the city, and political freedom, not to mention the nostalgia that pervades so many of the discussions of rural-urban differences, comes from the diminished functional relationship between existent social groups in industry or the community and the remote efficiency of the larger organizations created by modern planners. The derivative loss of meaning for the individual frequently becomes the moral background of vague and impotent reactions against technology and science, and of aggressive states of mind against the culture as a whole. In spatial terms the individual is obviously less isolated from his fellows in the large-scale housing project or in the factory than was his grandfather. What he has become isolated from is the sense of meaningful proximity to the major ends and purposes of his culture. With the relatively complete satisfaction of needs concerned with food, employment, and housing, a different order of needs begins to assert itself imperiously; and these have to do with spiritual belief and social status.

'The uneasiness, the malaise of our time,' writes C. Wright Mills, 'is due to this root fact: in our politics and economy, in family life and religion—in practically every sphere of our existence—the certainties of the eighteenth and nineteenth centuries have disintegrated or been destroyed and, at the same time, no new sanctions or justifications for the new routines we live, and must live, have taken hold . . . Among white-collar people, the malaise is deep-rooted; for the absence of any order of belief has left them morally defenseless as individuals and politically impotent as a group. Newly created in a harsh time of creation, white-collar man has no culture to lean upon except the contents of a mass society that has shaped him and seeks to manipulate him to its alien ends. For security's sake he must attach himself somewhere, but no communities or organizations seem to be thoroughly his.'

The quest for community will not be denied, for it springs from some of the powerful needs of human nature—needs for a clear sense of cultural purpose, membership, status, and continuity. Without these, no amount of mere material welfare will serve to arrest the developing sense of alienation in our society and the mounting preoccupation with the imperatives of community. To appeal to technological progress is futile. For what we discover is that rising standards of living, together with increases in leisure, actually intensify the disquietude and frustration that arise when cherished and proffered goals are without available means of fulfillment. 'Secular improvement that is taken for granted,' wrote Joseph Schumpeter, 'and coupled with individual insecurity that is acutely resented is of course the best recipe for breeding social unrest.'

The loss of old moral certainties and accustomed statuses is, however, only the setting of our problem. For, despite the enormous influence of nostalgia in human thinking, it is never the recovery of the institutionally old that is desired by most people. In any event, the quest for the past is as futile as is that of the future.

The real problem is not, then, the loss of old contexts but rather the failure of our present democratic and industrial scene to create new contexts of association and moral cohesion within which the smaller allegiances of men will assume both functional and psychological significance. It is almost as if the forces that weakened the old have remained to obstruct the new channels of association.

73

Civil Religion in America*

Robert N. Bellah

Kennedy's inaugural address of 20 January 1961 serves as an example and a clue with which to introduce this complex subject. That address began:

> We observe today not a victory of party but a celebration of freedom—symbolizing an end as well as a beginning—signifying renewal as well as change. For I have sworn before you and Almighty God the same solemn oath our forebears prescribed nearly a century and three quarters ago.
>
> The world is very different now. For man holds in his mortal hands the power to abolish all forms of human poverty and to abolish all forms of human life. And yet the same revolutionary beliefs for which our forebears fought are still at issue around the globe—the belief that the rights of man come not from the generosity of the state but from the hand of God.

And it concluded:

> Finally, whether you are citizens of America or of the world, ask of us the same high standards of strength and sacrifice that we shall ask of you. With a good conscience our only sure reward, with history the final judge of our deeds, let us go forth to lead the land we love, asking His blessing and His help, but knowing that here on earth God's work must truly be our own.

These are the three places in this brief address in which Kennedy mentioned the name of God. If we could understand why he mentioned God, the way in which he did it, and what he meant to say in those three references, we would understand much about American civil religion. But this is not a simple or obvious task, and American students of religion would probably differ widely in their interpretation of these passages.

Let us consider first the placing of the three references. They occur in the two opening paragraphs and in the closing paragraph, thus providing a sort of frame for the more concrete remarks that form the middle part of the speech. Looking beyond this particular speech, we would find that similar references to God are almost invariably to be found in the pronouncements of American presidents on solemn occasions, though usually not in the working messages that the president sends to Congress on various concrete issues. How, then, are we to interpret this placing of references to God?

It might be argued that the passages quoted reveal the essentially irrelevant role of religion in the very secular society that is America. The placing of the references in this speech as well as in public life generally indicates that religion has "only a ceremonial significance"; it gets only a sentimental nod which serves largely to placate the more unenlightened members of the

*"Civil Religion in America," Robert N. Bellah, *Daedalus* 96, 1 (1967): 1–21. Reprinted by permission of the MIT Press.

community, before a discussion of the really serious business with which religion has nothing whatever to do. A cynical observer might even say that an American president has to mention God or risk losing votes. A semblance of piety is merely one of the unwritten qualifications for the office, a bit more traditional than but not essentially different from the present-day requirement of a pleasing television personality.

But we know enough about the function of ceremonial and ritual in various societies to make us suspicious of dismissing something as unimportant because it is "only a ritual." What people say on solemn occasions need not be taken at face value, but it is often indicative of deep-seated values and commitments that are not made explicit in the course of everyday life. Following this line of argument, it is worth considering whether the very special placing of the references to God in Kennedy's address may not reveal something rather important and serious about religion in American life.

It might be countered that the very way in which Kennedy made his references reveals the essentially vestigial place of religion today. He did not refer to any religion in particular. He did not refer to Jesus Christ, or to Moses, or to the Christian church; certainly he did not refer to the Catholic Church. In fact, his only reference was to the concept of God, a word which almost all Americans can accept but which means so many different things to so many different people that it is almost an empty sign. Is this not just another indication that in America religion is considered vaguely to be a good thing, but that people care so little about it that it has lost any content whatever? Isn't Eisenhower reported to have said, "Our government makes no sense unless it is founded in a deeply felt religious faith—and I don't care what it is," and isn't that a complete negation of any real religion?

These questions are worth pursuing because they raise the issue of how civil religion relates to the political society, on the one hand, and to private religious organization, on the other. President Kennedy was a Christian, more specifically a Catholic Christian. Thus, his general references to God do not mean that he lacked a specific religious commitment. But why, then, did he not include some remark to the effect that Christ is the Lord of the world or some indication of respect for the Catholic Church? He did not because these are matters of his own private religious belief and of his relation to his own particular church; they are not matters relevant in any direct way to the conduct of his public office. Others with different religious views and commitments to different churches or denominations are equally qualified participants in the political process. The principle of separation of church and state guarantees the freedom of religious belief and association, but at the same time clearly segregates the religious sphere, which is considered to be essentially private, from the political one.

Considering the separation of church and state, how is a president justified in using the word *God* at all? The answer is that the separation of church and state has not denied the political realm a religious dimension. Although matters of personal religious belief, worship, and association are considered to be strictly private affairs, there are, at the same time, certain common elements of religious orientation that the great majority of Americans share. These have played a crucial role in the development of American institutions and still provide a religious dimension for the whole fabric of American life, including the political sphere. This public religious dimension is expressed in a set of beliefs, symbols, and rituals that I am calling the American civil religion. The inauguration of a president is an important ceremonial event in this religion. It reaffirms, among other things, the religious legitimation of the highest political authority.

Let us look more closely at what Kennedy actually said. First he said, "I have sworn before you and Almighty God the same solemn oath our forebears prescribed nearly a century and three quarters ago." The oath is the oath of office, including the acceptance of the obligation to uphold the Constitution. He swears it before the people (you) and God. Beyond the Constitution, then, the president's obligation extends not only to the people but to God. In American political theory, sovereignty rests, of course, with the people, but implicitly, and often explicitly, the ultimate sovereignty has been attributed to God. This is the meaning of the motto, "In God we trust," as well as the inclusion of the phrase "under God" in the pledge to the flag. What difference does it make that sovereignty belongs to God? Though the will of the people as expressed in majority vote is carefully institutionalized as the operative source of political authority, it is deprived of an ultimate significance. The will of the people is not itself the criterion of right and wrong. There is a higher criterion in terms of which this will can be judged; it is possible that the people may be wrong. The president's obligation extends to the higher criterion.

When Kennedy says that "the rights of man come not from the generosity of the state but from the hand of God," he is stressing this point again. It does not matter whether the state is the expression of the will of an autocratic monarch or of the "people"; the rights of man are more basic than any political structure and provide a point of revolutionary leverage from which any state structure may be radically altered. That is the basis for his reassertion of the revolutionary significance of America.

But the religious dimension in political life as recognized by Kennedy not only provides a grounding for the rights of man which makes any form of political absolutism illegitimate, it also provides a transcendent goal for the political process. This is implied in his final words that "here on earth God's work must truly be our own." What he means here is, I think, more clearly spelled out in a previous paragraph, the wording of which, incidentally, has a distinctly Biblical ring:

> Now the trumpet summons us again—not as a call to bear arms, though arms we need—not as a call to battle, though embattled we are—but a call to bear the burden of a long twilight struggle, year in and year out, "rejoicing in hope, patient in tribulation"—a struggle against the common enemies of man: tyranny, poverty, disease and war itself.

The whole address can be understood as only the most recent statement of a theme that lies very deep in the American tradition, namely the obligation, both collective and individual, to carry out God's will on earth. This was the motivating spirit of those who founded America, and it has been present in every generation since. Just below the surface throughout Kennedy's inaugural address, it becomes explicit in the closing statement that God's work must be our own. That this very activist and non-contemplative conception of the fundamental religious obligation, which has been historically associated with the Protestant position, should be enunciated so clearly in the first major statement of the first Catholic president seems to underline how deeply established it is in the American outlook. Let us now consider the form and history of the civil religious tradition in which Kennedy was speaking.

The Idea of a Civil Religion

The phrase *civil religion* is, of course, Rousseau's. In Chapter 8, Book 4, of *The Social Contract,* he outlines the simple dogmas of the civil religion: the existence of God, the life to come, the reward of virtue and the punishment of vice, and the exclusion of religious intolerance. All other religious opinions are outside the cognizance of the state and may be freely held by citizens. While the phrase *civil religion* was not used, to the best of my knowledge, by the founding fathers, and I am certainly not arguing for the particular influence of Rousseau, it is clear that similar ideas, as part of the cultural climate of the late-eighteenth century, were to be found among the Americans. For example, Franklin writes in his autobiography,

> I never was without some religious principles. I never doubted, for instance, the existence of the Deity; that he made the world and govern'd it by his Providence; that the most acceptable service of God was the doing of good to men; that our souls are immortal; and that all crime will be punished, and virtue rewarded either here or hereafter. These I esteemed the essentials of every religion; and, being to be found in all the religions we had in our country, I respected them all, tho' with different degrees of respect, as I found them more or less mix'd with other articles, which, without any tendency to inspire, promote or confirm morality, serv'd principally to divide us, and make us unfriendly to one another.

It is easy to dispose of this sort of position as essentially utilitarian in relation to religion. In Washington's Farewell Address (though the words may be Hamilton's) the utilitarian aspect is quite explicit:

> Of all the dispositions and habits which lead to political prosperity, Religion and Morality are indispensable supports. In vain would that man

> claim the tribute of Patriotism, who should labour to subvert these great Pillars of human happiness, these firmest props of the duties of men and citizens. The mere politician, equally with the pious man ought to respect and cherish them. A volume could not trace all their connections with private and public felicity. Let it simply be asked where is the security for property, for reputation, for life, if the sense of religious obligation *desert* the oaths, which are the instruments of investigation in Courts of Justice? And let us with caution indulge the supposition, that morality can be maintained without religion. Whatever may be conceded to the influence of refined education on minds of peculiar structure, reason and experience both forbid us to expect that National morality can prevail in exclusion of religious principle.

But there is every reason to believe that religion, particularly the idea of God, played a constitutive role in the thought of the early American statesmen.

Kennedy's inaugural pointed to the religious aspect of the Declaration of Independence, and it might be well to look at that document a bit more closely. There are four references to God. The first speaks of the "Laws of Nature and of Nature's God" which entitle any people to be independent. The second is the famous statement that all men "are endowed by their Creator with certain inalienable Rights." Here Jefferson is locating the fundamental legitimacy of the new nation in a conception of "higher law" that is itself based on both classical natural law and Biblical religion. The third is an appeal to "the Supreme Judge of the world for the rectitude of our intentions," and the last indicates "a firm reliance on the protection of divine Providence." In these last two references, a Biblical God of history who stands in judgment over the world is indicated.

The intimate relation of these religious notions with the self-conception of the new republic is indicated by the frequency of their appearance in early official documents. For example, we find in Washington's first inaugural address of 30 April 1789:

> It would be peculiarly improper to omit in this first official act my fervent supplications to that Almighty Being who rules over the universe, who presides in the councils of nations, and whose providential aids can supply every defect, that His benediction may consecrate to the liberties and happiness of the people of the United States a Government instituted by themselves for these essential purposes, and may enable every instrument employed in its administration to execute with success the functions allotted to his charge.
>
> No people can be bound to acknowledge and adore the Invisible Hand which conducts the affairs of man more than those of the United States. Every step by which we have advanced to the character of an independent nation seems to have been distinguished by some token of providential agency. . . .
>
> The propitious smiles of Heaven can never be expected on a nation that disregards the eternal rules of order and right which Heaven itself has ordained. . . . The preservation of the sacred fire of liberty and the destiny of the republican model of government are justly considered, perhaps, as *deeply,* as *finally,* staked on the experiment intrusted to the hands of the American people.

Nor did these religious sentiments remain merely the personal expression of the president. At the request of both Houses of Congress, Washington proclaimed on October 3 of that same first year as president that November 26 should be "a day of public thanksgiving and prayer," the first Thanksgiving Day under the Constitution.

The words and acts of the founding fathers, especially the first few presidents, shaped the form and tone of the civil religion as it has been maintained ever since. Though much is selectively derived from Christianity, this religion is clearly not itself Christianity. For one thing, neither Washington nor Adams nor Jefferson mentions Christ in his inaugural address; nor do any of the subsequent presidents, although not one of them fails to mention God. The God of the civil religion is not only rather "unitarian," he is also on the austere side, much more related to order, law, and right than to salvation and love. Even though he is somewhat deist in cast, he is by no means simply a watchmaker God. He is actively interested and involved in history, with a special concern for America. Here the analogy has much less to do with natural law than with ancient Israel; the equation of America with Israel in the idea of the "American Israel" is not infrequent. What was implicit in the words of Washington already quoted becomes explicit in Jefferson's second inaugural when he said: "I shall need, too, the favor of that Being in whose hands we are, who led our fathers, as Israel of old, from their native land and planted them in a country flowing with all the necessaries and comforts of life." Europe is Egypt; America, the promised land. God has led his people to establish a new sort of social order that shall be a light unto all the nations.

This theme, too, has been a continuous one in the civil religion. We have already alluded to it in the case of the Kennedy inaugural. We find it again in President Johnson's inaugural address:

> They came here—the exile and the stranger, brave but frightened—to find a place where a man could be his own man. They made a covenant with this land. Conceived in justice, written in liberty, bound in union, it was meant one day to inspire the hopes of all mankind; and it binds us still. If we keep its terms, we shall flourish.

What we have, then, from the earliest years of the republic is a collection of beliefs, symbols, and rituals with respect to sacred things and institutionalized in a collectivity. This religion—there seems no other word for it—while not antithetical to and indeed sharing much in common with Christianity, was neither sectarian nor in any specific sense Christian. At a time when the society was overwhelmingly Christian, it seems unlikely that this lack of Christian reference was meant to spare the feelings of the tiny non-Christian minority. Rather, the civil religion expressed what those who set the precedents felt was appropriate under the circumstances. It reflected their private as well as public views. Nor was the civil religion simply "religion in general." While generality was undoubtedly seen as a virtue by some, as in the quotation from Franklin above, the civil religion was specific enough when it came to the topic of America. Precisely because of this specificity, the civil religion was saved from empty formalism and served as a genuine vehicle of national religious self-understanding.

But the civil religion was not, in the minds of Franklin, Washington, Jefferson, or other leaders, with the exception of a few radicals like Tom Paine, ever felt to be a substitute for Christianity. There was an implicit but quite clear division of function between the civil religion and Christianity. Under the doctrine of religious liberty, an exceptionally wide sphere of personal piety and voluntary social action was left to the churches. But the churches were neither to control the state nor to be controlled by it. The national magistrate, whatever his private religious views, operates under the rubrics of the civil religion as long as he is in his official capacity, as we have already seen in the case of Kennedy. This accommodation was undoubtedly the product of a particular historical moment and of a cultural background dominated by Protestantism of several varieties and by the Enlightenment, but it has survived despite subsequent changes in the cultural and religious climate.

Civil War and Civil Religion

Until the Civil War, the American civil religion focused above all on the event of the Revolution, which was seen as the final act of the Exodus from the old lands across the waters. The Declaration of Independence and the Constitution were the sacred scriptures and Washington the divinely appointed Moses who led his people out of the hands of tyranny. The Civil War, which Sidney Mead calls "the center of American history" was the second great event that involved the national self-understanding so deeply as to require expression in the civil religion. In 1835, de Tocqueville wrote that the American republic had never really been tried, that victory in the Revolutionary War was more the result of British preoccupation elsewhere and the presence of a powerful ally than of any great military success of the Americans. But in 1861 the time of testing had indeed come. Not only did the Civil War have the tragic intensity of fratricidal strife, but it was one of the bloodiest wars of the nineteenth century; the loss of life was far greater than any previously suffered by Americans.

The Civil War raised the deepest questions of national meaning. The man who not only formulated but in his own person embodied its meaning for Americans was Abraham Lincoln. For him the issue was not in the first instance slavery but "whether that nation, or any nation so conceived, and so dedicated, can long endure." He had said in Independence Hall in Philadelphia on 22 February 1861:

> All the political sentiments I entertain have been drawn, so far as I have been able to draw them, from the sentiments which originated in and were given to the world from this Hall. I have never had a feeling, politically, that did not spring from the sentiments embodied in the Declaration of Independence.

The phrases of Jefferson constantly echo in Lincoln's speeches. His task was, first of all, to save the Union—not for America alone but for the meaning of America to the whole world so unforgettably etched in the last phrase of the Gettysburg Address.

But inevitably the issue of slavery as the deeper cause of the conflict had to be faced. In the second inaugural, Lincoln related slavery and the war in an ultimate perspective:

> If we shall suppose that American slavery is one of those offenses which, in the providence of God, must needs come, but which, having continued through His appointed time, He now wills to remove, and that He gives to both North and South this terrible war as the woe due to those by whom the offense came, shall we discern therein any departure from those divine attributes which the believers in a living God always ascribe to Him? Fondly do we hope, fervently do we pray, that this mighty scourge of war may speedily pass away. Yet, if God wills that it continue until all the wealth piled by the bondsman's two hundred and fifty years of unrequited toil shall be sunk, and until every drop of blood drawn with the lash shall be paid by another drawn with the sword, as was said three thousand years ago, so still it must be said "the judgements of the Lord are true and righteous altogether."

But he closes on a note if not of redemption then of reconciliation—"With malice toward none, with charity for all."

With the Civil War, a new theme of death, sacrifice, and rebirth enters the civil religion. It is symbolized in the life and death of Lincoln. Nowhere is it stated more vividly than in the Gettysburg Address, itself part of the Lincolnian "New Testament" among the civil scriptures. Robert Lowell has recently pointed out the "insistent use of birth images" in this speech explicitly devoted to "these honored dead": "brought forth," "conceived," "created," "a new birth of freedom." He goes on to say:

> The Gettysburg Address is a symbolic and sacramental act. Its verbal quality is resonance combined with a logical, matter of fact, prosaic brevity. . . . In his words, Lincoln symbolically died, just as the Union soldiers really died—and as he himself was soon really to die. By his words, he gave the field of battle a symbolic significance that it had lacked. For us and our country, he left Jefferson's ideals of freedom and equality joined to the Christian sacrificial act of death and rebirth. I believe this is a meaning that goes beyond sect or religion and beyond peace and war, and is now part of our lives as a challenge, obstacle and hope.

Lowell is certainly right in pointing out the Christian quality of the symbolism here, but he is also right in quickly disavowing any sectarian implication. The earlier symbolism of the civil religion had been Hebraic without being in any specific sense Jewish. The Gettysburg symbolism (". . . those who here gave their lives, that that nation might live") is Christian without having anything to do with the Christian church.

The symbolic equation of Lincoln with Jesus was made relatively early. Herndon, who had been Lincoln's law partner, wrote:

> For fifty years God rolled Abraham Lincoln through his fiery furnace. He did it to try Abraham and to purify him for his purposes. This made Mr. Lincoln humble, tender, forbearing, sympathetic to suffering, kind, sensitive, tolerant; broadening, deepening and widening his whole nature; making him the noblest and loveliest character since Jesus Christ. . . . I believe that Lincoln was God's chosen one.

With the Christian archetype in the background, Lincoln, "our martyred president," was linked to the war dead, those who "gave the last full measure of devotion." The theme of sacrifice was indelibly written into the civil religion.

The new symbolism soon found both physical and ritualistic expression. The great number of the war dead required the establishment of a number of national cemeteries. Of these, the Gettysburg National Cemetery, which Lincoln's famous address served to dedicate, has been overshadowed only by the Arlington National Cemetery. Begun somewhat vindictively on the Lee estate across the river from Washington, partly with the end that the Lee family could never reclaim it, it has subsequently become the most hallowed monument of the civil religion. Not only was a section set aside for the Confederate dead, but it has received the dead of each succeeding American war. It is the site of the one important new symbol to come out of World War I, the Tomb of the Unknown Soldier; more recently it has become the site of the tomb of another martyred president and its symbolic eternal flame.

Memorial Day, which grew out of the Civil War, gave ritual expression to the themes we have been discussing. As Lloyd Warner has so brilliantly analyzed it, the Memorial Day observance, especially in the towns and smaller cities of America, is a major event for the whole community involving a rededication to the martyred dead, to the spirit of sacrifice, and to the American vision. Just as Thanksgiving Day, which incidentally was securely institutionalized as an annual national holiday only under the presidency of Lincoln, serves to integrate the family into the civil religion, so Memorial Day has acted to integrate the local community into the national cult. Together with the less overtly religious Fourth of July and the more minor celebrations of Veterans Day and the birthdays of Washington and Lincoln, these two holidays provide an annual ritual calendar for the civil religion. The public-school system serves as a particularly important context for the cultic celebration of the civil rituals.

The Civil Religion Today

In reifying and giving a name to something that, though pervasive enough when you look at it, has gone on only semiconsciously, there is risk of severely distorting the data. But the reification and the naming have already begun. The religious critics of "religion in general," or of the "religion of the 'American Way of Life,'" or of "American Shinto" have really been talking about the civil religion. As usual in religious polemic, they take as criteria the best in their own religious tradition and as typical the worst in the tradition of the civil religion. Against these critics, I would argue that the civil religion at its best is a genuine apprehension of universal and transcendent religious reality as seen in or, one could almost say, as revealed through the experience of the American people. Like all religions, it has suffered various deformations and demonic distortions. At its best, it has neither been so general that it has lacked incisive relevance to the American scene nor so particular that it has placed American society above universal human values. I am not at all convinced that the leaders of the churches have consistently represented a higher level of religious insight than the spokesmen of the civil religion. Reinhold Niebuhr has this to say of Lincoln, who never joined a church and who certainly represents civil religion at its best:

> An analysis of the religion of Abraham Lincoln in the context of the traditional religion of his time and place and of its polemical use on the slavery issue, which corrupted religious life in the days before and during the Civil War, must lead to the conclusion that Lincoln's religious convictions were superior in depth and purity to those, not only of the political leaders of his day, but of the religious leaders of the era.

Perhaps the real animus of the religious critics has been not so much against the civil religion in itself but against its pervasive and dominating influence within the sphere of church religion. As S. M. Lipset has recently shown, American religion at least since the early-nineteenth century has been predominantly activist, moralistic, and social rather than contemplative, theological, or innerly spiritual. De Tocqueville spoke of American church religion as "a political institution which powerfully contributes to the maintenance of a democratic republic among the Americans" by supplying a strong moral consensus amidst continuous political change. Henry Bargy in 1902 spoke of American church religion as "la poésie du civisme."

It is certainly true that the relation between religion and politics in America has been singularly smooth. This is in large part due to the dominant tradition. As de Tocqueville wrote:

> The greatest part of British America was peopled by men who, after having shaken off the authority of the Pope, acknowledged no other religious supremacy: they brought with them into the New World a form of Christianity which I cannot better describe than by styling it a democratic and republican religion.

The churches opposed neither the Revolution nor the establishment of democratic institutions. Even when some of them opposed the full institutionalization of religious liberty, they accepted the final outcome with good grace and without nostalgia for an *ancien régime.* The American civil religion was never anticlerical or militantly secular. On the contrary, it borrowed selectively from the religious tradition in such a way that the average American saw no conflict between the two. In this way, the civil religion was able to build up without any bitter struggle with the church powerful symbols of national solidarity and to mobilize deep levels of personal motivation for the attainment of national goals.

Such an achievement is by no means to be taken for granted. It would seem that the problem of a civil religion is quite general in modern societies and that the way it is solved or not solved will have repercussions in many spheres. One needs only to think of France to see how differently things can go. The French Revolution was anticlerical to the core and attempted to set up an anti-Christian civil religion. Throughout modern French history, the chasm between traditional Catholic symbols and the symbolism of 1789 has been immense.

American civil religion is still very much alive. Just three years ago we participated in a vivid re-enactment of the sacrifice theme in connection with the funeral of our assassinated president. The American Israel theme is clearly behind both Kennedy's New Frontier and Johnson's Great Society. Let me give just one recent illustration of how the civil religion serves to mobilize support for the attainment of national goals. On 15 March 1965 President Johnson went before Congress to ask for a strong voting-rights bill. Early in the speech he said:

> Rarely are we met with the challenge, not to our growth or abundance, or our welfare or our security—but rather to the values and the purposes and the meaning of our beloved nation.
>
> The issue of equal rights for American Negroes is such an issue. And should we defeat every enemy, and should we double our wealth and conquer the stars and still be unequal to this issue, then we will have failed as a people and as a nation.
>
> For with a country as with a person, "What is a man profited, if he shall gain the whole world, and lose his own soul?"

And in conclusion he said:

> Above the pyramid on the great seal of the United States it says in Latin, "God has favored our undertaking."
>
> God will not favor everything that we do. It is rather our duty to divine his will. I cannot help but believe that He truly understands and that He really favors the undertaking that we begin here tonight.

The civil religion has not always been invoked in favor of worthy causes. On the domestic scene, an American-Legion type of ideology that fuses God, country, and flag has been used to attack nonconformist and liberal ideas and groups of all kinds. Still, it has been difficult to use the words of Jefferson and Lincoln to support special interests and undermine personal freedom. The defenders of slavery before the Civil War came to reject the thinking of the Declaration of Independence. Some of the most consistent of them turned against not only Jeffersonian democracy but Reformation religion; they dreamed of a South dominated by medieval chivalry and divine-right monarchy. For all the overt religiosity of the radical right today, their relation to the civil religious consensus is tenuous, as when the John Birch Society attacks the central American symbol of Democracy itself.

With respect to America's role in the world, the dangers of distortion are greater and the built-in safeguards of the tradition weaker. The theme of the American Israel was used, almost from the beginning, as a justification for the shameful treatment of the Indians so characteristic of our history. It can be overtly or implicitly linked to the idea of manifest destiny which has been used to legitimate several adventures in imperialism since the early-nineteenth century. Never has the danger been greater than today. The issue is not so much one of imperial expansion, of which we are accused, as of the tendency to assimilate all governments or parties in the world which support our immediate policies or call upon our help by invoking the notion of free institutions and democratic values. Those nations that are for the moment "on our side" become "the free world." A repressive and unstable military dictatorship in South Viet-Nam becomes "the free people of South Viet-Nam and their government." It is then part of the role of America as the New Jerusalem and "the last hope of earth" to defend such governments with treasure and eventually with blood. When our soldiers are actually dying, it becomes possible to consecrate the struggle further by invoking the great theme of sacrifice. For the majority of the American people who are unable to judge whether the people in South Viet-Nam (or wherever) are "free like us," such arguments are convincing. Fortunately President Johnson has been less ready to assert that "God has favored our undertaking" in the case of Viet-Nam than with respect to civil rights. But others are not so hesitant. The civil religion has exercised long-term pressure for the humane solution of our greatest domestic problem, the treatment of the Negro American. It remains to be seen how relevant it can become for our role in the world at large, and whether we can effectually stand for "the revolutionary beliefs for which our forebears fought," in John F. Kennedy's words.

The civil religion is obviously involved in the most pressing moral and political issues of the day. But it is also caught in another kind of crisis, theoretical and theological, of which it is at the moment largely unaware. "God" has clearly been a central symbol in the civil religion from the beginning and remains so today. This symbol is just as central to the civil religion as it is to Judaism or Christianity. In the late-eighteenth century this posed no problem; even Tom Paine, contrary to his detractors, was not an atheist. From left to right and regardless of church or sect, all could accept the idea of God. But today, as even *Time* has recognized, the meaning of the word *God* is by no means so clear or so obvious. There is no formal creed in the civil religion. We have had a Catholic president; it is conceivable that we could have a Jewish one. But could we have an agnostic president? Could a man with conscientious scruples about using the word *God* the way Kennedy and Johnson have used it be elected chief magistrate of our country? If the whole God symbolism requires reformulation, there will be obvious consequences for the civil religion, consequences perhaps of liberal alienation and of fundamentalist ossification that have not so far been prominent in this realm. The civil religion has been a point of articulation between the profoundest commitments of the Western religious and philosophical tradition and the common beliefs of ordinary Americans. It is not too soon to consider how the deepening theological crisis may affect the future of this articulation.

The Third Time of Trial

In conclusion it may be worthwhile to relate the civil religion to the most serious situation that we as Americans now face, what I call the third time of trial. The first time of trial had to do with the question of independence, whether we should or could run our own affairs in our own way. The second time of trial was over the issue of slavery, which in turn was only the most salient aspect of the more general problem of the full institutionalization of democracy within our country. This second problem we are still far from solving though we have some notable successes to our credit. But we have been overtaken by a third great problem which has led to a third great crisis, in the midst of which we stand. This is the problem of responsible action in a revolutionary world, a world seeking to attain many of the things, material and spiritual, that we have already attained. Americans have, from the beginning, been aware of the responsibility and the significance our republican experiment has for the whole world. The first internal political polarization in the new nation had to do with our attitude toward the French Revolution. But we were small and weak then, and "foreign entanglements" seemed to threaten our very survival. During the last century, our relevance for the world was not forgotten, but our role was seen as purely exemplary. Our democratic republic rebuked tyranny by merely existing. Just after World War I we were on the brink of taking a different role in the world, but once again we turned our back.

Since World War II the old pattern has become impossible. Every president since Roosevelt has been groping toward a new pattern of action in the world, one that would be consonant with our power and our responsibilities. For Truman and for the period dominated by John Foster Dulles that pattern was seen to be the great Manichaean confrontation of East and West, the confrontation of democracy and "the false philosophy of Communism" that provided the structure of Truman's inaugural address. But with the last years of Eisenhower and with the successive two presidents, the pattern began to shift. The great problems came to be seen as caused not solely by the evil intent of any one group of men, but as stemming from much more complex and multiple sources. For Kennedy, it was not so much a struggle against particular men as against "the common enemies of man: tyranny, poverty, disease and war itself."

But in the midst of this trend toward a less primitive conception of ourselves and our world, we have somehow, without anyone really intending it, stumbled into a military confrontation where we have come to feel that our honor is at stake. We have in a moment of uncertainty been tempted to rely on our overwhelming physical power rather than on our intelligence, and we have, in part, succumbed to this temptation. Bewildered and unnerved when our terrible power fails to bring immediate success, we are at the edge of a chasm the depth of which no man knows.

I cannot help but think of Robinson Jeffers, whose poetry seems more apt now than when it was written, when he said:

> Unhappy country, what wings you have! . . .
>
> Weep (it is frequent in human affairs), weep for the terrible magnificence of the means,
>
> The ridiculous incompetence of the reasons, the bloody and shabby
>
> Pathos of the result.

But as so often before in similar times, we have a man of prophetic stature, without the bitterness or misanthropy of Jeffers, who, as Lincoln before him, calls this nation to its judgment:

> When a nation is very powerful but lacking in self-confidence, it is likely to behave in a manner that is dangerous both to itself and to others.
>
> Gradually but unmistakably, America is succumbing to that arrogance of power which has afflicted, weakened and in some cases destroyed great nations in the past.
>
> If the war goes on and expands, if that fatal process continues to accelerate until America becomes what it is not now and never has been, a seeker after unlimited power and empire, then Vietnam will have had a mighty and tragic fallout indeed.
>
> I do not believe that will happen. I am very apprehensive but I still remain hopeful, and even confident, that America, with its humane and democratic traditions, will find the wisdom to match its power.

Without an awareness that our nation stands under higher judgment, the tradition of the civil religion would be dangerous indeed. Fortunately, the prophetic voices have never been lacking. Our present situation brings to mind the Mexican-American war that Lincoln, among so many others, opposed. The spirit of civil disobedience that is alive today in the civil rights movement and the opposition to the Viet-Nam war was already dearly outlined by Henry David Thoreau when he wrote, "If the law is of such a nature that it requires you to be an agent of injustice to another, then I say, break the law." Thoreau's words, "I would remind my countrymen that they are men first, and Americans at a late and convenient hour," provide an essential standard for any adequate thought and action in our third time of trial. As Americans, we have been well favored in the world, but it is as men that we will be judged.

Out of the first and second times of trial have come, as we have seen, the major symbols of the American civil religion. There seems little doubt that a successful negotiation of this third time of trial—the attainment of some kind of viable and coherent world order—would precipitate a major new set of symbolic forms. So far the flickering flame of the United Nations burns too low to be the focus of a cult, but the emergence of a genuine trans-national sovereignty would certainly change this. It would necessitate the incorporation of vital international symbolism into our civil religion, or, perhaps a better way of putting it, it would result in American civil religion becoming simply one part of a new civil religion of the world. It is useless to speculate on the form such a civil religion might take, though it obviously would draw on religious traditions beyond the sphere of Biblical religion alone. Fortunately, since the American civil religion is not the worship of the American nation but an understanding of the American experience in the light of ultimate and universal reality, the reorganization entailed by such a new situation need not disrupt the American civil religion's continuity. A world civil religion could be accepted as a fulfillment and not a denial of American civil religion. Indeed, such an outcome has been the eschatological hope of American civil religion from the beginning. To deny such an outcome would be to deny the meaning of America itself.

Behind the civil religion at every point lie Biblical archetypes: Exodus, Chosen People, Promised Land, New Jerusalem, Sacrificial Death and Rebirth. But it is also genuinely American and genuinely new. It has its own prophets and its own martyrs, its own sacred events and sacred places, its own solemn rituals and symbols. It is concerned that America be a society as perfectly in accord with the will of God as men can make it, and a light to all the nations.

It has often been used and is being used today as a cloak for petty interests and ugly passions. It is in need—as is any living faith—of continual reformation, of being measured by universal standards. But it is not evident that it is incapable of growth and new insight.

It does not make any decision for us. It does not remove us from moral ambiguity, from being, in Lincoln's fine phrase, an "almost chosen people." But it is a heritage of moral and religious experience from which we still have much to learn as we formulate the decisions that lie ahead.

74

A Normative Theory of Moral Community*

Philip Selznick

Many writers (and readers) are troubled by the fact that the idea of community is so elusive. There appears to be no clear consensus as to its central meaning.

It is not slipshod to speak of the European Economic Community, the Catholic community, the university community, the law school community, or the police as an occupational community. The main point here is that a framework of shared beliefs, interests, and commitments unites a set of *varied* groups and activities. Some are central, others peripheral, but all are connected by bonds that establish a common faith or fate, a personal identity, a sense of belonging, and a supportive structure of activities and relationships. The more pathways are provided for participation in diverse ways and touching multiple interests—for example, worshiping in Catholic churches, attending Catholic schools, contributing to Catholic charities, reading the Catholic press—the richer is the experience of community.

Treating community as a variable retains the threshold idea of comprehensiveness but does not commit us to a conventional criterion such as size or territoriality. Sociologists have often said that community necessarily presumes locality. Most "community studies," taking that for granted, focus on a particular village, town, or neighborhood, where (more or less) complete rounds of life can be observed. This makes sense, as a practical matter, because common residence is a congenial condition—perhaps the most congenial condition—for forming and sustaining community life. But communities can be formed in other ways as well; for example, on the basis of concerted activity and shared belief. In the interests of coherent theory, we should avoid confusing a congenial condition or a highly probable correlate with an essential or defining feature.

Thinking of community as variable allows for the possibility that special-purpose institutions may become communities or at least quasi-communities. This form of community occurs most readily when purpose is not very rigidly or narrowly conceived, when leeway is allowed for controversy over ends and means, and when participation is an important part of the individual's life within the organization. Thus community is more likely to develop in military or police organizations, which encourage a shared lifestyle, than in, say, marginal business firms where employment is sporadic, personnel turnover is

*Excerpts from *The Moral Commonwealth: Social Theory and the Promise of Community* by Philip Selznick.

high, training is unimportant, and work is highly routine and specialized. In other words, *the emergence of community depends on the opportunity for, and the impulse toward, comprehensive interaction, commitment, and responsibility.* These are variable outcomes; they require congenial conditions; but they are not necessarily peripheral or unimportant, even within special-purpose organizations.

This argument leaves intact the analytical distinction between community and special-purpose organization. The "pure" organization is an instrument for mobilizing human energies in disciplined, goal-directed ways. A community, by contrast, has generic functions but no special purpose. This distinction is one of the hardiest and most useful in sociological theory. The difference is often blurred in social reality, and we often want to move organizations *in the direction* of community, but the distinction remains a useful starting point for description and diagnosis.

Elements of Community

Although *a definition* of community is properly value-neutral, the *theory* we seek should be both normative and descriptive. We should be able to distinguish the better from the worse, not only according to some neutral criterion, such as "degree of social cohesion," but in the light of the best understanding we have of what makes for moral well-being. At the same time, we should pay close attention to the relevant descriptive sociology, that is, of the actual experience of living in communities. If it is to be effective as a guide to criticism and reconstruction, a normative model must build on that experience.

It has been said that community is a word that "seems never to be used unfavourably." That is surely an exaggeration, for the experience of community has many detractors who emphasize its potential for oppression. Nevertheless, the generally favorable usage is easy to understand when we remember that community—like culture, friendship, socialization, family life—is a prima facie good thing. Typically, communities provide settings within which people grow and flourish and within which subgroups are nourished and protected. This establishes a presumption of moral worth. The presumption is rebuttable on a showing that a given community is too narrow or attenuated to provide an effective framework for common life, or that it is too rigid and stultifying to serve the needs of personal and institutional development or too insular or self-destructive in its dealings with other communities, or that it is otherwise inadequate from the standpoint of critical morality. The same logic applies to our appreciation of family, friendship, law, and culture.

Thus understood, a normative theory of community is at once affirmative and critical—affirmative in that it explores, identifies, and embraces the positive contributions of community to human flourishing; critical in that it asks of a particular community how far, in what ways, and with what effects it deviates from a standard. The standard may allow for moral plurality, that is, for different but roughly equal renderings of the good community, but it should have enough bite to distinguish the better from the worse, the genuine from the spurious.

Any theory we propose must take into account the key values at stake in the construction and nurture of a community. These constitute a complex set of interacting variables: historicity, identity, mutuality, plurality, autonomy, participation, and integration. Each has limited and primitive forms; each is the basis of a more elaborated ideal.

Historicity. The bonds of community are strongest when they are fashioned from strands of shared history and culture. They are weak and precarious when they must depend on very general interests or abstract ideas. Furthermore, the character of a community largely reflects the particularities of custom, language, and institutional life; a heritage of significant events and crises; and such historically determined attributes as size, geography, and demography.

Historicity has prima facie moral worth. Rootedness and belonging make for individual well-being as well as commitment to others, and a sense of history is needed for sound collective judgment as to means and ends. Communities, like persons, can do better, and be better, if they understand their own possibilities and limits. To reach that understanding, however, brute particularity must be transcended. The quest is for principles latent in the community's culture and history. Once formulated, such principles become resources for internal dialogue. They are instruments of reflective morality, that is, they are authoritative standpoints from which to criticize and change specific beliefs, norms, and practices. At the same time, the principles express a distinctive ethos and a special experience.

Identity. A shared history tends to produce a sense of community, and this sense is manifested in loyalty, piety, and a distinctive identity. Every effort to create a community fosters such feelings and perceptions. A formed identity is the natural product of socialization, a process that is earned out not only in families but in most other institutions as well. When socialization is effective there is always some identification of self with others, with locality, and with association. The outcomes of socialization are highly variable, however. The mere fact that an identity-forming process is at work does not tell us how effective it is, nor does it say what kind of self—conformist or independent, supine or resourceful—is being produced.

Of all the elements of community, the moral worth of a formed identity is the most problematic. (This is one reason to avoid the common error of equating a *sense* of community with community itself.) Fixed identities—local, religious, ethnic—are likely to generate demands for self-affirmation that all too often lead to insularity and withdrawal. This parochialism is a chief source of virulent antagonisms. Hence the formation of identities can be destructive of community. The gains in security and self-esteem must be balanced against the loss of more comprehensive, more inclusive, more integrative attitudes.

Mutuality. Community begins with, and is largely supported by, the experience of interdependence and reciprocity. These very practical conditions account for the voluntary and rational components of community. If people and groups do not need each other, if nothing is to be gained from reciprocity and cooperation, community is not likely to emerge or to endure. For this necessary condition to be sufficient, however, mutuality cannot be very narrowly focused. It must go beyond impersonal exchange, beyond coordination for limited goals. To be effective in forming community, mutuality must implicate persons and groups as *unities* and not only in respect to segmental activities or roles. In the context of community, mutuality contemplates continuing relationships and high stakes.

The modern contract is a classic expression of baseline or bare-bones mutuality; hence it is difficult to sustain community on contract principles alone. At least there must be a significant departure from the principle of *limited* obligation in favor of more diffuse and open-ended duties; and the realities of association may require *unequal* contributions rather than a carefully balanced reciprocity. A zealous regard for specifying obligations in advance tends to close relations rather than open them, undermines trust, and limits contributions. Indeed, wherever continuity and concerted effort are prized, the (modern) contract model loses force and relevance. As we move to association, and from association to community, mutuality reaches beyond exchange to create more enduring bonds of interdependence, caring, and commitment. There is a transition, we may say, from reciprocity to solidarity, and from thereto fellowship.

Plurality. According to the pluralist and corporatist doctrines of Tocqueville, Lamennais, Gierke, and others, a community draws much of its vitality from "intermediate associations." Such associations are havens of protection and vehicles of meaningful participation. Through significant membership in corporate groups the individual's relation to the larger community can be extended and enriched. People lose the benefits of community when they are stripped of their group attachments and left naked before an impersonal or central authority. And the group structure of society generates countervailing forces to moderate the influence of any single power bloc.

Thus understood, plurality is a normative idea. It does not refer to every dispersal of power and commitment, every proliferation of interests, groups, and authorities. A healthy differentiation of institutions and of personal, family, ethnic, locality, and occupational groups depends on the capacity of each to preserve its own well-being within a framework of legitimacy, and without fracturing or fragmenting the social order.

Autonomy. Although pluralist thought has great merit, it also has a cardinal weakness: the assumption that individual well-being is effectively guaranteed by group autonomy and integrity. Pluralists have rightly emphasized that individuals need nurture, support, and group protection against external domination. But subsidiary groups can be oppressive, often more so than the state. Therefore pluralist theory must be modified as necessary to protect freedom *in* associations as well as freedom *of* association.

A concern for personal autonomy does not settle what freedoms are appropriate in the context at hand, nor does it assume that autonomy is equivalent to unconditional opportunity and choice. It does assume that the worth of community is measured by the contribution it makes to the flourishing of unique and responsible persons. As an attribute of selfhood and of self-affirmation, autonomy requires commitment as well as choice.

Participation. It is elementary that personal autonomy can be achieved only in and through social participation. But what *kind* of participation? Some kinds encourage rationality and self-determination; others undermine them. Some are egalitarian; others demand a spirit of subordination. The most rudimentary (and important) forms of communal participation have to do with the basic continuities of life: procreation, child-rearing, work, kinship, friendship. Participation in broader religious or political contexts builds on those continuities and tends to be distorted if they are weakened or absent. The mass mobilization of detached individuals is not a paradigm of communal participation. The lesson is that participation reflects and sustains community insofar as it entails multiple memberships and diverse commitments. The more compartmentalized, specialized, or single-minded the activity, the more limited is its contribution to the life of a community.

A flourishing community has high levels of participation: people are appropriately present, and expected to be present, on many different occasions and in many different roles and aspects. They are not *omni*present, however, nor are they asked to sacrifice their own most important concerns and connections. These are corollaries of what we earlier called "mediated" and "core" participation.

Integration. All the elements noted above require supportive institutions, norms, beliefs, and practices. These must exhibit enough coherence to sustain the foundations of a common life. We thus see the emergence of distinctively integrative political, legal, and cultural institutions. The quality of community depends, to a large extent, on the character of these institutions. How we perceive and construct the political and cultural order—whether as a tight system of integration and subordination or as a framework within which plurality and autonomy may flourish—becomes a central concern. There is, therefore, an intimate connection between democracy and community.

A fully realized community will have a rich and *balanced* mixture of all of these seven elements. We cannot ignore the givenness of received custom and decisive events, but the appeal to historicity must respect the other values, so far as they are affected. Similarly, the claims of plurality and autonomy must be balanced against those of mutuality and participation. In this normative theory, the moral quality of a community is measured by its ability to defend all the chief values at stake, to hold them in tension as necessary, and to encourage their refinement and elaboration.

It does not follow that any state of affairs less than a fully realized community is necessarily deficient from a moral point of view, any more than the morally best person must necessarily be the best-integrated or fully rounded. Different types of community—religious, political, occupational, institutional, international—will have different mixes of the main elements. A religious community may well give greater weight to historicity and mutuality than, say, an enterprise-based community will. And religious communities may differ among themselves in the weight they give to various forms and sources of fellowship. There is always room for debate as to the kind of community a group should be.

75

Communitarianism*

Amitai Etzioni

The age-old debate about what constitutes a good society has reintensified in the last decades. Religious fundamentalism has risen throughout the world, including in the West. Its champions are deeply concerned about the moral decay of their societies, which they often attribute to the influence of Western, or more generally modern, secular forces. To their way of thinking, individual rights have little or no standing. Fundamentalists argue that people thrive when they closely heed given religious laws. More moderate religious leaders and secular social conservatives are much more respectful of individual rights, but are nevertheless greatly and primarily concerned with the loss of virtues. They fear that barbarians are not at the gates but inside. For instance, they protest lurid rap songs much more than the severe beating of several African Americans by the police.

At the same time, libertarians and laissez-faire conservatives see the world awash with threats to individual liberties from expansive governments, religious fanatics, or power elites. Many of these individualists reject the very notion of a good society. Societies, they maintain, flourish when individuals are granted as much autonomy as possible. (The idea is expressed in more popular terms, in the often-repeated statement indicating that individuals should not be interfered with: "Don't mess with me.") They are much more likely to protest an unnecessary government regulation than face the moral issues raised by children having children.

It has been previously noted that these bodies of thought tend to center around the virtue of either liberty or order. Charles Taylor, for instance, points to a range of positions that "at one end give primacy to individual rights and freedom and, at the other, give highest priority to community life and the good of collectivities."

Among those ideologues and intellectuals largely concerned with social order (or their version of virtue), there are quite a few who are also concerned with liberty, and vice versa—among those whose thinking is focused on the defense of liberty, there are quite a few who are concerned with the social order. Both camps, however, tend to imply that the best way to sustain the "other" virtue is to attend to the one with which they are most concerned. They argue either that liberty is best sustained when order is firm, or that society is best ordered when liberty is maximized.

In contrast, the communitarian paradigm advanced here applies the notion of the golden rule

*Excerpts from *The New Golden Rule: Community and Morality in a Democratic Society* by Amitai Etzioni.

at the societal level, to characterize the good society as one that nourishes both social virtues and individual rights. I argue that a good society requires a carefully maintained equilibrium of order and autonomy, rather than the "maximization" of either.

To build my case, the following questions need to be answered:

1: Even if one ignores the extremists, what are the significant bodies of thought that center around order or autonomy but do not marry both? What are their arguments, and how may they be countered?

2: If one grants that all societies need to concern themselves with social order, one still must ask if the good society requires a special kind of order. If the answer is in the affirmative, what is that good order?

3: If one recognizes that all societies need to provide social foundations to sustain a significant measure of autonomy, what are the distinctive characteristics of autonomy in a good society?

4: What are the implications of the dual virtues of social order and autonomy for the old intellectual and ideological debate, which raged over the last 150 years, between those who champion free economies and those who favor extensive government controls, between conservatives and liberals?

5: To suggest that social order and autonomy must be held in a carefully crafted equilibrium still leaves open many questions concerning the relationship between these dual virtues. Is it true, as is often implied, that the more social order there is, the less liberty the members of the society have? And that the more liberties they take, the less social order there is? Can a society gain both more order and more liberty?

Many books have a subtext, often one that reflects a position with which they quarrel or from which they seek to differentiate themselves. Most communitarians have debated liberals, stressing that individuals are socially embedded and the inevitability of the social formulation of the good, and much that follows from that. I share this perspective. However, I am equally keen to engage the social conservatives. They pay insufficient attention, to put it mildly, to social and moral risks one faces when one promotes—above all, seeks to impose—virtue and conformity. The same charge had been previously made against communitarians ranging from Tönnies to contemporary Asian communitarians. (When in 1990 a new communitarian group was formed, many of those convened were concerned that they will be confused with previous conservative or collectivistic communitarians—hence the term "responsive communitarians" [responsive to individuals, that is] was created.) The communication position advanced here is deeply concerned with the balance between individual rights and social responsibilities, individuality and community, and autonomy and social order.

Methodological Notes

The paradigm developed here to explore the good society differs from many others in that it is more sociological, and thus empirical, and less normative (less prescriptive). While the discussion draws on political theory and social philosophy, these are not the main foundations of the argument. The sociological and empirical nature of my approach is similar to earlier statements by communitarians who pointed to the unrealistic assumptions made by libertarians (and those whom political theorists call "liberals") about the nature of the individual. In contrast to the libertarian perspective, communitarians have shown that individuals do not exist outside particular social contexts, and that it is erroneous to depict individuals as free agents. We are social animals, members in one another.

In the same sociological-empirical vein, it should be noted that while the term "communitarian" often brings to mind communities, and especially villages and small towns, this is a study of what makes any social entity, from a village to a group of nations, into more of a community. Community is a set of attributes, not a concrete place.

In trying to explore the nature of a good, communitarian society, the term "societal need" plays a pivotal role in the following discussion; it deserves a brief explication. The notion that societies have needs that must be addressed reflects the specific sociological approach applied here, which is known as functionalism. It explains the working of society by the contributions of the parts to the needs of the whole and the requirements a society must meet to maintain itself. For example, a society "needs" arrangements to ensure that as resources are depleted, they will be replenished.

We are used to thinking in terms of causality, and hence are often interested in what preceded what. In contrast, functional explanations tend to be ahistorical and therefore unconcerned with the originating circumstances of present conditions; they deal with factors that are contemporaneous, such as the observation that gated communities experience less violent crime. This is a valid observation even if one does not have the slightest notion about who erected the gates or why. Functional explanations rely primarily on elements that sustain one another, like bricks that hang together in an arch, instead of on cause-and-effect sequences.

Early functionalism was open to the charge that it contained a bias in favor of the status quo. It was assumed that whenever people did not conform to the dictates of their socially prescribed roles, they were "deviants." In this way all innovation and dissent could be characterized as endangering societal well-being. The functional paradigm applied in this book assumes that while certain *needs* are universal to all societies, there are always alternative *responses*. Instead of putting up gates, a community may fight crime by inviting those estranged from it to become members, and so on. True, these *alternatives* are never equivalent—they differ in their effectiveness. Societal needs do not dictate the specific ways a society must be designed; they only serve to indicate that satisfying basic societal needs—in one way or another—cannot be ignored, and that some ways make for a better society than others.

Thick Social Order—Fully Respectful of Autonomy

The Need for a Thick Social Order

All societies, whatever their virtue or lack thereof, must maintain some modicum of social order or they risk extinction. However, this is widely understood to mean the prevention of internal hostilities, ranging from violence among individuals to civil war among subgroups. In effect, all societies have a need for a much thicker social order, reflecting the fact that all societies promote some shared values, such as establishing a homeland (Israel for the Jews at its founding), seeking to develop a modern economy while sustaining socialism (Communist China in the early 1990s), or fostering its religion (Iran in the late 1980s). Hence, integral to the social order of all societies are at least some processes that mobilize some of their members' time, assets, energies, and loyalties to the *service of one or more common purposes.* (No assumption is made that a particular society is aware of these arrangements and makes them deliberately. A Spartan tribe, set on maintaining its warrior status, may not necessarily have a war mobilization board.)

Many of the old ideological and policy debates have been, in effect, about the question of how thick the social order ought to be. Social scientists keen on measuring thickness might use, as a first approximation, indicators such as the amount of tax exacted (as a proportion of the GNP); the size of the civil service as compared to the total labor force; the amount of time one is expected to spend serving the public (from performing jury duty to serving in the armed forces) and the community (for example, joining in anti-crime patrols); and the scope of regulations advanced in the name of the public good (e.g., do they encompass personal matters such as abortion or sodomy? do they also mandate certain private economic conduct?). We shall look at the proportion of values that are considered an integral part of the social order (and hence violating them is considered as undermining order) to those which members of the society are free to choose following their own normative commitments; this ratio is a particularly important indicator for differentiating various kinds of societies and paradigms.

The argument that there is a basic need for a thick social order may seem rather unremarkable, but it is contested by many individualists. Some libertarians challenge the very notions of a collective actor and societal needs. Jeremy Bentham wrote that society is a fiction. Margaret Thatcher proudly repeated this libertarian nostrum. Others seek to maximize liberty and minimize restrictions on it in name of the social order. James K. Glassman writes, "The big idea is to place human freedom above everything else." Lord Acton argued that "[l]iberty is not a means to a higher political end. It is itself the highest political end." Robert P. George notes critically that libertarians take an important truth, that freedom is essential to human dignity, and stretch it until it becomes a falsehood.

Most important, many libertarians and liberal individualists are troubled by social formulations of the common good that are a core part of thick social orders. They argue that each person should formulate his or her own virtue, and that public policies and mores should reflect only agreements that individuals voluntarily form.

Libertarians' and liberal individualists' subtext is a fear that collective formulations of morality will lead to judging as morally inferior those who are less able to live up to them. Libertarians often fear that this, in turn, will lead to discrimination, if not laws enforcing commitment to the shared good—i.e., to a violation of liberty, libertarianism's cardinal value.

A strong presentation of this approach by a contemporary philosopher is found in an influential book by Robert Nozick, *Anarchy, State, and Utopia.* Nozick writes: "[T]here is no *social entity* with a good that undergoes some sacrifice for its own good. There are only individual people, different individual people, with their own individual lives." Similarly Ronald Dworkin defines liberalism as the conviction that "political decisions must be, so far as possible, independent of any particular conception of the good life, or of what gives value to life."

And John Rawls writes at one point:

> [I]ndividuals find their good in different ways, and many things may be good for one person that would not be good for another. . . . In a well-ordered society [one that applies Rawls's theory of justice], then, the plans of life of individuals are different in the sense that these plans give prominence to different aims, and persons are left free to determine their good, the view of others being counted as merely advisory.

These points have been elaborated on often, especially in the debate between communitarians and liberal individualists. They have been the subject of an important and voluminous literature. They are not reiterated here. (For example, no attempt is made to revisit the often visited debate of communitarians with John Rawls.) The main point relevant to the discussion here is that while libertarians and liberal individualists do not ignore the need for social order, they not only champion a thin order but seek to limit the social order to one that is derived from and legitimated by individuals acting as free agents. In contrast, communitarians see a need for a social order that contains a set of shared values, to which individuals are taught they are obligated. Individuals may later question, challenge, rebel against, or even transform a given social order, but their starting point is a shared set of definitions of what is right versus what is wrong.

Communitarian Order: Largely Voluntary

Almost any form of social order may seem attractive to people engulfed by social anarchy, whether it stems from violent crime, tribal warfare, gangs, or widespread moral disorientation. People who have experienced civil war in Lebanon, Bosnia, or Sri Lanka, or who live in the crime-ridden parts of Moscow or Washington, D.C, are rather articulate supporters of this observation. A 1996 poll found that 77 percent of Russians think order is more important than democracy, while only 9 percent endorsed the opposite view. But not every social order makes for a good society *A good society requires an order that is aligned with the moral commitments of the members.* Other forms of social order generate high social and individual costs (such as withdrawal from work, abuse of alcohol and drugs, or a high incidence of psychosomatic illnesses), and lead to numerous attempts to evade, change, or escape such order.

The challenge for those who aspire to a good society is to form and sustain—or, if it has been lost, to regenerate—a social order that is considered legitimate by its members, not merely when it is established (as contract libertarians would have it) but continuously. The new golden rule requires that the tension between one's preferences and one's social commitments be reduced by increasing the realm of duties one affirms as moral responsibilities—not the realm of duties that are forcibly imposed but the realm of responsibilities one believes one should discharge and that one believes one is fairly called upon to assume. Much of what follows is dedicated to the question of how such a unique social order, one that is ultimately based on its members' voluntary compliance, can be sustained. I should say here by way of introduction that a voluntary order is not an oxymoron. If 1 believe firmly that a decent human being drives safely, respectful of the community mores—and many other members of my community share this belief—the traffic will be largely orderly, relying on our moral commitments. Several colleagues suggested that I avoid the term "order" and refer instead to "community"; they suggested that the former term has a disconcerting or conservative aura to it. Some particular forms of orders do, but not those, we shall see, that are an integral part of the good society.

The starting point for such an examination is the factual observation that all forms of social order draw to some extent on coercive means (such as police and jails), "utilitarian" means (economic incentives generated by public expenditures or subsidies), and normative means (appeals to values, moral education). Societies differ greatly, however, in the mix of means they employ. Totalitarian societies draw heavily on coercive means in ordering a very wide range of behavior; authoritarian societies maintain order in a similar manner, but for a significantly narrower range of behavior. Libertarian societies, which minimize the scope of the social order and seek to draw on the market even for public services (e.g., by privatizing garbage collection, welfare, schools, and even prison management), draw heavily on utilitarian means. The order of good communitarian societies relies heavily on normative means (education, leadership, consensus, peer pressure, pointing out role models, exhortation, and, above all, the moral voices of communities). In this sense, the social order of good societies is a moral order.

For a social order to be able to rely heavily on normative means requires that most members of the society, most of the time, *share a commitment to a set of core values,* and that most members, most of the time, will abide by the behavioral implications of these values because they believe in them, rather than being *forced* to comply with them. It is rather self-evident that high levels of violent crime and other forms of antisocial behavior are indications that a society's order is lacking; it is much less often recognized that a *large number of police officers, tax auditors, and inspectors also indicates a deficient moral order,* even if antisocial behavior is low. Indeed, this is exactly the point at which the kind of order implied by the phrase "law and order" and the communitarian notion of a social order differ most.

The needed good order will be served by restoration of the civil (or civic) society that many have called for recently, and is of merit in its own right, but by itself will not suffice to provide the kind of order a good society requires. "Civic order" is used to mean that people are civil to one another (that they do not demonize their opponents, are willing to compromise, conduct reasoned rather than impassioned discussions) and/or that a society should maintain a fabric of mediating institutions to protect individuals from the government. Or—that the government should heed the citizens' preferences. I agree that the civic order is part of the good order, but it is far too thin a concept; the civic order is often defined mainly in terms of procedure, limited to the political arena, or otherwise devoid of substantive values, as distinct from the concepts of good around which the social order of good societies is centered.

Once one grants that a good society requires a social order based on commitments to and the embodiment of specific virtues, one may well ask: How does such a conception of order differ from that championed by social conservatives? We shall see that the answer lies in the status of autonomy, in the scope of conduct that the social formulation of the good seeks to encompass, and in the means of enforcement.

Autonomy Fully Respectful of Order

Individualists and Unbounded Autonomy

Individualists' view that autonomy is the core virtue, not to be trumped by any other, mirrors their arguments against social formulation of the good: Individuals should be free to make their own choices (unless they harm other individuals). Reference is typically made to legal rights and freedom from government. Special significance is attributed to individuals' rights to have their lives protected and to control and use their property. This position is most explicitly embraced by libertarians and laissez-faire conservatives. While individualists do not deny in principle the need for curbing individuals, especially not when these limits are set socially and not by the government, in effect they tend to treat most specific claims on the individual with suspicion, if not hostility, at best with benign neglect, as we shall see.

Large parts of several social sciences are based in individualistic assumptions. These sciences assume that one can and should explain social phenomena in terms of the attributes and actions of individuals, and ignore or explicitly deny the importance of macro, historical, or cultural factors and forces. Individualism in social science is not a passing fad or a small branch. It has played a major role in psychology. Much of neoclassical economics, especially in the United States, is individualistic; so are public choice theory in political science, exchange sociology, and a significant part of legal studies (law and economics). The University of Chicago is a center for social science conducted within such an individualist paradigm; among the most often cited are Richard A. Epstein and Richard A. Posner. Terry Eastland is also referred to in this context, as is David Frum among younger writers.

Although individualists vary a great deal (for instance, even Mill's own position varies considerably from book to book), the rather familiar public philosophy and policy recommendations built on these divergent individualists' ideas are focused on one overarching concern: Can more of the public business (social security, public schools, police departments, prisons, tax collections) be privatized? Can private business be further deregulated? Can taxes be reduced and funds returned to private hands? Among the more radical libertarian ideas of ways to further curtail the state role are the abolition of border controls on immigration and a shutdown of the Food and Drug Administration. Some even suggest that criminal justice be replaced by civil justice, in which considerations of moral and social values are ignored and violators are punished by having to compensate their victims who bring suits against them. There is much less concern with the question of whether individual tastes and ambitions need to be balanced with concerns for the social order, either because it is assumed that such an order will arise automatically from the aggregation of individual acts (the invisible hand) or that, if individuals put their minds to it, they would heed the proper self-limitation. But there is no principled need for socially provided mores.

Civil libertarians are not usually considered in the same breath as other libertarians, although like other individualists they are strong champions of autonomy and are uncomfortable with the concept of social responsibility. Civil libertarians are concerned with rights and not duties; with entitlements and not with national service, tithes, and taxes. Above all, they oppose guidance by the government and, more indirectly by others, as to what one ought to do.

Strong individualists often define liberty as the right to choose. The same individualists, as an indication that they are not unmindful of the social order, tend to add that an individual is free to act only as long as he or she is causing no harm to others. However, the concept of harm is not a reliable guide. It is unclear whether it refers only to physical harm (in which cases violating someone's right to free speech, for instance, is not a "harm") or also includes psychological harm fin which case breaking up a romance might be prohibited). The level of harm that is to be avoided is also an unanswered issue. If all harm is to be avoided, individuals would lose practically all ability to act. For example, my operating an automobile might harm your ability to breathe pristine air. To the extent that the principle is interpreted to mean that the harm to others should not exceed the gain to ego, or not affect some Pareto, or some other theoretical distribution in an unfavorable manner, such determinations are impossible to make under most circumstances.

Socially Constructed Autonomy

The characterization of autonomy the good society requires does not treat it, as is often the case, as merely an individual virtue of persons who cherish freedom and who conduct themselves in ways that sustain that virtue. Reference here is to a societal attribute, an attribute of a society that provides structured opportunities and legitimation for individual and subgroup expression of their particular values, needs, and preferences. To signify that I deal with virtue as a societal and not a personal attribute, I will use the term "social virtue."

Socially constructed autonomy enhances the ability of the society to adapt to change, to be metastable. Providing structured opportunities for individual and subgroup expression balances a tendency of those in power to avoid making needed changes in social formations and public policies following changes in the external environment or in internal societal compositions. For societies to be stable, they must be metastable, that is, to keep the same overarching pattern, they must continue to remake themselves. (The difference between plain stability and metastability is often overlooked. It is akin to the difference between making repairs on a sailboat and converting a sailboat into a steamboat: It is still a boat which fulfills the same function and may have the same destination, but has a different structure. Thus, while a society needs some form of constructed autonomy if it is to successfully adapt and balance the dual virtues, the society may change profoundly the specific ways autonomy is constructed.)

Societies that exert high pressure on their members to conform, and thus constrict their members' autonomy, tend to suffer from a lack of adaptation. Japan is often reported to be a society that is highly conformist as well as one that has generated relatively few scientific or artistic breakthroughs as compared to Western societies. I will not try to determine whether these observations about Japan are valid; whatever the final data, the very debate serves to highlight the need for autonomy.

Totalitarian societies, which allow for even less autonomy, are typically even less adaptive. They tend to find out much later than those of democracies when their policies are erroneous. (While I apply terms that are often employed to characterize political regimes, such as democratic and authoritarian, they apply here to societal patterns. Thus, at issue is not merely the role of elections, legislatures, and such in the polity, but also the role of voluntary associations, and religious organizations, the treatment of the family, and many other societal factors.)

Furthermore, institutionalized autonomy allows a society to take into account that the members of society differ greatly in their capabilities and their specific environmental circumstances. To try to force them all to abide by the same rules (for instance, to insist that they all need to study calculus or a particular foreign language) sharply undercuts their ability to serve the society, aside from diminishing what they can do for themselves. This issue often arises in the area of education. Some societies control, on a national basis, the details of school curricula, while good societies leave much more room for local autonomy. The same issue is faced in numerous other areas of social policy.

Similar in importance is the opportunity for the expression of subgroup differences, whether these are mainly differences in values or are chiefly based on economic or power interests. Among the forms of governments, federalism has been touted as being more conducive to accommodating differences among subgroups than a unitary state. Discussions of devolution and of constitutional revisions to enhance federalism, suggestions to introduce a regional parliament in Scotland, and to enhance the rights of provinces in Canada and in many other countries—typically couched in legal, political, and institutional terms—are, in effect, discussions of how much autonomy to grant to various subgroups instead of holding them all to the same unitary, national standards. Moreover, the lines of subgroup autonomy are not limited to geographical or legal entities, such as states and local governments. Religious, racial, ethnic, or other subgroups all seek a measure of autonomy. The right not to work on Saturdays rather than on Sundays is a well-known case in point.

American public philosophy tends to base respect for autonomy not on societal needs but on the inalienable rights or the legal rights of the members of society, and the term "liberty" or "freedom" rather than autonomy is typically employed. I use the term "autonomy" to stress that it encompasses both what is typically considered as individual freedom and the needs for self-expression, innovation, creativity, and self-government as well as legitimation of the expression of subgroup differences.

Autonomy in the Good Society

Generals are often said to prepare to fight the last war rather than the next one. Western intellectuals, with long experience in confronting first authoritarianism, then totalitarianism, and more recently religious fundamentalism, are quite keenly aware of the dangers of excessive order, especially of the coercive variety. These intellectuals are less prepared to face the danger that ideologization of unbounded autonomy poses, as the champions of choice and self-expression undermine the moral taboos on antisocial behavior. A discussion of the difference between socially bounded and anarchic, unbounded autonomy highlights the kind of autonomy a good society requires.

While it is possible to think abstractly about individuals apart from a community, it must be noted that if individuals are actually deprived of the stable and positive affective attachments communities best provide, they exhibit very few of the attributes commonly associated with the notion of a freestanding person presumed by the individualist paradigm. Such individuals are unable to be reasonable and reasoning members of a civil society. Residents of large cities who live an isolated life in high-rise buildings and have no other sources of social attachments (e.g., at work) have been found to tend to be mentally unstable, impulsive, prone to suicide, and otherwise predisposed to mental and psychosomatic illnesses. Studies of inmates who have been isolated from the general prison population (compared to those who are allowed to remain integrated into the inmate groups and culture), and of people isolated in psychological experiments, further highlight the importance of the social fabric—of communal attachments—for individuality in general and the ability to reason and act freely in particular.

The extra step one needs to undertake is to note that not only are human beings social by nature but also that their sociability enhances their human and moral potential. Social thinking has to cease viewing communal attachments as cannonballs chained to inmates' legs, needed to maintain their stability but "encumbering." The social fabric sustains, nourishes, and enables individuality rather than diminishes it. True, as with all good things, from food to medications, an excess of sociability can cause major problems of its own. These include curtailing individual rights in the name of community needs; suppressing creativity in the name of conformity; and even suppresing a sense of self, losing I individuality in a mesh of familial or communal relations. But in good measure, communal attachments and individuality go hand-in-hand, enrich one another, and are not antagonistic. The self is enriched and, as we shall see, ennobled by being social; it is the asocial self that is held back by the *lack* of positive multiple attachments.

The greatest danger to autonomy arises when the social moorings of individuals are severed. The atomization of individuals or the reduction of communities to mobs, which result in the individual's loss of competence and self-identity, has historically generated societal conditions that led to totalitarianism, a grand loss of autonomy. Such atomization preceded the rise of totalitarian movements and governments in Russia after its defeat in the 1905 war with Japan, and in Germany in the 1920s following its defeat in World War I and the ruinous effects of runaway inflation and mass unemployment. Even when atomization is at levels lower than which a totalitarian regime would be "invited," the result is a high level of anomie, alienation, withdrawal, and antisocial behavior, as witnessed in major urban centers over the last decades.

The most common antidotes to mass society, already noted by Tocqueville as a cornerstone of civic society, are the "intermediary bodies" that stand between the individual and the state. It is often overlooked in this context that many of these bodies are not the vaunted voluntary associations, with their meager bonding power (from the March of Dimes to chess clubs), but communities, with their much stronger interpersonal attachments (especially ethnic, racial, and religious ones, as well as residential communities).

The communitarian paradigm, at least as advanced here, recognizes the need to nourish social attachments as part of the effort to maintain social order while ensuring that such attachments will not suppress all autonomous expressions. That is, a good society does not favor the social good over individual choices or vice versa; it favors societal formations that serve the two dual social virtues in careful equilibrium. We shall see that this societal pattern, in turn, requires: (a) a reliance mainly on education, leadership, persuasion, faith, and moral dialogues, rather than the law, for sustaining virtues; (b) defining a core of values that need to be promoted—a substantive core that is richer than those that make procedures meritorious; but (c) not a pervasive ideology or the kinds of religion that leave little room for autonomy.

In short, all bodies of thought and belief build on a primary concept. For individualists the cornerstone of a good society is the freestanding person; for social conservatives, it is a pervasive set of social virtues embodied in the society or state. For communitarians, it suffices as a first approximation to argue that a good society requires a balance between autonomy and order. And the order has to be of a special kind: voluntary and limited to core values rather than imposed or pervasive. And autonomy has to be contextuated within a social fabric of bonds and values rather than unbounded.

76

THE CIVILIZING PROCESS*

NORBERT ELIAS

On the one hand, the theory of civilization which the following study attempts to develop helps us to see the misleading image of man in what we call the modern age as less self-evident, and to detach ourselves from it, so that work can begin on an image of man oriented less by one's own feelings and the value judgments attached to them than by men as the actual objects of thought and observation. On the other hand, a critique of the modern image of man is needed for an understanding of the civilizing process. For in the course of this process the structure of individual human beings changes; they become "more civilized." And so long as we see the individual human being as by nature a closed container with an outer shell and a core concealed within it, we cannot comprehend how a civilizing process embracing many generations is possible, in the course of which the personality structure of the individual human being changes without the nature of human beings changing.

This must suffice here as an introduction to the reorientation of individual self-consciousness and to the resulting development of the image of man, without which any ability to conceive a civilizing process or a long-term process involving social and personality structures is largely blocked. So long as the concept of the individual is linked with the self-perception of the "ego" in a closed case, we can hardly conceive "society" as anything other than a collection of windowless monads. Concepts like "social structure," "social process," or "social development" then appear at best as artificial products of sociologists, as "ideal-typical" constructions needed by scientists to introduce some order, at least in thought, into what appears in reality to be a completely disordered and structureless accumulation of absolutely independent individual agents.

As can be seen, the actual state of affairs is the exact converse. The notion of individuals deciding, acting, and "existing" in absolute independence of one another is an artificial product of men which is characteristic of a particular stage in the development of their self-perception. It rests partly on a confusion of ideals and facts, and partly on a reification of individual self-control mechanisms—of the severance of individual affective impulses from the motor apparatus, from the direct control of bodily movements and actions.

This self-perception in terms of one's own isolation, of the invisible wall dividing one's own "inner" self from all the people and things "outside," takes on for a large number of people in the course of the modern age the same immediate force of conviction that the movement of the sun

*Excerpts from *The Civilizing Process: The History of Manners* by Norbert Elias, translated by Edmund Jephcott. Originally published in 1939.

around an earth situated at the center of the cosmos possessed in the Middle Ages. Like the geocentric picture of the physical universe earlier, the egocentric image of the social universe is certainly capable of being conquered by a more realistic, if emotionally less appealing picture. The emotion may or may not remain: it is an open question how far the feeling of isolation and alienation is attributable to ineptitude and ignorance in the development of individual self-controls, and how far to structural characteristics of advanced societies. Just as the public predominance of emotionally less appealing images of a physical universe not centered on the earth did not entirely efface the more private self-centered experience of the sun as circling around the earth, the ascendancy of a more objective image of man in public thinking may not necessarily efface the more private ego-centered experience of an invisible wall dividing one's own "inner world" from the world "outside." But it is certainly not impossible to dislodge this experience, and the image of man corresponding to it, from its self-evident acceptance in research in the human sciences. Here and in what follows one can see at least the beginnings of an image of man that agrees better with unhindered observations of human beings, and for this reason facilitates access to problems which, like those of the civilizing process or the state-building process, remain more or less inaccessible from the standpoint of the old image of man, or which, like the problem of the relation of individuals to society, continually give rise from that standpoint to unnecessarily complicated and never entirely convincing solutions.

The image of man as a "closed personality" is here replaced by the image of man as an "open personality" who possesses a greater or lesser degree of relative (but never absolute and total) autonomy vis-à-vis other people and who is, in fact, fundamentally oriented toward and dependent on other people throughout his life. The network of interdependencies among human beings is what binds them together. Such interdependencies are the nexus of what is here called the figuration, a structure of mutually oriented and dependent people. Since people are more or less dependent on each other first by nature and then through social learning, through education, socialization, and socially generated reciprocal needs, they exist, one might venture to say, only as pluralities, only in figurations. That is why, as was stated earlier, it is not particularly fruitful to conceive of men in the image of the individual man. It is more appropriate to envisage an image of numerous interdependent people forming figurations (i.e., groups or societies of different kinds) with each other. Seen from this basic standpoint, the rift in the traditional image of man disappears. The concept of the figuration has been introduced precisely because it expresses what we call "society" more clearly and unambiguously than the existing conceptual tools of sociology, as neither an abstraction of attributes of individuals existing without a society, nor a "system" or "totality" beyond individuals, but the network of inter-dependencies formed by individuals. It is certainly quite possible to speak of a social system formed of individuals. But the undertones associated with the concept of the social system in contemporary sociology make such an expression seem forced. Furthermore, the concept of the system is prejudiced by the associated notion of immutability.

What is meant by the concept of the figuration can be conveniently explained by reference to social dances. They are, in fact, the simplest example that could be chosen. One should think of a mazurka, a minuet, a polonaise, a tango, or rock 'n' roll. The image of the mobile figurations of interdependent people on a dance floor perhaps makes it easier to imagine states, cities, families, and also capitalist, communist, and feudal systems as figurations. By using this concept we can eliminate the antithesis, resting finally on different values and ideals, immanent today in the use of the words "individual" and "society." One can certainly speak of a dance in general, but no one will imagine a dance as a structure outside the individual or as a mere abstraction. The same dance figurations can certainly be danced by different people; but without a plurality of reciprocally oriented and dependent individuals, there is no dance. Like every other social figuration, a dance figuration is relatively independent of the specific individuals forming it here and now, but not of individuals as such. It would be absurd to say that dances are mental constructions abstracted from observations of individuals considered separately. The same applies to all other figurations. Just as the small dance figurations change—becoming now slower, now quicker—so too, gradually or more suddenly, do the large figurations which we call societies. The following study is concerned with such changes. Thus, the starting point of the study of the process of state formation is a figuration made up of numerous relatively small social units existing in free competition with one another. The investigation shows how and why this figuration changes. It demonstrates at the same time that there are explanations which do not have the character of causal explanations. For a change in a figuration is explained partly by the endogenous dynamic of the figuration itself, the immanent tendency of a figuration of freely competing units to form monopolies. The investigation therefore shows how in the course of centuries the original figuration changes into another, in which such great opportunities of monopoly power are linked with a single social position—kingship—that no occupant of any other social position within the network of interdependencies can compete with the monarch. At the same time, it indicates how the personality structures of human beings also change in conjunction with such figurational changes.

To detach oneself from the idea of oneself and of every individual human being as *homo clausus* is certainly not easy. But without detachment from this notion, one cannot possibly understand what is meant when a civilizing process is referred to as a transformation of individual structures. Similarly, it is not easy so to develop one's own imaginative capacity that one is able to think in figurations, and, moreover, in figurations whose normal characteristics include a tendency to change, sometimes even in a specific direction.

PART X

RACE AND GENDER

The thinkers whose writings compose this part are focused on understanding the inequities that arise from social identities based on race and gender. Sociological analyses of race, particularly those made by the African American sociologist W. E. B. Du Bois, hark back to the early 20th century—a time when, as he remarks, the biggest social problem facing the United States was *the problem of the color line*, racial segregation. Du Bois proposes, first, a social psychology that reveals the mental tension experienced by African Americans and, second, a policy proposal for improving the social situation of the African American community. The remaining readings—by feminist scholars Charlotte Perkins Gilman, Dorothy Smith, Patricia Hill Collins, and Judith Butler—discuss women's experiences: their unique ways of knowing, doing, and being. At the center of these sociological conceptualizations of gender is the oppression of women—of all races, ethnicities, social classes, and sexualities—by a hegemonic, misogynist culture.

The first reading, "The Veil and Double Consciousness," excerpted from the book *The Souls of Black Folk*, was first published in 1903 by W. E. B. Du Bois. Writing 40 years after emancipation, Du Bois contends that the problem of the color line is commonly expressed by the question, which whites routinely ask of Blacks, "How does it feel to be a problem?" According to Du Bois, the white world continuously reminds African Americans that they are different. This creates what Du Bois describes as a *veil*—a social division and a psychological perception—between Blacks and whites. It instills in Blacks a *double consciousness*, a self-awareness that is refracted through a white perspective and measured against a white standard. This split consciousness creates in African Americans a conflicted social self—one African, the other American, never being able to truly merge the two identities.

In his famous essay, "The Talented Tenth," Du Bois proposes a social experiment that he believes will advance the Black race: the education and development of *the talented tenth*—the top 10% in the African American community that consists of the best and most capable people. Every generation since colonial days, says Du Bois, has produced an elite class of knowledge and character comprising the talented tenth of Black men and women. These people are natural leaders of exceptional ability who must be provided with a broad-based education in colleges and universities. They require liberal training that gives them knowledge of the wider world and an understanding of social relations. Only through the talented tenth, who serve as reformers and role models, can the African American community develop materially, culturally, and socially.

Turning to issues of gender, Charlotte Perkins Gilman, in "The Economic Status of Women," first published in 1898, asserts that the relationship between men and women is essentially an economic relationship: Women are financially supported by men. At the time that Gilman was writing, women's work was limited to the domestic sphere and basically involved the more mundane activities of cooking, cleaning, and sewing. Because they had not been allowed to develop their economic activity, women could not contribute to economic progress. The making and management of industry, trade, commerce, and government was almost wholly the domain of men. In marriage, the wife was not the economic equal of her husband; she did not contribute financially to the partnership and thus could not be economically independent. Women were economically relevant only to the extent that their housework, which was not paid labor, enabled men to produce more wealth than they otherwise could. Women's *economic status*, their position relative to the exchange of goods and services, was that they were entirely dependent on men for their livelihood.

In "Feminist Standpoint Theory," Dorothy Smith proposes a *sociology for women*, one that conceptualizes society and social relations from the perspective of an embodied subject situated in a particular historical setting. Only in this way, says Smith, can the realities of women's unique experiences be understood and explained. *Feminist standpoint theory*, then, is a method for writing sociology from women's distinctive point of view. It is a sociology that reports the authentic words of real women speaking of the actualities of their everyday world. It is also a self-conscious sociology that produces "texts" read by a reader who, through the act of reading, attributes meaning to the particularities of women's daily lives. A sociology for women allows women to transcend what Smith calls the *ruling apparatus*—the impersonal forms of power and organization that are the domain of men—and to develop a sociological consciousness of their own.

In "Black Feminist Thought," Patricia Hill Collins specifically examines the experiences of *African American women*. As such, she regards *gender* simultaneously with *race* and *social class* as the three "interlocking systems of oppression" that have most profoundly affected Black women's lives. In addition to these three axes, Collins considers three levels at which Black women experience and resist domination: the biographical, the cultural, and the institutional. In placing Black women's subjectivity at the center of these six intersecting oppressions, what Collins calls the *matrix of domination*, she reveals how this holistic and integrative way of knowing can empower Black women. She asserts that by considering their own situated, subjugated standpoint, Black women become agents of knowledge. They produce *Black feminist thought*, which helps them to define their own experiences and actions and resist oppression.

In the final selection, "Performative Theory of Gender Acts," Judith Butler argues that gendered identity is an accomplishment. Determining gender *identity*, says Butler, involves a set of bodily gestures, movements, and styles that produces what appears to be an internal essence—a "true" masculinity or femininity. These gestures, movements, and styles are *performative*; they are given dramatic meaning. This internal essence does not have an ontological status; rather, it is a fabricated social fiction. What is created is the *illusion* of a natural gendered identity. But, in fact, gender is an attempt to *imitate* an unattainable ideal, of either "man" or "woman," that is socially constructed. Gender is not an essence; it is a performance.

77

The Veil and Double Consciousness*

W. E. B. Du Bois

Between me and the other world there is ever an unasked question: unasked by some through feelings of delicacy; by others through the difficulty of rightly framing it. All, nevertheless, flutter round it. They approach me in a half-hesitant sort of way, eye me curiously or compassionately, and then, instead of saying directly, How does it feel to be a problem? they say, I know an excellent colored man in my town; or, I fought at Mechanicsville; or, Do not these Southern outrages make your blood boil? At these I smile, or am interested, or reduce the boiling to a simmer, as the occasion may require. To the real question, How does it feel to be a problem? I answer seldom a word.

And yet, being a problem is a strange experience,—peculiar even for one who has never been anything else, save perhaps in babyhood and in Europe. It is in the early days of rollicking boyhood that the revelation first bursts upon one, all in a day, as it were. I remember well when the shadow swept across me. I was a little thing, away up in the hills of New England, where the dark Housatonic winds between Hoosac and Taghkanic to the sea. In a wee wooden schoolhouse, something put it into the boys' and girls' heads to buy gorgeous visiting-cards—ten cents a package—and exchange. The exchange was merry, till one girl, a tall newcomer, refused my card,—refused it peremptorily, with a glance. Then it dawned upon me with a certain suddenness that I was different from the others; or like, mayhap, in heart and life and longing, but shut out from their world by a vast veil. I had thereafter no desire to tear down that veil, to creep through; I held all beyond it in common contempt, and lived above it in a region of blue sky and great wandering shadows. That sky was bluest when I could beat my mates at examination-time, or beat them at a foot-race, or even beat their stringy heads. Alas, with the years all this fine contempt began to fade; for the words I longed for, and all their dazzling opportunities, were theirs, not mine. But they should not keep these prizes, I said; some, all, I would wrest from them. Just how I would do it I could never decide: by reading law, by healing the sick, by telling the wonderful tales that swam in my head,—some way. With other black boys the strife was not so fiercely sunny: their youth shrunk into tasteless sycophancy, or into silent hatred of the pale world about them and mocking distrust of everything white; or wasted itself in a bitter cry, Why did God make me an outcast and a stranger in mine own house? The shades of the prison-house closed round about us all; walls strait and stubborn to the whitest, but relentlessly narrow, tall, and

** Excerpts from *The Souls of Black Folk* by W.E.B. Du Bois.

unscalable to sons of night who must plod darkly on in resignation, or beat unavailing palms against the stone, or steadily, half hopelessly, watch the streak of blue above.

After the Egyptian and Indian, the Greek and Roman, the Teuton and Mongolian, the Negro is a sort of seventh son, born with a veil, and gifted with second-sight in this American world,—a world which yields him no true self-consciousness, but only lets him see himself through the revelation of the other world. It is a peculiar sensation, this double-consciousness, this sense of always looking at one's self through the eyes of others, of measuring one's soul by the tape of a world that looks on in amused contempt and pity. One ever *feels* his twoness,—an American, a Negro; two souls, two thoughts, two unreconciled strivings; two warring ideals in one dark body, whose dogged strength alone keeps it from being torn asunder.

The history of the American Negro is the history of this strife,—this longing to attain self-conscious manhood, to merge his double self into a better and truer self. In this merging he wishes neither of the older selves to be lost. He would not Africanize America, for America has too much to teach the world and Africa. He would not bleach his Negro soul in a flood of white Americanism, for he knows that Negro blood has a message for the world. He simply wishes to make it possible for a man to be both a Negro and an American, without being cursed and spit upon by his fellows, without having the doors of Opportunity closed roughly in his face.

This, then, is the end of his striving: to be a co-worker in the kingdom of culture, to escape both death and isolation, to husband and use his best powers and his latent genius. These powers of body and mind have in the past been strangely wasted, dispersed, or forgotten. The shadow of a mighty Negro past flits through the tale of Ethiopia the Shadowy and of Egypt the Sphinx. Through history, the powers of single black men flash here and there like falling stars, and die sometimes before the world has rightly gauged their brightness. Here in America, in the few days since Emancipation, the black man's turning hither and thither in hesitant and doubtful striving has often made his very strength to lose effectiveness, to seem like absence of power, like weakness. And yet it is not weakness,—it is the contradiction of double aims. The double-aimed struggle of the black artisan—on the one hand to escape white contempt for a nation of mere hewers of wood and drawers of water, and on the other hand to plough and nail and dig for a poverty-stricken horde—could only result in making him a poor craftsman, for he had but half a heart in either cause. By the poverty and ignorance of his people, the Negro minister or doctor was tempted toward quackery and demagogy; and by the criticism of the other world, toward ideals that made him ashamed of his lowly tasks. The would-be black *savant* was confronted by the paradox that the knowledge his people needed was a twice-told tale to his white neighbors, while the knowledge which would teach the white world was Greek to his own flesh and blood. The innate love of harmony and beauty that set the ruder souls of his people a-dancing and a-singing raised but confusion and doubt in the soul of the black artist; for the beauty revealed to him was the soul-beauty of a race which his larger audience despised, and he could not articulate the message of another people. This waste of double aims, this seeking to satisfy two unreconciled ideals, has wrought sad havoc with the courage and faith and deeds of ten thousand thousand people,—has sent them often wooing false gods and invoking false means of salvation, and at times has even seemed about to make them ashamed of themselves.

Away back in the days of bondage they thought to see in one divine event the end of all doubt and disappointment; few men ever worshipped Freedom with half such unquestioning faith as did the American Negro for two centuries. To him, so far as he thought and dreamed, slavery was indeed the sum of all villainies, the cause of all sorrow, the root of all prejudice; Emancipation was the key to a promised land of sweeter beauty than ever stretched before the eyes of wearied Israelites. In song and exhortation swelled one refrain—Liberty; in his tears and curses the God he implored had Freedom in his right hand. At last it came,—suddenly, fearfully, like a dream. With one wild carnival of blood and passion came the message in his own plaintive cadences:—

> "Shout, O children!
>
> Shout, you're free!
>
> For God has bought your liberty!"

Years have passed away since then,—ten, twenty, forty; forty years of national life, forty years of renewal and development, and yet the swarthy spectre sits in its accustomed seat at the Nation's feast. In vain do we cry to this our vastest social problem:—

"Take any shape but that, and my firm nerves

Shall never tremble!"

The Nation has not yet found peace from its sins; the freedman has not yet found in freedom his promised land. Whatever of good may have come in these years of change, the shadow of a deep disappointment rests upon the Negro people,—a disappointment all the more bitter because the unattained ideal was unbounded save by the simple ignorance of a lowly people.

The first decade was merely a prolongation of the vain search for freedom, the boon that seemed ever barely to elude their grasp,—like a tantalizing will-o'-the-wisp, maddening and misleading the headless host. The holocaust of war, the terrors of the Ku-Klux Klan, the lies of carpet-baggers, the disorganization of industry, and the contradictory advice of friends and foes, left the bewildered serf with no new watch-word beyond the old cry for freedom. As the time flew, however, he began to grasp a new idea. The ideal of liberty demanded for its attainment powerful means, and these the Fifteenth Amendment gave him. The ballot, which before he had looked upon as a visible sign of freedom, he now regarded as the chief means of gaining and perfecting the liberty with which war had partially endowed him. And why not? Had not votes made war and emancipated millions? Had not votes enfranchised the freedmen? Was anything impossible to a power that had done all this? A million black men started with renewed zeal to vote themselves into the kingdom. So the decade flew away, the revolution of 1876 came, and left the half-free serf weary, wondering, but still inspired. Slowly but steadily, in the following years, a new vision began gradually to replace the dream of political power,—a powerful movement, the rise of another ideal to guide the unguided, another pillar of fire by night after a clouded day It was the ideal of "book-learning" ; the curiosity, born of compulsory ignorance, to know and test the power of the cabalistic letters of the white man, the longing to know. Here at last seemed to have been discovered the mountain path to Canaan; longer than the highway of Emancipation and law, steep and rugged, but straight, leading to heights high enough to overlook life.

Up the new path the advance guard toiled, slowly, heavily, doggedly; only those who have watched and guided the faltering feet, the misty minds, the dull understandings, of the dark pupils of these schools know how faithfully, how piteously, this people strove to learn. It was weary work. The cold statistician wrote down the inches of progress here and there, noted also where here and there a foot had slipped or some one had fallen. To the tired climbers, the horizon was ever dark, the mists were often cold, the Canaan was always dim and far away. If, however, the vistas disclosed as yet no goal, no resting-place, little but flattery and criticism, the journey at least gave leisure for reflection and self-examination; it changed the child of Emancipation to the youth with dawning self-consciousness, self-realization, self-respect. In those somber forests of his striving his own soul rose before him, and he saw himself,—darkly as through a veil; and yet he saw in himself some faint revelation of his power, of his mission. He began to have a dim feeling that, to attain his place in the world, he must be himself, and not another. For the first time he sought to analyze the burden he bore upon his back, that dead-weight of social degradation partially masked behind a half-named Negro problem. He felt his poverty; without a cent, without a home, without land, tools, or savings, he had entered into competition with rich, landed, skilled neighbors. To be a poor man is hard, but to be a poor race in a land of dollars is the very bottom of hardships. He felt the weight of his ignorance,—not simply of letters, but of life, of business, of the humanities; the accumulated sloth and shirking and awkwardness of decades and centuries shackled his hands and feet. Nor was his burden all poverty and ignorance. The red stain of bastardy, which two centuries of systematic legal defilement of Negro women had stamped upon his race, meant not only the loss of ancient African chastity, but also the hereditary weight of a mass of corruption from white adulterers, threatening almost the obliteration of the Negro home.

A people thus handicapped ought not to be asked to race with the world, but rather allowed to give all its time and thought to its own social problems. But alas! while sociologists gleefully count his bastards and his prostitutes, the very soul of the toiling, sweating black man is darkened by the shadow of a vast despair. Men call the shadow prejudice, and learnedly explain it as the natural defence of culture against barbarism, learning against ignorance, purity against crime, the "higher" against the "lower" races. To which the Negro cries Amen! and swears that to so much of this strange prejudice as is founded on just homage to civilization, culture, righteousness, and progress, he humbly bows and meekly does obeisance. But before that nameless prejudice that leaps beyond all this he stands helpless, dismayed, and well-nigh speechless; before that personal disrespect and mockery, the ridicule and systematic humiliation, the distortion of fact and wanton license of fancy, the cynical ignoring of the better and the boisterous welcoming of the worse, the all-pervading desire to inculcate disdain for everything black, from Toussaint to the devil,—before this there rises a sickening despair that would disarm and discourage any nation save that black host to whom "discouragement" is an unwritten word.

But the facing of so vast a prejudice could not but bring the inevitable self-questioning, self-disparagement, and lowering of ideals which ever accompany repression and breed in an atmosphere of contempt and hate. Whisperings and portents came borne upon the four winds: Lo! we are diseased and dying, cried the dark hosts; we cannot write, our voting is vain; what need of education, since we must always cook and serve? And the Nation echoed and enforced this self-criticism, saying: Be content to be servants, and nothing more; what need of higher culture for half-men? Away with the black man's ballot, by force or fraud,—and behold the suicide of a race! Nevertheless, out of the evil came something of good,—the more careful adjustment of education to real life, the clearer perception of the Negroes' social responsibilities, and the sobering realization of the meaning of progress.

So dawned the time of *Sturm und Drang:* storm and stress to-day rocks our little boat on the mad waters of the world-sea; there is within and without the sound of conflict, the burning of body and rending of soul; inspiration strives with doubt, and faith with vain questionings. The bright ideals of the past,—physical freedom, political power, the training of brains and the training of hands,—all these in turn have waxed and waned, until even the last grows dim and overcast. Are they all wrong,—all false? No, not that, but each alone was over-simple and incomplete,—the dreams of a credulous race-childhood, or the fond imaginings of the other world which does not know and does not want to know our power. To be really true, all. these ideals must be melted and welded into one. The training of the schools we need to-day more than ever,—the training of deft hands, quick eyes and ears, and above all the broader, deeper, higher culture of gifted minds and pure hearts. The power of the ballot we need in sheer self-defence,—else what shall save us from a second slavery? Freedom, too, the long-sought, we still seek,—the freedom of life and limb, the freedom to work and think, the freedom to love and aspire. Work, culture, liberty,—all these we need, not singly but together, not successively but together, each growing and aiding each, and all striving toward that vaster ideal that swims before the Negro people, the ideal of human brotherhood, gained through the unifying ideal of Race; the ideal of fostering and developing the traits and talents of the Negro, not in opposition to or contempt for other races, but rather in large conformity to the greater ideals of the American Republic, in order that some day on American soil two world-races may give each to each those characteristics both so sadly lack. We the darker ones come even now not altogether empty-handed: there are to-day no truer exponents of the pure human spirit of the Declaration of Independence than the American Negroes; there is no true American music but the wild sweet melodies of the Negro slave; the American fairy tales and folk-lore are Indian and African; and, all in all, we black men seem the sole oasis of simple faith and reverence in a dusty desert of dollars and smartness. Will America be poorer if she replace her brutal dyspeptic blundering with light-hearted but determined Negro humility? or her coarse and cruel wit with loving jovial good-humor? or her vulgar music with the soul of the Sorrow Songs?

Merely a concrete test of the underlying principles of the great republic is the Negro Problem, and the spiritual striving of the freedmen's sons is the travail of souls whose burden is almost beyond the measure of their strength, but who bear it in the name of an historic race, in the name of this the land of their fathers' fathers, and in the name of human opportunity.

78

The Talented Tenth*

W. E. B. Du Bois

The Negro race, like all races, is going to be saved by its exceptional men. The problem of education, then, among Negroes must first of all deal with the Talented Tenth; it is the problem of developing the Best of this race that they may guide the Mass away from the contamination and death of the Worst, in their own and other races. Now the training of men is a difficult and intricate task. Its technique is a matter for educational experts, but its object is for the vision of seers. If we make money the object of man-training, we shall develop money-makers but not necessarily men; if we make technical skill the object of education, we may possess artisans but not, in nature, men. Men we shall have only as we make manhood the object of the work of the schools—intelligence, broad sympathy, knowledge of the world that was and is, and of the relation of men to it—this is the curriculum of that Higher Education which must underlie true life. On this foundation we may build bread winning, skill of hand and quickness of brain, with never a fear lest the child and man mistake the means of living for the object of life.

If this be true—and who can deny it—three tasks lay before me; first to show from the past that the Talented Tenth as they have risen among American Negroes have been worthy of leadership; secondly, to show how these men may be educated and developed; and thirdly, to show their relation to the Negro problem.

You misjudge us because you do not know us. From the very first it has been the educated and intelligent of the Negro people that have led and elevated the mass, and the sole obstacles that nullified and retarded their efforts were slavery and race prejudice; for what is slavery but the legalized survival of the unfit and the nullification of the work of natural internal leadership? Negro leadership, therefore, sought from the first to rid the race of this awful incubus that it might make way for natural selection and the survival of the fittest. In colonial days came Phillis Wheatley and Paul Cuffe striving against the bars of prejudice; and Benjamin Banneker, the almanac maker, voiced their longings.

Then came Dr. James Derham, who could tell even the learned Dr. Rush something of medicine, and Lemuel Haynes, to whom Middlebury College gave an honorary A. M. in 1804. These and others we may call the Revolutionary group of distinguished Negroes—they were persons of marked ability, leaders of a Talented Tenth, standing conspicuously among the best of their

*Excerpts from *The Negro Problem* by Booker T. Washington et al. New York: James Pott & Company, 1903.

time. They strove by word and deed to save the color line from becoming the line between the bond and free, but all they could do was nullified by Eli Whitney and the Curse of Gold. So they passed into forgetfulness.

But their spirit did not wholly die; here and there in the early part of the century came other exceptional men. Some were natural sons of unnatural fathers and were given often a liberal training and thus a race of educated mulattoes sprang up to plead for black men's rights. There was Ira Aldridge, whom all Europe loved to honor; there was that Voice crying in the Wilderness, David Walker, and saying:

"I declare it does appear to me as though some nations think God is asleep, or that he made the Africans for nothing else but to dig their mines and work their farms, or they cannot believe history, sacred or profane. I ask every man who has a heart, and is blessed with the privilege of believing—Is not God a God of justice to all his creatures?"

This was the wild voice that first aroused Southern legislators in 1829 to the terrors of abolitionism.

In 1831 there met that first Negro convention in Philadelphia, at which the world gaped curiously but which bravely attacked the problems of race and slavery, crying out against persecution and declaring that "Laws as cruel in themselves as they were unconstitutional and unjust, have in many places been enacted against our poor, unfriended and unoffending brethren (without a shadow of provocation on our part), at whose bare recital the very savage draws himself up for fear of contagion—looks noble and prides himself because he bears not the name of Christian." Side by side this free Negro movement, and the movement for abolition, strove until they merged into one strong stream. Too little notice has been taken of the work which the Talented Tenth among Negroes took in the great abolition crusade. From the very day that a Philadelphia colored man became the first subscriber to Garrison's "Liberator," to the day when Negro soldiers made the Emancipation Proclamation possible, black leaders worked shoulder to shoulder with white men in a movement, the success of which would have been impossible without them. There was Purvis and Remond, Pennington and Highland Garnett, Sojourner Truth and Alexander Crummel, and above all, Frederick Douglass—what would the abolition movement have been without them? They stood as living examples of the possibilities of the Negro race, their own hard experiences and well wrought culture said silently more than all the drawn periods of orators—they were the men who made American slavery impossible.

Where were these black abolitionists trained? Some, like Frederick Douglass, were self-trained, but yet trained liberally; others, like Alexander Crummell and McCune Smith, graduated from famous foreign universities. Most of them rose up through the colored schools of New York and Philadelphia and Boston, taught by college-bred men like Russworm, of Dartmouth, and college-bred white men like Neau and Benezet.

After emancipation came a new group of educated and gifted leaders: Langston, Bruce and Elliot, Greener, Williams and Payne. Through political organization, historical and polemic writing and moral regeneration, these men strove to uplift their people. It is the fashion of to-day to sneer at them and to say that with freedom Negro leadership should have begun at the plow and not in the Senate—a foolish and mischievous lie; two hundred and fifty years that black serf toiled at the plow and yet that toiling was in vain till the Senate passed the war amendments; and two hundred and fifty years more the half-free serf of to-day may toil at his plow, but unless he have political rights and righteously guarded civic status, he will still remain the poverty-stricken and ignorant plaything of rascals, that he now is. This all sane men know even if they dare not say it.

And so we come to the present—a day of cowardice and vacillation, of strident wide-voiced wrong and faint hearted compromise; of double-faced dallying with Truth and Right. Who are to-day guiding the work of the Negro people? The "exceptions" of course. And yet so sure as this Talented Tenth is pointed out, the blind worshippers of the Average cry out in alarm: "These are exceptions, look here at death, disease and crime—these are the happy rule." Of course they are the rule, because a silly nation made them the rule: Because for three long centuries this people lynched Negroes who dared to be brave, raped black women who dared to be virtuous, crushed dark-hued youth who dared to be ambitious, and encouraged and made to flourish servility and lewdness and apathy. But not even this was able to crush all manhood and chastity and aspiration from black folk. A saving remnant continually survives and persists, continually aspires, continually shows itself in thrift and ability and character. Exceptional it is to be sure, but this is its chiefest promise; it shows the capability of Negro blood, the promise of black men. Do Americans ever stop to reflect that there are in this land a million men of Negro blood, well-educated, owners of homes, against the honor of whose womanhood no breath was ever raised, whose men occupy positions of trust and usefulness, and who, judged by any standard, have reached the full measure of the best type of modern European culture? Is it fair, is it decent, is it Christian to ignore these facts of the Negro problem, to belittle such aspiration, to nullify such leadership and seek to crush these people back into the mass out of which by toil and travail, they and their fathers have raised themselves?

Can the masses of the Negro people be in any possible way more quickly raised than by the effort and example of this aristocracy of talent and character? Was there ever a nation on God's fair earth civilized from the bottom upward? Never; it is, ever was and ever will be from the top downward that culture filters. The Talented Tenth rises and pulls all that are worth the saving up to their vantage ground. This is the history of human progress; and the two historic mistakes which have hindered that progress were the thinking first that no more could ever rise save the few already risen; or second, that it would better the unrisen to pull the risen down.

How then shall the leaders of a struggling people be trained and the hands of the risen few strengthened? There can be but one answer: The best and most capable of their youth must be schooled in the colleges and universities of the land. We will not quarrel as to just what the university of the Negro should teach or how it should teach it—I willingly admit that each soul and each race-soul needs its own peculiar curriculum. But this is true: A university is a human invention for the transmission of knowledge and culture from generation to generation, through the training of quick minds and pure hearts, and for this work no other human invention will suffice, not even trade and industrial schools.

All men cannot go to college but some men must; every isolated group or nation must have its yeast, must have for the talented few centers of training where men are not so mystified and befuddled by the hard and necessary toil of earning a living, as to have no aims higher than their bellies, and no God greater than Gold. This is true training, and thus in the beginning were the favored sons of the freedmen trained. Out of the colleges of the North came, after the blood of war, Ware, Cravath, Chase, Andrews, Bumstead and Spence to build the foundations of knowledge and civilization in the black South.

Where ought they to have begun to build? At the bottom, of course, quibbles the mole with his eyes in the earth. Aye! truly at the bottom, at the very bottom; at the bottom of knowledge, down in the very depths of knowledge there where the roots of justice strike into the lowest soil of Truth. And so they did begin; they founded colleges, and up from the colleges shot normal schools, and out from the normal schools went teachers, and around the normal teachers clustered other teachers to teach the public schools; the college trained in Greek and Latin and mathematics, 2,000 men; and these men trained full 50,000 others in morals and manners, and they in turn taught thrift and the alphabet to nine millions of men, who to-day hold $300,000,000 of property. It was a miracle—the most wonderful peace-battle of the 19th century, and yet to-day men smile at it, and in fine superiority tell us that it was all a strange mistake; that a proper way to found a system of education is first to gather the children and buy them spelling books and hoes; afterward men may look about for teachers, if haply they may find them; or again they would teach men Work, but as for Life—why, what has Work to do with Life, they ask vacantly.

Was the work of these college founders successful; did it stand the test of time? Did the college graduates, with all their fine theories of life, really live? Are they useful men helping to civilize and elevate their less fortunate fellows? Let us see. Omitting all institutions which have not actually graduated students from a college course, there are to-day in the United States thirty-four institutions giving something above high school training to Negroes and designed especially for this race.

Three of these were established in border States before the War; thirteen were planted by the Freedmen's Bureau in the years 1864–1869;

nine were established between 1870 and 1880 by various church bodies; five were established after 1881 by Negro churches, and four are state institutions supported by United States' agricultural funds. In most cases the college departments are small adjuncts to high and common school work. As a matter of fact six institutions—Atlanta, Fisk, Howard, Shaw, Wilberforce and Leland, are the important Negro colleges so far as actual work and number of students are concerned. In all these institutions, seven hundred and fifty Negro college students are enrolled. In grade the best of these colleges are about a year behind the smaller New England colleges and a typical curriculum is that of Atlanta University. Here students from the grammar grades, after a three years' high school course, take a college course of 136 weeks. One-fourth of this time is given to Latin and Greek; one-fifth, to English and modem languages; one-sixth, to history and social science; one-seventh, to natural science; one-eighth to mathematics, and one-eighth to philosophy and pedagogy.

In addition to these students in the South, Negroes have attended Northern colleges for many years. As early as 1826 one was graduated from Bowdoin College, and from that time till to-day nearly every year has seen elsewhere, other such graduates. They have, of course, met much color prejudice. Fifty years ago very few colleges would admit them at all. Even to-day no Negro has ever been admitted to Princeton, and at some other leading institutions they are rather endured than encouraged. Oberlin was the great pioneer in the work of blotting out the color line in colleges, and has more Negro graduates by far than any other Northern college.

The most interesting question, and in many respects the crucial question, to be asked concerning college-bred Negroes, is: Do they earn a living? It has been intimated more than once that the higher training of Negroes has resulted in sending into the world of work, men who could find nothing to do suitable to their talents. Now and then there comes a rumor of a colored college man working at menial service, etc. Fortunately, returns as to occupations of college-bred Negroes, gathered by the Atlanta conference, are quite full—nearly sixty per cent, of the total number of graduates.

This enables us to reach fairly certain conclusions as to the occupations of all college-bred Negroes.

Over half are teachers, a sixth are preachers, another sixth are students and professional men; over 6 per cent, are farmers, artisans and merchants, and 4 per cent, are in government service.

These figures illustrate vividly the function of the college-bred Negro. He is, as he ought to be, the group leader, the man who sets the ideals of the community where he lives, directs its thoughts and heads its social movements. It need hardly be argued that the Negro people need social leadership more than most groups; that they have no traditions to fall back upon, no long established customs, no strong family ties, no well defined social classes. All these things must be slowly and painfully evolved. The preacher was, even before the war, the group leader of the Negroes, and the church their greatest social institution. Naturally this preacher was ignorant and often immoral, and the problem of replacing the older type by better educated men has been a difficult one. Both by direct work and by direct influence on other preachers, and on congregations, the college-bred preacher has an opportunity for reformatory work and moral inspiration, the value of which cannot be overestimated.

It has, however, been in the furnishing of teachers that the Negro college has found its peculiar function. Few persons realize how vast a work, how mighty a revolution has been thus accomplished. To furnish five millions and more of ignorant people with teachers of their own race and blood, in one generation, was not only a very difficult undertaking, but a very important one, in that, it placed before the eyes of almost every Negro child an attainable ideal. It brought the masses of the blacks in contact with modern civilization, made black men the leaders of their communities and trainers of the new generation. In this work college-bred Negroes were first teachers, and then teachers of teachers. And here it is that the broad culture of college work has been of peculiar value. Knowledge of life and its wider meaning, has been the point of the Negro's deepest ignorance, and the sending out of teachers whose training has not been simply for bread winning, but also for human culture, has been of inestimable value in the training of these men.

In earlier years the two occupations of preacher and teacher were practically the only ones open to the black college graduate. Of later years a larger diversity of life among his people, has opened new avenues of employment.

The problem of training the Negro is to-day immensely complicated by the fact that the whole question of the efficiency and appropriateness of our present systems of education, for any kind of child, is a matter of active debate, in which final settlement seems still afar off. Consequently it often happens that persons arguing for or against certain systems of education for Negroes, have these controversies in mind and miss the real question at issue. The main question, so far as the Southern Negro is concerned, is: What under the present circumstance, must a system of education do in order to raise the Negro as quickly as possible in the scale of civilization? The answer to this question seems to me clear: It must strengthen the Negro's character, increase his knowledge and teach him to earn a living. Now it goes without saying, that it is hard to do all these things simultaneously or suddenly, and that at the same time it will not do to give all the attention to one and neglect the others; we could give black boys trades, but that alone will not civilize a race of ex-slaves; we might simply increase their knowledge of the world, but this would not necessarily make them wish to use this knowledge honestly; we might seek to strengthen character and purpose, but to what end if this people have nothing to eat or to wear? A system of education is not one thing, nor does it have a single definite object. nor is it a mere matter of schools. Education is that whole system of human training within and without the school house walls, which molds and develops men. If then we start out to train an ignorant and unskilled people with a heritage of bad habits, our system of training must set before itself two great aims—the one dealing with knowledge and character, the other part seeking to give the child the technical knowledge necessary for him to earn a living under the present circumstances. These objects are accomplished in part by the opening of the common schools on the one, and of the industrial schools on the other. But only in part, for there must also be trained those who are to teach these schools—men and women of knowledge and culture and technical skill who understand modern civilization, and have the training and aptitude to impart it to the children under them. There must be teachers, and teachers of teachers, and to attempt to establish any sort of a system of common and industrial school training, without *first* (and I say *first* advisedly) without *first* providing for the higher training of the very best teachers, is simply throwing your money to the winds. School houses do not teach themselves—piles of brick and mortar and machinery do not send out *men*. It is the trained, living human soul, cultivated and strengthened by long study and thought, that breathes the real breath of life into boys and girls and makes them human, whether they be black or white, Greek, Russian or American. Nothing, in these latter days, has so dampened the faith of thinking Negroes in recent educational movements, as the fact that such movements have been accompanied by ridicule and denouncement and decrying of those very institutions of higher training which made the Negro public school possible, and make Negro industrial schools thinkable. It was Fisk, Atlanta, Howard and Straight, those colleges born of the faith and sacrifice of the abolitionists, that placed in the black schools of the South the 30,000 teachers and more, which some, who depreciate the work of these higher schools, are using to teach their own new experiments. If Hampton, Tuskegee and the hundred other industrial schools prove in the future to be as successful as they deserve to be, then their success in training black artisans for the South, will be due primarily to the white colleges of the North and the black colleges of the South, which trained the teachers who to-day conduct these institutions. There was a time when the American people believed pretty devoutly that a log of wood with a boy at one end and Mark Hopkins at the other, represented the highest ideal of human training. But in these eager days it would seem that we have changed all that and think it necessary to add, a couple of saw-mills and a hammer to this outfit, and, at a pinch, to dispense with the services of Mark Hopkins.

I would not deny, or for a moment seem to deny, the paramount necessity of teaching the Negro to work, and to work steadily and skillfully; or seem to depreciate in the slightest degree the important part industrial schools must play in the accomplishment of these ends, but I *do* say, and insist upon it, that it is industrialism drunk with its vision of success, to imagine that its own work can be accomplished without providing for the training of broadly cultured men and women to teach its own teachers, and to teach the teachers of the public schools.

But I have already said that human education is not simply a matter of schools; it is much more a matter of family and group life—the training of one's home, of one's daily companions, of one's social class. Now the black boy of the South moves in a black world—a world with its own leaders, its own thoughts, its own ideals. In this world he gets by far the larger part of his life training, and through the eyes of this dark world he peers into the veiled world beyond. Who guides and determines the education which he receives in his world? His teachers here are the group-leaders of the Negro people—the physicians and clergymen, the trained fathers and mothers, the influential and forceful men about him of all kinds; here it is, if at all, that the culture of the surrounding world trickles through and is handed on by the graduates of the higher schools. Can such culture training of group leaders be neglected? Can we afford to ignore it? Do you think that if the leaders of thought among Negroes are not trained and educated thinkers, that they will have no leaders? On the contrary a hundred half-trained demagogues will still hold the places they so largely occupy now, and hundreds of vociferous busy-bodies will multiply. You have no choice; either you must help furnish this race from within its own ranks with thoughtful men of trained leadership, or you must suffer the evil consequences of a headless misguided rabble.

I am an earnest advocate of manual training and trade teaching for black boys, and for white boys, too. I believe that next to the founding of Negro colleges the most valuable addition to Negro education since the war, has been industrial training for black boys. Nevertheless, I insist that the object of all true education is not to make men carpenters, it is to make carpenters men; there are two means of making the carpenter a man, each equally important: the first is to give the group and community in which he works, liberally trained teachers and leaders to teach him and his family what life means; the second is to give him sufficient intelligence and technical skill to make him an efficient workman; the first object demands the Negro college and college-bred men—not a quantity of such colleges, but a few of excellent quality; not too many college-bred men, but enough to leaven the lump, to inspire the masses, to raise the Talented Tenth to leadership; the second object demands a good system of common schools, well-taught, conveniently located and properly equipped.

The Sixth Atlanta Conference truly said in 1901:

"We call the attention of the Nation to the fact that less than one million of the three million Negro children of school age, are at present regularly attending school, and these attend a session which lasts only a few months.

"We are to-day deliberately rearing millions of our citizens in ignorance, and at the same time limiting the rights of citizenship by educational qualifications. This is unjust. Half the black youth of the land have no opportunities open to them for learning to read, write and cipher. In the discussion as to the proper training of Negro children after they leave the public schools, we have forgotten that they are not yet decently provided with public schools.

"Propositions are beginning to be made in the South to reduce the already meagre school facilities of Negroes. We congratulate the South on resisting, as much as it has, this pressure, and on the many millions it has spent on Negro education. But it is only fair to point out that Negro taxes and the Negroes' share of the income from indirect taxes and endowments have fully repaid this expenditure, so that the Negro public school system has not in all probability cost the white taxpayers a single cent since the war.

"This is not fair. Negro schools should be a public burden, since they are a public benefit. The Negro has a right to demand good common school training at the hands of the States and the Nation since by their fault he is not in position to pay for this himself."

What is the chief need for the building up of the Negro public school in the South? The Negro race in the South needs teachers to-day above all else. This is the concurrent testimony of all who know the situation. For the supply of this great demand two things are needed—institutions of higher education and money for school houses and salaries. It is usually assumed that a hundred or more institutions for Negro training are to-day turning out so many teachers and college-bred men that the race is threatened with an over-supply.

This is sheer nonsense. There are to-day less than 3,000 living Negro college graduates in the United States, and less than 1,000 Negroes in college. Moreover, in the 164 schools for Negroes, 95 per cent, of their students are doing elementary and secondary work, work which should be done in the public schools. Over half the remaining 2,157 students are taking high school studies. The mass of so-called "normal" schools for the Negro, are simply doing elementary common school work, or, at most, high school work, with a little instruction in methods. The Negro colleges and the post-graduate courses at other institutions are the only agencies for the broader and more careful training of teachers. The work of these institutions is hampered for lack of funds. It is getting increasingly difficult to get funds for training teachers in the best modern methods, and yet all over the South, from State Superintendents, county officials, city boards and school principals comes the wail, "We need TEACHERS!" and teachers must be trained. As the fairest minded of all white Southerners, Atticus G. Haygood, once said: "The defects of colored teachers are so great as to create an urgent necessity for training better ones. Their excellencies and their successes are sufficient to justify the best hopes of success in the effort, and to vindicate the judgment of those who make large investments of money and service, to give to colored students opportunity for thoroughly preparing themselves for the work of teaching children of their people."

The truth of this has been strikingly shown in the marked improvement of white teachers in the South. Twenty years ago the rank and file of white public school teachers were not as good as the Negro teachers. But they, by scholarships and good salaries, have been encouraged to thorough normal and collegiate preparation, while the Negro teachers have been discouraged by starvation wages and the idea that any training will do for a black teacher. If carpenters are needed it is well and good to train men as carpenters. But to train men as carpenters, and then set them to teaching is wasteful and criminal; and to train men as teachers and then refuse them living wages, unless they become carpenters, is rank nonsense.

We need Negro teachers for the Negro common schools, and we need first-class normal schools and colleges to train them. This is the work of higher Negro education and it must be done.

Further than this, after being provided with group leaders of civilization, and a foundation of intelligence in the public schools, the carpenter, in order to be a man, needs technical skill. This calls for trade schools. Now trade schools are not nearly such simple things as people once thought. The original idea was that the "Industrial" school was to furnish education, practically free, to those willing to work for it; it was to "do" things—i.e.: become a center of productive industry, it was to be partially, if not wholly, self-supporting, and it was to teach trades. Admirable as were some of the ideas underlying this scheme, the whole thing simply would not work in practice; it was found that if you were to use time and material to teach trades thoroughly, you could not at the same time keep the industries on a commercial basis and make them pay. Many schools started out to do this on a large scale and went into virtual bankruptcy. Moreover, it was found also that it was possible to teach a boy a trade mechanically, without giving him the full educative benefit of the process, and vice versa, that there was a distinctive educative value in teaching a boy to use his hands and eyes in carrying out certain physical processes, even though he did not actually learn a trade. It has happened, therefore, in the last decade, that a noticeable change has come over the industrial schools. In the first place the idea of commercially remunerative industry in a school is being pushed rapidly to the background. There are still schools with shops and farms that bring an income, and schools that use student labor partially for the erection of their buildings and the furnishing of equipment. It is coming to be seen, however, in the education of the Negro, as clearly as it has been seen in the education of the youths the world over, that it is the *boy* and not the material product, that is the true object of education. Consequently the object of the industrial school came to be the thorough training of boys regardless of the cost of the training, so long as it was thoroughly well done.

Even at this point, however, the difficulties were not surmounted. In the first place modern industry has taken great strides since the war, and the teaching of trades is no longer a simple matter. Machinery and long processes of work have greatly changed the work of the carpenter, the ironworker and the shoemaker. A really efficient workman must be to-day an intelligent man who has had good technical training in addition to thorough common school, and perhaps even higher training. To meet this situation the industrial schools began a further development; they established distinct Trade Schools for the thorough training of better class artisans, and at the same time they sought to preserve for the purposes of general education, such of the simpler processes of elementary trade learning as were best suited therefor. In this differentiation of the Trade School and manual training, the best of the industrial schools simply followed the plain trend of the present educational epoch. A prominent educator tells us that, in Sweden, "In the beginning the economic conception was generally adopted, and everywhere manual training was looked upon as a means of preparing the children of the common people to earn their living. But gradually it came to be recognized that manual training has a more elevated purpose, and one, indeed, more useful in the deeper meaning of the term. It came to be considered as an educative process for the complete moral, physical and intellectual development of the child."

Thus, again, in the manning of trade schools and manual training schools we are thrown back upon the higher training as its source and chief support. There was a time when any aged and wornout carpenter could teach in a trade school. But not so to-day.

Men of America, the problem is plain before you. Here is a race transplanted through the criminal foolishness of your fathers. Whether you like it or not the millions are here, and here they will remain. If you do not lift them up, they will pull you down. Education and work are the levers to uplift a people. Work alone will not do it unless inspired by the right ideals and guided by intelligence. Education must not simply teach work—it must teach Life. The Talented Tenth of the Negro race must be made leaders of thought and missionaries of culture among their people. No others can do this work and Negro colleges must train men for it. The Negro race, like all other races, is going to be saved by its exceptional men.

79

The Economic Status of Women*

Charlotte Perkins Gilman

We are the only animal species in which the female depends on the male for food, the only animal species in which the sex-relation is also an economic relation. With us an entire sex lives in a relation of economic dependence upon the other sex, and the economic relation is combined with the sex-relation. The economic status of the human female is relative to the sex-relation.

In studying the economic position of the sexes collectively, the difference is most marked. As a social animal, the economic status of man rests on the combined and exchanged services of vast numbers of progressively specialized individuals. The economic progress of the race, its maintenance at any period, its continued advance, involve the collective activities of all the trades, crafts, arts, manufactures, inventions, discoveries, and all the civil and military institutions that go to maintain them. The economic status of any race at any time, with its involved effect on all the constituent individuals, depends on their world-wide labors and their free exchange. Economic progress, however, is almost exclusively masculine. Such economic processes as women have been allowed to exercise are of the earliest and most primitive kind. Were men to perform no economic services save such as are still performed by women, our racial status in economics would be reduced to most painful limitations.

To take from any community its male workers would paralyze it economically to a far greater degree than to remove its female workers. The labor now performed by the women could be performed by the men, requiring only the setting back of many advanced workers into earlier forms of industry; but the labor now performed by the men could not be performed by the women without generations of effort and adaptation. Men can cook, clean, and sew as well as women; but the making and managing of the great engines of modern industry, the threading of earth and sea in our vast systems of transportation, the handling of our elaborate machinery of trade, commerce, government,—these things could not be done so well by women in their present degree of economic development.

This is not owing to lack of the essential human faculties necessary to such achievements, nor to any inherent disability of sex, but to the

*Excerpts from *Women and Economics: A Study of the Economic Relation Between Men and Women as a Factor in Social Evolution* by Charlotte Perkins Gilman, with a new Introduction by Michael Kimmel and Amy Aronson.

present condition of woman, forbidding the development of this degree of economic ability. The male human being is thousands of years in advance of the female in economic status. Speaking collectively, men produce and distribute wealth; and women receive it at their hands. As men hunt, fish, keep cattle, or raise corn, so do women eat game, fish, beef, or corn. As men go down to the sea in ships, and bring coffee and spices and silks and gems from far away, so do women partake of the coffee and spices and silks and gems the men bring.

The economic status of the human race in any nation, at any time, is governed mainly by the activities of the male: the female obtains her share in the racial advance only through him.

Studied individually, the facts are even more plainly visible, more open and familiar. From the day laborer to the millionnaire, the wife's worn dress or flashing jewels, her low roof or her lordly one, her weary feet or her rich equipage,—these speak of the economic ability of the husband. The comfort, the luxury, the necessities of life itself, which the woman receives, are obtained by the husband, and given her by him. And, when the woman, left alone with no man to "support" her, tries to meet her own economic necessities, the difficulties which confront her prove conclusively what the general economic status of the woman is. None can deny these patent facts,—that the economic status of women generally depends upon that of men generally, and that the economic status of women individually depends upon that of men individually, those men to whom they are related. But we are instantly confronted by the commonly received opinion that, although it must be admitted that men make and distribute the wealth of the world, yet women earn their share of it as wives. This assumes either that the husband is in the position of employer and the wife as employee, or that marriage is a "partnership," and the wife an equal factor with the husband in producing wealth.

Economic independence is a relative condition at best. In the broadest sense, all living things are economically dependent upon others,—the animals upon the vegetables, and man upon both. In a narrower sense, all social life is economically interdependent, man producing collectively what he could by no possibility produce separately. But, in the closest interpretation, individual economic independence among human beings means that the individual pays for what he gets, works for what he gets, gives to the other an equivalent for what the other gives him. I depend on the shoemaker for shoes, and the tailor for coats; but, if I give the shoemaker and the tailor enough of my own labor as a house-builder to pay for the shoes and coats they give me, I retain my personal independence. I have not taken of their product, and given nothing of mine. As long as what I get is obtained by what I give, I am economically independent.

Women consume economic goods. What economic product do they give in exchange for what they consume? The claim that marriage is a partnership, in which the two persons married produce wealth which neither of them, separately, could produce, will not bear examination. A man happy and comfortable can produce more than one unhappy and uncomfortable, but this is as true of a father or son as of a husband. To take from a man any of the conditions which make him happy and strong is to cripple his industry, generally speaking. But those relatives who make him happy are not therefore his business partners, and entitled to share his income.

Grateful return for happiness conferred is not the method of exchange in a partnership. The comfort a man takes with his wife is not in the nature of a business partnership, nor are her frugality and industry. A housekeeper, in her place, might be as frugal, as industrious, but would not therefore be a partner. Man and wife are partners truly in their mutual obligation to their children,—their common love, duty, and service. But a manufacturer who marries, or a doctor, or a lawyer, does not take a partner in his business, when he takes a partner in parenthood, unless his wife is also a manufacturer, a doctor, or a lawyer. In his business, she cannot even advise wisely without training and experience. To love her husband, the composer, does not enable her to compose; and the loss of a man's wife, though it may break his heart, does not cripple his business, unless his mind is affected by grief. She is in no sense a business partner, unless she contributes capital or experience or labor, as a man would in like relation. Most men would hesitate very seriously before entering a business partnership with any woman, wife or not.

If the wife is not, then, truly a business partner, in what way does she earn from her husband the food, clothing, and shelter she receives at his hands? By house service, it will be instantly replied. This is the general misty idea upon the subject,—that women earn all they get, and more, by house service. Here we come to a very practical and definite economic ground. Although not producers of wealth, women serve in the final processes of preparation and distribution. Their labor in the household has a genuine economic value.

For a certain percentage of persons to serve other persons, in order that the ones so served may produce more, is a contribution not to be overlooked. The labor of women in the house, certainly, enables men to produce more wealth than they otherwise could; and in this way women are economic factors in society. But so are horses. The labor of horses enables men to produce more wealth than they otherwise could. The horse is an economic factor in society. But the horse is not economically independent, nor is the woman. If a man plus a valet can perform more useful service than he could minus a valet, then the valet is performing useful service. But, if the valet is the property of the man, is obliged to perform this service, and is not paid for it, he is not economically independent.

The labor which the wife performs in the household is given as part of her functional duty, not as employment. The wife of the poor man, who works hard in a small house, doing all the work for the family, or the wife of the rich man, who wisely and gracefully manages a large house and administers its functions, each is entitled to fair pay for services rendered.

To take this ground and hold it honestly, wives, as earners through domestic service, are entitled to the wages of cooks, housemaids, nursemaids, seamstresses, or housekeepers, and to no more. This would of course reduce the spending money of the wives of the rich, and put it out of the power of the poor man to "support" a wife at all, unless, indeed, the poor man faced the situation fully, paid his wife her wages as house servant, and then she and he combined their funds in the support of their children. He would be keeping a servant: she would be helping keep the family. But nowhere on earth would there be "a rich woman" by these means. Even the highest class of private housekeeper, useful as her services are, does not accumulate a fortune. She does not buy diamonds and sables and keep a carriage. Things like these are not earned by house service.

But the salient fact in this discussion is that, whatever the economic value of the domestic industry of women is, they do not get it. The women who do the most work get the least money, and the women who have the most money do the least work. Their labor is neither given nor taken as a factor in economic exchange. It is held to be their duty as women to do this work; and their economic status bears no relation to their domestic labors, unless an inverse one. Moreover, if they were thus fairly paid,—given what they earned, and no more,—all women working in this way would be reduced to the economic status of the house servant. Few women—or men either—care to face this condition. The ground that women earn their living by domestic labor is instantly forsaken, and we are told that they obtain their livelihood as mothers. This is a peculiar position. We speak of it commonly enough, and often with deep feeling, but without due analysis.

In treating of an economic exchange, asking what return in goods or labor women make for the goods and labor given them,—either to the race collectively or to their husbands individually,—what payment women make for their clothes and shoes and furniture and food and shelter, we are told that the duties and services of the mother entitle her to support.

If this is so, if motherhood is an exchangeable commodity given by women in payment for clothes and food, then we must of course find some relation between the quantity or quality of the motherhood and the quantity and quality of the pay. This being true, then the women who are not mothers have no economic status at all; and the economic status of those who are must be shown to be relative to their motherhood. This is obviously absurd. The childless wife has as much money as the mother of many,—more; for the children of the latter consume what would otherwise be hers; and the inefficient mother is no less provided for than the efficient one. Visibly, and upon the face of it, women are not maintained in economic prosperity proportioned to their motherhood. Motherhood bears no relation to their economic status. Among primitive races, it is true,—in the patriarchal period, for instance,—there was some truth in this position. Women being of no value whatever save as bearers of children, their favor and indulgence did bear direct relation to maternity;

and they had reason to exult on more grounds than one when they could boast a son. To-day, however, the maintenance of the woman is not conditioned upon this. A man is not allowed to discard his wife because she is barren. The claim of motherhood as a factor in economic exchange is false to-day. But suppose it were true. Are we willing to hold this ground, even in theory? Are we willing to consider motherhood as a business, a form of commercial exchange? Are the cares and duties of the mother, her travail and her love, commodities to be exchanged for bread?

It is revolting so to consider them; and, if we dare face our own thoughts, and force them to their logical conclusion, we shall see that nothing could be more repugnant to human feeling, or more socially and individually injurious, than to make motherhood a trade. Driven off these alleged grounds of women's economic independence; shown that women, as a class, neither produce nor distribute wealth; that women, as individuals, labor mainly as house servants, are not paid as such, and would not be satisfied with such an economic status if they were so paid; that wives are not business partners or co-producers of wealth with their husbands, unless they actually practise the same profession; that they are not salaried as mothers, and that it would be unspeakably degrading if they were,—what remains to those who deny that women are supported by men? This (and a most amusing position it is),—that the function of maternity unfits a woman for economic production, and, therefore, it is right that she should be supported by her husband.

The ground is taken that the human female is not economically independent, that she is fed by the male of her species. In denial of this, it is first alleged that she is economically independent,—that she does support herself by her own industry in the house. It being shown that there is no relation between the economic status of woman and the labor she performs in the home, it is then alleged that not as house servant, but as mother, does woman earn her living. It being shown that the economic status of woman bears no relation to her motherhood, either in quantity or quality, it is then alleged that motherhood renders a woman unfit for economic production, and that, therefore, it is right that she be supported by her husband. Before going farther, let us seize upon this admission,—that she *is* supported by her husband.

Without going into either the ethics or the necessities of the case, we have reached so much common ground: the female of genus homo is supported by the male. Whereas, in other species of animals, male and female alike graze and browse, hunt and kill, climb, swim, dig, run, and fly for their livings, in our species the female does not seek her own living in the specific activities of our race, but is fed by the male.

Now as to the alleged necessity. Because of her maternal duties, the human female is said to be unable to get her own living. As the maternal duties of other females do not unfit them for getting their own living and also the livings of their young, it would seem that the human maternal duties require the segregation of the entire energies of the mother to the service of the child during her entire adult life, or so large a proportion of them that not enough remains to devote to the individual interests of the mother.

Such a condition, did it exist, would of course excuse and justify the pitiful dependence of the human female, and her support by the male. As the queen bee, modified entirely to maternity, is supported, not by the male, to be sure, but by her co-workers, the "old maids," the barren working bees, who labor so patiently and lovingly in their branch of the maternal duties of the hive, so would the human female, modified entirely to maternity, become unfit for any other exertion, and a helpless dependant.

Is this the condition of human motherhood? Does the human mother, by her motherhood, thereby lose control of brain and body, lose power and skill and desire for any other work? Do we see before us the human race, with all its females segregated entirely to the uses of motherhood, consecrated, set apart, specially developed, spending every power of their nature on the service of their children?

We do not. We see the human mother worked far harder than a mare, laboring her life long in the service, not of her children only, but of men; husbands, brothers, fathers, whatever male relatives she has; for mother and sister also; for the church a little, if she is allowed; for society, if she is able; for charity and education and reform,—working in many ways that are not the ways of motherhood.

It is not motherhood that keeps the housewife on her feet from dawn till dark; it is house service, not child service. Women work longer and harder than most men, and not solely in maternal duties. The savage mother carries the burdens, and does all menial service for the tribe. The peasant mother toils in the fields, and the workingman's wife in the home. Many mothers, even now, are wage-earners for the family, as well as bearers and rearers of it. And the women who are not so occupied, the women who belong to rich men,—here perhaps is the exhaustive devotion to maternity which is supposed to justify an admitted economic dependence. But we do not find it even among these. Women of ease and wealth provide for their children better care than the poor woman can; but they do not spend more time upon it themselves, nor more care and effort. They have other occupation.

In spite of her supposed segregation to maternal duties, the human female, the world over, works at extra-maternal duties for hours enough to provide her with an independent living, and then is denied independence on the ground that motherhood prevents her working!

If this ground were tenable, we should find a world full of women who never lifted a finger save in the service of their children, and of men who did *all* the work besides, and waited on the women whom motherhood prevented from waiting on themselves. The ground is not tenable. A human female, healthy, sound, has twenty-five years of life before she is a mother, and should have twenty-five years more after the period of such maternal service as is expected of her has been given. The duties of grandmotherhood are surely not alleged as preventing economic independence.

The working power of the mother has always been a prominent factor in human life. She is the worker *par excellence,* but her work is not such as to affect her economic status. Her living, all that she gets,—food, clothing, ornaments, amusements, luxuries,—these bear no relation to her power to produce wealth, to her services in the house, or to her motherhood. These things bear relation only to the man she marries, the man she depends on,—to how much he has and how much he is willing to give her. The women whose splendid extravagance dazzles the world, whose economic goods are the greatest, are often neither houseworkers nor mothers, but simply the women who hold most power over the men who have the most money. The female of genus homo is economically dependent on the male. He is her food supply.

80

Feminist Standpoint Theory*

Dorothy E. Smith

The fulcrum of a sociology for women is the standpoint of the subject. A sociology for women preserves the presence of subjects as knowers and as actors. It does not transform subjects into the objects of study or make use of conceptual devices for eliminating the active presence of subjects. Its methods of thinking and its analytic procedures must preserve the presence of the active and experiencing subject. A sociology is a systematically developed knowledge of society and social relations. The knower who is construed in the sociological texts of a sociology for women is she whose grasp of the world *from where she stands* is enlarged thereby. For actual subjects situated in the actualities of their everyday worlds, a sociology for women offers an understanding of how those worlds are organized and determined by social relations immanent in and extending beyond them.

Methods of thinking could, I suppose, be described as "theories," but to do so is to suggest that I am concerned with formulations that will explain phenomena, when what I am primarily concerned with is how to conceptualize or how to constitute the textuality of social phenomena. I am concerned with how to *write* the social, to make it visible in sociological texts, in ways that will explicate a problematic, the actuality of which is immanent in the everyday world. In part what is meant by methods of thinking will emerge in the course of the chapter. This is an exploration rather than an account of a destination. We are in search of conceptual practices with which to explicate the actual social relations disclosed in investigation and analysis. We are looking, in other words, for methods and principles for generating sociological texts, for selecting syntax and indexical forms preserving the presence of subjects in our accounts, in short for methods of *writing* sociology. Such methods must recognize that the subject of our sociological texts exists outside them, that, as Marx says, "The real subject [matter] retains its autonomous existence outside the head just as before." Or perhaps we go further than Marx in insisting that both subject matter and the "head" that theorizes it as well as its theorizing are enfolded in the existence of our subject matter. A sociology for women must be conscious of its necessary indexicality and hence that its meaning remains to be completed by a reader who is situated just as she is—a particular woman reading somewhere at a particular time amid the particularities of her everyday world—and that it is the capacity of our sociological texts, as she enlivens them, to reflect upon, to expand, and to enlarge her grasp of the world she reads in, and that is the world that completes the meaning of the text as she reads.

So this chapter is concerned with how to write a sociology that will do this. It does not go so far as the practicalities of how to do it. That will be a later topic. Here the focus is on those aspects of standard methods of thinking sociologically that deny us the presence of subjects and on formulating alternatives and suggesting how we might proceed in exploring the everyday world from the standpoint of women.

To avoid potential misunderstanding, I should state first what I do not mean by the standpoint of women. A sociology for women should not be mistaken for an ideological position that represents women's oppression as having a determinate character and takes up the analysis of social forms with a view to discovering in them the lineaments of what the ideologist already supposes that she knows. The standpoint of women therefore as I am deploying it here cannot be equated with perspective or worldview. It does not universalize a particular experience. It is rather a method that, at the outset of inquiry, creates the space for an absent subject, and an absent experience that is to be filled with the presence and spoken experience of actual women speaking of and in the actualities of their everyday worlds.

I explored issues for women arising from a culture and politics developed almost exclusively by men and written from the standpoint of men and not of women. This statement was as true of intellectual and scientific discourses as of TV commercials. To begin with, therefore, we had to discover *how* to take the standpoint of women. We did not know—there were no precedents—how to view the world from where we were. We discovered that what we had known as *our* history was not in fact ours at all but theirs. We discovered the same of our sociology. We had not realized what and who was not there in the texts in which we had learned to understand ourselves. Becoming a feminist in these contexts means taking this disjuncture up deliberately as an enterprise. The very forms of our oppression require a deliberate remaking of our relations with others and of these the relations of our knowledge must be key, for the dimensions of our oppression are only fully revealed in discoveries that go beyond what direct experience will teach us. But such a remaking cannot be prejudged, for in the very nature of the case we cannot know in advance what we will discover, what we will have to learn, and how it will be conceptualized. Remaking, in the context of intellectual enterprise, is itself a course of inquiry.

The exclusion of women is not the only one. The ruling apparatus is an organization of class and as such implicates dominant classes. The working class is excluded from the ruling apparatus. It also excludes the many voices of women and men of color, of native peoples, and of homosexual women and men. From different standpoints different aspects of the ruling apparatus and of class come into view. But, as I have argued the standpoint of women is distinctive and has distinctive implications for the practice of sociology as a systematically developed consciousness of society.

I proposed women's standpoint as one situated outside textually mediated discourses in the actualities of our everyday lives. This is a standpoint designed in part by our exclusion from the making of cultural and intellectual discourse and the strategies of resorting to our experience as the ground of a new knowledge, a new culture. But it is also designed by an organization of work that has typically been ours, for women's work, as wives, secretaries, and in other ancillary roles, has been that which anchors the impersonal and objectified forms of action and relations to particular individuals, particular local places, particular relationships. Whatever other part women play in the social division of labor, they have been assigned and confined predominantly to work roles mediating the relation of the impersonal and objectified forms of action to the concrete local and particular worlds in which all of us necessarily exist.

The standpoint of women therefore directs us to an "embodied" subject located in a particular actual local historical setting. Her world presents itself to her in its full particularity—the books on her shelves, the Cowichan sweaters she has bought for her sons' birthdays, the Rainforest chair she bought three years ago in a sale, the portable computer she is using to write on, the eighteenth-century chair, made of long-since-exhausted Caribbean mahogany, one of a set of four given her by her mother years ago—each is particularized by insertion into her biography and projects as well as by its immediacy in the now in which she writes. The abstracted constructions of discourse or bureaucracy are accomplishments in and of her everyday world. Her reading and writing are done in actual locations at actual times and under definite material conditions. Though discourse, bureaucracy, and the exchange of money for commodities create forms of social relations that transcend the local and particular, they are constituted, created, and practiced always *within* the local and particular. It is the special magic of the ubiquity of text and its capacity to manifest itself as the same in diverse multiple settings that provide for the local practices of transcendence.

A standpoint in the everyday world is the fundamental grounding of modes of knowing developed in a ruling apparatus. The ruling apparatus is that familiar complex of management, government administration, professions, and intelligentsia, as well as the textually mediated discourses that coordinate and interpenetrate it. Its special capacity is the organization of particular actual places, persons, and events into generalized and abstracted modes vested in categorial systems, rules, laws, and conceptual practices. The former thereby become subject to an abstracted and universalized system of ruling mediated by texts. A mode of ruling has been created that transcends local particularities but at the same time exists only in them. The ruling apparatus of this loosely coordinated collection of varied sites of power has been largely if not exclusively the sphere of men. From within its textual modes the embodied subject and the everyday world as its site are present only as object and never as subject's standpoint. But from the standpoint of women whose work has served to complete the invisibility of the actual as the locus of the subject, from the standpoint of she who stands at the beginning of her work, the grounding of an abstracted conceptual organization of ruling comes into view as a product in and of the everyday world.

Sociology is part of the ruling apparatus. Its relevances and subtending organization are given by the relation of the ruling apparatus to the social world it governs. The institutional forms of ruling constitute its major topics—the sociology of organizations, of education, of health, of work, of mental illness, of deviance, of law, of knowledge, and the like. The organization of sociological thinking and knowledge is articulated to this institutional structure. It pioneers methods of thinking and the systematics of articulating particular actualities to a generalized conceptual order that serves it. To a significant extent, sociology has been busy clarifying, organizing, mapping, and extending the relations of the institutional forms of ruling to the actualities of their domains.

Women's lives have been outside or subordinate to the ruling apparatus. Its conceptual practices do not work for us in the development of a sociological consciousness of our own. The grid of political sociology, the sociology of the family, of organizations, of mental illness, of education, and so forth, does not map the unknown that extends before us as what is to be discovered and explored; it does not fit when we ask how we should organize a sociology beginning from the standpoint of women. We start, as we must, with women's experience (for what other resource do we have?); the available concepts and frameworks do not work because they have already posited a subject situated outside a local and actual experience, a particularized knowledge of the world. Women are readily made the objects of sociological study precisely because they have not been its subjects. Beneath the apparent gender neutrality of the impersonal or absent subject of an objective sociology is the reality of the masculine author of the texts of its tradition and his membership in the circle of men participating in the division of the labor of ruling. The problem confronted here is how to do a sociology that is for women and that takes women as its subjects and its knowers when the methods of thinking, which we have learned as sociologists as the methods of producing recognizably sociological texts, reconstruct us as objects.

If we begin where people are actually located in that independently existing world outside texts, we begin in the particularities of an actual everyday world. As a first step in entering that standpoint into a textually mediated discourse, we constitute the everyday world as our problematic. We do so by interesting ourselves in its opacity for we cannot understand how it is organized or comes about by remaining within it. The concept of problematic transfers this opacity to the level of discourse. It directs attention to a possible set of questions that have yet to be posed or of puzzles that are not yet formulated as such but are "latent" in the actualities of our experienced worlds. The problematic of the everyday world is an explicit discursive formulation of an actual property of the organization of the everyday world. I am talking about a reality as it arises for those who live it—the reality, for example, that effects arise that do not originate in it. Yet I *am talking* (or rather writing) about it. I am entering it into discourse. The term "problematic" enters an actual aspect of the organization of the everyday world (as it is ongoingly produced by actual individuals) into a systematic inquiry. It responds to our practical ignorance of the determinations of our local worlds so long as we look for them within their limits. In this sense the puzzle or puzzles are really there. Hence an inquiry defined by such a problematic addresses a problem of how we are related to the worlds we live in. We may not experience our ignorance as such, but we are nonetheless ignorant.

The problematic, located by our ignorance of how our everyday worlds are shaped and determined by relation and forces external to them, must not be taken to imply that we are dopes or dupes. Within our everyday worlds, we are expert practitioners of their quiddity, of the way they are just the way they are. Our everyday worlds are in part our own accomplishments, and our special and expert knowledge is continually demonstrated in their ordinary familiarity and unsurprising ongoing presence. But how they are knitted into the extended social relations of a contemporary capitalist economy and society is not discoverable with them. The relations among multiple everyday worlds and the accomplishment of those relations within them create a dynamic organization that, in the context of contemporary capitalism, continually feeds change through to our local experience. In the research context this means that so far as their everyday worlds are concerned, we rely entirely on what women tell us, what people tell us, about what they do and what happens. But we cannot rely upon them for an understanding of the relations that shape and determine the everyday. Here then is our business as social scientists for the investigation of these relations and the exploration of the ways they are present in the everyday are and must be a specialized enterprise, a work, the work of a social scientist.

The contemporary feminist critique has emphasized problems in the relationship between researcher and "subject" and has proposed and practiced methods of interview that do not objectify the research "other." Important as such methods are, they are not in themselves sufficient to ground a feminist sociology. Changes in the relationship of researcher and "subjects" do not resolve the kinds of problems we have been discussing. They are not solutions so long as the sociological methods of thinking and analysis objectify what our "subjects" have told us about their lives. We are restricted to the descriptive, to allowing the voices of women's experience to be heard, unless we can go beyond what our respondents themselves have to tell us. Important as it has been and is to hear the authentic speaking of women, it is not sufficient to ground and guide a sociological inquiry. The development of a feminist method in sociology has to go beyond our interviewing practices and our research relationships to explore methods of thinking that will organize our inquiry and write our sociological texts so as to preserve the presence of actual subjects while exploring and explicating the relations in which our everyday worlds are embedded.

81

Black Feminist Thought*

Patricia Hill Collins

Black feminist thought demonstrates Black women's emerging power as agents of knowledge. By portraying African-American women as self-defined, self-reliant individuals confronting race, gender, and class oppression, Afrocentric feminist thought speaks to the importance that knowledge plays in empowering oppressed people. One distinguishing feature of Black feminist thought is its insistence that both the changed consciousness of individuals and the social transformation of political and economic institutions constitute essential ingredients for social change. New knowledge is important for both dimensions of change.

Knowledge is a vitally important part of the social relations of domination and resistance. By objectifying African-American women and recasting our experiences to serve the interests of elite white men, much of the Eurocentric masculinist worldview fosters Black women's subordination. But placing Black women's experiences at the center of analysis offers fresh insights on the prevailing concepts, paradigms, and epistemologies of this worldview and on its feminist and Afrocentric critiques. Viewing the world through a both/and conceptual lens of the simultaneity of race, class, and gender oppression and of the need for a humanist vision of community creates new possibilities for an empowering Afrocentric feminist knowledge. Many Black feminist intellectuals have long thought about the world in this way because this is the way we experience the world.

Afrocentric feminist thought offers two significant contributions toward furthering our understanding of the important connections among knowledge, consciousness, and the politics of empowerment. First, Black feminist thought fosters a fundamental paradigmatic shift in how we think about oppression. By embracing a paradigm of race, class, and gender as interlocking systems of oppression, Black feminist thought reconceptualizes the social relations of domination and resistance. Second, Black feminist thought addresses ongoing epistemological debates in feminist theory and in the sociology of knowledge concerning ways of assessing "truth." Offering subordinate groups new knowledge about their own experiences can be empowering. But revealing new ways of knowing that allow subordinate groups to define their own reality has far greater implications.

Paradigmatic Shifts: Domination and Resistance

Reconceptualizing Race, Class, and Gender as Interlocking Systems of Oppression

"What *I* really feel is radical is trying to make coalitions with people, who are different from you," maintains Barbara Smith. "I feel it is radical to be dealing with race and sex and class and sexual identity all at one time. I think *that* is really radical because it has never been done before." Black feminist thought fosters a fundamental paradigmatic shift that rejects additive approaches to oppression. Instead of starting with gender and then adding in other variables such as age, sexual orientation, race, social class, and religion, Black feminist thought sees these distinctive systems of oppression as being part of one overarching structure of domination. Viewing relations of domination for Black women for any given sociohistorical context as being structured via a system of interlocking race, class, and gender oppression expands the focus of analysis from merely describing the similarities and differences distinguishing these systems of oppression and focuses greater attention on how they interconnect. Assuming that each system needs the others in order to function creates a distinct theoretical stance that stimulates the rethinking of basic social science concepts.

Afrocentric feminist notions of family reflect this reconceptualization process. Black women's experiences as bloodmothers, othermothers, and community othermothers reveal that the mythical norm of a heterosexual, married couple, nuclear family with a nonworking spouse and a husband earning a "family wage" is far from being natural, universal, and preferred but instead is deeply embedded in specific race and class formations. Placing African-American women in the center of analysis not only reveals much-needed information about Black women's experiences but also questions Eurocentric masculinist perspectives on family.

Black women's experiences and the Afrocentric feminist thought rearticulating them also challenge prevailing definitions of community. Black women's actions in the struggle for group survival suggest a vision of community that stands in opposition to that extant in the dominant culture. The definition of community implicit in the market model sees community as arbitrary and fragile, structured fundamentally by competition and domination. In contrast, Afrocentric models of community stress connections, caring, and personal accountability. As cultural workers, African-American women have rejected the generalized ideology of domination advanced by the dominant group in order to conserve Afrocentric conceptualizations of community. Denied access to the podium, Black women have been unable to spend time theorizing about alternative conceptualizations of community. Instead, through daily actions African-American women have *created* alternative communities that empower.

This vision of community sustained by African-American women in conjunction with African-American men addresses the larger issue of reconceptualizing power. The type of Black women's power discussed here does resemble feminist theories of power which emphasize energy and community. However, in contrast to this body of literature whose celebration of women's power is often accompanied by a lack of attention to the importance of power as domination, Black women's experiences as mothers, community othermothers, educators, church leaders, labor union centerwomen, and community leaders seem to suggest that power as energy can be fostered by creative acts of resistance.

The spheres of influence created and sustained by African-American women are not meant solely to provide a respite from oppressive situations or a retreat from their effects. Rather, these Black female spheres of influence constitute potential sanctuaries where individual Black women and men are nurtured in order to confront oppressive social institutions. Power from this perspective is a creative power used for the good of the community, whether that community is conceptualized as one's family, church community, or the next generation of the community's children.

By making the community stronger, African-American women become empowered, and that same community can serve as a source of support when Black women encounter race, gender, and class oppression.

Rethinking Black women's activism uncovers a new vision of Black women's empowerment that is distinct from existing models of power as domination. Black women have not conceptualized our quest for empowerment as one of replacing elite white male authorities with ourselves as benevolent Black female ones. Instead, African-American women have overtly rejected theories of power based on domination in order to embrace an alternative vision of power based on a humanist vision of self-actualization, self-definition, and self-determination.

It is important to develop analyses of contemporary social phenomena that explore the connections among race, class, and gender oppression and use new reconceptualizations of family, community, and power in doing so. Such analyses must retain the creative tension between the specificity needed to study the workings of race, class, and gender in Black women's lives and generalizations about these systems created by cross-cultural and transhistorical research.

Approaches that assume that race, gender, and class are interconnected have immediate practical applications. For example, African-American women continue to be inadequately protected by Title VII of the Civil Rights Act of 1964. The primary purpose of the statute is to eradicate all aspects of discrimination. But judicial treatment of Black women's employment discrimination claims has encouraged Black women to identify race *or* sex as the so-called primary discrimination. "To resolve the inequities that confront Black women," counsels Scarborough, "the courts must first correctly conceptualize them as 'Black women,' a distinct class protected by Title VII." Such a shift, from protected categories to protected classes of people whose Title VII claims might be based on more than two discriminations, would work to alter the entire basis of current antidiscrimination efforts.

Reconceptualizing phenomena such as the rapid growth of female-headed households in African-American communities would also benefit from a race-, class-, and gender-inclusive analysis. Case studies of Black women heading households must be attentive to racially segmented local labor markets and community patterns, to changes in local political economies specific to a given city or region, and to established racial and gender ideology for a given location. This approach would go far to deconstruct Eurocentric, masculinist analyses that implicitly rely on controlling images of the matriarch or the welfare mother as guiding conceptual premises. This level of specificity could lead to generalizations about how race, class, and gender as interlocking phenomena produce an increase in female-headed households in national and international contexts. Revised definitions of family and community refocus attention on cross-cultural patterns of this household structure, especially those stimulated by changes in the international division of labor, and offer new visions of race- and class-inclusive analyses of Black women's gender experiences. Black feminist thought that rearticulates experiences such as these fosters an enhanced theoretical understanding of how race, gender, and class oppression are part of a single, historically created system.

The Matrix of Domination

Additive models of oppression are firmly rooted in the either/or dichotomous thinking of Eurocentric, masculinist thought. One must be either Black or white in such thought systems—persons of ambiguous racial and ethnic identity constantly battle with questions such as "what are you, anyway?" This emphasis on quantification and categorization occurs in conjunction with the belief that either/or categories must be ranked. The search for certainty of this sort requires that one side of a dichotomy be privileged while its other is denigrated. Privilege becomes defined in relation to its other.

Replacing additive models of oppression with interlocking ones creates possibilities for new paradigms. The significance of seeing race, class, and gender as interlocking systems of oppression is that such an approach fosters a paradigmatic shift of thinking inclusively about other oppressions, such as age, sexual orientation, religion, and ethnicity. Race, class, and gender represent the three systems of oppression that most heavily affect African-American women. But these systems and the economic, political, and ideological conditions that support them may not be the most fundamental oppressions, and they certainly affect many more groups than Black women. Other people of color, Jews, the poor, white women, and gays and lesbians have all had similar ideological justifications offered for their subordination. All categories of humans labeled Others have been equated to one another, to animals, and to nature.

Placing African-American women and other excluded groups in the center of analysis opens up possibilities for a both/and conceptual stance, one in which all groups possess varying amounts of penalty and privilege in one historically created system. In this system, for example, white women are penalized by their gender but privileged by their race. Depending on the context, an individual may be an oppressor, a member of an oppressed group, or simultaneously oppressor and oppressed.

Adhering to a both/and conceptual stance does not mean that race, class, and gender oppression are interchangeable. For example, whereas race, class, and gender oppression operate on the social structural level of institutions, gender oppression seems better able to annex the basic power of the erotic and intrude in personal relationships via family dynamics and within individual consciousness. This may be because racial oppression has fostered historically concrete communities among African-Americans and other racial/ethnic groups. These communities have stimulated cultures of resistance. While these communities segregate Blacks from whites, they simultaneously provide counter-institutional buffers that subordinate groups such as African-Americans use to resist the ideas and institutions of dominant groups. Social class may be similarly structured. Traditionally conceptualized as a relationship of *individual* employees to their employers, social class might be better viewed as a relationship of *communities* to capitalist political economies. Moreover, significant overlap exists between racial and social class oppression when viewing them through the collective lens of family and community. Existing community structures provide a primary line of resistance against racial and class oppression. But because gender cross-cuts these structures, it finds fewer comparable institutional bases to foster resistance.

Embracing a both/and conceptual stance moves us from additive, separate systems approaches to oppression and toward what I now see as the more fundamental issue of the social relations of domination. Race, class, and gender constitute axes of oppression that characterize Black women's experiences within a more generalized matrix of domination. Other groups may encounter different dimensions of the matrix, such as sexual orientation, religion, and age, but the overarching relationship is one of domination and the types of activism it generates.

bell hooks labels this matrix a "politic of domination" and describes how it operates along interlocking axes of race, class, and gender oppression. This politic of domination

> refers to the ideological ground that they share, which is a belief in domination, and a belief in the notions of superior and inferior, which are components of ail of those systems. For me it's like a house, they share the foundation, but the foundation is the ideological beliefs around which notions of domination are constructed.

Johnella Butler claims that new methodologies growing from this new paradigm would be "non-hierarchical" and would "refuse primacy" to either race, class, gender, or ethnicity, demanding instead a recognition of their matrix-like interaction". Race, class, and gender may not be the most fundamental or important systems of oppression, but they have most profoundly affected African-American women. One significant dimension of Black feminist thought is its potential to reveal insights about the social relations of domination organized along other axes such as religion, ethnicity, sexual orientation, and age. Investigating Black women's particular experiences thus promises to reveal much about the more universal process of domination.

Multiple Levels of Domination

In addition to being structured along axes such as race, gender, and social class, the matrix of domination is structured on several levels. People experience and resist oppression on three levels: the level of personal biography; the group or community level of the cultural context created by race, class, and gender; and the systemic level of social institutions. Black feminist thought emphasizes all three levels as sites of domination and as potential sites of resistance.

Each individual has a unique personal biography made up of concrete experiences, values, motivations, and emotions. No two individuals occupy the same social space; thus no two biographies are identical. Human ties can be freeing and empowering, as is the case with Black women's heterosexual love relationships or in the power of motherhood in African-American families and communities. Human ties can also be confining and oppressive. Situations of domestic violence and abuse or cases in which controlling images foster Black women's internalized oppression represent domination on the personal level. The same situation can look quite different depending on the consciousness one brings to interpret it.

This level of individual consciousness is a fundamental area where new knowledge can generate change. Traditional accounts assume that power as domination operates from the top down by forcing and controlling unwilling victims to bend to the will of more powerful superiors. But these accounts fail to account for questions concerning why, for example, women stay with abusive men even with ample opportunity to leave or why slaves did not kill their owners more often. The willingness of the victim to collude in her or his own victimization becomes lost. They also fail to account for sustained resistance by victims, even when chances for victory appear remote. By emphasizing the power of self-definition and the necessity of a free mind, Black feminist thought speaks to the importance African-American women thinkers place on consciousness as a sphere of freedom. Black women intellectuals realize that domination operates not only by structuring power from the top down but by simultaneously annexing the power as energy of those on the bottom for its own ends. In their efforts to rearticulate the standpoint of African-American women as a group, Black feminist thinkers offer individual African-American women the conceptual tools to resist oppression.

The cultural context formed by those experiences and ideas that are shared with other members of a group or community which give meaning to individual biographies constitutes a second level at which domination is experienced and resisted. Each individual biography is rooted in several overlapping cultural contexts—for example, groups defined by race, social class, age, gender, religion, and sexual orientation. The cultural component contributes, among other things, the concepts used in thinking and acting, group validation of an individual's interpretation of concepts, the "thought models" used in the acquisition of knowledge, and standards used to evaluate individual thought and behavior. The most cohesive cultural contexts are those with identifiable histories, geographic locations, and social institutions. For Black women African-American communities have provided the location for an Afrocentric group perspective to endure.

Subjugated knowledges, such as a Black women's culture of resistance, develop in cultural contexts controlled by oppressed groups. Dominant groups aim to replace subjugated knowledge with their own specialized thought because they realize that gaining control over this dimension of subordinate groups' lives simplifies control. While efforts to influence this dimension of an oppressed group's experiences can be partially successful, this level is more difficult to control than dominant groups would have us believe. For example, adhering to externally derived standards of beauty leads many African-American women to dislike their skin color or hair texture. Similarly, internalizing Eurocentric gender ideology leads some Black men to abuse Black women. These are cases of the successful infusion of the dominant group's specialized thought into the everyday cultural context of African-Americans. But the long-standing existence of a Black women's culture of resistance as expressed through Black women's relationships with one another, the Black women's blues tradition, and the voices of contemporary African-American women writers all attest to the difficulty of eliminating the cultural context as a fundamental site of resistance.

Domination is also experienced and resisted on the third level of social institutions controlled by the dominant group: namely, schools, churches, the media, and other formal organizations. These institutions expose individuals to the specialized thought representing the dominant group's standpoint and interests. While such institutions offer the promise of both literacy and other skills that can be used for individual empowerment and social transformation, they simultaneously require docility and passivity. Such institutions would have us believe that the theorizing of elites constitutes the whole of theory. The existence of African-American women thinkers such as Maria Stewart, Sojourner Truth, Zora Neale Hurston, and Fannie Lou Hamer who, though excluded from and/or marginalized within such institutions, continued to produce theory effectively opposes this hegemonic view. Moreover, the more recent resurgence of Black feminist thought within these institutions, the case of the outpouring of contemporary Black feminist thought in history and literature, directly challenges the Eurocentric masculinist thought pervading these institutions.

Resisting the Matrix of Domination

Domination operates by seducing, pressuring, or forcing African-American women and members of subordinated groups to replace individual and cultural ways of knowing with the dominant group's specialized thought. As a result, suggests Audre Lorde, "the true focus of revolutionary change is never merely the oppressive situations which we seek to escape, but that piece of the oppressor which is planted deep within each of us." Or as Toni Cade Bambara succinctly states, "revolution begins with the self, in the self."

Lorde and Bambara's suppositions raise an important issue for Black feminist intellectuals and for all scholars and activists working for social change. Although most individuals have little difficulty identifying their own victimization within some major system of oppression—whether it be by race, social class, religion, physical ability, sexual orientation, ethnicity, age or gender—they typically fail to see how their thoughts and actions uphold someone else's subordination. Thus white feminists routinely point with confidence to their oppression as women but resist seeing how much their white skin privileges them. African-Americans who possess eloquent analyses of racism often persist in viewing poor white women as symbols of white power. The radical left fares little better. "If only people of color and women could see their true class interests," they argue, "class solidarity would eliminate racism and sexism." In essence, each group identifies the oppression with which it feels most comfortable as being fundamental and classifies all others as being of lesser importance. Oppression is filled with such contradictions because these approaches fail to recognize that a matrix of domination contains few pure victims or oppressors. Each individual derives varying amounts of penalty and privilege from the multiple systems of oppression which frame everyone's lives.

A broader focus stresses the interlocking nature of oppressions that are structured on multiple levels, from the individual to the social structural, and which are part of a larger matrix of domination. Adhering to this inclusive model provides the conceptual space needed for each individual to see that she or he is *both* a member of multiple dominant groups *and* a member of multiple subordinate groups. Shifting the analysis to investigating how the matrix of domination is structured along certain axes—race, gender, and class being the axes of investigation for African-American women—reveals that different systems of oppression may rely in varying degrees on systemic versus interpersonal mechanisms of domination.

Empowerment involves rejecting the dimensions of knowledge, whether personal, cultural, or institutional, that perpetuate objectification and dehumanization. African-American women and other individuals in subordinate groups become empowered when we understand and use those dimensions of our individual, group, and disciplinary ways of knowing that foster our humanity as fully human subjects. This is the case when Black women value our self-definitions, participate in a Black women's activist tradition, invoke an Afrocentric feminist epistemology as central to our worldview, and view the skills gained in schools as part of a focused education for Black community development. C. Wright Mills identifies this holistic epistemology as the "sociological imagination" and identifies its task and its promise as a way of knowing that enables individuals to grasp the relations between history and biography within society. Using one's standpoint to engage the sociological imagination can empower the individual. "My fullest concentration of energy is available to me," Audre Lorde maintains, "only when I integrate all the parts of who I am, openly, allowing power from particular sources of my living to flow back and forth freely through all my different selves, without the restriction of externally imposed definition."

Epistemological Shifts: Dialogue, Empathy, and Truth

Black Women as Agents of Knowledge

Living life as an African-American woman is a necessary prerequisite for producing Black feminist thought because within Black women's communities thought is validated and produced with reference to a particular set of historical, material, and epistemological conditions.

African-American women who adhere to the idea that claims about Black women must be substantiated by Black women's sense of our own experiences and who anchor our knowledge claims in an Afrocentric feminist epistemology have produced a rich tradition of Black feminist thought.

Traditionally such women were blues singers, poets, autobiographers, storytellers, and orators validated by everyday Black women as experts on a Black women's standpoint. Only a few unusual African-American feminist scholars have been able to defy Eurocentric masculinist epistemologies and explicitly embrace an Afrocentric feminist epistemology. Consider Alice Walker's description of Zora Neale Hurston:

> In my mind, Zora Neale Hurston, Billie Holiday, and Bessie Smith form a sort of unholy trinity. Zora *belongs* in the tradition of black women singers, rather than among "the literati." . . . Like Billie and Bessie she followed her own road, believed in her own gods, pursued her own dreams, and refused to separate herself from "common" people.

Zora Neale Hurston is an exception for prior to 1950, few African-American women earned advanced degrees and most of those who did complied with Eurocentric masculinist epistemologies. Although these women worked on behalf of Black women, they did so within the confines of pervasive race and gender oppression. Black women scholars were in a position to see the exclusion of African-American women from scholarly discourse, and the thematic content of their work often reflected their interest in examining a Black women's standpoint. However, their tenuous status in academic institutions led them to adhere to Eurocentric masculinist epistemologies so that their work would be accepted as scholarly. As a result, while they produced Black feminist thought, those African-American women most likely to gain academic credentials were often least likely to produce Black feminist thought that used an Afrocentric feminist epistemology.

An ongoing tension exists for Black women as agents of knowledge, a tension rooted in the sometimes conflicting demands of Afrocentricity and feminism. Those Black women who are feminists are critical of how Black culture and many of its traditions oppress women. For example, the strong pronatal beliefs in African-American communities that foster early motherhood among adolescent girls, the lack of self-actualization that can accompany the double-day of paid employment and work in the home, and the emotional and physical abuse that many Black women experience from their fathers, lovers, and husbands all reflect practices opposed by African-American women who are feminists. But these same women may have a parallel desire as members of an oppressed racial group to affirm the value of that same culture and traditions. Thus strong Black mothers appear in Black women's literature, Black women's economic contributions to families is lauded, and a curious silence exists concerning domestic abuse.

As more African-American women earn advanced degrees, the range of Black feminist scholarship is expanding. Increasing numbers of African-American women scholars are explicitly choosing to ground their work in Black women's experiences, and, by doing so, they implicitly adhere to an Afrocentric feminist epistemology. Rather than being restrained by their both/and status of marginality, these women make creative use of their outsider-within status and produce innovative Afrocentric feminist thought. The difficulties these women face lie less in demonstrating that they have mastered white male epistemologies than in resisting the hegemonic nature of these patterns of thought in order to see, value, and use existing alternative Afrocentric feminist ways of knowing.

In establishing the legitimacy of their knowledge claims, Black women scholars who want to develop Afrocentric feminist thought may encounter the often conflicting standards of three key groups. First, Black feminist thought must be validated by ordinary African-American women who, in the words of Hannah Nelson, grow to womanhood "in a world where the saner you are, the madder you are made to appear". To be credible in the eyes of this group, scholars must be personal advocates for their material, be accountable for the consequences of their work, have lived or experienced their material in some fashion, and be willing to engage in dialogues about their findings with ordinary, everyday people. Second, Black feminist thought also must be accepted by the community of Black women scholars. These scholars place varying amounts of importance on rearticulating a Black women's standpoint using an Afrocentric feminist epistemology. Third, Afrocentric feminist thought within academia must be prepared to confront Eurocentric masculinist political and epistemological requirements.

The dilemma facing Black women scholars engaged in creating Black feminist thought is that a knowledge claim that meets the criteria of adequacy for one group and thus is judged to be an acceptable knowledge claim may not be translatable into the terms of a different group. Using the example of Black English, June Jordan illustrates the difficulty of moving among epistemologies:

> You cannot "translate" instances of Standard English preoccupied with abstraction or with nothing/nobody evidently alive into Black English. That would warp the language into uses antithetical to the guiding perspective of its community of users. Rather you must first change those Standard English sentences, themselves, into ideas consistent with the person-centered assumptions of Black English.

Although both worldviews share a common vocabulary, the ideas themselves defy direct translation.

For Black women who are agents of knowledge, the marginality that accompanies outsider-within status can be the source of both frustration and creativity. In an attempt to minimize the differences between the cultural context of African-American communities and the expectations of social institutions, some women dichotomize their behavior and become two different people. Over time, the strain of doing this can be enormous. Others reject their cultural context and work against their own best interests by enforcing the dominant group's specialized thought. Still others manage to inhabit both contexts but do so critically, using their outsider-within perspectives as a source of insights and ideas. But while outsiders within can make substantial contributions as agents of knowledge, they rarely do so without substantial personal cost. "Eventually it comes to you," observes Lorraine Hansberry, "the thing that makes you exceptional, if you are at all, is inevitably that which must also make you lonely."

Once Black feminist scholars face the notion that, on certain dimensions of a Black women's standpoint, it may be fruitless to try and translate ideas from an Afrocentric feminist epistemology into a Eurocentric masculinist framework, then other choices emerge. Rather than trying to uncover universal knowledge claims that can withstand the translation from one epistemology to another (initially, at least), Black women intellectuals might find efforts to rearticulate a Black women's standpoint especially fruitful. Rearticulating a Black women's standpoint refashions the concrete and reveals the more universal human dimensions of Black women's everyday lives. "I date all my work," notes Nikki Giovanni, "because I think poetry, or any writing, is but a reflection of the moment. The universal comes from the particular." bell hooks maintains, "my goal as a feminist thinker and theorist is to take that abstraction and articulate it in a language that renders it accessible—not less complex or rigorous—but simply more accessible." The complexity exists; interpreting it remains the unfulfilled challenge for Black women intellectuals.

Situated Knowledge, Subjugated Knowledge, and Partial Perspectives

"My life seems to be an increasing revelation of the intimate face of universal struggle," claims June Jordan:

> You begin with your family and the kids on the block, and next you open your eyes to what you call your people and that leads you into land reform into Black English into Angola leads you back to your own bed where you lie by yourself, wondering if you deserve to be peaceful, or trusted or desired or left to the freedom of your own unfaltering heart. And the scale shrinks to the size of a skull: your own interior cage.

Lorraine Hansberry expresses a similar idea: "I believe that one of the most sound ideas in dramatic writing is that in order to create the universal, you must pay very great attention to the specific. Universality, I think, emerges from the truthful identity of what is". Jordan and

Hansberry's insights that universal struggle and truth may wear a particularistic, intimate face suggest a new epistemological stance concerning how we negotiate competing knowledge claims and identify "truth."

The context in which African-American women's ideas are nurtured or suppressed matters. Understanding the content and epistemology of Black women's ideas as specialized knowledge requires attending to the context from which those ideas emerge. While produced by individuals, Black feminist thought as situated knowledge is embedded in the communities in which African-American women find ourselves.

A Black women's standpoint and those of other oppressed groups is not only embedded in a context but exists in a situation characterized by domination. Because Black women's ideas have been suppressed, this suppression has stimulated African-American women to create knowledge that empowers people to resist domination. Thus Afrocentric feminist thought represents a subjugated knowledge. A Black women's standpoint may provide a preferred stance from which to view the matrix of domination because, in principle, Black feminist thought as specialized thought is less likely than the specialized knowledge produced by dominant groups to deny the connection between ideas and the vested interests of their creators. However, Black feminist thought as subjugated knowledge is not exempt from critical analysis, because subjugation is not grounds for an epistemology.

Despite African-American women's potential power to reveal new insights about the matrix of domination, a Black women's standpoint is only one angle of vision. Thus Black feminist thought represents a partial perspective. The overarching matrix of domination houses multiple groups, each with varying experiences with penalty and privilege that produce corresponding partial perspectives, situated knowledges, and, for clearly identifiable subordinate groups, subjugated knowledges. No one group has a clear angle of vision. No one group possesses the theory or methodology that allows it to discover the absolute "truth" or, worse yet, proclaim its theories and methodologies as the universal norm evaluating other groups' experiences. Given that groups are unequal in power in making themselves heard, dominant groups have a vested interest in suppressing the knowledge produced by subordinate groups. Given the existence of multiple and competing knowledge claims to "truth" produced by groups with partial perspectives, what epistemological approach offers the most promise?

Dialogue and Empathy

Western social and political thought contains two alternative approaches to ascertaining "truth." The first, reflected in positivist science, has long claimed that absolute truths exist and that the task of scholarship is to develop objective, unbiased tools of science to measure these truths. But Afrocentric, feminist, and other bodies of critical theory have unmasked the concepts and epistemology of this version of science as representing the vested interests of elite white men and therefore as being less valid when applied to experiences of other groups and, more recently, to white male recounting of their own exploits. Earlier versions of standpoint theories, themselves rooted in a Marxist positivism, essentially reversed positivist science's assumptions concerning whose truth would prevail. These approaches suggest that the oppressed allegedly have a clearer view of "truth" than their oppressors because they lack the blinders created by the dominant group's ideology. But this version of standpoint theory basically duplicates the positivist belief in one "true" interpretation of reality and, like positivist science, comes with its own set of problems.

Relativism, the second approach, has been forwarded as the antithesis of and inevitable outcome of rejecting a positivist science. From a relativist perspective all groups produce specialized thought and each group's thought is equally valid. No group can claim to have a better interpretation of the "truth" than another. In a sense, relativism represents the opposite of scientific ideologies of objectivity. As epistemological stances, both positivist science and relativism minimize the importance of specific location in influencing a group's knowledge claims, the power inequities among groups that produce subjugated knowledges, and the strengths and limitations of partial perspective.

The existence of Black feminist thought suggests another alternative to the ostensibly objective norms of science and to relativism's claims that groups with competing knowledge claims are equal. In this volume I placed Black women's subjectivity in the center of analysis and examined the interdependence of the everyday, taken-for-granted knowledge shared by African-American women as a group, the more specialized knowledge produced by Black women intellectuals, and the social conditions shaping both types of thought. This approach allowed me to describe the creative tension linking how sociological conditions influenced a Black women's standpoint and how the power of the ideas themselves gave many African-American women the strength to shape those same sociological conditions. I approached Afrocentric feminist thought as situated in a context of domination and not as a system of ideas divorced from political and economic reality. Moreover, I presented Black feminist thought as subjugated knowledge in that African-American women have long struggled to find alternative locations and techniques for articulating our own standpoint. In brief, I examined the situated, subjugated standpoint of African-American women in order to understand Black feminist thought as a partial perspective on domination.

This approach to Afrocentric feminist thought allows African-American women to bring a Black women's standpoint to larger epistemological dialogues concerning the nature of the matrix of domination. Eventually such dialogues may get us to a point at which, claims Elsa Barkiey Brown, "all people can learn to center in another experience, validate it, and judge it by its own standards without need of comparison or need to adopt that framework as their own". In such dialogues, "one has no need to 'decenter' anyone in order to center someone else; one has only to constantly, appropriately, 'pivot the center' ".

Those ideas that are validated as true by African-American women, African-American men, Latina lesbians, Asian-American women, Puerto Rican men, and other groups with distinctive standpoints, with each group using the epistemological approaches growing from its unique standpoint, thus become the most "objective" truths. Each group speaks from its own standpoint and shares its own partial, situated knowledge. But because each group perceives its own truth as partial, its knowledge is unfinished. Each group becomes better able to consider other groups' standpoints without relinquishing the uniqueness of its own standpoint or suppressing other groups' partial perspectives. "What is always needed in the appreciation of art, or life," maintains Alice Walker, "is the larger perspective. Connections made, or at least attempted, where none existed before, the straining to encompass in one's glance at the varied world the common thread, the unifying theme through immense diversity". Partiality and not universality is the condition of being heard; individuals and groups forwarding knowledge claims without owning their position are deemed less credible than those who do.

Dialogue is critical to the success of this epistemological approach, the type of dialogue long extant in the Afrocentric call-and-response tradition whereby power dynamics are fluid, everyone has a voice, but everyone must listen and respond to other voices in order to be allowed to remain in the community. Sharing a common cause fosters dialogue and encourages groups to transcend their differences.

Existing power inequities among groups must be addressed before an alternative epistemology such as that described by Elsa Barkiey Brown or Alice Walker can be utilized. The presence of subjugated knowledges means that groups are not equal in making their standpoints known to themselves and others. "Decentering" the dominant group is essential, and relinquishing privilege of this magnitude is unlikely to occur without struggle. But still the vision exists, one encompassing "coming to believe in the possibility of a variety of experiences, a variety of ways of understanding the world, a variety of frameworks of operation, without imposing consciously or unconsciously a notion of the norm".

The Politics of Empowerment

African-American women have been victimized by race, gender, and class oppression. But portraying Black women solely as passive, unfortunate recipients of racial and sexual abuse stifles notions that Black women can actively work to change our circumstances and bring about changes in our lives. Similarly, presenting African-

American women solely as heroic figures who easily engage in resisting oppression on all fronts minimizes the very real costs of oppression and can foster the perception that Black women need no help because we can "take it."

Black feminist thought's emphasis on the ongoing interplay between Black women's oppression and Black women's activism presents the matrix of domination as responsive to human agency. Such thought views the world as a dynamic place where the goal is not merely to survive or to fit in or to cope; rather, it becomes a place where we feel ownership and accountability. The existence of Afrocentric feminist thought suggests that there is always choice, and power to act, no matter how bleak the situation may appear to be. Viewing the world as one in the making raises the issue of individual responsibility for bringing about change. It also shows that while individual empowerment is key, only collective action can effectively generate lasting social transformation of political and economic institutions.

In 1831 Maria Stewart asked, "How long shall the fair daughters of Africa be compelled to bury their minds and talents beneath a load of iron pots and kettles?". Stewart's response speaks eloquently to the connections between knowledge, consciousness, and the politics of empowerment:

> Until union, knowledge and love begin to flow among us. How long shall a mean set of men flatter us with their smiles, and enrich themselves with our hard earnings; their wives' fingers sparkling with rings, and they themselves laughing at our folly? Until we begin to promote and patronize each other. . . . Do you ask, what can we do? Unite and build a store of your own. . . . Do you ask where is the money? We have spent more than enough for nonsense, to do what building we should want.

82

Performative Theory of Gender Acts*

Judith Butler

In *Discipline and Punish* Foucault challenges the language of internalization as it operates in the service of the disciplinary regime of the subjection and subjectivation of criminals. Although Foucault objected to what he understood to be the psychoanalytic belief in the "inner" truth of sex in *The History of Sexuality*, he turns to a criticism of the doctrine of internalization for separate purposes in the context of his history of criminology. In a sense, *Discipline and Punish* can be read as Foucault's effort to rewrite Nietzsche's doctrine of internalization in *On the Genealogy of Morals* on the model of *inscription*. In the context of prisoners, Foucault writes, the strategy has been not to enforce a repression of their desires, but to compel their bodies to signify the prohibitive law as their very essence, style, and necessity. That law is not literally internalized, but incorporated, with the consequence that bodies are produced which signify that law on and through the body; there the law is manifest as the essence of their selves, the meaning of their soul, their conscience, the law of their desire. In effect, the law is at once fully manifest and fully latent, for it never appears as external to the bodies it subjects and subjectivates. Foucault writes:

> It would be wrong to say that the soul is an illusion, or an ideological effect. On the contrary, it exists, it has a reality, it is produced permanently *around, on, within*, the body by the functioning of a power that is exercised on those that are punished (my emphasis).

The figure of the interior soul understood as "within" the body is signified through its inscription *on* the body, even though its primary mode of signification is through its very absence, its potent invisibility. The effect of a structuring inner space is produced through the signification of a body as a vital and sacred enclosure. The soul is precisely what the body lacks; hence, the body presents itself as a signifying lack. That lack which *is* the body signifies the soul as that which cannot show. In this sense, then, the soul is a surface signification that contests and displaces the inner/outer distinction itself, a figure of interior psychic space inscribed *on* the body as a social signification that perpetually renounces itself as such. In Foucault's terms, the soul is not imprisoned by or within the body, as some Christian imagery would suggest, but "the soul is the prison of the body."

The redescription of intrapsychic processes in terms of the surface politics of the body implies a corollary redescription of gender as the disciplinary production of the figures of fantasy through the play of presence and absence on the body's surface, the construction of the gendered body through a series of exclusions and denials, signifying absences. But what determines the manifest and latent text of the body politic? What is the prohibitive law that generates the corporeal stylization of gender, the fantasied and fantastic figuration of the body? We have already considered the incest taboo and the prior taboo against homosexuality as the generative moments of gender identity, the prohibitions that produce identity along the culturally intelligible grids of an idealized and compulsory heterosexuality. That disciplinary production of gender effects a false stabilization of gender in the interests of the heterosexual construction and regulation of sexuality within the reproductive domain. The construction of coherence conceals the gender discontinuities that run rampant within heterosexual, bisexual, and gay and lesbian contexts in which gender does not necessarily follow from sex, and desire, or sexuality generally, does not seem to follow from gender—indeed, where none of these dimensions of significant corporeality express or reflect one another. When the disorganization and disaggregation of the field of bodies disrupt the regulatory fiction of heterosexual coherence, it seems that the expressive model loses its descriptive force. That regulatory ideal is then exposed as a norm and a fiction that disguises itself as a developmental law regulating the sexual field that it purports to describe.

According to the understanding of identification as an enacted fantasy or incorporation, however, it is clear that coherence is desired, wished for, idealized, and that this idealization is an effect of a corporeal signification. In other words, acts, gestures, and desire produce the effect of an internal core or substance, but produce this *on the surface* of the body, through the play of signifying absences that suggest, but never reveal, the organizing principle of identity as a cause. Such acts, gestures, enactments, generally construed, are *performative* in the sense that the essence or identity that they otherwise purport to express are *fabrications* manufactured and sustained through corporeal signs and other discursive means. That the gendered body is performative suggests that it has no ontological status apart from the various acts which constitute its reality. This also suggests that if that reality is fabricated as an interior essence, that very inferiority is an effect and function of a decidedly public and social discourse, the public regulation of fantasy through the surface politics of the body, the gender border control that differentiates inner from outer, and so institutes the "integrity" of the subject. In other words, acts and gestures, articulated and enacted desires create the illusion of an interior and organizing gender core, an illusion discursively maintained for the purposes of the regulation of sexuality within the obligatory frame of reproductive heterosexuality. If the "cause" of desire, gesture, and act can be localized within the "self" of the actor, then the political regulations and disciplinary practices which produce that ostensibly coherent gender are effectively displaced from view. The displacement of a political and discursive origin of gender identity onto a psychological "core" precludes an analysis of the political constitution of the gendered subject and its fabricated notions about the ineffable interiority of its sex or of its true identity.

If the inner truth of gender is a fabrication and if a true gender is a fantasy instituted and inscribed on the surface of bodies, then it seems that genders can be neither true nor false, but are only produced as the truth effects of a discourse of primary and stable identity. In *Mother Camp: Female Impersonators in America,* anthropologist Esther Newton suggests that the structure of impersonation reveals one of the key fabricating mechanisms through which the social construction of gender takes place. I would suggest as well that drag fully subverts the distinction between inner and outer psychic space and effectively mocks both the expressive model of gender and the notion of a true gender identity. Newton writes:

> At its most complex, [drag] is a double inversion that says, "appearance is an illusion." Drag says [Newton's curious personification] "my 'outside' appearance is feminine, but my essence 'inside' [the body] is masculine." At the same time it symbolizes the opposite inversion; "my

> appearance 'outside' [my body, my gender] is masculine but my essence 'inside' [myself] is feminine."

Both claims to truth contradict one another and so displace the entire enactment of gender significations from the discourse of truth and falsity.

The notion of an original or primary gender identity is often parodied within the cultural practices of drag, cross-dressing, and the sexual stylization of butch/femme identities. Within feminist theory, such parodic identities have been understood to be either degrading to women, in the case of drag and cross-dressing, or an uncritical appropriation of sex-role stereotyping from within the practice of heterosexuality, especially in the case of butch/femme lesbian identities. But the relation between the "imitation" and the "original" is, I think, more complicated than that critique generally allows. Moreover, it gives us a clue to the way in which the relationship between primary identification—that is, the original meanings accorded to gender—and subsequent gender experience might be re-framed. The performance of drag plays upon the distinction between the anatomy of the performer and the gender that is being performed. But we are actually in the presence of three contingent dimensions of significant corporeality: anatomical sex, gender identity, and gender performance. If the anatomy of the performer is already distinct from the gender of the performer, and both of those are distinct from the gender of the performance, then the performance suggests a dissonance not only between sex and performance, but sex and gender, and gender and performance. As much as drag creates a unified picture of "woman" (what its critics often oppose), it also reveals the distinctness of those aspects of gendered experience which are falsely naturalized as a unity through the regulatory fiction of heterosexual coherence. *In imitating gender, drag implicitly reveals the imitative structure of gender itself—as well as its contingency.* Indeed, part of the pleasure, the giddiness of the performance is in the recognition of a radical contingency in the relation between sex and gender in the face of cultural configurations of causal unities that are regularly assumed to be natural and necessary. In the place of the law of heterosexual coherence, we see sex and gender denaturalized by means of a performance which avows their distinctness and dramatizes the cultural mechanism of their fabricated unity.

The notion of gender parody defended here does not assume that there is an original which such parodic identities imitate. Indeed, the parody is of the very notion of an original; just as the psychoanalytic notion of gender identification is constituted by a fantasy of a fantasy, the transfiguration of an Other who is always already a "figure" in that double sense, so gender parody reveals that the original identity after which gender fashions itself is an imitation without an origin. To be more precise, it is a production which, in effect—that is, in its effect—postures as an imitation. This perpetual displacement constitutes a fluidity of identities that suggests an openness to resignification and recontextualization; parodic proliferation deprives hegemonic culture and its critics of the claim to naturalized or essentialist gender identities. Although the gender meanings taken up in these parodic styles are clearly part of hegemonic, misogynist culture, they are nevertheless denaturalized and mobilized through their parodic recontextualization. As imitations which effectively displace the meaning of the original, they imitate the myth of originality itself. In the place of an original identification which serves as a determining cause, gender identity might be reconceived as a personal/cultural history of received meanings subject to a set of imitative practices which refer laterally to other imitations and which, jointly, construct the illusion of a primary and interior gendered self or parody the mechanism of that construction.

According to Fredric Jameson's "Postmodernism and Consumer Society," the imitation that mocks the notion of an original is characteristic of pastiche rather than parody:

> Pastiche is, like parody, the imitation of a peculiar or unique style, the wearing of a stylistic mask, speech in a dead language: but it is a neutral practice of mimicry, without parody's ulterior motive, without the satirical impulse, without laughter, without that still latent feeling that there exists something *normal* compared to which what

is being imitated is rather comic. Pastiche is blank parody, parody that has lost it humor.

The loss of the sense of "the normal," however, can be its own occasion for laughter, especially when "the normal," "the original" is revealed to be a copy, and an inevitably failed one, an ideal that no one *can* embody. In this sense, laughter emerges in the realization that all along the original was derived.

Parody by itself is not subversive, and there must be a way to understand what makes certain kinds of parodic repetitions effectively disruptive, truly troubling, and which repetitions become domesticated and recirculated as instruments of cultural hegemony. A typology of actions would clearly not suffice, for parodic displacement, indeed, parodic laughter, depends on a context and reception in which subversive confusions can be fostered. What performance where will invert the inner/outer distinction and compel a radical rethinking of the psychological presuppositions of gender identity and sexuality? What performance where will compel a reconsideration of the *place* and stability of the masculine and the feminine? And what kind of gender performance will enact and reveal the performativity of gender itself in a way that destabilizes the naturalized categories of identity and desire.

If the body is not a "being," but a variable boundary, a surface whose permeability is politically regulated, a signifying practice within a cultural field of gender hierarchy and compulsory heterosexuality, then what language is left for understanding this corporeal enactment, gender, that constitutes its "interior" signification on its surface? Sartre would perhaps have called this act "a style of being," Foucault, "a stylistics of existence." And in my earlier reading of Beauvoir, I suggest that gendered bodies are so many "styles of the flesh." These styles all never fully self-styled, for styles have a history, and those histories condition and limit the possibilities. Consider gender, for instance, as *a corporeal style*, an "act," as it were, which is both intentional and performative, where "*performative*" suggests a dramatic and contingent construction of meaning.

Wittig understands gender as the workings of "sex," where "sex" is an obligatory injunction for the body to become a cultural sign, to materialize itself in obedience to a historically delimited possibility, and to do this, not once or twice, but as a sustained and repeated corporeal project. The notion of a "project," however, suggests the originating force of a radical will, and because gender is a project which has cultural survival as its end, the term *strategy* better suggests the situation of duress under which gender performance always and variously occurs. Hence, as a strategy of survival within compulsory systems, gender is a performance with clearly punitive consequences. Discrete genders are part of what "humanizes" individuals within contemporary culture; indeed, we regularly punish those who fail to do their gender right. Because there is neither an "essence" that gender expresses or externalizes nor an objective ideal to which gender aspires, and because gender is not a fact, the various acts of gender create the idea of gender, and without those acts, there would be no gender at all. Gender is, thus, a construction that regularly conceals its genesis; the tacit collective agreement to perform, produce, and sustain discrete and polar genders as cultural fictions is obscured by the credibility of those productions—and the punishments that attend not agreeing to believe in them; the construction "compels" our belief in its necessity and naturalness. The historical possibilities materialized through various corporeal styles are nothing other than those punitively regulated cultural fictions alternately embodied and deflected under duress.

Consider that a sedimentation of gender norms produces the peculiar phenomenon of a "natural sex" or a "real woman" or any number of prevalent and compelling social fictions, and that this is a sedimentation that over time has produced a set of corporeal styles which, in reified form, appear as the natural configuration of bodies into sexes existing in a binary relation to one another. If these styles are enacted, and if they produce the coherent gendered subjects who pose as their originators, what kind of performance might reveal this ostensible "cause" to be an "effect"?

In what senses, then, is gender an act? As in other ritual social dramas, the action of gender requires a performance that is *repeated*. This repetition is at once a reenactment and reexperiencing of a set of meanings already socially established; and it is the mundane and ritualized form of their legitimation. Although there are individual bodies that enact these significations by becoming stylized into gendered modes, this "action" is a public action. There are temporal and collective dimensions to these actions, and their public character is not inconsequential; indeed, the performance is effected with the strategic aim of maintaining gender within its binary frame—an aim that cannot be attributed to a subject, but, rather, must be understood to found and consolidate the subject.

Gender ought not to be construed as a stable identity or locus of agency from which various acts follow; rather, gender is an identity tenuously constituted in time, instituted in an exterior space through a *stylized repetition of acts.* The effect of gender is produced through the stylization of the body and, hence, must be understood as the mundane way in which bodily gestures, movements, and styles of various kinds constitute the illusion of an abiding gendered self. This formulation moves the conception of gender off the ground of a substantial model of identity to one that requires a conception of gender as a constituted social *temporality.* Significantly, if gender is instituted through acts which are internally discontinuous, then the *appearance of substance* is precisely that, a constructed identity, a performative accomplishment which the mundane social audience, including the actors themselves, come to believe and to perform in the mode of belief. Gender is also a norm that can never be fully internalized; "the internal" is a surface signification, and gender norms are finally phantasmatic, impossible to embody. If the ground of gender identity is the stylized repetition of acts through time and not a seemingly seamless identity, then the spatial metaphor of a "ground" will be displaced and revealed as a stylized configuration, indeed, a gendered corporealization of time. The abiding gendered self will then be shown to be structured by repeated acts that seek to approximate the ideal of a substantial ground of identity, but which, in their occasional *dis*continuity, reveal the temporal and contingent groundlessness of this "ground." The possibilities of gender transformation are to be found precisely in the arbitrary relation between such acts, in the possibility of a failure to repeat, a de-formity, or a parodic repetition that exposes the phantasmatic effect of abiding identity as a politically tenuous construction.

If gender attributes, however, are not expressive but performative, then these attributes effectively constitute the identity they are said to express or reveal. The distinction between expression and performativeness is crucial. If gender attributes and acts, the various ways in which a body shows or produces its cultural signification, are performative, then there is no preexisting identity by which an act or attribute might be measured; there would be no true or false, real or distorted acts of gender, and the postulation of a true gender identity would be revealed as a regulatory fiction. That gender reality is created through sustained social performances means that the very notions of an essential sex and a true or abiding masculinity or femininity are also constituted as part of the strategy that conceals gender's performative character and the performative possibilities for proliferating gender configurations outside the restricting frames of masculinist domination and compulsory heterosexuality.

Genders can be neither true nor false, neither real nor apparent, neither original nor derived. As credible bearers of those attributes, however, genders can also be rendered thoroughly and radically *incredible.*

PART XI

Systems and Networks

The sociologists whose writings are considered in this part produced their theories in reference to their view of society as either a system or a network. Niklas Luhmann and Jürgen Habermas were much influenced by Talcott Parson's idea of society as being a system made of differentiated and interrelated structures. However, after this common starting point, they both depart considerably from Parsons's focus on functional differentiation to give greater consideration to system self-reference, in the case of Luhmann, and to intersubjective communication, in the case of Habermas. Immanuel Wallerstein also utilizes the basic notion of a system but augments his theory with a critical analysis of capitalism. In contrast, Manuel Castells and Bruno Latour rely on the notion of a network. While the theoretical constructs of a system and a network share several conceptual commonalities, network theory pays particular attention to relational ties and *nodes*, or converging points of information around which these ties are patterned.

According to Niklas Luhmann, a *system* refers to any entity that draws and maintains a boundary that distinguishes it from its external environment. In "Autopoietic Systems," he argues that a system is *autopoietic*—that is, it reproduces itself (self-producing), regulates itself (self-regulating), and continually refers to itself by distinguishing itself from its environment (self-referential). The distinction between system and environment points to the *relations* between information-processing *elements* that constitute the system. According to Luhmann, *complexity* occurs when every element is related to every other element. Because *social* systems are systems of meaningful *communication*, they are able to reduce complexity by selecting only a limited amount of information.

In the reading "Lifeworld and Social System," Jürgen Habermas also considers the notions of system and communication. But he makes a case for conceptualizing society simultaneously as a *social system*—an integrated, differentiated, and self-maintaining structure—and as a *lifeworld*—the everyday world involving three interrelated structural components and their processes: *culture* and its reproduction, *society* and its solidarity, and *personality* and its socialization. In the lifeworld, individuals are involved in *communicative action*, or the rational consensus of individuals arrived at through their shared interpretation of a situation in reference to the subjective, objective, and social (or intersubjective) spheres. Thus, whereas a social system is understood from the perspective of a detached external observer, a lifeworld is understood from the perspective of interpreting, interacting participants. For Habermas, the "fundamental problem of social theory" is to connect the conceptual analyses proposed by a social system (functional coordination) and a lifeworld (mutual understanding).

Immanuel Wallerstein applies the concept of social system to the global level to explain the historical development of capitalism as a world economy. As such, he introduces the notion of world system. As Wallerstein explains in "World-Systems Analysis," a *world system* is a total social system, with boundaries, structures, rules, classes, status groups, and integration. Further, the world system is an economic entity with an international division of labor. One type of world system, which contains several political structures of varying strengths and is the product of modern capitalism, is the *world-economy*. The wealthy countries of the capitalist world-economy, with strong central governments and pronounced national identities, Wallerstein calls *core-states*. In interdependent relation to core-states are the semi-peripheral and peripheral areas, each of which exist in different states of development. *Semi-peripheral areas* of the world system consist of countries that are relatively weaker, politically, economically, and militarily, and that function as buffers between the core-states and the peripheral areas. *Peripheral areas* consist of countries that are the weakest, politically, economically, and militarily. They are dependent on the core for capital and are exploited by the core for their labor and raw materials.

In "The Network Society," Manuel Castells depicts society not as a system but as a network. He popularized the concept of the *network society*, by which he means a complex social structure of communication composed of interconnected nodes. These nodes process and recombine information that enables individuals and organizations to interact anywhere, anytime. Electronic communication technologies, such as the Internet, not only eradicate space-time barriers but also give rise to new forms of social organization and interaction. Whereas societies had previously been characterized by industrialism, early 21st-century societies, says Castells, are characterized by *informationalism*. This refers to the heightened capacity of information processing made possible by communication and biological technologies. While industrialism depended on electricity for its economic productivity, informationalism depends on electronically processed information networks.

Bruno Latour uses the term *network* differently than does Castells, who treats it as an entity with a structure. For Latour, networks do not have a structure. Rather, they are a complex web of actors or *actants*; they are *actant-networks*. Networks are coherent wholes consisting of clusters of heterogeneous actants (human and nonhuman) that create meaning. Social networks, for Latour, consist of actual actors and their concrete relations. In "Actor-Network-Theory," Latour conveys the methodology of *actor-network-theory*, or ANT, in the form of a fictional dialogue between a professor and a student writing a PhD dissertation on organizations. The professor tells the inquiring student that ANT is an analytical method about how to *describe* new and changing networks. Latour regards networks as "thick" texts, which means that they provide multiple forms of information and thus *transform* all descriptions of them. Their ultimate description is based on how the social scientist *writes* about them.

83

Autopoietic Systems*

Niklas Luhmann

The theory of self-referential systems maintains that systems can differentiate only by self-reference, which is to say, only insofar as systems refer to themselves (be this to elements of the same system, to operations of the same system, or to the unity of the same system) in constituting their elements and their elemental operations. To make this possible, systems must create and employ a description of themselves; they must at least be able to use the difference between system and environment within themselves, for orientation and as a principle for creating information. Therefore self-referential closure is possible only in an environment, only, under ecological conditions. The environment is a necessary correlate of self-referential operations because these out of all operations cannot operate under the premise of solipsism (one could even say because everything that is seen as playing a role in the environment must be introduced by means of distinction). The (subsequently classical) distinction between "closed" and "open" systems is replaced by the question of how self-referential closure can create openness.

Here too one comes to a "sublation" [*Aufhebung*] of the older basic difference into a more complex theory, which now enables one to speak about the introduction of self-descriptions, self-observations, and self-simplifications within systems. One can now distinguish the system environment difference as seen from the perspective of an observer (e.g., that of a scientist) from the system/environment difference as it is used within the system itself, the observer, in turn, being conceivable himself only as a self-referential system. Reflexive relationships of this type don't just revolutionize the classical subject-object epistemology, don't just dedogmatize and "naturalize" the theory of science: they also produce a very much more complex understanding of their object via a very much more complex theory design.

In the theory of self-referential systems everything that belongs to the system (including any possible apex, boundaries, or surpluses) is included in self-production and thereby demystified for the observer. This admits developments that can make systems theory interesting for sociology in new ways.

The state of research does not allow us to begin with a report of assured results and to incorporate these results as "applied systems research" into sociology. It does enable us, however, to intensify

*Excerpts from *Social Systems* by Niklas Luhmann, Translated by John Bednarz, Jr., with Dick Baecker.

the basic concepts beyond what is common in the literature and at the same time to introduce them into a context that takes into consideration the problems that interest sociological research and the experiences it has encountered.

1. There is agreement within the discipline today that the point of departure for all systems-theoretical analysis must be the *difference between system and environment.* Systems are oriented by their environment not just occasionally and adaptively, but structurally, and they cannot exist without an environment. They constitute and maintain themselves by creating and maintaining a difference from their environment, and they use their boundaries to regulate this difference. Without difference from an environment, there would not even be self-reference, because difference is the functional premise of self-referential operations. In this sense *boundary* maintenance is system maintenance.

2. As a paradigm, the difference between system and environment forces systems theory to replace the difference between the whole and its parts with a theory of system differentiation. System differentiation is nothing more than the repetition of system formation within systems. Further system/environment differences can be differentiated within systems. The entire system then acquires the function of an "internal environment" for these subsystems, indeed, for each subsystem in its own specific way. The system /environment difference is therefore duplicated; the entire system multiplies itself as a multiplicity of system/environment differences. Every difference between subsystem and internal environment is the entire system—but only from different perspectives. Therefore system differentiation is a process of increasing complexity that greatly affects what can be observed as the unity of the entire system.

3. The switch to the difference between system and environment has profound consequences for understanding causality. The line that separates system and environment cannot be understood as isolating and combining the "most important" causes in the system. Instead, it cuts through causal connections. The question is: From what perspective? System and environment constantly collaborate, producing every effect—if only because in the domain of social systems no communication can be achieved without the consciousness of psychic systems. Therefore we must clarify why and how causality is distributed over system and environment.

Without prematurely offering criteria for such a distribution, we can at least formulate the problem more precisely and connect it to other aspects of systems theory. We can do this via the concept of *production* (and its derivatives: reproduction, self-reproduction, and autopoiesis). We will speak of production if *some* but *not all* causes that are necessary for specific effects can be employed under the control of a system.

4. The difference between system and environment must be distinguished from a second, equally constitutive difference: namely, the difference between element and relation. Here, as previously, we must conceive the unity of the difference as constitutive. Just as there are no systems without environments or environments without systems, there are no elements without relational connections or relations without elements. Therefore there are two different possibilities for viewing the decomposition of a system. One aims to form subsystems (or, more precisely, internal system/environment relations) within the system. The other decomposes systems into elements and relations. In the former, rooms compose a house; in the latter, cinderblocks, beams, nails, and so forth do. The first kind of decomposition is carried out as a theory of system differentiation. The other ends up in a theory of system complexity. Only this distinction makes it meaningful and nontautological to say that system complexity increases with an increase in differentiation or with a change in the form of differentiation.

5. Out of the relation among elements emerges the centrally important systems-theoretical concept of *conditioning.* Systems are not merely relations (in the plural!) among elements. The connections among relations must also somehow be regulated. This regulation employs the basic form of conditioning. That is to say, a determinate relation among elements is realized only under the condition that something else is or is not the case. Whenever we speak of "conditions" or "conditions of possibility" (in the epistemological sense), this is what we mean.

6. Next, we would like to introduce the problem of *complexity* and then resume the analysis of system/environment relations together with

the enrichments that result from considering this concept.

If one starts out from this basic conceptual (but systems-related) difference between element and relation, then one immediately sees that, when the number of elements that must be held together *in a system or for a system as its environment* increases, one very quickly encounters a threshold where it is no longer possible to relate every element to every other one. A definition of complexity follows from this: we will call an interconnected collection of elements "complex" when, because of immanent constraints in the elements' connective capacity, it is no longer possible at any moment to connect every element with every other element. The concept of "immanent constraint" refers to the internal complexity of the elements, which is not at the system's disposal, yet which makes possible their "capacity for unity." In this respect, complexity is a self-conditioning state of affairs: the fact that elements must already be constituted as complex in order to function as a unity for higher levels of system formation limits their connective capacity and thus reproduces complexity as an unavoidable condition on every higher level of system formation. Leaping ahead, we may hint at the fact that this self-reference of complexity is then "internalized" as the self-reference of systems.

One must distinguish the incomprehensible complexity in a system (or its environment) that would result if one connected everything with everything else, from determinately structured complexity, which can only be selected contingently. And one must distinguish environmental complexity (in both forms) from system complexity (again in both forms); the system complexity is always lesser and must compensate by exploiting its contingency, that is, by its pattern of selections. In both cases the *difference* between two complexities is the real principle compelling (and therefore giving form to) selection; and if one does not speak of states, but rather of operations, then both cases are the *reduction of complexity*, namely, the reduction of one complexity by another.

From the viewpoint of this necessity for reduction (which follows from complexity), a second concept of complexity has been developed. In this second sense, complexity is a measure for indeterminacy or lack of information. Viewed in this way, it is the information that the system lacks fully to grasp and to describe its environment (environmental complexity) or itself (system complexity). From the perspective of individual elements—for example, specific actions or information processing by systems—complexity is relevant only in this second sense, thus only as a horizon within which selections are made. And this second version can be used in meaning systems to re-introduce the system's complexity within the system: as a concept, as an unknown and therefore effective quantity, as a factor of anxiety, as the concept of uncertainty or risk, as problems of planning and decision, or as an excuse. The distinction between both concepts of complexity points to the fact that systems cannot grasp their own complexity (even less that of their environment) and yet can problematize it. The system produces and reacts to an unclear picture of itself.

7. This amalgamation of the problematic of complexity and systems analysis is confirmed by a more precise interpretation of the function of system boundaries. Systems have boundaries. This is what distinguishes the concept of system from that of structure. Boundaries cannot be conceived without something "beyond"; thus they presuppose the reality of a beyond and the possibility of transcendence. In common understanding, they have the double function of separating and connecting system and environment. This double function can be clarified by means of the distinction between element and relation, a clarification that at the same time returns us to the thematic of complexity. As soon as boundaries are defined sharply, elements must be attributed either to the system or to the environment. Yet relations between system and environment can exist. Thus a boundary separates elements, but not necessarily relations. It separates events, but lets causal effects pass through.

This long-established and indisputable concept of boundary is the prerequisite for newer developments in systems theory, which no longer interpret the distinction between open and closed systems as an opposition of types but rather regard it as a relationship of intensification. Using boundaries, systems can open and close at the same time, separating internal interdependencies from system/environment interdependencies and relating both to each other.

8. The conceptual distinction between (the concept of) system and (the concept of) complexity is central to the following analyses, because they concern complex systems.

Complex systems must adapt not only to their environments but also to their own complexity. They must cope with internal improbabilities and inadequacies. They must develop mechanisms that build precisely on those failings, such as mechanisms that reduce deviant behavior, behavior that becomes possible only when there are dominant basic structures. Complex systems are forced to adapt to themselves, in the double sense of adapting to their own complexity. This is the only way to explain why systems cannot seamlessly follow the changes in their environments, but rather must make allowances for different adaptive viewpoints and ultimately collapse because of self-adaptation.

The concept of *selection* also changes when one considers complex systems. Selection can no longer be conceived as carried out by a subject, as analogous with action. It is a subjectless event, an operation that is triggered by establishing a difference. Difference does not determine what must be selected, only that a selection must be made. Above all, the system/environment difference seems to be what obliges the system to force itself, through its own complexity, to make selections. Thus the theory of self-referential systems has been prepared for in the semantic range of "adaptation" as well as in that of "selection."

9. The next central theme to be addressed is *self-reference*. It has attracted rapidly growing attention in the most recent systems research, where it has also gone under the names self-organization and autopoiesis.

One can call a system self-referential if it itself constitutes the elements that compose it as functional unities and runs reference to this self-constitution through all the relations among these elements, continuously reproducing its self-constitution in this way.

Autopoiesis does not necessarily presuppose that the environment of a system is completely devoid of the types of operations by which the system reproduces itself. In the environments of living organisms there are other living organisms, in the environments of consciousnesses, other consciousnesses. But in both cases the system's own process of reproduction can be used only internally. One cannot use it to knit together system and environment, to tap another life or another consciousness and transfer it into one's own system. (Organ transplants are a mechanical intervention and not a case that we exclude here, namely, one in which life procures life, as life, for itself.) With social systems, this situation differs in two ways. On the one hand, there is no communication outside the communication system of society. This system is the only one employing this type of operation, and to that extent it is, as a matter of fact, necessarily closed. On the other, this does not hold for all other social systems. They must define their specific mode of operation or determine their identity by reflection to be able to regulate which internal meaning-units enable the self-reproduction of the system and thus are repeatedly to be reproduced.

10. Self-reference presupposes a principle that one could call multiple constitution. We will treat this idea in more detail from the perspective of "double contingency."

In other words, the system contains, as complexity, a surplus of possibilities, which it self-selectively reduces. This reduction is carried out through communicative processes, and therefore the system needs a "mutualistic" basic organization—that is, attribution of its elements to complexes that are capable of communication.

11. One of the most important consequences of the transition to a theory of self-referential systems concerns the operative level, or system processes. On the level of elements, self-reference means that these connect up by referring back to one another and that interconnections or processes thereby become possible. But this can occur only if the types of element are sufficiently similar. Therefore, to cite an extreme case, no system unity can exist between mechanical and conscious operations, between chemical operations and those that communicate meaning.

Thus autopoietic reproduction depends on an adequate homogeneity of system operations, and these define the unity of a determinate type of system. Of course, one can comprehend and observe things from other perspectives; but one cannot observe self-referential system constitution if one does not hold to the type of process and system thus given.

12. From self-referential system relationships, an immense extension of the boundaries of structural adaptability and of the corresponding scope of system-internal communication can be induced. The principle of this extension can best be conceived by starting with the concept of information. Information occurs whenever a selective event (of an external or internal kind) works selectively within the system, namely, can select the system's states.

The system can perceive impulses from without as information—which is to say, as the experience of difference—and can in this way bring about an effect. Such systems, which procure causality for themselves, can no longer be "causally explained" (except in the reductive schema of an observer), not because their complexity is impenetrable, but on logical grounds. They presuppose themselves as the production of their self-production.

84

Lifeworld and Social System*

Jürgen Habermas

This distinction between a *social integration* of society, which takes effect in action orientations, and a *systemic integration,* which reaches through and beyond action orientations, calls for a corresponding differentiation in the concept of society itself. No matter whether one starts with Mead from basic concepts of social interaction or with Durkheim from basic concepts of collective representation, in either case society is conceived from the perspective of acting subjects as the *lifeworld of a social group.* In contrast, from the observer's perspective of someone not involved, society can be conceived only as a *system of actions* such that each action has a functional significance according to its contribution to the maintenance of the system.

One can join the system concept of society with the life world concept, as Mead did. He related the natural or objective meanings that the biologist ascribes to the *behavior of an organism* in the system of its species-specific environment to the semanticized meanings of the corresponding *actions* as these become accessible to the actor himself within his lifeworld. As we have seen, Mead reconstructs the emergence of the sociocultural world as the transition to a stage, first, of symbolically mediated interaction and, then, of linguistically mediated interaction. In the process, natural meanings resulting from the significance of specific items in the functional circuit of animal behavior are transformed into symbolic meanings at the intentional disposition of participants in interactions. The object domain is changed by this process of semanticization, so that the ethological model of a self-regulating system, according to which every event or state is ascribed a meaning on the basis of its functional significance, is gradually replaced by the communication-theoretic model, according to which actors orient their actions by their own interpretations. Of course, this latter model of the life world would be *adequate* for human societies only if that process of semanticization absorbed *all* "natural" meanings—that is, if *all* systemic interconnections in which interactions stand were brought into the horizon of the lifeworld and thereby into the intuitive knowledge of participants. This is a bold assumption, but it is an empirical matter that should not be *pre*decided at an analytical level by a conception of society set out in action-theoretical terms.

Every theory of society that is restricted to communication theory is subject to limitations that must be observed. The concept of the

*Excerpts from *Theory of Communicative Action, Vol 2, LIfeworld and System: A Critique of Functionalist Reason* by Jurgen Habermas, translated by Thomas McCarthy.

life-world that emerges from the conceptual perspective of communicative action has only limited analytical and empirical range. I would therefore like to propose (1) that we conceive of societies *simultaneously* and lifeworlds. This concept proves itself in (2) a theory of social evolution that separates the rationalization of the lifeworld from the growing complexity of societal systems so as to make the connection Durkheim envisaged between forms of social integration and stages of system differentiation tangible, that is, susceptible to empirical analysis.

I should like to begin by (*A*) making clear how the lifeworld is related to those three worlds on which subjects acting with an orientation to mutual understanding base their common definitions of situations, (*B*) I will then elaborate upon the concept of the lifeworld present as a context in communicative action and relate it to Durkheim's concept of the collective consciousness. Certainly it is not a concept that can be put to empirical use without further ado. (*C*) The concepts of the lifeworld normally employed in interpretive [*versteben-den*] sociology are linked with everyday concepts that are, to begin with, serviceable only for the narrative presentation of historical events and social circumstances. (*D*) An investigation of the functions that communicative action takes on in maintaining a structurally differentiated world originates from within this horizon. In connection with these functions, we can clarify the necessary conditions for a rationalization of the lifeworld. (*E*) This takes us to the limit of theoretical approaches that identify society with the lifeworld. I shall therefore propose that we conceive of society simultaneously as a system and as a lifeworld.

A.—In examining the ontological presuppositions of teleological, normatively regulated, and dramaturgical action, I distinguished three different actor-world relations that a subject can take up to something in a world—to something that either obtains or can be brought about in the one objective world, to something recognized as obligatory in the social world supposedly shared by all the members of a collective, or to something that other actors attribute to the speaker's own subjective world (to which he has privileged access). These actor-world relations turn up again in the pure types of action oriented to mutual understanding. By attending to the modes of language use, we can clarify what it means for a speaker, in performing one of the standard speech acts, to take up a pragmatic relation

- to something in the objective world (as the totality of entities about which true statements are possible); or
- to something in the social world (as the totality of legitimately regulated interpersonal relations); or
- to something in the subjective world (as the totality of experience to which a speaker has privileged access and which he can express before a public);

such that what the speech act refers to appears to the speaker as something objective, normative, or subjective. In introducing the concept of communicative action, I pointed out that the pure types of action oriented to mutual understanding are merely limit cases. In fact, communicative utterances are always embedded in various world relations at the same time. Communicative action relies on a cooperative process of interpretation in which participants relate simultaneously to something in the objective, the social, and the subjective worlds, even when they *the matically stress only one* of the three components in their utterances. Speaker and hearer use the reference system of the three worlds as an interpretive framework within which they work out their common situation definitions.

B.—Up to now we have conceived of action in terms of dealing with situations. The concept of communicative action singles out above all two aspects of this situation management: the *teleological aspect* of realizing one's aims (or carrying out one's plan of action) and the *communicative aspect* of interpreting a situation and arriving at some agreement. In communicative action participants pursue their plans cooperatively on the basis of a shared definition of the situation. If a shared definition of the situation has first to be negotiated, or if efforts to come to some agreement within the framework of shared situation definitions fail, the attainment of consensus, which is normally a condition for pursuing goals, can itself become an end. In any case, the *success* achieved by teleological action and the *consensus* brought about by acts of reaching understanding are the criteria for whether a situation has been dealt with successfully or not.

A *situation* represents a segment of the lifeworld delimited in relation to a theme.

If we understand lifeworld analysis as an attempt to describe reconstructively, from the internal perspective of members, what Durkheim called the *conscience collective*, then the standpoint from which he viewed the structural transformation of collective consciousness could also prove to be instructive for a phenomenological investigation. We could then understand the differentiation processes he observed as follows: the lifeworld loses its prejudgmental power over everyday communicative practice to the degree that actors owe their mutual understanding to *their own* interpretative performances. Durkheim understands the process of the differentiation of the lifeworld as a separation of culture, society, and personality. We now have to introduce and explain these as structural components of the lifeworld.

C.—The *everyday concept of the lifeworld*; it is by this means that communicative actors locate and date their utterances in social spaces and historical times. In the communicative practice of everyday life, persons do not only encounter one another in the attitude of participants; they also give narrative presentations of events that take place in the context of their lifeworld. *Narration* is a specialized form of constative speech that serves to describe sociocultural events and objects. Actors base their narrative presentations on a lay concept of the "world," in the sense of the everyday world or lifeworld, which defines the totality of states of affairs that can be reported in true stories.

Under the functional aspect of *mutual understanding*, communicative action serves to transmit and renew cultural knowledge; under the aspect of *coordinating action*, it serves social integration and the establishment of solidarity; finally under the aspect of *socialization*, communicative action serves the formation of personal identities. The symbolic structures of the lifeworld are reproduced by way of the continuation of valid knowledge, stabilization of group solidarity, and socialization of responsible actors. The process of reproduction connects up new situations with the existing conditions of the lifeworld; it does this in the *semantic* dimension of meanings or contents (of the cultural tradition), as well as in the dimensions of *social space* (of socially integrated groups), and *historical time* (of successive generations). Corresponding to these processes of *cultural reproduction*, *social integration*, and *socialization* are the structural components of the lifeworld: culture, society, person.

I use the term *culture* for the stock of knowledge from which participants in communication supply themselves with interpretations as they come to an understanding about something in the world. I use the term *society* for the legitimate orders through which participants regulate their memberships in social groups and thereby secure solidarity. By *personality* I understand the competences that make a subject capable of speaking and acting, that put him in a position to take part in processes of reaching understanding and thereby to assert his own identity. The dimensions in which communicative action extends comprise the semantic field of symbolic contents, social space, and historical time. The interactions woven into the fabric of every communicative practice constitute the medium through which culture, society, and person get reproduced. These reproduction processes cover the symbolic structures of the lifeworld. We have to distinguish from this the maintenance of the material substratum of the lifeworld.

D.—Once one has drawn these distinctions, a question arises concerning the contribution of the individual reproduction processes to maintaining the structural components of the lifeworld. If culture provides sufficient valid knowledge to cover the given need for mutual understanding in a lifeworld, the contributions of cultural reproduction to maintaining *the two other* components consist, on the one hand, in *legitimations* for existing institutions and, on the other hand, in *socialization patterns* for the acquisition of generalized competences for action. If society is sufficiently integrated to cover the given need for coordination in a lifeworld, the contribution of the integration process to maintaining the *two other* components consist, on the one hand, in *legitimately regulated social memberships* of individuals and, on the other, in moral duties or *obligations:* the central stock of cultural values institutionalized in legitimate orders is incorporated into a normative reality that is, if not criticism-proof, at least resistant to criticism and to this extent beyond the reach of continuous testing by action oriented to reaching understanding. If, finally personality systems have developed such strong identities that they can deal on a realistic basis with the situations that come up in their lifeworld, the contribution of socialization processes to maintaining *the other two* components consists, on the one hand, in *interpretive accomplishments* and, on the other, in *motivations for actions that conform to norms* (see Figure 1).

We can now reformulate this idea as follows: the further the structural components of the lifeworld and the processes that contribute to maintaining them get differentiated, the more interaction contexts come under conditions of rationally motivated mutual understanding, that is of consensus formation that rests *in the end* on the authority of the better argument.

My guiding idea is that, on the one hand, the dynamics of development are steered by imperatives issuing from problems of self-maintenance, that is, problems of materially reproducing the lifeworld; but that, on the other hand, this societal development draws upon structural *possibilities* and is subject to structural *limitations* that, with the rationalization of the lifeworld, undergo systematic change in dependence upon corresponding learning processes. Thus the systems-theoretical perspective is relativized by the fact that the rationalization of the lifeworld leads to a directional variation of the structural patterns defining the maintenance of the system.

E.—If we understand the integration of society exclusively as *social integration*, we are opting for a conceptual strategy that, as we have seen, starts from communicative action and construes society as a lifeworld. It ties social-scientific analysis to the internal perspective of members of social groups and commits the investigator to hermeneutically connect up his own understanding with that of the participants. The reproduction of society then appears to be the maintenance of the symbolic structures of the lifeworld. Problems of material reproduction are not simply filtered out of this perspective; maintenance of the

FIGURE 1 Contributions of Reproductive Process to Maintaining the Structural Components of the Lifeworld

Structural Components / Reproduction Processes	Culture	Society	Personality
Cultural Reproduction	Interpretive Schemes Fit for Consensus (“Valid Knowledge”)	Legitimations	Socialization Patterns Educational Goals
Social Integration	Obligations	Legitimately Ordered Interpersonal Relations	Social Memberships
Socialization	Interpretive Accomplishments	Motivations for Actions that Conform to Norms	Interactive Capabilities (“Personal Identity”)

material substratum of the lifeworld is a necessary condition for maintaining its symbolic structures. But processes of material reproduction come into view only from the perspective of acting subjects who are dealing with situations in a goal-directed manner; what gets filtered out are all the counterintuitive aspects of the nexus of societal reproduction. This limitation suggests an immanent critique of the hermeneutic idealism of interpretive sociology.

If, on the other hand, we understand the integration of society exclusively as *system integration*, we are opting for a conceptual strategy that presents society after the model of a self regulating system. It ties social-scientific analysis to the external perspective of an observer and poses the problem of interpreting the concept of a system in such a way that it can be applied to interconnections of action. We shall examine the foundations of social scientific systems research; for now I want only to note that action systems are considered to be a special case of living systems. Living systems are understood as open systems, which maintain themselves vis-à-vis an unstable and hypercomplex environment through interchange processes across their boundaries. States of the system are viewed as fulfilling functions with respect to its maintenance.

However, the conceptualization of societies cannot be so smoothly linked with that of organic systems, for, unlike structural patterns in biology, the structural patterns of action systems are not accessible to [purely external] observation; they have to be gotten at hermeneutically that is, from the internal perspective of participants. The entities that are to be subsumed under systems-theoretical concepts from the external perspective of an observer must be identified beforehand as the lifeworlds of social groups and understood in their symbolic structures. The inner logic of the symbolic reproduction of the lifeworld, which we discussed from the standpoints of cultural reproduction, social integration, and socialization, results in *internal limitations* on the reproduction of the societies we view from the outside as boundary-maintaining systems. Because they are structures of a lifeworld, the structures important for the maintenance of a [social] system, those with which the identity of a society stands or falls, are accessible only to a reconstructive analysis that begins with the members' intuitive knowledge.

The fundamental problem of social theory is how to connect in a satisfactory way the two conceptual strategies indicated by the notions of 'system' and 'lifeworld'.

85

WORLD-SYSTEMS ANALYSIS*

IMMANUEL WALLERSTEIN

In order to describe the origins and initial workings of a world system, I have had to argue a certain conception of a world-system. A world-system is a social system, one that has boundaries, structures, member groups, rules of legitimation, and coherence. Its life is made up of the conflicting forces which hold it together by tension and tear it apart as each group seeks eternally to remold it to its advantage. It has the characteristics of an organism, in that it has a life-span over which its characteristics change in some respects and remain stable in others. One can define its structures as being at different times strong or weak in terms of the internal logic of its functioning.

What characterizes a social system in my view is the fact that life within it is largely self-contained, and that the dynamics of its development are largely internal. The reader may feel that the use of the term "largely" is a case of academic weaseling. I admit I cannot quantify it. Probably no one ever will be able to do so, as the definition is based on a counterfactual hypothesis: If the system, for any reason, were to be cut off from all external forces (which virtually never happens), the definition implies that the system would continue to function substantially in the same manner. Again, of course, substantially is difficult to convert into hard operational criteria. Nonetheless the point is an important one and key to many parts of empirical analyses. Perhaps we should think of self-containment as a theoretical absolute, a sort of social vacuum, rarely visible and even more implausible to create artificially, but still and all a socially-real asymptote, the distance from which is somehow measurable.

Using such a criterion, it is contended here that most entities usually described as social systems—"tribes," communities, nation-states—are not in fact total systems. Indeed, on the contrary, we are arguing that the only real social systems are, on the one hand, those relatively small, highly autonomous subsistence economies not part of some regular tribute-demanding system and, on the other hand, world-systems. These latter are to be sure distinguished from the former because they are relatively large; that is, they are in common parlance "worlds." More precisely, however, they are defined by the fact that their self-containment as an economic-material entity is based on extensive division of labor and that they contain within them a multiplicity of cultures.

It is further argued that thus far there have only existed two varieties of such world-systems:

---

*Excerpts from *The Modern World-System I: Capitalist Agriculture and the Origins of the European World-Economy in the Sixteenth Century* by Immanuel Wallerstein.

world-empires, in which there is a single political system over most of the area, however attenuated the degree of its effective control; and those systems in which such a single political system does not exist over all, or virtually all, of the space. For convenience and for want of a better term, we are using the term "world-economy," to describe the latter.

Finally, we have argued that prior to the modern era, world-economies were highly unstable structures which tended either to be converted into empires or to disintegrate. It is the peculiarity of the modern world-system that a world-economy has survived for 500 years and yet has not come to be transformed into a world-empire—a peculiarity that is the secret of its strength.

This peculiarity is the political side of the form of economic organization called capitalism. Capitalism has been able to flourish precisely because the world-economy has had within its bounds not one but a multiplicity of political systems.

I am not here arguing the classic case of capitalist ideology that capitalism is a system based on the noninterference of the state in economic affairs. Quite the contrary! Capitalism is based on the constant absorption of economic loss by political entities, while economic gain is distributed to "private" hands. What I am arguing rather is that capitalism as an economic mode is based on the fact that the economic factors operate within an arena larger than that which any political entity can totally control. This gives capitalists a freedom of maneuver that is structurally based. It has made possible the constant economic expansion of the world-system, albeit a very skewed distribution of its rewards. The only alternative world-system that could maintain a high level of productivity and change the system of distribution would involve the reintegration of the levels of political and economic decision-making. This would constitute a third possible form of world-system, a socialist world government. This is not a form that presently exists, and it was not even remotely conceivable in the sixteenth century.

The historical reasons why the European world-economy came into existence in the sixteenth century and resisted attempts to transform it into an empire have been expounded at length. We shall not review them here. It should however be noted that the size of a world-economy is a function of the state of technology, and in particular of the possibilities of transport and communication within its bounds. Since this is a constantly changing phenomenon, not always for the better, the boundaries of a world-economy are ever fluid.

We have defined a world-system as one in which there is extensive division of labor. This division is not merely functional—that is, occupational—but geographical. That is to say, the range of economic tasks is not evenly distributed throughout the world-system. In part this is the consequence of ecological considerations, to be sure. But for the most part, it is a function of the social organization of work, one which magnifies and legitimizes the ability of some groups within the system to exploit the labor of others, that is, to receive a larger share of the surplus.

While, in an empire, the political structure tends to link culture with occupation, in a world-economy the political structure tends to link culture with spatial location. The reason is that in a world-economy the first point of political pressure available to groups is the local (national) state structure. Cultural homogenization tends to serve the interests of key groups and the pressures build up to create cultural-national identities.

This is particularly the case in the advantaged areas of the world-economy—what we have called the core-states. In such states, the creation of a strong state machinery coupled with a national culture, a phenomenon often referred to as integration, serves both as a mechanism to protect disparities that have arisen within the world-system, and as an ideological mask and justification for the maintenance of these disparities.

World-economies then are divided into core-states and peripheral areas. I do not say peripheral *states* because one characteristic of a peripheral area is that the indigenous state is weak, ranging from its nonexistence (that is, a colonial situation) to one with a low degree of autonomy (that is, a neo-colonial situation).

There are also semiperipheral areas which are in between the core and the periphery on a series of dimensions, such as the complexity of economic activities, strength of the state machinery, cultural integrity, etc. Some of these areas had been core-areas of earlier versions of a given world-economy. Some had been peripheral areas that were later promoted, so to speak, as a result of the changing geopolitics of an expanding world-economy.

The semiperiphery, however, is not an artifice of statistical cutting points, nor is it a residual category. The semiperiphery is a necessary structural element in a world-economy. These areas play a role parallel to that played, *mutatis mutandis,* by middle trading groups in an empire. They are collection points of vital skills that are often poetically unpopular. These middle areas (like middle groups in an empire) partially deflect the political pressures which groups primarily located in peripheral areas might otherwise direct against core-states and the groups which operate within and through their state machineries. On the other hand, the interests primarily located in the semiperiphery are located outside the political arena of the core-states, and find it difficult to pursue the ends in political coalitions that might be open to them were they in the same political arena.

The division of a world-economy involves a hierarchy of occupational tasks, in which tasks requiring higher levels of skill and greater capitalization are reserved for higher-ranking areas. Since a capitalist world-economy essentially rewards accumulated capital, including human capital, at a higher rate than "raw" labor power, the geographical maldistribution of these occupational skills involves a strong trend toward self-maintenance. The forces of the marketplace reinforce them rather than undermine them. And the absence of a central political mechanism for the world-economy makes it very difficult to intrude counteracting forces to the maldistribution of rewards.

Hence, the ongoing process of a world-economy tends to expand the economic and social gaps among its varying areas in the very process of its development. One factor that tends to mask this fact is that the process of development of a world-economy brings about technological advances which make it possible to expand the boundaries of a world-economy. In this case, particular regions of the world may change their structural role in the world-economy, to their advantage, even though the disparity of reward between different sectors of the world-economy as a whole may be simultaneously widening. It is in order to observe this crucial phenomenon clearly that we have insisted on the distinction between a peripheral area of a given world-economy and the external arena of the world-economy. The external arena of one century often becomes the periphery of the next—or its semiperiphery. But then too core-states can become semiperipheral and semiperipheral ones peripheral.

While the advantages of the core-states have not ceased to expand throughout the history of the modern world-system, the ability of a particular state to remain in the core sector is not beyond challenge. The hounds are ever to the hares for the position of top dog. Indeed, it may well be that in this kind of system it is not structurally possible to avoid, over a long period of historical time, a circulation of the elites in the sense that the particular country that is dominant at a given time tends to be replaced in this role sooner or later by another country.

We have insisted that the modern world-economy is, and only can be, a capitalist world-economy. It is for this reason that we have rejected the appellation of "feudalism" for the various forms of capitalist agriculture based on coerced labor which grow up in a world-economy. Furthermore, although this has not been discussed, it is for this same reason that we will regard with great circumspection and prudence the claim that there exist in the twentieth century socialist national economies within the framework of the world-economy (as opposed to socialist movements controlling certain state-machineries within the world-economy).

If world-systems are the only real social systems (other than truly isolated subsistence economies), then it must follow that the emergence, consolidation, and political roles of classes and status groups must be appreciated as elements of this *world*-system. And in turn it follows that one of the key elements in analyzing a class or a status-group is not only the state of its self-consciousness but the geographical scope of its self-definition.

Classes always exist potentially *(an sich)*. The issue is under what conditions they become class-conscious *(für sich)*, that is, operate as a group in the politico-economic arenas and even to some extent as a cultural entity. Such self-consciousness is a function of conflict situations. But for upper strata open conflict, and hence overt consciousness, is always *faute de mieux*. To the extent that class boundaries are not made explicit, to that extent it is more likely that privileges be maintained.

Since in conflict situations, multiple factions tend to reduce to two by virtue of the forging of alliances, it is by definition not possible to have three or more (conscious) classes. There obviously can be a multitude of occupational interest groups which may organize themselves to operate within the social structure. But such groups are really one variety of status-groups, and indeed often overlap heavily with other kinds of status-groups such as those defined by ethnic, linguistic, or religious criteria.

To say that there cannot be three or more classes is not however to say that there are always two. There may be none, though this is rare and transitional. There may be one, and this is most common. There may be two, and this is most explosive.

We say there may be only one class, although we have also said that classes only actually exist in conflict situations, and conflicts presume two sides. There is no contradiction here. For a conflict may be defined as being between one class, which conceives of itself as the universal class, and all the other strata. This has in fact been the usual situation in the modern world-system. The capitalist class (the *bourgeoisie*) has claimed to be the universal class and sought to organize political life to pursue its objectives against two opponents. On the one hand, there were those who spoke for the maintenance of traditional rank distinctions despite the fact that these ranks might have lost their original correlation with economic function. Such elements preferred to define the social structure as a non-class structure. It was to counter this ideology that the bourgeoisie came to operate as a class conscious of itself.

The European world-economy of the sixteenth century tended overall to be a one-class system. It was the dynamic forces profiting from economic expansion and the capitalist system, especially those in the core-areas, who tended to be class-conscious, that is to operate within the political arena as a group defined primarily by their common role in the economy. This common role was in fact defined somewhat broadly from a twentieth-century perspective. It included persons who were farmers, merchants, and industrialists. Individual entrepreneurs often moved back arid forth between these activities in any case, or combined them. The crucial distinction was between these men, whatever their occupation, principally oriented to obtaining profit in the world market, and the others not so oriented.

The "others" fought back in terms of their status privileges—those of the traditional aristocracy, those which small farmers had derived from the feudal system, those resulting from guild monopolies that were outmoded. Under the cover of cultural similarities, one can often weld strange alliances. Those strange alliances can take a very activist form and force the political centers to take account of them. Or they can take a politically passive form that serves well the needs of the dominant forces in the world-system. The triumph of Polish Catholicism as a cultural force was a case in point.

The details of the canvas are filled in with the panoply of multiple forms of status-groups, their particular strengths and accents. But the grand sweep is in terms of the process of class formation. And in this regard, the sixteenth century was indecisive. The capitalist strata formed a class that survived and gained *droit de cité*, but did not yet triumph in the political arena.

The evolution of the state machineries reflected precisely this uncertainty. Strong states serve the interests of some groups and hurt those of others. From however the standpoint of the world-system as a whole, if there is to be a multitude of political entities (that is, if the system is not a world-empire), then it cannot he the case that all these entities be equally strong. For if they were, they would he in the position of blocking the effective operation of transnational economic entities whose locus were in another state. It would then follow that the world division of labor would be impeded, the world-economy decline and eventually the world-system fall apart.

It also cannot be that, *no* state machinery is strong. For in such a case the capitalist strata would have no mechanisms to protect their interests, guaranteeing their properly rights, assuring various monopolies, spreading losses among the larger population, etc.

It follows then that the world-economy develops a pattern where state structures are relatively strong in the core areas and relatively weak in the periphery. Which areas play which roles is in many ways accidental. What is necessary is that in some areas the state machinery be far stronger than in others.

What do we mean by a strong state machinery? We mean strength vis-à-vis other states within the world-economy including other core-states, and strong vis-à-vis local political units within the boundaries of the state. In effect, we mean a sovereignty that is *de facto* as well as *de jure*. We also mean a state that is strong vis-à-vis any particular social group within the state. Obviously, such groups vary in the amount of pressure they can bring to bear upon the state. And obviously certain combinations of these groups control the state. It is not that the state is a neutral arbiter. But the state is more than a simple vector of given forces, if only because many of these forces are situated in more than one state or are defined in terms that have little correlation with state boundaries.

A strong state then is a partially autonomous entity in the sense that it has a margin of action available to it wherein it reflects the compromises of multiple interests, even if the bounds of these margins are set by the existence of some groups of primordial strength. To be a partially autonomous entity, there must be a group of people whose direct interests are served by such an entity: state managers and a state bureaucracy.

Such groups emerge within the framework of a capitalist world-economy because a strong state is the best choice between difficult alternatives for the two groups that are strongest in political, economic, and military terms: the emergent capitalist strata, and the old aristocratic hierarchies.

For the former, the strong state in the form of the "absolute monarchies" was a prime customer, a guardian against local and international brigandage, a mode of social legitimation, a preemptive protection against the creation of strong state barriers elsewhere. For the latter, the strong state represented a brake on these same capitalist strata, an upholder of status conventions, a maintainer of order, a promoter of luxury.

No doubt both nobles and bourgeois found the state machineries to be a burdensome drain of funds, and a meddlesome unproductive bureaucracy. But what options did they have? Nonetheless they were always restive and the immediate politics of the world-system was made up of the pushes and pulls resulting from the efforts of both groups to insulate themselves from what seemed to them the negative effects of the state machinery.

A state machinery involves a tipping mechanism. There is a point where strength creates more strength. The tax revenue enables the state to have a larger and more efficient civil bureaucracy and army which in turn leads to greater tax revenue—a process that continues in spiral form. The tipping mechanism works in other direction too—weakness leading to greater weakness. In between these two tipping points lies the politics of state-creation. It is in this arena that the skills of particular managerial groups make a difference. And it is because of the two tipping mechanisms that at certain points a small gap in the world-system can very rapidly become a larger one.

In those states in which the state machinery is weak, the state managers do not play the role of coordinating a complex industrial–commercial–agricultural mechanism. Rather they simply become one set of landlords amidst others, with little claim to legitimate authority over the whole.

These tend to be called traditional rulers. The political struggle is often phrased in terms of tradition versus change. This is of course a grossly misleading and ideological terminology. It may in fact be taken as a general sociological principle that, at any given point of time, what is thought to be traditional is of more recent origin than people generally imagine it to be, and represents primarily the conservative instincts of some group threatened with declining social status. Indeed, there seems to be nothing which emerges and evolves as quickly as a "tradition" when the need presents itself.

In a one-class system, the "traditional" is that in the name of which the "others" fight the class-conscious group. If they can encrust their values by legitimating them widely, even better by enacting them into legislative barriers, they thereby change the system in a way favorable to them.

The traditionalists may win in some states, but if a world-economy is to survive, they must lose more or less in the others. Furthermore, the gain in one region is the counterpart of the loss in another.

This is not quite a zero-sum game, but it is also inconceivable that all elements in a capitalist world-economy shift their values in a given direction simultaneously. The social system is built on having a multiplicity of value systems within it, reflecting the specific functions groups and areas play in the world division of labor.

We have not exhausted here the theoretical problems relevant to the functioning of a world-economy. We have tried only to speak to those illustrated by the early period of the world-economy in creation, to wit, sixteenth-century Europe. Many other problems emerged at later stages.

In the sixteenth century, Europe was like a bucking bronco. The attempt of some groups to establish a world-economy based on a particular division of labor, to create national states in the core areas as politico-economic guarantors of this system, and to get the workers to pay not only the profits but the costs of maintaining the system was not easy. It was to Europe's credit that it was done, since without the thrust of the sixteenth century the modern world would not have been born and, for all its cruelties, it is better that it was born than that it had not been.

It is also to Europe's credit that it was not easy, and particularly that it was not easy because the people who paid the short-run costs screamed lustily at the unfairness of it all. The peasants and workers in Poland and England and Brazil and Mexico were all rambunctious in their various ways. As R. H. Tawney says of the agrarian disturbances of sixteenth-century England: "Such movements are a proof of blood and sinew and of a high and gallant spirit. . . . Happy the nation whose people has not forgotten how to rebel."

The mark of the modern world is the imagination of its profiteers and the counter-assertiveness of the oppressed. Exploitation and the refusal to accept exploitation as either inevitable or just constitute the continuing antinomy of the modern era, joined together in a dialectic which was far from reached its climax in the twentieth century.

86

The Network Society*

Manuel Castells

A network society is a society whose social structure is made of networks powered by microelectronics-based information and communication technologies. By social structure, I understand the organizational arrangements of humans in relations of production, consumption, reproduction, experience, and power expressed in meaningful communication coded by culture. A network is a set of interconnected nodes. A node is the point where the curve intersects itself. A network has no center, just nodes. Nodes may be of varying relevance for the network. Nodes increase their importance for the network by absorbing more relevant information, and processing it more efficiently. The relative importance of a node does not stem from its specific features but from its ability to contribute to the network's goals. However, all nodes of a network are necessary for the network's performance. When nodes become redundant or useless, networks tend to reconfigure themselves, deleting some nodes, and adding new ones. Nodes only exist and function as components of networks. The network is the unit, not the node.

"Communication networks are the patterns of contact that are created by flows of messages among communicators through time and space". So, networks process flows. Flows are streams of information between nodes circulating through the channels of connection between nodes. A network is defined by the program that assigns the network its goals and its rules of performance. This program is made up of codes that include valuation of performance and criteria for success or failure. To alter the outcomes of the network, a new program (a set of compatible codes) will have to be installed in the network—from outside the network. Networks cooperate or compete with each other. Cooperation is based on the ability to communicate between networks. This ability depends on the existence of codes of translation and inter-operability between the networks (protocols of communication), and on access to connection points (switches). Competition depends on the ability to outperform other networks by superior efficiency in performance or in cooperation capacity. Competition may also take a destructive form by disrupting the switches of competing networks and/or interfering with their communication protocols.

Networks work on a binary logic: inclusion/exclusion. Within the network, distance between nodes tends to zero, as networks follow the logic of small worlds' properties: they are able to connect to the entire network and communicated networks

*Excerpts from *The Network Society: A Cross-Cultural Perspective* edited by Manuel Castells.

from any node in the network by sharing protocols of communication. Between nodes in the network and those outside the network distance is infinite, since there is no access unless the program of the network is changed. Thus, networks are self-reconfigurable, complex structures of communication that ensure, at the same time, unity of purpose and flexibility of its execution by the capacity to adapt to the operating environment.

Networks, however, are not specific to twenty-first century societies or, for that matter, to human organization. Networks constitute the fundamental pattern of life, of all kinds of life. As Fritjof Capra writes "the network is a pattern that is common to all life. Wherever we see life, we see networks". In social life, social networks analysts have for a long time investigated the dynamic of social networks at the heart of social interaction and the production of meaning, leading to the formulation of a systematic theory of communication networks. Furthermore, in terms of social structure, archaeologists and historians of antiquity have forcefully reminded us that the historical record shows the pervasiveness and relevance of networks as the backbone of societies, thousands of years ago, in the most advanced ancient civilizations in several regions of the planet. Indeed, if we transfer the notion of globalization to the geography of the ancient world, as determined by available transportation technologies, there was globalization of a sort in antiquity, as societies depended for their livelihood, resources, and power on the connectivity of their main activities to networks transcending the limits of their locality.

The ability of networks to introduce new actors and new contents in the process of social organization, with relative independence of the power centers, increased over time with technological change, and, more precisely, with the evolution of communication technologies. This was particularly the case with the possibility of relying on a distributed energy network that characterized the advent of the industrial revolution: railways, ocean liners, and the telegraph constituted the first infrastructure for a quasi-global network with self-reconfiguring capacity. However, industrial society (both in its capitalist and its statist versions) was predominantly structured around large-scale, vertical production organizations and extremely hierarchical state apparatuses, in some instances evolving into totalitarian systems. This is to say that early, electrically based communication technologies were not powerful enough to equip networks with autonomy in all their nodes, as this autonomy would have required multidirectionality and a continuous flow of interactive information processing. But it also means that the availability of proper technology is a necessary, but not sufficient condition for the transformation of the social structure. It was only under the conditions of a mature industrial society that autonomous projects of organizational networking could emerge. When they did, they could use the potential of microelectronics-based communication technologies.

Networks became the most efficient organizational form as a result of three major features of networks that benefited from the new technological environment: flexibility, scalability, and survivability.

- Flexibility: networks can reconfigure according to changing environments, keeping their goals while changing their components. They go around blocking points in communication channels to find new connections.
- Scalability: they can expand or shrink in size with little disruption.
- Survivability: because they have no center, and can operate in a wide range of configurations, networks can resist attacks on their nodes and codes because the codes of the network are contained in multiple nodes that can reproduce the instructions and find new ways to perform. So, only the physical ability to destroy the connecting points can eliminate the network.

At the core of the technological change that unleashed the power of networks was the transformation of information and communication technologies, based on the microelectronics revolution that took place in the 1940s and 1950s. It constituted the foundation of a new technological paradigm, consolidated in the 1970s, mainly in the United States, and rapidly diffused throughout the world, ushering in what I have characterized, descriptively, as the information age.

William Mitchell, in an important and well-documented book, has retraced the evolving logic of information and communication technology throughout history as a process of expansion and augmentation of the human body and the human mind; a process that, in the early twenty-first century, is characterized by the explosion of portable machines that provide ubiquitous wireless communication and computing capacity. This enables social units (individuals or organizations) to interact anywhere, anytime, while relying on a support infrastructure that manages material resources in a distributed information power grid. With the advent of nanotechnology and the convergence between microelectronics and biological processes and materials, the boundaries between human life and machine life are blurred, so that networks extend their interaction from our inner self to the whole realm of human activity, transcending barriers of time and space. Neither Mitchell nor I indulge in science fiction scenarios as a substitute for analysis of the techno-social transformation process. But it is essential, precisely for the sake of analysis, to emphasize the role of technology in the process of social transformation, particularly when we consider the central technology of our time, communication technology, which relates to the heart of the specificity of the human species: conscious, meaningful communication.

It is because of available electronic information and communication technologies that the network society can deploy itself fully, transcending the historical limits of networks as forms of social organization and interaction. This approach is different from the conceptual framework that defines our societies as information or knowledge societies. To be blunt, I believe that this is an empirical and theoretical error. But let me advance the argument.

The reason, very simply, is that, as far as we can trust the historical record, all known societies are based on information and knowledge as the source of power, wealth, and meaning. Information has not much value per se without the knowledge to recombine it for a purpose. And knowledge is, of course, relative to each culture and society. So, knowledge of metallurgy or the technology of sailing or Roman law were the essential means of information and knowledge on which military power, administrative efficiency, the control of resources, and, ultimately, wealth and the rules for its distribution were based. So, if information and knowledge are the key factors for power and wealth in *all* societies, it is misleading to conceptualize our society as such, even if, for the practical reason of making communication easier, I gave in to the fashion of the times in my labels by characterizing our historical period as the "information age." What we actually mean, and what I always meant, is that our society is characterized by the power embedded in information technology, at the heart of an entirely new technological paradigm, which I called informationalism. Yet printing is also a most important information technology, and it has been around for quite a while, particularly in China. And we do not usually consider the post-printing societies as information societies.

So, what is actually new, both technologically and socially, is a society built around microelectronics-based information technologies. To which I add biological technologies based on genetic engineering, as they also refer to the decoding and recoding of the information of living matter. Furthermore, information technologies can be more properly labeled as communication technologies, since information that is not communicated ceases to be relevant. The early emphasis on information technology, semantically separated from communication, reflected, in fact, the logic of stand-alone electronic devices and computers. This is outdated, at least since the deployment of the Arpanet, more than three decades ago. It is also a reflection of the division of the world of communication technology between computers, telecommunications, and the broadcast media. Again, this is a distinction that has a relative justification in the business and institutions that organize each domain, but is senseless in technological terms. Thus, what is specific to our world is the extension and augmentation of the body and mind of human subjects in networks of interaction powered by microelectronics-based, software-operated, communication technologies. These technologies are increasingly diffused throughout the entire realm of human activity by growing miniaturization. They are converging with new genetic engineering technologies able to reprogram the communication networks of living matter. It is on this basis that a new social structure is expanding as the foundation of our society; the network society.

Informationalism: The Technological Paradigm of the Network Society

Technology, understood as material culture, is a fundamental dimension of social structure and social change. Technology is usually defined as the use of scientific knowledge to set procedures for performance in a reproducible manner. It evolves in interaction with other dimensions of society, but it has its own dynamics, linked to the conditions of scientific discovery, technological innovation, and application and diffusion in society at large. Technological systems evolve incrementally, but this evolution is punctuated by major discontinuities, as Stephen J. Gould has convincingly argued for the history of life. These discontinuities are marked by technological revolutions that usher in a new technological paradigm. The notion of paradigm was proposed by Thomas Kuhn to explain the transformation of knowledge by scientific revolutions, and imported into the social and economic formations of technology by Christopher Freeman and Carlota Perez. A paradigm is a conceptual pattern that sets the standards for performance. It integrates discoveries into a coherent system of relationships characterized by its synergy; that is, by the added value of the system vis-à-vis its individual components. A technological paradigm organizes a series of technological discoveries around a nucleus and a system of relationships that enhance the performance of each specific technology.

Informationalism is the technological paradigm that constitutes the material basis of early twenty-first century societies. Over the last quarter of the twentieth century of the Common Era it replaced and subsumed industrialism as the dominant technological paradigm. Industrialism, associated with the industrial revolution, is a paradigm characterized by the systemic organization of technologies based on the capacity to generate and distribute energy by human-made machines without depending on the natural environment—albeit they use natural resources as an input for the generation of energy. Energy is a primary resource for all activities, and by transforming energy generation, and the ability to distribute it to any location and to portable applications, humankind became able to increase its power over nature, taking charge of the conditions for its own existence (not necessarily a good thing, as the historical record of the twentieth-century shows). Around the energy nucleus of the industrial revolution, technologies clustered and converged in various fields, from chemical engineering and metallurgy to transportation, telecommunications, and, ultimately, life sciences and their applications.

A similar structuration of scientific knowledge and technological innovation is taking place under the new paradigm of informationalism. To be sure, industrialism does not disappear. It is subsumed by informationalism. Informationalism presupposes industrialism, as energy, and its associated technologies are still a fundamental component of all processes. Informationalism is a technological paradigm based on the augmentation of the human capacity of information processing and communication made possible by the revolutions in microelectronics, software, and genetic engineering. Computers and digital communications are the most direct expressions of this revolution. Indeed, microelectronics, software, computation, telecommunications, and digital communication as a whole, are all components of the same integrated system. Thus, in strict terms, the paradigm should be called "electronic informational-communicationalism." Reasons of clarity and economy suggest, however, that it is better to keep the concept of informationalism, as it is already widely employed and resonates in close parallel to industrialism. As information and communication are the most fundamental dimensions of human activity and organization, a revolutionary change in the material conditions of their performance affects the entire realm of human activity.

However, what is specific to this new system of information and communication technologies that sets it apart from historical experience? I propose that what makes this paradigm unique in relation to previous historical developments of information and communication technologies (such as printing, the telegraph, or the non-digital telephone) are, in essence, three major, distinctive features of the technologies at the heart of the system:

- their self-expanding processing and communicating capacity in terms of volume, complexity, and speed;
- their ability to recombine on the basis of digitization and recurrent communication;
- their distributing flexibility through interactive, digitized networking.

Let me elaborate on these features. I will do it separately for the two fundamental, and originally distinct, fields—digital electronics and genetic engineering—before considering their interaction.

Digital electronics technologies allow for an historically unprecedented increase in the capacity to process information, not only in the volume of information, but in the complexity of the operations involved, and in the speed of processing, including the speed of communication. However, how much is "much more" compared with previous information-processing technologies? How do we know that there is a revolution characterized by a giant leap forward in processing capacity?

One factor in the answer to this fundamental question is empirical. The history of electronics information and communication technologies in the past three decades shows an exponential increase in processing power, coupled with an equally dramatic decrease in the cost per operation, precisely the mark of a technological revolution, as documented by Paul David for the industrial revolution. Whatever measures we take in terms of integration of circuitry in microelectronics, of speed and volume in telecommunications, in computing power measured from megabytes to terabytes, and in the management of complex operations per lines of software code, they all show an unprecedented rate of technological change in the information and communication field.

Thus, in the first three decades of the information and communication technology revolution we have observed the self-generated, expansive capacity of new technologies to process information; current limits of integration, programming, and networking capacity are likely to be superseded by new waves of innovation in the making; and if and when the limits of the processing power of these technologies are reached, a new technological paradigm will emerge—under forms and with technologies that we cannot imagine today, except in science fiction scenarios, or in the innovative dreams of the usual suspects.

Secondly, digital technologies are also characterized by their ability to recombine information on the basis of recurrent, interactive communication. This is what I call the hypertext, in the tradition of Ted Nelson and Tim Berners-Lee. One of the key contributions of the Internet is its potential ability to link up everything digital from everywhere and to recombine it. Indeed, the original design of the World Wide Web by Berners-Lee had two functions: a browser and an editor. The commercial and bureaucratic practice of the World Wide Web has largely reduced its use, for most people, to a browser and information provider, connected to an e-mail system. Yet, from shared art creation to the political agora of the anti-globalization movement, and to joint engineering of networked corporate labs, the Internet is quickly becoming a medium of interactive communication beyond the cute, but scarcely relevant practice of chat rooms (increasingly made obsolete by SMSs and other wireless, instant communication systems). The added value of the Internet over other communication media is its capacity to recombine in chosen time information products and information processes to generate a new output, which is immediately processed in the Net, in an endless process of production of information, communication, and feedback in real time or chosen time. This is crucial because recombination is the source of innovation, and innovation is at the root of economic productivity, cultural creativity, and political power-making. Indeed, while the generation of new knowledge always required the application of theory to recombined information, the ability to experiment in real time with the results of the recombination, coming from a multiplicity of sources, considerably extends the realm of knowledge generation. It also allows increasing connections between different fields of knowledge and their applications—precisely the source of knowledge innovation in Kuhn's theory of scientific revolutions.

The third feature of new information and communication technologies is their flexibility, which allows the distribution of processing power in various contexts and applications, such as business firms, military units, the media, public services (such as health or distance education), political activity, and personal interaction. Software developments, such as Java and Jini languages, powered the distributive networks. And wireless communications made the multiplication of points of communication possible almost at the level of each individual—except, of course, for the majority of the population of the planet on the other side of the digital divide, a major social issue to which I will return in my analysis of the network society. So, it is not only a matter of the density of the communication network, but also of its flexibility, and of its ability to be integrated in all the sites and contexts of the human environment. As Mitchell writes "wireless connections and portable access devices create continuous fields of presence that may extend throughout buildings, outdoors, and into public space as well as private. This has profound implications for the locations and spatial distributions of all human activities that depend, in some way, upon access to information." It is this spatial transformation that I have tried to capture under the concept of the space of flows, which interacts with the traditional space of places, so that the new spatial structure associated with informationalism, is not placeless, but is made up of networks connecting places by information and communication flows.

Under the informational paradigm, the capacity for any communicating subject to act on the communication network gives people and organizations the possibility of reconfiguring the network according to their needs, desires, and projects. Yet (and this is fundamental) the reconfiguring capacity for each subject depends on the pattern of power present in the configuration of the network.

I will elaborate more succinctly on the second component of the information and communication technology revolution: *genetic engineering*. I consider its potential consequences as more far reaching than those already induced by the digital revolution in the structure and dynamics of society. This is because it affects the programs of life, and therefore the basis of our existence. However, its effects have been less diffused throughout the entire social structure because of the nature of its implications which have led to institutional resistance to their application; and also because its true breakthroughs required further advancements in the digital revolution, whose technologies are essential for the qualitative development of biological research (as was shown by the decisive role played by massive, parallel computing in the elaboration of the Human Genome Project).

While genetic engineering is often considered as an independent process from the information technology revolution, it is not. First, from an analytical perspective, these technologies are obviously information technologies, focused on the decoding and actual reprogramming of DNA, the code of living matter. And since biologists know that cells do not work in isolation, the real issue is to understand their networks of communication. Thus, genetic engineering is both an information and a communication technology, very much as digital electronics.

Secondly, there is a direct, methodological connection between the two revolutions. Computer models, and computing power, are the tools of trade in genetic engineering nowadays, so that microbiologists, bio-engineers, electrical engineers, chemical engineers, and computer scientists are all essential components of the daring teams attempting to unearth the secrets of life—and in some cases to play God. On the other hand, bio-chips and DNA-based chemically operated computing processes are the foundations of a new form of digital processing and molecular electronics, leading the way to the diffusion of nanotechnology, and, eventually, to the spread of nanobots, in a whole range of applications, including the repair and maintenance of the human body.

Thirdly, there is a theoretical convergence between the two technological fields around the analytical paradigm based on networking, complexity, self-organization, and emergent properties, as illustrated some time ago by the work of visionary teams of researchers at the Santa Fe Institute and as theorized by Fritjof Capra.

Genetic engineering technologies are also characterized by their self-expanding processing capacity, by their ability to recombine through communication networks, and by the flexibility of their distributive power. To be more specific, the existence of the Human Genome Map, and, increasingly, of genetic maps of specific parts of our body, as well as of a number of species and subspecies, raises the possibility of cumulative knowledge in the field of genetic engineering, leading to the understanding of processes that were beyond the realm of observation. In other words, better targeted, new, meaningful experiments become possible as knowledge progresses and fills the empty spaces of the model.

Secondly, the recombining ability of genetic engineering technologies is critical, as it is in the uses of digital communication and information processing. The first generation of genetic engineering applications largely failed because cells were manipulated as isolated entities, without a full understanding of their context, and of their place in the networks of life. Research has shown that cells are defined in their function by their relationship to others. Their DNA structure is meaningless outside the context of their specific interactions. So, interacting networks of cells, communicating through their codes, rather than isolated sets of instructions, are the object of genetic recombination strategies. Emergent properties are associated with networks of genes, and are identified by simulation models, only later validated by clinical experiments.

Finally, the promise of genetic engineering is precisely its ability to reprogram different codes and their protocols of communication in different areas of different bodies (or systems) of different species. Transgenic research and self-regenerative processes in living organisms are the frontiers of genetic engineering. Genetic drugs, which will at some time be delivered by nanotechnology-produced devices, are intended to induce in the body the capability of self-programming by living organisms: this is the ultimate expression of distributed information-processing power by communication networks.

It was on the foundations of informationalism that the network society gradually emerged as a new form of social organization of human activity in the last lap of the twentieth century. Without the capacity provided by this new technological paradigm, the network society would not be able to operate, just as industrial society could not fully expand without the use of electricity.

87

Actor-Network-Theory*

Bruno Latour

An office at the London School of Economics on a dark Tuesday afternoon in February before moving upstairs to the *Beaver* for a pint. A quiet but insistent knock is heard. A student peers into the office.

Student: Am I bothering you?

Professor: Not at all. These are my office hours. Come in, have a seat.

S: Thank you.

P: So . . . I take it that you are a bit lost?

S: Well, yes. I am finding it difficult, I have to say, to apply Actor Network Theory to my case study on organizations.

P: No wonder! It isn't applicable to anything.

S: But we were taught . . . I mean . . . it seems like hot stuff around here. Are you saying it's useless?

P: It might be useful, but only if it does not 'apply' to something.

S: Sorry, but are you playing some sort of Zen trick here? I have to warn you that I'm just a straight Organization Studies doctoral student, so don't expect . . . I'm not too much into French stuff either, just read a bit of *Thousand Plateaus* but couldn't make much sense of it . . .

P: Sorry, I wasn't trying to say anything cute. Just that ANT is first of all a *negative* argument. It does not say anything positive on any state of affairs.

S: So what can it do for me?

P: The best it can do for you is to say something like, 'When your informants mix up organization, hardware, psychology, and politics in one sentence, don't break it down first into neat little pots; try to follow the link they make among those elements that would have looked completely incommensurable if you had followed normal procedures.' That's all. ANT can't tell you positively what the link is.

S: So why is it called a 'theory' if it says nothing about the things we study?

P: It's a theory, and a strong one I think, but about *how* to study things, or rather how *not* to study them—or rather, how to let the actors have some room to express themselves.

S: Do you mean that other social theories don't allow that?

P: In a way, yes, and because of their very strengths: they are good at saying *substantive* things about what the social world is made of. In most cases that's fine; the ingredients are known; their repertoire should be kept short. But that doesn't work when things are changing fast. Nor is it good for organization studies, information studies, marketing, science and technology studies or management studies, where boundaries are so terribly fuzzy. New topics, that's what you need ANT for.

S: But my agents, 1 mean the people I am studying at the company, they form a lot of networks. They are connected to a lot of other things, they are all over the place . . .

P: But see, that's the problem! You don't need Actor-Network to say that. Any available social theory would do. It's a waste of time for you to pick such an outlandish argument simply to show that your informants are 'forming a network'.

S; But they are! They form a network. Look, I have been tracing their connections: computer chips, standards, schooling, money, rewards, countries, cultures, corporate boardrooms, everything. Haven't I described a network in your sense?

P: Not necessarily. I agree this is terribly confusing, and it's largely our fault—the word we invented is a pretty horrible one. But you should not confuse the network that is drawn by the description and the network that is used to make the description.

S: Come again?

P: Surely you'd agree that drawing *with* a pencil is not the same thing as drawing the *shape* of a pencil. It's the same with this ambiguous word: network. With Actor-Network you may describe something that doesn't at all look like a network—an individual state of mind, a piece of machinery, a fictional character; conversely, you may describe a network—subways, sewages, telephones—which is not all drawn in an 'Actor-Networky' way. You are simply confusing the object with the method. ANT is a method, and mostly a negative one at that; it says nothing about the *shape* of what is being described with it.

S: This is confusing! But my company executives, are they not forming a nice, revealing, powerful network?

P: Maybe, I mean, surely they are—but so what?

S: Then I can study them with Actor-Network-Theory!

P: Again, maybe yes, but maybe not. It depends entirely on what *you yourself* allow your actors (or rather, your actants) to do. Being connected, being interconnected, or being heterogeneous is not enough. It all depends on the sort of action that is flowing from one to the other, hence the words 'net' and 'work'. Really, we should say 'work-net' instead of 'network'. It's the work, and the movement, and the flow, and the changes that should be stressed. But now we are stuck with 'network' and everyone thinks we mean the World Wide Web or something like that.

S: Do you mean to say that once I have shown that my actors are related in the shape of a network, I have not yet done an ANT study?

P: That's exactly what I mean: ANT is more like the name of a pencil or a brush than the name of a specific shape to be drawn or painted.

S: But when I said ANT was a tool and asked you if it could be applied, you objected!

P: Because it's not a tool, or rather, because tools are never 'mere' tools ready to be applied: they always modify the goals you had in mind. That's what 'actor' means. Actor Network (I agree the name is silly) allows you to produce some *effects* that you would not have obtained by some other social theory. That's all that I can vouch for. It's a very common experience. Just try to draw with a lead pencil or with charcoal, you will feel the difference; and cooking tarts with a gas oven is not the same as with an electric one.

S: But that's not what my supervisor wants. He wants a frame in which to put my data.

P: If you want to store more data, buy a bigger hard disk.

S: He always says: 'Student, you need a framework.'

P: Maybe your supervisor is in the business of selling pictures! It's true that frames are nice for showing: gilded, white, carved, baroque, aluminum, etc. But have you ever met a painter who began his masterpiece by first choosing the frame? That would be a bit odd, wouldn't it?

S: You're playing with words. By 'frame' I mean a theory, an argument, a general point, a concept—something for making sense of the data. You always need one.

P: No you don't! Tell me, if some X is a mere 'case of' Y, what is more important to study: X that is the special case or Y which is the rule?

S: Probably Y . . .but X too, just to see if it's really an application of . . . well, both I guess.

P: I would bet on Y myself, since X will not teach you anything new. If something is simply an 'instance of' some other state of affairs, go study this state of affairs instead. A case study that needs a frame in addition, well, it is a case study that was badly chosen to begin with!

S: But you always need to put things into a context, don't you?

P: I have never understood what context meant, no. A frame makes a picture look nicer, it may direct the gaze better, increase the value, allows to date it, but it doesn't add anything to the picture. The frame, or the context, is precisely the sum of factors that make no difference to the data, what is common knowledge about it. If I were you, I would abstain from frameworks altogether. Just describe the state of affairs at hand.

S: 'Just describe'. Sorry to ask, but is this not terribly naive? Is this not exactly the sort of empiricism, or realism, that we have been warned against? I thought your argument was, um, more sophisticated than that.

P: Because you think description is easy? You must be confusing it, I guess, with strings of cliches. For every hundred books of commentaries and arguments, there is only one of description. To describe, to be attentive to the concrete state of affairs, to find the uniquely adequate account of a given situation, I myself have always found this incredibly demanding.

S: I have to say that I'm lost here. We have been taught that there are two types of sociology, the interpretative and the objectivist. Surely you don't want to say you are of the objectivist type?

P: You bet I am! Yes, by all means.

S: You? But we have been told you were something of a relativist! You have been quoted as saying that even the natural sciences are not objective. Surely you are for interpretative sociology, for viewpoints, multiplicity of standpoints and all that.

P: I have no real sympathy for interpretative sociologies. No. On the contrary, I firmly believe that sciences are objective—what else could they be? They're all about objects, no? What I have said is simply that objects might look a bit more complicated, folded, multiple, complex, and entangled than what the 'objectivist', as you say, would like them to be.

S: But that's exactly what 'interpretative' sociologies argue, no?

P: Oh no, not at all. They would say that *human* desires, *human* meanings, *human* intentions, etc., introduce some 'interpretive flexibility' into a world of inflexible objects, of 'pure causal relations', of 'strictly material connections'. That's not at all what I am saying. I would say that this computer here on my desk, this screen, this keyboard are objects made of multiple layers, exactly as much as you sitting here are: your body, your language, your worries. It's the object itself that adds multiplicity, or rather the thing, the 'gathering'. When you speak of hermeneutics, no matter which precaution you take, you always expect the second shoe to drop: someone inevitably will add: 'But of course there *also* exists "natural," "objective" things that are "not" interpreted'

S: That's just what I was going to say! There are not only objective realities, but also subjective ones! This is why we need both types of social theories . . .

P: See? That's the inevitable trap: 'Not only . . . but also'. Either you extend the argument to everything, but then it becomes useless—'interpretation' becomes another synonym for 'objectivity'—or else you limit it to one aspect of reality, the human, and then you are stuck—since objectivity is always on the other side of the fence. And it makes no difference if the other side is considered richer or poorer; it's out of reach anyway.

S: But you wouldn't deny that you also possess a standpoint, that ANT is situated as well, that you also add another layer of interpretation, a perspective?

P: No, why would 1 'deny' it? But so what? The great thing about a standpoint is that you can stand on it and modify it! Why would I be 'stuck with' it? From where they are on earth, astronomers have a limited perspective. Take for instance Greenwich, the Observatory down the river from here. Have you been there? It's a beautiful place. And yet, they have been pretty good at shifting this perspective, through instruments, telescopes, satellites. They can now draw a map of the distribution of galaxies in the whole universe. Pretty good, no? Show me one standpoint and I will show you two dozen ways to shift out of it. Listen: all this opposition between 'standpoint' and 'view from nowhere', you can safely forget. And also this difference between 'interpretative' and 'objectivist'. Leave hermeneutics aside and go back to the object—or rather, to the thing.

S: But I am always limited to my situated viewpoint, to my perspective, to my own subjectivity?

P: Of course you are! But what makes you think that 'having a viewpoint' means 'being limited' or especially 'subjective'? When you travel abroad and you follow the sign 'Belvedere 1.5 km' 'Panorama', 'Bella vista', when you finally reach the breath-taking site, in what way is this proof of your 'subjective limits'? It's the thing itself, the valley, the peaks, the roads, that offer you this grasp, this handle, this take. The best proof is that, two meters lower, you see nothing because of the trees and two meters higher, you see nothing because of a parking lot. And yet you have the same limited 'subjectivity' and you transport with you exactly the very same 'standpoint'! If you can have many points of views on a statue, it's because the statue itself is in three-dimensions and *allows* you, yes, allows you to move around it. If something supports many viewpoints, it's just that it's highly complex, intricately folded, nicely organized, and beautiful, yes, *objectively* beautiful.

S: But certainly nothing is objectively beautiful—beauty has to be subjective . . . taste and color, relative . . . I am lost again. Why would we spend so much time in this school fighting objectivism then? What you say can't be right.

P: Because the things people call 'objective' are most of the time the clichés of matters of facts. We don't have a very good description of anything: of what a computer, a piece of software, a formal system, a theorem, a company, a market is. We know next to nothing of what this thing you're studying, an *organization*, is. How would we be able to distinguish it from human emotions? So, there are two ways to criticize objectivity: one is by going *away* from the object to the subjective human viewpoint. But the other direction is the one I am talking about: back to the object. Positivists don't *own* objectivity. A computer described by Alan Turing is quite a bit richer and more interesting than the ones described by *Wired* magazine, no? As we saw in class yesterday, a soap factory described by Richard Powers in *Gain* is much livelier than what you read in Harvard case studies. The name of the game is to get back to empiricism.

S: Still, I am limited to my own view.

P: Of course you are, but again, so what? Don't believe all that crap about being 'limited' to one's perspective. All of the sciences have been inventing ways to *move* from one standpoint to the next, from one frame of reference to the next, for God's sake: that's called relativity.

S: Ah! So you confess you are a relativist!

P: But of course, what else could 1 be? If I want to be a scientist and reach objectivity, I have to be able to travel from one frame of reference to the next, from one standpoint to the next. Without those displacements, I would be limited to my own narrow point of view for good.

S: So you associate objectivity with relativism?

P: 'Relativity', yes, of course. All the sciences do the same. Our sciences do it as well.

S: But what is *our* way to change our standpoints?

P: I told you, we are in the business of descriptions. Everyone else is trading on clichés. Enquiries, survey, fieldwork, archives, polls, whatever—we go, we listen, we learn, we practice, we become competent, we change our views. Very simple really: it's called inquiries. Good inquiries always produce a lot of new descriptions.

S: But I have lots of descriptions already! I'm drowning in them. That's just my problem. That's why I'm lost and that's why I thought it would be useful to come to you. Can't ANT help me with this mass of data? I need a framework!

P: 'My Kingdom for a frame!' Very moving; I think I understand your desperation. But no, ANT is pretty useless for that. Its main tenet is that actors themselves make everything, including their own frames, their own theories, their own contexts, their own metaphysics, even their own ontologies. So the direction to follow would be more descriptions I am afraid.

S: But descriptions are too long. 1 have to *explain* instead.

P: See? This is where I disagree with most of the training in the social sciences.

S: You would disagree with the need for social sciences to provide an explanation for the data they accumulate? And you call yourself a social *scientist* and an objectivist!

P: I'd say that if your description needs an explanation, it's not a good description, that's all. Only bad descriptions need an explanation. It's quite simple really. What is meant by a 'social explanation' most of the time? Adding another actor to provide those already described with the energy necessary to act. But if you have to add one, then the network was not complete. And if the actors already assembled do not have enough energy to act, then they are not 'actors' but mere intermediaries, dopes, puppets. They do nothing, so they should not be in the description anyhow. I have never seen a good description in need of an explanation. But I have read countless bad descriptions to which nothing was added by a massive addition of 'explanations'. And ANT did not help.

S: This is very distressing. I should have known—the other students warned me not to touch ANT stuff even with a long pole. Now you are telling me that I shouldn't even try to explain anything!

P: I did not say that. I simply said that either your explanation is relevant and, in practice, this means you are adding a new agent to the description—the network is simply longer than you thought—or it's not an actor that makes any difference and you are merely adding something irrelevant which helps neither the description nor the explanation. In that case, throw it away.

S: But all my colleagues use them. They talk about 'IBM corporate culture', 'British isolationism', 'market pressure', 'self-interest'. Why should I deprive myself of those contextual explanations?

P: You can keep them as shorthand or to quickly fill in the parts of your picture that make no difference to you, but don't believe they explain anything. At best they apply equally to all your actors, which means they are probably superfluous since they are unable to introduce a difference among them. At worst, they drown all the new interesting actors in a diluvium of older ones. Deploy the content with all its connections and you will have the context in addition.

As Rem Koolhaas said, 'context stinks'. It's simply a way of stopping the description when you are tired or too lazy to go on.

S: But that's exactly my problem: to stop. I have to complete this doctorate. I have just eight more months. You always say 'more descriptions' but this is like Freud and his cures: indefinite analysis. When do you stop? My actors are all over the place! Where should I go? What is a complete description?

P: Now that's a good question because it's a practical one. As I always say: a good thesis is a thesis that is done. But there is another way to stop than just by 'adding an explanation' or 'putting it into a frame'.

S: Tell me it then.

P: You stop when you have written your 50,000 words or whatever is the format here, I always forget.

S: Oh! That's really great. So my thesis is finished when it's completed. So helpful, really, many thanks. I feel so relieved now.

P: Glad you like it! No seriously, don't you agree that any method depends on the size and type of texts you promised to deliver?

S: But that's a *textual* limit, it has nothing to do with method.

P: See? That's again why I dislike the way doctoral students are trained. Writing texts has *everything* to do with method. You write a text of so many words, in so many months, based on so many interviews, so many hours of observation, so many documents. That's all.

You do nothing more.

S: But I do more than that. I learn, I study, I explain, I criticize, I . . .

P: But all those grandiose goals, you achieve them through a text, don't you?

S: Of course, but it's a tool, a medium, a way of expressing myself.

P: There is no tool, no medium, only mediators. A text is thick. That's an ANT tenet, if any.

S: Sorry, Professor, I told you, I have never been into French stuff; I can write in C and even C ++, but I don't do Derrida, semiotics, any of it. I don't believe the world is made of words and all of that . . .

P: Don't try to be sarcastic. It doesn't suit the engineer in you. And anyway I don't believe that either. You ask me how to stop and I am just telling you that the best you will be able to do, as a PhD student, is to *add* a text—which will have been read by your advisors, maybe a few of your informants, and three or four fellow doctoral students—to a given state of affairs. Nothing fancy in that: just plain realism. One solution for how to stop is to 'add a framework', an 'explanation'; the other is to put the last word in the last chapter of your damn thesis.

S; I have been trained in the sciences! I am a systems engineer—I am not coming to Organization Studies to abandon that. I am willing to add flow charts, institutions, people, mythologies, and psychology to what I already know. I am even prepared to be 'symmetric' as you teach us about those various factors. But don't tell me that science is about telling nice stories. This is the difficulty with you. One moment you are completely objectivist, perhaps even a naive realist —'just describe'—and the other you are completely relativist—'tell some nice stories and run'. Is this not so terribly French?

P: And that would make you so terribly what? Don't be silly. Who talked about 'nice stories'? Not me. I said you were *writing* a PhD thesis. Can you deny that? And then I said that this so-many-words-long PhD thesis—which will be the only lasting result of your stay among us—is thick.

S: Meaning?

P: Meaning that it's not just a transparent windowpane, transporting without deformation some information about your study. 'There is no in-formation, only trans-formation.' I assume that you agree with this ANT slogan? Well, then this is surely also true of your PhD thesis, no?

S: Maybe, but in what sense does it help me to be more scientific, that's what I want to know. I don't want to abandon the ethos of science.

P: Because this text, depending on the way it's written, will *or will not* capture the actor-network you wish to study. The text, in our discipline, is not a story, not a nice story. Rather, it's the functional equivalent of a laboratory. It's a place for trials, experiments, and simulations. Depending on what happens in it, there is or there is not an actor and there is or there is not a network being traced. And that depends entirely on the precise ways in which it is written—and every single new topic requires a new way to be handled by a text. Most texts are just plain dead. Nothing happens in them.

S: But no one mentions 'text' in our program. We talk about studying the organization, not 'writing' about it.

P: That's what I am telling you: you are being badly trained! Not teaching social science doctoral students to *write* their PhDs is like not teaching chemists to do laboratory experiments. That's why I am teaching nothing but writing nowadays. I keep repeating the same mantra: 'describe, write, describe, write.'

S: The problem is that's not what my supervisor wants! He wants my case studies to 'lead to some useful generalization'. He does not want 'mere description'. So even if I do what you want, I will have one nice description of one state of affairs, and then what? I still have to put it into a frame, find a typology, compare, explain, generalize. That's why I'm starting to panic.

P: You should panic only if your actors were not doing that constantly as well, actively, reflexively, obsessively. They, too, compare; they, too, produce typologies; they, too, design standards; they, too spread their machines as well as their organizations, their ideologies, their states of mind. Why would you be the one doing the intelligent stuff while they would act like a bunch of morons? What they do to expand, to relate, to compare, to organize is what you have to describe as well. It's not another layer that you would have to add to the 'mere description'. Don't try to shift from description to explanation: simply *go on with* the description. What your own ideas are about your company is of no interest whatsoever compared to how this bit of the company itself has managed to spread.

S: But if my people don't act, if they don't actively compare, standardize, organize, generalize, what do I do? I will be stuck! I won't be able to add any other explanations.

P: You are really extraordinary! If your actors don't act, they will leave no trace whatsoever. So you will have no information at all. So you will have nothing to say.

S You mean when there is no trace I should remain silent?

P: Incredible! Would you raise this question in any of the natural sciences? It would sound totally silly. It takes a social scientist to claim that they can go on explaining even in the absence of any information! Are you really prepared to make up data?

S: No, of course not, but still I want . . .

P: Good, at least you are more reasonable than some of our colleagues. No trace left, thus no information, thus no description, then no talk. *Don't fill it in.* It's like a map of a country in the 16th century: no one went there or no one came back, so for God's sake, leave it blank! *Terra incognita.*

S: But what about invisible entities acting in some hidden ways?

P: If they act, they leave some trace. And then you will have some information, then you can talk about them. If not, just shut up.

S: But what if they are repressed, denied, silenced?

P: Nothing on earth allows you to say they are there without bringing in the *proof* of their presence. That proof might be indirect, farfetched, complicated, but you need it. Invisible things are invisible. Period. If they make other things move, and you can document those moves, then they are visible.

S: Proof? What is a proof anyway? Isn't that terribly positivistic?

P: I hope so, yes. What's so great about saying that things are acting whose existence you can't prove? I am afraid you are confusing social theory with conspiracy theory—although these days most of critical social science comes down to that.

S: But if I add nothing, I simply repeat what actors say.

P: What would be the use of adding invisible entities that act without leaving any trace and make no difference to any state of affairs?

S: But I have to make the actors learn something they didn't know; if not, why would I study them?

P: You social scientists! You always baffle me. If you were studying ants, instead of ANT, would you expect ants to *learn* something from your study? Of course not. They are the teachers, you learn from them. You explain what they do to you for your own benefit, or for that of other entomologists, not for them, who don't care one bit. What makes you think that a study is always supposed to teach things to the people being studied?

S: But that's the whole idea of the social sciences! That's why I'm here at the school: to criticize the ideology of management, to debunk the many myths of information technology, to gain a critical edge over all the technical hype, the ideology of the market. If not, believe me, I would still be in Silicon Valley, and I would be making a lot more money—well, maybe not now, since the bubble burst . . . But anyway, I have to provide some reflexive understanding to the people . . .

P: . . . Who of course were not reflexive before you came to honor them with your study!

S: In a way, yes. I mean, no. They did things but did not know why . . . What's wrong with that?

P: What's wrong is that it's so terribly cheap. Most of what social scientist call 'reflexivity' is just a way of asking totally irrelevant questions to people who ask other questions for which the analyst does not have the slightest answer! Reflexivity is not a birthright you transport with you just because you are at the LSE! You and your informants have different concerns—when they intersect it's a miracle. And miracles, in case you don't know, are rare.

S: But if I have nothing to add to what actors say, I won't be able to be critical.

P: See, one moment you want to explain and play the scientist, while the next moment you want to debunk and criticize and play the militant . . .

S: I was going to say: one moment you are a naive realist—back to the object—and the next you say that you just write a text that adds nothing but simply trails behind your proverbial 'actors themselves'. This is totally apolitical. No critical edge that I can see.

P: Tell me, Master Debunker, how are you going to gain a 'critical edge' over your actors? I am eager to hear this.

S: Only if I have a framework. That's what I was looking for in coming here, but obviously ANT is unable to give me one.

P: And I am glad it doesn't. I assume this framework of yours is hidden to the eyes of your informants and revealed by your study?

S: Yes, of course. That should be the added value of my work, not the description since everyone already knows that. But the explanation, the context, that's something they have no time to see, the typology. You see, they are too busy to think. That's what I can deliver. By the way, I have not told you yet, at the company, they are ready to give me access to their files.

P: Excellent, at least they are interested in what you do. It's a good beginning. But you are not claiming that in your six months of fieldwork, you can by yourself, just by writing a few hundred pages, produce more knowledge than those 340 engineers and staff that you have been studying?

S: Not 'more' knowledge but different. Yes, I hope I can. Shouldn't I strive exactly for that? Is this not why I am in this business?

P: I am not sure what business you are in, but how *different* is the knowledge you produce from theirs, that's the big question.

S: It's the same kind of knowledge as all the sciences, the same way of explaining things: by going from the case at hand to the cause. And once I know the cause, I can generate the effect as a consequence. What's wrong with that? It's like asking what will happen to a pendulum that has been moved far from the equilibrium. If I know Galileo's law, I don't even need to look at any concrete pendulum anymore; I know exactly what will happen—provided I forget the perturbations, naturally.

P: Naturally! So what you are hoping for is that your explanatory framework will be to your case study what Galileo's law is to the fall of the pendulum—minus the perturbations.

S: Yes, I guess so, though less precisely scientific. Why? What's wrong with that?

P: Nothing. It would be great, but is it feasible? It means that, whatever a given concrete pendulum does, it will add no new information to the law of falling bodies. The law holds *in potentia* everything there is to know about the pendulum's state of affairs. The concrete case is simply, to speak like a philosopher, the 'realization of a potential' that was already there.

S: Isn't that an ideal explanation?

P: That's just the problem. It's an ideal squared: the ideal of an ideal explanation. I doubt somewhat that your company's subsidiary behaves that way. And I am pretty confident that you can't produce the law of its behavior that will allow you to deduce everything as the realization *in concreto* of what was already there potentially.

S: Minus the perturbations . . .

P: Yes, yes, yes, this goes without saying. Your modesty is admirable.

S: Are you making fun of me here? Striving for that sort of framework seems feasible to me.

P: But even it were, would it be desirable? See, what you are really telling me is that the actors in your description make *no difference whatsoever*. They have simply realized a potential—apart from minor deviations—which means they are not actors at all: they simply carry the force that comes through them. So, my dear Student, you have been wasting your time describing people, objects, sites that are nothing, in effect, but passive intermediaries since they do nothing on their own. Your fieldwork has been simply wasted. You should have gone directly to the cause.

S: But that's what a science is for! Just that: finding the hidden structure that explains the behavior of those agents you thought were doing something but in fact are simply placeholders for something else.

P: So you are a structuralist! You've finally come out of the closet. Placeholders, isn't that what you call actors? And you want to do Actor Network Theory at the same time! That's stretching the limits of eclecticism pretty far!

S: Why can't I do both? Certainly if ANT has any scientific content, it has to be structuralist.

P: Have you realized that there is the word 'actor' in actor-network? Can you tell me what sort of action a placeholder does in a structuralist explanation?

S: That's easy, it fulfills a function. This is what is so great about structuralism, if I have understood it correctly. Any other agent in the same position would be forced to do the same.

P: So a placeholder, by definition, is entirely *substitutable* by any other?

S: Yes, that's what I am saying.

P: But that's also what is so implausible and what makes it radically incompatible with ANT. In my vocabulary, an actor that makes no difference is not an actor at all. An actor, if words have any meaning, is exactly what is *not* substitutable. It's a unique event, totally irreducible to any other, except, that is, if you render one commensurable with another one by some process of standardization—but even that requires a *third* actor, a third event.

S: So you are telling me that ANT is not a science!

P: Not a structuralist science, that's for sure.

S: That's the same thing, any science . . .

P: No! Organization Studies, Science and Technology Studies, Business Studies, Information Studies, Sociology, Geography, Anthropology, whatever the field, they cannot rely, by definition, on any structuralist explanation since information is transformation.

S: 'Systems of transformations', that's exactly what structuralism is about!

P: No way, my friend, since in structuralism nothing is really transformed, it's simply *combined*. You don't seem to fathom the abyss that exists between it and ANT. A structure is just a network on which you have only very sketchy information. It's useful when you are pressed for time, but don't tell me it's more scientific. If I want to have actors in my account, they have to do things, not to be placeholders; if they *do* something, they have to make a difference. If they make no difference, drop them, start the description anew. You want a science in which there is no object.

S: You and your stories. Eventful stories, that's what you want! I am talking about explanation, knowledge, critical edge, not writing scripts for soap operas on Channel 4!

P: I was getting to that. You want your bundle of a few hundred pages to make a difference, no? Well then, you have to be able to prove that your description of what people do, when it comes back to them, *does* make a difference to the way they were doing things. Is this what you call having a 'critical edge'?

S: I guess so, yes.

P: But you would agree that it wouldn't do to provide them with an irrelevant appeal to causes that make no difference to what they do because they are too general?

S: Of course not. I was talking about *real* causalities.

P: But those won't do either because if they existed, which I doubt very much they do, they would have no other effect than transforming your informants into the placeholders of other actors, which you call function, structure, grammar, etc. In effect, they wouldn't be actors anymore but dopes, puppets—and even that would be quite unfair to puppets. Anyway, you are making actors out to be nothing: at best they could add some minor perturbations like the concrete pendulum that only adds slight wobbles.

S: Huh?

P: Now you have to tell me what is so politically great about transforming those you have studied into hapless, 'actless' placeholders for hidden functions that you, and you only, can see and detect?

S: Hmm, you have a way of turning things upside down. Now I am not so sure. If actors become aware of what is imposed on them, if they become more conscious, more reflexive, then is their consciousness not raised somewhat? They can now take their fate into their own hands. They become more enlightened, no? If so, I would say that now, and in part thanks to me, they are more active now, more complete actors.

P: *Bravo, bravissimo*! So an actor for you is some fully determined agent, plus a placeholder for a function, plus a bit of perturbation, plus some consciousness provided by enlightened social scientists? Horrible, simply horrible. And you want to apply ANT to these people! After you have reduced them from actors to placeholders, you want to add insult to injury and generously bring to those poor blokes the reflexivity they had before and that you have taken away by treating them in a structuralist way! Magnificent! They were actors *before* you came in with your 'explanation'. Don't tell me that it's your study that might make them so. Great job, Student! Bourdieu could not have done better.

S: You might not like Bourdieu very much, but at least he was a real scientist, and even better, he was politically relevant. As far as I can tell, your ANT is neither.

P: Thanks. I have been studying the links between science and politics for about thirty years, so I am hard to intimidate with talks of which science is 'politically relevant'.

S: I have learned not to be intimidated by arguments of authority, so your thirty years of study makes no difference to me.

P: *Touché*. But your question was: 'What can I do with ANT?' I answered it: no structuralist explanation. The two are completely incompatible. Either you have actors who realize potentialities and thus are not actors at all, or you describe actors who are rendering virtualities actual (this is Deleuze's parlance by the way) and which require very specific texts. Your connection with those you study requires very specific protocols to work—I guess this is what you would call 'critical edge' and 'political relevance'.

S: So where do we differ? You, too, want to have a critical edge.

P: Yes, maybe, but I am sure of one thing: it's not automatic and most of the time it will fail. Two hundred pages of interviews, observations, etc. will not make any difference whatsoever. To be relevant requires another set of extraordinary circumstances. It's a rare event. It requires an incredibly imaginative protocol. It requires something as miraculous as Galileo with his pendulum or Pasteur with his rabies virus.

S: So what should I do? Pray for a miracle? Sacrifice a chicken?

P: But why do you want your tiny little text to be automatically more relevant to those who might be concerned by it (or not) than say a huge laboratory of natural sciences? Look at how much it takes for Intel™ chips to become relevant for mobile phones! And you want everyone to have a label 'LSE™ inside' at no cost at all? To become relevant you need extra work.

S: Just what I need, the prospect of even more work!

P: But that's the whole point: if an argument is automatic, across the board, all-purpose, then it can't possibly be scientific. It's simply irrelevant.

If a study is really scientific, then it could have failed.

S: Great reassurance, nice of you to remind me that I can fail my thesis!

P: You are contusing science with mastery. 'Being able to lose the phenomenon is essential to scientific practice' Tell me, can you imagine one single topic to which Bourdieu's critical sociology, which you are so fond of, could possibly *not* apply?

S: But I can't imagine one single topic to which ANT would apply!

P: Beautiful, you are so right, that's exactly what 1 think.

S: That was not meant as a compliment.

P: But I take it as a true one! An application of anything is as rare as a good text of social science.

S: May I politely remark that, for all your exceedingly subtle philosophy of science, you have yet to tell me how to write one.

P: You were so eager to add frames, context, structure to your 'mere descriptions', how would you have listened to me?

S: But what's the difference between a good and a bad ANT text?

P: Now, that's a good question! Answer: the same as between a good and a bad laboratory. No more, no less.

S: Well, okay, um, thanks. It was nice of you to talk to me. But I think after all, instead of ANT, I was thinking of using Luhmann's system theory as an underlying framework—that seems to hold a lot of promise, 'autopoiesis' and all that. Or maybe I will use a bit of both.

P: Hmmm . . .

S: Don't you like Luhmann?

P-. I would leave aside all 'underlying frameworks' if I were you.

S: But your sort of 'science', from what I see, means breaking all the rules of social science training.

P: I prefer to break them and follow my actors. As you said, I am, in the end, a naive realist, a positivist.

S: You know what would be real nice? Since no one around here seems to understand what ANT is, you should write an introduction to it. That would ensure our teachers know what it is and then, if I may say without being rude, they might not try to push us too hard into it, if you see what I mean . . .

P: So it's really that bad?

S: See, I'm just a PhD student, but you're a professor. You have published a lot. You can afford to do things that I can't. 1 have to listen to my supervisor. I simply can't follow your advice too far.

P: Why come to me then? Why try to use ANT?

S: For the last half hour, I have to confess, I've been wondering the same thing . . .

PART XII

LATE MODERNITY AND POSTMODERNITY

The sociological theories discussed up to this point—extending generally from the mid-19th century to the mid-20th century—were explicitly involved in understanding society and the social self in the era of *modernity*. Notwithstanding the numerous intellectual conflicts, tensions, and dilemmas that characterized these theories, Marx, Weber, Le Bon, Parsons, Lukács, Mead, Goffman, and the others relied on certain core presuppositions. These presuppositions—articulated as rationalization, social order, collective mind, civic solidarity, power differentials, the coherent self, and so forth—were, by the second half of the 20th century, being challenged by major societal transformations. These transformations in knowing, doing, and being marked the beginning of an emerging society—described variously as *postindustrial*, *late modern*, and *postmodern*—that called for new forms of theorizing. The new theories had to take into account the paradoxes and contradictions and the risks and globalizing trends of the bourgeoning society. But they also had to conceptually transcend the old boundaries of space and time and eradicate the established distinctions between the macro and micro, the subjective and objective aspects of social reality.

We begin with Alain Touraine, who maintains that the conception of society as a system of order that dominates actors, which was popular during the period of industrialization, must now be abandoned. In the reading "Sociological Intervention," he urges sociologists to instead study the social relations of participants in social movements. In a *postindustrial society* (a term coined by Touraine), where power relations, conflicts, and negotiations create temporary and unstable situations, it is more important to study how society changes rather than how it functions. As such, Touraine proposes a method of research, *sociological intervention*, that allows sociologists to insert themselves as researchers in studying the innovative and conflictual actions of participants in social movements. Researchers engage in sociological intervention when they help these participants undertake group self-analysis in an effort to reveal underlying structures and relationships in their social movements. This new, engaged sociology and this new focus on the participants of social movements ends the classical separation between system and actor and between researcher and subject. It also ends the opposition between the macrolevel and microlevel of social analysis.

Anthony Giddens goes further than Touraine in endeavoring to abolish the traditional theoretical polarization between macro and micro—between a structural sociological approach and an interpretative one. In "Structuration Theory," he maintains that rather than focus exclusively on the individual actor or on some type of societal totality, *structuration theory* examines social activities as they are reproduced across space and time. These durable activities are *recursive*, which is to say that they are continually recreated by social actors through the very conditions that make these activities possible.

This production and reproduction of social activities requires that actors engage in three conscious processes: *reflexive monitoring*, that they routinely review their behavior and social circumstances and expect others to do the same; *rationalization*, that they articulate reasons for their behavior; and *motivation*, that they have certain wants that prompt their behavior. Further, all actors have *agency*, the power to act (or not to act) in different ways to influence social conditions. But agency depends on *structure*, or those institutions that make it possible for similar social activities to exist across time and space, with its social rules and resources. As actors draw upon these rules and resources, they reproduce their daily activities. For Giddens, structure and agency do not signify a distinct dualism between macrolevel forces and microlevel activities; rather, they represent a mutually dependent *duality*.

In "Ontological Security, Existential Anxiety, and Self-Identity," Giddens turns to an examination of the self and society in the period of *late modernity*. He contends that even while individuals engage in the conscious processes of reflexive monitoring, rationalization, and motivation when carrying out everyday activities, they also engage in a "nonconscious" form of knowing that he calls practical consciousness. *Practical consciousness* involves the bracketing of trivial events so that individuals can focus on the tasks at hand and thus prevent psychological overwhelm, or anxiety. Practical consciousness serves to anchor people's existential feelings of *ontological security*—their coherent sense of "being in the world." Ontological security, says Giddens, is psychologically developed early in life through *basic trust* in others. Relations of trust provide a practical consciousness that helps individuals bracket events that could pose risks to them, including threats to their self-identity. Giddens describes *self-identity* as an ongoing self-consciousness experienced by the individual as a feeling of biographical continuity. In circumstances of tension and strain, self-identity is temporarily compromised—split—and ontological security is disrupted.

In the reading "Habitus," Pierre Bourdieu proposes a concept that is somewhat similar to Giddens's concept of practical consciousness. For Bourdieu, *habitus* refers to a set of nonconscious acquired dispositions—categories of perception, thought, and action—that are based on historical experiences and are aimed at practical ends. Habitus can neither be understood solely in objective, structural terms, as patterned social practices, nor solely in subjective, agentic terms, as conscious free will. Indeed, like structuration, the concept of habitus interrelates structure and agency. Habitus, according to Bourdieu, can only be explained by relating the past life experiences of their production with the current, actual conditions of their realization. The dispositions of habitus are durable but not unchanging; they are both structured and structuring.

According to Ulrich Beck, in "The Risk Society," late modernity has given rise to a *risk-distributing society*. It distributes risks—associated with ecological and high-tech hazards that threaten health, property, and profit—according to the pattern of a class society: Just as wealth accumulates at the top, so does risk amass at the bottom. Late modernity marks the period of transition from a *scarcity society*, where people are preoccupied with meeting their basic needs, to a *risk society*, where people are increasingly concerned with maintaining their safety. They experience insecurity because of world-threatening events with catastrophic potential. These risks are matters of nuclear and chemical production—climate change, deforestation, toxins in foods, ozone depletion, nuclear waste, oil spills, and so forth—and are consequences of overproduction, modernization, and globalization. Risks transcend space and time; not only are they global in scope, they will also affect future generations. Being at risk has become the way of being in the world of late modernity.

In "Liquid Modernity," originally published in 2000, Zygmunt Bauman uses the metaphor of *fluidity* to understand the new but continuing stage of modernity. Some characteristics of *liquids* (one variety of fluids) are that they are prone to change their shape, they do not settle into space, and they move with the flow of time. In short, liquids are extraordinarily mobile and changeable. According to Baumann, the main project of the early or *solid* stage of modernity was to dissolve the premodern structures and replace them with a rational, predictable, and permanent social order. But in the later stage of modernity—which he calls *liquid modernity*—stable structures are harder to rely upon. This is because there now exist numerous contradicting and nonregulating forms and patterns—and identities—that are undergoing constant and relentless change. Due largely to instantaneous electronic communications and high-speed travel, liquid social life attains a "nomadic" quality that does not adhere to time and space and therefore contributes to globalization.

Roland Robertson takes up the issue of *globalization*, or the homogenization of world society, in the selection titled "Global Modernities." Here, he states that the notion that there exists a contradiction between the *local*, or particular, and the *global*, or universal, was popularized by the thesis that globalization is a consequence of the worldwide diffusion of modernity. Thus was promoted the idea that the global is in opposition to the local. But in Roberson's view, local assertions of identity and culture are largely produced in global terms. Indeed, it is through the convergence that occurs between a variety of diverse communities and a plurality of cultures that globalization is produced. Robertson suggests replacing the tendentious and vague concept of globalization with the term *glocalization*, referring to what he describes as the concurrent interpenetration between the global and the local. Thus, rather than regard the global as being in tension with the local (which can refer to home, community, or locality), the global should be seen as *including* the local. In late modernity, globalization and localization make each other possible.

Jean-François Lyotard shifts from what the aforementioned theorists have referred to as the age of late or ongoing modernity to instead consider a close examination of *postmodernity*. In "The Postmodern Condition," Lyotard begins with the premise that there are two competing kinds of knowledge: scientific and narrative. In the *modern* context, scientific knowledge—which must be legitimated by the scientific community through consensus as a truth-value—underwent a legitimation crisis. The *postmodern*, by contrast, is depicted as a network of flexible *language games*, including knowledge games. As such, the two modern views of society—as a stable system or as a conflicting duality—and their respective forms of knowledge—the positivist and the critical/interpretivist—are no longer acceptable. Furthermore, there exists an incredulity toward comprehensive theoretical approaches, or *grand narratives* (such as, for example, the belief in the totality and unity of all knowledge or the belief in the emancipation of humanity). Instead, postmodern society is formed through many competing *small narratives*, and neither scientific knowledge nor narrative knowledge can be evaluated on the basis of the other's criteria of competence. Postmodern scientific knowledge, with its nonrationality, indeterminism, and paradoxes, must be legitimated not through the consensus of truth-value but through *paralogy*, the ongoing production of new ideas.

Another view of the postmodern condition is offered by Jean Baudrillard in "Hyperreality." Here, Baudrillard states that in postmodern culture, *simulation*, an imitation of something, involves the production of a copy without the original. Because the simulated copy now precedes and determines the original object, it is no longer possible to distinguish the fake from the original. Simulating mental illness is itself a mental illness. *Simulacra* are images whose meaning is lost in the representation. The Byzantine icon becomes more real than the divine identity that it initially represented. It is now its own pure simulacrum because it has no relation to any reality whatsoever. Theme parks and reality television shows create imaginary worlds that conceal the imaginary aspects of the larger society. These constructions of media culture give the impression that the larger society is the "real" reality, when, in fact, they are all on the same ontological footing: Theme parks and reality shows are as real as society. Postmodernity, for Baudrillard, produces a culture in which what is believed to be reality is itself a simulacrum of reality; it is a state of *hyperreality*.

88

Sociological Intervention*

Alain Touraine

The creation of the International Society of Political Psychology is a particularly appropriate occasion to examine afresh the relationship in the social sciences between the situation and the actor; in other words to redefine the specific object of these sciences. We are still to some extent the heirs of an intellectual tradition which has long defined this object with a simplicity which seemed self-explanatory: is not society the object of social sciences?

We may use different terms when dealing with societies other than our own modern industrial one, but they all play the same role. The nineteenth century used the word *civilization* to refer to concrete historical units which were defined not so much in terms of an activity as in terms of a spirit, which was usually expressed mainly in terms of religion. And when we study preliterate communities we consider them primarily as cultures, as quasi-stable systems of internal and external exchanges. The word *society* is more usually employed for historical entities which are defined in terms of the action which they exert on themselves rather than by their values and their stability. Its use has spread with the growth of the modern state, of its law and regulations, and with the development of national consciousness. But the difference between cultures or civilizations and societies is that the former, because they are systems of social reproduction or of social control, do not distinguish between the actor and the social system. Society on the contrary is defined in terms of a social order which is actively imposed upon a set of human beings.

This leads to a separation between the social system, which is perceived as the "spirit" of the laws *(L' esprit des Lois)* to use Montesquieu's title, and the actors who are thought of as the raw material which is organized by the law, which brings order to disorder. In the vocabulary of classicism, society is reason, whereas the actors are moved by passions. Hence the importance of education which, for social philosophy, is the equivalent of socialization, defined as internalization of the rules of conduct which enable us to live in society. The classical concept of society leads to a complete separation between the system and the actor, akin to the distinction which exists between public life and private life, or between male and female. Politics is then identified with man and psychology with woman. The former is the domain of calculation and reason, even reason of state; in the latter, feeling and emotion are predominant. This classical image of

*"The Voice and the Eye: On the Relationship between Actors and Analysts," Alain Touraine, *Political Psychology* 2, 1 (1980): 3–14. Reproduced with permission of Blackwell Publishing Ltd.

society strangely reappears in some contemporary Marxist authors. They are returning to a definition of society as a social order, or, to use the vocabulary of Althusser, as the ideological instruments of the state, probably because the institutionalization of industrial conflict has made it more difficult to put open class conflict at the center of our image of society. N. Poulantzas, for example, insists on the need to distinguish between the level of social structure, (that is the mode of production considered as an overall system) and the level of action which he considers to be subject to constant changes and hence less important. Similarly, historians who have been influenced by Marxism have distinguished between history in depth, which deals with the cultural and material bases of society, and the history of events, which deals with the actors. Whether these authors consider material resources or cultural values as the background of society is of little importance. The main point is that in every case the actor is located in the realm of contingency and therefore in a less important position than that accorded to the system and to the structure underlying it.

This devaluation of the actor has led us to define social sciences as the study of institutions. The latter were defined as the normative regulation of functional activities. Society was therefore seen as a living being, and theories about society conveyed an image of society as paterfamilias, or as "The Prince"—the latter being incarnated either in the King or in the Republic. Generally speaking, order is considered a creative and pacifying force while the actor symbolizes violence and disorder; but sometimes, as for example in the writings of J.J. Rousseau, order is, on the contrary, considered as a force of oppression and contrasted with the state of nature which is the world of community and equality. In both cases, the opposition nature-society, which corresponds to the opposition actor-system, gives a central role to the state and the laws which ensure, for better or for worse, the transition from the state of nature to the state of society.

The Ambiguities Inherent in the Discovery of Social Relations

Sociology was born with the critique of this conception of society, when order was no longer opposed to disorder, or spirit to nature, and when society was defined not as a unifying principle but as a network of relations among social actors. Beginning with Hegel, the idea of civil society becomes distinct from that of the state, and it triumphs with the rise of the industrial bourgeoisie. This is explained by the fact that the intervention of society on itself has gone beyond the world of trade and the circulation of goods, which was regulated by laws and political measures, and has entered the world of work organization. All the analysts of the making of industrial society, from Adam Smith to Ure, or from Saint-Simon to Marx, have commented on this. Industry is primarily an authoritarian change in the forms of work organization. It is not defined by the use of machines (the best known examples of rationalization are those of Taylor and do not involve a single machine) but as the breaking down, the measurement and the redefinition of the elements of the productive process so as to improve the productivity of the workshop.

Any progress in industry is therefore fundamentally linked to the transformation of the social relations of production. Social life is centered round problems of work and production and no longer those of space and legislation. Society was defined as a system of production. Industrialization in Great Britain, and later in Western Europe, was so brutal and unprecedented that social thinking was long concerned uniquely with its origins and attributes. But just as social relations seemed to be becoming the main object of analysis, a new type of appeal to a metasocial principle as an explanation of social life began once again to obscure them. The opposition of order to disorder, or of reason to nature, was over. But social thinkers opposed modernity, complexity, and exchange to tradition, experience, and custom as successive stages of evolution. The concept of society is then broken down into social relations, that is, the world of the actors and historical development as evolution from the simple to the complex, which can be found in the writings of Darwin, Spencer, Durkheim, and Talcott Parsons (whose death has so recently bereaved us). When the concept of society is no longer seen as a unifying principle in the analysis of the social situation, the concept of evolution replaces it and maintains the distance between the system and the actors. This dualism seems to be inherent in all sociological writings which originate in a reflection on industrial society. For Auguste Comte, Durkheim, and the functionalists, evolution is defined in natural, material terms. Take, for example, the importance which Durkheim gives to the density of social interactions and more recently the definitions of modernization given by Deutsch, Germani, or Lipset. On the contrary, social relations are defined by them in terms of values, or moral integration or disintegration. On the other hand, the Weberian tradition maintains a cultural definition of the orientations of action while it observes the progress of instrumental rationality at the level of social relations. Finally, Marx emphasized the opposition between social relations dominated by profit and exploitation and the natural evolution of the forces of production, leaving no room at either level for values.

Thus, all of the three main classical schools draw a sharp separation between social relations and historical evolution. Weberian Kantism opposes the noumenon to the phenomenon. Marx reciprocates by opposing the necessary and desirable course of evolution to the irrationality of social relations dominated by contradiction. Finally, Durkheim, while admiring modernity and secularization, is alarmed (as was de Tocqueville before him) by the destruction of social bonds and insists on the need to recreate, in particular through education, the moral unity of society.

Thus, the evolutionists did away with the concept of society but reconstructed it in another form. Today, we must reject interpretations as vigorously as the first sociologists rejected those of the 17th and 18th centuries.

In our century social thinking is dominated by a deep transformation of the relationship between politics and history, and therefore between the actor and the system. Contemporary societies can no longer be situated historically, because they produce their history. The concept of development is replacing the concept of evolution. It was fitting that the International Sociological Association chose as the title for its recent congress "the paths of development." The plural excludes any recourse to the type of evolutionism that dominated social thinking from Auguste Comte to Talcott Parsons. Today it is impossible to believe that different types of societies follow one another in a linear progression, that socialism will follow capitalism, and that division of labor, secularization, and rationalization will carry on indefinitely. Growth and crises, wars and revolutions, fascism, communism, nationalism, and even welfare states are evidences of the capacity of our societies to upset their very existence, and to transform their economies and their organization in the name of ideas and as a result of a way of seizing and using power. Social organization can no longer be thought of as a train, with the economy, or inversely with ideas as the engine. This new experience spans the whole of the planet and not just the "developed" countries, but it leads to two rather different directions in the developed and in the developing countries.

Let us consider first the case of societies which are moving beyond the industrial economy. In most aspects of social life, and not only in the production of goods, they appear to be dominated by decision-making centers and large organizations that impose on the population a certain type of consumption and therefore of social behavior. This in return leads to the creation of countermodels of consumption. These models reject the definition of demands by the system of supply and appeal to needs that can be defined as natural or basic but also, and more significantly, as the expression of a desire for personal and collective autonomy—in a word, for self-management. Thus the whole of what used to be defined as institutions becomes networks of power relationships and a scene for new protest movements. The cultural movements or innovations and the social crises, which have been even more frequent in the past 15 years in the United States than in Western Europe or in Japan, have dealt the final blow in the destruction of the concept of society. Instead of the idea that the university is an instrument for the development of rational thinking, or of the opposite idea that it is merely a means of reproducing social inequalities, the idea is gradually spreading that knowledge itself is a source of power and can be produced, transmitted, and utilized in different ways according to the political situation. Similarly, a discussion on public health has begun, which has demonstrated that hospital organization and drug industry or, on the contrary, anticapitalist or antitechnocratic movements can define health in different terms and build different health policies. Especially in countries in which social security expenditures have reached a very high level, the simple idea of a continuous progress of medical care has been abandoned. But the most far-reaching change is the tendency to end the distinction between public and private life, that is between society and nature. This has been hastened by the women's movement based on modern methods of birth control and of the recent increase in the participation of women in the labor force, especially at the higher levels. As I said, the distinction between the system and the actor, between order and nature, was classically manifested by the distinction between male and female. During the period of industrialization, the opposition between money, machines, and arms on the one hand, and family life on the other hand was still that of male and female. Women hardly ever entered the decision-making centers of the industrial economy. The women's movements, by rejecting this separation and the subordinate position in which they were imprisoned, have made a crucial contribution towards the elimination of all explanations of social action which resort to a transcendental, metasocial principle. They have contributed to reducing what is referred to as "society" to a network of social relations between actors who are involved in conflicts about the social and political control of cultural resources.

Henceforth, society is no longer a unifying principle, but the end product of social conflicts and of the main cultural orientations which are the issues at stake in the social conflicts. Society is no longer an essence, but an event. Likewise, an organization appears to be only an unstable and provisional state of relations between social groups which possess or do not possess authority within defined limits. A society is merely an ever-changing combination of latent or manifest conflicts, of negotiations, of imposed domination, and of violence. One cannot understand the actor by studying the society to which he belongs. To understand how the categories of social behavior are constructed we must begin with the actors and the conflicts which oppose them and through which society produces itself. The outcome of this basic conflict is the partial institutionalization.

At last sociology can completely do away with the concept of society. A biologist, Francois Jacob, has written that modern biology originated when biologists stopped asking questions about life and started studying living beings. Similarly, sociology really begins when sociologists reject society as a concept and devote themselves entirely to the study of social relations.

This in turn puts an end to any opposition between functionalists and interactionists and to any separation between the system and the actor. The actors are not motivated by a search for pleasure or interest and must not be analyzed "psychologically." Neither should the system be defined historically or in terms of principles or objective laws. The actors are ultimately defined by their position within the struggle for the control of cultural patterns through which a collectivity molds its relations with its environment. I therefore propose that the concept of society be completely disregarded in sociological analysis and that this term be used solely to describe specific historical entities, such as the "American society" or even the "industrial society."

The Self-Production of Society

The sociologist becomes easily enthusiastic about changes which reveal the originality and the necessity of his approach. He looks everywhere for conflicting processes of self-production of society. At times he feels at one with the new protest movements; more usually his affinities lie with the new forms of democracy which are attempting to force their way into grounds which were formerly dominated by tradition or principles. He likes to think that his research contributes to the extension of democracy because the illusion of order is being replaced by the reality of discussion, conflict, and negotiation. In short the sociologist demonstrates that society is a political arena. But as he scales the heights of the Capitol, the Tarpeian rock looms before him. From a society characterized by action, innovation, and conflict, we move suddenly to the complete opposite—to a society characterized by a restrictive and repressive social order. In large parts of the world this order is imposed by a totalitarian state which speaks in the name of national and social movements, as well as in the name of economic development. We, the sociologists, who have consistently fought for the civil society against the state and against all the forces of social and moral control, suddenly find ourselves surrounded by states with unrestricted power. Events like the communist revolutions from Petrograd to Peking and from Havana to Phnom Penh, which had been perceived by many of us as the most tremendous production of societies by popular mass political and social forces, became, under our very eyes, Gulag, gang of four, cult of personality or genocide. Mass movements are tending increasingly to give birth to fundamentalist movements, be they Muslim or otherwise, and to states with unrestricted powers. In our own countries, the capacity for innovation and conflict seems to be suppressed by the concentration of power and the diffusion of a consumers' mentality which discourages any active intervention. Even the development of defensive professional unions or leagues, which proliferate in the shadows of the technobureaucracy, contributes to the decline of what Proudhon used to call "political capacity."

The increasing control of society over itself and the development of mass politics themselves can very well lead not to more active societies but to the division of the world between conformity and terror, and ultimately to the destruction of all social relations and to a total state control. When confronted with the rise of Nazi totalitarianism, the philosophers of the Frankfurt School, from Horkheimer to Marcuse, given the dramatically obvious impotency of the social forces, were compelled to invoke the Waning out Reason. Today Jurgen Habermas anxiously asks himself and us whether it is possible that civil society, the *Öffentlichkeit* with its origins in the England and France of the seventeenth and eighteenth centuries, might disappear. The dissidents, who oppose Communist regimes, no longer reason in terms of class struggle, even when they say they are Marxists, but in terms of the right of man, as opposed to the absolute state. They also appeal to the cultural experience which has marked them most intensely and most personally, in reaction to the abstract, arbitrary world which Solzhenitsyn, Bukovki, or Zinoviev describe.

When the sociologist describes society as networks of actors, one can be tempted to believe that he has been dazzled by a bright light which is gradually fading and does not notice the deepening shadow of the states which surround it. It may be that the ending of "society" does not liberate the social actors; would it not be more correct to say that it brings us back to the domination of empires and to the reinforcement of social control, of propaganda, and of repression? This is in effect the question which we have inherited from de Tocqueville. And we sociologists, are not we disappearing with the object of our studies from an increasing number of areas of the world, after having believed, in the light of decolonization and revolutions, that all the parts of the world were going to become actors of their own transformation?

I shall not conclude on such a pessimistic note but at least retain the idea that the sociologist is of necessity engaged in the struggle for the recognition and the expression of social relationships in opposition to the domination of social order, especially when the latter is totalitarian. This idea leads us into the second part of this reflection in which we must no longer ask "what do you think?" but "what is to be done?" It reminds us that the object of our study is never visible to us. It is constantly hidden and repressed by power and its counterpart, violence. Instead of seeing social relationships everywhere, we mainly see systems of prohibition and revolts or concentration camps. To be able to study social behavior we must first fight for the liberation of actors and social relations. This attitude, apart from being politically or morally praiseworthy, is useful to us because it helps us to set up research methods which are suited to our new representation of social facts.

The Study of Social Movements

After having defined the object of our research by making a comparison with other representations of social facts, we must define in the same way a method to study it by opposing it to other ways of studying social behavior. Above all, we must emphasize the differences which exist between methods as far as the relationship between the researcher and the actor is concerned.

From Studies of the Consumption of Society to Studies of the Production of Society

We have all studied choices which are predetermined by social organization. We reduce then the actor to the roles given him by his various statuses in society. We show that the rich are more conservative and the poor more reformist or that the most highly educated are more culturally innovative than the others. These studies of how social resources are consumed, whether they bear on commercial, political, or educative behavior, place the observer in a position of neutrality. He only intervenes in order to constitute aggregates and categories and to relate behavior to a situation. Both behavior and situation are more or less directly defined as forms and levels of social participation.

But we cannot limit ourselves to these studies of social consumption. Even when they explain the responses given, they do not enable us to understand why the questions took a particular form. They tell us why a specific social category tends to vote more frequently Democrat than Republican. They do not explain why the voters have to choose between Republicans and Democrats rather than between Monarchists and Trotskyites. Whence the importance of a second type of research, which deals with the production of the categories of practice, and especially with decision-making processes. Considerable progress has been made recently in the study of urban or industrial policies. The situation here no longer preexists the intervention of the actors. On the contrary, the situation seems to be the result of their intervention and of their relative influence. The researcher here is forced to intervene more directly than in the studies of consumption since not all the elements of a decision leave a trace in the form of a written document or a visible effect. He feeds back information to his informants and provokes a reaction among the actors by informing them of the actions or the attitudes of other actors. Sometimes he organizes simulations.

But the moment has now come to go beyond consumption studies and decision-making studies and to enter the world of the self-production of society. Let us consider directly the central conflicts, in which social forces fight for the control of investment, of knowledge, and of the patterns of ethical behavior. For example, in industrial, capitalist society, private businessmen and industrial workers oppose each other in an attempt to assign a specific social orientation to the values of industrial society, to its beliefs in progress, in work, in the deferred gratification pattern, in historical explanation, in organization. Both sides accept these basic tenets, but they attempt to give them different social forms, which can be schematically termed capitalist and socialist. The entrepreneurs and the workers in their respective movements are the two leading actors in an industrial society. The mode of production, distribution, and consumption is shaped by the outcome of their conflicts and negotiations. Each of these actors is aware that his struggle for power makes him a producer of society and not merely a consumer of it.

But the question is: how should we study these actors? The researcher who thinks of them as consumers, whose behavior manifests a given degree of social participation, would be completely mistaken. It is necessary to side with the actor, his values and his aims. But then another danger arises, which is as serious as the previous one. The sociological analysis may be confused with the ideology of the actor: however, it is imperative that it remains separate because ideology is the definition of a social situation by the actor who is involved in it, whereas the sociological analysis is the explanation of the actor by the social relationship in which he is involved.

Sociology has not given much thought to this fundamental difficulty. Most of the books which deal with collective behavior or social movements limit themselves either to conveying the intentions and ideology of the actors, or to reducing action to patterns of consumption and adaptation. The literature on the labor movement, for example, in its attempt to explain strikes, either concentrates on an objective analysis of the general economic situation or just comments on the reformist or revolutionary statements made by political and trade union organizations. It could be said that the study of collective behavior, whose outcome is of the greatest social importance, is the weakest chapter in sociology, and, still worse, the field in which the study of the social system and that of the actors are kept most strictly apart when they should be more closely united here than anywhere else. What is the point of thinking that society is engaged in a process of self-production through its cultural orientations and its social conflicts if one is not capable of studying the actors who are collectively involved in these innovative and conflictual actions?

The Actor as Self-Analyst

This question brings two complementary answers to mind since it comes up against two obstacles. In the first place, the actor must be recognized as such: this immediately places the sociologist in a new situation. It is not enough to say that, if one wishes to study the labor movement, the black movement, or the women's movement, there is no point in using surveys and questionnaires since social movements are not answers to questions but constructions of a social field. It can be easily accepted that research on collective action must be carried out by means of the study of groups of actors, even when the movement examined has an individualist ideology, as is usually the case with the action of economic leaders. But the main point is that the actor must take part in the research as an actor and not as a subject for observation or experimentation. If, in his own eyes, our research does not have a positive function for his action, either he refuses to participate in it, or, if he does not do so, he just plays the game and his real orientations are covered by ideological rationalizations. All this rules out the classical separation between action and research. In his relationship with the researcher, the actor must behave as an actor; the researcher cannot be a referee, still less a judge.

But before we examine the problems that face the researchers in this situation let's look more closely at the role of the actor in research. Two methodological principles can be formulated. In the first place, the actor must be studied as much as possible within the context of social relationships which are meaningful to him. Should we not remind ourselves that, since our main object of study is social relations, we ought to concentrate more on these in our observations and experiments and less on situations or behavior? For example, we should not study the labor movement but study directly the social relations of production, always bearing in mind that these relations are relations between actors who are at the same time opposed to each other socially, and oriented towards the same cultural values. If, however, one takes as a starting point a study of union members, one must immediately observe them in interaction with executives, civil servants, labor lawyers and with all the other social actors whom they themselves recognize as belonging to the same field of action.

Secondly, it is imperative to respect another fundamental principle of sociological analysis, namely, that there can be no role without consciousness of it and consequently no class without class-consciousness, although class consciousness may not lead directly to class action. The nearer one comes to the highest level of collective behavior, which corresponds to the *self-production of society,* the more important it becomes to respect the analysis which the actor makes of his action. The object of the analysis should not be the behavior of the actor but the analysis which the actor makes of his own behavior and of the behavior of his social partners. In the method of research which I term *sociological intervention,* the first and the most obvious of the researcher's roles is to continually push the actor to conduct this self-analysis, while continuing to be an actor. It is the actor's ability to conduct this analysis which best informs us about the nature of his actions, since this ability increases as one goes from behavior that can be defined as *production of society.* To sum up, the intervention consists first of all in studying collective actors as actors in their relations with their social partners and through the analysis of these relations which they themselves conduct. That requires a long interaction between actors and researchers—more than a hundred hours in my own practice. Quite different from extensive surveys, this approach is still more different from the classical Marxist approach. The latter reduces the labor movement, for example, to a sign of the contradictions of capitalism, a sign which can only be interpreted by those intellectuals who are the trustees of a scientific theory of history. On the contrary, I consider that social relations oppose value oriented actors who try to control in opposite ways the same cultural field.

The Intervention of the Researcher

This self-analysis of the actor cannot be entirely freed from ideology. If it were, the actor would stop being an actor and would become a sociologist—which is in effect what happens when a movement is assailed with doubts and a feeling of helplessness. The actor therefore requires a mediator, who enables him to be confronted with a more elaborate analysis of his own behavior while remaining himself an actor. How can the researcher play this role? How can he avoid either being an ideologist or destroying the actor by observing him as a dead butterfly? I think that he can do this by representing for the actor the highest possible meaning of his action. This constitutes the central proposal of the method which I am putting before you. Let's consider the case of antinuclear militants who oppose the construction of nuclear power plants. They are afraid of accidents or of contamination, or they criticize the economic and technical arguments of the spokesmen for the nuclear industry. But the researcher introduces the hypothesis that this defensive action bears the seeds of a new form of class struggle, the defense of a population against technocracy and that at the same time it contains elements of cultural innovation since it introduces values and consumption patterns which are appropriate to the postindustrial society in the making. The researcher in no way states that this highest possible meaning is in fact historically the most effective. He does not say that antinuclear actions are actually capable of becoming an organized political movement with the capacity to attack centers of power. But he presents to the actors the highest possible meaning of their collective action in such a way as to ensure that the actors react to it. All collective actions involve, directly or indirectly, a struggle for power, together with other kinds of social relations. The nature of collective action can be determined by the way in which the actors react to the image put by the sociologist of its highest components. When faced with this very abstract and very general interpretation of their action, the actors are far from their ideology, which interprets a concrete historical situation. They are as far removed as possible from their practical activity, and this disequilibrium forces them to look for a deeper significance of their action. The researcher, by placing himself as far away as possible from the practical interpretation of the action, leaves room for the analysis. The actors, by responding to the researcher's hypothesis, define their own place in it. If we were to compare the situation with that of an oil refinery, we could speak here of the cracking of collective behavior.

The sociologist in no way identifies himself with the actual struggle of the actor or with his ideology. Nor is he a neutral observer incapable of interacting with the actor without destroying him. He acts as an agent in the analysis of the actor and his intervention enables him to advance his own analysis. This role of the researcher is very far from the cold objectivity of the sociological tradition. But it is even further from the identification with the actor which the different types of militant research or action-research propose. The researcher aims at knowledge while the actor's aim is action. But the researcher is not neutral. He hopes that the actor will be capable of acting at the highest possible level. Like the psychotherapist who wishes to help his patient to control his behavior and to liberate him from anxiety, the sociologist wishes here to help the actor liberate himself from the constraints of a situation which is imposed upon him and to participate in the conflictual *self-production of society* because it is only through the struggle of the actors that the object of sociological analysis, the social relations themselves, can be discovered, beneath thick layers of dominant ideologies which hide aims and conflicts. Action and analysis are allied against order and ideology.

Analysis and Action: Permanent Sociology

This definition of his role leads the sociologist to verify his hypotheses by studying the effects of his analysis on the behavior of the actors. The actor, using the sociologist's analysis obtains, from the observed consequences of his action, confirmation or refutation of this analysis. He transmits the results to the sociologist and asks him to change his hypotheses if necessary. More simply, the sociologist observes whether the actors react in a predictable manner to situations that correspond to different levels of collective action. By doing so we enter a two-way process between action and analysis which could go on for ever. This is why I have named the second part of the research, which follows the intervention itself, *permanent sociology*. In the case of the study that we are completing at the moment, which deals with the antinuclear movement in France, this phase of permanent sociology has been going on for more than a year now and we expect it to continue for several years after the publication of our book.

As a closing remark about the method that I have briefly presented, and which is described in greater detail in my recent book *The Voice and the Eye (La voix et le regard),* I want to emphasize that it implies a deep transformation of the relationship observed between the analyst and the observed actor. Psychologists are accustomed to this double role of analyst and intervener. Sociologists preferred to keep their distance because they remained convinced that the object they were studying was society. They saw a clear division of labor between themselves and social psychologists who devoted themselves to the study of actors in social situations and especially in groups. The approach that I am attempting to develop differs both from the psychological study of groups and particularly from group-centered groups, and from the analysis of situations or social trends. It seems to be appropriate for the study of collective behavior, which questions most directly cultural orientations and power structure. But this method should not be limited to the study of protest movements. We are devoting our first six-year program to these movements, but I shall attempt to gradually extend the application of the method to other data by turning my attention to three different fields: First, ruling class movements because management should be considered as a social movement, exactly as much as unionism; second, movements which are oriented toward the control of the process of societal change, for example of industrialization, especially in developing countries; and finally, diluted or indirect forms of protest movements which are generally classified as riots, disorder, deviance, or even mental illness. My first research program, which I began in 1976, deals with the student movement, the antinuclear movement, a regionalist movement, labor unions, and the women's movement. The study of the student movement has just been published. The one on the antinuclear movement is finished, and we are now in the midst of our study of the regionalist movement. These studies are carried out in France for practical reasons but I should here like to express my deep interest in training research teams and in conducting research with these in other countries, especially where sociologists are independent and creative.

I trust that this research and the spirit in which it is carried out will help to increase our capacity for innovation and conflict and will contribute to the development of new forms of direct democracy. When power was in the hands of the Prince, the nation attempted to elect its representatives to vote for taxes and to thereby control the most important decisions. When power was personified in the factory owners, the labor unions created a more direct form of democracy. Now that almost all the spheres of our life are dominated by technostructures, there is a need to further the development of social movements that are no longer transmission belts for political parties and that go beyond lobbies and interest groups.

Our active participation in this new advance of democracy will support our search for knowledge. It is not by keeping our distances from creative social action and by taking for granted the present forms of social organization that we shall reach a better knowledge of social life and free it from ideological and social pressures. To the contrary, we would thus make ourselves responsible for identifying a social system with its power structure. The abstract character of certain formulations should not prevent us from seeing that they were 10 or 20 years later, to a large extent, an expression of the dominant ideology of the times. By perceiving as directly as possible relationships, conflicts, and social movements, we will be able to free ourselves from ideologies and to discover the central object of our research, that is to understand how a human group, acting upon itself through symbolic systems, investment and ethical patterns, produces, through conflicts for the social control of these actions, the categories of its social and cultural organization.

Since the actors in the drama of industrial society are gradually disappearing from the state of history, while new actors and new issues that represent postindustrial society are only beginning to appear, we often have the impression of living in a historical vacuum. This impression is heightened by the decline of dominant ideologies, either in the West or in the East. This explains why, at the moment, a semiotical conception of social life, which sees signs where sociologists look for social relations, is so influential. I can understand why so many observers see in present day societies only signs of bureaucracy, mass consumption, nationalism, or totalitarianism. But it is already too late to accept such a pessimistic image. From many places we hear again voices of anger and hope; they announce the coming of new debates and new struggles. I feel myself very remote from those, Marxists or not, who reduce society to a system of domination and to the reproduction of this domination, and very close to those, Marxists or not, who are sensitive to innovations and to new forms of social struggle. I also listen to those who try to impose new forms of power and who invent new ideologies that break with those of the former ruling classes. I would like us sociologists to waste no more time on reliving the struggles of the 19th century and not to yield to the false idea that actors have disappeared from our societies, either because these are totally submitted to a central power or on the contrary because all conflicts are disrupted by permanent changes. I would like sociology to realize that new dramas and new social movements are being born in many parts of the world. These include places where totalitarianism seemed to have drowned out their voices, where nationalism seemed to preclude any social discussion, as well as places where the complexity of organizations and the rapidity of changes seemed to make the formation of struggles in general more difficult. If we succeed in thus redefining our role, we shall give sociology a legitimacy which it is no longer sure of possessing. The concept of society gave it a legitimacy which has become more dangerous than useful. Today we must start with the conviction that the study of social relations, conceived as primarily created by social movements, is linked with the permanent fight for freedom and against nonsocial explanations and legitimizations of social order.

We can play a recognized role in our society if we first succeed in ending the separation between the system and the actors, and between politics and psychology because domination and repression have always been ideologically based on these dichotomies. And in doing so we will give its full importance to the study of political psychology which brings us together today.

89

Structuration Theory*

Anthony Giddens

The differences between the structural and hermeneutic perspectives on social science have often been taken to be epistemological, whereas they are in fact also ontological. What is at issue is how the concepts of action, meaning and subjectivity should be specified and how they might relate to notions of structure and constraint. If interpretative sociologies are founded, as it were, upon an imperialism of the subject, functionalism and structuralism propose an imperialism of the social object. One of my principal ambitions in the formulation of structuration theory is to put an end to each of these empire-building endeavours. The basic domain of study of the social sciences, according to the theory of structuration, is neither the experience of the individual actor, nor the existence of any form of societal totality, but social practices ordered across space and time. Human social activities, like some self-reproducing items in nature, are recursive. That is to say, they are not brought into being by social actors but continually recreated by them via the very means whereby they express themselves as actors. In and through their activities agents reproduce the conditions that make these activities possible. However, the sort of 'knowledgeability' displayed in nature, in the form of coded programmes, is distant from the cognitive skills displayed by human agents. It is in the conceptualizing of human knowledgeability and its involvement in action that I seek to appropriate some of the major contributions of interpretative sociologies. In structuration theory a hermeneutic starting-point is accepted in so far as it is acknowledged that the description of human activities demands a familiarity with the forms of life expressed in those activities.

It is the specifically reflexive form of the knowledgeability of human agents that is most deeply involved in the recursive ordering of social practices. Continuity of practices presumes reflexivity, but reflexivity in turn is possible only because of the continuity of practices that makes them distinctively 'the same' across space and time. 'Reflexivity' hence should be understood not merely as 'self-consciousness' but as the monitored character of the ongoing flow of social life. To be a human being is to be a purposive agent, who both has reasons for his or her activities and is able, if asked, to elaborate discursively upon those reasons (including lying about them). But terms such as 'purpose' or 'intention', 'reason', 'motive' and so on have to be treated with caution, since their usage in the philosophical literature has very often been associated with a hermeneutical voluntarism, and because they extricate

*Excerpt from *The Constitution of Society: Outline of the Theory of Structuration* by Anthony Giddens.

human action from the contextuality of time-space. Human action occurs as a *durée*, a continuous flow of conduct, as does cognition. Purposive action is not composed of an aggregate or series of separate intentions, reasons and motives. Thus it is useful to speak of reflexivity as grounded in the continuous monitoring of action which human beings display and expect others to display. The reflexive monitoring of action depends upon rationalization, understood here as a process rather than a state and as inherently involved in the competence of agents. An ontology of time-space as constitutive of social practices is basic to the conception of structuration, which *begins* from temporality and thus, in one sense, 'history'.

This approach can draw only sparingly upon the analytical philosophy of action, as 'action' is ordinarily portrayed by most contemporary Anglo-American writers. 'Action' is not a combination of 'acts': 'acts' are constituted only by a discursive moment of attention to the *durée* of lived-through experience. Nor can 'action' be discussed in separation from the body, its mediations with the surrounding world and the coherence of an acting self. What I call a *stratification model* of the acting self involves treating the reflexive monitoring, rationalization and motivation of action as embedded sets of processes. The rationalization of action, referring to 'intentionality' as process, is, like the other two dimensions, a routine characteristic of human conduct, carried on in a taken-for-granted fashion. In circumstances of interaction—encounters and episodes—the reflexive monitoring of action typically, and again routinely, incorporates the monitoring of the setting of such interaction.

The Agent, Agency

The stratification model of the agent can be represented as in Figure 1. The reflexive monitoring of activity is a chronic feature of everyday action and involves the conduct not just of the individual but also of others. That is to say, actors not only monitor continuously the flow of their activities and expect others to do the same for their own; they also routinely monitor aspects, social and physical, of the contexts in which they move. By the rationalization of action, I mean that actors—also routinely and for the most part without fuss—maintain a continuing 'theoretical understanding' of the grounds of their activity.

I distinguish the reflexive monitoring and rationalization of action from its motivation. If reasons refer to the grounds of action, motives refer to the wants which prompt it. However, motivation is not as directly bound up with the continuity of action as are its reflexive monitoring or rationalization. Motivation refers to potential for action rather than to the mode in which action is chronically carried on by the agent. Motives tend to have a direct purchase on action only in relatively unusual circumstances, situations which in some way break with the routine. For the most part motives supply overall plans or programmes—'projects', in Schutz's term—within which a range of conduct is enacted. Much of our day-to-day conduct is not directly motivated.

While competent actors can nearly always report discursively about their intentions in, and reasons for, acting as they do, they cannot necessarily do so of their motives.

These concepts all refer to the agent. What of the nature of agency? This can be connected with a further issue. The *durée* of day-to-day life occurs as a flow of intentional action. However, acts have unintended consequences; and, as indicated in Figure 1, unintended consequences may systematically feed back to be the unacknowledged conditions of further acts. Thus one of the regular consequences of my speaking or writing

Figure 1

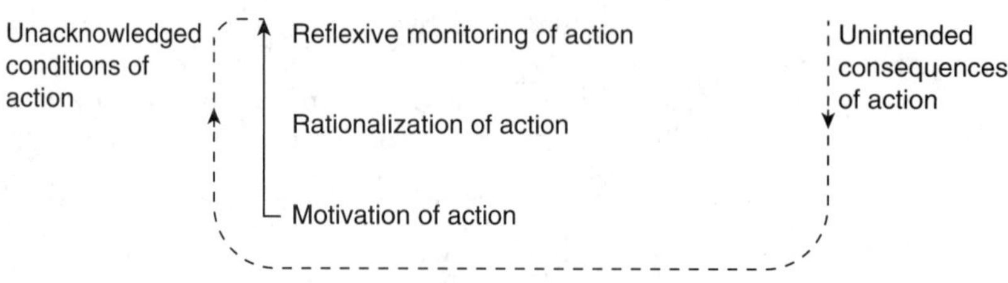

English in a correct way is to contribute to the reproduction of the English language as a whole. My speaking English correctly is intentional; the contribution I make to the reproduction of the language is not. But how should we formulate what unintended consequences are?

Agency refers not to the intentions people have in doing things but to their capability of doing those things in the first place (which is why agency implies power: cf. the Oxford English Dictionary definition of an agent, as 'one who exerts power or produces an effect'). Agency concerns events of which an individual is the perpetrator, in the sense that the individual could, at any phase in a given sequence of conduct, have acted differently. Whatever happened would not have happened if that individual had not intervened. Action is a continuous process, a flow, in which the reflexive monitoring which the individual maintains is fundamental to the control of the body that actors ordinarily sustain throughout their day-to-day lives. I am the author of many things I do not intend to do, and may not want to bring about, but none the less *do*. Conversely, there may be circumstances in which I intend to achieve something, and do achieve it, although not directly through my agency. Take the example of the spilled coffee. Supposing an individual, A, were a malicious spirit and played a practical joke by placing the cup on a saucer at such an angle that, when picked up, it would be very likely to spill. Individual B picks up the coffee, and it duly spills over. It would be right to say that what A did brought the incident about, or at least contributed to its coming about. But A did not spill the coffee; B did. Individual B, who did not intend to spill the coffee, spilled the coffee; individual A, who did intend that the coffee should be spilled, did not spill it.

Philosophers have used up a great deal of ink attempting to analyse the nature of intentional activity. But from the point of view of the social sciences, it is hard to exaggerate the importance of the unintended consequences of intentional conduct.

A second type of circumstance upon which the social analyst might focus is one in which, instead of a pattern of unintended consequences initiated by a single event, there is a pattern resulting from a complex of individual activities. Here a definite 'end result' is taken as the phenomenon to be explained, and that end result is shown to derive as an unintended consequence from an aggregate of courses of intentional conduct.

The third type of context in which unintended consequences may be traced out is that pointed to by Merton: where the interest of the analyst is in the mechanisms of reproduction of institutionalized practices. Here the unintended consequences of action form the acknowledged conditions of further action in a non-reflexive feedback cycle (causal loops). I have pointed out that it is not enough to isolate functional relations in order to explain why such feedback occurs. How, then, does it happen that cycles of unintended consequences feed back to promote social reproduction across long periods of time? In a general way, this is not difficult to analyse. Repetitive activities, located in one context of time and space, have regularized consequences, unintended by those who engage in those activities, in more or less 'distant' time-space contexts. What happens in this second series of contexts then, directly or indirectly, influences the further conditions of action in the original context. To understand what is going on no explanatory variables are needed other than those which explain why individuals are motivated to engage in regularized social practices across time and space, and what consequences ensue. The unintended consequences are regularly 'distributed' as a by-product of regularized behaviour reflexively sustained as such by its participants.

Agency and Power

To be able to 'act otherwise' means being able to intervene in the world, or to refrain from such intervention, with the effect of influencing a specific process or state of affairs. This presumes that to be an agent is to be able to deploy (chronically, in the flow of daily life) a range of causal powers, including that of influencing those deployed by others. Action depends upon the capability of the individual to ' make a difference' to a pre-existing state of affairs or course of events. An agent ceases to be such if he or she loses the capability to 'make a difference', that is, to exercise some sort of power.

Resources (focused via signification and legitimation) are structured properties of social systems, drawn upon and reproduced by knowledgeable agents in the course of interaction.

Power is not intrinsically connected to the achievement of sectional interests. In this conception the use of power characterizes not specific types of conduct but all action, and power is not itself a resource. Resources are media through which power is exercised, as a routine element of the instantiation of conduct in social reproduction. We should not conceive of the structures of domination built into social institutions as in some way grinding out 'docile bodies' who behave like the automata suggested by objectivist social science. Power within social systems which enjoy some continuity over time and space presumes regularized relations of autonomy and dependence between actors or collectivities in contexts of social interaction. But all forms of dependence offer some resources whereby those who are subordinate can influence the activities of their superiors. This is what I call the *dialectic of control* in social systems.

Structure, Structuration

Let me now move to the core of structuration theory: the concepts of 'structure', 'system' and 'duality of structure'.

Structure refers, in social analysis, to the structuring properties allowing the 'binding' of time-space in social systems, the properties which make it possible for discernibly similar social practices to exist across varying spans of time and space and which lend them 'systemic' form. To say that structure is a 'virtual order' of transformative relations means that social systems, as reproduced social practices, do not have 'structures' but rather exhibit 'structural properties' and that structure exists, as time-space presence, only in its instantiations in such practices and as memory traces orienting the conduct of knowledgeable human agents. This does not prevent us from conceiving of structural properties as hierarchically organized in terms of the time-space extension of the practices they recursively organize. The most deeply embedded structural properties, implicated in the reproduction of societal totalities, I call *structural principles*. Those practices which have the greatest time-space extension within such totalities can be referred to as *institutions*.

One of the main propositions of structuration theory is that the rules and resources drawn upon in the production and reproduction of social action are at the same time the means of system reproduction (the duality of structure).

Let us regard the rules of social life, then, as techniques or generalizable procedures applied in the enactment/reproduction of social practices.

Those types of rule which are of most significance for social theory are locked into the reproduction of institutionalized practices, that is, practices most deeply sedimented in time-space.

Most of the rules implicated in the production and reproduction of social practices are only tacitly grasped by actors: they know how to 'go on'. *The discursive formulation of a rule is already an interpretation of it*, and, as I have noted, may in and of itself alter the form of its application. Among rules that are not just discursively formulated but are formally codified, the type case is that of laws.

The structuring qualities of rules can be studied in respect, first of all, of the forming, sustaining, termination and reforming of encounters. Although a dazzling variety of procedures and tactics are used by agents in the constitution and reconstitution of encounters, probably particularly significant are those involved in the sustaining of ontological security.

The most important aspects of structure are rules and resources recursively involved in institutions. Institutions by definition are the more enduring features of social life. In speaking of the structural properties of social systems I mean their institutionalized features, giving 'solidity' across time and space. I use the concept of 'structures' to get at relations of transformation and mediation which are the 'circuit switches' underlying observed conditions of system reproduction.

The Duality of Structure

Let me summarize the argument thus far. Structure, as recursively organized sets of rules and resources, is out of time and space, save in its instantiations and co-ordination as memory traces, and is marked by an 'absence of the subject'. The social systems in which structure is recursively implicated, on the contrary, comprise the situated activities of human agents, reproduced across time and space. Analysing the structuration of social systems means studying the modes in which such systems, grounded in the knowledgeable activities of situated actors who draw upon rules and resources in the diversity of action contexts, are produced and reproduced in interaction. Crucial to the idea of structuration is the theorem of the duality of structure, which is logically implied in the arguments portrayed above. The constitution of agents and structures are not two independently given sets of phenomena, a dualism, but represent a duality. According to the notion of the duality of structure, the structural properties of social systems are both medium and outcome of the practices they recursively organize. Structure is not 'external' to individuals: as memory traces, and as instantiated in social practices, it is in a certain sense more 'internal' than exterior to their activities in a Durkheimian sense. Structure is not to be equated with constraint but is always both constraining and enabling. This, of course, does not prevent the structured properties of social systems from stretching away, in time and space, beyond the control of any individual actors. Nor does it compromise the possibility that actors' own theories of the social systems which they help to constitute and reconstitute in their activities may reify those systems. The reification of social relations, or the discursive 'naturalization' of the historically contingent circumstances and products of human action, is one of the main dimensions of ideology in social life.

According to structuration theory, the moment of the production of action is also one of reproduction in the contexts of the day-to-day enactment of social life. This is so even during the most violent upheavals or most radical forms of social change. It is not accurate to see the structural properties of social systems as 'social products' because this tends to imply that pre-constituted actors somehow come together to create them. In reproducing structural properties to repeat a phrase used earlier, agents also reproduce the conditions that make such action possible. Structure has no existence independent of the knowledge that agents have about what they do in their day-to-day activity. Human agents always know what they are doing on the level of discursive consciousness under some description. However, what they do may be quite unfamiliar under other descriptions, and they may know little of the ramified consequences of the activities in which they engage.

The duality of structure is always the main grounding of continuities in social reproduction across time-space. It in turn presupposes the reflexive monitoring of agents in, and as constituting, the *durée* of daily social activity. But human knowledgeability is always bounded. The flow of action continually produces consequences which are unintended by actors, and these unintended consequences also may form unacknowledged conditions of action in a feedback fashion. Human history is created by intentional activities but is not an intended project; it persistently eludes efforts to bring it under conscious direction. However, such attempts are continually made by human beings, who operate under the threat and the promise of the circumstance that they are the only creatures who make their 'history' in cognizance of that fact.

Structure(s)	*System(s)*	*Structuration*
Rules and resources, or sets of transformation relations, organized as properties of social systems	Reproduced relations between actors or collectivities, organized as regular social practices	Conditions governing the continuity or transmutation of structures, and therefore the reproduction of social systems

90

Ontological Security, Existential Anxiety, and Self-Identity*

Anthony Giddens

All human beings continuously monitor the circumstances of their activities as a feature of doing what they do, and such monitoring always has discursive features. In other words, agents are normally able, if asked, to provide discursive interpretations of the nature of, and the reasons for, the behaviour in which they engage.

The knowledgeability of human agents, however, is not confined to discursive consciousness of the conditions of their action. Many of the elements of being able to 'go on' are carried at the level of practical consciousness, incorporated within the continuity of everyday activities. Practical consciousness is integral to the reflexive monitoring of action, but it is 'non-conscious', rather than unconscious. Most forms of practical consciousness could not be 'held in mind' during the course of social activities, since their tacit or taken-for-granted qualities form the essential condition which allows actors to concentrate on tasks at hand. Yet there are no cognitive barriers separating discursive and practical consciousness, as there are divisions between the unconscious and consciousness taken generically. Unconscious modes of cognition and emotional governance, as a matter of definition, specifically resist being brought into consciousness, and appear there only in a distorted or transposed way.

Ontological Security and Trust

Practical consciousness is the cognitive and emotive anchor of the feelings of *ontological security* characteristic of large segments of human activity in all cultures. The notion of ontological security ties in closely to the tacit character of practical consciousness—or, in phenomenological terms, to the 'bracketings' presumed by the 'natural attitude' in everyday life. On the other side of what might appear to be quite trivial aspects of day-to-day action and discourse, chaos lurks. And this chaos is not just disorganisation, but the loss of a sense of the very reality of things and of other persons.

To live our lives, we normally take for granted issues which, as centuries of philosophical enquiry have found, wither away under the sceptical gaze. Such issues include those quite properly called existential, whether posed on the level of philosophical analysis, or on a more practical level by individuals passing through a period of psychological crisis. They are questions of time, space, continuity and identity. In the natural attitude, actors take for granted existential parameters of their activity that are sustained, but in no way 'grounded' by the interactional conventions they observe. Existentially, these presume a tacit acceptance of the categories of duration and extension, together with the identity of objects, other persons and—particularly important for this study—the self.

To investigate such matters on the level of abstract philosophical discussion is, of course, quite different from actually 'living' them. The chaos that threatens on the other side of the ordinariness of everyday conventions can be seen psychologically as *dread* in Kierkegaard's sense: the prospect of being overwhelmed by anxieties that reach to the very roots of our coherent sense of 'being in the world'. Practical consciousness, together with the day-to-day routines reproduced by it, help bracket such anxieties not only, or even primarily, because of the social stability that they imply, but because of their constitutive role in organising an 'as if' environment in relation to existential issues. They provide modes of orientation which, on the level of practice, 'answer' the questions which could be raised about the frameworks of existence. It is of central importance to the analysis which follows to see that the anchoring aspects of such 'answers' are emotional rather than simply cognitive. How far different cultural settings allow a 'faith' in the coherence of everyday life to be achieved through providing symbolic interpretations of existential questions is, as we shall see below, very important. But cognitive frames of meaning will not generate that faith without a corresponding level of underlying emotional commitment—whose origins, I shall argue, are largely unconscious. Trust, hope and courage are all relevant to such commitment.

How is such faith achieved in terms of the psychological development of the human being? What creates a sense of ontological security that will carry the individual through transitions, crises and circumstances of high risk? Trust in the existential anchorings of reality in an emotional, and to some degree in a cognitive, sense rests on confidence in the reliability of persons, acquired in the early experiences of the infant. What Erik Erikson, echoing D. W. Winnicott, calls 'basic trust' forms the original nexus from which a combined emotive-cognitive orientation towards others, the object-world, and self-identity, emerges. The experience of basic trust is the core of that specific 'hope' of which Ernst Bloch speaks, and is at origin of what Tillich calls 'the courage to be'. As developed through the loving attentions of early caretakers, basic trust links self-identity in a fateful way to the appraisals of others. The mutuality with early caretakers which basic trust presumes is a substantially unconscious sociality which precedes an 'I' and a 'me', and is a prior basis of any differentiation between the two.

Basic trust is connected in an essential way to the interpersonal organisation of time and space. An awareness of the separate identity of the parenting figures originates in the emotional acceptance of *absence*: the 'faith' that the caretaker will return, even though she or he is no longer in the presence of the infant. Basic trust is forged through what Winnicott calls the 'potential space' (actually, a phenomenon of time-space) which relates, yet distances, infant and prime caretaker. Potential space is created as the means whereby the infant makes the move from omnipotence to a grasp of the reality principle. 'Reality' here, however, should not be understood simply as a given object-world, but as a set of experiences organised constitutively through the mutuality of infant and caretakers.

The trust which the child, in normal circumstances, vests in its caretakers, I want to argue, can be seen as a sort of *emotional inoculation* against existential anxieties—a protection against future threats and dangers which allows the individual to sustain hope and courage in the face of whatever debilitating circumstances she or he might later confront. Basic trust is a screening-off device in relation to risks and dangers in the surrounding settings of action and interaction. It is the main emotional support of a defensive carapace or *protective cocoon* which all normal individuals carry around with them as the means whereby they are able to get on with the affairs of day-to-day life.

The sustaining of life, in a bodily sense as well as in the sense of psychological health, is inherently subject to risk. The fact that the behaviour of human beings is so strongly influenced by mediated experience, together with the calculative capacities which human agents possess, mean that every human individual could (in principle) be overwhelmed by anxieties about risks which are implied by the very business of living. That sense of 'invulnerability' which blocks off negative possibilities in favour of a generalised attitude of hope derives from basic trust. The protective cocoon is essentially a sense of 'unreality' rather than a firm conviction of security: it is a bracketing, on the level of practice, of possible events which could threaten the bodily or psychological integrity of the agent. The protective barrier it offers may be pierced, temporarily or more permanently, by happenings which demonstrate as real the negative contingencies built into all risk. Which car driver, passing by the scene of a serious traffic accident, has not had the experience of being so sobered as to drive more slowly—for a few miles—afterwards? Such an example is one which demonstrates—not in a counterfactual universe of abstract possibilities, but in a tangible and vivid way—the risks of driving, and thereby serves temporarily to pull apart the protective cocoon. But the feeling of relative invulnerability soon returns and the chances are that the driver then tends to speed up again.

All individuals develop a framework of ontological security of some sort, based on routines of various forms. People handle dangers, and the fears associated with them, in terms of the emotional and behavioural 'formulae' which have come to be part of their everyday behaviour and thought. Anxiety also differs from fear in so far as it concerns (unconsciously) perceived threats to the integrity of the security system of the individual. The analysis of anxiety worked out by Harry Stack Sullivan, rather than that of Freud himself, is very useful here. Sullivan emphasises that the need for a sense of security emerges very early on in the life of the child, and is 'much more important in the human being than the impulses resulting from a feeling of hunger, or thirst'.

Like Winnicott and Erikson, Sullivan stresses that the infant's early sense of security comes from the nurturance of the caretaking agents—which he interprets in terms of the infant's sensitivity to parental approval or disapproval. Anxiety is felt through a—real or imagined—sensing of a caretaker's disapproval long before the development of consciously formed responses to the disapprobation of the other. Anxiety is felt as a 'cosmic' experience related to the reactions of others and to emerging self-esteem. It attacks the core of the self once a basic security system is set up, which is why it is so difficult for the individual to objectify it. Rising anxiety tends to threaten awareness of self-identity, since awareness of the self in relation to constituting features of the object-world becomes obscured. It is only in terms of the basic security system, the origin of the sense of ontological security, that the individual has the experience of self in relation to a world of persons and objects organised cognitively through basic trust.

The prime existential question which the infant 'answers' in the course of early psychological development concerns *existence itself*: the discovery of an ontological framework of 'external reality'. When Kierkegaard analyses anxiety—or elemental dread—as 'the struggle of being against non-being', he points directly to this issue. To 'be' for the human individual, is to have ontological awareness. This is not the same as awareness of self-identity, however closely the two may be related in the developing experience of the infant. The 'struggle of being against non-being' is the perpetual task of the individual, not just to 'accept' reality, but to create ontological reference points as an integral aspect of 'going on' in the contexts of day-to-day life. Existence is a mode of being-in-the-world in Kierkegaard's sense. In 'doing' everyday life, all human beings 'answer' the question of being; they do it by the nature of the activities they carry out. As with other existential questions such 'answers' are lodged fundamentally on the level of behaviour.

Another type of existential question concerns precisely: *self-identity*. But what exactly is self-identity? Since the self is a somewhat amorphous phenomenon, self-identity cannot refer merely to its persistence over time in the way philosophers might speak of the 'identity' of objects or things. The 'identity' of the self, in contrast to the self as a generic phenomenon, presumes reflexive awareness. It is what the individual is conscious 'of' in the term 'self-consciousness'. Self-identity, in other words, is not something that is just given, as a result of the continuities of the individual's action-system, but something that has to be routinely created and sustained in the reflexive activities of the individual.

Self-identity is not a distinctive trait, or even a collection of traits, possessed by the individual. It is *the self as reflexively understood by the person in terms of her or his biography.* Identity here still presumes continuity across time and space: but self-identity is such continuity as interpreted reflexively by the agent. This includes the cognitive component of personhood. To be a 'person' is not just to be a reflexive actor, but to have a concept of a person (as applied both to the self and others). What a 'person' is understood to be certainly varies across cultures, although there are elements of such a notion that are common to all cultures. The capacity to use 'I' in shifting contexts, characteristic of every known culture, is the most elemental feature of reflexive conceptions of personhood.

A normal sense of self-identity is the obverse of these characteristics. A person with a reasonably stable sense of self-identity has a feeling of biographical continuity which she is able to grasp reflexively and, to a greater or lesser degree, communicate to other people. That person also, through early trust relations, has established a protective cocoon which 'filters out', in the practical conduct of day-to-day life, many of the dangers which in principle threaten the integrity of the self. Finally, the individual is able to accept that integrity as worthwhile. There is sufficient self-regard to sustain a sense of the self as 'alive'—within the scope of reflexive control, rather than having the inert quality of things in the object-world.

How far normal appearances can be carried on in ways consistent with the individual's biographical narrative is of vital importance for feelings of ontological security. All human beings, in all cultures, preserve a division between their self-identities and the 'performances' they put on in specific social contexts. But in some circumstances the individual might come to feel that the whole flow of his activities is put on or false. An established routine, for one reason or another, becomes invalid. For instance, a husband may conceal from his wife the fact that he is having an affair and plans to divorce her. Ordinary routines then become false performances, staged routines from which the person feels a certain distance—the individual has to continue with ordinary appearances by acting as though nothing were up. What is habitually structured into practical consciousness becomes contrived, and probably unconsciously problematic. Playing the part of the dutiful husband in effect represents a false persona, but not one that seriously compromises the individual's own self-image.

Where the dissociation is more thoroughgoing, and less contextual, however, a more severe dislocation is likely to result. A person feels he is continually acting out most or all routines, rather than following them for valid reasons. If Laing is correct, such a situation characteristically leads to an 'unembodied' self. Most people are absorbed in their bodies, and feel themselves to be a unified body and self. Too radical a discrepancy between accepted routines and the individual's biographical narrative creates what Laing (following Winnicott) calls a false self—in which the body appears as an object or instrument manipulated by the self from behind the scenes. Disentanglement from the body—or perhaps a complete merging of self and body—in the form of spiritual ecstasy, is a common ideal of the world's religions, and appears there in a positive light. But when this dissociation happens as an unwanted feature of personality, it expresses existential anxieties impinging directly upon self-identity.

Disembodiment in more minor versions is a characteristic feature of disruptions in ontological security experienced by everyone in tensionful situations of daily life. The splitting is a temporary reaction to a danger which passes, not a chronic dissociation. It is not fanciful to discern a close connection between Winnicott, Laing and Lacan on this point. For if the hypothesis of the mirror stage is valid, perception of the body as separate—in the imaginary—is central to the formation of self-identity at a particular phase of child development. A narrative of self-identity cannot begin until this phase is transcended; or, more accurately, the emergence of such a narrative is the means of its transcendence. Against this backdrop, it is not surprising that, in circumstances of strain, feelings of separation from the body should be common. The individual enters a temporary schizoid state, and becomes detached from what the body is doing or what is being done to it.

Mirror image and self can effectively become reversed in more pronounced and semi-permanent schizoid personalities. The experience of agency is withdrawn from the body and attached to a fantasy world of narrative biography, separated from the intersecting of the imaginary and the reality principle upon which ordinary social activity depends. Self-identity is no longer integrated with the day-to-day routines in which the person is involved. The individual may in fact feel invisible to others, since the body in action ceases to be the 'vehicle of the self'.

91

HABITUS*

PIERRE BOURDIEU

The conditionings associated with a particular class of conditions of existence produce *habitus*, systems of durable, transposable dispositions, structured structures predisposed to function as structuring structures, that is, as principles which generate and organize practices and representations that can be objectively adapted to their outcomes without presupposing a conscious aiming at ends or an express mastery of the operations necessary in order to attain them. Objectively "regulated" and "regular" without being in any way the product of obedience to rules, they can be collectively orchestrated without being the product of the organizing action of a conductor.

Unlike scientific estimations, which are corrected after each experiment according to rigorous rules of calculation, the anticipations of the *habitus*, practical hypotheses based on past experience, give disproportionate weight to early experiences. Through the economic and social necessity that they bring to bear on the relatively autonomous world of the domestic economy and family relations, or more precisely, through the specifically familial manifestations of this external necessity (forms of the division of labour between the sexes, household objects, modes of consumption, parent-child relations, etc.), the structures characterizing a determinate class of conditions of existence produce the structures of the *habitus*, which in their turn are the basis of the perception and appreciation of all subsequent experiences.

The *habitus*, a product of history, produces individual and collective practices—more history—in accordance with the schemes generated by history. It ensures the active presence of past experiences, which, deposited in each organism in the form of schemes of perception, thought, and action, tend to guarantee the "correctness" of practices and their constancy over time, more reliably than all formal rules and explicit norms. This system of dispositions—a present past that tends to perpetuate itself into the future by reactivation in similarly structured practices, an internal law through which the law of external necessities, irreducible to immediate constraints, is constantly exerted—is the principle of the continuity and regularity which objectivism sees in social practices without being able to account for it; and also of the regulated transformations that cannot be explained either by the extrinsic, instantaneous determinisms of mechanistic sociologism or by the purely internal but equally instantaneous determination of spontaneist subjectivism. Overriding the spurious opposition between the forces inscribed in an earlier state of the system,

*Excerpts from *The Logic of Practice* by Pierre Bourdieu, Translated by Richard Nice.

outside the body, and the internal forces arising instantaneously as motivations springing from free will, the internal dispositions—the internalization of externality—enable the external forces to exert themselves, but in accordance with the specific logic of the organisms in which they are incorporated, i.e., in a durable, systematic, and non-mechanical way. As an acquired system of generative schemes, the *habitus* makes possible the free production of all the thoughts, perceptions, and actions inherent in the particular conditions of its production—and only those. Through the *habitus*, the structure of which it is the product governs practice, not along the paths of a mechanical determinism, but within the constraints and limits initially set on its inventions.

Because they tend to reproduce the regularities immanent in the conditions in which their generative principle was produced while adjusting to the demands inscribed as objective potentialities in the situation as defined by the cognitive and motivating structures that constitute the *habitus*, practices cannot be deduced either from the present conditions which may seem to have provoked them or from the past conditions which have produced the *habitus*, the durable principle of their production. They can therefore only be accounted for by relating the social conditions in which the *habitus* that generated them was constituted, to the social conditions in which it is implemented, that is, through the scientific work of performing the interrelationship of these two states of the social world that the *habitus* performs, while concealing it, in and through practice. The "unconscious," which enables one to dispense with this interrelating, is never anything other than the forgetting of history which history itself produces by realizing the objective structures that it generates in the quasi-natures of *habitus*.

The *habitus*—embodied history, internalized as a second nature and so forgotten as history—is the active presence of the whole past of which it is the product. As such, it is what gives practices their relative autonomy with respect to external determinations of the immediate present. This autonomy is that of the past, enacted and acting, which, functioning as accumulated capital, produces history on the basis of history and so ensures the permanence in change that makes the individual agent a world within the world. The *habitus* is a spontaneity without consciousness or will, opposed as much to the mechanical necessity of things without history in mechanistic theories as it is to the reflexive freedom of subjects "without inertia" in rationalist theories.

The objective homogenizing of group or class *habitus* that results from homogeneity of conditions of existence is what enables practices to be objectively harmonized without any calculation or conscious reference to a norm and mutually adjusted in the absence of any direct interaction or, *a fortiori*, explicit co-ordination. The interaction itself owes its form to the objective structures that have produced the dispositions of the interacting agents, which continue to assign them their relative positions in the interaction and elsewhere.

Sociology treats as identical all biological individuals who, being the products of the same objective conditions, have the same *habitus*. A social class (in-itself)—a class of identical or similar conditions of existence and conditionings—is at the same time a class of biological individuals having the same *habitus*, understood as a system of dispositions common to all products of the same conditionings. Though it is impossible for all (or even two) members of the same class to have had the same experiences, in the same order, it is certain that each member of the same class is more likely than any member of another class to have been confronted with the situations most frequent for members of that class. Through the always convergent experiences that give a social environment its physiognomy, with its "closed doors," "dead ends," and "limited prospects," the objective structures that sociology apprehends in the form of probabilities of access to goods, services, and powers, inculcate the "art of assessing likelihoods," as Leibniz put it, of anticipating the objective future, in short, the "sense of reality," or realities, which is perhaps the best-concealed principle of their efficacy.

Only in imaginary experience (in the folk tale, for example), which neutralizes the sense of social realities, does the social world take the form of a universe of possibles equally possible for any possible subject. Agents shape their aspirations according to concrete indices of the accessible and the inaccessible, of what is and is not "for us," a division as fundamental and as fundamentally recognized as that between the sacred and the profane. The pre-emptive rights on the future that are defined by law and by the monopolistic right to certain possibles that it confers are merely the explicitly guaranteed form of the whole set of appropriated chances through which the power relations of the present project themselves into the future, from where they govern present dispositions, especially those towards the future. In fact, a given agent's practical relation to the future, which governs his present practice, is defined in the relationship between, on the one hand, his *habitus* with its temporal structures and dispositions towards the future, constituted in the course of a particular relationship to a particular universe of probabilities, and on the other hand a certain state of the chances objectively offered to him by the social world. The relation to what is possible is a relation to power; and the sense of the probable future is constituted in the prolonged relationship with a world structured according to the categories of the possible (for us) and the impossible (for us), of what is appropriated in advance by and for others and what one can reasonably expect for oneself. The *habitus* is the principle of a selective perception of the indices tending to confirm and reinforce it rather than transform it, a matrix generating responses adapted in advance to all objective conditions identical to or homologous with the (past) conditions of its production; it adjusts itself to a probable future which it anticipates and helps to bring about because it reads it directly in the present of the presumed world, the only one it can ever know. It is thus the basis of what Marx calls "effective demand" (as opposed to "demand without effect," based on need and desire), a realistic relation to what is possible, founded on and therefore limited by power. This disposition, always marked by its (social) conditions of acquisition and realization, tends to adjust to the objective chances of satisfying need or desire, inclining agents to "cut their coats according to their cloth," and so to become the accomplices of the processes that tend to make the probable a reality.

92

The Risk Society*

Ulrich Beck

In advanced modernity the social production of *wealth* is systematically accompanied by the social production of *risks*. Accordingly, the problems and conflicts relating to distribution in a society of scarcity overlap with the problems and conflicts that arise from the production, definition and distribution of techno-scientifically produced risks.

This change from the logic of wealth distribution in a society of scarcity to the logic of risk distribution in late modernity is connected historically to (at least) two conditions. First, it occurs—as is recognizable today—where and to the extent that *genuine material need* can be objectively reduced and socially isolated through the development of human and technological productivity, as well as through legal and welfare-state protections and regulations. Second, this categorical change is likewise dependent upon the fact that in the course of the exponentially growing productive forces in the modernization process, hazards and potential threats have been unleashed to an extent previously unknown.

To the extent that these conditions occur, one historical type of thinking and acting is relativized or overridden by another. The concepts of 'industrial' or 'class society', in the broadest sense of Marx or Weber, revolved around the issue of how socially produced wealth could be distributed in a socially unequal and *also* 'legitimate' way. This overlaps with the new *paradigm of risk society* which is based on the solution of a similar and yet quite different problem. How can the risks and hazards systematically produced as part of modernization be prevented, minimized, dramatized, or channeled? Where they do finally see the light of day in the shape of 'latent side effects', how can they be limited and distributed away so that they neither hamper the modernization process nor exceed the limits of that which is 'tolerable'—ecologically, medically, psychologically and socially?

We are therefore concerned no longer exclusively with making nature useful, or with releasing mankind from traditional constraints, but also and essentially with problems resulting from techno-economic development itself. Modernization is becoming *reflexive*; it is becoming its own theme. Questions of the development and employment of technologies (in the realms of nature, society and the personality) are being eclipsed by questions of the political and

*Excerpts from *Risk Society: Towards a New Modernity* by Ulrich Beck, Translated by Mark Ritter. First published 1986 in German as *Risikogesellschaft: Auf dem Weg in eine andere Moderne.*

economic 'management' of the risks of actually or potentially utilized technologies—discovering, administering, acknowledging, avoiding or concealing such hazards with respect to specially defined horizons of relevance. The promise of security grows with the risks and destruction and must he reaffirmed over and over again to an alert and critical public through cosmetic or real interventions in the techno-economic development.

Both 'paradigms' of inequality are systematically related to definite periods of modernization. The distribution of socially produced wealth and related conflicts occupy the foreground so long as obvious material need, the 'dictatorship of scarcity', rules the thought and action of people (as today in large parts of the so-called Third World). Under these conditions of 'scarcity society', the modernization process takes place with the claim of opening the gates to hidden sources of social wealth with the keys of techno-scientific development. These promises of emancipation from undeserved poverty and dependence underlie action, thought and research in the categories of social inequality, from the class through the stratified to the individualized society.

In the welfare states of the West a double process is taking place now. On the one hand, the struggle for one's 'daily bread' has lost its urgency as a cardinal problem overshadowing everything else, compared to material subsistence in the first half of this century and to a Third World menaced by hunger. For many people problems of 'overweight' take the place of hunger. This development, however, withdraws the legitimizing basis from the modernization process, the struggle against obvious scarcity, for which one was prepared to accept a few (no longer completely) unseen side effects.

Parallel to that, the knowledge is spreading that the sources of wealth are 'polluted' by growing 'hazardous side effects'. This is not at all new, but it has remained unnoticed for a long time in the efforts to overcome poverty. This dark side is also gaining importance through the overdevelopment of productive forces. In the modernization process, more and more *destructive* forces are also being unleashed, forces before which the human imagination stands in awe. Both sources feed a growing critique of modernization, which loudly and contentiously determines public discussions.

In systematic terms, sooner or later in the continuity of modernization the social positions and conflicts of a 'wealth-distributing' society begin to be joined by those of a 'risk-distributing' society. In West Germany we have faced the beginning of this transition since the early 1970s at the latest—that is my thesis. That means that two types of topics and conflicts overlap here. We do not *yet* live in a risk society, but we also no longer live *only* within the distribution conflicts of scarcity societies. To the extent that this transition occurs, there will be a real transformation of society which will lead us out of the previous modes of thought and action.

Can the concept of risk carry the theoretical and historical significance which is demanded of it here? Is this not a primeval phenomenon of human action? Are not risks already characteristic of the industrial society period, against which they are being differentiated here? It is also true that risks are not an invention of modernity. Anyone who set out to discover new countries and continents—like Columbus—certainly accepted '*risks*'. But these were *personal risks*, not global dangers like those that arise for all of humanity from nuclear fission or the storage of radioactive waste. In that earlier period, the word 'risk' had a note of bravery and adventure, not the threat of self-destruction of all life on Earth.

Forests have also been dying for some centuries now—first through being transformed into fields, then through reckless overcutting. But the death of forests today occurs *globally*, as the *implicit* consequence of industrialization—with quite different social and political consequences. Heavily wooded countries like Norway and Sweden, which hardly have any pollutant-intensive industries of their own, are also affected. They have to settle up the pollution accounts of other highly industrialized countries with dying trees, plants and animal species.

It is reported that sailors who fell into the Thames in the early nineteenth century did not drown, but rather choked to death inhaling the foul-smelling and poisonous fumes of this London sewer. A walk through the narrow streets of a medieval city would also have been like running the gauntlet for the nose. 'Excrement piles up everywhere, in the streets, at the turnpikes, in the carriages . . . The facades of Parisian houses are decomposing from urine . . . the socially organized constipation threatens to pull all of Paris into the process of putrescent decomposition'. It is nevertheless striking that hazards in those days assaulted the nose or the eyes and were thus perceptible to the senses, while the risks of civilization today typically *escape perception* and are localized in the sphere of *physical and chemical formulas* (e.g. toxins in foodstuffs or the nuclear threat).

Another difference is directly connected to this. In the past, the hazards could be traced back to an *under*supply of hygienic technology. Today they have their basis in industrial *over*production. The risks and hazards of today thus differ in an essential way from the superficially similar ones in the Middle Ages through the global nature of their threat (people, animals and plants) and through their modern causes. They are risks of *modernization.* They are a *wholesale product* of industrialization, and are systematically intensified as it becomes global.

The concept of risk is directly bound to the concept of reflexive modernization. *Risk* may be defined as a *systematic way of dealing with hazards and insecurities induced and introduced by modernization itself.* Risks, as opposed to older dangers, are consequences which relate to the threatening force of modernization and to its globalization of doubt. They are *politically reflexive.*

Risks, in this meaning of the word, are certainly as old as that development itself. The immiseration of large parts of the population—the 'poverty risk'—kept the nineteenth century holding its breath. 'Threats to skills' and 'health risks' have long been a theme of automation processes and the related social conflicts, protections (and research). It did take some time and struggle to establish social welfare state norms and minimize or limit these kinds of risk politically. Nevertheless, the ecological and high-tech risks that have upset the public for some years now, which will be the focus of what follows, have a new quality. In the afflictions they produce they are no longer tied to their place of origin—the industrial plant. By their nature they endanger all forms of life on this planet. The normative bases of their calculation—the concept of accident and insurance, medical precautions, and so on—do not fit the basic dimensions of these modern threats. Atomic plants, for example, are not privately insured or insurable. Atomic accidents are accidents no more (in the limited sense of the word 'accident'). They outlast generations. The affected even include those not yet alive at the time or in the place where the accident occurred but born years later and long distances away.

This means that the calculation of risk as it has been established so far by science and legal institutions *collapses.* Dealing with these consequences of modern productive and destructive forces in the normal terms of risk is a false but nevertheless very effective way of legitimizing them. Risk scientists normally do so as if there is not the gap of a century between the local accidents of the nineteenth century and the often creeping, catastrophic potentials at the end of the twentieth century. Indeed, if you distinguish between calculable and non-calculable threats, under the surface of risk calculation new kinds of *industrialized, decision-produced incalculablities and threats* are spreading within the globalization of high-risk industries, whether for warfare or welfare purposes. Max Weber's concept of 'rationalization' no longer grasps this late modern reality, produced by successful rationalization. *Along with the growing capacity of technical options [Zweckrationalität] grows the incalculability of their consequences.* Compared to these global consequences, the hazards of primary industrialization indeed belonged to a different age. The dangers of highly developed nuclear and chemical productive forces abolish the foundations and categories according to which we have thought and acted to this point, such as space and time, work and leisure time, factory and nation state, indeed even the borders between continents. To put it differently, in the risk society the unknown and unintended consequences come to be a dominant force in history and society.

The social architecture and political dynamics of such potentials for self-endangerment in civilization will occupy the center of these discussions. The argument can be set out in five theses:

(1) Risks such as those produced in the late modernity differ essentially from wealth. By risks I mean above all radioactivity, which completely evades human perceptive abilities, but

also toxins and pollutants in the air, the water and foodstuffs, together with the accompanying short- and long-term effects on plants, animals and people. They induce systematic and often *irreversible* harm, generally remain *invisible*, are based on *causal interpretations*, and thus initially only exist in terms of the (scientific or anti-scientific) *knowledge about them*. They can thus be changed, magnified, dramatized or minimized within knowledge, and to that extent they are particularly *open to social definition and construction*. Hence the mass media and the scientific and legal professions in charge of defining risks become key social and political positions.

(2) Some people are more affected than others by the distribution and growth of risks, that is, *social risk positions* spring up. In some of their dimensions these follow the inequalities of class and strata positions, but they bring a fundamentally different distributional logic into play. Risks of modernization sooner or later also strike those who produce or profit from them. They contain a *boomerang effect*, which breaks up the pattern of class and national society. Ecological disaster and atomic fallout ignore the borders of nations. Even the rich and powerful are not safe from them. These are hazards not only to health, but also to legitimation, property and profit. *Connected* to the recognition of modernization risks are *ecological devaluations and expropriations*, which frequently and systematically enter into contradiction to the profit and property interests which advance the process of industrialization. Simultaneously, risks produce *new international inequalities*, firstly between the Third World and the industrial states, secondly among the industrial states themselves. They undermine the order of national jurisdictions. In view of the universality and supra-nationality of the circulation of pollutants, the life of a blade of grass in the Bavarian Forest ultimately comes to depend on the making and keeping of international agreements. Risk society in this sense is a world risk society.

(3) Nevertheless, the diffusion and commercialization of risks do not break with the logic of capitalist development completely, but instead they raise the latter to a new stage. There are always losers but also winners in risk definitions. The space between them varies in relation to different issues and power differentials. Modernization risks from the winners' points of view are *big business*. They are the insatiable demands long sought by economists. Hunger can be sated, needs can be satisfied, but *civilization* risks are a *bottomless barrel of demands*, unsatisfiable, infinite, self-producible. One could say along with Luhmann that with the advent of risks, the economy becomes 'self-referential', independent of the surrounding satisfaction of human needs. But that means: with the economic exploitation of the risks it sets free, industrial society produces the hazards and the political potential of the risk society.

(4) One can *possess* wealth, but one can only be *afflicted* by risks; they are, so to speak, *ascribed* by civilization. [Bluntly, one might say: in class and stratification positions being determines consciousness, while in risk positions *consciousness determines being*.] Knowledge gains a new political significance. Accordingly the political potential of the risk society must be elaborated and analyzed in a sociological theory of the origin and diffusion of *knowledge about risks*.

(5) Socially recognized risks, as appears clearly in the discussions of forest destruction, contain a peculiar political explosive: *what was until now considered unpolitical becomes political—the elimination of the causes in the industrialization process itself.* Suddenly the public and politics extend their rule into the private sphere of plant management—into product planning and technical equipment. What is at stake in the public dispute over the definition of risks is revealed here in an exemplary fashion: not just secondary health problems for nature and mankind, but the *social, economic and political consequences of these side effects*—collapsing markets, devaluation of capital, bureaucratic checks on plant decisions, the opening of new markets, mammoth costs, legal proceedings and loss of face, in smaller or larger increments—a smog alarm, a toxic spill, etc.—what thus emerges in risk society is the *political potential of catastrophes*. Averting and managing these can include a *reorganization of power and authority*. Risk society is a *catastrophic* society. In it the exceptional condition threatens to become the norm.

93

Liquid Modernity*

Zygmunt Bauman

'Fluidity' is the quality of liquids and gases. What distinguishes both of them from solids, as the *Encyclopaedia Britannica* authoritatively informs us, is that they 'cannot sustain a tangential, or shearing, force when at rest' and so undergo 'a continuous change in shape when subjected to such a stress'.

> This continuous and irrecoverable change of position of one part of the material relative to another part when under shear stress constitutes flow, a characteristic property of fluids. In contrast, the shearing forces within a solid, held in a twisted or flexed position, are maintained, the solid undergoes no flow and can spring back to its original shape.

Liquids, one variety of fluids, owe these remarkable qualities to the fact that their 'molecules are preserved in an orderly array over only a few molecular diameters'; while 'the wide variety of behaviour exhibited by solids is a direct result of the type of bonding that holds the atoms of the solid together and of the structural arrangements of the atoms'. 'Bonding', in turn, is a term that signifies the stability of solids—the resistance they put up 'against separation of the atoms'.

So much for the *Encyclopaedia Britannica*—in what reads like a bid to deploy 'fluidity' as the leading metaphor for the present stage of the modern era.

What all these features of fluids amount to, in simple language, is that liquids, unlike solids, cannot easily hold their shape. Fluids, so to speak, neither fix space nor bind time. While solids have clear spatial dimensions but neutralize the impact, and thus downgrade the significance, of time (effectively resist its flow or render it irrelevant), fluids do not keep to any shape for long and are constantly ready (and prone) to change it; and so for them it is the flow of time that counts, more than the space they happen to occupy: that space, after all, they fill but 'for a moment'. In a sense, solids cancel time; for liquids, on the contrary, it is mostly time that matters. When describing solids, one may ignore time altogether; in describing fluids, to leave time out of account would be a grievous mistake. Descriptions of fluids are all snapshots, and they need a date at the bottom of the picture.

Fluids travel easily. They 'flow', 'spill', 'run out', 'splash', 'pour over', 'leak', 'flood', 'spray', 'drip', 'seep', 'ooze'; unlike solids, they are not easily stopped—they pass around some obstacles, dissolve some others and bore or soak their way through others still. From the meeting with solids they emerge unscathed, while the solids they have met, if they stay solid, are changed—get moist or drenched. The extraordinary mobility of fluids is what associates them with the idea of 'lightness'. There are liquids which, cubic inch for cubic inch, are heavier than many solids, but we are inclined nonetheless to visualize them all as lighter, less 'weighty' than everything solid. We associate 'lightness' or 'weightlessness' with mobility and inconstancy: we know from practice that the lighter we travel the easier and faster we move.

These are reasons to consider 'fluidity' or 'liquidity' as fitting metaphors when we wish to grasp the nature of the present, in many ways *novel*, phase in the history of modernity.

I readily agree that such a proposition may give a pause to anyone at home in the 'modernity discourse' and familiar with the vocabulary commonly used to narrate modern history. Was not modernity a process of 'liquefaction' from the start? Was not 'melting the solids' its major pastime and prime accomplishment all along? In other words, has modernity not been 'fluid' since its inception?

These and similar objections are well justified, and will seem more so once we recall that the famous phrase 'melting the solids', when coined a century and a half ago by the authors of *The Communist Manifesto*, referred to the treatment which the self-confident and exuberant modern spirit awarded the society it found much too stagnant for its taste and much too resistant to shift and mould for its ambitions—since it was frozen in its habitual ways. If the 'spirit' was 'modern', it was so indeed in so far as it was determined that reality should be emancipated from the 'dead hand' of its own history—and this could only be done by melting the solids (that is, by definition, dissolving whatever persists over time and is negligent of its passage or immune to its flow). That intention called in turn for the 'profaning of the sacred': for disavowing and dethroning the past, and first and foremost 'tradition'—to wit, the sediment and residue of the past in the present; it thereby called for the smashing of the protective armour forged of the beliefs and loyalties which allowed the solids to resist the 'liquefaction'.

Let us remember, however, that all this was to be done not in order to do away with the solids once and for all and make the brave new world free of them for ever, but to clear the site for *new and improved solids*; to replace the inherited set of deficient and defective solids with another set, which was much improved and preferably perfect, and for that reason no longer alterable. When reading de Tocqueville's *Ancien Régime*, one might wonder in addition to what extent the 'found solids' were resented, condemned and earmarked for liquefaction for the reason that they were already rusty, mushy, coming apart at the seams and altogether unreliable. Modern times found the pre-modern solids in a fairly advanced state of disintegration; and one of the most powerful motives behind the urge to melt them was the wish to discover or invent solids of—for a change—*lasting* solidity, a solidity which one could trust and rely upon and which would make the world predictable and therefore manageable.

The first solids to be melted and the first sacreds to be profaned were traditional loyalties, customary rights and obligations which bound hands and feet, hindered moves and cramped the enterprise.

To set earnestly about the task of building a new (truly solid!) order, it was necessary to get rid of the ballast with which the old order burdened the builders. 'Melting the solids' meant first and foremost shedding the 'irrelevant' obligations standing in the way of rational calculation of effects; as Max Weber put it, liberating business enterprise from the shackles of the family—household duties and from the dense tissue of ethical obligations; or, as Thomas Carlyle would have it, leaving solely the 'cash nexus' of the many bonds underlying human mutuality and mutual responsibilities. By the same token, that kind of 'melting the solids' left the whole complex network of social relations unstuck—bare, unprotected, unarmed and exposed, impotent to resist the business-inspired rules of action and business-shaped criteria of rationality, let alone to compete with them effectively.

That fateful departure laid the field open to the invasion and domination of (as Weber put it) instrumental rationality, or (as Karl Marx articulated it) the determining role of economy: now the 'basis' of social life gave all life's other realms the status of 'superstructure'—to wit, an artefact of the 'basis' whose sole function was to service its smooth and continuing operation. The melting of solids led to the progressive untying of economy from its traditional political, ethical and cultural entanglements. It sedimented a new order, defined primarily in economic terms. That new order was to be more 'solid' than the orders it replaced, because—unlike them—it was immune to the challenge from non-economic action. Most political or moral levers capable of shifting or reforming the new order have been broken or rendered too short, weak or otherwise inadequate for the task. Not that the economic order, once entrenched, will have colonized, re-educated and converted to its ways the rest of social life; that order came to dominate the totality of human life because whatever else might have happened in that life has been rendered irrelevant and ineffective as far as the relentless and continuous reproduction of that order was concerned.

That stage in modernity's career has been well described by Claus Offe (in 'The Utopia of the Zero Option', first published in 1987 in *Praxis International*): 'complex' societies 'have become rigid to such an extent that the very attempt to reflect normatively upon or renew their "order," that is, the nature of the coordination of the processes which take place in them, is virtually precluded by dint of their practical futility and thus their essential inadequacy'. However free and volatile the 'subsystems' of that order may be singly or severally, the way in which they are intertwined is 'rigid, fatal, and sealed off from any freedom of choice'. The overall order of things is not open to options; it is far from clear what such options could be, and even less clear how an ostensibly viable option could be made real in the unlikely case of social life being able to conceive it and gestate. Between the overall order and every one of the agencies, vehicles and stratagems of purposeful action there is a cleavage—a perpetually widening gap with no bridge in sight.

Contrary to most dystopian scenarios, this effect has not been achieved through dictatorial rule, subordination, oppression or enslavement; nor through the 'colonization' of the private sphere by the 'system'. Quite the opposite: the present-day situation emerged out of the radical melting of the fetters and manacles rightly or wrongly suspected of limiting the individual freedom to choose and to act. *Rigidity of order is the artefact and sediment of the human agents' freedom.* That rigidity is the overall product of 'releasing the brakes': of deregulation, liberalization, 'flexibilization', increased fluidity, unbridling the financial, real estate and labour markets, easing the tax burden, etc. (as Offe pointed out in 'Binding, Shackles, Brakes', first published in 1987); or (to quote from Richard Sennett's *Flesh and Stone*) of the techniques of 'speed, escape, passivity'—in other words, techniques which allow the system and free agents to remain radically disengaged, to by-pass each other instead of meeting. If the time of systemic revolutions has passed, it is because there are no buildings where the control desks of the system are lodged and which could be stormed and captured by the revolutionaries; and also because it is excruciatingly difficult, nay impossible, to imagine what the victors, once inside the buildings (if they found them first), could do to turn the tables and put paid to the misery that prompted them to rebel. One should be hardly taken aback or puzzled by the evident shortage of would-be revolutionaries: of the kind of people who articulate the desire to change their individual plights as a project of changing the order of society.

The task of constructing a new and better order to replace the old and defective one is not presently on the agenda—at least not on the agenda of that realm where political action is supposed to reside. The 'melting of solids', the permanent feature of modernity, has therefore acquired a new meaning, and above all has been redirected to a new target—one of the paramount effects of that redirection being the dissolution of forces which could keep the question of order and system on the political agenda. The solids whose turn has come to be thrown into the melting pot and which are in the process of being melted at the present time, the time of fluid modernity, are the bonds which interlock individual choices in collective projects and actions—the patterns of communication and co-ordination between individually conducted life policies on the one hand and political actions of human collectivities on the other.

In an interview given to Jonathan Rutherford on 3 February 1999, Ulrich Beck (who a few years earlier coined the term 'second modernity' to connote the phase marked by the modernity 'turning upon itself', the era of the *soi-disant* 'modernization of modernity') speaks of 'zombie categories' and 'zombie institutions' which are 'dead and still alive'. He names the family, class and neighbourhood as the foremost examples of that new phenomenon. The family, for instance:

> Ask yourself what actually is a family nowadays? What does it mean? Of course there are children, my children, our children. But even parenthood, the core of family life, is beginning to disintegrate under conditions of divorce . . . [G]randmothers and grandfathers get included and excluded without any means of participating in the decisions of their sons and daughters. From the point of view of their grandchildren the meaning of grandparents has to be determined by individual decisions and choices.

What is happening at present is, so to speak, a redistribution and reallocation of modernity's 'melting powers'. They affected at first the extant institutions, the frames that circumscribed the realms of possible action-choices, like hereditary estates with their no-appeal-allowed allocation-by-ascription. Configurations, constellations, patterns of dependency and interaction were all thrown into the melting pot, to be subsequently recast and refashioned; this was the 'breaking the mould' phase in the history of the inherently transgressive, boundary-breaking, all-eroding modernity. As for the individuals, however—they could be excused for failing to notice; they came to be confronted by patterns and figurations which, albeit 'new and improved', were as stiff and indomitable as ever.

Indeed, no mould was broken without being replaced with another; people were let out from their old cages only to be admonished and censured in case they failed to relocate themselves, through their own, dedicated and continuous, truly life-long efforts, in the ready-made niches of the new order: in the *classes*, the frames which (as uncompromisingly as the already dissolved *estates*) encapsulated the totality of life conditions and life prospects and determined the range of realistic life projects and life strategies. The task confronting free individuals was to use their new freedom to find the appropriate niche and to settle there through conformity: by faithfully following the rules and modes of conduct identified as right and proper for the location.

It is such patterns, codes and rules to which one could conform, which one could select as stable orientation points and by which one could subsequently let oneself be guided, that are nowadays in increasingly short supply. It does not mean that our contemporaries are guided solely by their own imagination and resolve and are free to construct their mode of life from scratch and at will, or that they are no longer dependent on society for the building materials and design blueprints. But it does mean that we are presently moving from the era of pre-allocated 'reference groups' into the epoch of 'universal comparison', in which the destination of individual self-constructing labours is endemically and incurably underdetermined, is not given in advance, and tends to undergo numerous and profound changes before such labours reach their only genuine end: that is, the end of the individual's life.

These days patterns and configurations are no longer 'given', let alone 'self-evident'; there are just too many of them, clashing with one another and contradicting one another's commandments, so that each one has been stripped of a good deal of compelling, coercively constraining powers. And they have changed their nature and have been accordingly reclassified: as items in the inventory of individual tasks. Rather than preceding life-politics and framing its future course, they are to follow it (follow *from* it), to be shaped and reshaped by its twists and turns. The liquidizing powers have moved from the 'system' to 'society', from 'politics' to 'life-policies'—or have descended from the 'macro' to the 'micro' level of social cohabitation.

Ours is, as a result, an individualized, privatized version of modernity, with the burden of pattern-weaving and the responsibility for failure falling primarily on the individual's shoulders. It is the patterns of dependency and interaction whose turn to be liquefied has now come. They are now malleable to an extent unexperienced by, and unimaginable for, past generations; but like all fluids they do not keep their shape for long. Shaping them is easier than keeping them in shape. Solids are cast once and for all. Keeping fluids in shape requires a lot of attention, constant vigilance and perpetual effort—and even then the success of the effort is anything but a foregone conclusion.

It would be imprudent to deny, or even to play down, the profound change which the advent of 'fluid modernity' has brought to the human condition. The remoteness and unreachability of systemic structure, coupled with the unstructured, fluid state of the immediate setting of life-politics, change that condition in a radical way and call for a rethinking of old concepts that used to frame its narratives. Like zombies, such concepts are today simultaneously dead and alive. The practical question is whether their resurrection, albeit in a new shape or incarnation, is feasible; or—if it is not—how to arrange for their decent and effective burial.

Modernity means many things, and its arrival and progress can be traced using many and different markers. One feature of modern life and its modern setting stands out, however, as perhaps that 'difference which make[s] the difference'; as the crucial attribute from which all other characteristics follow. That attribute is the changing relationship between space and time.

Modernity starts when space and time are separated from living practice and from each other and so become ready to be theorized as distinct and mutually independent categories of strategy and action, when they cease to be, as they used to be in long pre-modern centuries, the intertwined and so barely distinguishable aspects of living experience, locked in a stable and apparently invulnerable one-to-one correspondence. In modernity, time has *history*, it has history because of the perpetually expanding 'carrying capacity' of time—the lengthening of the stretches of space which units of time allow to 'pass', 'cross', 'cover'—or *conquer*. Time acquires history once the speed of movement through space (unlike the eminently inflexible space, which cannot be stretched and would not shrink) becomes a matter of human ingenuity, imagination and resourcefulness.

The very idea of speed (even more conspicuously, that of acceleration), when referring to the relationship between time and space, *assumes* its variability, and it would hardly have any meaning at all were not that relation truly changeable, were it an attribute of inhuman and pre-human reality rather than a matter of human inventiveness and resolve, and were it not reaching far beyond the narrow range of variations to which the natural tools of mobility—human or equine legs—used to confine the movements of pre-modern bodies. Once the distance passed in a unit of time came to be dependent on technology, on artificial means of transportation, all extant, inherited limits to the speed of movement could be in principle transgressed. Only the sky (or, as it transpired later, the speed of light) was now the limit, and modernity was one continuous, unstoppable and fast accelerating effort to reach it.

Thanks to its newly acquired flexibility and expansiveness, modern time has become, first and foremost, the weapon in the conquest of space. In the modern struggle between time and space, space was the solid and stolid, unwieldy and inert side, capable of waging only a defensive, trench war—being an obstacle to the resilient advances of time. Time was the active and dynamic side in the battle, the side always on the offensive: the invading, conquering and colonizing force. Velocity of movement and access to faster means of mobility steadily rose in modern times to the position of the principal tool of power and domination.

Michel Foucault used Jeremy Bentham's design of Panopticon as the archmetaphor of modern power. In Panopticon, the inmates were tied to the place and barred from all movement, confined within thick, dense and closely guarded walls and fixed to their beds, cells or workbenches. They could not move because they were under watch; they had to stick to their appointed places at all times because they did not know, and had no way of knowing where at the moment their watchers—free to move at will—were. The surveillants' facility and expediency of movement was the warrant of their domination; the inmates' 'fixedness to the place' was the most secure and the hardest to break or loose of the manifold bonds of their subordination. Mastery over time was the secret of the managers' power—and immobilizing their subordinates in space through denying them the right to move and through the routinization of the time-rhythm they had to obey was the principal strategy in their exercise of power. The pyramid of power was built out of velocity, access to the means of transportation and the resulting freedom of movement.

Panopticon was a model of mutual engagement and confrontation between the two sides of the power relationship. The managers' strategies of guarding their own volatility and routinizing the flow of time of their subordinates merged into one. But there was tension between the two tasks. The second task put constraints on the first—it tied the 'routinizers' to the place within which the objects of time routinization had been confined. The routinizers were not truly and fully free to move: the option of 'absentee landlords' was, practically, out of the question.

Panopticon is burdened with other handicaps as well. It is an expensive strategy: conquering space and holding to it as well as keeping its residents in the surveilled place spawned a wide range of costly and cumbersome administrative tasks. There are buildings to erect and maintain in good shape, professional surveillants to hire and pay, the survival and working capacity of the inmates to be attended to and provided for. Finally, administration means, willy-nilly, taking responsibility for the overall well-being of the place, even if only in the name of well-understood self-interest—and responsibility again means being bound to the place. It requires presence, and engagement, at least in the form of a perpetual confrontation and tug-of-war.

What prompts so many commentators to speak of the 'end of history', of post-modernity, 'second modernity' and 'surmodernity', or otherwise to articulate the intuition of a radical change in the arrangement of human cohabitation and in social conditions under which life-politics is nowadays conducted, is the fact that the long effort to accelerate the speed of movement has presently reached its 'natural limit'. Power can move with the speed of the electronic signal—and so the time required for the movement of its essential ingredients has been reduced to instantaneity. For all practical purposes, power has become truly *exterritorial*, no longer bound, not even slowed down, by the resistance of space (the advent of cellular telephones may well serve as a symbolic 'last blow' delivered to the dependency on space: even the access to a telephone socket is unnecessary for a command to be given and seen through to its effect. It does not matter any more where the giver of the command is—the difference between 'close by' and 'far away', or for that matter between the wilderness and the civilized, orderly space, has been all but cancelled.) This gives the power-holders a truly unprecedented opportunity: the awkward and irritating aspects of the panoptical technique of power may be disposed of. Whatever else the present stage in the history of modernity is, it is also, perhaps above all, *post-Panoptical*. What mattered in Panopticon was that the people in charge were assumed always to 'be there', nearby, in the controlling tower. What matters in post-Panoptical power-relations is that the people operating the levers of power on which the fate of the less volatile partners in the relationship depends can at any moment escape beyond reach —into sheer inaccessibility.

The end of Panopticon augurs *the end of the era of mutual engagement*: between the supervisors and the supervised, capital and labour, leaders and their followers, armies at war. The prime technique of power is now escape, slippage, elision and avoidance, the effective rejection of any territorial confinement with its cumbersome corollaries of order-building, order-maintenance and the responsibility for the consequences of it all as well as of the necessity to bear their costs.

This new technique of power has been vividly illustrated by the strategies deployed by the attackers in the Gulf and Jugoslav wars. The reluctance to deploy ground forces in the conduct of war was striking; whatever the official explanations might have implied, that reluctance was dictated not only by the widely publicized 'body-bag' syndrome. Engaging in a ground combat was resented not just for its possible adverse effect on domestic politics, but also (perhaps mainly) for its total uselessness and even counter-productivity as far as the goals of war are concerned. After all, the conquest of territory with all its administrative and managerial consequences was not just absent from the list of the objectives of war actions, but it was an eventuality meant to be by all means avoided, viewed with repugnance as another sort of 'collateral damage', this time inflicted on the attacking force itself.

Blows delivered by stealthy fighter planes and 'smart' self-guided and target-seeking missiles—delivered by surprise, coming from nowhere and immediately vanishing from sight—replaced the territorial advances of the infantry troops and the effort to dispossess the enemy of its territory—to take over the land owned, controlled and administered by the enemy. The attackers definitely wished no longer to be 'the last on the battlefield' after the enemy ran or was routed. Military force and its 'hit and run' war-plan prefigured, embodied and portended what was really at stake in the new type of war in the era of liquid modernity: not the conquest of a new territory, but crushing the walls which stopped the flow of new, fluid global powers; beating out of the enemy's head the desire to set up his own rules, and so opening up the so-far barricaded and walled-off, inaccessible space to the operations of the other, non-military, arms of power. War today, one may say (paraphrasing Clausewitz's famous formula), looks increasingly like a 'promotion of global free trade by other means'.

Jim MacLaughlin has reminded us recently (in *Sociology* 1/99) that the advent of the modern era meant, among other things, the consistent and systematic assault of the 'settled', converted to the sedentary way of life, against nomadic peoples and the nomadic style of life, starkly at odds with the territorial and boundary preoccupations of the emergent modern state. Ibn Khaldoun could in the fourteenth century sing the praise of nomadism, which brings peoples 'closer to being good than settled peoples because they. . .are more removed from all the evil habits that have infected the hearts of the settlers'—but the practice of feverish nation- and nation-state-building which shortly afterwards started in earnest all over Europe put the 'soil' firmly above the 'blood' when laying the foundations of the new legislated order and codifying the citizens' rights and duties. The nomads, who made light of the legislators' territorial concerns and blatantly disregarded their zealous efforts of boundary-drawing, were cast among the main villains in the holy war waged in the name of progress and civilization. Modern 'chronopolitics' placed them not just as inferior and primitive beings, 'underdeveloped' and in need of thorough reform and enlightenment, but also as backward and 'behind time', suffering from 'cultural lag', lingering at the lower rungs of the evolutionary ladder, and unforgivably slow or morbidly reluctant to climb it to follow the 'universal pattern of development'.

Throughout the solid stage of the modern era, nomadic habits remained out of favour. Citizenship went hand in hand with settlement, and the absence of 'fixed address' and 'statelessness' meant exclusion from the law-abiding and law-protected community and more often than not brought upon the culprits legal discrimination, if not active prosecution. While this still applies to the homeless and shifty 'underclass', which is subject to the old techniques of panoptical control (techniques largely abandoned as the prime vehicle of integrating and disciplining the bulk of the population), the era of unconditional superiority of sedentarism over nomadism and the domination of the settled over the mobile is on the whole grinding fast to a halt. We are witnessing the revenge of nomadism over the principle of territoriality and settlement. In the fluid stage of modernity, the settled majority is ruled by the nomadic and exterritorial elite. Keeping the roads free for nomadic traffic and phasing out the remaining check-points has now become the meta-purpose of politics, and also of wars, which, as Clausewitz originally declared, are but 'extension of politics by other means'.

The contemporary global elite is shaped after the pattern of the old-style 'absentee landlords'. It can rule without burdening itself with the chores of administration, management, welfare concerns, or, for that matter, with the mission of 'bringing light', 'reforming the ways', morally uplifting, 'civilizing' and cultural crusades. Active engagement in the life of subordinate populations is no longer needed (on the contrary, it is actively avoided as unnecessarily costly and ineffective)—and so the 'bigger' is not just not 'better' any more, but devoid of rational sense. It is now the smaller, the lighter, the more portable that signifies improvement and 'progress'. Travelling light, rather than holding tightly to things deemed attractive for their reliability and solidity—that is, for their heavy weight, substantiality and unyielding power of resistance—is now the asset of power.

Holding to the ground is not that important if the ground can be reached and abandoned at whim, in a short time or in no time. On the other hand, holding too fast, burdening one's bond with mutually binding commitments, may prove positively harmful and the new chances crop up elsewhere. Rockefeller might have wished to make his factories, railroads and oilrigs big and bulky and own them for a long, long time to come (for eternity, if one measures time by the duration of human or human family life). Bill Gates, however, feels no regret when parting with possessions in which he took pride yesterday; it is the mind-boggling speed of circulation, of recycling, ageing, dumping and replacement which brings profit today—not the durability and lasting reliability of the product. In a remarkable reversal of the millennia-long tradition, it is the high and mighty of the day who resent and shun the durable and cherish the transient, while it is those at the bottom of the heap who—against all odds—desperately struggle to force their flimsy and paltry, transient possessions to last longer and render durable service. The two meet nowadays mostly on opposite sides of the jumbo-sales or used-car auction counters.

The disintegration of the social network, the falling apart of effective agencies of collective action is often noted with a good deal of anxiety and bewailed as the unanticipated 'side effect' of the new lightness and fluidity of the increasingly mobile, slippery, shifty, evasive and fugitive power. But social disintegration is as much a condition as it is the outcome of the new technique of power, using disengagement and the art of escape as its major tools. For power to be free to flow, the world must be free of fences, barriers, fortified borders and checkpoints. Any dense and tight network of social bonds, and particularly a territorially rooted tight network, is an obstacle to be cleared out of the way. Global powers are bent on dismantling such networks for the sake of their continuous and growing fluidity, that principal source of their strength and the warrant of their invincibility. And it is the falling apart, the friability, the brittleness, the transcience, the until-further-noticeness of human bonds and networks which allow these powers to do their job in the first place.

Were the intertwined trends to develop unabated, men and women would be reshaped after the pattern of the electronic mole, that proud invention of the pioneering years of cybernetics immediately acclaimed as the harbinger of times to come: a plug on castors, scuffling around in a desperate search for electrical sockets to plug into. But in the coming age augured by cellular telephones, sockets are likely to be declared obsolete and in bad taste as well as offered in ever shrinking quantity and ever shakier quality. At the moment, many electric power suppliers extol the advantages of plugging into their respective networks and vie for the favours of the socket-seekers. But in the long run (whatever 'the long run' means in the era of instantaneity) sockets are likely to be ousted and supplanted by disposable batteries individually bought in the shops and on offer in every airport kiosk and every service station along the motorway and country road.

This seems to be a dyotopia made to the measure of liquid modernity—one fit to replace the fears recorded in Orwellian and Huxleyan-style nightmares.

94

GLOBAL MODERNITIES*

ROLAND ROBERTSON

According to *The Oxford Dictionary of New Words* the term 'glocal' and the process noun 'glocalization' are 'formed by telescoping *global* and *local* to make a blend'. Also according to the *Dictionary* that idea has been 'modelled on Japanese *dochakuka* (deriving from *dochaku* "living on one's own land"), originally the agricultural principle of adapting one's farming techniques to local conditions, but also adopted in Japanese business for *global localization,* a global outlook adapted to local conditions' (emphasis in original). More specifically, the terms 'glocal' and 'glocalization' became aspects of business jargon during the 1980s, but their major locus of origin was in fact Japan, a country which has for a very long time strongly cultivated the spatio-cultural significance of Japan itself and where the general issue of the relationship between the particular and the universal has historically received almost obsessive attention. By now it has become, again in the words of *The Oxford Dictionary of New Words*, 'one of the main marketing buzzwords of the beginning of the nineties'.

The idea of glocalization in its business sense is closely related to what in some contexts is called, in more straightforwardly economic terms, micro-marketing: the tailoring and advertising of goods and services on a global or near-global basis to increasingly differentiated local and particular markets. Almost needless to say, in the world of capitalistic production for increasingly global markets the adaptation to local and other particular conditions is not simply a case of business responses to existing global variety—to civilizational, regional, societal, ethnic, gender and still other types of differentiated consumers—as if such variety or heterogeneity existed simply 'in itself'. To a considerable extent micro-marketing—or, in the more comprehensive phrase, glocalization—involves *the construction* of increasingly differentiated consumers, the 'invention' of 'consumer traditions' (of which tourism, arguably the biggest 'industry' of the contemporary world, is undoubtedly the most clear-cut example). To put it very simply, diversity sells. From the consumer's point of view it can be a significant basis of cultural capital formation. This, it should be emphasized, is not its only function. The proliferation of, for example, 'ethnic' supermarkets in California and elsewhere does to a large extent cater not so much to difference for the sake of difference, but to the desire for the familiar and/or to nostalgic wishes. On the other hand, these too can also be bases of cultural capital formation.

It is not my purpose here to delve into the comparative history of capitalistic business practices. Thus the accuracy of the etymology concerning 'glocalization' provided by *The Oxford Dictionary of New Words* is not a crucial issue. Rather I want to use the general idea of glocalization to make a number of points about the global–local problematic. There is a widespread tendency to regard this problematic as straightforwardly involving a polarity, which assumes its most acute form in the claim that we live in a world of local assertions *against* globalizing trends, a world in which the very idea of locality is sometimes cast as a form of opposition or resistance to the hegemonically global (or one in which the assertion of 'locality' or *Gemeinschaft* is seen as the pitting of subaltern 'universals' against the 'hegemonic universal' of dominant cultures and/or classes). An interesting variant of this general view is to be found in the replication of the German culture–civilization distinction at the global level: the old notion of ('good') culture is pitted against the ('bad') notion of civilization. In this traditional German perspective local culture becomes, in effect, national culture, while civilization is given a distinctively global, world-wide colouring.

We have, in my judgement, to be much more subtle about the dynamics of the production and reproduction of difference and, in the broadest sense, locality. Speaking in reference to the local–cosmopolitan distinction, Hannerz has remarked that for locals diversity 'happens to be the principle which allows all locals to stick to their respective cultures'. At the same time, cosmopolitans largely depend on 'other people' carving out 'special niches' for their cultures. Thus 'there can be no cosmopolitans without locals'. This point has some bearing on the particular nature of the intellectual interest in and the approach to the local–global issue. In relation to Hannerz's general argument, however, we should note that in the contemporary world, or at least in the West, the current counter-urbanization trend, much of which in the USA is producing 'fortress communities', proceeds in terms of the standardization of locality, rather than straightforwardly in terms of 'the principle of difference'.

In any case, we should become much more historically conscious of the various ways in which the deceptively modern, or postmodern, problem of the relationship between the global and the local, the universal and the particular, and so on, is not by any means as unique to the second half of the twentieth century as many would have us believe. This is clearly shown in Greenfeld's recent study of the origins of nationalism in England, France, Germany, Russia and America. With the notable exception, of English nationalism, she shows that the emergence of all national identities—such constituting 'the most common and salient form of particularism in the modern world'—developed as a part of an 'essentially international.

The more extreme or adamant claims concerning the contemporary uniqueness of these alleged opposites is a refraction of what some have called the nostalgic paradigm in Western social science. It is a manifestation of the not always implicit world view that suggests that we—the global we—once lived in and were distributed not so long ago across a multitude of ontologically secure, collective 'homes'. Now, according to this narrative—or, perhaps, a metanarrative—our sense of home is rapidly being destroyed by waves of (Western?) 'globalization'. In contrast I maintain—although I can present here only part of my overall argument—that globalization has involved the reconstruction, in a sense the production, of 'home', 'community' and 'locality'. To that extent the local is not best seen, at least as an analytic or interpretative departure point, as a counterpoint to the global. Indeed it can be regarded, subject to some qualifications, as *an aspect* of globalization. One part of my argument which must remain underdeveloped in the immediate context is that we are being led into the polar-opposite way of thinking by the thesis that globalization is a direct 'consequence of modernity'. In this perspective Weber's 'iron cage' is globalized. Moreover, in this view there could never have been any kind of globalization without the instrumental rationality often taken to be the hallmark of modernity (a rationality which, it is readily conceded, Giddens sees as carrying both disabling *and* reflexive enabling possibilities).

Thus the notion of glocalization actually conveys much of what I myself have previously written about globalization. From my own analytic and interpretative standpoint the concept of globalization has involved the simultaneity and the interpenetration of what are conventionally called the global and the local, or—in more abstract vein—the universal and the particular. (Talking strictly of my own position in the current debate about and the discourse of globalization, it may even become necessary to substitute the term 'glocalization' for the contested term 'globalization' in order to make my argument more precise.) I certainly do not wish to fall victim, cognitive or otherwise, to a particular brand of current marketing terminology. Insofar as we regard the idea of glocalization as simply a capitalistic business term (of apparent Japanese origin) then I would of course reject it as, *inter alia,* not having sufficient analytic-interpretative leverage. On the other hand, we are surely coming to recognize that seemingly autonomous economic terms frequently have deep cultural roots. In the Japanese and other societal cases the cognitive and moral 'struggle' even to recognize the economic domain as relatively autonomous has never really been 'won'. In any case, we live in a world which increasingly acknowledges the quotidian conflation of the economic and the cultural. But we inherited from classical social theory, particularly in its German version in the decades from about 1880 to about 1920, a view that talk of 'culture' and 'cultivation' was distinctly at odds with 'materialism' and the rhetoric of economics and instrumental rationality.

My deliberations in this chapter on the local–global problematic hinge upon the view that contemporary conceptions of locality are largely produced in something like global terms, but this certainly does not mean that all forms of locality are thus substantively homogenized (notwithstanding the standardization, for example, of relatively new suburban, fortress communities). An important thing to recognize in this connection is that there is an increasingly globe-wide discourse of locality, community, home and the like. One of the ways of considering the idea of *global culture* is in terms of its being constituted by the increasing interconnectedness of many local cultures both large and small, although I certainly do not myself think that global culture is entirely constituted by such interconnectedness. In any case we should be careful *not to equate the communicative and interactional connecting of such cultures*—including very asymmetrical forms of such communication and interaction, as well as 'third cultures' of mediation—*with the notion of homogenization of all cultures.*

I have in mind the rapid, recent development of a relatively autonomous discourse of 'intercultural communication'. This discourse is being promoted by a growing number of professionals, along the lines of an older genre of 'how to' literature. So it is not simply a question of social and cultural theorists talking about cultural difference and countervailing forces of homogenization. One of the 'proper objects' of study here is the phenomenon of 'experts' who specialize in the 'instrumentally rational' promotion of intercultural communication. These 'experts' have in fact a vested interest in the promotion and protection of variety and diversity. Their jobs and their profession depend upon the expansion and reproduction of heterogeneity. The same seems to apply to strong themes in modern American business practice.

We should also be more interested in the conditions for the production of cultural pluralism—as well as geographical pluralism. Let me also say that the idea of locality, indeed of globality, is very relative. In spatial terms a village community is of course local relative to a region of a society, while a society is local relative to a civilizational area, and so on.

Relativity also arises in temporal terms. Contrasting the well-known pair consisting of locals and cosmopolitans, Hannerz has written that 'what was cosmopolitan in the early 1940s may be counted as a moderate form of localism by now'. I do not in the present context get explicitly involved in the problem of relativity (or relativism). But sensitivity to the problem does inform much of what I say.

There are certain conditions that are currently promoting the production of concern with the local-global problematic within the academy. King has addressed an important aspect of this. In talking specifically of the spatial compression dimension of globalization he remarks on the increasing numbers of 'protoprofessionals from so-called "Third World" societies' who are travelling to 'the core' for professional education. The educational sector of 'core' countries 'depends increasingly on this input of students from the global periphery'. It is the experience of 'flying round the world and needing schemata to make sense of what they see' on the one hand, and encountering students from all over the world in the classroom on the other, which forms an important experiential basis for academics of what King calls totalizing and global theories. I would maintain, however, that it is *interest in 'the local'* as much as the 'totally global' which is promoted in this way.

The Local in the Global? The Global in the Local?

In one way or another the issue of the relationship between the 'local' and the 'global' has become increasingly salient in a wide variety of intellectual and practical contexts. In some respects this development hinges upon the increasing recognition of the significance of space, as opposed to time, in a number of fields of academic and practical endeavour. The general interest in the idea of postmodernity, whatever its limitations, is probably the most intellectually tangible manifestation of this. The most well known maxim—virtually a cliché—proclaimed in the diagnosis of 'the postmodern condition' is of course that 'grand narratives' have come to an end, and that we are now in a circumstance of proliferating and often competing narratives. In this perspective there are no longer any stable accounts of dominant change in the world. This view itself has developed, on the other hand, at precisely the same time that there has crystallized an increasing interest in the world as a whole as a single place. (Robbins also notes this, in specific reference to geographers.) As the sense of temporal unidirectionality has faded so, on the other hand, has the sense of 'representational' space within which all kinds of narratives may be inserted expanded. This of course has increasingly raised in recent years the vital question as to whether the apparent collapse—and the 'deconstruction'—of the heretofore dominant social-evolutionist accounts of implicit or explicit world history are leading rapidly to a situation of chaos or one in which, to quote Giddens, 'an infinite number of purely idiosyncratic "histories" can be written'. Giddens claims in fact that *we can* make generalizations about 'definite episodes of historical transition'. However, since he also maintains that 'modernity' on a global scale has amounted to a rupture with virtually all prior forms of life he provides no guidance as to how history or histories might actually be done.

In numerous contemporary accounts, then, globalizing trends are regarded as in tension with 'local' assertions of identity and culture. Thus ideas such as the global *versus* the local, the global *versus* the 'tribal', the international *versus* the national, and the universal *versus* the particular are widely promoted. For some, these alleged oppositions are simply puzzles, while for others the second part of each opposition is seen as a reaction against the first. For still others they are contradictions. In the perspective of contradiction the tension between, for example, the universal and the particular may be seen either in the dynamic sense of being a relatively progressive source of overall change or as a modality which preserves an existing global system in its present state. We find both views in Wallerstein's argument that the relation between the universal and the particular is basically a product of expanding world-systemic capitalism. Only what Wallerstein calls anti-systemic movements—and then only those which effectively challenge its 'metaphysical presuppositions'—can move the world beyond the presuppositions of its present (capitalist) condition. In that light we may regard the contemporary proliferation of 'minority discourses' as being encouraged by the presentation of a 'world-system'. Indeed, there is much to suggest that adherents to minority discourses have, somewhat paradoxically, a special liking for Wallersteinian or other 'totalistic' forms of world-systems theory. But it must also be noted that many of the enthusiastic participants in the discourse of 'minorities' describe their intellectual practice in terms of the *singular*, minority discourse. This suggests that there is indeed a potentially *global* mode of writing and talking on behalf of, or at least about, minorities.

Barber (1992) argues that 'tribalism' and 'globalism' have become what he describes as the two axial principles of our time. In this he echoes a very widespread view of 'the new world (dis) order'. I chose to consider his position because it is succinctly stated and has been quite widely disseminated. Barber sees these two principles as inevitably in tension—a 'McWorld' of homogenizing globalization *versus* a 'Jihad world' of particularizing 'lebanonization'. (He might well now say 'balkanization'.) Barber is primarily interested in the bearing which each of these supposedly clashing principles have on the prospects for democracy. That is certainly a very important matter, but I am here only directly concerned with the global–local debate.

Like many others, Barber defines globalization as the opposite of localization. He argues that 'four imperatives make up the dynamic of McWorld; a market imperative, a resource imperative, an information-technology imperative, and an ecological imperative'. Each of these contributes to 'shrinking the world and diminishing the salience of national borders' and together they have 'achieved a considerable victory over factiousness and particularism, and not least over their most virulent traditional form—nationalism'. Remarking that 'the Enlightenment dream of a universal rational society has to a remarkable degree been realized', Barber emphasizes that that achievement has, however, been realized in commercialized, bureaucratized, homogenized and what he calls 'depoliticized' form. Moreover, he argues that it is a very incomplete achievement because it is 'in competition with forces of global breakdown, national dissolution, and centrifugal corruption'. While notions of localism, locality and locale do not figure explicitly in Barber's essay they certainly diffusely inform it.

There is no good reason, other than recently established convention in some quarters, to define globalization largely in terms of homogenization. Of course, anyone is at liberty to so define globalization, but I think that there is a great deal to be said against such a procedure. Indeed, while each of the imperatives of Barber's McWorld appear superficially to suggest homogenization, when one considers them more closely, they each have a local, diversifying aspect. I maintain also that it makes no good sense to define the global as if the global excludes the local. In somewhat technical terms, defining the global in such a way suggests that the global lies beyond all localities, as having systemic properties over and beyond the attributes of units within a global system. This way of talking flows along the lines suggested by the macro–micro distinction, which has held much sway in the discipline of economics and has recently become a popular theme in sociology and other social sciences.

Without denying that the world-as-a-whole has some systemic properties beyond those of the 'units' within it, it must be emphasized, on the other hand, that such units themselves are to a large degree constructed in terms of extra-unit processes and actions, in terms of increasingly global dynamics. For example, nationally organized societies—and the 'local' aspirations for establishing yet more nationally organized societies—are not simply units within a global context or texts within a context or intertext. Both their existence, and particularly the form of their existence, is largely the result of extra-societal—more generally, extra-local—processes and actions. If we grant with Wallerstein and Greenfeld that 'the national' is a 'prototype of the particular' we must, on the other hand, also recognize that the nation-state—more generally, the national society—is in a crucial respect a *cultural idea* (as Greenfeid herself seems to acknowledge). Much of the apparatus of contemporary nations, of the national-state organization of societies, including *the form* of their particularities—the construction of their unique identities—is very similar across the entire world in spite of much variation in levels of 'development'. This is, perhaps, the most tangible of contemporary sites of the interpenetration of particularism and universalism.

Before coming directly to the contemporary circumstance, it is necessary to say a few words about globalization in a longer, historical perspective. One can undoubtedly trace far back into human history developments involving the expansion of chains of connectedness across wide expanses of the earth. In that sense 'world formation' has been proceeding for many hundreds, indeed thousands, of years. At the same time, we can undoubtedly trace through human history periods during which the consciousness of the potential for world 'unity' was in one way or another particularly acute. One of the major tasks of students of globalization is, as I have said, to comprehend *the form* in which the present, seemingly rapid shifts towards a highly interdependent world was structured. I have specifically argued that that form has been centred upon four main elements of the global-human condition: societies, individuals, the international system of societies, and humankind. It is around the changing relationships between, different emphases upon and often conflicting interpretations of these aspects of human life that the contemporary world as a whole has crystallized. So in my perspective the issue of what is to he included under the notion of the global is treated very comprehensively. The global is not in and of itself counterposed to the local. Rather, what is often referred to as the local is essentially included within the global.

In this respect globalization, defined in its most general sense as the compression of the world as a whole, involves the linking of localities. But it also involves the 'invention' of locality, in the same general sense as the idea of the invention of tradition (Hobsbawm and Ranger, 1983), as well as its 'imagination'. There is indeed currently something like an 'ideology of home' which has in fact come into being partly in response to the constant repetition and global diffusion of the claim that we now live in a condition of homelessness or rootlessness; as if in prior periods of history the vast majority of people lived in 'secure' and homogenized locales. Two things, among others, must be said in objection to such ideas. First, the form of globalization has involved considerable emphasis, at least until now, on the cultural homogenization of nationally constituted societies; but, on the other hand, prior to that emphasis, which began to develop at the end of the eighteenth century, what McNeill calls polyethnicity was normal. Second, the phenomenological diagnosis of the generalized homelessness of modern man and woman has been developed as if 'the same people are behaving and interpreting at the same time in the same broad social process'; whereas there is in fact much to suggest that it is increasingly global expectations concerning the relationship between individual and society that have produced both routinized and 'existential' selves. On top of that, (the very ability to identify 'home', directly or indirectly, is contingent upon the (contested) construction and organization of interlaced categories of space and time.

But it is not my purpose here to go over this ground again, but rather to emphasize the significance of certain periods prior to the second half of the twentieth century when the possibilities for a single world seemed at the time to be considerable, but also problematic. Developing research along such lines will undoubtedly emphasize a variety of areas of the world and different periods. But as far as relatively recent times are concerned, I would draw attention to two arguments, both of which draw attention to rapid extension of communication across the world as a whole and thematize the central issue of changing conceptions of time-and-space. Johnson has in his book, *The Birth of the Modern,* argued that 'world society'—or 'international society in its totality'—largely crystallized in the period 1815–30. Here the emphasis is upon the crucial significance of the Congress of Vienna which was assembled following Bonaparte's first abdication in 1814. According to Johnson, the peace settlement in Vienna, following what was in effect the first world war, was 'reinforced by the powerful currents of romanticism sweeping through the world. . . . Thus was established 'an international order which, in most respects, endured for a century'. Regardless of its particular ideological bent, Johnson's book is important because he does attempt not merely to cover all continents of the world but also to range freely over many aspects of life generally, not just world politics or international relations. He raises significant issues concerning the development of consciousness of the world as a whole, which was largely made possible by the industrial and communicative revolution on the one hand, and the Enlightenment on the other.

Second (and, regardless of the issue of the periodization of globalization, more important), Kern has drawn attention to the crucial period of 1880–1918, in a way that is particularly relevant to the present set of issues. In his study of the *Culture of Time and Space* Kern's most basic point is that in the last two decades of the nineteenth century and the first twenty years or so of the twentieth century very consequential shifts took place with respect to both our sense of space and time. There occurred, through international negotiations and technological innovations, a standardization of time–space which was inevitably both universal and particular: world time organized in terms of particularistic space, in a sense the co-ordination of objectiveness and subjectiveness. In other words, homogenization went hand in hand with heterogenization. They made each other possible. It was in this period that 'the world' became locked into a particular *form* of a strong shift to unicity. It was during this time that the four major 'components' of globalization which I have previously specified were given formidable concreteness. Moreover, it was in the late-nineteenth century that there occurred a big spurt in the organized attempts to link localities on an international or ecumenical basis.

An immediate precursor of such was the beginning of international exhibitions in the mid-nineteenth century, involving the internationally organized display of particular national 'glories' and achievements. The last two decades of the century witnessed many more such international or cross-cultural ventures, among them the beginnings of the modern religious ecumenical movement, which at one and the same time celebrated difference and searched for commonality within the framework of an emergent culture for 'doing' the relationship between the particular and the, certainly not uncontested, universal. An interesting example of the latter is provided by the International Youth Hostel movement, which spread quite rapidly and not only in the northern hemisphere. This movement attempted on an organized international, or global, basis to promote the cultivation of communal, 'back to nature' values. Thus at one and the same time particularity was valorized but this was done on an increasingly globe-wide, pan-local basis.

The present century has seen a remarkable proliferation with respect to the 'international' organization and promotion of locality. A very pertinent example is provided by the current attempts to organize globally the promotion of the rights and identities of native, or indigenous, peoples. This was a strong feature, for example, of the Global Forum in Brazil in 1992, which, so to say, surrounded the official United Nations 'Earth Summit'. Another is the attempt by the World Health Organization to promote 'world health' by the reactivation and, if need be, the invention of 'indigenous' local medicine. It should be stressed that these are only a few examples taken from a multifaceted trend.

Glocalization and the Cultural Imperialism Thesis

Some of the issues which I have been raising are considered from a very different angle in Appiah's work on the viability of Pan-Africanism. Appiah's primary theme is 'the question of how we are to think about Africa's contemporary cultures in the light of the two main external determinants of her recent history—European and Afro-New World conceptions of Africa—and of her own endogenous cultural traditions'. His contention is that the 'ideological decolonization' which he seeks to effect can only be made possible by what he calls finding a 'negotiable middle way' between endogenous 'tradition' and 'Western' ideas, both of the latter designations being placed within quotation marks by Appiah himself. He objects strongly to what he calls the racial and racist thrusts of much of the Pan-American idea, pointing out that insofar as Pan-Africanism makes assumptions about the racial unity of all Africans, then this derives in large part from the experience and memory of non-African ideas about Africa and Africans which were prevalent in Europe and the USA during the latter part of the nineteenth century. Speaking specifically of the idea of the 'decolonization' of African literature, Appiah insists, I think correctly, that in much of the talk about decolonization we find what Appiah himself calls (again within quotation marks) a 'reverse discourse':

> The pose of repudiation actually presupposes the cultural institutions of the West and the ideological matrix in which they, in turn, are imbricated. Railing against the cultural hegemony of the West, the nativists are of its party without knowing it.... (D)efiance is determined less by 'indigenous' notions of resistance than by the dictates of the West's own Herderian legacy—its highly elaborated ideologies of national autonomy, of language and literature as their cultural substrate. Native nostalgia, in short is largely fueled by that Western sentimentalism so familiar after Rousseau; few things, then, are less native than nativism in its current form.

Appiah's statement facilitates the explication of a particularly important point. It helps to demonstrate that much of the conception of contemporary locality and indigeneity is itself historically contingent upon *encounters* between one civilizational region and another. Within such interactions, many of them historically imperialistic, has developed a sense of particularistic locality. But the latter is in large part a consequence of the increasingly global 'institutionalization' of the expectation and construction of local particularism. Not merely is variety continuously produced and reproduced in the contemporary world, that *variety is largely an aspect of the very dynamics which a considerable number of commentators interpret as homogenization.* So in this light we are again required to come up with a more subtle interpretation than is usually offered in the general debate about locality and globality.

Some important aspects of the local—global issue are manifested in the general and growing debate about and the discourse of cultural imperialism. There is of course a quite popular intellectual view which would have it that the entire world is being swamped by Western—more specifically, American—culture. This view has undoubtedly exacerbated recent French political complaints about American cultural imperialism, particularly within the context of GATT negotiations. There are, on the other hand, more probing discussions of and research on this matter. For starters, it should be emphasized that the virtually overwhelming evidence is that even 'cultural messages' which emanate directly from 'the USA' are *differentially* received and interpreted; that 'local' groups 'absorb' communication from the 'centre' in a great variety of ways. Second, we have to realize that the major alleged producers of 'global culture'—such as those in Atlanta (CNN) and Los Angeles (Hollywood)—increasingly tailor their products to a differentiated global market (which they partly construct). For example, Hollywood attempts to employ mixed, 'multinational' casts of actors and a variety of 'local' settings when it is particularly concerned, as it increasingly is, to get a global audience. Third, there is much to suggest that seemingly 'national' symbolic resources are in fact increasingly available for differentiated global interpretation and consumption. For example, in a recent discussion of the staging of Shakespeare's plays, Billington notes that in recent years Shakespeare has been subject to wide-ranging cultural interpretation and staging. Shakespeare no longer belongs to England. Shakespeare has assumed a universalistic significance; and we have to distinguish in this respect between Shakespeare as representing Englishness and Shakespeare as of 'local-cum-global' relevance. Fourth, clearly many have seriously underestimated the flow of ideas and practices from the so-called Third World to the seemingly dominant societies and regions of the world.

Much of global 'mass culture' is in fact impregnated with ideas, styles and genres concerning religion, music, art, cooking, and so on. In fact the whole question of what will 'fly' globally and what will not is a very important question in the present global situation. We know of course that the question of what 'flies' is in part contingent upon issues of power; but we would be very ill-advised to think of this simply as a matter of the hegemonic extension of Western modernity. As Tomlinson has argued, 'local cultures' are, in Sartre's phrase, *condemned to freedom*. And their global participation has been greatly (and politically) underestimated. At this time 'freedom' is manifested particularly in terms of the social construction of identity-and-tradition, by the appropriation of cultural traditions. Although, as I have emphasized, this reflexiveness is typically undertaken along relatively standardized global-cultural lines. (For example, in 1982 the UN fully recognized the existence of indigenous peoples. In so doing it effectively established *criteria* in terms of which indigenous groups could and should identify themselves and be recognized formally. There are national parallels to this, in the sense that some societies have legal criteria for ethnic groups and cultural traditions.)

Then there is the question of diversity at the local level. This issue has been raised in a particularly salient way by Balibar, who talks of *world spaces*. The latter are places in which the world-as-a-whole is potentially inserted. The general idea of world-space suggests that we should consider the local as a 'micro' manifestation of the global—in opposition, *inter alia*, to the implication that the local indicates enclaves of cultural, ethnic, or racial homogeneity. Where, in other words, is *home* in the late-twentieth century? Balibar's analysis—which is centred on contemporary Europe—suggests that in the present situation of global complexity, the idea of home has to be divorced analytically from the idea of locality. There may well be groups and categories which equate the two, but that doesn't entitle them or their representatives to project their perspective onto humanity as a whole. In fact there is much to suggest that the senses of home and locality are contingent upon alienation from home and/or locale. How else could one have (reflexive) consciousness of such? We talk of the mixing of cultures, of polyethnicity, but we also often underestimate the significance of what Lila Abu-Lughod calls 'halfies'. As Geertz has said, 'like nostalgia, diversity is not what it used to be'. One of the most significant aspects of contemporary diversity is indeed the complication it raises for conventional notions of culture. We must be careful not to remain in thrall to the old and rather well established view that cultures are organically binding and sharply bounded. In fact Lila Abu-Lughod opposes the very idea of culture because it seems to her to deny the importance of 'halfies', those who combine in themselves as individuals a number of cultural, ethnic and gendered features. This issue is closely related to the frequently addressed theme of global hybridization, even more closely to the idea of creolization.

Conclusion: Sameness and Difference

My emphasis upon the significance of the concept of glocalization has arisen mainly from what I perceive to be major weaknesses in much of the employment of the term 'globalization'. In particular, I have tried to transcend the tendency to cast the idea of globalization as inevitably in tension with the idea of localization. I have instead maintained that globalization—in the broadest sense, the compression of the world—has involved and increasingly involves the creation and the incorporation of locality, processes which themselves largely shape, in turn, the compression of the world as a whole. Even though we are, for various reasons, likely to continue to use the concept of globalization, it might well be preferable to replace it for certain purposes with the concept of glocalization. The latter concept has the definite advantage of making the concern with space as important as the focus upon temporal issues. At the same time emphasis upon the global condition—that is, upon globality—further constrains us to make our analysis and interpretation of the contemporary world both spatial and temporal, geographical as well as historical.

Systematic incorporation of the concept of glocalization into the current debate about globalization is of assistance with respect to the issue of what I have called form. The form of globalization has specifically to do with the way in which the compression of the world is, in the broadest sense, structured. This means that the issue of the form of globalization is related to the ideologically laden notion of world order. However, I want to emphasize strongly that insofar as this is indeed the case, my own effort here has been directed only at making sense of two *seemingly* opposing trends: homogenization and heterogenization. These simultaneous trends are, in the last instance, complementary and interpenetrative; even though they certainly can and do collide in concrete situations. Moreover, glocalization can be—in fact, is—used strategically, as in the strategies of glocalization employed by contemporary TV enterprises seeking global markets (MTV, then CNN, and now others). Thus we should realize that in arguing that the current form of globalization involves what is best described as glocalization I fully acknowledge that there are many different modes of practical glocalization. Thus, even though much of what I said in this chapter has been hinged upon the Japanese conception of glocalization, I have in fact generalized that concept so as, in principle, to encompass the world as a whole. In this latter perspective the Japanese notion of glocaiization appears as a *particular version* of a very general phenomenon.

An important issue which arises from my overall discussion has to do with the ways in which, since the era of the nation-state began in the late eighteenth century, the nation-state itself has been a major agency for the production of diversity and hybridization. Again, it happens to be the case that Japan provides the most well-known example of what Westney calls cross-societal emulation, most clearly during the early Meiji period. I would, however, prefer the term, selective incorporation in order to describe the very widespread tendency for nation-states to 'copy' ideas and practices from other societies—to engage, in varying degrees of systematicity, in projects of importation and hybridization. So, even though I have emphasized that the cultural idea of the nation-state is a 'global fact', we also should recognize that nation-states have, particularly since the late nineteenth century, been engaged in selective learning from other societies, each nation-state thus incorporating a different mixture of 'alien' ideas.

There is still another factor in this brief consideration of 'hybridized national cultures'. This is the phenomenon of cultural nationalism. Yet again, this concept has emerged in particular reference to Japan. On the basis of a discussion of *nihonjinron* (the discourse on and of Japanese uniqueness), Yoshino argues that *nihonjinron* has, in varying degrees, been a common practice. Specifically, modern nations have tended to promote discourses concerning their own unique difference, a practice much encouraged in and by the great globalizing thrusts of the late nineteenth and early twentieth centuries. In this respect what is sometimes these days called strategic essentialism—mainly in reference to liberation movements of various kinds—is much older than some may think. It is in fact an extension and generalization of a long drawn-out process.

Finally, in returning to the issue of form, I would argue that no matter how much we may speak of global disorder, uncertainty and the like, generalizations and theorizations of such are inevitable. We should not entirely conflate the empirical issues with the interpretative-analytical ones. Speaking in the latter vein we can conclude that the form of globalization is currently being reflexively reshaped in such a way as to increasingly make projects of glocalization the constitutive features of contemporary globalization.

95

THE POSTMODERN CONDITION*

JEAN-FRANÇOIS LYOTARD

Scientific knowledge does not represent the totality of knowledge; it has always existed in addition to, and in competition and conflict with, another kind of knowledge, which I will call narrative in the interests of simplicity (its characteristics will be described later). I do not mean to say that narrative knowledge can prevail over science, but its model is related to ideas of internal equilibrium and conviviality next to which contemporary scientific knowledge cuts a poor figure, especially if it is to undergo an exteriorization with respect to the "knower" and an alienation from its user even greater than has previously been the case. The resulting demoralization of researchers and teachers is far from negligible; it is well known that during the 1960s, in all of the most highly developed societies, it reached such explosive dimensions among those preparing to practice these professions—the students—that there was noticeable decrease in productivity at laboratories and universities unable to protect themselves from its contamination. Expecting this, with hope or fear, to lead to a revolution (as was then often the case) is out of the question: it will not change the order of things in postindustrial society overnight. But this doubt on the part of scientists must be taken into account as a major factor in evaluating the present and future status of scientific knowledge.

It is all the more necessary to take it into consideration since—and this is the second point—the scientists' demoralization has an impact on the central problem of legitimation. I use the word in a broader sense than do contemporary German theorists in their discussions of the question of authority. Take any civil law as an example: it states that a given category of citizens must perform a specific kind of action. Legitimation is the process by which a legislator is authorized to promulgate such a law as a norm. Now take the example of a scientific statement: it is subject to the rule that a statement must fulfill a given set of conditions in order to be accepted as scientific. In this case, legitimation is the process by which a "legislator" dealing with scientific discourse is authorized to prescribe the stated conditions (in general, conditions of internal consistency and experimental verification) determining whether a statement is to be included in that discourse for consideration by the scientific community.

The parallel may appear forced. But as we will see, it is not. The question of the legitimacy of science has been indissociably linked to that of the legitimation of the legislator since the time of Plato. From this point of view, the right to decide what is true is not independent of the right to decide what is just, even if the statements consigned to these two authorities differ in nature. The point is that there is a strict interlinkage between the kind of language called science and the kind called ethics and politics: they both stem from the same perspective, the same "choice" if you will—the choice called the Occident.

When we examine the current status of scientific knowledge—at a time when science seems more completely subordinated to the prevailing powers than ever before and, along with the new technologies, is in danger of becoming a major stake in their conflicts—the question of double legitimation, far from receding into the background, necessarily comes to the fore. For it appears in its most complete form, that of reversion, revealing that knowledge and power are simply two sides of the same question: who decides what knowledge is, and who knows what needs to be decided? In the computer age, the question of knowledge is now more than ever a question of government.

The Nature of the Social Bond: The Modern Alternative

If we wish to discuss knowledge in the most highly developed contemporary society, we must answer the preliminary question of what methodological representation to apply to that society. Simplifying to the extreme, it is fair to say that in principle there have been, at least over the last half-century, two basic representational models for society: either society forms a functional whole, or it is divided in two. An illustration of the first model is suggested by Talcott Parsons (at least the postwar Parsons) and his school, and of the second, by the Marxist current (all of its component schools, whatever differences they may have, accept both the principle of class struggle and dialectics as a duality operating within society).

The alternative seems clear: it is a choice between the homogeneity and the intrinsic duality of the social, between functional and critical knowledge. But the decision seems difficult, or arbitrary.

It is tempting to avoid the decision altogether by distinguishing two kinds of knowledge. One, the positivist kind, would be directly applicable to technologies bearing on men and materials, and would lend itself to operating as an indispensable productive force within the system. The other—the critical, reflexive, or hermeneutic kind—by reflecting directly or indirectly on values or aims, would resist any such "recuperation."

The Nature of the Social Bond: The Postmodern Perspective

I find this partition solution unacceptable. I suggest that the alternative it attempts to resolve, but only reproduces, is no longer relevant for the societies with which we are concerned and that the solution itself is still caught within a type of oppositional thinking that is out of step with the most vital modes of postmodern knowledge. As I have already said, economic "redeployment" in the current phase of capitalism, aided by a shift in techniques and technology, goes hand in hand with a change in the function of the State: the image of society this syndrome suggests necessitates a serious revision of the alternate approaches considered. For brevity's sake, suffice it to say that functions of regulation, and therefore of reproduction, are being and will be further withdrawn from administrators and entrusted to machines. Increasingly, the central question is becoming who will have access to the information these machines must have in storage to guarantee that the right decisions are made. Access to data is, and will continue to be, the prerogative of experts of all stripes. The ruling class is and will continue to be the class of decision makers. Even now it is no longer composed of the traditional political class, but of a composite layer of corporate leaders, high-level administrators, and the heads of the major professional, labor, political, and religious organizations.

What is new in all of this is that the old poles of attraction represented by nation-states, parties, professions, institutions, and historical traditions are losing their attraction. And it does not look as though they will be replaced, at least not on their former scale. The Trilateral Commission is not a popular pole of attraction. "Identifying" with the great names, the heroes of contemporary history, is becoming more and more difficult. Dedicating oneself to "catching up with Germany," the life goal the French president [Giscard d'Estaing at the time this book was published in France] seems to be offering his countrymen, is not exactly exicting. But then again, it is not exactly a life goal. It depends on each individual's industriousness. Each individual is referred to himself. And each of us knows that our *self* does not amount to much.

This breaking up of the grand Narratives leads to what some authors analyze in terms of the dissolution of the social bond and the disintegration of social aggregates into a mass of individual atoms thrown into the absurdity of Brownian motion. Nothing of the kind is happening: this point of view, it seems to me, is haunted by the paradisaic representation of a lost "organic" society.

A *self* does not amount to much, but no self is an island; each exists in a fabric of relations that is now more complex and mobile than ever before. Young or old, man or woman, rich or poor, a person is always located at "nodal points" of specific communication circuits, however tiny these may be. Or better: one is always located at a post through which various kinds of messages pass. No one, not even the least privileged among us, is ever entirely powerless over the messages that traverse and position him at the post of sender, addressee, or referent. One's mobility in relation to these language game effects (language games, of course, are what this is all about) is tolerable, at least within certain limits (and the limits are vague); it is even solicited by regulatory mechanisms, and in particular by the self-adjustments the system undertakes in order to improve its performance. It may even be said that the system can and must encourage such movement to the extent that it combats its own entropy; the novelty of an unexpected "move," with its correlative displacement of a partner or group of partners, can supply the system with that increased performativity it forever demands and consumes.

It should now be clear from which perspective I chose language games as my general methodological approach. I am not claiming that the *entirety* of social relations is of this nature—that will remain an open question. But there is no need to resort to some fiction of social origins to establish that language games are the minimum relation required for society to exist: even before he is born, if only by virtue of the name he is given, the human child is already positioned as the referent in the story recounted by those around him, in relation to which he will inevitably chart his course. Or more simply still, the question of the social bond, insofar as it is a question, is itself a language game, the game of inquiry. It immediately positions the person who asks, as well as the addressee and the referent asked about: it is already the social bond.

What is needed if we are to understand social relations in this manner, on whatever scale we choose, is not only a theory of communication, but a theory of games which accepts agonistics as a founding principle. In this context, it is easy to see that the essential element of newness is not simply "innovation." Support for this approach can be found in the work of a number of contemporary sociologists, in addition to linguists and philosophers of language.

This "atomization" of the social into flexible networks of language games may seem far removed from the modern reality, which is depicted, on the contrary, as afflicted with bureaucratic paralysis. The objection will be made, at least, that the weight of certain institutions imposes limits on the games, and thus restricts the inventiveness of the players in making their moves. But I think this can be taken into account without causing any particular difficulty.

In the ordinary use of discourse—for example, in a discussion between two friends—the interlocutors use any available ammunition, changing games from one utterance to the next: questions, requests, assertions, and narratives are launched pell-mell into battle. The war is not without rules, but the rules allow and encourage the greatest possible flexibility of utterance.

From this point of view, an institution differs from a conversation in that it always requires supplementary constraints for statements to be declared admissible within its bounds. The constraints function to filter discursive potentials, interrupting possible connections in the communication networks: there are things that should not be said. They also privilege certain classes of statements (sometimes only one) whose predominance characterizes the discourse of the particular institution: there are things that should be said, and there are ways of saying them. Thus: orders in the army, prayer in church, denotation in the schools, narration in families, questions in philosophy, performativity in businesses. Bureaucratization is the outer limit of this tendency.

However, this hypothesis about the institution is still too "unwieldy": its point of departure is an overly "reifying" view of what is institutionalized. We know today that the limits the institution imposes on potential language "moves" are never established once and for all (cvcn if they have been formally defined). Rather, the limits are themselves the stakes and provisional results of language strategies, within the institution and without. Examples: Does the university have a place for language experiments (poetics)? Can you tell stories in a cabinet meeting? Advocate a cause in the barracks? The answers are clear: yes, if the university opens creative workshops; yes, if the cabinet works with prospective scenarios; yes, if the limits of the old institution are displaced. Reciprocally, it can be said that the boundaries only stabilize when they cease to be stakes in the game.

This, I think, is the appropriate approach to contemporary institutions of knowledge.

The Pragmatics of Narrative Knowledge

Knowledge [*savoir*] in general cannot be reduced to science, nor even to learning [*connaissance*]. Learning is the set of statements which, to the exclusion of all other statements, denote or describe objects and may be declared true or false. Science is a subset of learning. It is also composed of denotative statements, but imposes two supplementary conditions on their acceptability: the objects to which they refer must be available for repeated access, in other words, they must be accessible in explicit conditions of observation; and it must be possible to decide whether or not a given statement pertains to the language judged relevant by the experts.

But what is meant by the term *knowledge* is not only a set of denotative statements, far from it. It also includes notions of "know-how," "knowing how to live," "how to listen" [*savoir-faire, savoir-vivre, savoir-écouter*], etc. Knowledge, then, is a question of competence that goes beyond the simple determination and application of the criterion of truth, extending to the determination and application of criteria of efficiency (technical qualification), of justice and/ or happiness (ethical wisdom), of the beauty of a sound or color (auditory and visual sensibility), etc. Understood in this way, knowledge is what makes someone capable of forming "good" denotative utterances, but also "good" prescriptive and "good" evaluative utterances.... It is not a competence relative to a particular class of statements (for example, cognitive ones) to the exclusion of all others. On the contrary, it makes "good" performances in relation to a variety of objects of discourse possible: objects to be known, decided on, evaluated, transformed. .... From this derives one of the principal features of knowledge: it coincides with an extensive array of competence-building measures and is the only form embodied in a subject constituted by the various areas of competence composing it.

Another characteristic meriting special attention is the relation between this kind of knowledge and custom. What is a "good" prescriptive or evaluative utterance, a "good" performance in denotative or technical matters? They are all judged to be "good" because they conform to the relevant criteria (of justice, beauty, truth, and efficiency respectively) accepted in the social circle of the "knower's" interlocutors. The early philosophers called this mode of legitimating statements opinion. The consensus that permits such knowledge to be circumscribed and makes it possible to distinguish one who knows from one who doesn't (the foreigner, the child) is what constitutes the culture of a people.

It is fair to say that there is one point on which all of the investigations agree, regardless of which scenario they propose to dramatize and understand the distance separating the customary state of knowledge from its state in the scientific age: the preeminence of the narrative form in the formulation of traditional knowledge. Some study this form for its own sake; others see it as the diachronic costume of the structural operators that, according to them, properly constitute the knowledge in question; still others bring to it an "economic" interpretation in the Freudian sense of the term. All that is important here is the fact that its form is narrative. Narration is the quintessential form of customary knowledge, in more ways than one.

A narrative tradition is also the tradition of the criteria defining a threefold competence —"know-how," "knowing how to speak," and "knowing how to hear" [*savoir-faire, savoir-dire, savoir-entendre*]—through which the community's relationship to itself and its environment is played out. What is transmitted through these narratives is the set of pragmatic rules that constitutes the social bond.

By way of a simplifying fiction, we can hypothesize that, against all expectations, a collectivity that takes narrative as its key form of competence has no need to remember its past. It finds the raw material for its social bond not only in the meaning of the narratives it recounts, but also in the act of reciting them. The narratives' reference may seem to belong to the past, but in reality it is always contemporaneous with the act of recitation. It is the present act that on each of its occurrences marshals in the ephemeral temporality inhabiting the space between the "I have heard" and the "you will hear."

Narratives, as we have seen, determine criteria of competence and/or illustrate how they are to be applied. They thus define what has the right to be said and done in the culture in question, and since they are themselves a part of that culture, they are legitimated by the simple fact that they do what they do.

The Pragmatics of Scientific Knowledge

1. Scientific knowledge requires that one language game, denotation, be retained and all others excluded. A statement's truth-value is the criterion determining its acceptability.

2. Scientific knowledge is in this way set apart from the language games that combine to form the social bond. Unlike narrative knowledge, it is no longer a direct and shared component of the bond. But it is indirectly a component of it, because it developes into a profession and gives rise to institutions, and in modern societies language games consolidate themselves in the form of institutions run by qualified partners (the professional class). The relation between knowledge and society (that is, the sum total of partners in the general agonistics, excluding scientists in their professional capacity) becomes one of mutual exteriority. A new problem appears—that of the relationship between the scientific institution and society.

Drawing a parallel between science and nonscientific (narrative) knowledge helps us understand, or at least sense, that the former's existence is no more—and no less—necessary than the latter's. Both are composed of sets of statements; the statements are "moves" made by the players within the framework of generally applicable rules; these rules are specific to each particular kind of knowledge, and the "moves" judged to be "good" in one cannot be of the same type as those judged "good" in another, unless it happens that way by chance.

It is therefore impossible to judge the existence or validity of narrative knowledge on the basis of scientific knowledge and vice versa: the relevant criteria are different. All we can do is gaze in wonderment at the diversity of discursive species, just as we do at the diversity of plant or animal species. Lamenting the "loss of meaning" in postmodernity boils down to mourning the fact that knowledge is no longer principally narrative. Such a reaction does not necessarily follow. Neither does an attempt to derive or engender (using operators like development) scientific knowledge from narrative knowledge, as if the former contained the latter in an embryonic state.

Delegitimation

In contemporary society and culture—postindustrial society, postmodern culture—the question of the legitimation of knowledge is formulated in different terms. The grand narrative has lost its credibility, regardless of what mode of unification it uses, regardless of whether it is a speculative narrative or a narrative of emancipation.

The decline of narrative can be seen as an effect of the blossoming of techniques and technologies since the Second World War, which has shifted emphasis from the ends of action to its means; it can also be seen as an effect of the redeployment of advanced liberal capitalism after its retreat under the protection of Keynesianism during the period 1930-60, a renewal that has eliminated the communist alternative and valorized the individual enjoyment of goods and services.

The "crisis" of scientific knowledge, signs of which have been accumulating since the end of the nineteenth century, is not born of a chance proliferation of sciences, itself an effect of progress in technology and the expansion of capitalism. It represents, rather, an internal erosion of the legitimacy principle of knowledge. There is erosion at work inside the speculative game, and by loosening the weave of the encyclopedic net in which each science was to find its place, it eventually sets them free.

It in no way follows that they are reduced to barbarity. What saves them from it is their knowledge that legitimation can only spring from their own linguistic practice and communicational interaction. Science "smiling into its beard" at every other belief has taught them the harsh austerity of realism.

Postmodern Science as the Search for Instabilities

As previously indicated, the pragmatics of scientific research, especially in its search for new methods of argumentation, emphasizes the invention of new "moves" and even new rules for language games. We must now take a closer look at this aspect of the problem, which is of decisive importance in the present state of scientific knowledge. We could say, tongue in cheek, that scientific knowledge is seeking a "crisis resolution" —a resolution of the crisis of determinism. Determinism is the hypothesis upon which legitimation by performativity is based: since performativity is defined by an input/ output ratio, there is a presupposition that the system into which the input is entered is stable; that system must follow a regular "path" that it is possible to express as a continuous function possessing a derivative, so that an accurate prediction of the output can be made.

Such is the positivist "philosophy" of efficiency. I will cite a number of prominent examples as evidence against it to facilitate the final discussion of legitimation. Briefly, the aim is to demonstrate on the basis of a few exhibits that the pragmatics of postmodern scientific knowledge per se has little affinity with the quest for performativity.

I made the point that the striking feature of postmodern scientific knowledge is that the discourse on the rules that validate it is (explicitly) immanent to it. What was considered at the end of the nineteenth century to be a loss of legitimacy and a fall into philosophical "pragmatism" or logical positivism was only an episode, from which knowledge has recovered by including within scientific discourse the discourse on the validation of statements held to be laws. As we have seen, this inclusion is not a simple operation, but gives rise to "paradoxes" that are taken extremely seriously and to "limitations" on the scope of knowledge that are in fact changes in its nature.

The metamathematical research that led to Gödel's theorem is a veritable paradigm of how this change in nature takes place. But the transformation that dynamics has undergone is no less exemplary of the new scientific spirit, and it is of particular interest here because it compels us to reconsider a notion that, as we have seen, figures prominently in the discussion of performance, particularly in the domain of social theory: the notion of system.

The idea of performance implies a highly stable system because it is based on the principle of a relation, which is in theory always calculable, between heat and work, hot source and cold source, input and output. This idea comes from thermodynamics. It is associated with the notion that the evolution of a system's performance can be predicated if all of the variables are known. The ideal fulfillment of this condition is clearly expressed in Laplace's fiction of the "demon:" he knows all of the variables determining the state of the universe at a moment *t*, and can thus predict its state at a moment $t'>t$. This fiction is sustained by the principle that physical systems, including the system of systems called the universe, follow regular patterns, with the result that their evolution traces a regular path and gives rise to "normal" continuous functions (and to futurology . . .).

The advent of quantum mechanics and atomic physics has limited the range of applicability of this principle in two ways, the respective implications of which differ in scope. First, a complete definition of the initial state of a system (or all the independent variables) would require an expenditure of energy at least equivalent to that consumed by the system to be defined. A layman's version of the de facto impossibility of ever achieving a complete measure of any given state of a system is provided in a note by Borges. An emperor wishes to have a perfectly accurate map of the empire made. The project leads the country to ruin—the entire population devotes all its energy to cartography.

Brillouin's argument leads to the conclusion that the idea (or ideology) of perfect control over a system, which is supposed to improve its performance, is inconsistent with respect to the law of contradiction: it in fact lowers the performance level it claims to raise. This inconsistency explains the weakness of state and socioeconomic bureaucracies: they stifle the systems or subsystems they control and asphyxiate themselves in the process (negative feedback). The interest of such an explanation is that it has no need to invoke any form of legitimation outside the system itself (for example, the freedom of human agents inciting them to rise up against excessive authority). Even if we accept that society is a system, complete control over it, which would necessitate an exact definition of its initial state, is impossible because no such definition could ever be effected.

But this limitation only calls into question the practicability of exact knowledge and the power that would result from it. They remain possible in theory. Classical determinism continues to work within the framework of the unreachable—but conceivable—limit of the total knowledge of a system.

The conclusion we can draw from this research (and much more not mentioned here) is that the continuous differentiable function is losing its preeminence as a paradigm of knowledge and prediction. Postmodern science—by concerning itself with such things as undecidables, the limits of precise control, conflicts characterized by incomplete information, *"fracta,"* catastrophes, and pragmatic paradoxes—is theorizing its own evolution as discontinuous, catastrophic, nonrectifiable, and paradoxical. It is changing the meaning of the word *knowledge*, while expressing how such a change can take place. It is producing not the known, but the unknown. And it suggests a model of legitimation that has nothing to do with maximized performance, but has as its basis difference understood as paralogy.

A game theory specialist whose work is moving in this same direction said it well: "Wherein, then, does the usefulness of game theory lie? Game theory, we think, is useful in the same sense that any sophisticated theory is useful, namely as a generator of ideas." P. B. Medawar, for his part, has stated that "*having ideas* is the scientist's highest accomplishment," that there is no "scientific method," and that a scientist is before anything else a person who "tells stories." The only difference is that he is duty bound to verify them.

Legitimation by Paralogy

Let us say at this point that the facts we have presented concerning the problem of the legitimation of knowledge today are sufficient for our purposes. We no longer have recourse to the grand narratives—we can resort neither to the dialectic of Spirit nor even to the emancipation of humanity as a validation for postmodern scientific discourse. But as we have just seen, the little narrative [*petit récit*] remains the quintessential form of imaginative invention, most particularly in science. In addition, the principle of consensus as a criterion of validation seems to be inadequate. It has two formulations. In the first, consensus is an agreement between men, defined as knowing intellects and free wills, and is obtained through dialogue. This is the form elaborated by Habermas, but his conception is based on the validity of the narrative of emancipation. In the second, consensus is a component of the system, which manipulates it in order to maintain and improve its performance. It is the object of administrative procedures, in Luhmann's sense. In this case, its only validity is as an instrument to be used toward achieving the real goal, which is what legitimates the system—power.

This summary makes it easy to see that systems theory and the kind of legitimation it proposes have no scientific basis whatsoever; science itself does not function according to this theory's paradigm of the system, and contemporary science excludes the possibility of using such a paradigm to describe society.

In this context, let us examine two important points in Luhmann's argument. On the one hand, the system can only function by reducing complexity, and on the other, it must induce the adaptation of individual aspirations to its own ends. The reduction in complexity is required to maintain the system's power capability. If all messages could circulate freely among all individuals, the quantity of the information that would have to be taken into account before making the correct choice would delay decisions considerably, thereby lowering performativity. Speed, in effect, is a power component of the system.

The objection will be made that these molecular opinions must indeed be taken into account if the risk of serious disturbances is to be avoided, Luhmann replies—and this is the second point—that it is possible to guide individual aspirations through a process of "quasi-apprenticeship," "free of all disturbance," in order to make them compatible with the system's decisions. The decisions do not have to respect individuals' aspirations: the aspirations have to aspire to the decisions, or at least to their effects. Administrative procedures should make individuals "want" what the system needs in order to perform well It is easy to see what role telematics technology could play in this.

It cannot be denied that there is persuasive force in the idea that context control and domination are inherently better than their absence. The performativity criterion has its "advantages." It excludes in principle adherence to a metaphysical discourse; it requires the renunciation of fables; it demands clear minds and cold wills; it replaces the definition of essences with the calculation of interactions; it makes the "players" assume responsibility not only for the statements they propose, but also for the rules to which they submit those statements in order to render them acceptable. It brings the pragmatic functions of knowledge clearly to light, to the extent that they seem to relate to the criterion of efficiency: the pragmatics of argumentation, of the production of proof, of the transmission of learning, and of the apprenticeship of the imagination.

It also contributes to elevating all language games to self-knowledge, even those not within the realm of canonical knowledge. It tends to jolt everyday discourse into a kind of metadiscourse: ordinary statements are now displaying a propensity for self-citation, and the various pragmatic posts are tending to make an indirect connection even to current messages concerning them. Finally, it suggests that the problems of internal communication experienced by the scientific community in the course of its work of dismantling and remounting its languages are comparable in nature to the problems experienced by the social collectivity when, deprived of its narrative culture, it must reexamine its own internal communication and in the process question the nature of the legitimacy of the decisions made in its name.

From the beginning of this study, I have emphasized the differences (not only formal, but also pragmatic) between the various language games, especially between denotative, or knowledge, games and prescriptive, or action, games. The pragmatics of science is centered on denotative utterances, which are the foundation upon which it builds institutions of learning (institutes, centers, universities, etc.). But its postmodern development brings a decisive "fact" to the fore: even discussions of denotative statements need to have rules. Rules are not denotative but prescriptive utterances, which we are better off calling metaprescriptive utterances to avoid confusion (they prescribe what the moves of language games must be in order to be admissible). The function of the differential or imaginative or paralogical activity of the current pragmatics of science is to point out these metaprescriptives (science's "presuppositions") and to petition the players to accept different ones. The only legitimation that can make this kind of request admissible is that it will generate ideas, in other words, new statements.

Social pragmatics does not have the "simplicity" of scientific pragmatics. It is a monster formed by the interweaving of various networks of heteromorphous classes of utterances (denotative, prescriptive, performàtive, technical, evaluative, etc.). There is no reason to think that it would be possible to determine metaprescriptives common to all of these language games or that a revisable consensus like the one in force at a given moment in the scientific community could embrace the totality of metaprescriptions regulating the totality of statements circulating in the social collectivity. As a matter of fact, the contemporary decline of narratives of legitimation—be they traditional or "modern" (the emancipation of humanity, the realization of the Idea)—is tied to the abandonment of this belief. It is its absence for which the ideology of the "system," with its pretensions to totality, tries to compensate and which it expresses in the cynicism of its criterion of performance.

For this reason, it seems neither possible, nor even prudent, to follow Habermas in orienting our treatment of the problem of legitimation in the direction of a search for universal consensus through what he calls *Diskurs*, in other words, a dialogue of argumentation.

This would be to make two assumptions. The first is that it is possible for all speakers to come to agreement on which rules or metaprescriptions are universally valid for language games, when it is clear that language games are heteromorphous, subject to heterogeneous sets of pragmatic rules.

The second assumption is that the goal of dialogue is consensus. But as I have shown in the analysis of the pragmatics of science, consensus is only a particular state of discussion, not its end. Its end, on the contrary, is paralogy. This double observation (the heterogeneity of the rules and the search for dissent) destroys a belief that still underlies Habermas's research, namely, that humanity as a collective (universal) subject seeks its common emancipation through the regularization of the "moves" permitted in all language games and that the legitimacy of any statement resides in its contributing to that emancipation.

It is easy to see what function this recourse plays in Habermas's argument against Luhmann. *Diskurs* is his ultimate weapon against the theory of the stable system. The cause is good, but the argument is not. Consensus has become an outmoded and suspect value. But justice as a value is neither outmoded nor suspect. We must thus arrive at an idea and practice of justice that is not linked to that of consensus.

A recognition of the heteromorphous nature of language games is a first step in that direction. This obviously implies a renunciation of terror, which assumes that they are isomorphic and tries to make them so. The second step is the principle that any consensus on the rules defining a game and the "moves" playable within it *must* be local, in other words, agreed on by its present players and subject to eventual cancellation. The orientation then favors a multiplicity of finite meta-arguments, by which I mean argumentation that concerns metaprescriptives and is limited in space and time.

This orientation corresponds to the course that the evolution of social interaction is currently taking; the temporary contract is in practice supplanting permanent institutions in the professional, emotional, sexual, cultural, family, and international domains, as well as in political affairs. This evolution is of course ambiguous: the temporary contract is favored by the system due to its greater flexibility, lower cost, and the creative turmoil of its accompanying motivations—all of these factors contribute to increased operativity. In any case, there is no question here of proposing a "pure" alternative to the system: we all now know, as the 1970s come to a close, that an attempt at an alternative of that kind would end up resembling the system it was meant to replace. We should be happy that the tendency toward the temporary contract is ambiguous: it is not totally subordinated to the goal of the system, yet the system tolerates it. This bears witness to the existence of another goal within the system: knowledge of language games as such and the decision to assume responsibility for their rules and effects. Their most significant effect is precisely what validates the adoption of rules—the quest for paralogy.

We are finally in a position to understand how the computerization of society affects this problematic. It could become the "dream" instrument for controlling and regulating the market system, extended to include knowledge itself and governed exclusively by the performativity principle. In that case, it would inevitably involve the use of terror. But it could also aid groups discussing metaprescriptives by supplying them with the information they usually lack for making knowledgeable decisions. The line to follow for computerization to take the second of these two paths is, in principle, quite simple: give the public free access to the memory and data banks. Language games would then be games of perfect information at any given moment. But they would also be nonzero-sum games, and by virtue of that fact discussion would never risk fixating in a position of minimax equilibrium because it had exhausted its stakes. For the stakes would be knowledge (or information, if you will), and the reserve of knowledge—language's reserve of possible utterances—is inexhaustible. This sketches the outline of a politics that would respect both the desire for justice and the desire for the unknown.

96

Hyperreality*

Jean Baudrillard

If once we were able to view the Borges fable in which the cartographers of the Empire draw up a map so detailed that it ends up covering the territory exactly (the decline of the Empire witnesses the fraying of this map, little by little, and its fall into ruins, though some shreds are still discernible in the deserts—the metaphysical beauty of this ruined abstraction testifying to a pride equal to the Empire and rotting like a carcass, returning to the substance of the soil, a bit as the double ends by being confused with the real through aging)—as the most beautiful allegory of simulation, this fable has now come full circle for us, and possesses nothing but the discrete charm of second-order simulacra.

Today abstraction is no longer that of the map, the double, the mirror, or the concept. Simulation is no longer that of a territory, a referential being, or a substance. It is the generation by models of a real without origin or reality: a hyperreal. The territory no longer precedes the map, nor does it survive it. It is nevertheless the map that precedes the territory—*precession of simulacra*—that engenders the territory, and if one must return to the fable, today it is the territory whose shreds slowly rot across the extent of the map. It is the real, and not the map, whose vestiges persist here and there in the deserts that are no longer those of the Empire, but ours. *The desert of the real itself.*

The Divine Irreference of Images

To dissimulate is to pretend not to have what one has. To simulate is to feign to have what one doesn't have. One implies a presence, the other an absence. But it is more complicated than that because simulating is not pretending: "Whoever fakes an illness can simply stay in bed and make everyone believe he is ill. Whoever simulates an illness produces in himself some of the symptoms" (Littré). Therefore, pretending, or dissimulating, leaves the principle of reality intact: the difference is always clear, it is simply masked, whereas simulation threatens the difference between the "true" and the "false," the "real" and the "imaginary." Is the simulator sick or not, given that he produces "true" symptoms? Objectively one cannot treat him as being either ill or not ill. Psychology and medicine stop at this point, forestalled by the illness's henceforth undiscoverable truth. For if

*Excerpts from *Selected Writings* by Jean Baudrillard, Translated by Sheila Faria Glaser.

any symptom can be "produced," and can no longer be taken as a fact of nature, then every illness can be considered as simulatable and simulated, and medicine loses its meaning since it only knows how to treat "real" illnesses according to their objective causes. Psychosomatics evolves in a dubious manner at the borders of the principle of illness. As to psychoanalysis, it transfers the symptom of the organic order to the unconscious order: the latter is new and taken for "real" more real than the other—but why would simulation be at the gates of the unconscious? Why couldn't the "work" of the unconscious be "produced" in the same way as any old symptom of classical medicine? Dreams already are.

Certainly, the psychiatrist purports that "for every form of mental alienation there is a particular order in the succession of symptoms of which the simulator is ignorant and in the absence of which the psychiatrist would not be deceived." This (which dates from 1865) in order to safeguard the principle of a truth at all costs and to escape the interrogation posed by simulation—the knowledge that truth, reference, objective cause have ceased to exist. Now, what can medicine do with what floats on either side of illness, on either side of health, with the duplication of illness in a discourse that is no longer either true or false? What can psychoanalysis do with the duplication of the discourse of the unconscious in the discourse of simulation that can never again be unmasked, since it is not false either?

What can the army do about simulators? Traditionally it unmasks them and punishes them, according to a clear principle of identification. Today it can discharge a very good simulator as exactly equivalent to a "real" homosexual, a heart patient, or a madman. Even military psychology draws back from Cartesian certainties and hesitates to make the distinction between true and false, between the "produced" and the authentic symptom. "If he is this good at acting crazy, it's because he is." Nor is military psychology mistaken in this regard: in this sense, all crazy people simulate, and this lack of distinction is the worst kind of subversion. It is against this lack of distinction that classical reason armed itself in all its categories. But it is what today again outflanks them, submerging the principle of truth.

Beyond medicine and the army, favored terrains of simulation, the question returns to religion and the simulacrum of divinity: "I forbade that there be any simulacra in the temples because the divinity that animates nature can never be represented." Indeed it can be. But what becomes of the divinity when it reveals itself in icons, when it is multiplied in simulacra? Does it remain the supreme power that is simply incarnated in images as a visible theology? Or does it volatilize itself in the simulacra that, alone, deploy their power and pomp of fascination—the visible machinery of icons substituted for the pure and intelligible Idea of God? This is precisely what was feared by Iconoclasts, whose millennial quarrel is still with us today. This is precisely because they predicted this omnipotence of simulacra, the faculty simulacra have of effacing God from the conscience of man, and the destructive, annihilating truth that they allow to appear—that deep down God never existed, that only the simulacrum ever existed, even that God himself was never anything but his own simulacrum—from this came their urge to destroy the images. If they could have believed that these images only obfuscated or masked the Platonic Idea of God, there would have been no reason to destroy them. One can live with the idea of distorted truth. But their metaphysical despair came from the idea that the image didn't conceal anything at all, and that these images were in essence not images, such as an original model would have made them, but perfect simulacra, forever radiant with their own fascination. Thus this death of the divine referential must be exorcised at all costs.

One can see that the iconoclasts, whom one accuses of disdaining and negating images, were those who accorded them their true value, in contrast to the iconolaters who only saw reflections in them and were content to venerate a filigree God. On the other hand, one can say that the icon worshipers were the most modern minds, the most adventurous, because, in the guise of having God become apparent in the mirror of images, they were already enacting his death and his disappearance in the epiphany of his representations (which, perhaps, they already knew no longer represented anything, that they were purely a game, but that it was therein the great game lay—knowing also that it is dangerous to unmask images, since they dissimulate the fact that there is nothing behind them).

This was the approach of the Jesuits, who founded their politics on the virtual disappearance of God and on the worldly and spectacular manipulation of consciences—the evanescence of God in the epiphany of power—the end of transcendence, which now only serves as an alibi for a strategy altogether free of influences and signs. Behind the baroqueness of images hides the eminence grise of politics.

This way the stake will always have been the murderous power of images, murderers of the real, murderers of their own model, as the Byzantine icons could be those of divine identity. To this murderous power is opposed that of representations as a dialectical power, the visible and intelligible mediation of the Real. All Western faith and good faith became engaged in this wager on representation: that a sign could refer to the depth of meaning, that a sign could be exchanged for meaning and that something could guarantee this exchange—God of course. But what if God himself can be simulated, that is to say can be reduced to the signs that constitute faith? Then the whole system becomes weightless, it is no longer itself anything but a gigantic simulacrum—not unreal, but a simulacrum, that is to say never exchanged for the real, but exchanged for itself, in an uninterrupted circuit without reference or circumference.

Such is simulation, insofar as it is opposed to representation. Representation stems from the principle of the equivalence of the sign and of the real (even if this equivalence is Utopian, it is a fundamental axiom). Simulation, on the contrary, stems from the Utopia of the principle of equivalence, *from the radical negation of the sign as value*, from the sign as the reversion and death sentence of every reference. Whereas representation attempts to absorb simulation by interpreting it as a false representation, simulation envelops the whole edifice of representation itself as a simulacrum,

Such would be the successive phases of the image:

> it is the reflection of a profound reality;
> it masks and denatures a profound reality;
> it masks the *absence* of a profound reality;
> it has no relation to any reality whatsoever: it is its own pure simulacrum.

In the first case, the image is a *good* appearance—representation is of the sacramental order. In the second, it is an evil appearance—it is of the order of maleficence. In the third, it plays at being an appearance—it is of the order of sorcery. In the fourth, it is no longer of the order of appearances, but of simulation.

The transition from signs that dissimulate something to signs that dissimulate that there is nothing marks a decisive turning point. The first reflects a theology of truth and secrecy (to which the notion of ideology still belongs). The second inaugurates the era of simulacra and of simulation, in which there is no longer a God to recognize his own, no longer a Last Judgment to separate the false from the true, the real from its artificial resurrection, as everything is already dead and resurrected in advance.

When the real is no longer what it was, nostalgia assumes its full meaning. There is a plethora of myths of origin and of signs of reality—a plethora of truth, of secondary objectivity, and authenticity. Escalation of the true, of lived experience, resurrection of the figurative where the object and substance have disappeared. Panic-stricken production of the real and of the referential, parallel to and greater than the panic of material production: this is how simulation appears in the phase that concerns us—a strategy of the real, of the neoreal and the hyperreal that everywhere is the double of a strategy of deterrence.

The Hyperreal and the Imaginary

Disneyland is a perfect model of all the entangled orders of simulacra. It is first of all a play of illusions and phantasms: the Pirates, the Frontier, the Future World, etc. This imaginary world is supposed to ensure the success of the operation. But what attracts the crowds the most is without a doubt the social microcosm, the *religious*, miniaturized pleasure of real America, of its constraints and joys. One parks outside and stands in line inside, one is altogether abandoned at the exit. The only phantasmagoria in this imaginary world lies in the tenderness and warmth of the crowd, and in the sufficient and excessive number of gadgets necessary to create the multitudinous effect. The contrast with the absolute solitude of the parking lot—a veritable concentration camp—is total. Or, rather: inside, a whole panoply of gadgets magnetizes the crowd in directed flows—outside, solitude is directed at a single gadget: the automobile. By an extraordinary coincidence (but this derives without a doubt from the enchantment inherent to this universe), this frozen, childlike world is found to have been conceived and realized by a man who is himself now cryogenized: Walt Disney, who awaits his resurrection through an increase of 180 degrees centigrade.

Thus, everywhere in Disneyland the objective profile of America, down to the morphology of individuals and of the crowd, is drawn. All its values are exalted by the miniature and the comic strip. Embalmed and pacified. Whence the possibility of an ideological analysis of Disneyland (L. Marin did it very well in *Utopiques, jeux d'espace* [Utopias, play of space]): digest of the American way of life, panegyric of American values, idealized transposition of a contradictory reality. Certainly. But this masks something else and this "ideological" blanket functions as a cover for a *simulation of the third order*: Disneyland exists in order to hide that it is the "real" country, all of "real" America that is Disneyland (a bit like prisons are there to hide that it is the social in its entirety, in its banal omnipresence, that is carceral). Disneyland is presented as imaginary in order to make us believe that the rest is real, whereas all of Los Angeles and the America that surrounds it are no longer real, but belong to the hyperreal order and to the order of simulation. It is no longer a question of a false representation of reality (ideology) but of concealing the fact that the real is no longer real, and thus of saving the reality principle.

The imaginary of Disneyland is neither true nor false, it is a deterrence machine set up in order to rejuvenate the fiction of the real in the opposite camp. Whence the debility of this imaginary, its infantile degeneration. This world wants to be childish in order to make us believe that the adults are elsewhere, in the "real" world, and to conceal the fact that true childishness is everywhere—that it is that of the adults themselves who come here to act the child in order to foster illusions as to their real childishness.

Disneyland is not the only one, however. Enchanted Village, Magic Mountain, Marine World: Los Angeles is surrounded by these imaginary stations that feed reality, the energy of the real to a city whose mystery is precisely that of no longer being anything but a network of incessant, unreal circulation—a city of incredible proportions but without space, without dimension. As much as electrical and atomic power stations, as much as cinema studios, this city, which is no longer anything but an immense scenario and a perpetual pan shot, needs this old imaginary like a sympathetic nervous system made up of childhood signals and faked phantasms.

Disneyland: a space of the regeneration of the imaginary as waste-treatment plants are elsewhere, and even here. Everywhere today one must recycle waste, and the dreams, the phantasms, the historical, fairylike, legendary imaginary of children and adults is a waste product, the first great toxic excrement of a hyperreal civilization. On a mental level, Disneyland is the prototype of this new function. But all the sexual, psychic, somatic recycling institutes, which proliferate in California, belong to the same order. People no longer look at each other, but there are institutes for that. They no longer touch each other, but there is contactotherapy. They no longer walk, but they go jogging, etc. Everywhere one recycles lost faculties, or lost bodies, or lost sociality, or the lost taste for food. One reinvents penury, asceticism, vanished savage naturalness: natural food, health food, yoga. Marshall Sahlins's idea that it is the economy of the market, and not of nature at all, that secretes penury, is verified, but at a secondary level: here, in the sophisticated confines of a triumphal market economy is reinvented a penury/sign, a penury/simulacrum, a simulated behavior of the underdeveloped (including the adoption of Marxist tenets) that, in the guise of ecology, of energy crises and the critique of capital, adds a final esoteric aureole to the triumph of an esoteric culture. Nevertheless, maybe a mental catastrophe, a mental implosion and involution without precedent lies in wait for a system of this kind, whose visible signs would be those of this strange obesity, or the incredible coexistence of the most bizarre theories and practices, which correspond to the improbable coalition of luxury, heaven, and money, to the improbable luxurious materialization of life and to undiscoverable contradictions.

The End of the Panopticon

It is still to this ideology of lived experience—exhumation of the real in its fundamental banality, in its radical authenticity—that the American TV verité experiment attempted on the Loud family in 1971 refers: seven months of uninterrupted shooting, three hundred hours of nonstop broadcasting, without a script or a screenplay the odyssey of a family, its dramas, its joys, its unexpected events, nonstop—in short, a "raw" historical document, and the "greatest television performance, comparable, on the scale of our day-to-day life, to the footage of our landing on the moon." It becomes more complicated because this family fell apart during the filming: a crisis erupted, the Louds separated, etc. Whence that insoluble controversy: was TV itself responsible? What would have happened *if TV hadn't been there*?

More interesting is the illusion of filming the Louds as *if TV weren't there*. The producer's triumph was to say: "They lived as if we were not there." An absurd, paradoxical formula—neither true nor false: Utopian. The "as if we were not there" being equal to "as if you were there." It is this Utopia, this paradox that fascinated the twenty million viewers, much more than did the "perverse" pleasure of violating someone's privacy In the "verite" experience it is not a question of secrecy or perversion, but of a sort of frisson of the real, or of an aesthetics of the hyperreal, a frisson of vertiginous and phony exactitude, a frisson of simultaneous distancing and magnification, of distortion of scale, of an excessive transparency. The pleasure of an excess of meaning, when the bar of the sign falls below the usual waterline of meaning: the nonsignifier is exalted by the camera angle. There one sees what the real never was (but "as if you were there"), without the distance that gives us perspectival space and depth vision (but "more real than nature"). Pleasure in the microscopic simulation that allows the real to pass into the hyperreal. (This is also somewhat the case in porno, which is fascinating more on a metaphysical than on a sexual level.)

Besides, this family was already hyperreal by the very nature of its selection: a typical ideal American family, California home, three garages, five children, assured social and professional status, decorative housewife, upper-middle-class standing. In a way it is this statistical perfection that dooms it to death. Ideal heroine of the American way of life, it is, as in ancient sacrifices, chosen in order to be glorified and to die beneath the flames of the medium, a modern *fatum*. Because heavenly fire no longer falls on corrupted cities, it is the camera lens that, like a laser, comes to pierce lived reality in order to put it to death. "The Louds: simply a family who agreed to deliver themselves into the hands of television, and to die by it," the director will say. Thus it is a question of a sacrificial process, of a sacrificial spectacle offered to twenty million Americans. The liturgical drama of a mass society.

TV verité. A term admirable in its ambiguity, does it refer to the truth of this family or to the truth of TV? In fact, it is TV that is the truth of the Louds, it is TV that is true, it is TV that renders true. Truth that is no longer the reflexive truth of the mirror, nor the perspectival truth of the panoptic system and of the gaze, but the manipulative truth of the test that sounds out and interrogates, of the laser that touches and pierces, of computer cards that retain your preferred sequences, of the genetic code that controls your combinations, of cells that inform your sensory universe. It is to this truth that the Loud family was subjected by the medium of TV, and in this sense it amounts to a death sentence (but is it still a question of truth?).

End of the panoptic system. The eye of TV is no longer the source of an absolute gaze, and the ideal of control is no longer that of transparency. This still presupposes an objective space (that of the Renaissance) and the omnipotence of the despotic gaze. It is still, if not a system of confinement, at least a system of mapping. More subtly, but always externally, playing on the opposition of seeing and being seen, even if the panoptic focal point may be blind.

Something else in regard to the Louds. "You no longer watch TV, it is TV that watches you (live)," or again: "You are no longer listening to Don't Panic, it is Don't Panic that is listening to you"—a switch from the panoptic mechanism of surveillance (*Discipline and Punish* [*Surveiller et punir*]) to a system of deterrence, in which the distinction between the passive and the active is abolished. There is no longer any imperative of submission to the model, or to the gaze "YOU are the model!" "YOU are the majority" Such is the watershed of a hyperreal sociality, in which the real is confused with the model, as in the statistical operation, or with the medium, as in the Louds' operation. Such is the last stage of the social relation, ours, which is no longer one of persuasion (the classical age of propaganda, of ideology, of publicity, etc.) but one of deterrence: "YOU are information, you are the social, you are the event, you are involved, you have the word, etc." An about-face through which it becomes impossible to locate one instance of the model, of power, of the gaze, of the medium itself, because *you* are always already on the other side. No more subject, no more focal point, no more center or periphery: pure flexion or circular inflexion. No more violence or surveillance: only "information," secret virulence, chain reaction, slow implosion, and simulacra of spaces in which the effect of the real again comes into play.

We are witnessing the end of perspectival and panoptic space (which remains a moral hypothesis bound up with all the classical analyses on the "objective" essence of power), and thus to the *very abolition of the spectacular*. Television, for example in the case of the Louds, is no longer a spectacular medium. We are no longer in the society of the spectacle, of which the situationists spoke, nor in the specific kinds of alienation and repression that it implied. The medium itself is no longer identifiable as such, and the confusion of the medium and the message (McLuhan) is the first great formula of this new era. There is no longer a medium in the literal sense: it is now intangible, diffused, and diffracted in the real, and one can no longer even say that the medium is altered by it.

ABOUT THE EDITOR

A. Javier Treviño is the author and editor of several books including *The Social Thought of C. Wright Mills* (SAGE, 2012), *Investigating Social Problems* (SAGE, 2014) and *C. Wright Mills and the Cuban Revolution: An Exercise in the Art of Sociological Imagination* (University of North Carolina Press, 2017). He has served as President of the Justice Studies Association (2000–2002) and as President of the Society for the Study of Social Problems (2010–2011). He was a Visiting Research Fellow at the University of Sussex, UK (2006), a Fulbright Scholar to the Republic of Moldova (2009), and since 2014 has been a Visiting Professor in Social and Political Theory at the University of Innsbruck, Austria.